Expressionist Utopias

Dokumente der Wirklichkeit

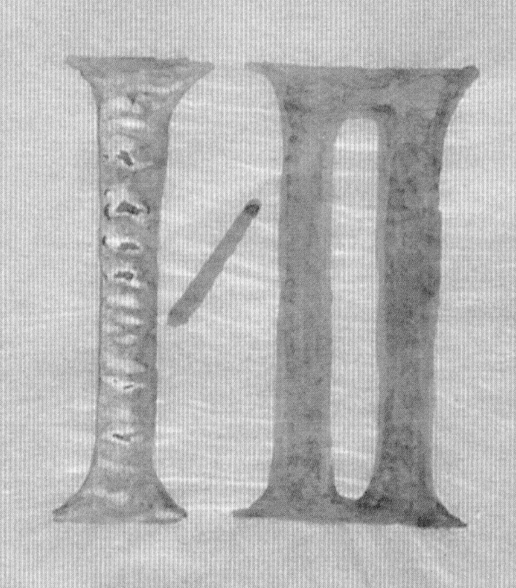

Expressionist Utopias

Paradise ✢ Metropolis ✢ Architectural Fantasy

Timothy O. Benson

with contributions by

Edward Dimendberg

David Frisby

Reinhold Heller

Anton Kaes

Iain Boyd Whyte

University of California Press

Berkeley ✢ Los Angeles ✢ London

LOS ANGELES COUNTY MUSEUM OF ART

Hannah Höch
Raum für ein Kabarett,
1924–25
(Room for a cabaret)
Cat. no. 91

Los Angeles County Museum of Art
October 21, 1993–January 2, 1994
Published by the Los Angeles County Museum of Art,
5905 Wilshire Boulevard, Los Angeles, California 90036, and
University of California Press, Berkeley and Los Angeles, California.

This book was published in conjunction with the exhibition *Expressionist Utopias: Paradise, Metropolis, Architectural Fantasy,* which was organized by the Los Angeles County Museum of Art and made possible by grants from the National Endowment for the Arts, the National Endowment for the Humanities, the Federal Republic of Germany, the Harry and Yvonne Lenart Charitable Foundation, and the Andrew W. Mellon Foundation.

Edited by Karen Jacobson
Designed by Robin Weiss
Text composed in Electra and Bank Gothic by On Line Topography, San Francisco
Display type composed in Koch Antiqua on a Macintosh IIcx
Printed by Insync Media, Inglewood, California

Frontispiece:
Oskar Schlemmer
Utopia: Dokumente der Wirklichkeit, 1921
(Utopia: Documents of reality)
Cat. no. 190

Library of Congress Cataloging-in-Publication Data

Benson, Timothy O., 1950–
Expressionist utopias : paradise, metropolis, architectural fantasy/ Timothy O. Benson ; with contributions by David Frisby . . . [et al.].
p. cm. – (Weimar and now ; 29)
Originally published: Los Angeles : Los Angeles County Museum of Art, 1993
Published in conjunction with an exhibition held at the Los Angeles County Museum of Art Oct. 21, 1993–Jan. 2, 1994.
Includes bibliographical references and index.
ISBN 0-520-23003-5 (pbk. : alk. paper)
1. Expressionism (Art)—Germany—Exhibitions. 2. Art, German—Exhibitions. 3. Art, Modern—20th century—Germany—Exhibitions. I. Frisby, David. II. Los Angeles County Museum of Art. III. Title. IV. Series.
N6868.5.E9 B46 2001
709'.43' 07479494—dc21 00-067624

Contents

Foreword

Expressionist Utopias: Paradise, Metropolis, Architectural Fantasy* examines an often overlooked aspect of German Expressionist art. In the first decades of the twentieth century Expressionist artists and architects produced images of a new architecture and of planned cities where harmonious and just social conditions prevailed. Their visionary prints, drawings, and watercolors conveyed their conviction that the betterment of the world would have to begin with changes within themselves, their art, and existing social institutions. However unrealizable these projects may have been, they suggested a more humane vision of what might be accomplished from which we can still draw inspiration.

Presented in 1993, the exhibition *Expressionist Utopias* further enhanced the museum's important commitment to German heritage through such exhibitions as *German Expressionism 1915–1925: The Second Generation*, *The Apocalyptic Landscapes of Ludwig Meidner*, and more recently *Nolde: The Painter's Prints* and *Exiles and Emigrés: The Flight of European Artists from Hilter*. The opening of the museum's Robert Gore Rifkind Center for German Expressionist Studies in 1987 provided an unparalleled resource, drawn upon by its curator, Timothy Benson, in organizing *Expressionist Utopias*. This exhibition joins an evolving tradition of innovative exhibitions mounted by the museum exploring challenging facets of art and culture while pioneering new approaches to installation and presentation that has included *Art and Technology*, *The Avant-Garde in Russia, 1910–1930: New Perspectives*, *German Expressionist Sculpture*, and *"Degenerate Art": The Fate of the Avant-Garde in Nazi Germany*.

We are delighted to be able to reissue this exhibition catalogue with a new chapter by Edward Dimendberg and Wolf D. Prix documenting the stunning and provocative installation created for *Expressionist Utopias* by the vanguard Viennese architectural firm Coop Himmelblau, directed by Prix and Helmut Swiczinsky. The architects' sensitive interpretation of the multifaceted nature of utopian aspirations, so central to the exhibition's concept, resulted in a marriage of curatorial intention and architectural assertion of spatial ambiguity that was recognized by the International Association of Art Critics with its annual "Best Architecture Show" award. The installation deeply challenged many previously unquestioned assumptions about exhibition space and the presentation of art objects—issues now at the forefront as museums plan permanent spaces that can be flexible and versatile yet aesthetically engaging.

This expanded second edition of *Expressionist Utopias* is indebted to former Director of Publications Garrett White, Managing Editor Stephanie Emerson, Susan Landesmann at Susan Landesmann Design, Ingrid Wassermann at Coop Himmelblau, Charlene Woodcock at the University of California Press, Teri Roseman and Insync Media, and Ollie Zad and Appleton Paper.

Hermann Finsterlin
Geometrische Durch-dringungen, 1922–23
(Geometric penetrations)
Cat. no. 33

The exhibition, along with its educational programs and related events, was made possible by the generous support of the National Endowment for the Humanities and the National Endowment for the Arts. Additional support was received from the Federal Republic of Germany, the Harry and Yvonne Lenart Charitable Foundation, and the Andrew W. Mellon Foundation. We are especially indebted to the many lenders of often-fragile materials listed on page 334, whose generosity was essential to the realization of this project.

ANDREA L. RICH
President and Director
Los Angeles County Museum of Art

Introduction

Conjoining the words *Expressionist* and *utopia* produces a conundrum, as neither term easily lends itself to definition. While utopia is a vital ingredient of nearly all social ideologies—be they political, religious, ethical, or aesthetic—it is not so much a fixed ideal as a mediation between the ideal and the real, a means of propelling thought forward, of helping it transcend what already is. As an embodiment or vision of what might be, utopia defines itself through opposition to its historical context, thereby gaining a strong social resonance. Like human aspiration or artistic creativity, it depends for its survival on being protean, on defiantly eluding the containment of fixed or exhaustive definitions.

While Expressionism is also difficult to define, most historians agree that it was less an artistic or literary style than a socially dynamic cultural movement driven by the forward-looking ideology of modernism. Running its course in Germany between roughly 1905 and 1920, with echoes lingering into the 1920s, Expressionism offers a historical frame through which we may follow the changing manifestations of utopia within a modernist movement. Thus, while *Expressionist Utopias: Paradise, Metropolis, Architectural Fantasy* attempts to trace these embodiments of an alternative, potential reality, it also seeks to define the broader role of the metaphor of utopia within the ideology of modernism.

During the tumultuous period between the turn of the century and the dawn of the Weimar era, Germany endured extreme social disjunction brought on by galloping industrialization, the horrific world war that such industrialization made possible, and the social and economic instability that followed. The architectural fantasies at the center of this exhibition represent a response to these conditions, expressing the faith among artists and architects in the power of aesthetic activity to shape a better world. The utopian architects of the Gläserne Kette (Crystal chain), a group assembled by Bruno Taut in 1919, attempted to restore the image of a humanity at home in the cosmos through architectural invention. With sources ranging from the religious tradition of the Apocalypse to the secular hymns of a new pantheism, their fantasies also embodied an elemental search for universal rhythms and structural principles in images such as idealized agrarian communities and futuristic worlds dependent on miraculous advances in technology for their creation or discovery.

These visionary works, which had reverberations in architecture throughout the Weimar era, cannot be understood without considering prewar Expressionist antecedents, especially the portrayals of a natural paradise by the artists of the Dresden Brücke (Bridge) and the Munich Blaue Reiter (Blue rider). Expressionist architectural fantasies also responded to the urban phase of early Expressionism, centered in Berlin just prior to World War I. The man-made metropolis was ambivalently viewed as both a "second nature" and an antipode to the natural paradise. While the architects' fantasies were often unbuildable, they succeeded in transforming the earlier Expressionists' expectations of

Wenzel Hablik
Untitled, 1909
Cat. no. 55

Wassily Kandinsky
Postkarte für die Bauhaus-Ausstellung, 1923
(Postcard for the Bauhaus exhibition)
Cat. no. 104

a rediscovered natural paradise into the promise of a constructed cultural utopia, thus preparing the way for the pragmatism that entered art and architecture in the 1920s.

As social stability returned with the dawn of the Weimar era, an ironic anti-utopian attitude took hold among the members of the Gläserne Kette and their avant-garde associates (including some of the Berlin Dadaists). In the "machine aesthetic" that grew out of this reaction, cultural criticism was conjoined with a functionalism that supplanted the more rhapsodic aspects of the utopians' earlier musings. This turn toward pragmatism and incipient Constructivism was also reflected in the Bauhaus aesthetic and related *Gesamtkunstwerk* (total work of art) stage productions, yet nostalgic and exotic variations of utopia continued to flourish in the mass medium of film.

The exhibition is grouped into five interrelated sections representative of the roughly chronological progression from arcadian to man-made utopias: Paradise, Metropolis, Architectural Fantasy, Anti-Utopia, and Film and Stage. Correspondingly in the catalogue my introductory essay on the utopia metaphor as an essential, if protean, component of modernist ideology is followed by Reinhold Heller's examination of how the Brücke artists sought to integrate art and life, using paradise imagery of the nude in both nature and the studio to help create an alternative community. Abhorring Enlightenment rationalism and empiricism, the Expressionists evoked Romantic pantheism in their pursuit of the sublime. Despite the decline of the landscape genre and the rejection of traditional religious imagery, art became the principal arena for the revelatory enactment of utopian visions. Through art, as David Frisby shows, Expressionist utopias could be situated even in the contradictory context of the metropolis, that phenomenon of industrialization that enticed and repelled a generation attuning itself to the condition of modernity. Drawing the parallels between Expressionist depictions of the metropolis and the sociological writings of Ferdinand Tönnies, Max Weber, Georg Simmel, and others, Frisby shows how art could embody a utopian vision of the future imbedded in the fragmentary present.

Similarly, in his interrogation and rejection of the received view of Expressionist architecture as an isolated and irrational interlude in the forward march of modern functionalism, Iain Boyd Whyte shows how the sublime, associated with nature during the Romantic period, became linked with the processes and products of industrialization, including the great cities it made possible. In its confrontation with the unportrayable, the sublime was joined with the concept of utopia, both in grand architectural schemes and in morally conceived alternative communities. The fate of utopia, as Anton Kaes suggests in his discussion of Fritz Lang's *Metropolis*, was balanced precariously between the progressive and dangerously repressive tendencies of modernism. Drawing on ideas developed by the utopian architects during the 1910s, *Metropolis* evoked the spectacle of the rationalized secular word of high capitalism in its complex relationship with religion, irrationality, and spirituality, remnants of an earlier era. Kaes examines the film's controversial reconciliation of these two worlds in terms of the contradictory nature of modernity.

As much as any modernist movement, Expressionism was held together by an elastic web of social exchange in which issues were discussed in letters, articles, manifestos, and books. The Appendix of this volume presents an overview of this exchange, including a sampling of the Gläserne Kette's utopian correspondence. To aid the reader in understanding this interaction and the careers of the participants, the Catalogue of the Exhibition includes biographies of the artists and architects whose work is represented.

Despite their diversity, the many manifestations of the Expressionist revival of utopia examined in this exhibition responded to the same dilemma: Could a transcendent artistic experience lead to an actual utopia, or was it merely an escape from social constraints and economic realities that would first have to be resolved before a utopia could even be imagined? Ernst Bloch came to the conclusion that art derives its essential validity from its ability both to confront reality critically and to propose an alternative vision. Through this utopian function of affirmation and negation, art can inform humanity about the future in terms entirely of the present, offering a glimpse of destiny rooted in the immediacy of aesthetic experience.

TIMOTHY O. BENSON
Curator
Robert Gore Rifkind Center for German Expressionist Studies

TIMOTHY O. BENSON

Fantasy and Functionality: The Fate of Utopia

CAN ONE DRAW HAPPINESS? WE CAN ALL LIVE IT AND BUILD IT. UTOPIA? IS NOT UTOPIA THE "CERTAIN" AND THE "REAL," SWIMMING IN THE MIRE OF ILLUSION AND INDOLENT HABIT! IS NOT THE CONTENT OF OUR ASPIRATIONS THE TRUE PRESENT, RESTING ON THE ROCK OF FAITH AND KNOWLEDGE![1]

THE PARADOXES OF UTOPIA

This passage from architect Bruno Taut's book *Die Auflösung der Städte* (The dissolution of the cities, 1920; see fig. 1) appears amid crystalline and spiral forms like an oracle of creation. An illustrated prophecy of a peaceful humanity living in harmony with nature, *Die Auflösung der Städte* embodies the urgent hopes of a generation of German artists, architects, and literati who, having survived a catastrophic decade of war and revolution, now seemed on the threshold of a prosperous reconstruction promised by the Weimar era. In Germany—as in Russia, where Wassily Kandinsky in 1920 called for "the building of an international house of art," to be called "The Great Utopia"[2]— architecture had become a captivating metaphor for a socialist political and cultural transformation.

In Berlin during the political turmoil of early 1919, Taut and architect Walter Gropius organized an exhibition of "unknown architects" in order to draw creative minds into the rebuilding effort. In the exhibition pamphlet Taut declared: "We call upon all those who believe in the future. All strong longing for the future is architecture in the making. One day there will be a world-view, and then there will also be its sign, its crystal—architecture."[3] The exhibition took place under the auspices of the Arbeitsrat für Kunst (Working council for art), an organization of artists, writers, and architects in Berlin that—like the Novembergruppe (November group), the Rat geistiger Arbeiter (Council of intellectual workers), and similar groups—modeled itself on the revolutionary soldiers' and sailors' soviets that sprang up during the fall of Kaiser Wilhelm II's regime in November 1918. Full of grand ambitions, the group advocated the abolition of the academies and destruction of old monuments in favor of the nationalization of the theaters, the unification of the arts, and the building of a new community based on collaboration between the intelligentsia and the proletariat (see Appendix). Just as the building of cathedrals provided a social and economic locus during the Middle Ages, architecture would help restore social order in the modern era. As Gropius exhorted, "Let us together will, think out, create the new idea of architecture. . . the creative conception of the cathedral of the future."[4]

Gropius's and Taut's heady idealism became increasingly untenable, however, in the face of the hardships imposed on a defeated Germany by the June 1919 Treaty of Versailles. Following the brutal suppression of the left-wing Spartacists by the coalition socialist government earlier that year, members of the avant-garde who had once viewed themselves as seers leading the way to the future became disillusioned.[5] Expressionism seemed moribund even to some of its staunchest past supporters.[6]

By 1920 this increasingly critical self-appraisal within the avant-garde was apparent in the ironic comment Taut added to the title page of *Die Auflösung der Städte*: "Nur eine Utopie und eine kleine Unterhaltung" (only a utopia and a little diversion). In German, as in English, *utopia* has negative as well as positive connotations, often associated with

1
Bruno Taut
Kann man das Glück zeichnen?
1920
(Can one draw happiness?)
Illustration from *Die Auflösung der Städte*, p. 30
See cat. no. 234

impracticality, an "idea without real foundations," a "disappointment," or merely a "dream of the future."[7] Originating in 1516 in Sir Thomas More's dialogue on the strengths and weaknesses of a perfect society, the term *utopia* also encompasses anti-utopia and thus can serve as an invigorating ideological battleground and a resilient, flexible metaphor for humanity's hopes for social, artistic, and spiritual renewal.[8] More contrived the name of the imaginary island of his perfect state with deliberate ambiguity and humor: the Greek *ou*, meaning "not," and *topos*, meaning "a place," also suggests *eutopia*, "a good place."[9] Here lay the challenge of making perfection real. Yet *what* utopia (and its inescapable antipode, anti-utopia) means is inseparable from *how* and *when* it means, that is, from the way a given culture finds an image of its desired destiny.

Following antecedents ranging from Plato and the Old Testament prophets to Saint Augustine and Girolamo Savonarola, More introduced an ironic genre that seemed to anticipate the chorus of mocking anti-utopian parodies that swiftly succeeded it. With the French Revolution this genre was extended in social and political thought to embrace a concept of historical development. Now displaced into the future, utopia was linked to the present by governing principles: for the utopian socialists Saint-Simon, Charles Fourier, and Etienne Cabet, an inherently good *code de la nature*; for Robert Owen, a rationalist social model based on moral conduct; for Karl Marx and Friedrich Engels, a Hegelian pattern of dialectical development. Throughout its subsequent evolution—the anarchists Mikhail Bakunin, Peter Kropotkin, and Max Stirner being most significant for the German Expressionists—utopia could not avoid contact with concrete reality.

If the social circumstances in which Taut and his colleagues developed their utopian visions were unprecedented, their quest for an authentic experience "in the true present," from which they might project a utopian future, was deeply rooted in Expressionist ideology. Thus they were indebted less to earlier architecture than to the turn-of-the-century enthusiasm in Germany for a return to nature and a cultivation of pure, subjective experience. Eschewing the rationalism and empiricism that they associated with industrialization, artists around 1900 hoped to find in nature signatures or traces of forces that might reshape the world for the betterment of humanity. Consequently they spoke more of *Geist* (spirit), *Fühlen* (feeling), and *Wollen* (will)—literary critic Kurt Pinthus's trinity—than of the utopia they might produce."[10] While sharing the reform spirit of the populist Wandervogel (founded in 1901) and Jugendbewegung (Youth movement, founded in 1906) groups, the avant-garde was more interested in the German mystical tradition of Meister Eckhart (1260/62–1327?) and Jakob Böhme (1575–1624), as well as in non-Western and esoteric religions, including Hinduism, Buddhism, theosophy, and Rosicrucianism. Espousing at the same time anarchist political views, they formed groups such as Gustav Landauer's Neue Gemeinschaft (New society, founded in 1900) and Sozialistischer Bund (Socialist group, founded in 1908), and Erich Mühsam's Gruppe Anarchist (Anarchist group, founded with Landauer in 1908).[11]

Although they adopted the revolutionary rhetoric of Bakunin, Kropotkin, Stirner, and Pierre-Joseph Proudhon, most artists and intellectuals did not share the practical concerns of contemporary political movements and the materialist Marxian tenets that the German Socialists, for example, had endorsed with their adoption of the Erfurt program in 1891. Preferring artistic inspiration and philosophical absolutes, German artists and writers could overcome their social alienation and political despair only through dreams of a unified ethical, political, and aesthetic revolution. A neo-Kantian revival in German academic circles at the turn of the century offered a doctrine of sovereign power vested in the

2
Heinrich Vogeler
Die sieben Schalen des Zorns (Offenbarung Johannis), 1918
(The Seven Bowls of Wrath [Revelation to John])
Cat. no. 217

imagination *(Einbildungskraft)*, which not only could shape perception and consciousness but also was believed capable of changing the world.[12]

The artists and writers who were published in the leading Expressionist journals *Der Sturm* (The storm), *Die Aktion* (Action), and *Die weissen Blätter* (The white papers) shared this missionary belief in the power of the creative will. A favorite utopian metaphor was *der neue Mensch* (the new man) in whom Geist—meaning inspired intellect or spirit, a variant of neo-Kantian "critical consciousness"—reaches its purest form.[13] Masculine-gendered in German thought, Geist, embodied in the new man, manifested the highest potential for human creativity in defiance of the "outer" world of materialist forces and inert matter (given, by contrast, the feminine gender).[14]

In tandem with the new man, the Expressionists desired an art of "the new form," in which the creative will might function analogously and, as the philosopher Ernst Bloch speculated in *Die weissen Blätter*, furnish preutopian suggestions.[15] Kurt Hiller insisted that "just copying down the existing" was "counterrevolutionary," while a subjective art might embody the revolutionary in its very confrontation with reality. As Theodor Adorno later said of utopia, "By concretizing itself as something false, it always points at the same time to what should be"; that is, "the true thing defines itself via the false thing."[16]

THE VANISHING NATURAL PARADISE AND THE AUTONOMY OF ART

The early Expressionists' quest for a utopian future began in a nostalgic return to the past, as much an attempt to find a lost paradise as to build a new world. They shared the ideals expressed in a motto of the Wandervogel—"the beautiful earth and human becoming are for the Wandervogel everything"[17]—while following Friedrich Nietzsche's dictum: "The domestication (the culture) of man does not go deep—where it does it at once becomes degeneration.... The savage... is a return to nature—and in a certain sense his recovery,

3
Erich Heckel
Badende am Teich, 1912
(Bathers at the pond)
Cat. no. 82

4
Oskar Kokoschka
Das Mädchen Li und ich, 1906–8
(The girl Li and I)
Cat. no. 121

his cure from culture."[18] Their escape from the rigidity of Wilhelmine culture assumed what Oskar Pfister, writing in 1920, called a "stage of transition," during which "the road to progress is possible only through the detour of such a regression."[19] This notion of an *Übergang* (going over) by means of an *Untergang* (going under) is explicit in the passage from Nietzsche's *Also sprach Zarathustra* (Thus spoke Zarathustra, 1883), supposedly invoked by Karl Schmidt-Rottluff as the source for the name of the group he formed in 1905 with Fritz Bleyl, Erich Heckel, and Ernst Ludwig Kirchner, his fellow architecture students at the technical college in Dresden: "What is great in man is that he is a bridge and not a goal: what can be loved in man is that he is a going-over and a going-under."[20]

The Brücke's manifesto emphasized freedom from the cultural establishment and celebrated a communal association around the natural form-giving force, or "will," which would lead the way to the future (see Appendix). These ideas were embodied in the group's idealized portrayals of nude figures in nature in a style derived from Postimpressionism and devoid of the trappings of classical mythology and the historicism of the academic tradition. Carrying on the age-old tradition equating beauty, nudity, and truth, Heckel's *Badende am Teich* (Bathers at the pond, 1912; fig. 3) transforms the rustic environs of the Moritzburg Ponds, near Dresden, into a primordial, timeless setting in which progress is abstracted as pure vital force. The celebration of the nude and youth as emblems of natural regeneration was common in Jugendstil periodicals (including *Pan*, *Jugend* [Youth], and *Die Schönheit* [Beauty]) and was put into practice by adherents of *Freikörperkultur* (nudism) and *Bodenreform* (land reform) as a radical, albeit often politically conservative, escape from modern civilization into the purity of nature.[21] Kirchner's presentation of sexually mixed groups of nudes in his *Mit Schilf werfende Badende* (Bathers tossing reeds, 1910; fig. 79), however, defied the gender segregation practiced in most nudist colonies, while his eroticism offended bourgeois morality.[22] He extolled the nude as nothing less than "the foundation of all pictorial art," and the Brücke artists adopted the nude as a symbol, situating themselves socially and historically as a spiritual and utopian alternative.[23]

Sexuality was regarded as a subversive force throughout the movement. The Dionysian view of sexual love as a means of transcendence was espoused in Stanislaw Przybyszewski's writings in *Der Sturm* and played a role in the festivities of Stefan George's circle in Munich, as may be reflected in Kandinsky's Garden of Love series (see fig. 70).[24] By Contrast Viennese artist Oskar Kokoschka savored longing in the idyllic paradise of *Das Mädchen Li und ich* (The girl Li and I, 1906–8; fig. 4) in his book *Die träumenden Knaben* (The dreaming boys).

The Expressionists' natural paradise was conceived as a source of spiritual renewal providing clues to a spontaneous artistic formal language. Harking back to German Romanticism, the idea that pure form alone could transcend imitation and reveal the forces operating behind nature was voiced in the Jugendstil periodicals.[25] Friedrich von Schiller's

notion of the landscape as a vehicle for indefinite sensations evoked through formal composition, for example, was conveyed in *Pan*, where a new art of "harmonic melody" was described in which "lines and colors" could be "metaphysically more effective" than representation.[26] As the Expressionist apologist Paul Fechter wrote in 1914: "Appearance is subordinate to the will to form [*Ausdruckswillen*].... Nature yields its hitherto governing role to the human soul, to the artist."[27] Behind the nostalgic portrayal of paradise lay the pursuit of genesis and a fascination with origination, especially in the unconscious. Hermann Obrist, whose school Kirchner attended in 1903–4, devoted his book of pedagogical essays on art and architecture, *Neue Möglichkeiten in der bildenden Kunst* (New possibilities in the visual arts, 1903), to the proposition that "we must again become what earlier humans were: creative," recommending that we do "everything unconscious and natural."[28]

The Brücke artists cultivated the unconscious in the "spontaneous" technomorphic processes of making woodcuts where "natural" qualities might be found.[29] In Heckel's

5
Erich Heckel
Kniende am Stein, 1913
(Woman kneeling near a rock)
Cat. no. 84

6
Franz Marc
Zaubriger Moment: Blatt 21 des "Skizzenbuchs aus dem Felde," 1915
(Magical moment: Page 21 from "Sketchbook from the field")
Cat. no. 132

7
Johannes Molzahn
Sternendröhnen, 1919
(Roar of the stars)
Cat. no. 157

Kniende am Stein (Woman kneeling near a rock, 1913; fig. 5) and *Badende am Teich*, for example, accidental marks resulting from the physical process of gouging and splintering the wood surface are mingled with autographic tracings and descriptive signs. Seeking contact with the formative forces of nature, the Expressionists participated in what the sociologist and cultural critic Georg Simmel envisioned as a struggle between "unformed life" and "cultural forms"—for him the essential crisis of modern culture.[30] As it gradually departed from natural appearances, the Expressionist paradise became more emphatically embodied in cultural signs representing change.

A program for the symbolic representation of a coming spiritual age was launched by the Munich Blaue Reiter (Blue rider) group, founded by Kandinsky and Franz Marc in 1911. According to Marc, their goal was "to create out of their work *symbols* for their own time, symbols that belong on the altars of a future spiritual religion, symbols behind which the technical heritage cannot be seen." The means to the utopian "Great Spiritual Epoch" were spelled out by Kandinsky in his essay "Über die Formfrage" (On the problem of form) as "two roads" through art to the future: "The Great Abstraction" and "The Great Realism." Like Alexej von Jawlensky, Marianne von Werefkin, and others in his circle, Kandinsky was deeply interested in the Symbolists (especially Arnold Böcklin and Maurice Maeterlinck) and in Rudolf Steiner's anthroposophy.[31]

Kandinsky articulated a theory of abstract art as a universal language of spiritual revelation in *Über das Geistige in der Kunst* (Concerning the spiritual in art, 1912), an essential chapter of which won the admiration of Bruno Taut when it appeared in *Der Sturm*.[32] Kandinsky's *Paradies* (Paradise, 1911–12; fig. 70) shows how his progression toward abstraction began in a "method" of veiling imagery derived from Maeterlinck's poetry, so

that "the object is not itself seen" but "exercises a direct impression on the soul."[33] As is also evident in the works of Marc and Johannes Molzahn (see figs. 6, 7), Kandinsky was moving toward the creation within his art of a "spiritual atmosphere" for humanity's "tragic collision between matter and spirit," where "displacement" and "instability" would offer a "precognition of the path of Truth."[34] Drawn to the gloom of Maeterlinck's poetry and the apocalyptic disintegration in Blaue Reiter colleague Alfred Kubin's illustrated anti-utopian novel *Die andere Seite* (The other side, 1909), he created an apocalyptic yet immaterial atmosphere in which his progressively abstracted grammar of form and color seems to generate a space continuous in all directions, denying the subject-object antithesis.[35] He believed that historical progress was governed by "the operation of law," wherein destiny is determined by "the abstract spirit."[36] Moreover, "like the work of nature, the work of art is subordinated to the same law, that of construction," which reaches an advanced stage in the portfolio Kleine Welten (Small worlds, 1922; see fig. 8) and in *Fröhlicher Aufstieg* (Joyful ascension, 1923; fig. 9).[37]

Motivated by "the mystical inner construction, which is the great problem of our generation,"[38] Marc sought to present an image continually in the process of becoming in his pantheistic *Geburt der Pferde* (The birth of horses, 1913; fig. 10). For Marc the *Naturbild* (image of nature) had to be destroyed in order "to show the powerful laws that are at work behind the beautiful appearances." While believing that "nature is everywhere, in us and outside us," he also saw art as autonomous, calling it "the most audacious removal from nature and 'naturalness,' the bridge into the realm of the spirit" and "something that is not entirely nature."[39] As Kandinsky said of one of Marc's paintings, "The natural impossibility of a red horse demands a correspondingly unnatural milieu in which this horse is placed."[40]

Paul Klee was in Munich in the autumn of 1911 and became closely associated with the newly formed Blaue Reiter. He was influenced by Kandinsky's prophetic proto-Constructivist "Malerei als reine Kunst" (Painting as pure art) throughout the decade, as can be seen in his "Creative Credo" (1920), in which he contends that "art is an analogy of creation."[41] Klee saw himself continuing the Romantic tradition of Caspar David Friedrich, Philipp Otto Runge, and the physician, philosopher, and landscape painter Carl Gustav Carus.[42] Influenced by Goethe's scientific endeavors, Carus saw nature as a text written by God to be "translated" by art and science.[43] Klee's *Zahlenbaumlandschaft* (Number-tree landscape, 1919; fig. 11) embodies this view of the world as a hieroglyph and art as the lost medieval *theoria*, the totality of truth, beauty, and spirit. For Klee, "art does not reproduce what is visible, instead, it makes visible."[44]

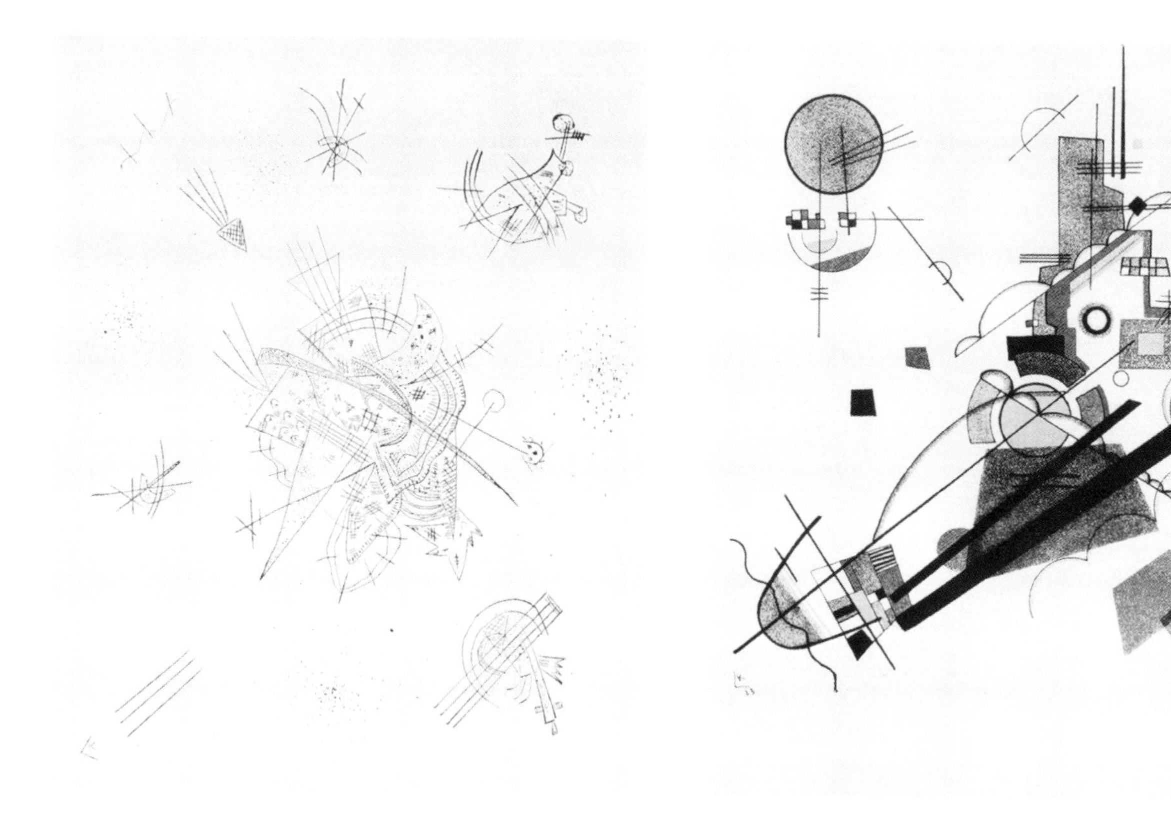

8
Wassily Kandinsky
Kleine Welten X, 1922
(Small worlds X)
Cat. no. 102

9
Wassily Kandinsky
Fröhlicher Aufstieg, 1923
(Joyful ascension)
Cat. no. 103

The Expressionists had taken the path that their Romantic predecessors had established in landscape, which led inevitably toward abstraction. The Romantics yearned for what Friedrich Schlegel called an "infinite unity" with the cosmos, wherein no duality would remain; mind and matter would be one. But if, as Novalis wrote, "all that is visible rests on an invisible foundation," then the landscape exists, as Friedrich Schelling said, only "in the eye of the beholder." Attaining Goethe's "silent feeling of the sublime [*Erhaben*]... solitude, absence, seclusion" meant the pursuit of a vanishing canvas, or what one scholar has called an "art without a subject."[45]

Although Friedrich created an idealized nature of the sort admired by Rainer Maria Rilke, he usually retained a mediating human presence.[46] Heckel and Schmidt-Rottluff, by contrast, allowed the self to be absorbed in the form-giving forces of nature in the ambiguous forms of *Sonnenaufgang* (Sunrise, 1914; fig. 12) and *Bucht im Mondschein* (Bay in moonlight, 1914; fig. 13). As critic Paul Westheim affirmed, landscape was no longer relevant to modern art in the same way that it had been to realism and Impressionism. The new landscape "possibly says nothing about how a piece of the world appears;

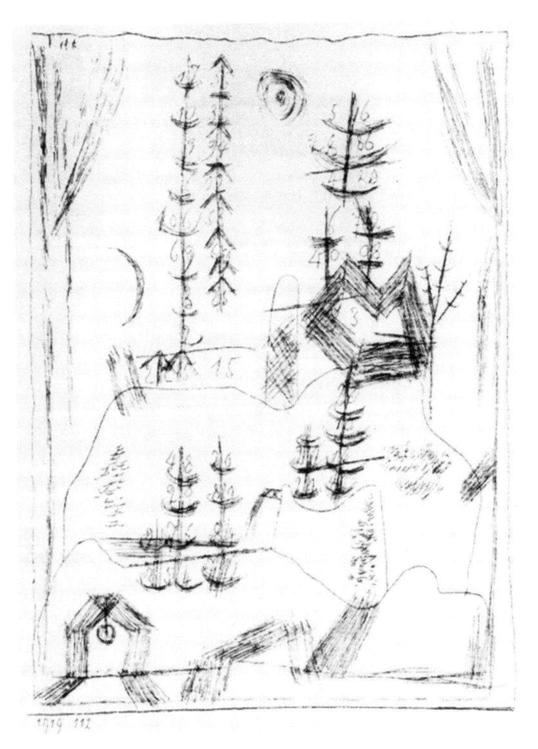

10
Franz Marc
Geburt der Pferde, 1913
(The birth of horses)
Cat. no. 131

11
Paul Klee
Zahlenbaumlandschaft, 1919
(Number-tree landscape)
Cat. no. 116

but [speaks] through something entirely immediate: Through its functional values it possibly speaks of angst and terror, of want and craving, of joy and goodness, of sublimity and eternity. If Munch, Nolde, Kirchner, Heckel, Meidner, and many others still paint landscapes, then it has to do most essentially with these."[47] Westheim's emphasis on emotions driven by the desire for unity and totality is very much like Simmel's explanation of "mood" [*Stimmung*] as experienced in the immediacy of seeing and feeling, corresponding with the "inner quality" of nature. For Simmel everything called culture consists of a series of self-sufficient images created, or "made," in the dynamic forming process of life and the unifying force of the soul [*Seele*].[48]

Perhaps more than any of the other Expressionists' landscapes, Heckel's show how all but the last vestiges of referentiality could vanish into subjectively formed images in an autonomous art. His *Sonnenaufgang*, with its disk set against calm sky and water, has been seen as imparting a mood of hope.[49] In his *Kniende am Stein* signs of the physical process of cutting the block blend into the crystalline evocation of the sky and chalk cliffs of the Baltic coastline near Osterholz. The huge rock, a feature at which Heckel marveled, is reminiscent of Friedrich's wilderness altars.

Representation is virtually engulfed by autonomous organic forms that seem to establish their own compositional rules in Schmidt-Rottluff's *Bucht im Mondschein*. By abandoning halftones in favor of forceful contrasts, rejecting illusionist perspective, and creating absolute, nonobjective forms, he advanced the Expressionist landscape toward its final departure from its Romantic antecedents. The irregular forms of the shoreline are constructed through regularized procedures and a limited vocabulary of similar shapes, all approximating rather than describing a visual reality. According to Carl Einstein, the true experience of art is attained by creating an "equation" (*Gleichung*) or "equivalent" (*Äquivalent*). Schmidt-Rottluff's forms allow mass to be absorbed into flatter equivalents as they take on autonomous qualities, becoming increasingly arbitrary and following the organic, constructive principles of composition, thus affirming Einstein's claim that perception is not passive, but the "creation of concrete organisms."[50]

THE 'WORLD CITY' AS SECOND NATURE

THE TIME HAS COME AT LAST TO START PAINTING OUR REAL HOMELAND, THE BIG CITY WHICH WE ALL LOVE SO MUCH.
LUDWIG MEIDNER[51]

During the urban phase of Expressionism, beginning in Berlin during the early 1910s, a utopian vision was articulated by the artists and literati who frequented cafés such as the Café des Westens and the Romanische Café, contributed to *Der Sturm* and *Die Aktion*, and formed literary associations such as Hiller's Neue Club (New club). Change would come from within an avant-garde "utopian synod of intellectuals," as Hiller titled a lecture given at a meeting of the Neue Club in 1910.[52]

Having originated Expressionism in the provinces, artists were gradually drawn into the cosmopolitan milieu. Kirchner, Schmidt-Rottluff, and Heckel arrived in Berlin in late 1911 at the urging of Max Pechstein, who had lived there since 1908. Former Brücke member Emil Nolde was spending his winters in Berlin, while Kokoschka arrived in 1910 as the principal artist for *Der Sturm*, mounting his first solo exhibition at Paul Cassirer's gallery. Many contemporary art trends, such as Futurism and Cubism, were not represented at the modern art galleries owned by Cassirer, Fritz Gurlitt, and I. B. Neumann, finding a venue only with the opening of Herwarth Walden's Sturm gallery in 1910. The New Secession, founded by Pechstein and Georg Tappert in the same year, offered an exhibition venue for the Brücke and more than twenty other artists who had been rejected by the Impressionist-oriented Berlin Secession.

12
Erich Heckel
Sonnenaufgang, 1914
(Sunrise)
Cat. no. 86

13
Karl Schmidt-Rottluff
Bucht im Mondschein, 1914
(Bay in moonlight)
Cat. no. 194

14
George Grosz
Vorstadt, 1915–16
(Suburb)
Cat. no. 49

15
Wilhelm Plünnecke
Untitled (factory), 1919
Cat. no. 174

Just as they had sought spiritual and artistic renewal in nature, the Expressionists continued their search for paradise in the city. Even prior to moving to Berlin, the Brücke artists had begun to portray the Dresden suburbs (see fig. 76) as well as Hamburg harbor and other urban prospects, regarding them as just as much a part of the landscape as the rural scenes at Dangast, Fehmarn, and Nidden. They used painterly means derived from Vincent van Gogh and Henri Matisse to discover what architect August Endell called "the beauty of the city as nature."[53] With Peter Behrens, Hermann Mathesius, and Bruno Paul, Endell was part of a circle of Berlin architects who were bringing a new functionalism into building design based on their experiences in the Werkbund in Munich. Endell's appreciation of the beauty of the metropolis marked a significant departure from the prevailing view among more traditional architects and critics, who regarded the rapidly expanding German capital as an affront to natural beauty. Walther Rathenau, for example, disdainfully dismissed Berlin as a "Chicago on the Spree." The influential critic Karl Scheffler derided it as "the capital…of all modern ugliness."[54]

Yet there was already a growing appreciation for the city in German Impressionist circles. In his introductory essay for a portfolio of lithographic views of the Berlin suburbs by German Impressionist Rudolf Grossmann, novelist Georg Hermann discerned an essentially new kind of urban beauty. So extraordinary was "the rare essence of the metropolis" that it "exists beyond all laws known to earth." Hermann's cosmic *Weltstadt* (world city) superseded both the prosaic eighteenth-century *König-* or *Residenzstadt* (royal city) and the industrialized nineteenth-century *Bürgerstadt* of officialdom and the bourgeoisie: "Nature departs with its old [laws] and the city comes with its new laws."[55] Grossmann, Meidner, Schmidt-Rottluff, and later George Grosz (see fig. 14) and Wilhelm Plünnecke (see figs. 15, 92) shared Hermann's delight in how the surrounding countryside was arbitrarily cut up by the tentacles of the new infrastructures of transportation, communication, and housing for a mushrooming population.

As the Expressionists became more interested in the contrast between the artificial and the natural, they abandoned the panoramic suburban "landscape" in favor of the movement and intensity of urban streets. In this they were inspired by the works of Umberto Boccioni and the Italian Futurists, which were exhibited at the Sturm gallery in 1912, and by the Futurist manifestos then appearing in *Der Sturm*. Meidner called for a sensual immersion in the urban spectacle: "Let's paint what is close to us, our city world [*Stadt-Welt*]! the wild streets."[56] His fusion of the words *city* and *world* captures the singular surging cosmos of his hallucinatory "apocalyptic" cityscapes, where people and houses seem to disintegrate into tilting faceted planes and cascading rhythms (see fig. 16). Kirchner's *Frauen am Potsdamer Platz* (Women at Potsdamer Platz, 1914–15; fig. 17), Carlo Mense's *Strasse mit Fahnen* (Street with flags, 1913; fig. 89), and Otto Möller's *Berliner Expression* (undated; fig. 19) further convey the transitoriness of Endell's "street as living being," where the movement of vehicles and masses of people produce "mere appearances,"

16
Ludwig Meidner
Strasse im Wilmersdorf, 1913
(Street in Wilmersdorf)
Cat. no. 134

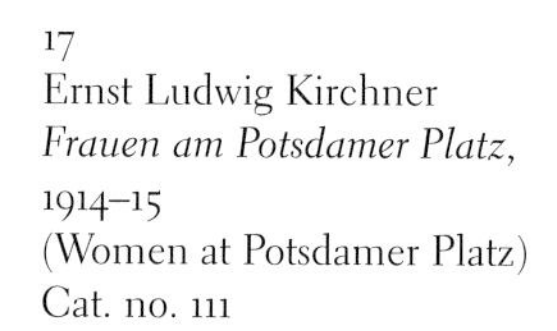

17
Ernst Ludwig Kirchner
Frauen am Potsdamer Platz,
1914–15
(Women at Potsdamer Platz)
Cat. no. 111

18
Ernst Ludwig Kirchner
Potsdamer Platz
(Berlin Street Scene)
Colored chalk
25½ x 19 in. (64.8 x 48.3cm)
Courtesy of the Busch-Reisinger Museum, Harvard University Art Museums, Association Fund

19
Otto Möller
Berliner Expression
(Berlin expression)
Cat. no. 153

"autonomous organizations," not of "inner connections" but of outward forms. Having studied Immanuel Kant's philosophy and Theodor Lipps's empathy theory, Endell situated the beauty of the city in the instantaneity of the present: "Seeing as such is pleasurable."[57] Yet while he called for an autonomous art devoid of allegory, rhetoric, or historical reference, his admiration for French Impressionism was not shared by Kirchner, Meidner, and Mense.[58] Meidner repudiated "the dissolving of contours" and the "vagueness and fuzziness of Impressionism" in his endeavor to convey the street as a "bombardment of whizzing rows of windows, of screeching lights between vehicles of all kinds and a thousand jumping spheres, scraps of human beings, advertising signs, and shapeless color."[59]

Urban Expressionism corresponds to the mode of perception imposed on the individual by the conditions of the city as expounded upon by Simmel, the influential sociologist whose lectures attracted Ernst Bloch, Julius Meier-Graefe, and Georg Lukács. In his essay "Die Grossstädte und das Geistesleben" (The metropolis and mental life, 1903), Simmel presented the psychological character of the urban individual as defined by an "intensification of nervous stimulation" so extreme that brutally assaulted nerves exhaust "their last reserves of strength."[60] The individual creates "an organ protecting him against...his external environment," using rational calculation tied to the external aspects of "practical life," such as the quantification of social exchange through the money economy (the subject of his earlier book *Die Philosophie des Geldes* [The philosophy of money, 1900]) and the coordination of simultaneous events in precisely measured time. The clocks in Möller's *Berliner Expression* and Mense's *Strasse mit Fahnen* may allude to the "strictest punctuality" without which "the whole structure would break down into an inextricable chaos."[61]

Simmel recognized the immense burden imposed on the spatial and temporal dimensions of the imagination by rationality and functionality, which relegated the individual to what the Expressionist playwright Ludwig Rubiner called an "island existence." Hiller, agreeing with Simmel, sought to regain a lost universal and harmonious "totality" of the objective and subjective faculties not through a Rousseauian return to a simple, "natural" existence, nor through the intellect, but rather through a subjective absorption of lost qualitative experiences.[62] If, in the words of Expressionist poet Franz Werfel, "the world begins in man," then the task of envisioning a utopia meant situating the self and finding a shared formal language in which hopes and aspirations could be expressed.[63]

The task of urban Expressionism was to regain "those irrational, instinctive, sovereign traits and impulses" that Simmel believed metropolitan life excluded. Kirchner recognized that "any objective [pictorial] construction is futile, since a passing taxi, a bright or dark evening dress transforms the entire laboriously achieved construction."[64] Avoiding "an exact reconstruction" of his impressions, he began his *Fünf Kokotten* (Five tarts, 1914–15; fig. 93) and *Frauen am Potsdamer Platz* with spontaneous notations made "directly from nature"—what he later called "hieroglyphs"—which he regularized and abstracted until they served the constructive principles of composition (see fig. 18).[65] The steep perspective, distortion of scale, and disjointed suggestions of buildings in the woodcut *Potsdamer Platz* disorient the viewer, conveying a disunified and decentered experience of the self. To be sure, the portrayal of the exploitative, dehumanizing institution of prostitution, which the metropolis and its money economy make possible, functions as an anti-utopian critique. Yet Kirchner also presents humanity affirmatively, as a vital and instinctual presence "belonging" in its surroundings. His eroticized relocation of the paradise imagery of the Brücke to an urban setting affords the sense of community essential for a utopia.[66]

A more overtly negative view of the metropolis as a new Babylon is conveyed in the

20
Paul Gangolf
Seiltänzerin, c. 1922
(Tightrope walker)
Cat. no. 36

21
George Grosz
Strasse, 1915–16
(Street)
Cat. no. 51

22
Otto Dix
Elektrische, 1920
(Streetcar)
Cat. no. 15

darkened city of Paul Gangolf's *Seiltänzerin* (Tightrope walker, c. 1922; fig. 20) and *Strassenszene* (Street scene, 1925; fig. 100) as well as in the urban jungle of Grosz's *Strasse* (Street, 1915–16; fig. 21).[67] Grosz's collagelike, jumbled compositions, like Otto Dix's *Elektrische* (Streetcar, 1920; fig. 22), suggest the fragmentary mode of urban consciousness conveyed by the staccato rhythms of the "simultaneous" poetry of August Stramm and Jacob van Hoddis. These artists and poets present heterogeneous arrays of images and use discontinuity as a formal principle, thus satisfying an essential prerequisite for any modern utopian construct: defining the collective norms of perception and consciousness as those of the modern psyche in its urban setting.[68] Just as Simmel believed that the individual, given greater independence by the anonymity of urban existence, was able to project the self "temporally and spatially,"[69] Expressionist writers such as Einstein, neo-Kantian philosopher Salomo Friedländer, Otto Gross, and Franz Jung found affirmative value in the dissolution of the individual into the apparent disorder of the world. Einstein's novel *Bebuquin; oder, Die Dilettanten des Wunders* (Bebuquin; or, the dilettantes of wonder, 1912) portrays the mind as fragmented and capable of attaining unity only as part of a communal vision.[70] Friedländer extols the "new man," or "universal world-person," as the vessel of "magic," "utopia, " "the perpetual motion machine," and "inexhaustible power"—an *Erdkaise*r (earth-emperor) of "presentism," who, as "the synthesis of the world," is an "eternal present."[71]

In the indifference attained in the immediacy of the present, moreover, lay potentially constructive principles. Whereas Simmel saw individuality created through "differentiation" of the individual and his products, Friedländer stated in his *Schöpferische Indifferenz* (Creative indifference, 1918) that even willful acts were "automatic, like mechanisms," so

that all culture was the result of "creative indifference."[72] As the Dadaists later recognized, the machine metaphor provided an ironic distance from which one could launch a social critique (see figs. 57, 171). Meanwhile a far greater disruption occurred as the world the Expressionists knew came to an end with the outbreak of war in August 1914.

ARCHITECTURAL UTOPIAS

Behrens's statement, accompanied by a drawing of a gleaming domed building of monumental proportions, reflects the fervor with which architects embraced the task of rebuilding as a vanquished Germany emerged from the war (see fig. 23).[73] The broadside "Für das neue Deutschland" (For the new Germany; see Appendix) was circulated during the election of delegates to the Weimar assembly in January 1919, a period of euphoria within the avant-garde.[74] The Arbeitsrat für Kunst had gone even further in its chiliastic espousal of architecture as "the direct carrier of spiritual forces, molder of the sensibilities of the general public" in Taut's "Architektur-Programm" (Program for architecture; see Appendix). Its call for the dissolution of the boundaries between architecture, painting, and sculpture was conveyed in a bold woodcut, probably by Arbeitsrat member Pechstein (fig. 25), presenting personifications of the three arts erecting a building against a background of stars and abstract shapes suggesting the cosmic forces of creation. The arts would be the mediators of the "complete revolution in the spiritual realm [that] will create this architecture."[75] Enthusiasm for architecture predominates in the responses of some twenty-eight artists, patrons, and critics to a questionnaire seeking a "common basis" among the Arbeitsrat members during the spring of 1919 (see Appendix). Obrist's response is rhapsodic: "[Utopia] is, in fact, the only thing that survives. Let us then live in Utopia, let us

ERECT ON THE DEBRIS OF THE VANISHED AGE STAND THE EMBLEMS OF THE NEW. LET US CAST DOUBT ASIDE, SET TO WORK, AND BUILD THAT BRIGHT EDIFICE.

PETER BEHRENS
JANUARY 13, 1919

23
Für das neue Deutschland,
1919
(For the new Germany)
Cat. no. 227

24
Peter Behrens
Cover for *Das Plakat*, 1920
Cat. no. 6

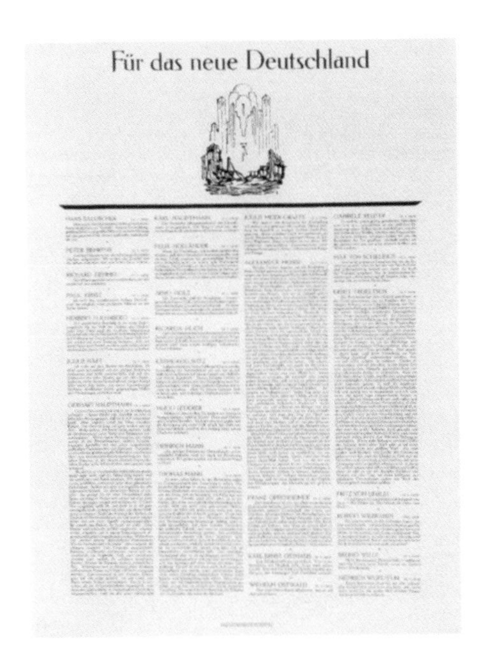
Für das neue Deutschland

25
Attributed to Max Pechstein
Cover for *Arbeitsrat Für Kunst Berlin*, 1919 (Z 6)
Cat. no. 172

26
Lyonel Feininger
Kathedrale, 1919
(Cathedral)
Cat. no. 23

27
Gerhard Marcks
Landschaft mit Turmarchitekturen, 1919
(Landscape with tower architecture)
Cat. no. 133

28
Hermann Finsterlin
Traum aus Glas, 1920
(Glass Dream)
Cat. no. 26

fabricate plans, castles in Spain."[76] César Klein describes a coastal city of "gigantic silos" and "enormous double archways," with a central town hall—a "sculptural creation" with grottos, fountains, and pavilions.

Divisive political events pushed these utopian visions ever farther from realization, The murders of radical socialists Karl Liebknecht and Rosa Luxemburg, the repression of Berlin street demonstrations, and the deaths of Landauer and socialist leader Kurt Eisner in connection with the military suppression of the Bavarian Socialist Councils Republic were among the events of early 1919 causing Gropius, Taut, and critic Adolf Behne to seek radical alternatives to both party politics and the traditional institutions of museums, academies, and building commissions. The Arbeitsrat für Kunst rallied around the notion of an architectural project that would function somewhat like the medieval *Bauhütte*, or lodge, where an enlightened "conspiratorial brotherhood" would work directly with proletarian craftsmen to create a spiritually uplifting environment based around a *Volkshaus* (people's house).[77] The image of such a "cathedral of socialism" would soon become closely associated with the Bauhaus (see fig. 26), the school of art and design whose directorship Gropius assumed in 1919.[78] With no prospects for realizing such a grandiose scheme, Gropius and Taut instead organized the *Ausstellung für unbekannte Architekten* (Exhibition of unknown architects) in April 1919 at the most progressive gallery in Berlin, I. B. Neumann's Graphisches Kabinett, located on the decidedly unproletarian Kurfürstendamm.

An uncompromising stance against functionalism was conveyed both in the pamphlet that served as the exhibition catalogue and in many of the architectural fantasies on display (see Appendix), most living up to Gropius's exhortation to "*build in imagination [Phantasie]*, unconcerned about technical difficulties." If, as Behne declared, "utopian [is]

29
Jefim Golyscheff
Untitled, 1918
Cat. no. 38

30
Paul Gösch
Untitled (fantasy architecture), c. 1921
Cat. no. 42

the idea of a collaborative effort by architects, sculptors, and painters to erect great models pointing to the future,"[79] then the exhibition succeeded in its inclusion of fantasies by the sculptor Gerhard Marcks (see fig. 27) and theater sets by Klein, as well as paintings and sculpture. And if, as Gropius insisted, the exhibition was to present "watersheds between dream and reality,"[80] then the doughlike organic forms of painter Hermann Finsterlin's *Traum aus Glas* (Glass dream, 1920; fig. 28) and Jefim Golyscheff's crystalline labyrinths (see fig. 29) were among the "sensations of the exhibition."[81] Golyscheff's drawings had been solicited by Gropius as "ultimate examples of what we want: utopia," and his works garnered critical praise for their use of "glass and reinforced concrete, the favored materials of the modern architectural poets."[82] Although some were dismissed by critics as "architectural fantasy without architecture," most of the works in the exhibition were appreciated as uninhibited fantasies,[83] among the most successful, childlike images by Paul Gösch which belied his architectural training (see fig. 30).

Not unexpectedly, given the Expressionists' devotion to the sublime and the pantheistic attitudes of Romanticism,[84] their utopian fantasies were assumed to be in harmony with the formative forces of nature as manifested in the unconscious. One critic observed that Golyscheff's environments went beyond the anthropomorphic to the unconscious.[85] Finsterlin generated architectural forms through unconscious, undirected scribbling, which he then refined (see figs. 32, 33), a gestural technique also used by architects Erich Mendelsohn and Bruno Taut. Although not represented in the exhibition, Mendelsohn was one of the members of the Arbeitsrat who actually brought a building to completion. His Einsteinturm (Einstein tower, 1919–21; figs. 36, 37) demonstrated the elastic properties of new materials. Sketches related to the project were exhibited at Paul Cassirer's gallery in late 1919.[86]

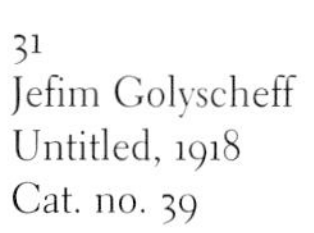

31
Jefim Golyscheff
Untitled, 1918
Cat. no. 39

32
Hermann Finsterlin
Architekturentwürfe
(Architectural sketches)
Cat. no. 35

33
Hermann Finsterlin
Grundriss, Serie III, Blatt 7, c. 1922
(Ground plan, series III, sheet 7)
Cat. no. 29

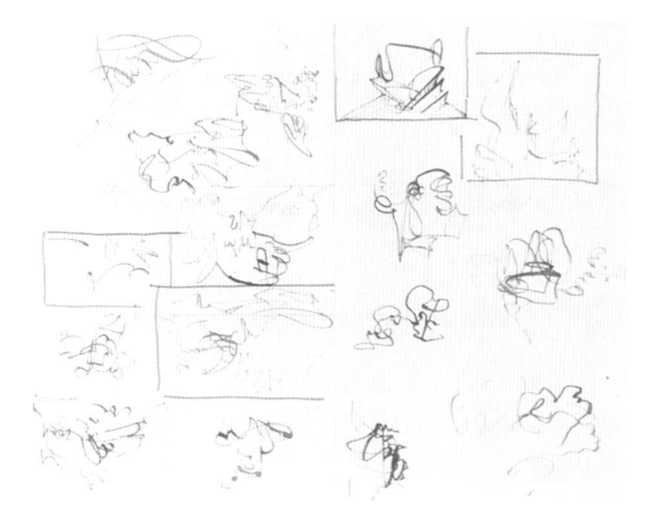

34
Erich Mendelsohn
Skizze für ein Bahnhofsgebäude—Perspektive, 1914
(Sketch for a railroad station—perspective)
Cat. no. 140

37
Erich Mendelsohn
Einsteinturm, Potsdam, 1919–21

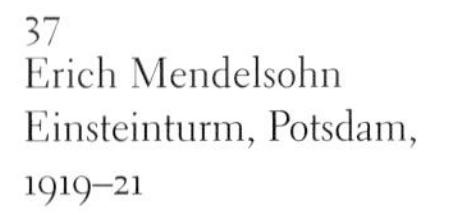

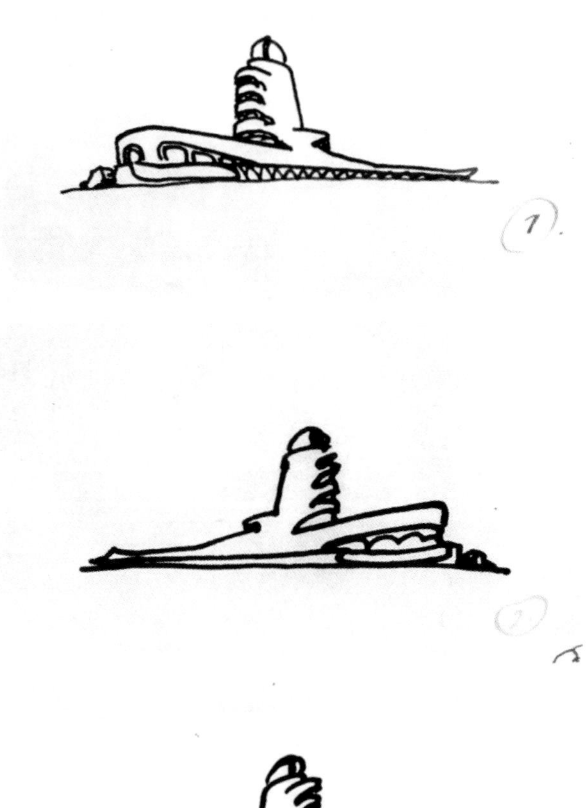

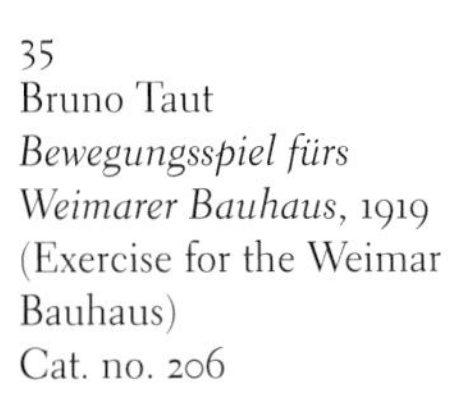

35
Bruno Taut
Bewegungsspiel fürs Weimarer Bauhaus, 1919
(Exercise for the Weimar Bauhaus)
Cat. no. 206

36
Erich Mendelsohn
Einsteinturm: Drei Skizzenblätter mit je einer Perspektive (von Nordwesten und Nordosten) in verschiedenen Fassungen, 1920
(Einstein tower: Three sketches with one perspective each [from northwest and northeast] in different versions)
Cat. no. 143

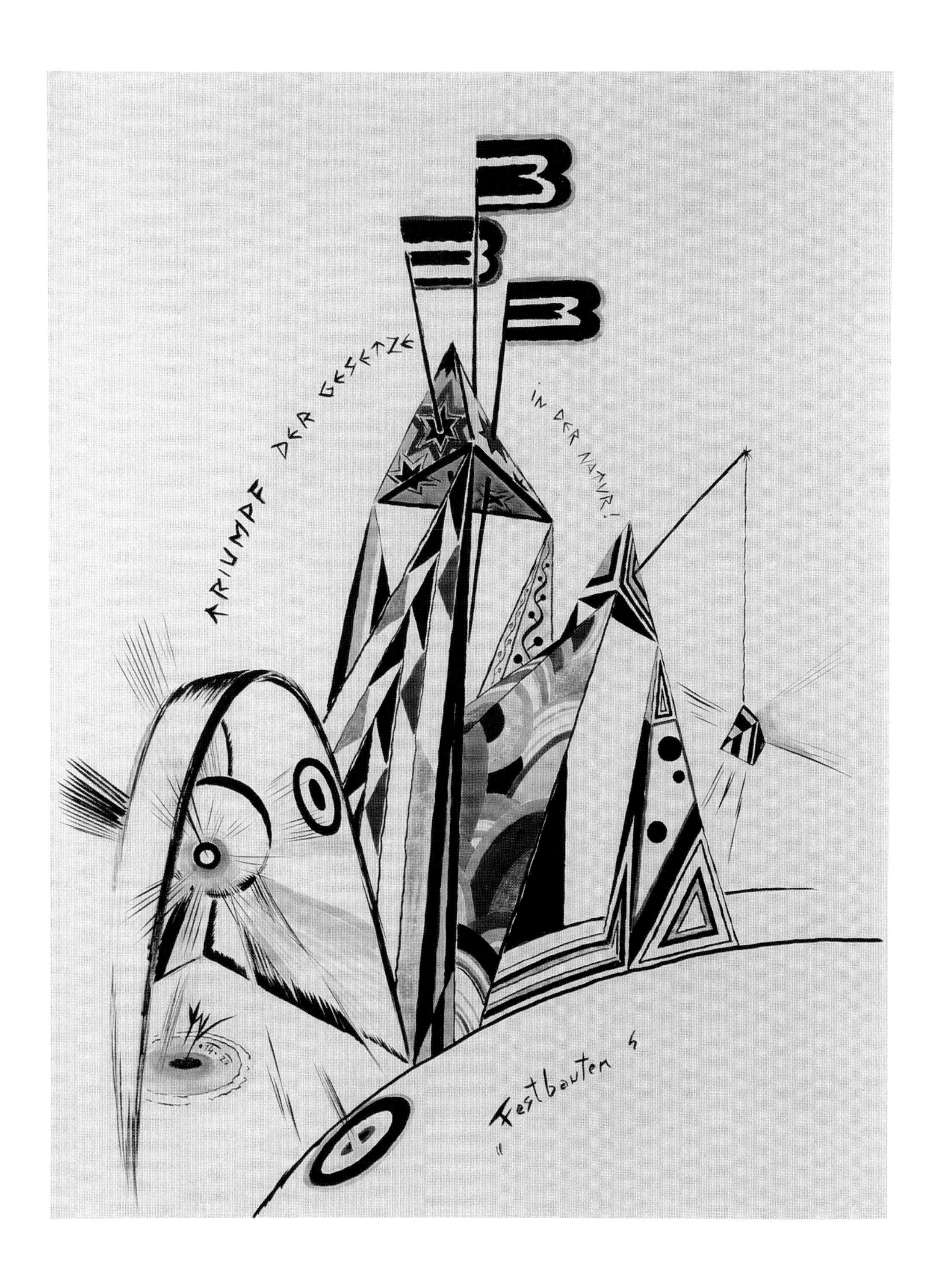
TRIUMPF DER GESETZE
IN DER NATUR!
"Festbauten"

38
Wenzel Hablik
Festbauten: "Triumpf der Gesetze in der Natur!" 1920
(Festival buildings: "Triumph of the laws of nature!")
Cat. no. 59

Wenzel Hablik, who inscribed such statements as "trust only in nature and respect her laws"[87] and "triumph of the laws of nature" (see fig. 38) across his crystalline fantasies, had treated architecture as a creation of nature a decade earlier in his portfolio of twenty etchings entitled Schaffende Kräfte (Creative forces, 1909; see fig. 39). His representations of thrusting geological formations, cresting waves, and billowing clouds of air and mist producing crystal caverns and castles hark back to the Romantic image of the *Bergkristall* (mountain crystal).[88] Hablik studied at the Vienna school of applied arts around the turn of the century, and his works reflect the Jugendstil conception of architectural forms as conveyors of significance and emotion, as well as his fascination with crystals (see fig. 40).

Crystalline castles nestled in the mountains also appeared in the 1904 book *Architektur-Skizzen* (Architectural sketches) by Hermann Billing, teacher of Hans Luckhardt and Max Taut (Bruno Taut's brother [see fig. 43]). The crystal remained a popular metaphor for the unity of material nature and the immaterial spirit among Expressionist artists and writers, partly as a result of the writings of the influential monist philosopher and Darwinian biologist Ernst Haeckel, whose *Kristallseelen* (Crystal souls) was published in 1917.[89] Wilhelm Worringer believed that "transcendental art sets out with the aim of de-organicising the organic...in the world of the inorganic. This led...to rigid lines, to inert crystalline form."[90] A dominant motif in the works of Carl Krayl, Moriz Melzer, and Rudolf Schwarz (see figs. 117, 41, 42), crystalline forms linger on in Hablik's 1925 *Museum im Hochgebirge* (Museum in the high mountains; fig. 44) from the portfolio Cyklus Architektur—Utopie (Architectural cycle—utopia) and appeared throughout the few built examples of Expressionist architecture, for example, Bruno Taut's seminal Glashaus (Glass house; see figs. 120, 121) for the 1914 Werkbund exhibition in Cologne and Gropius's monument to the March dead (see figs. 45, 46).[91] Taut's Glashaus combined the basic elements of his earlier paintings (nature, water, cosmos) and emphasized light, air, water, and, above all, glass, for Behne the "most bodiless, most elementary, most flexible material."[92] The inert crystalline "topos" of the Romantic Bergkristall, where "sublime, profound silence" venerates the cosmos, was described in a short prose piece by poet Paul Scheerbart included in Taut's utopian book *Die Stadtkrone* (The city-crown, 1919) and reflected in Taut's *Alpine Architektur* (Alpine architecture, 1919; see figs. 113, 114).[93]

Nature was also evoked in Finsterlin's organic "form play," based on the natural formations of caves, bones, sand dunes, and plants (see fig. 132). The use of organic forms had prewar antecedents in the work of Henry van de Velde and in Rudolf Steiner's Goetheanum of 1913 (see fig. 47). Steiner, who was not trained as an architect, profoundly influenced several of the Expressionists, including Finsterlin, Hablik, and Kandinsky, through his occult world view of anthroposophy. His architecture was derived from his many spheres of activity (including mathematics, literature, and philosophy) and the principle of "organic development, " which affects linear movement, sculptural form, and the metamorphosis of form.[94]

In mid-1919, after the unknown architects exhibition, political stability began to return with the enactment of a Weimar constitution that left many of the conservative forces in power. This brought an end to chiliastic expectations for social change within the avant-garde.[95] Yet none of the ambitions of the Arbeitsrat had been realized; nor were there financial resources for building. Hoping to keep the ambitions of the "imaginary architects" alive, Taut formed a pseudo-Masonic secret society of a select group of twelve members (see Appendix). The playwright and poet Alfred Brust, who had not been an

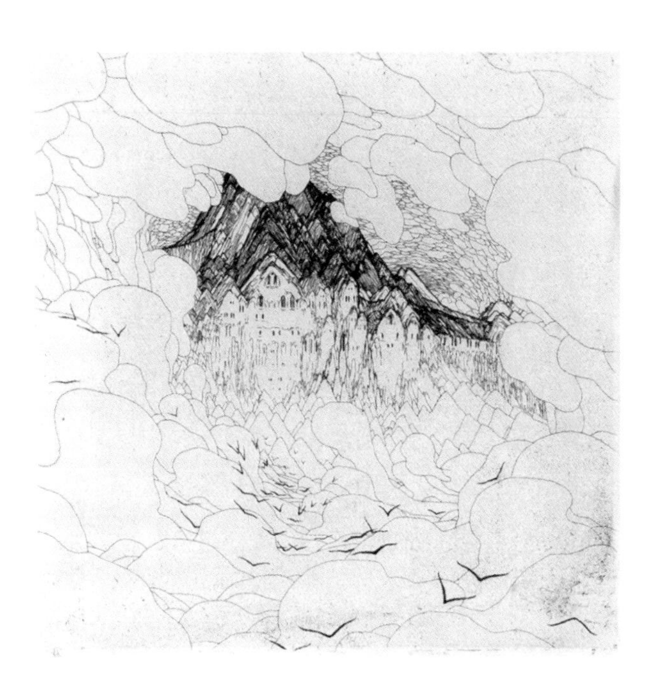

39
Wenzel Hablik
Untitled, 1909
Cat. no. 57

40
Wenzel Hablik
Kristallschloss, 1903
(Crystal castle)
Cat. no. 52

Arbeitsrat member, also joined and provided the name *Gläserne Kette* (Crystal chain), using glass as a metaphor of transcendence and alluding to the members' exchange of ideas through written correspondence. Because the Gläserne Kette participants resided throughout Germany, they circulated essays, drawings, designs, and letters, often as photostat or carbon copies. These rudimentary forms of printmaking could produce exquisite results (see fig. 48). All the participants used pseudonyms—Taut was *Glas* (glass); Luckhardt, *Zacken* (spikes); Krayl, *Anfang* (beginning); Finsterlin, *Prometh* (Prometheus); and Gropius, *Mass* (measure or proportion)—which lent an occult aura to the proceedings, especially when the aliases appeared in the periodical *Frühlicht* (Daybreak). These publications, however, were the result of strategic decisions; as Taut proclaimed: "We must guard the bud carefully. Therefore no great 'actions.' Only occasional publications."[96]

From Taut's first letter the group was imbued with the Nietzschean idea of a select humanity, the self-elected community espoused earlier by Landauer. They would "do all the hard groundwork…[for] those who will come *after* us."[97] While projects ranging from Hablik's collaborative Bible-like book to a jointly produced spectacular fairy-tale film spanning two thousand years were proposed,[98] the main unifying ambition remained a large-scale architectural project, "the Idea," a building "of such dimensions that it could be achieved only by an army of workers fired by the joy of creation" (see Appendix). This project would be a "monument to the new law" and the belief prevailed, especially in the writings of Hablik and Taut (see fig. 175), that entrusting it to the laws of nature would guarantee that technology would be found to resolve any technical difficulties. One of Hablik's drawings of this time is inscribed "Provoke the engineers, and they'll create wonders for you. Trust only in nature and respect her laws," while another bears the inscription "Technical things are never impossible as long as they are based on the laws of nature. The laws of nature were also once utopian."[99] Similarly Taut's cult of science combined "religious interpretation, astronomy, and astrology" since "technology is only a slave."[100]

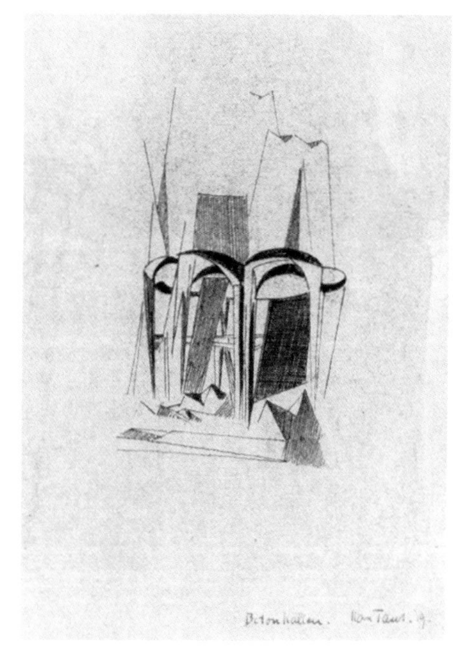

41
Moriz Melzer
Untitled (abstract composition), c. 1919
Cat. no. 138

42
Rudolf Schwarz
Gloria, c. 1920
Cat. no. 199

43
Max Taut
Betonhallen, c. 1919
(Concrete halls)
Cat. no. 213

44
Wenzel Hablik
Museum im Hochgebirge, 1925
(Museum in the high mountains)
Cat. no. 68

The Gläserne Kette's activities culminated in *Neues Bauen* (New building), an exhibition of drawings held in May 1920 under the auspices of the Arbeitsrat at Neumann's Graphisches Kabinett. An accompanying pamphlet entitled *Ruf zum Bauen* (see Appendix) included Behne's essay rejecting current plans for low-income housing (architects should devote themselves to the "higher duty of building the house of the future") and the text of Bruno Taut's *Der Weltbaumeister* (The universal master builder, 1920; see figs. 122, 123, and Appendix), an "architectural drama for symphonic music" conveying the idea of a cosmic force shaping nature and architectural form.[101] The synesthetic theme was continued in architect Hans Scharoun's "Gedanken zum Theaterraum" (Thoughts on theatrical space; see Appendix), while Hans Hansen expanded on Taut's "city-crown" idea of a utopian community dispersed around a central building (see Appendix). Scheerbart's influence was apparent in a proto-Constructivist tendency emerging among the utopian architects.[102] His 1914 *Glasarchitektur* (Glass architecture) is quoted in Behne's essay: "Our culture is to a certain extent the product of our architecture. If we want our culture to rise to a higher level, we are obliged, for better or worse, to change our architecture."[103]

Taut had earlier located the principles for such a transformation in Expressionist painting. In a 1914 article in *Der Sturm*, entitled "Eine Notwendigkeit" (A necessity; see Appendix), he found in the "purely synthetic and abstract" paintings of Kandinsky, Marc, Robert Delaunay, and Alexander Archipenko not only a synthesis of painting, sculpture, and architecture but also a constructive approach: "On every side there is talk of the construction of images." A "structural intensity" would be realized in the glass, iron, and concrete of the new architecture: "The edifice of ideal architecture that the new art already represents must manifest itself in a visible building. And it is a necessity that this happen."

A decided shift toward pragmatism and functionality had begun throughout the German avant-garde by 1920, when even Taut was engaged in plans for a housing estate at Ruhland. The term *utopia* was now becoming a liability, leading him to state in one of the

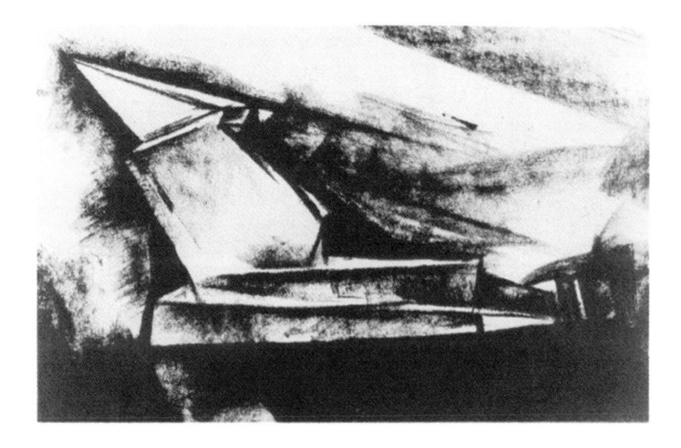

last Gläserne Kette letters: "Long live Utopia!... Hurrah!... In a word, I no longer want to draw Utopias 'in principio,' but absolutely palpable Utopias that 'stand with both feet on the ground" (see Appendix). This pragmatism marks a rejection of the illustration of utopias in favor of an aesthetic of embodiment, the testing of an epochal "locating" or reification of the "no place." Transcending literary genres and historicist concepts, utopia was now taking on the epistemological, rather than nostalgic, purpose of discovering and embodying knowledge. Fragmentary traces or signatures could offer clues for the realization of a utopian future, even if, as thinkers from Kant to Jean-François Lyotard have claimed, the impossibility of realizing a utopia in art leads back to an awareness of the sublime.[104]

As the writings of Ernst Bloch demonstrate, the fates of utopia and the avant-garde had become intertwined. Social conditions in Germany in the late 1910s had placed avant-garde artists and writers in an uncomfortable position between *Politischen* (political activists who viewed art about future conditions as escapist) and *Geistigen* (artists and literati, often of mystical inclination, who sought to get beyond both materialism and the "bloodless intellect," but whose elitism could blind them to social realities).[105] With both camps having fallen short of their goals, the credibility of the avant-garde as seers guiding a "movement" was at stake. Bloch was a well-read intellectual who had trained as a musician, studied sociology under Simmel (with Georg Lukács), and had subscribed to the Marxist view that social conditions were defined by the material conditions of the present. He espoused a solution that combined mystical and material concerns in *Geist der Utopie* (Spirit of utopia, 1918; see Appendix) and "Über das noch nicht bewusste Wissen" (On

45
Walter Gropius
Grabdenkmal der Märzgefallenen, 1923
(Grave monument to the March dead, Weimar)
Cat. no. 47

46
Walter Gropius
Grabdenkmal der Märzgefallenen, Weimar, 1922

47
Rudolf Steiner
Goetheanum, Dornach, Switzerland, 1913

48
Wenzel Hablik
Siedlungsanlage einer Familie,
c. 1920
(Family housing plan)
Cat. no. 62

49
Jefim Golyscheff
Ip'erioum, c. 1918
Watercolor, ink, and collage
7 7/8 x 10 3/4 in. (20.0 x 27.3 cm)
Arturo Schwarz collection,
Milan

50
John Heartfield and
George Grosz
Leben und Treiben in Universal-City, um 12 Uhr 5 Mittags, c. 1919
(Life and times in universal city at five past noon)
Cat. no. 79

preconscious knowledge, 1919; see Appendix). Artists, he believed, could convey a "not-yet-conscious" foretaste of a "still unknown, inchoate utopia" in harmony with the forces of nature in the immediacy of aesthetic experience.[106] Although far more incomplete and fragmentary than nostalgic projections of the future, such clues to a utopia were far more securely validated in the authenticity of being.[107] The raison d'être of art was regained in its function as the embodiment of a subjective knowledge of future perfection.

The Dadaists, and some of the Arbeitsrat members associated with them, soon took a similar functionalist approach while embracing the fragmentary conditions of modernity. Beginning where the Cubist collage and objet trouvé left off, they developed the new medium of photomontage (see figs. 137, 167). For them, as for Bloch, the heterogeneous residue of the surrounding culture still held mystical value,[108] at the same time affording a critical means of disrupting the syntax and cohesiveness of established culture. The Dadaists critiqued the Expressionists' utopias in heterotopias, to borrow, Michel Foucault's word for "counter-sites, a kind of effectively enacted utopia in which the real sites...that can be found within the culture, are simultaneously represented, contested, and inverted."[109]

Utopian visions of a great German architecture were parodied in Johannes Baader's assemblage *Das grosse Plasto-Dio-Dada-Drama* (The great plasto-dio-Dada-drama, 1920; see fig. 177), a "Dadaist monumental architecture" accompanied by a satirical manifesto (see Appendix), which was shown at the *Erste internationale Dada-Messe* (First international Dada fair; see fig. 50) in Berlin in 1920. The collage technique lent itself to a deconstructive appraisal of utopian aspirations in Golyscheff's *Ip'erioum* (c. 1918; fig. 49), which presents the optimistic *Ja!* clipped from the cover of the 1919 publication *Ja! Stimmen des Arbeitsrates für Kunst in Berlin* (Yes! Voices of the Arbeitsrat für Kunst in Berlin) amid other bits of cultural debris: clippings from Dada publications, a photograph of street marchers, an ink box wrapper, a button, and paper currency. But there were constructive principles to be found in this fragmentary and disjunctive world as well. Just as nature uses simple elements to build complex structures, Golyscheff, Raoul Hausmann, Krayl, Taut, and Schwarz (see figs. 51, 52) all deliberately constructed architectonic images from a reductive, elemental vocabulary. Hausmann generated concrete poetry from the disorder of chance (his poem "Ip'erioum" appears in Golyscheff's collage), while Baader derived imaginary architectural schemes from random forms (see fig. 53).[110] Likewise the combination of play and elemental structuring in children's use of building blocks

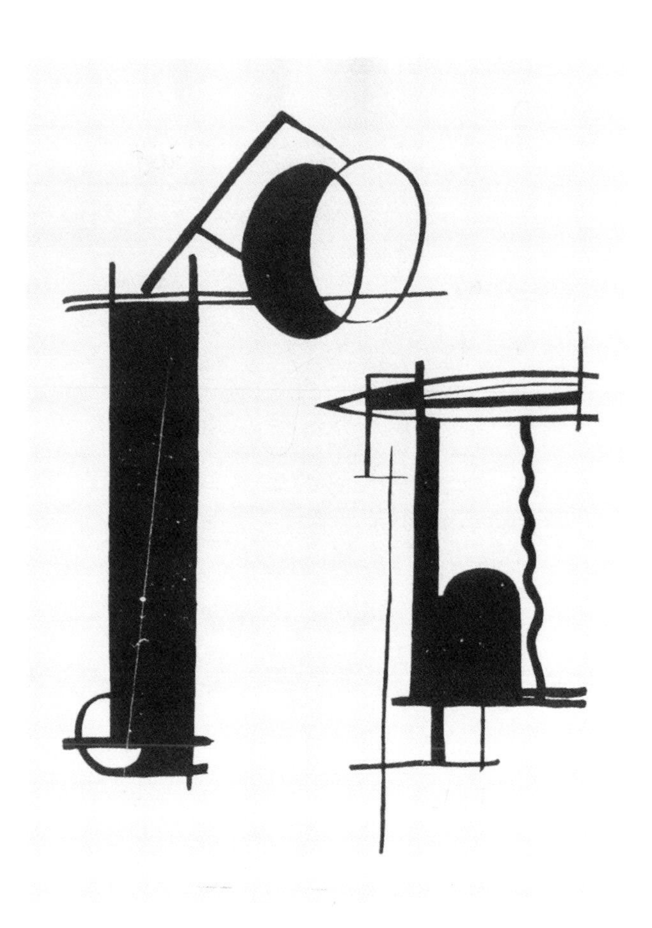

51
Raoul Hausmann
Abstrakte Bildidee (Andruck aus den "Dadaco"), 1919
(Abstract picture idea [Dadaco proof])
Cat. no. 74

52
Carl Krayl
Einen Licht Gruss aus meinem Sternenhaus, 1920
(Light greetings from my star house)
Cat. no. 124

53
Johannes Baader
Architektur für Svoboda (Andruck aus dem "Dadaco"), 1919
(Architecture for Svoboda [Dadaco proof])
Cat. no. 4

inspired Taut's *Dandanah, the Fairy Palace* (1919; fig. 54), Finsterlin's *Das Stilspiel* 1921 (The style game, 1921, 1922; fig. 55), and his highly systematic *Didym-Durchdringungen geometrischer Körper* (Didym-penetrations of geometric bodies, 1922–23; fig. 56).[111]

In an ironic combination of the fragmentary and the functional, the machine metaphor became popular around 1920 as a critique of utopian perfection. Thought processes became mechanical calculations in Hausmann's *Elasticum* (1920; fig. 171) and *Mechanischer Kopf: Der Geist unserer Zeit* (Mechanical head: The spirit of our time, c. 1921; fig. 161), and even nature was taken over by the machine in Hannah Höch's *Mechanischer Garten* (Mechanical garden, 1920; fig. 57). This critique of functionalist perfection harks back to Scheerbart's influential book *Das Perpetuum Mobile* (The perpetual motion machine, 1910), in which the machine is a metaphor for an ironic, dysfunctional utopia that never comes about, despite the determined fantasy and invention of the narrator-protagonist. Molzahn blended the pantheistic cosmic forms of his earlier *Schöpfung* (Creation, 1917; fig. 69) into the world of mechanical processes in his portfolio Zeit-Taster: Eine kleine Kollektion utopisch-phantastischer Maschinen und Apparate (Time-feeler: A small collection of utopian fantastic machines and apparatuses, 1921; see figs. 58, 170). Despite its parody of utopianism, the "role" of Dadaism, by Hausmann's own declaration, had a familiar utopian ring: Dadaism was "a form of transition," using "the concrete" and "satire" to get beyond the "sea of new form" and "cathedral style" in which Expressionism had become grounded.[112] No longer the apocalyptic transformation of Heinrich Vogeler's *Die sieben Schalen des Zorns (Offenbarung Johannis)* (The Seven Bowls of Wrath [Revelation to John], 1918; fig. 2),[113] the path to the future was to be discerned in the efficient functioning of processes created and set in motion by humans in collaboration with natural laws and principles. The "technician…the designer of machines…the scientific experimenter" of Hausmann's "Lob des Konventionellen" (In praise of the conventional; see Appen-

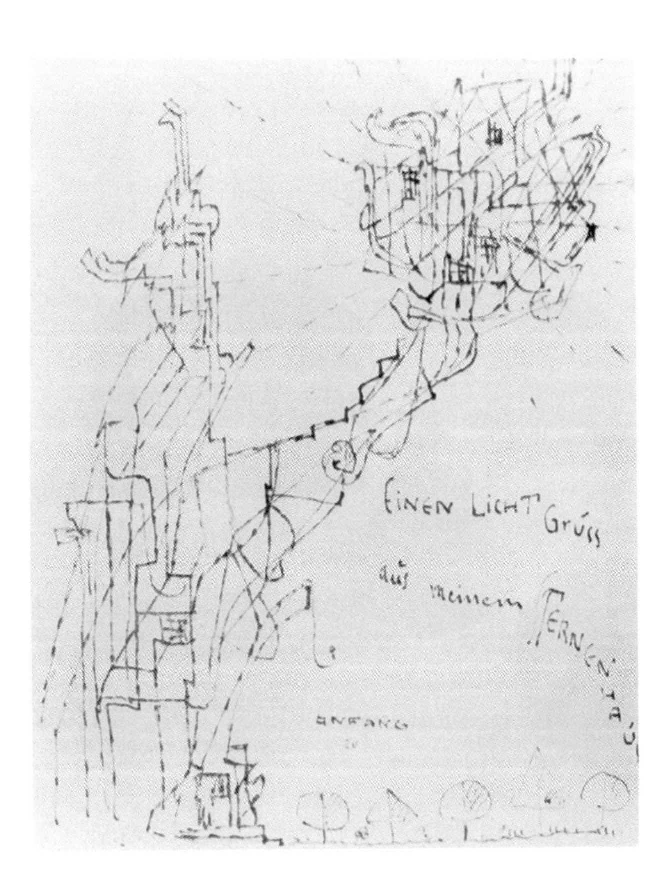

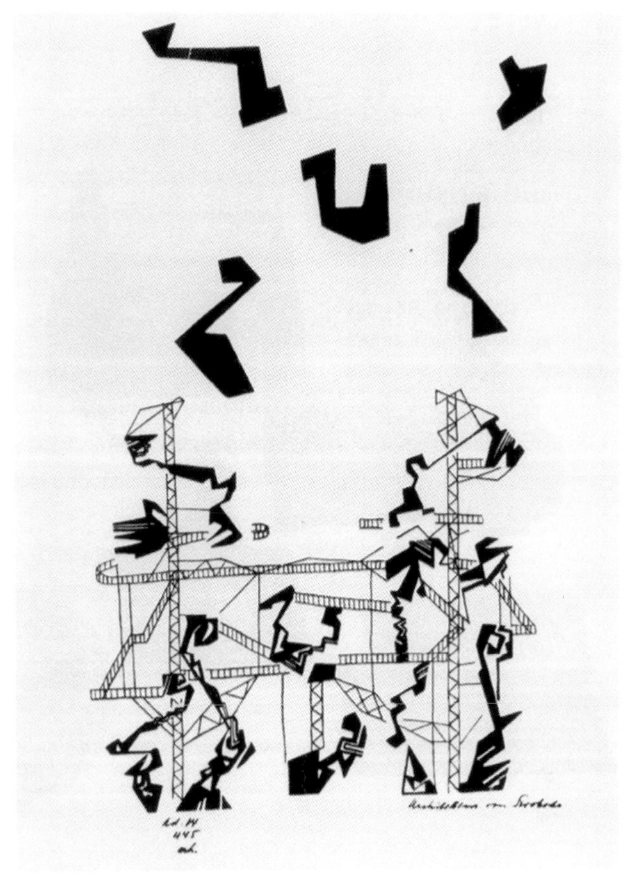

54
Bruno Taut
Dandanah, The Fairy Palace
1919
Cat. no. 207

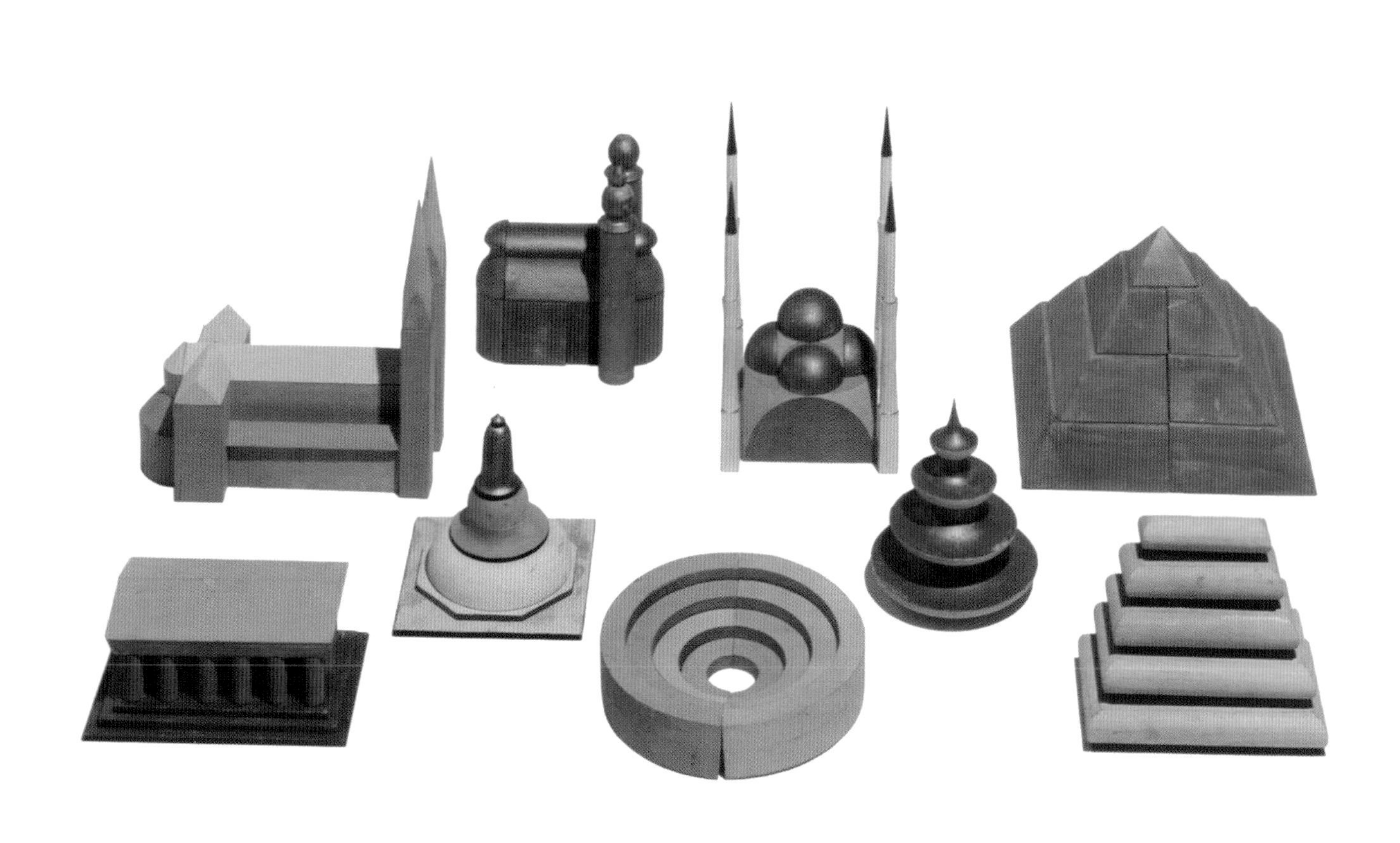

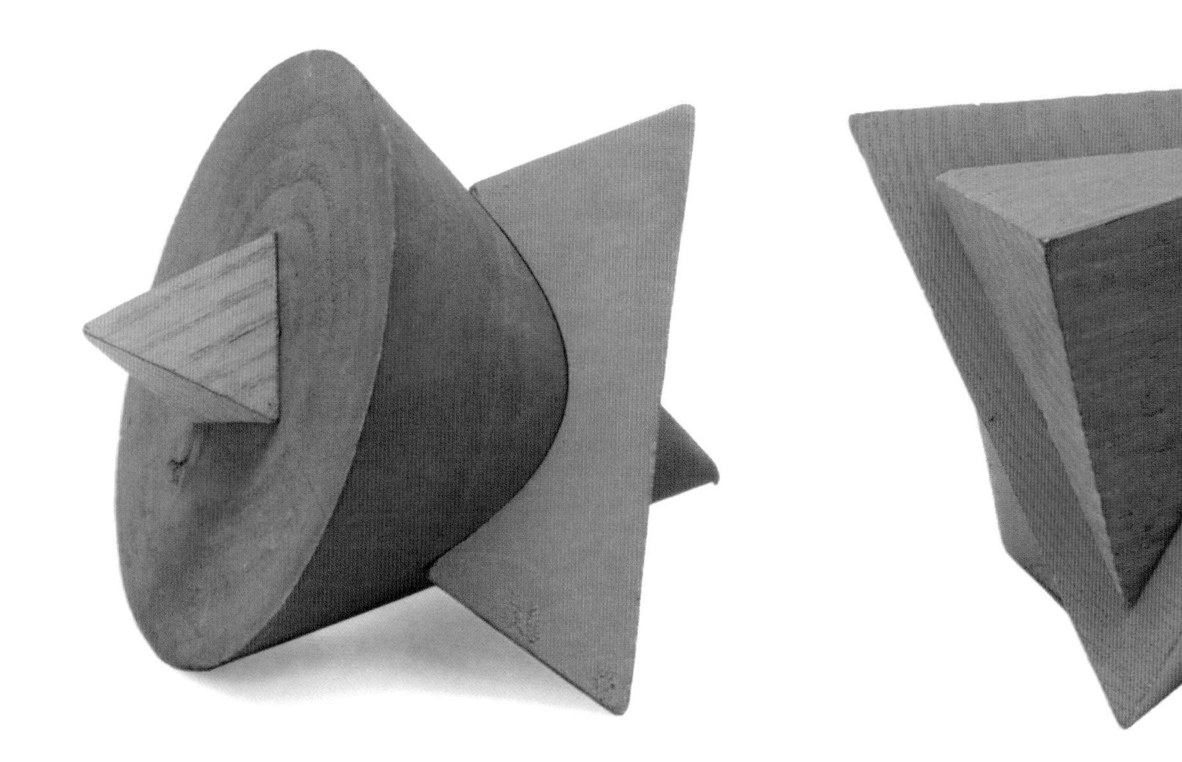

dix) and his watercolor *Die Ingenieure* (The engineers, 1920; fig. 59) immerses himself in the immediacy of the present to decipher the clues to the future and construct a new world.

Despite the new pragmatism and the concurrent "end of Expressionism" being decreed by its former defenders around 1920, architectural utopias continued to thrive in film and on the stage, both art forms having come late to Expressionism. With the arrival of Oskar Schlemmer and Lothar Schreyer at the Bauhaus in 1921, a revival of autonomous art as the setting for utopian visions was provided by the Bauhaus stage. Recognizing the emphasis on architecture throughout the Bauhaus, Schlemmer commented: "Because of our economic depression we may possibly not be able to build for a long time. There are no great assignments for the utopian fantasies of the moderns. There is space for this in the illusionary world of the theater."[114]

At a time when Taut was attempting to realize his *Glanzwelt* (glistening world) of the imagination on the stage,[115] Schlemmer was presenting a new totality of humanity, space, abstraction, and movement in his *Triadisches Ballett* (Triadic ballet). In 1926 Bauhaus student Andor Weininger produced his *Mechanische Bühnen-Revue* (Mechanical stage revue; see fig. 140), a *Gesamtkunstwerk* (total work of art) in which light, sound, and motion are blended. Such experiments continued throughout the 1920s, leading to Roman Clemens's *"Russisches": Bühnenbild zum "Spiel aus Form, Farbe, Licht und Ton"* ("Russian": Stage design for "Play of form, color, light, and sound"; fig. 141), Kandinsky's designs for Modest Mussorgski's *Pictures at an Exhibition* (see fig. 143), and Arnold Schoenberg's design for his musical drama *Die glückliche Hand* (The fortunate hand; see fig. 60), which departs even further from theatrical convention toward a total synesthesia of light and sound.

The film medium afforded an imaginary realm in which the fantasies of several of the Expressionist architects reached fruition. Hans Poelzig, whose baroque tendencies had earlier been seen in his revamping of the Grosses Schauspielhaus in Berlin (see figs. 61, 62), also created the grottolike Jewish ghetto in Paul Wegener's *Der Golem* (The golem, 1920). By contrast neither his ambitious project for the Salzburg Festspielhaus nor his plan for a way chapel were realized (see figs. 63, 64). Grand set designs such as those of Erich Kettelhut for Fritz Lang's film *Metropolis* were the only possible realization of the Expressionist architects' dreams of urban skyscrapers (see figs. 138, 151).

UTOPIA AND MODERNISM

We have seen how the concept of utopia is both paradoxical and productive in its inherent challenge to make from the imaginary "no place" an actual "good place." Utopia functioned within modernism as a continuous, constructive means of self-critical renewal, an enactment of the central tenet of the avant-garde: creative artistic endeavors can embody hope and prepare the way for better conditions for humanity. The quest for utopia had a corresponding conservative side, rooted in religious, philosophic, and literary traditions that were being challenged by the new social and cultural conditions of modernity. Clues to a utopia depended on a distanced and autonomous nature or art, both assumed to be fully experienced only in aesthetic contemplation. Conditions of modernization threatened this distance, especially the heterogeneous and fragmentary experience of the metropolis. The increasing social dislocation and the commodification of cultural exchange so well described by Simmel endangered the essential mission of an avant-garde that saw itself as based in historical progress and embodying the future in works of art.

55
Hermann Finsterlin
Das Stilspiel 1921, 1922
(The style game, 1921)
Cat. no. 30

56
Hermann Finsterlin
Didym-Durchdringungen geometrischer Körper, 1922–23
(Didym-penetrations of geometric bodies)
Cat. no. 32

With unprecedented resilience, however, utopian visions reconciled the increasing hegemony of the present and the growing rejection of the "no place" of the future, countering a disjunctive reality with principles of building and structuring derived from art and nature, and eventually accommodating that reality with a resolute pragmatism. Ironically this reaction against the utopias of the past was both the salvation of the avant-garde and the death knell for the fantasies that had sustained its mission during modernism's darkest days. A better world could no longer be sought in the timeless and placeless realms imagined in the Gläserne Kette correspondence but instead would be built, for better or worse, in the modern industrialized culture of the Weimar era. As events unfolding into our time have brought a clearer recognition of what was at stake, we may begin to hear the resounding truth in these words from Behne's review of the unknown architects exhibition: "A utopia is...no laughing matter."[116]

57
Hannah Höch
Mechanischer Garten, 1920
(Mechanical garden)
Cat. no. 88

58
Johannes Molzahn
Zeit-Taster: Eine kleine Kollektion utopisch-phantastischer Maschinen und Apparate, 1921
(Time-feeler: A small collection of utopian fantastic machines and apparatuses)
Cat. no. 158

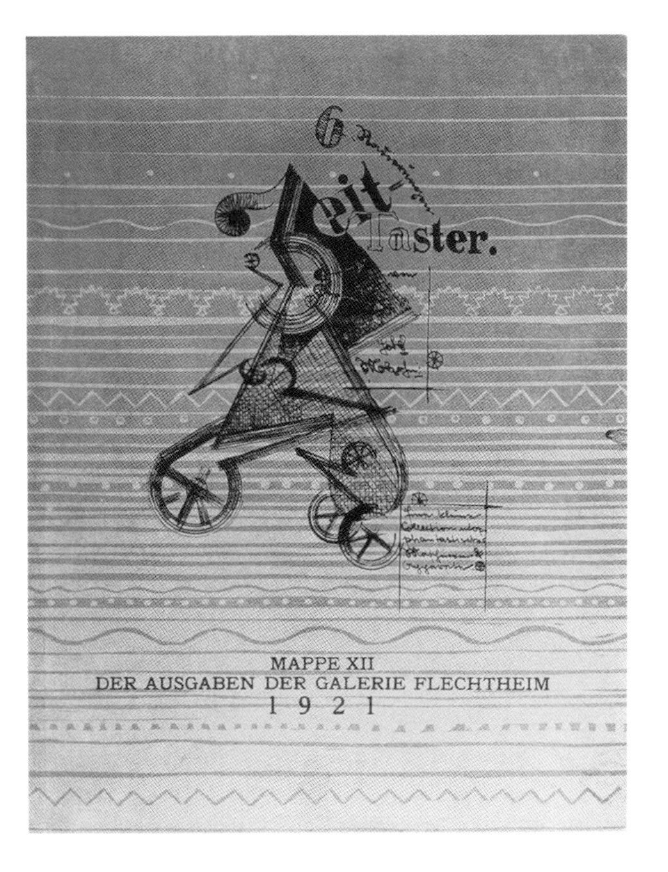

59
Raoul Hausmann
Die Ingenieure, 1920
(The engineers)
Watercolor on paper
13 7/8 x 9 5/16 in. (35.2 x 23.7 cm)
Arturo Schwarz collection,
Milan

60
Arnold Schoenberg
Szenenentwurf für "Die glückliche Hand": 2. Bild: "Beleuchtungsquelle"
(Sketch for "The fortunate hand": Scene 2, "The source of light")
Cat. no. 196

61
Karl Hubbuch
Probe im Grossen Schauspielhaus, 1922
(Rehearsal in the Grosses Schauspielhaus)
Cat. no. 93

62
Hans Poelzig
Grosses Schauspielhaus, Berlin, 1919

NOTES

1. Bruno Taut, *Die Auflösung der Städte; oder, Die Erde, eine gute Wohnung* (Hagen: Folkwang, 1920), p. 30 (translation by Iain Boyd Whyte); for a complete translation, see *Dissolution of the Cities*, in F. Borsi and G. K. König, *Architettura dell'espressionismo* (Genoa: Vitali e Ghianda, 1967), p. 288.

2. Wassily Kandinsky, "The Great Utopia," in *Kandinsky: Complete Writings on Art*, ed. Kenneth C. Lindsay and Peter Vergo, vol. 1 (Boston: G. K. Hall, 1982), pp. 444–48.

3. Walter Gropius, in *Ausstellung für unbekannte Architekten*, exh. cat. (Berlin: Graphisches Kabinett I. B. Neumann, 1919), unpaginated; translated in Ulrich Conrads, ed., *Programs and Manifestoes on Twentieth-Century Architecture*, trans. Michael Bullock (Cambridge: MIT Press, 1971), p. 47.

4. Ibid., p. 46.

5. Although the term *avant-garde* was not widely used in Germany at this time, it is, as Theda Shapiro has stated, "the only accurate generic term available" for the self-proclaimed "foreseers" of modernism (see *Painters and Politics: The European Avant-Garde and Society, 1900–1925* [New York: Elsevier, 1976], pp. xiv–xv). For a thorough history of German avant-garde institutions and their political involvement at the end of World War I, see Joan Weinstein, *The End of Expressionism: Art and the November Revolution in Germany, 1918–1919* (Chicago: University of Chicago Press, 1990).

6. For example, Wilhelm Worringer, Iwan Goll, and Paul Hatvani; see Paul Raabe, ed., *Expessionismus: Der Kampf um eine literarische Bewegung* (Zurich: Arche, 1987), pp. 173–86.

7. Wolfgang Müller, ed., *Duden Bedeutungswörterbuch* (Mannheim: Bibliographisches Institut, 1985), s.v. "Utopie."

8. Ruth Levitas, *The Concept of Utopia* (Syracuse: Syracuse University Press, 1990), p. 3. On anti-utopia, see Hans Ulrich Seeber, "Bemerkungen zum Begriff 'Gegenutopie,'" in Klaus L. Berghahn and Hans Ulrich Seeber, eds., *Literarische Utopien von Morus bis zur Gegenwart* (Königstein: Athenäum, 1983), pp. 163–71.

9. See Oxford English Dictionary, s. v. "utopia," "eutopia"; Levitas, *Concept of Utopia*, p. 2; Frank E. Manuel and Fritzie P. Manuel, *Utopian Thought in the Western World* (Cambridge, Mass.: Belknap, 1979), p. 1.

10. Kurt Pinthus, "Zur jüngsten Dichtung," *Die weissen Blätter* 2 (December 1915): 1502–10; see also Barbara Drygulski Wright, "Expressionist Utopia: The Pursuit of Objectless Politics," Ph.D. diss., University of California, Berkeley, 1977, p. 17.

11. See Roy F. Allen, *Literary Life in German Expressionism and the Berlin Circles* (Göppingen: Kümmerle, 1974); Walter Fähnders, *Anarchismus und Literatur: Ein vergessenes Kapitel deutscher Literaturgeschichte zwischen 1890 und 1910* (Stuttgart: Metzler, 1987), pp. 171–87.

12. Iain Boyd Whyte, "The Politics of Expressionist Architecture," *Architectural Association Quarterly* 12, no. 3 (1980): 11–17; see also Barbara Drygulski Wright, "Sublime Ambition: Art, Politics, and Ethical Idealism in the Cultural Journals of German Expressionism," in *Passion and Rebellion: The Expressionist Heritage*, ed. Stephen Eric Bronner and Douglas Kellner (New York: Universe Books, 1983), pp. 82–112.

13. Although "der neue Mensch" could be rendered as "the new human being," the translation "the new man" more accurately reflects the gendered attitudes of the Expressionist generation; for a discussion of this complex issue, see Barbara Drygulski Wright, "'New Man,' Eternal Woman: Expressionist Responses to German Feminism," *German Quarterly* 40 (Fall 1987): 587.

14. Paul Hatvani, "Versuch über den Expressionismus," *Die Aktion* 7, nos. 11–12 (1917): cols. 146–50.

15. Walter H. Sokel, *The Writer in Extremis: Expressionism in Twentieth-Century German Literature* (Stanford, Calif.: Stanford University Press, 1959), p. 227; Ernst Bloch, "Über das noch nicht bewusste Wissen," *Die weissen Blätter* 6 (August 1919): 365.

16. Kurt Hiller, "Philosophy des Ziels," *Das Ziel* 1 (1916): 193; Ernst Bloch, *The Utopian Function of Art and Literature* (Cambridge: MIT Press, 1988), p. 12.

17. Quoted in Corona Hepp, *Avantgarde: Moderne Kunst, Kulturkritik und Reformbewegungen nach der Jahrhundertwende* (Munich: Deutscher Taschenbuch Verlag, 1987), p. 22.

18. Quoted in Jill Lloyd, "Primitivism and Modernity: An Expressionist Dilemma," in *German Art in the Twentieth Century: Painting and Sculpture, 1905–1985*, exh. cat. (Munich: Prestel, 1985), p. 110.

19. Oskar Pfister, *Expressionism in Art: Its Psychological and Biological Basis* (1920), p. 195; quoted in Donald Gordon, "German Expressionism," in *"Primitivism" in Twentieth-Century Art: Affinity of the Tribal and the Modern*, exh. cat., ed. William Rubin (New York: Museum of Modern Art, 1984), vol. 2, p. 369.

20. Friedrich Nietzsche, *Also sprach Zarathustra: Ein Buch für alle und Keinen* (Frankfurt: Insel, 1982), p. 16; see also Staatliche Museen, *Expressionisten: Die Avantgarde in Deutschland, ,1905–1920*, exh. cat. [East Berlin: Henschel, 1986), pp. 28–29, where it is suggested that Schmidt-Rottluff might have thought of the term spontaneously.

21. See Harald Szeemann, ed., *Monte Verità–Berg der Wahrheit: Lokale Anthropologie als Beitrag zur Wiederentdeckung einer neuzeitlichen sakralen Topographie*, exh. cat. (Zurich: Kunsthaus Zurich, 1978); Jill Lloyd, "The Brücke Bathers: Back to Nature," in *German Expressionism: Primitivism and Modernity* (New Haven, Conn.: Yale University Press, 1991), pp. 102–29.

22. Lloyd, "Brücke Bathers," p. 112; on Kirchner's progression from the erotic to symbolic "nature imagery," see "Die Gestaltung des Verhältnisses zur Frau," in *E. L. Kirchner: Druckgraphik*, 1905–1936, exh. cat. (Hamburg: Kunstverein, 1978), pp. 66–74.

23. Ernst Ludwig Kirchner, *Chronik KG Brücke* (1913). When "passive" memberships in the Brücke were offered in 1906 as a means of cultivating an otherwise absent sympathetic audience, membership privileges for the twelve-mark annual fee included the remarkable *Jahresmappe*, an annual portfolio of original prints. Nearly half the twenty-six prints that make up the seven Jahresmappen feature nudes.

24. Stanislaw Przybyszewski, "Das Geschlecht," parts 1, 2, *Der Sturm* 6, nos. 31, 32 (1910): 521; see Rose-Carol Washton Long, "Kandinsky's Vision of Utopia as a Garden of Love," *Art Journal* 43 (Spring 1983): 50–60.

25. On the Brücke artists' interest in Jugendstil, see Frances Carey and Antony Griffiths, *The Print in Germany, 1880–1933: The Age of Expressionism*, exh. cat. (London: British Museum, 1984), p. 29; Zdenek Felix, ed., *Erich Heckel, 1883–1970: Gemälde, Aquarelle, Zeichnungen und Graphik*, exh. cat. (Munich: Haus der Kunst, 1983), pp. 43–44.

26. Friedrich von Schiller, "Über Matthissons Gedichte," in *Werke: Nationalausgabe*, vol. 22 (Weimar: Böhlau, 1958), p, 273; A. H. Schmitz, quoted in Leopold Reidemeister, "Die 'Brücke' im Spiegel der Zeitschriftenkritik," *Brücke-Archiv*, no. 1 (1967): 41. See Alice Kuzniar, "The Vanishing Canvas: Notes on German Romantic Landscape Aesthetics," *German Studies Review* 11 (October 1988): 361.

27. Paul Fechter, *Der Expressionismus* (Munich: R. Piper, 1920), p. 22; see also Donald Gordon, *Expressionism: Art and Idea* (New Haven, Conn.: Yale University Press, 1987), pp. 176–77.

28. Lloyd, *German Expression ism*, p. 5; Hermann Obrist, *Neue Möglichkeiten in der bildenden Kunst: Essays* (Leipzig: Eugen Diederichs, 1903), pp. 96–97.

29. Jill Lloyd discusses how these words were being used to describe tribal art in 1903; see "Primitivism and Modernity," p. 106, n. 6.

30. Georg Simmel, *The Conflict in Modern Culture and Other Essays*, ed. and trans. K. Peter Etzkorn (New York: Teachers College Press, 1968), pp. 17, 25.

31. Franz Marc, "The 'Savages' of Germany," in *The Blaue Reiter Almanac*, ed. Klaus Lankheit (New York: Viking, 1974), p. 64 (originally published as "Die 'Wilden' Deutschlands," in *Der blaue Reiter* [Munich: Piper, 1912], pp. 5–7); Wassily Kandinsky, "On the Problem of Form," in *Theories of Modern Art*, ed. Hershel Chipp (Berkeley and Los Angeles: University of California Press, 1971), pp. 159–60 (originally published as "Über die Formfrage," in *Der blaue Reiter*, pp. 74–100); for an example of Kandinsky's admiration of the European symbolists as well as various Russian authors, see "Whither the 'New' Art?" (1911), in *Kandinsky: Complete Writings on Art*, vol. 1, pp. 98–104.

32. *Wassily Kandinsky, Concerning the Spiritual in Art*, trans. M. T. H. Sadler (New York: Dover, 1977); originally published as *Über das Geistige in der Kunst* (Munich: R. Piper, 1911); see Rose-Carol Washton Long, "Expressionism, Abstraction, and the Search for Utopia in Germany," *The Spiritual in Art: Abstract Painting, 1890–1985*, exh. Cat. (Los Angeles: Los Angeles County Museum of Art, 1986), p. 206.

63
Hans Poelzig
Festspielhaus Salzburg, erste Fassung: Zuschauerraum, 1920–21
(Salzburg festival hall, first version: Auditorium)
Cat. no. 177

64
Hans Poelzig
Modell für eine Wegkapelle, 1921
(Model for a way chapel)
Cat. no. 179

33. Kandinsky, *Concerning the Spiritual*, p. 15; see also Rose-Carol Washton Long, "Kandinsky's Abstract Style: The Veiling of Apocalyptic Folk Imagery," *Art Journal* 34 (Spring 1975): 217–28

34. Kandinsky, *Concerning the Spiritual*, p, 14; idem, "Whither the 'New Art,'" p. 103.

35. Kandinsky, *Concerning the Spiritual*, p. 14; see Donald R. Benson, "Kandinsky's Dramatic Reconstruction of Pictorial Space," *Annals of Scholarship* 4 (Fall 1986): 110–21.

36. Wassily Kandinsky, "Second Exhibition of the Editors of the Blaue Reiter" (1912), in *Complete Writings*, vol. 1, p. 228; idem, "On the Question of Form," in Lankheit, *Blaue Reiter Almanac*, p. 149.

37. Wassily Kandinsky, "Malerei als reine Kunst," *Der Sturm* 4, no. 178–79 (1913): 98–99; translated in *Complete Writings*, vol. 1, p. 350.

38. Franz Marc, "Spiritual Treasures," in Lankheit, *Blaue Reiter Almanac*, p. 59.

39. Franz Marc, "Die konstruktiven Ideen der neuen Malerei," *Pan* 2 (21 March 1912): 527–31; idem, "Die neue Malerei," Pan 2 (7 March 1912): 468–71. Both articles are reprinted in Klaus Lankheit, ed., *Franz Marc: Schriffen* (Cologne: DuMont, 1978), pp. 108, 104.

40. Quoted in Ulrich Finke, *German Painting from Romanticism to Expressionism* (London: Thames and Hudson, 1974), p. 198.

41. Klee mentions Kandinsky's "Malerei als reine Kunst" in a diary entry of 24 September 1918 (see Richard Sheppard, "Kandinsky's Early Aesthetic Theory," *Journal of European Studies* 5 [1975]: 19–40); Paul Klee, "Creative Credo," in Werner Schmalenbach, *Paul Klee: The Düsseldorf Collection* (Munich: Prestel, 1986), p. 24; for another translation, see Victor H. Miesel, ed., *Voices of German Expressionism* (Englewood Cliffs, N.J.: Prentice Hall, 1970), p. 87; Klee's essay was untitled when it was first published in Kasimir Edschmid, *Schöpferische Konfession*, Tribune des Kunst und Zeit, no. 13 (Berlin: E. Reiss, 1920), pp. 28–40.

42. Schmalenbach, *Paul Klee*, p. 24.

43. Rainer Piepmeier, "Das Ende der ästhetischen Kategorie 'Landschaft,'" *Westfälische Forschungen: Mitteilungen des Provinzialinstitutes für westfälische Landes- und Volksforschung des Landesverbandes Westfalen-Lippe* 30 (1980): 23.

44. Klee, "Creative Credo," in Miesel, *Voices*, p. 83.

45. Novalis, "Studien zur bildenden Kunst," in *Schriften: Die Werke Friedrich von Hardenbergs*, ed. Paul Kluckhohn and Richard Samuel, vol. 2, *Das philosophische Werk I* (Stuttgart: Kohlhammer, 1960), p. 650; Friedrich Wilhelm Joseph Schelling, *Philosophie der Kunst* (Darmstadt; Wissenschaftliche Buchgesellschaft, 1966). p. 138. See also Kuzniar, "The Vanishing Canvas."

46. Rainer Maria Rilke, *Sämtliche Werke*, ed. Ruth Sieber-Rilke (Wiesbaden: Insel, 1955–66), vol. 5, p. 520. In his 1902 essay on landscape, Rilke recommended that the artist not paint "an impression" or a "human interpretation," for nature was "as foreign to man as the unexplored forest of an undiscovered island." A corresponding art must be "almost hostile…in order to give our existence new meaning."

47. Paul Westheim, "Die Landschaft," *Das Kunstblatt*, no. 1 (January 1920): 7, 17–18.

48. Georg Simmel, "Philosophie der Landschaft," in *Brücke und Tür: Essays des Philosophen zur Geschichte, Religion, Kunst und Gesellschaft*, ed. Michael Landmann (Stuttgart: K. F. Koehler, 1957), p. 140.

49. Leopold Reidemeister, "Der frühe Holzschnitt Erich Heckels," in *Erich Heckel, 1883–1970: Der frühe Holzschnitt*, exh. cat. (Berlin: Brücke Museum, 1983), p. 10.

50. Carl Einstein, *Negerplastik* (Leipzig: Verlag der Weissen Blätter, 1915), p. xx; idem, "Totalität," *Die Aktion* 4, no. 16 (1914): col. 346.

51. Ludwig Meidner, "An Introduction to Painting Big Cities," in Miesel, *Voices*, p. 111; originally published as "Anleitung zum Malen von Grossstadtbildern," in "Das neue Programm," *Kunst und Künstler* 12 (March 1914): 299–314.

52. Hiller's lecture "Utopische Synode der Geister" was announced on the program for the Neopathetisches Cabaret, sponsored by Der Neue Club on 9 November 1910; reproduced in Nina Schneider, *Georg Heym: Der Städte Schultern knacken: Bilder, Texte, Dokumente* (Zurich: Arche, 1987), p. 70.

53. August Endell, *Die Schönheit der grossen Stadt* (Stuttgart: Strecker und Schröder, 1908), p. 31. The work of van Gogh had been presented at the Salon Richter in Dresden in 1908 and in a large exhibition at Paul Cassirer's gallery in Berlin in 1910. Matisse was exhibited at Cassirer's at the end of 1908.

54. [Walter Rathenau], "Die schönste Stadt der Welt," *Die Zukunft* 26 (1899); reprinted in *Impressionen* (Leipzig, 1902), pp. 137–63; see also Lothar Müller, "The Beauty of the Metropolis: Toward an Aesthetic Urbanism in Turn-of-the-Century Berlin," in *Berlin: Culture and Metropolis*, ed. Charles W. Haxthausen and Heidrun Suhr (Minneapolis: University of Minnesota Press, 1990), pp. 39–40; Karl Scheffler, *Berlin: Ein Stadtschicksal* (Berlin: Erich Reiss, 1910), p. 200.

55. Georg Hermann, in Rudolf Grossmann, Um Berlin (Berlin: Paul Cassirer, 1912); reprinted in *Pan* 2, no. 2 (1911–12): 1101–6.

56. Meidner, "Introduction to Painting Big Cities," p. 114.

57. Endell, *Schönheit*, pp. 65, 67, 37.

58. On Endell's theory of vision, see Müller, "Beauty of the Metropolis," pp. 37–57.

59. Meidner, "Introduction to Painting Big Cities," p. 111.

60. Georg Simmel, "The Metropolis and Mental Life," in *The Sociology of Georg Simmel*, ed. Kurt H. Wolff, trans. Hans Gerth (Glencoe, Ill.: Free Press, 1950), pp. 410, 414; originally published as "Die Grossstädte und das Geistesleben," in *Die Grossstadt*, special issue of *Jahrbuch der Gehe-Stiftung zu Dresden* 9 (1903): 185–206.

61. Simmel, "Metropolis and Mental Life," pp. 410, 412.

62. Ludwig Rubiner, "Uff… die Psychoanalyse," *Die Aktion* 3, no. 23 (1913), cols. 565–68; Kurt Hiller, "Über Kultur" (1909), in *Die Weisheit der Langeweile: Eine Zeit- und Streitschrift*, vol. 1 (Leipzig: Kurt Wolff, 1913), p. 49ff.; discussed in Allen, *Literary Life*, pp. 192–96.

63. Quoted in Westheim, "Die Landschaft," p. 7.

64. Simmel, "Metropolis and Mental Life," p. 413; Ernst Ludwig Kirchner, "Die Arbeit E. L. Kirchners," in Eberhard W. Kornfeld, *Ernst Ludwig Kirchner: Nachzeichnung seines Lebens* (Bern: Kornfeld, 1979), p. 341; translated in Charles W. Haxthausen, "'A New Beauty': Ernst Ludwig Kirchner's Images of Berlin," in Haxthausen and Suhr, *Berlin*, pp. 66–67.

65. Kirchner discusses the role of hieroglyphs in his graphic techniques in [Louis de Marsalle], "Über Kirchners Graphik," *Genius* 3, no. 2 (1921): 250–63; translated in Miesel, *Voices*, p. 26.

66. See Rosalyn Deutsche, "Alienation in Berlin: Kirchner's Street Scenes," *Art in America* 71 (January 1983): 64–72; for an interpretation of Kirchner's eroticization of the city, see Haxthausen, "New Beauty," pp. 58–94.

67. See Hanne Bergius, "Berlin als Hure Babylon," in *Die Metropole: Industriekultur in Berlin im 20. Jahrhundert*,

ed. Jochen Boberg, Tilman Fichter, and Eckhart Gillen, Industriekultur deutscher Städte und Regionen (Munich: C. H. Beck, 1986), pp. 102–19.

68. Silvio Vietta, "Grossstadtwahrnehmung und ihre literarische Darstellung: Expressionistischer Reihungsstil und Collage," *Deutsche Vierteljahrsschrift für Literaturwissenschaft und Geistesgeschichte* 48 (May 1974): 354–73.

69. Simmel, "Metropolis and Mental Life," p. 419.

70. Carl Einstein, *Bebuquin; oder, Die Dilettanten des Wunders* (Berlin: Verlag der Wochenschrift "Die Aktion," 1912).

71. Salomo Friedländer, "Absolutismus," *Der Sturm* 4 (January 1914): 162; idem, "Präsentismus: Rede des Erdkaisers an die Menschen," *Der Sturm* 3, no. 144–45 (1913): 253–54. Friedländer had graduated from the University of Jena in 1902 with a dissertation on Schopenhauer and Kant's *Critique of Pure Reason*.

72. Simmel, "Metropolis and Mental Life," p. 420; Salomo Friedländer, *Schöpferische Indifferenz* (Munich: Müller, 1918), pp. xxi, xxiii. The book was begun in 1912 (see Eberhard Roters, "Big-City Expressionism: Berlin and German Expressionism, " in *Expressionism: A German Intuition, 1905–1920*, exh. cat. [New York: Solomon R. Guggenheim Museum, 1980], p. 245).

73. The drawing may be attributed to Behrens on the basis of its similarity to his cover for a 1920 issue of *Das Plakat* (see fig. 24).

74. The largest winners were the Social Democratic Party, with 163 of the 421 seats at stake at the constitutional convention; the Catholic Center Party; with 89 seats; and the Democratic Party, with 75 seats. The Independent Socialists, to which many artists owed their allegiance, won only 22 seats, while the Communists boycotted the elections altogether.

75. Bruno Taut, "A Programme for Architecture," in Conrads, *Programs and Manifestoes*, P. 41.

76. Ulrich Conrads and Hans G. Sperlich, *The Architecture of Fantasy: Utopian Building and Planning in Modern Times*, ed. and trans. Christiane C. Collins and George R. Collins (New York: Praeger, 1962), p. 139.

77. Gropius's ideas, presented in an address on 22 March 1919, survive in the Bauhaus-Archiv in Berlin; see Iain Boyd Whyte, ed. and trans., *The Crystal Chain Letters: Architectural Fantasies by Bruno Taut and His Circle* (Cambridge: MIT Press, 1985), p. 2. On Gropius's position and his role in the internal dynamics of the Arbeitsrat für Kunst, see Weinstein, *End of Expressionism*, pp. 66–67; Iain Boyd Whyte, *Bruno Taut and the Architecture of Activism* (Cambridge: Cambridge University Press, 1982), pp. 123–30.

78. At the time of Gropius's contract negotiations in early 1919, the school was emerging as the successor to the school of fine art and the school of applied arts in Weimar. The name *Bauhaus* was adopted later that year.

79. Adolf Behne, "Zur Einführung in die Ausstellung 'Für unbekannte Architekten,'" in *Sozialistische Monatshefte* 25 (28 April 1919): 422–23; reprinted in Manfred Schlösser, ed., *Arbeitsrat für Kunst, Berlin, 1918–1921*, exh. cat. (Berlin: Akademie der Künste, 1980), pp. 92–93.

80. Schlösser, *Arbeitsrat für Kunst*, p. 90; translated in Conrads, *Programs and Manifestoes*, p. 46.

81. Kurt Gerstenberg, "Revolution in der Architektur," *Der Cicerone* 11 (May 1919): 255–57; reprinted in Schlösser, *Arbeitsrat für Kunst*, pp. 94–95.

82. Joan Ockman, "Reinventing Jefim Golyscheff: Lives of a Minor Modernist," *Assemblage* 11 (April 1990): 75; John Schikowski, "Architekturträume," *Vorwärts*, 29 March 1919; translated in Whyte, *Bruno Taut*, p. 137.

83. Paul Westheim, "Architektonische Phantasien," *Frankfurter Zeitung*, 30 April 1919; reprinted in Schlösser, *Arbeitsrat für Kunst*, pp. 93–94; Gerstenberg, "Revolution in der Architektur," in Schlösser, *Arbeitsrat für Kunst*.

84.. On the romantic theory of the imagination, see August K. Wiedmann, *Romantic Roots in Modern Art: Romanticism and Expressionism, a Study in Comparative Aesthetics* (Old Woking, England: Gresham Books, 1979), pp. 100ff.

85. Gerstenberg, "Revolution in der Architektur," in Schlösser, *Arbeitsrat für Kunst*, pp. 94–95.

86. Dennis Sharp, *Modern Architecture and Expressionism* (New York: George Braziller, 1967), p. 113.

87. Whyte, *Letters*, ill. p. 30.

88. Eugene Santomasso, "Wenzel Hablik: The 'Schaffende Kräfte' Folio and Its Relationship to Expressionist Aims and Ideals," *Architectural Association Quarterly* 12, no. 3 (1980): 25–38.

89. Hermann Billing, *Architektur-Skizzen* (Stuttgart, 1904); see Wolfgang Pehnt, *Expessionist Architecture in Drawings* (New York: Van Nostrand Reinhold, 1985), ill. p. 9; Ernst Haeckel, *Kristallseelen: Studien über das anorganische Leben* (Leipzig: Alfred Kröner, 1917).

90. Wilhelm Worringer, *Abstraction and Empathy*, trans. Michael Bullock (New York: International Universities Press, 1967), pp. 133–34; originally published as *Abstraktion und Einfühlung: Ein Beitrag zur Stilpsychologie* (Munich: R. Piper, 1911); see also Roland März, "Dac Kristallinische im deutschen Espressionismus: Feininger, Klee und andere," *Bildende Kunst*, no. 3 (1987): 111–12, Regine Prange, *Das Kristalline als Kunstsymbol: Bruno Taut und Paul Klee* (Hildesheim: Georg Olms, 1991), p. 29ff.

91. Other examples include Wassili Luckhardt and Rudolf Belling's advertising sign on the Avus in Berlin (1922–23) and the Lunapark structures Albulabahn (1920) and Der gläserne See (The glass sea, 1921); see Whyte, *Bruno Taut*, pp. 218–20.

92. Adolf Behne, "Gedanken über Kunst und Zweck, dem Glashaus gewidmet," *Kunstgewerbeblatt*, n.s., 27 (October 1915): 4; translated and discussed by Rosemarie Haag

Bletter, in "The Interpretation of the Glass Dream: Expressionist Architecture and the History of the Crystal Metaphor," *Journal of the Society of Architectural Historians* 40 (March 1981): 34. The relationship of Taut's early painting to his entire oeuvre is discussed in Manfred Speidel, "Farbe und Licht: Zum malerischen Werk von Bruno Taut / Colour and Light: On Bruno Taut's Oeuvre as a Painter," *Daidalos*, no. 45 (15 September 1992): 117–35.

93. Paul Scheerbart, "Das neue Leben: Architektonische Apokalypse," in Bruno Taut, *Die Stadtkrone* (Jena: Eugen Diederichs, 1919), pp. 9–15; on the crystal "topos," see Prange, *Das Kristalline*, p. 345.

94. As discussed by Kenneth Bayes in Sharp, *Modern Architecture*, p. 149.

95. The Weimar constitution was ratified on 31 July 1919, becoming law on 11 August.

96. Bruno Taut, letter of 27 December 1919, in Whyte, *Letters*, p. 28.

97. Ibid., pp. 19, 154.

98. See Bruno Taut's letter of 8 July 1920 and his undated letter "The Shoes of Fortune" and Hablik's response of 22 July 1920 (ibid., pp. 118–22, 122–25).

99. Ibid., p. 30; for inscription on Hablik's ink drawing *Fliegende Siedlung* (Flying settlement, 1907–14), see *Wenzel Hablik: Attraverso l'espressionismo / Wenzel Hablik: Expressionismus und Utopie*, exh. cat. (Florence: Museo Mediceo, Palazzo Medici Riccardi, 1989), ill. p. 55; translated in Anthony Tischhauser, "Wenzel Hablik: Crystal Utopias," *Architectural Association Quarterly* 12, no. 3 (1980): 20.

100. Taut, *Dissolution of the Cities*, p. 283; idem, Alpine Architecture, in Borsi and König, *Architettura dell' espressionismo*, p. 267; originally published as *Alpine Architektur* (Hagen: Folkwang, 1919).

101. *Ruf zum Bauen* (Berlin: Wasmuth, 1920); reprinted in Schlösser, *Arbeitsrat für Kunst*, pp. 77–80.

102. As is argued by Rosemarie Haag Bletter, in "Paul Scheerbart's Architectural Fantasies," *Journal of the Society of Architectural Historians* 34 (May 1975): 83–97.

103. Paul Scheerbart, *Glass Architecture* (published in the same volume with Bruno Taut, *Alpine Architecture*), ed. Dennis Sharp, trans. James Palmer (New York: Praeger, 1972), p. 41; originally published as *Glasarchitektur* (Berlin: Verlag "Der Strum," 1914).

104. See Jean-François Lyotard, "Complexity and the Sublime," ICA *Documents 4: Postmodernism* (London Institute for Contemporary Art, 1986), pp. 10–11; for a discussion of these tendencies in relation to Expressionism, see Jochen Schulte-Sasse, "Carl Einstein; or, The Postmodern Transformation of Modernism," *Modernity and the Text: Revisions of German Modernism*, ed. Andreas Huyssen and David Bathrick (New York: Columbia University Press, 1989) pp. 36–59.

105. Michael Stark, *Für und wider den Expressionismus: Die Entstehung der Intellektuellendebatte in der deutschen Literaturgeschichte* (Stuttgart: Metzler, 1982), p. 29.

106. Bloch, "Über das noch nicht bewusste Wissen," p. 365; on Bloch's eventual philosophical reconciliation of humanity and nature, see Peter J. Brenner, "Aspekte und Probleme der neueren Utopiediskussion in der Philosophie," in *Utopieforschung: Interdisziplinäre Studien zur neuzeitlichen Utopie*, vol. 1, ed. Wilhelm Vosskamp (Stuttgart: Metzler, 1982), p. 14.

107. See Fredric Jameson, "Ernst Bloch and the Future," in *Marxism and Form* (Princeton, N.J.: Princeton University Press, 1971), pp. 116–59.

108. See Timothy O. Benson, "Mysticism, Materialism, and the Machine in Berlin Dada," *Art Journal* 46 (Spring 1987): 46–55.

109. Michel Foucault, "Of Other Spaces," *Diacritics* 16 (Spring 1986): 24.

110. Hausmann's poem appears in its entirety in *Der Dada*, no. 1 (June 1919): 2, from which Golyscheff clipped it.

111. Other modern artists and architects, including Klee and Frank Lloyd Wright, have expressed their indebtedness to childhood experiences with building blocks (see Bonnie Yochelson, "Paul Klee and Architecture," *Marsyas* 20 [1979–80]: 61–70).

112. Raoul Hausmann, "Objektive Betrachtung der Rolle des Dadaismus," *Der Kunsttopf*, no. 4 (October 1920): 62–68; reprinted in Raoul Hausmann, *Bilanz der Feierlichkeit: Texte bis 1933*, ed. Michael Erlhoff, vol. 1 (Munich: Text und Kritik, 1982), pp. 108–13.

113. For a discussion of Vogeler's cosmic theory, see Heinrich Wiegand Petzet, *Von Worpswede nach Moskau: Heinrich Vogeler, ein Künstler zwischen den Zeiten* (Cologne: DuMont, 1977), pp. 138–39.

114. Oskar Schlemmer, letter of 14 June 1921 to Otto Meyer Amden, in Dirk Scheper, Oskar Schlemmer: *Das triadische Ballett und die Bauhausbühne*, Schriftenreihe der Akademie der Künste, no. 20 (Berlin: Akademie der Künste, 1988), p. 32.

115. Bruno Taut, "Zum neuen Theaterbau," *Das hohe Ufer 1* (August 1919): 204–8. In 1920 Taut proposed a performance of his *Weltbaumeister* in Darmstadt, which, however, never materialized. In 1921 he created the stage designs for a performance of Schiller's *Die Jungfrau von Orleans* at the Deutsches Theater in Berlin (see Whyte, *Bruno Taut*, pp. 209–12).

116. Behne, "Zur Einführung," in Schlösser, *Arbeitsrat für Kunst*, pp. 92–93.

65
Erich Heckel
Stehendes Kind, 1910
(Standing child)
Cat. no. 80

66
Franz Marc
Versöhnung, 1912
(Reconciliation)
Cat. no. 130

67
Wassily Kandinsky
Orientalisches, 1911
(Oriental)
Cat. no. 100

68
Erich Heckel
Parksee, 1914
(Lake in a park)
Cat. no. 85

69
Johannes Molzahn
Schöpfung, 1917
(Creation)
Cat. no 154

70
Wassily Kandinsky
Paradies, 1911–12
(Paradise)
Cat. no. 101

71
Heinrich Campendonk
Adam und Eva, c. 1925
(Adam and Eve)
Cat. no. 12

72
Otto Mueller
Adam und Eva, 1920–23
(Adam and Eve)
Cat. no. 167

73
Max Beckmann
Adam und Eva, 1917
(Adam and Eve)
Cat. no. 5

74
Richard Seewald
Paradies, 1914
(Paradise)
Cat. no. 204

REINHOLD HELLER

Bridge to Utopia: The Brücke as Utopian Experiment

A MAP OF THE WORLD THAT DOES NOT INCLUDE UTOPIA IS NOT WORTH EVEN GLANCING AT, FOR IT LEAVES OUT THE ONE COUNTRY AT WHICH HUMANITY IS ALWAYS LANDING.
OSCAR WILDE[1]

In its brief founding manifesto of 1905 (see Appendix), the Dresden Expressionist artists' group Brücke (Bridge)[2] projected a vision of an ideal future, one in which established powers would be supplanted by youth. In shared values of youth, community would be found. Youth and its art would represent "freedom of movement," intellectual as well as physical, so as to permit "direct and authentic" expression of those unconscious or subconscious forces and desires in which artistic productivity resides. Authenticity, freedom, and youth were the hallmarks of a new age, not only of artists but also of their admirers, who would form the nucleus of a transformed humanity. The Brücke would be its initial attempt at realization, an experiment in an alternative communal life-style conceived by artists.

Other than the sparse testimony of the manifesto, the Brücke provided no texts that formulated a utopian society, a vision of an ideal communal future. Nor is there evidence such as books in the artists' libraries which suggests direct contact with the utopian visions recorded by numerous authors since Plato and Sir Thomas More. Neither the noun *utopia* nor the adjective *utopian* appears in the public pronouncements or private correspondence of the artists. Similarly, insofar as utopian desires demand political action to approach fulfillment, the Brücke artists, like most German cultural figures of the time, openly joined no organized political or social movement, supported no political party or organization, and remained outside the actualities of German political life prior to the conflagration of World War I.[3] If we seek to identify the group's utopian convictions, it must be through a kind of archaeological investigation into the life and milieu of the organization and its functions, which extracts utopia from the artists' portrayals of their experiences and visions. Prints, drawings, paintings, and sculptures, as well as the practices of the artists themselves, are the texts and traces of the Brücke's utopian vision, its "dream of a true and just ordering of life."[4]

The Brücke's utopian engagement was not directed at society at large, but at art, culture, and the lives of artists, at the realms of *Geist*—the spirit, soul, and imagination—not at pragmatic *Macht*, or power. Like all attempts to realize utopia, the Brücke's was rooted in opposition to established society and its institutions. The group projected a hoped-for future, a counterimage of a transformed and perfected reality rooted in community and friendship, but it provided no systematic map or blueprint, only enticing, albeit sketchy associations and implications that must be retrieved through critical interpretation.

THE BRÜCKE'S COMMUNAL UTOPIA

In his *Chronik KG Brücke* (Chronicle of the artists' group Brücke, 1913; see fig. 75), Ernst Ludwig Kirchner recalled how he, Erich Heckel, Karl Schmidt-Rottluff, and Fritz Bleyl had come together some ten years earlier, informally at first, then, after 1905, as a

Im Jahre 1902 lernten sich die Maler Bleyl und Kirchner in Dresden kennen. Durch seinen Bruder, einen Freund von Kirchner, kam Heckel hinzu. Heckel brachte Schmidt-Rottluff mit, den er von Chemnitz her kannte. In Kirchners Atelier kam man zum Arbeiten zusammen. Man hatte hier die Möglichkeit, den Akt, die Grundlage aller bildenden Kunst, in freier Natürlichkeit zu studieren. Aus dem Zeichnen auf dieser Grundlage ergab sich das allen gemeinsame Gefühl, aus dem Leben die Anregung zum Schaffen zu nehmen und sich dem Erlebnis unterzuordnen. In einem Buch "Odi profanum" zeichneten und schrieben die einzelnen nebeneinander ihre Ideen nieder und verglichen dadurch ihre Eigenart. So wuchsen sie ganz von selbst zu einer Gruppe zusammen, die den Namen "Brücke" erhielt. Einer regte den andern an. Kirchner brachte den Holzschnitt aus Süddeutschland mit, den er, durch die alten Schnitte in Nürnberg angeregt, wieder aufgenommen hatte. Heckel schnitzte wieder Holzfiguren; Kirchner bereicherte diese Technik in den seinen durch die Bemalung und suchte in Stein und Zinnguss den Rhythmus der geschlossenen Form. Schmidt-Rottluff machte die ersten Lithos auf dem Stein. Die erste Ausstellung der Gruppe fand in eigenen Räumen in Dresden statt; sie fand keine Anerkennung. Dresden gab aber durch die landschaftlichen Reize und seine alte Kultur viele Anregung. Hier fand "Brücke" auch die ersten kunstgeschichtlichen Stützpunkte in Cranach, Beham und andern deutschen Meistern des Mittelalters. Bei Gelegenheit einer Ausstellung von Amiet in Dresden wurde dieser

75
Ernst Ludwig Kirchner
Page from *Chronik KG Brücke* (1913) with two woodcuts by Kirchner
Los Angeles County Museum of Art
The Robert Gore Rifkind Center for German Expressionist Studies

76
Karl Schmidt-Rottluff
Berliner Strasse in Dresden,
1909
Cat. no. 193

formally registered artists' organization that modestly identified its purpose as "the arrangement of modern art exhibitions":[5]

> *They met in Kirchner's studio to work together. Here there existed the opportunity to study the nude, the foundation of all pictorial art, in free and natural motion. From our drawings...there developed the communal sense that we should derive the inspiration for our work from life itself and should submit ourselves to its direct experience.... Each individual drew and wrote down his ideas next to those of the others, and in this comparative way they discovered what they had in common. Thus, naturally and without force, they developed into a group, which received the name* Brücke. *Each inspired the other.*[6]

What Kirchner described in his mixed first- and third-person narrative was the spontaneous, unhampered evolution of mutually supportive individuals into a consciously cohesive group, a community of friends united by shared concerns. As each member contributed to the common goal, the artists melded into a new collective that operated as an evolving, experimental alternative to the ossified system of artistic production and support that existed in Dresden and throughout the German Empire.

The Brücke was formed as a means of coalescing opposition to "established older powers" (see Appendix). These powers are readily identifiable as the interlinked organizations of the academies, their allied art schools, and the *Kunstgenossenschaft* (art union).[7] Founded in 1856 as a pan-German professional organization, the state-supported Allgemeine deutsche Kunstgenossenschaft (General German art union) and its local branches (known as *Kunstverein* or *Künstlerverein*, art or artists' associations), which consolidated their power during the late nineteenth century, essentially served as a union and licensing organization, granting professional recognition to individuals as artists. Its members worked as instructors at the art academies, and it sponsored collective exhibitions for its membership, thus controlling access to the marketplace as well as to the very profession of artist. With artistic values rooted in the past, committed to the preservation of accepted standards and to the maintenance of commercial privilege, the academies and Kunstgenossenschaft were an institutionalized obstacle to innovation, originality, and independence. They forced young artists into their mold or effectively destroyed them. For reform-oriented artists such as the members of the Brücke, there was no accommodation.

Well before the Brücke's formal founding in 1905, artists repeatedly rebelled against the powerful art institutions of German-speaking Europe, most notably against the academies before the emergence of the Kunstgenossenschaft. As early as 1796, in a pioneering proclamation of artistic independence, the painter Asmus Jakob Carstens passionately announced, "I belong, not to the Berlin academy, but to humanity." He demanded the freedom to develop his talent according to his own convictions and to choose his own prototypes, free from the academy's control: "I never promised to place myself at the service of the academy as a lifelong serf."[8] Similar sentiments were later voiced by the Viennese painter Ferdinand Georg Waldmüller, who also complained about the debilitating effects of the academic straitjacket: "Freedom is the essence, the soul of art. True artists can be formed only by instruction that is free from every imposed style, free from all pedantry in its formal aspects, free from all bureaucratic supervision, free from all demands from the state.... It is a fact of history that the spirit of art withered with the emergence of academic study."[9]

On June 7, 1905, Erich Heckel rented an empty butcher's shop in Dresden's Friedrichstadt section, at Berliner Strasse 60, to function as the Brücke's communal studio, where together the artists could develop their skills and their art free from the discipline of the academy, using nonprofessional models (see fig. 76). The models at the academy and the technical college in Dresden, where Bleyl, Heckel, and Kirchner had studied architecture, assumed standardized poses often derived from antique and Renaissance statuary and held the poses for long periods of time to permit detailed drawing. The Brücke's untutored models, in contrast, posed informally, constantly changing their positions. As Bleyl recalled:

> *Since the drawing after the nude practiced at the technical college was too academically conceived, it failed to satisfy us, and we decided to sponsor classes for sketching the nude on our own. For this, a gracefully lithe model made herself available for us, a pretty girl with a friendly and compliant nature and with a wonderfully symmetrical build, with her body just at the brink of maturity. She had the wonderfully melodious name of Isabella. Without any sign of effort—and she never tired of this—she was able to surprise and enchant us with ever new, unself-consciously natural nude poses. Only a quarter hour was allowed for any one pose. That necessitated quick comprehension and rapid execution of a few courageous lines, and after two hours' work we were quite exhausted. But then we all sat together with Isabella in merry company and drank a cup of tea.*[10]

Freedom from the academy marked a first step toward the realization of the Brücke's utopian desires, as it had for earlier artists.

The major component of the Brücke's utopian demands—the dream of absolute freedom, independence, and autonomy for art as well as artists—was a reformulation of Waldmüller's and Carstens's demands for emancipation from the existing system of artistic production and consumption. When Carstens and Waldmüller rejected externally imposed instruction and prototypes as inimical to the emergence of an authentic art, they spoke as individuals and as mature artists, perhaps struggling, but with established careers and reputations. The Brücke artists, in contrast, acted communally and were at the very beginning of their artistic careers. As they began to develop their painting skills autodidactically, they put into practice earlier demands for the free development of artists outside the imposed discipline of the academies. By rejecting already established styles and methods, they sought to retain the spontaneity of their naive vision, to develop their natural perception rather than submit to imposed artifice, and thereby to gain access to the truth of what they saw. They began, according to Kirchner's *Chronik*, without preconceived notions of artistic style and vocabulary and sought to develop their art through shared experience and observation, working side by side as journeymen, guided only by nature and their responses to it. The truth and innocence of nature, both in terms of what they depicted—"natural" models unhampered by fashion or tradition—and how they worked—"natural" artists unhampered by academic discipline or limiting prototypes—functioned as a utopian moral principle, a manifestation of artistic and existential freedom.

"In 1903 Brücke organized into a cooperative association in order to forge a path for the strivings of the new German art," the group proclaimed in 1910 in a brief statement of its history and ideals.[11] The emphasis on communal and cooperative existence was a constant in the Brücke's proclamations, from the 1905 *Programm* to Kirchner's 1913 *Chronik*, and was reflected in the group's 1908 exhibition poster. Like the group's ideal of freedom and autonomy, this utopian sense of equality and interdependence, this belief that a new community would emerge through shared experience founded in shared needs and shared natures, followed nineteenth-century models.

The first and most noted of these prototypical fraternities was the group of six young painters—Johann Conrad Hottinger, Johann Friedrich Overbeck, Franz Pforr, Josef Sutter, Ludwig Vogel, and Josef Wintergerst—who joined together in 1809 as the Lukasbund (League of Saint Luke) in formal recognition of the communal identity that had emerged after they first met in 1808 at the Vienna academy. As would later be true for the Brücke, opposition to academic teaching and contemporary art practice united them: "Slavish study at the academies leads nowhere.... One learns to paint a remarkable fold of drapery, to draw a figure properly, learns perspective, architecture, in short everything learnable, and yet no true painter emerges. There is one thing missing in all newer paintings, although it may well be that it is considered only incidental—*heart, soul, feeling!*"[12] Communal interaction would give rise to a new shared identity:

> *On July 10th of last year [1809] we celebrated our first anniversary with an evening meal. During this, we discussed the current state of art, we all felt intensely how low it had sunk, and almost simultaneously we all offered to do whatever we could for its restoration. We grasped each other's hands and a bond was formed that, we hope, shall remain firm. We also agreed as far as possible to present every painting that we completed to the collected membership; if,*

after a nonpartisan examination, it was found to be worthy, then it should be marked with our sign. This consists of a small label on which Saint Luke is depicted. [13]

Individual was subsumed into community, which withdrew from the turmoil of the mundane world. The artists adopted a monastic life devoted to art, avoided the temptations of society and possessions, and moved from Vienna to Rome, where they lived and worked together in the secularized monastery of San Isidoro (and received the name by which they are best known, the Nazarenes).[14]

Patterns of utopian social critique, especially the formation of an alternative community in opposition to established society, the rejection of contemporary art practices, and the establishment of mutually agreed upon "natural" standards for interactive work as a means of renewing art: the ideas that we associate with the Brücke were first espoused by the Nazarenes and were later adapted by other artists' groups during the nineteenth century, notably the Pre-Raphaelite Brotherhood in London in 1848.[15] Although the Pre-Raphaelites set out to emulate the Nazarenes' neoreligious art, in dramatic contrast to the Brücke's secular orientation, they did provide a prototype for the Dresden artists. Like the Brücke, the Pre-Raphaelites lived in a modern metropolis, a center of capitalist industry and commerce. They too chose to remain in that urban environment, to address its middle-class audiences and patrons, even to allow its presence and life to enter their imagery from time to time, though always in the guise of a moralizing critique. And just as the Brücke published programs, catalogues, annual print portfolios, and posters, thereby making its aesthetic and work known to a wider public, the London artists recognized the modern need for propaganda, extending the reach of their reform efforts by issuing the illustrated periodical *The Germ* in 1849–50.

Although the Pre-Raphaelites' practices mirror aspects of the Brücke's efforts at utopian reform and the linked desire for natural artistic expression (for example, the belief that "a kindred simplicity should regulate our ambition…[along with the insistence on] the naïve traits of frank expression and unaffected grace"[16]), the English artists did not seek to function as an alternative to existing art institutions. Participation in the Royal Academy's annual exhibitions marked their activity, as did the effort to overcome negative response by enlisting the partisan pen and voice of John Ruskin in letters to newspapers, critical essays, and public lectures. Nonetheless their model of formally organizing for the purpose of mutual support and the development of a communal art vocabulary inspired later artists to plan similar experiments, as when Vincent van Gogh in 1888 imagined a "Studio of the South" in Arles, where he, Paul Gauguin, Emile Bernard, and other Post-Impressionist artists could live and work together. Indeed this desire to flee the major urban and industrial centers in order to recover a more "authentic" human existence, which was shared by many artists in the late nineteenth century, owes much to the Pre-Raphaelites' effort to revive medieval and Elizabethan art and life in their paintings, thereby proposing an idyllic utopian alternative to the blight of contemporary London, Liverpool, or Manchester.

The idea of projecting a utopian past into the present was taken a step further by William Morris, whose anti-industrial arts and crafts movement attempted to regain for labor the nobility and freedom, the satisfying linkage of producer and product, that he associated with the medieval economy. A description of the Morris and Company textile workshop at Merton Abbey in Surrey in 1891, well removed from metropolitan England, calls forth an arcadian vision of beauty and harmony:

77
Ernst Ludwig Kirchner's studio in Dresden, 1910
Photograph by Kirchner

> *A garden with an age-old wall, verdant meadows and shady trees at the edge of a clear brook. Within it, the work sheds, stretched out and with low roofs, and a mill wheel that slowly turns in a circle. Long strips of patterned cotton cloth wash gently in the water; dense strands of glowing yarns, fresh from their indigo bath, play in the winds. Dyers and printers glide around silently. Within the house there are neither steam-powered machines nor mass production. A few hand looms for silk and woolen cloths, looms for knotting rugs and Gobelin tapestries, a room for printing patterns on cloth, the dyers' rooms, and the studio for glass painting. Over it all, an air as if from a past age, an atmosphere of peace, even of leisure, in which the worker is not hounded to death but can pause for breath and also enjoy some of the beauty of our earth. That was Merton Abbey.*[17]

The wistful account of Merton Abbey's peaceful, utopian world is taken from an early German history of the European arts and crafts movement, written as the Brücke was being founded. The history was an effort to link Morris's arcadian counterreality to the ideology of social democracy, to nineteenth-century utopian socialism, and to Karl Marx's demand that utopian yearning be transformed into systematic science and concrete reality, into praxis.[18] The Brücke's utopian experiment has a certain kinship with such Social Democratic histories of reform in the applied arts, sharing their advocacy of truth to nature as a foundation for artistic practice and their interest in efforts to create an alternative culture of artists and artisans whose work would be "good in the sense of the employed material and the technical execution."[19]

Morris's dream of an art-generated scientific communist utopia, described in his visionary novel *News from Nowhere* (1891), was applied in a less systematic fashion by other German proponents of an alternative society. Focusing on his condemnations of the capitalist city, on the "disgraceful contrast" that existed "between the fields where beasts live and the streets where men live,"[20] these reformers linked his praise of the value of craftsmanship in premodern society with the virulent antiurbanism of Julius Langbehn and other prophets of "cultural despair."[21] During the 1890s a number of utopian communities were established in Germany. These idyllic garden communes, with paradisiacal names such as Eden and Monte Verità, were formed outside Germany's despised, rapidly expanding cities as "blossoming oas[es] in the midst of the capitalist desert and its ugliness, corruption, and bodily degeneration...a first fully ripened fruit of liberal socialism."[22] As their vegetarian settlers tilled the communally owned land, harvested the fruits of ecologically cultivated orchards, and sold home-grown foods for support, these self-sufficient land reform communes provided a utopian alternative to both capitalism and Marxist socialism, a romantic-agrarian "third way," in which the individual would be liberated as community was created. The vices of a materialistic modern society would find no welcome in these settlements: "Eden is the first and only 'dry' community in Germany. Alcohol sale is not permitted. In Eden no butcher shop, no tobacco shop, no pornography, no modern cinema, no nightclubs, no betting parlors, no gambling clubs are allowed to open.... Prostitution and sexually transmitted diseases are unknown in Eden."[23]

Less drastic in their conception and regulation than the utopian garden settlements, largely rejecting their asceticism but indisputably related to them, were the numerous artists' colonies that German artists founded in fishing and farming villages. Imitating the painters of the Barbizon school as well as William Morris, these artists added another dimension to the confusing, amorphous, and ungrounded ideological complex of the third way. Thus a young writer who participated in Munich's alienated literary and artistic

78
Erich Heckel
Szene im Wald, 1910
(Scene in the woods)
Cat. no. 81

bohemia of the 1890s recorded: "We, a small group of poets and artists, wanted to move to [the medieval town of] Visby on the Swedish island Gotland, in order to write poems, paint, print books, and weave tapestries." The settlement would be organized according to "purely aesthetic principles."[24] In these sheltered agrarian communities, far removed from profit-oriented urban society, producing the furnishings and decorations as well as the shelter and nourishment their colonies needed, artists sought to translate their visions of social and artistic reform into reality and to rediscover a primordial unity with nature. Artworks, artists, community, environment, and nature were fused into a utopian *Gesamtkunstwerk*, an integrated work of art employing its human members as its constructive medium.

In the village of Worpswede, amid the peat bogs and moors north of Bremen, the painters Hans am Ende, Fritz Mackensen, Otto Modersohn, Fritz Overbeck, Carl Vinnen,

79
Ernst Ludwig Kirchner
Mit Schilf werfende Badende, 1910
(Bathers tossing reeds)
Cat. no. 109

and Heinrich Vogeler joined together as the Künstlervereinigung Worpswede (Worpswede artists' alliance) in 1895. The artists lived and painted together, designing and constructing their own houses and furnishings in the manner of Morris's arts and crafts designs. In their utopian withdrawal from urban existence and in their embrace of northern Germany's landscape—the "truth" of nature that contrasted with the "falseness" of the city—they hoped to create a new art, an idyllic vision inspired by the land and soil. Worpswede's artists were repeatedly awarded gold medals at art exhibitions and received consistent critical praise for the "profound truth" of their work. "This is not simply a copying of what might be found to appeal externally," one critic wrote, "but a becoming one with surrounding nature, an organic emergence of the artwork from the spirit of the land and the people."[25] For young German artists such as the members of the Brücke, Worpswede's communal rejection of urban art institutions could not but function as an example to be emulated in other cooperative ventures.

Artists' communities were set up not only in the countryside but within the expanding urban milieu of imperial Germany as well. Thus in Darmstadt Grand Duke Ernst Ludwig of Hesse-Darmstadt founded the Mathildenhöhe artists' colony in 1899 on a hill overlooking the old city. A new, enclosed suburban village and exhibition site emerged, a "free creative community" that would encourage "joy in work and striving for the ideal" by means of "collegial work together"; there would be no hierarchy, no subordination, but total freedom and equality for the Darmstadt-Mathildenhöhe community.[26] Artists purchased subsidized ground on which to build houses and studios whose harmonious Jugendstil design would contrast with the surrounding urban landscape, with its lack of unity and planning and its functional, commercial, utilitarian, and historicist structures. A utopian alternative to the modern city, a "beautiful city," would be set up right next to it:

We must build a city, an entire city!... In the entire layout and down to the smallest detail everything will be controlled by the same spirit. The streets and the gardens and the palaces and the huts and the tables and the chairs and the lights and the spoons will be expressions of the same sensibility. But in the center, like a temple in a sacred grove, will be the House of Work, at one and the same time a studio for artists and a workshop for the craftsmen, where now the artist shall always be close to the calming, orderly process of the craft, and the craftsman shall always be close to the liberating and purifying presence of art, until such a time as artist and worker fuse into a single personality![27]

A life and environment of beauty, with no discord to disrupt the communal life and activity of the artists and craftsmen: this was the ideal that the Mathildenhöhe artists' colony strove for in its effort to reform by means of example, by means of actualized utopian prototype.

Without outside sponsorship, lacking the resources of Worpswede or Mathildenhöhe or the large and devoted membership of Eden, the Brücke artists nonetheless approximated some of their efforts. If they could not shape the external environment of Dresden, they could determine the internal form of the studio at Berliner Strasse 60. Even if Kirchner's pronouncements about his own leadership are problematic, and clearly contrary to the sense of fraternity and equality that guided the Brücke's formation, his *Chronik* records the artists' efforts to shape an environment that corresponded to their concept of an anti-bourgeois utopia and art: "Heckel and Kirchner attempted to bring the new painting into harmony with an interior space. Kirchner equipped his rooms with wall paintings and tapestries, on which Heckel worked too."[28] Decorations employing their new Expressionist vocabulary brought their art into their environment, thereby incorporating life itself into a new totality of artistic vision (see fig. 77). The artists also made their own utensils and furnishings, frequently emulating the non-European, "natural" forms of African and Oceanic furnishings and sculpture and also applying the concept of the Jugendstil Gesamtkunstwerk that the Mathildenhöhe artists' colony propagated.

The division between high and applied art, one of the hallmarks of postmedieval European culture, was erased. Entry into the Brücke's studio signified entry into a world removed from the early twentieth-century proletarian and industrial surroundings of Dresden-Friedrichstadt, from the middle-class world of the artists' origins and patrons, and from the world of official exhibitions and academic studios. It provided an antithetical "other" to the life and civilization of Germany, a realm of artistic freedom and invention, a temporary utopian retreat and counterreality.

THE BRÜCKE AND THE UTOPIA OF NATURE

In establishing and furnishing their Dresden studio, the Brücke artists translated their art into utopian praxis. The murals and tapestries in the studio as well as the other paintings, sculptures, drawings, and prints produced by the artists made visible and extended the group's vision of utopia. The utopia of an artist's life, the utopia of the studio, and the utopia of the images melded into one another, as Kirchner later recalled:

The manner of the development of the objects of our external life, from the first appliquéd tablecloth in the first Dresden studio to the completed harmonic space in the Berlin studios of the individual artists, consists of a single uninter-

> *rupted, logical process of intensification, which went hand in hand with the painterly development of the paintings and graphics and sculptures. The first bowl that was carved because it was impossible to buy one that appealed to us transferred its plastic form to the surface-oriented form of the paintings, and kneaded into personal form, through and through, down to the last stroke, were the most varied techniques. The love that the painter felt for the girl* [Mädchen] *who was his companion and helper was transferred to the carved figure, ennobled itself through its proximity into a painting, and then once more mediated between a specific form of chair or table and the life habits of the human model. In this simple example our manner of producing art can be seen.... Primary for the artists was free drawing from free people in free naturalness.... We painted and drew hundreds of sheets of paper each day, interrupted by talk and play; painters became models and vice versa. The painters learned by means of constant attempts to draw naked boys and girls and young men, whom they drew drawing. All the events of the day were made part of memory in that way. The studio became a home to the people who were being drawn: They learned from the artists, the artists from them. Directly and richly, the pictures absorbed life.*[29]

Kirchner's diary, which repeats aspects of his characterization of the Brücke's life and history in the 1913 *Chronik* (and which, like the *Chronik*, was partially motivated by a desire to minimize the role of Pechstein while maximizing his own), describes the foundation of an experimental utopian community of artists. Art, its manifestations and its making, influenced all aspects of the men's life and work together, shaping their environment as well as their interpersonal contacts and relationships. In art, in the content and structure of its imagery, the Brücke's utopian vision was made manifest; in art life was absorbed, transformed, and projected back into life.

The Brücke's belief that art had the potential to mold and anticipate a future perfected humanity is rooted in eighteenth-century German idealism, notably the aesthetics of Immanuel Kant and their development by the poet-philosopher Friedrich von Schiller. Art, rather than being a secondary or incidental aspect of social and political life, was fundamental, as Schiller wrote in 1793, during the French Revolution: "Usefulness and practicality are the great idol of our time, which is adored by all powers and which all talents should serve.... I hope to convince you that [art and aesthetics are] alien not so much to the needs, but rather only to the taste of our time, and indeed that we are obliged precisely to take the path through aesthetics in order to solve the actual political question, for it is through beauty that we arrive at freedom."[30] Like the Brücke artists, Schiller made freedom the goal of his aesthetic utopian vision, with art serving as mediator between imperfect present and utopian future. Art, by visualizing an ideal beauty (which necessarily invokes freedom, since lack of freedom counters the ideal), projects an alternate reality. Thus in the imagined imagery of art, a prototype for a utopian future is consciously presented.[31] The image world of the Brücke's paintings, drawings, prints, sculpture, and furnishings corresponded to the one they attempted to realize in their communal life and working methods.

Linked to the preeminence of freedom in the Brücke's writings and mode of organization is the concept of nature, which varies in meaning, referring both to the outdoors,

80
Max Pechstein
Tanzende und Badende am Waldteich, 1912 (L 149)
(Dancers and bathers at a forest pond)
Cat. no. 171

the landscape, and "uncivilized" settings, and to essence, the fundamental and defining aspects of a thing rather than accidental accretions. In both senses nature exists as the antithesis to the artifice of civilization, to imposed laws and structures that alter what is fundamental or true. Nature is whatever is God-created rather than man-created, and thus the more human civilization removed itself from it, the more unnatural, unwholesome, and unauthentic humanity became, according to this pattern of thought, with the urban, capitalist, industrial civilization of modernity being the ultimate manifestation of this process. When Kirchner wrote of how the community of the Brücke evolved without force, organically, he argued for the group's "naturalness," its emergence from free and natural interaction, in contrast to the imposed regulation of modern civilization and its institutions.[32]

The Brücke's yearning for nature in all its ramifications was shared by numerous other Germans, mostly members of the educated middle classes and the lower ranks of the aristocracy, notably those seeking third-way alternatives. As the most evident and imposing artefact of modern civilization, the city was regarded as an anti-utopia through which utopia could be defined:

Forget the city with its labor and work, its sweat, its fumes and odors and afflictions. Forget the high house walls, the stone pavements of the streets, the narrow rooms where you forgot how to breathe and broke yourself of the habit of looking, of gazing at vitally growing life, at the dome of heaven, at the blue horizon of the landscape, at the lush greenness of the meadow, at the colorful glory of the flowers. Close your eyes. What do you see? Do you still feel the pressure of the ceiling in your room, do you still pass through narrow alleys between high house walls, with the hard stones beneath your feet? Then wander farther away from the city.[33]

81
Erich Heckel
Ballspielende, 1912
(Ball players)
Cat. no. 83

The open land, nature unblemished by, urban intrusion, provided the antidote to the dehumanizing effects of the city, and immersion in nature, even if only temporary, was a necessary and hygienic corrective to the "nervous hysteria" of sunless, smoke- and dust-filled city life: "In addition to a daily change of air, a weekly one (Sunday excursion), and finally a semiannual, or at least annual, extensive change of air must take place.... We respond with glad approval to school trips to the country during summertime, the convalescence stations and recovery homes in the mountains,...vacation colonies, etc., since these will aid many, even if not everyone, in gaining access to the benefits of a change of air to restore their health."[34] The Brücke artists' frequent excursions to the countryside near Dresden or to the North Sea—even as they steadfastly remained city dwellers, never seeking to set up a Worpswede-like rural colony—provided a "change of air." They shared the life reform movement's belief in the benefits of fresh air, sunlight, pure water, and the land. In the Brücke's utopia nature was a healer.[35]

"Naturally we worked outdoors a lot, directly before nature," recalled Fritz Bleyl of the Brücke's early years, "for example, at the Räcknitz Heights or on the shores of the River Elbe—as far upstream as Pillnitz-Pirna, downstream as far as the Meissen area—and from time to time in the area around Moritzburg."[36] Small towns or landscaped parks, the areas Bleyl mentions, were easily reachable by streetcar or train from Dresden and were popular destinations for the daylong family excursions that the life reform movement advocated (see fig. 78). Similarly Kirchner's *Chronik* is punctuated by itemizations of the artists' trips to various villages and parks, as if they marked major stations in the group's artistic development: "Schmidt-Rottluff went with [Emil Nolde] to Alsen. Later Schmidt-Rottluff and Heckel went to Dangast. The brisk air of the North Sea gave rise to a monumental impressionism.... Kirchner and Pechstein went to Gollverode.... Heckel and Kirchner went to the Moritzburg Ponds.... Schmidt-Rottluff worked on perfecting his color rhythm in Dangast.... Pechstein joined Heckel in Dangast...[then] both of them came to Kirchner at Moritzburg."

Nature healed and re-formed the inhabitants of the urban anti-utopia as they sought to give form to their art-driven utopian vision. The landscape they entered, moreover, was the landscape of the city dweller, the landscape of *Erholung*, of recovery, relaxation, and contrast. Nature here was disciplined and cultivated for the inhabitants of Germany's spreading metropolises; it was within ready reach to offer its salutary forces to receptive visitors. It was not, however, nature in its most dramatic form. The Brücke's sketches and paintings of the Dresden years do not depict the picturesque views of rugged mountains and valleys that would have been available somewhat farther from Dresden, in the area known as Saxon Switzerland; nor do they show the vistas along the shores of the Elbe. Rather than portraying the "untouched" nature that might be found in a primeval paradise or in the anthropomorphic views of the Romantic painters, they depicted nature that knew the presence of humanity, evidenced by village houses and streets, for example. They show nature tamed, no longer a threat, but not yet overpowered and despoiled by urban expansion. Nestled in gently sloping, verdant hills, mirrored in its peaceful waters, the products of human presence are in utopian harmony with nature.

Nature is also presented as shelter and as recuperative power in the other major grouping of Brücke landscape representations, in which the human presence becomes overt. While scenes of workers in fields or travelers along paths were produced, they function as incidental contrasts to the motif that generally occupied the artists' attention. When Kirchner wrote in the *Chronik* of visiting the Moritzburg Ponds with Heckel and Pechstein during the summers of 1909, 1910, and 1911, he noted that their purpose was "to study the nude in the open air," and he identified the nude as "the foundation of all pictorial arts." One of the artists' goals in establishing their communal studio was to depict the nude and its "free and natural motion," an opportunity that the art schools had denied them. In the nude resided the concept of freedom and the related concept of nature, the two primary components of the Brücke's utopian vision.

The artists' recollections of these summer sojourns, and those of their friends, present an idyllic life free from pain and worry. The appearance of an occasional policeman to object to the immodesty of naked bathers provided an almost necessary anti-utopian counterpoint recalling the limits and rules of society. As Pechstein recounted:

> *When we were together in Berlin [in 1910], I agreed with Heckel and Kirchner that we three would work at the ponds around Moritzburg, near Dresden. We already knew the landscape...and we knew that the possibility was there to paint the nude undisturbed in open nature.... We had to find two or three people who were not professional models and thus would reveal to us movements unhindered by studio discipline.... We were also in luck as far as the weather was concerned: not a single rainy day.... We painter fellows would*

82
Ernst Ludwig Kirchner
Spielende nackte Menschen unter Bäumen, 1910
(Nudes playing under trees)
Oil on canvas
30⁵⁄16 x 35¹⁄16 in.
(77.0 x 89.0 cm)
Leingabe aus Privatbesitz bei den Bayerische Staatsgemäldesammlungen, Munich

Umfang acht Seiten — Einzelbezug 15 Pfennig

DER STURM

WOCHENSCHRIFT FÜR KULTUR UND DIE KÜNSTE

Herausgeber und Schriftleiter: HERWARTH WALDEN

JAHRGANG 1912 — BERLIN JANUAR 1912 — NUMMER 93

Inhalt: KURT HILLER: Der Sinn des Lebens und die Reichstagswahl / TRUST: Zwischen Weihnachten und Neujahr / FJODOR SSOLLOGUB: Die weisen Jungfrauen / ELSE LASKER-SCHÜLER: Briefe nach Norwegen / J. A.: Humoristen / MAX PECHSTEIN: Erlegung des Festbratens / Originalholzschnitt

Max Pechstein: Erlegung des Festbratens / Originalholzschnitt

83
Max Pechstein
Erlegung des Festbratens, 1911
(H 131)
(Killing of the banquet roast)
Cat. no. 170

move out early in the mornings, loaded down with our gear, behind us the models carrying bags full of stuff to eat and drink. We lived in absolute harmony, worked and bathed. If the counterpoint of a male model was lacking, then one of us three would fill the gap.... Each of us produced numerous sketches, drawings, and pictures. [37]

An account by Gustav Schiefler, the retired Hamburg jurist who became one of the Brücke's major benefactors and defenders, written in 1918, likewise transports the trips to the Moritzburg Ponds to a realm of artistic perfection:

For several months they settled with numerous models at one of the ponds in the environs of Dresden and spent days there, as much as the climate permitted, naked in the open air. A small tree-covered island...provided a kind of campsite, and so apparently they led a life similar to that of some wild primeval tribe. What Gauguin had sought in the South Seas, they produced for themselves in immediate proximity to the metropolis. The sketches that were made there in endless number are the documents of this original experiment, and since everything that the artists learned during the previous years came to fruition in them, we find artistic achievements of a high order among them. Nonetheless, it was not until the winter months that the final consequences were drawn in the reworking of the motifs in paintings.[38]

The Brücke's faith in the nude was linked to their faith in the reformative function of their art. The naked women and men absorbing the health-giving rays of the sun represented a nudist utopia (see figs. 79, 80, 81).

Along with the other reform movements that preached a return to nature and the land, nudism gained a significant following in Germany, beginning in the 1890s. Nakedness—according to one of its most vocal spokesmen, Heinrich Pudor—signified health and vitality and would preserve youth, eventually leading to immortality.[39] "Light-air baths" were advocated, exposing the body to open air and sunlight, and "light-air-sports-baths" were constructed in the cities, so that even within the urban milieu the city-infected bodies of the citizens, strictly segregated by gender, could be presented to the regenerative experience of movement, light, and air unhindered by the unnatural stricture of clothing. Nude beaches, enclosed by wooden fences mandated to be two and a half meters tall and without knotholes, were established along the North and Baltic seas and near cities, on the shores of rivers and wooded ponds, in "naturist colonies," frequently subdivided according to various ideological or religious allegiances.[40] The call to "bathe in light, air, and sun" was transforming or re-forming at least a small part of the German population into a synthesized *Lichtluftgeschöpf*, a creation produced by sunlight and air.

The Brücke's celebration of the nude body, while certainly an expression of the belief that the human figure is the supreme subject of art, was likewise such an effort to recover a utopian "naturalness" that civilization attempted to deny. The painted celebrations of bathers at the Moritzburg Ponds, in which figures communed with trees and water or interacted in joyful and uninhibited play (see fig. 82), were extensions of the ideal life that the Brücke attempted to create, a utopia that emphasized informal human interaction and communication, play, and art while filtering out everything else. The images of naked women and men walking in the woods, playing with bows and arrows, reclining in hammocks or on blankets, frolicking among the reeds and bulrushes by the lakes, or making

84
Otto Mueller
Knabe zwischen Blattpflanzen, 1912
(Youth seated between Large plants)
Cat. no. 165

sketches, refer to the traditional iconography of the Golden Age but proclaim their modernity by means of a style that rejects the retrospective attitudes of traditional Golden Age depictions (see figs. 83, 84, 85). Utopia, as the Brücke conceived of it, was rooted in the present, and their vision of a life devoid of care and dominated by joy and pleasure was addressed to contemporary viewers.

Although the Brücke's images, like the nudists' celebration of the benefits of light, sun, and open air, highlighted the benefits of nature and granted it an empathic subjective force, nature and the landscape were in a fundamental sense incidental to the images. The natural setting not only acted as a foil and an antidote to the city where the artists lived and worked but was also an alternate studio, an extension of the utopian work environment that the artists had created in Dresden.

Initially the Brücke's Dresden studio, where they invited other artists to join them in depicting the nude, functioned as did most teaching studios, with a work space furnished with easels and a platform on which a model posed. The two worlds, those of the artist and his subject, remained separate, coming together only briefly for tea after the sketching session was completed, as Bleyl recalled. As Heckel and Kirchner began to paint scenes on the walls and carve studio furnishings, however, the distinction began to dissolve. The studio itself became the locus and motif of their independent works, with models viewed and depicted specifically in the enhanced studio environment.

Kirchner recalled in 1923 that the Brücke "theory" of art involved a persistent exploration in which a motif was transferred from medium to medium, from painting to sculpture to print to furniture in multiple combinations, variations, and directions so that the world of

85
Otto Mueller
Badende, 1920
(Bathers)
Cat. no. 166

the artwork and the world surrounding it were conceptually and visually fused, becoming extensions of each other. Utopia became simultaneously no place—an unlocatable site, in the sense of Thomas More's invented Greek word, somewhere between studio and painting—and every place, as painted image and three-dimensional environment became intertwined. Judging from the paintings and drawings, this process of transformation came to completion late in 1909, when the studio setting, with its paintings, tapestries, chairs, stools, and couches, began to compete with the figure as the central subject of the artists' works (see fig. 86).[41] Chronologically this coincides with the increased focus on bathers and other figures in nature, so that the two utopias—one outdoors, the other indoors—merge. In the Brücke's portrayals of models in front of tapestries and wall paintings that include landscape settings, moreover, the worlds of nature and the studio cease to be distinguishable and again become an ambiguous utopian site (see fig. 65). It was to the studio that the artists and models returned each evening from their daily summer excursions, and it was in the studio that the paintings that synthesize outdoor impressions were produced later in the year, as nature became inhospitable.[42]

The studio offered the model of an alternative society with art and freedom (and subsumed in freedom, naturalness or nature) as its guiding principles. The images of figures in the studio reveal a progressive transformation. Initially the artists followed relatively traditional practices in which models were posed—and any held pose, even the fifteen-minute ones the Brücke advocated, results in stiffness and artificiality—against a neutral background. Setting is insignificant or arbitrary. It is a construct of the picture's own world and thus distances itself from the world in which the artist works as well as that of the

86
Ernst Ludwig Kirchner
Interieur II, 1911
(Interior II)
Ink
13 3/16 x 11 1/4 in.
(33.5 x 28.5 cm)
Brücke-Museum, Berlin

87
Ernst Ludwig Kirchner
Atelierszene (Besucher im Atelier), c. 1910–11
(Studio scene [visitor in the studio])
Ink
16 5/16 x 13 9/16 in.
(41.5 x 34.5 cm)
Kupferstichkabinett, Staatliche Museen zu Berlin, Preussischer Kulturbesitz

viewer. The repetition of the studio environment in the paintings, the inclusion of paintings in the environment, this fluidly dialectical process that Kirchner described, placed the figures in an extension of the artist's milieu, so that the world within the painting no longer differed from the world outside it. Such an injection of the studio world into the paintings and drawings extended further as the models ceased to pose and began to move freely, nude or clothed, about the studio (see fig. 87). Scenes of conversations, games, and dances alternated with scenes of women reclining, sitting, standing, or bathing, usually facing the artist. A greater informality and spontaneity entered the Brücke paintings, which as a result functioned as a more appropriate sign of the life the artists sought to represent. This informality, moreover, was derived from familiarity, as the models either lived in the studio with the artists or spent much of their time there. The world within the pictures ceased to be an artificial construct, invented and unfamiliar, and became a souvenir rendition of the mundane bohemian milieu, the utopian everyday of the studio.

If Kirchner's recollection is considered, the conceptual fusion between artist, image, and milieu was also testimony to the sexual and amorous relationships between the Brücke painters and their models. As the artists depicted the women they loved, Kirchner argued, their paintings reflected that emotional link. Whether or not this contention is accepted, the scenes of naked models interacting with their artist companions, who were themselves sometimes naked, or reclining languorously alone are sexually charged. Whereas the nudist movement argued puritanically that habitual nakedness reduces sexual stimulation and saw the body largely in terms of skin, rather than flesh or sexual organs and signs,[43] the Brücke saw the human body as a site of pleasure and the celebration of sexuality. Whether mature, with heavy breasts and accented pubic hair, or pubescent, with breast buds and hairless bodies, the Brücke's female models displayed a conscious sexuality (see fig. 65). The men depicted often responded with rising penises, or this response was suggested by the inclusion within the paintings and prints of the scenes of loving couples that proliferated on the studio walls. The freedom of utopia and its celebration of nature were projected into and from the bodies of the women and men who inhabited the Brücke's studio.[44]

TAKING LEAVE OF UTOPIA

There was no predetermined schema according to which the Brücke's artistic utopia was shaped. Its configuration emerged through its evolution after the artists began to sketch nudes together in 1903, and it can be recognized only in terms of their interaction and the images they produced until they left Dresden for Berlin in 1911. While their concretely formed utopian experiment lacks direct correlation to utopian texts, the Brücke artists, like other visionaries, accented concepts of freedom, nature, and the future, basing their art as well as their community on them.[45] But utopia is also elusive. The word *utopia* means nowhere, and for the Brücke too it was situated in a netherworld somewhere between the world of the studio and the world of the images, with the two intermingling into a utopian otherworld, especially in the artists' later nostalgic recollections. The utopian community that was sought in Dresden failed the test of its transplant to Berlin, where the group ejected Pechstein for exhibiting independently, substituted Otto Mueller for him, and finally splintered apart as Kirchner attempted to chronicle its history in 1912. The Brücke artists continued to explore utopian imagery in their separate studios that emulated the decor of the one in Dresden, in depictions of nudes and landscapes and interiors, but the community in which it originated ceased to exist. Utopia, even imperfect, was nowhere.

NOTES

1. Oscar Wilde, "The Soul of Man under Socialism," in *The Complete Works of Oscar Wilde*, rev. ed. (London: Collins, 1966), p. 35. Wilde's essay, originally published in 1890, appeared in 1904 in German translation in the anthology *Der Sozialismus und die Seele des Menschen, Aus dem Zuchthaus zu Reading, Aesthetisches Manifest*, trans. Hedwig Lachmann and Gustav Landauer (Berlin: K. S. A. Juncker, 1904).

2. Although the group's name is generally rendered in English-language texts as *Die Brücke* or *The Bridge*, the use of the definite article has no precedent in Brücke posters, publications, or letters. The artists were at all times careful to refer to themselves collectively as Brücke or by their more formal, legal title, *Künstlergruppe Brücke* (Artists' group bridge). The difference in connotation is significant. The name *Brücke* reflects the group's view of itself as a means of passage from the present to the future. Use of a definite article suggests that the group regarded itself as the *only* bridge to the future. Its members, however, were receptive to various alternatives to existing cultural institutions, and they made no claim to exclusivity in their approach to art. See Reinhold Heller, introduction to *Brücke: German Expressionist Prints from the Granvil and Marcia Specks Collection*, exh. cat. (Evanston, Ill.: Mary and Leigh Block Gallery, Northwestern University, 1988).

3. Notable exceptions to this are Max Pechstein, who actively supported the Social Democratic Party after World War I, and Emil Nolde (insofar as his brief membership in the Brücke during 1906–7 identifies him with the group), who joined the North Schleswig National Socialist Party in 1920. Significantly, however, such demonstrative party allegiance dates to the years after 1918 and does not characterize the attitudes of even these two artists prior to World War I.

4. Max Horkheimer, "Anfänge der bürgerlichen Geschichtsphilosophie" (1930), in *Anfänge der bürgerlichen Geschichtsphilosophie: Hegel und das Problem der Metaphysik, Montaigne und die Funktion der Skepsis* (Frankfurt: S. Fischer, 1971), p. 9.

5. Willy Oskar Dressler, ed., *Kunsthandbuch*, vol. 1 (Berlin: E. Wasmuth, 1906), p. 232.

6. Ernst Ludwig Kirchner, Chronik KG Brücke (1913), as translated by Reinhold Heller, in *Brücke: German Expressionist Prints*, p. 16.

7. Concerning the Kunstgenossenschaft and other artists' associations in Germany, see Heinrich Dieters, *Geschichte der Allgemeinen deutschen Kunstgenossenschaft* (Düsseldorf, 1903); Karin Brommenschenkel, "Berliner Kunst- und Künstlervereine des 19. Jahrhunderts bis zum Weltkrieg," Ph.D. diss., Friedrich-Wilhelms-Universität, Berlin, 1942; Nicolaas Teeuwisse, *Vom Salon zur Secession: Berliner Kunstleben zwischen Tradition und Aufbruch zur Moderne, 1871–1900* (Berlin: Deutscher Verlag für Kunstwissenschaft, 1986).

8. Asmus Jakob Carstens to Minister Friedrich von Heinitz, 20 February 1796, in Carl Ludwig Fernow, *Leben des Künstlers Asmus Jakob Carstens: Ein Beitrag zur Kunstgeschichte des 18. Jahrhunderts* (Leipzig: Hartknoch, 1806), p. 204; for a translation of the central paragraph of Carstens's frequently cited letter, see *Neo-Classicism and Romanticism, 1750–1850*, vol. 1, *Enlightenment and Revolution*, ed. Lorenz Eitner, Sources and Documents in the History of Art Series (Englewood Cliffs, N.J.: Prentice Hall, 1970), p. 109.

9. Ferdinand Georg Waldmüller to Freiherr Carl von Bruck, after 1860, in *Künstlerbriefe aus dem neunzehnten Jahrhundert*, comp. Else Cassirer (Berlin: Bruno Cassirer, 1923), p. 263.

10. Fritz Bleyl, "Erinnerungen," in Lothar Günther Buchheim, *Die Künstlergemeinschaft Brücke* (Feldafing: Buchheim, 1956), p. 38; for a slightly different text, substantively the same in terms of the recollected situation, see "Aus den 'Erinnerungen' von Fritz Bleyl," in *Bildnisse der "Brücke"-Künstler von einander*, ed. Hans Wentzel (Stuttgart: Philipp Reclam, 1961), pp. 23–29; Hans Wentzel, "Fritz Bleyl, Gründungsmitglied der 'Brücke,'" *Kunst in Hessen und am Mittelrhein*, no. 8 (1968): 89–105.

11. Introduction to *Katalog zur Ausstellung der K.G. "Brücke"* (Dresden: Galerie Arnold, 1910), unpaginated.

12. Letter from Friedrich Overbeck to his father, 1808, in Margaret Howitt, *Friedrich Overbeck: Sein Leben und Schaffen*, vol. 1 (Freiburg:

Herder'schen Verlagsbuchhandlung, 1866), pp. 71–72, as cited in Eckart Klessmann, *Die deutsche Romantik* (Cologne: DuMont, 1979), pp. 53–54.

13. Franz Pforr to Johann David Passavant, 21 March 1810, in Fritz Herbert Lehr, *Die Blütezeit romantischer Bildkunst: Franz Pforr, der Meister des Lukasbunds* (Marburg: Kunstgeschichtliches Seminar der Universität Marburg, 1924), p. 41; see also the translation by Lorenz Eitner, pp. 33–34.

14. For an extensive discussion of the League of Saint Luke, its artists, and their work, see Keith Andrews, *The Nazarenes: A Brotherhood of German Painters* (Oxford: Clarendon Press, 1964).

15. For a consideration of the link between the Nazarenes and the Pre-Raphaelites, see William Vaughan, *German Romanticism and English Art* (New Haven, Conn.: Yale University Press, 1979).

16. William Holman Hunt, *Pre-Raphaelitism and the Pre-Raphaelite Brotherhood* (London: Macmillan, 1905; New York: AMS Press, 1967), p. 108.

17. Heinrich Waentig, *Wirtschaft und Kunst: Eine Untersuchung über Geschichte und Theorie der modernen Kunstgewerbebewegung* (Jena: Gustav Fischer, 1909), pp. 79–80.

18. Significantly William Morris's utopian novel *News from Nowhere; or, An Epoch of Rest, Being Some Chapters from a Utopian Romance* was published in German translation with a preface by Wilhelm Liebknecht, a leader of the Marxist Social Democratic Party of Germany; the translator was his wife, Natalie Reh Liebknecht.

19. Waentig, *Wirtschaft und Kunst*, p. 296.

20. William Morris, "The Lesser Arts," in *The Collected Works of William Morris*, vol. 12 (London: Longmans, Green and Co., 1915), p. 25.

21. Fritz Stern, *The Politics of Cultural Despair: A Study in the Rise of the Germanic Ideology* (Berkeley and Los Angeles: University of California Press, 1961).

22. Franz Oppenheimer, *Erlebtes, Erstrebtes, Erreichtes: Lebenserinnerungen* (Düsseldorf: J. Melzer, 1964), as cited in Gabriele Riedle, "Paradies sucht Zukunft," *Die Zeit* (Hamburg), 18 September 1992, overseas edition, p. 22. According to Riedle, the Obstbausiedlung Eden (orchard settlement Eden), founded in 1893, still exists today near Oranienburg, north of Berlin, with 340 houses and fifteen hundred inhabitants. Concerning the garden city, land reform, and commune movements in Germany, see also Ulrich Linse, ed., *Zurück, o Mensch, zur Mutter Erde: Landkommunen in Deutschland*, 1890–1933 (Munich: Deutscher Taschenbuch Verlag, 1983); Kristiana Hartmann, *Deutsche Gartenstadtbewegung: Kulturpolitik und Lebensreform* (Munich: Deutscher Taschenbuch Verlag, 1976). For a pioneering, highly critical analysis of the garden city movement, see George L. Mosse, "Germanic Utopias," in *The Crisis of German Ideology: Intellectual Origins of the Third Reich* (New York: Grosset and Dunlap, 1964; New York: Schocken, 1981), pp. 108–25.

23. Walter Eberding, "35 Jahre Obstbausiedlung Eden," in *Biologische Heilkunst*. no. 17 (1928), cited in Janos Frecot, Johann Friedrich Geist, and Diethart Kerbs, *Fidus, 1868–1948: Zur ästhetischen Praxis bürgerlicher Fluchtbewegung* (Munich: Rogner und Bernhard, 1972), p. 37.

24. Arthur Holitscher, "Die Münchner Zeit: Erinnerungen," in *Die neue Rundschau* 35 (March 1924): 390.

25. *Worpswede, eine deutsche Künstlerkolonie um 1900*, exh. cat. (Bremen: Kunsthalle Bremen, 1980), pp. 83–84.

26. *Darmstädter Tagesblatt*, 21 July 1899, cited by Annette Wolde, "Der ökonomische Hintergrund der Künstlerkolonie," in *Ein Dokument deutscher Kunst: Darmstadt, 1901-1976*, exh. cat., vol. 5 (Darmstadt: Mathildenhöhe, 1976–77), p. 49.

27. Josef Maria Olbrich (1901), cited by Eva Huber, "Die Darmstädter Künstlerkolonie: Anspruch und Verwirklichung ihrer künstlerischen Zielsetzung," in *Ein Dokument deutscher Kunst*, p. 60.

28. Kirchner, *Chronik*, p. 16. There is disagreement among historians of the Brücke as to whether it was Kirchner or Heckel who first began to make wall paintings. Contrary to Kirchner's recollection in the *Chronik*, the evidence of sketches and photographs suggests that Heckel may have begun wall decorations early in 1909. Moreover photographs thought to have been taken in the studio at Berliner Strasse 60, and dated as early as 1908, have recently been shown to have been taken in the studio at Berliner Strasse 80 after November 1909 (see Jill Lloyd, *German Expressionism: Primitivism and Modernity* [New Haven, Conn.: Yale University Press, 1991], pp. 23–24). While this revised dating of the photographs seems probable, no absolute evidence for it has been found so far.

29. Ernst Ludwig Kirchner, 6 March 1923, in Lothar Grisebach, *E. L. Kirchners Davoser Tagebuch* (Cologne: DuMont, 1968), p. 78. The word *Mädchen* might also be translated as "girlfriend" or possibly "young woman." The women who were the Brücke painters' lovers in Dresden ranged in age from the late teens to early twenties. The role of women in the Brücke's utopia is discussed later in this essay.

30. Friedrich von Schiller, "Über die ästhetische Erziehung des Menschen in einer Reihe von Briefen," in *Werke in drei Bänden*, vol. 2 (Munich: Hanser, 1966), p. 447.

31. "The importance of beauty consists for [Schiller] in the possibility the aesthetic experience affords of a practical apprenticeship for the real political and social freedom to come. In art, consciousness prepares itself for a change in the world itself and at the same time learns to make demands on the real world which hasten that change: for the experience of the imaginary offers (in an imaginary mode) that total satisfaction of the personality and of Being in the light of which the real world stands condemned, in the light of which the Utopian idea, the revolutionary blueprint, may be conceived" (Frederic Jameson, *Marxism and Form: Twentieth-Century Dialectical Theories of Literature* [Princeton, N. J.: Princeton University Press, 1971], p. 90).

32. While there are numerous similarities between the implied thought processes of the Brücke artists and those of such "prophets of cultural despair" as Paul Lagarde and Julius Langbehn, whose thought Fritz Stern has characterized (see note 20 above), the tendency to draw an absolute equation that has characterized much recent scholarship on Expressionism should be resisted. Similarly, while the Brücke's concepts clearly manifest the culture-civilization antithesis that originated in German idealism, their ambivalence toward "civilization" demands to be included in an analysis of their thought.

33. Heinrich Pudor, *Kathechismus der Nackt-Kultur: Leitfaden für Sonnenbäder und Nacktpflege* (Berlin-Steglitz: Kraft und Schönheit, 1906), p. 6.

34. M. Platen, *Die neue Heilmethode: Lehrbuch der naturgemässen Lebensweise, der Gesundheitspflege und der naturgemässen Heilweise*, vol. 1 (Berlin, 1913), pp. 442–43, cited in *"Wir sind nackt und nennen uns Du": Von Lichtfreunden und Sonnenkämpfern: Eine Geschichte der Freikörperkultur*, ed. Michael Andritzky and Thomas Rautenberg (Giessen: Anabas, 1989), p. 15.

35. Aspects of the Brücke's nature worship are discussed by Jill Lloyd, in "The *Brücke* Bathers: Back to Nature," in *German Expressionism*, pp. 102–29. While her account parallels mine in many respects, it does not recognize the utopian quality of the Brücke's nature ideology.

36. "Aus den 'Erinnerungen' von Fritz Bleyl," p. 25.

37. Max Pechstein, *Erinnerungen*, ed. Leopold Reidemeister (Wiesbaden: Limes Verlag, 1960), pp. 41–44.

38. Gustav Schiefler, "Erich Heckels graphisches Werk," *Das Kunstblatt* 2, no. 9 (1918): 283.

39. Heinrich Pudor, *Nackt-Kultur*, vol. 3, *Die Probleme des Lebens und der Zeugung* (Berlin-Steglitz, 1907), cited in Andritzky and Rautenberg, *"Wir sind nackt,"* p. 19. For a brief summary of Pudor's ideology, with an emphasis on his radical nationalism and anti-Semitism, see Frecot, Geist, and Kerbs, *Fidus*, 1868–1948, pp. 48–50. The Brücke's affinities with nudism are discussed extensively in Lloyd, "The *Brücke* Bathers"; the parallel was first drawn by Charles S. Kessler ("Sun Worship and Anxiety: Nature, Nakedness, and Nihilism in German Expressionist Painting," *Magazine of Art* 45 [November 1952]:304–12).

40. For an overview of the development of nudism in Germany, see Andritzky and Rautenberg, *"Wir sind nackt."*

41. Basing her dating for the studio furnishings on various documents in which they are either mentioned or, before 1909, significantly not mentioned, Jill Lloyd argues likewise that the studio decorations were produced in 1909 (*German Expressionism*, p. 23).

42. Although the Brücke's paintings and prints of bathers are usually dated to the time they depict, i.e., the summer months, as if the artists were Impressionist plein-air painters, evidence suggests that the works were actually produced from sketches during the winter months. The finished works of the Brücke depict recollections and memories, not a scene in the process of being witnessed (see Heller, *Brücke*, pp. 50–51).

43. Andritzky and Rautenberg, *"Wir sind nackt,"* pp. 18–20.

44. That this "utopia" was conceived and generated for and by men, with women serving subsidiary roles as "companions and helpers," in Kirchner's words, is readily recognizable. Not only are the women depicted largely in terms of their relationship to men or displaying themselves for men, but women were never depicted performing the "male" act of making art. Although some of the Brücke's models did make drawings during the sketching sessions, the artists never represented them doing so or even performing such tasks as weaving rugs or sewing tapestries for the studios. Artistic work and creativity, according to the visual record of the Brücke's imagery, was not "women's work," and this would seem to imply a perception of women as inferior to their male counterparts within the context of the group's utopian vision.

45. If a comparison must be made between the Brücke's perception of an improved society without imposed authority and discipline, with a celebration of nature and nonmonogamous love, with a free communism and an individualistic socialism, and with art as the driving force behind the emergence of utopia, it should be with the unsystematic ideas of utopia presented in Oscar Wilde's essay "The Soul of Man under Socialism" (see note 1 above). Since the German translation of this essay was included in the same volume as "The Ballad of Reading Gaol," for which Heckel made a series of woodcuts in 1907, it is even possible (but not demonstrable) that the artists knew this text. I am not arguing that Wilde influenced the Brücke, however, only for kinship between his ideas and those that shaped the Brücke.

Galerie Berinson, Berlin

88
Marianne Brandt
Unsere irritierende Grossstadt, 1926
(Our irritating metropolis)
Cat. no. 11

89
Carl Mense
Strasse mit Fahnen, 1913
(Street with flags)
Cat. no. 146

90
Ludwig Meidner
Wannsee Bahnhof, 1913
(Wannsee train station)
Cat. no. 135

91
Ernst Ludwig Kirchner
Stadtbahnbogen, 1915
(Tramway arch)
Cat. no. 113

92
Wilhelm Plünnecke
Häuser, Bäume, Menschen, 1919
(Houses, trees, people)
Cat. no. 173

HÄUSER BÄUME
MENSCHEN
Zehn Steindrucke
von
WILHELM PLÜNNECKE
FRIEDRICH DEHNE VERLAG LEIPZIG

DAVID FRISBY

Social Theory, the Metropolis, and Expressionism

In 1863, in his essay "Le peintre de la vie moderne" (The painter of modern life), Charles Baudelaire defined modernity as "the transitory, the fleeting, the fortuitous, the half of art whose other half is the eternal and the immutable."[1] The painter of modern life was to focus on the transitory, fleeting, and fortuitous dimensions of modern experience, which was viewed by Baudelaire as specifically metropolitan. Modernity was both a quality of modern life and a new aesthetic object. Subsequent avant-garde movements would share this concern with "the fundamentally new object whose force lies solely in the fact that it is new, regardless of how repulsive and wretched it may be."[2]

According to Baudelaire, the aesthetic representation of "the ephemeral, contingent newness of the present" should not capture an eternal element but rather "the age, its fashions, its morals, its emotions." The modern painter must grasp the "rapid movement" that we find "in trivial life, in the daily metamorphosis of external things." Within "the landscapes of the great city—landscapes of stone, caressed by the mist or buffeted by the sun," the modern painter must capture "*the outward show of life*...[and] express at once the attitude and the gesture of human beings." Like Poe's "Man of the Crowd," the artist of modern life must be a "passionate lover of crowds and incognitos," with a capacity to view the present, however trivial, anew. The artist as "passionate spectator" must "set up house in the heart of the multitude, amid the ebb and flow of the movement, in the midst of the fugitive and the infinite." The act of plunging oneself into "the multiplicity of life" forces the artist "to become one flesh with the crowd," to enter into it "as though it were an immense reservoir of electrical energy."[3]

But this immersion in the dynamic flux of the metropolitan crowd, in the latest fashions as the transitory heraldry of the absolutely new, and this marveling at "the amazing harmony of life in the capital cities" does not exhaust Baudelaire's tasks for the modern artist.[4] In his own works—*Les fleurs du mal* (Flowers of evil) or *Le spleen de Paris* (Paris spleen)—he attempts to capture "the savagery that lurks in the midst of civilization," its "living monstrosities," and, not least, the "sickly population which swallows the dust of the factories, breathes in particles of cotton, and lets its tissues be permeated by white lead, mercury and all the poisons needed for the production of masterpieces."[5]

Baudelaire's delineation of modernity and his call for artists to capture our experience of it concentrate upon newness, everyday urban existence, the crowd, and the dynamic movement of the metropolis. Aesthetic representations of such experiences of modernity must confront the full impact and consequences of modern existence: the problems of representing the discontinuous and disintegrating experience of time as transitory, space as indefinite, and causality as replaced by fortuitous or arbitrary constellations. This problematization of our modern experience, and the attendant implications for human individ-

93
Ernst Ludwig Kirchner
Fünf Kokotten, 1914–15
(Five tarts)
Cat. no. 112

uality and subjectivity, is evident in all modern aesthetic movements. Each feels itself to be modern in a new and different manner and proclaims so in its manifestos. All modernist movements have provided aesthetic representations of a "new" object, one viewed and experienced in a new manner, and have applied new methods and techniques to this object. No modernist movement has asserted that it is merely another artistic style; each is always a radical break with the past, with earlier modes of experience and representation. Expressionism too saw itself this way. As Friedrich Huebner insisted, "Expressionism is more; it signifies a change of epoch [*Zeitwende*]." Expressionism, like other modernist movements, offers new possibilities; it "believes in the all-possible. It is the world view of utopia. It places human beings once more at the center of creation."[6]

Such a retrospective view of Expressionism as a cultural movement does little, however, to illuminate its aesthetic focus. Certainly a crucial site of modernity in Expressionist art is the metropolis. Overstating somewhat, Jost Hermand argues: "Expressionism was, from the very outset, a modernistic, avant-garde, metropolitan art.... Indeed, Expressionism was—despite the many tendencies pushing into the biological, mystical, utopian, primal—the first real metropolitan art in Germany...and thus found its logical center in Berlin."[7] Aside from pointing to the significance of other centers (Dresden and Munich, among others), one could also elaborate on the diverse nature of Expressionist representations of the metropolis. For instance, Reinhold Heller has questioned "whether the simple dichotomy of an Expressionist anti-urban versus a non-Expressionist celebration of the city is truly viable," suggesting such variations as the panoramic dead city (Egon Schiele), the city of animated architecture and deanimated persons (Ludwig Meidner), or a "focus on the city's inhabitants while subordinating architectural setting" (Ernst Ludwig Kirchner [see fig. 93]).[8] Sharing the Futurists' celebration of the city at night, the Expressionists often took darkness as a theme. But equally compelling in many Expressionist images is the manner in which the spectator is *in* the street, *in* the crowd, *in* the tumult of the metropolis, rather than viewing the city from a distance, from above, from outside, as a landscape (see fig. 94).

Indeed this inclusion of the spectator in the frame of the street—thereby destroying the perspective of the flaneur posited by Baudelaire and the very conception of a passive spectator—and his or her participation in the dynamic of the metropolis were precisely the avowed aims of some Expressionists. As Meidner stated in his 1914 manifesto: "The time has come at last to start painting our real homeland, the big city which we all love so much. Our feverish hands should race across countless canvases, let them be as large as frescoes, sketching the glorious and the fantastic, the monstrous and dramatic—streets, railroad stations, factories, and towers."[9]

According to Meidner, the Expressionist's aim is not to paint in the Impressionist or Jugendstil manner, but rather to "achieve a deeper insight into reality." In confronting metropolitan reality, the artist must address three dimensions of representation: light, viewpoint, and the application of the straight line. Whereas Impressionists saw light everywhere, Expressionists saw "weight, darkness, and static matter." Between the canyons of high buildings is "a tumult of light and dark." Furthermore, "light sets everything in space into motion. The towers, houses, lanterns appear suspended or swimming in air." The viewpoint, rather than perspective, is "the most intense part of the picture and the climax of the design." It can be located anywhere but preferably below the middle of the picture. It is important that "all things...are clear, sharp and unmystical." But while distant objects are in perspective, "the houses next to us—we see them with only half an eye—they seem

94
Ludwig Meidner
Wögende Menge, 1913
(Surging crowd)
Cat. no. 136

to totter and collapse.... Gables, smokestacks, windows are dark, chaotic masses, fantastically foreshortened and ambiguous." Opposing both Impressionist and decorative tendencies, modern artists, as "contemporaries of the engineer...see beauty in straight lines and geometric forms." The straight line is crucial for portraying cities: "Are not our big city landscapes all battlefields filled with mathematical shapes. What triangles, quadrilaterals, polygons, and circles rush out at us in the streets."

Meidner calls upon his younger colleagues to "flood all our exhibitions with big-city pictures."[10] Yet it was not only visual artists who demanded a return to the reality and utopian potential of the metropolis. In his essay "Rede für die Zukunft" (A speech for the future, 1918), the writer Kurt Pinthus also pleaded for an appreciation of the metropolis:

> *The flight from the cities into nature will no longer be preached, for the stone-filled city is not the symbol of ugliness and inhumanity, no longer the asylum of impoverishment, but as a contrast to the given extended countryside, it is formed by human beings, the work of our hands, the raised-up temple of community, whose boisterous rhythm unites us. Here there beats in all houses and streets the empathic heart of fellow human beings, here the eternally moving spirit calls up the deed.* [11]

Yet not all Expressionist artists responded in equal measure to such calls, and their attitudes toward the metropolis, like those of others before them, often remained deeply ambivalent.

Just as the association of German Expressionism with new representations of the metropolis hides both the extent of preoccupation with nonmetropolitan themes and the diversity of responses to the metropolis, so the treatment of the metropolis by German social the-

95
George Grosz
Mondnacht, 1915–16
(Moonlit night)
Cat. no. 48

orists and commentators also reveals an ambivalence and sometimes hostility to urban experience. Such responses range from an identification of the metropolis with the most negative features of society, through the city as the site and exemplar of an ugly civilization, the city as the potential source of positive aesthetic representations, to the metropolis as the necessary site for aesthetic modernisms. Many of these responses to metropolitan experience in social theory anticipate and certainly illuminate dimensions of Expressionist representations of the big city.

At the most general level the oppositions between community and society and culture and civilization were already widely disseminated in the decade of Expressionist production, from 1910 to 1920. So too was the positive view of community, culture, creativity, and authentic values, and the negative view of society, civilization, conventionality, and inauthentic values. Such a juxtaposition found articulate expression in sociologist Ferdinand Tönnies's *Gemeinschaft und Gesellschaft* (Community and society), first published in 1887 and reprinted many times subsequently.[12] There Tönnies—who hated cities, especially Berlin—explored the tendency for the emergence of modern society to be associated with the destruction of community. He regarded society as "a transitional and superficial phenomenon." Whereas "community is old, society is *new*, as a phenomenon and as a name." One goes into society "as into a *strange* country," into a "mechanical aggregate and artefact."[13] Society is characterized by contractual exchange relations, hostility, and indifference. The act of exchange is "performed by individuals who are alien to each other, have nothing in common with one another, and confront each other in an essentially antagonistic and even hostile manner."[14] Society thus produces a multiplicity of relations between individuals who "remain nevertheless independent of one another and devoid of mutual familiar relationships."[15] The dominance of *Gesellschaft* is accelerated by contemporary processes such as urbanization, and the highest form of societal tendencies is the metropolis.

In contrast all the "creative, formative and contributive activity of human beings" that is "akin to art" belongs to community (*Gemeinschaft*).[16] Decrying modern society's rationalization and its degradation of "everything—objects and humans alike—to the level of means," Tönnies, in later editions of his work, looked for alternative collective structures such as cooperatives (1912) and cooperative production (1922). It is not difficult to read into his work the search for a new community, even a nostalgia for lost communal social forms as an antidote to the negativity of modern societal processes. This utopian community grounded in authentic social relations could be the site of genuine creativity, of "spiritual friendship," itself "a kind of invisible place, a mystical city and gathering, vitalized by both an artistic intuition and a creative will."[17]

Similar conceptions of a utopian community abounded in Expressionist writings. Yet the conception of the metropolis as exemplar of an inauthentic society was often associated with its recognition as a legitimate source of artistic inspiration.[18] In other words, the horror of the *moral* order of the metropolis could exist side by side with a fascination with its *aesthetic* order, despite its ugliness. Flowers of evil blossom in the metropolis, as Baudelaire testified.

96
Lyonel Feininger
Das Tor, 1912
(The gate)
Cat. no. 21

97
Martel Schwichtenberg
Torsäule, c. 1915–18
(Portal Column)
Cat. no. 202

Yet those who argued for recognition of the aesthetic attraction of the metropolis had to confront not merely the powerful antiurbanist tendencies in German society—be they the ideological idylls of a vanished village existence; the various back-to-nature movements; or the retreat to moral, artistic, or religious communities in the countryside—but also the powerful representation of German cities, and not least Berlin, as fundamentally ugly compared with other European cities. Like many of the other urban centers of the German empire, Berlin had experienced massive expansion and extensive industrialization following unification in 1871. Its population at unification was more than three-quarters of a million, but by 1895 it had reached 1.7 million and, a decade later, stood at more than 2 million. By 1920 the population of greater Berlin was approaching 4 million, an expansion fed by mass migrations, particularly from the east.[19] At the same time successive phases of building and reconstruction for industrial development and transportation networks within a short period of time created substantial differences in population density, in turn heightening inequities, class divisions, and urban impoverishment.

Berlin's dramatic expansion into a major metropolis, even its elevation to a *Weltstadt* (world city), symbolized by the Berlin Trade Exhibition of 1896, meant that it was a thoroughly modern city.[20] The 1912 Baedeker guide proclaimed: "Though Berlin does not compete in antiquity or historical interest with the other great European capitals, its position as the metropolis of the German empire...invests it with high importance, in addition to *its special and characteristic interest as the greatest purely modern city in Europe*."[21]

Berlin's pure modernity was, however, often viewed as purely modern ugliness. The author of an anonymous article entitled "Die schönste Stadt der Welt" (The most beautiful city in the world), published in *Die Zukunft* (The future) in 1899, ironically contrasted London, Paris, and New York with Berlin, "the parvenu of big cities and the big city of parvenus." The city's claim to be a metropolis rested on its status as "the factory city that no one knows. which is perhaps the greatest in the world." Its architecture is characterized by a chaotic juxtaposition of historicist styles: "One feels oneself to be in a fevered dream...[in] the major thoroughfares of the west. Here an Assyrian temple structure, adjacent a patrician house from Nuremberg, farther along a piece of Versailles, then reminiscences of Broadway, Italy, Egypt—dreadful premature births of polytechnic beer fantasies. A thousand misunderstood forms spring out of the walls of these petit bourgeois dwellings." And although a city does not necessarily need beautiful buildings if it has the advantage of a striking natural setting, when it has none of these it requires "a significant and well-planned street perspective." To achieve this would require the "planned destruction" of the existing city and the creation (clearly in a manner reminiscent of Baron Haussmann's reorganization of Paris) of that which Berlin lacks: "air, free prospect, perspective."[22]

The essay's author, Walther Rathenau, abandoned such aesthetic reflections for moral and quasi-religious ones in later works such as *Zur Mechanik des Geistes* (On the mechanics of the spirit, 1913), reprinted nineteen times by 1925.

> *The sites of soullessness are terrifying. The wanderer who approaches the metropolis in the twilight from the depths of the country experiences a descent into open tracts of misfortune. Once one has stepped through the atmosphere of effluence, dwelling blocks open up like dark rows of teeth and close off the sky.... The spaces behind the glass panes are filled, their inscriptions shimmering in white-blue arc light. "Big bar," "hairdressing salon," "candy shop," "boot paradise," "cinema, " "installment business, " "world bazaar"— these are the places of consumption....*
>
> *This is the nighttime image of those cities that are praised and applauded as places of happiness, of longing, of intoxication, of the intellect, that depopulate the countryside, that kindle the desire of those excluded to the point of criminality.*[23]

There is little doubt that Rathenau's metropolis is Berlin, portrayed in quasi-Expressionist rhetoric. Yet it is possible to discern views of the city that run counter to this pessimistic image and to the popular negative contrast between Berlin and Vienna, between civilization and culture. Occasionally it was the potential of the modern metropolis that was applauded. In *Ecce Poeta* (1912) Egon Friedell insists that "we must become Americans" in order to become "good Europeans":

> *Berlin is a wonderful modern machine hall, a giant electric motor that, with incredible precision, speed, and energy, brings forth a wealth of complex mechanical products of labor. It is true: this machine at present has no soul. The life of Berlin is the life of a cinematograph theater, the life of a virtuoso-constructed* homme-machine *[man-machine]. But that is enough for a start. Berlin is in the awkward adolescent years of a coming culture.... Berlin's examples of tastelessness are at least modern tastelessness, and they are always better than the most tasteless unmodern, because in them the possibilities for development are located.*[24]

Friedell's futurist metaphors of the machine and the electric motor as positive symbols of modernity and his reference to the cinema are characteristic of the dynamic interpretation of the metropolis that was taken up by the Expressionists. So too is his insistence that despite everything the future lies with modernity.

Four years earlier, in his *Die Schönheit der grossen Stadt* (The beauty of the big city, 1908), the artist and architect August Endell likewise argued for a "love of today and here," criticizing those who shrink from the present through a return to nature.[25] In particular he maintained that despite the deficiencies and ugliness of modern big cities, they contain inexhaustible sources of life and, if we view them in a new light, beauty. The significance of Endell's aesthetics of modern urban life lies in his insistence that utopian traces of beauty can be found in the here and now of the metropolis.

The relationship between the economy and modern culture was investigated by several social theorists, including the sociologist and economist Werner Sombart, who examined the economic transformation of modern culture.

> *The distinctive nature of our technology, the distinctive nature of our social communal living, in large valleys of stone and upon hills of stone, glass, and iron, have brought about a situation in which between ourselves and living nature...a mountain of dead masses of material has piled up that has quite specifically given our intellectual life its characteristic features, A new cultural foundation has thereby been created: the stone pavement; out of it a new culture has emerged: asphalt culture.*

This culture creates "a species of human being that leads its life with no genuine affinity with living nature...a species with pocket watches, umbrellas, rubber shoes, and electric light: an artificial species." Even when this urban mass escapes the valleys of stone, it "hardly enters into an inner relationship with nature," for the nature it confronts is its own creation; the "so-called sense of nature is indeed really a product of the cities." The interaction of mass (of things and people) and change (increasing tempo) creates a leveling of cultural qualities, even "a kind of average person," and the insecurity of all external conditions of life "has also made the inner core of human beings *unstable, restless, and hurried*." This condition also affects artists and writers since "they receive from outside a thousandfold impressions, are so bombarded with stimuli that they too find it increasingly difficult to realize their personal, distinctive nature. For example, if our rich, dazzling age is not capable of developing a distinctive architectural style, is this not due to the fact that a style no longer has the time to establish itself?"[26]

Sombart had earlier developed such themes with respect to the effects of technology on culture at the First German Sociological Association Conference in Frankfurt in 1910.[27] They elicited a reply from the sociologist Max Weber, who drew attention to the interaction among technology, the metropolis, and modern culture. The question, he maintains, of whether "modern *technology [Technik]*, in the commonly understood sense of the word, stands in some relationship to formal-aesthetic values must be answered...in the *affirmative*." He defines a relationship between modern technology and aesthetics using the example of the metropolis and its world of things:

> *Quite specific formal values in our modern artistic culture could indeed only be born due to the existence of the modern* metropolis...*with its streetcars, subway, electrical and other lighting, shop windows, concert halls and*

> *restaurants, cafés, smokestacks, masses of stone, and all the wild dance of tones and impressions of color, the impressions that have their affect on sexual fantasy and the experiences of variations in psychic makeup, that affect the hungry rabble through all kinds of apparently inexhaustible possibilities of life-style and happiness.*[28]

The objects of metropolitan existence not only provide subject matter for modern artistic endeavors but also penetrate the forms of their representation. Although Weber mentions Stefan George and Emile Verhaeren in passing, his thesis is more appropriate to an emergent Expressionist movement, with its emphasis on an objective, disjointed culture of metropolitan technology and its attendant "fantasies," " dreams," and "intensive forms of intoxication."

Weber expands upon his thesis with regard to other features of the modern metropolis and modern artistic representation:

> *I believe that it is quite impossible that certain formal values of modern painting could ever have been realized without the...absolutely distinctive impression made by the modern metropolis, hitherto never offered to human eyes before in the whole of history, forceful by day but totally overwhelming by night. And since what is* visible*—and this alone is of concern here—in each and every modern metropolis receives its specific quality not from property relations and social constellations, but rather primarily from modern technology, so here indeed is a point at which technology purely as such has very far-reaching significance for artistic culture.*[29]

The belief in the total autonomy of modern technology, which Weber did not share, is a significant dimension of some Expressionist critiques of modern society. The preface to Kurt Pinthus's anthology of Expressionist poetry, *Menschheitsdämmerung* (Twilight of humanity, 1919), with its ambiguous title (*Dämmerung* refers to both dusk and dawn), contains the following assertion: "One feels ever more certainly the impossibility of a humanity that has made itself totally dependent upon its own creations, upon its science, its technology, statistics, trade and industry, upon a hypertrophied communal order of bourgeois and conventional utility."[30] Somewhat less dramatically, Georg Simmel's essay "Die Grossstädte und das Geistesleben" (The metropolis and mental life, 1903) commences: "The deepest problems of modern life derive from the claim of the individual to preserve the autonomy and individuality of his existence in the face of overwhelming social forces, of historical heritage, of external culture, and of the technique of life.... An inquiry into the inner meaning of specifically modern life and its products...must seek to solve the equation which structures like the metropolis set up between the individual and the super-individual contents of life."[31]

Such thematic affinities should not be surprising since, for many of his contemporaries, Simmel possessed an instinct for the times that allowed him to anticipate positions that were not yet fully articulated. Writing in 1920, Huebner, for instance, names only Nietzsche and Simmel as philosophical precursors of Expressionism: "In philosophy Georg Simmel prepared the ground for the new mode of thought...with his elaboration of the concepts of 'form,' 'self,' and 'life.'[32]" Thus Simmel's essay on the metropolis and other analyses of

98
Fritz Levy
Grossstadt, c. 1920
(Metropolis)
Cat. no. 126

the city are relevant to our understanding of the experiential foundations of Expressionist representations of the big city.

For Simmel the metropolis is "not a spatial entity with sociological consequences, but a sociological entity that is formed spatially." Human interaction is experienced as different relational ways of filling in space. He highlights a number of spatial forms confronted in interaction: the exclusiveness or uniqueness of space (such as districts of cities); boundaries of space (as in spatial framing, the picture frame, the enclosing boundary of darkness); the fixing of social forms in space (including the rendezvous—whose significance "lies, on the one hand, in the tension between punctuality and the fleeting nature of the occurrence and its spatio-temporal fixing, on the other"—and the individualizing of space, as in the numbering of houses); spatial proximity and distance (including the abstraction and indifference of the spatially proximate in the metropolis); and finally movement in space (the traveler, the stranger, and the dynamic of metropolitan interactions).[33]

The metropolis is not merely the focal point of social differentiation and the complex intersection of social networks but is also the location of more indefinite collectivities such as crowds. The openness of the city, facilitating the intersection of diverse social strata, can be contrasted with the relative isolation and social distance manifested by the "concentrated minority" in the ghetto. The intersection of social groups and individuals in the metropolis generates spatial constellations that foster a total indifference to one's fellow human beings. The development of boundaries and social distance in the metropolis is of fundamental significance in understanding social interaction and patterns of network formation in the city.

Perhaps the most striking dimension of Simmel's analysis of the metropolis lies in his examination of the psychological consequences of the endlessly dynamic interaction of networks, things, individuals, and images within "the genuine showplace of this culture." He elaborates on "the atrophy of individual culture and the hypertrophy of objective culture" through the tendency of each to develop a relative autonomy, with objective culture possessing a "unity and autonomous self-sufficiency" and subjective culture emerging out of "the subjectivism of modern times" and its attendant "dissociation" and "retreat" from objective culture. Nowhere is this apparently autonomous objective culture more evident than in the metropolis, where individuals are faced with "the rapid and unbroken change in external stimuli" that they experience "with every crossing of the street, with the speed and diversity of professional and social life" as "the rapid crowding of changing images, the sharp discontinuity in the grasp of a single glance, and the unexpectedness of onrushing impressions."[34] This experience of modernity as a stream of ever-changing, discontinuous, and diverse impressions is depicted in Expressionist streetscapes (see figs. 100, 101, 102).

The "particularly abstract existence" of the metropolis, however, originates in part in the very labyrinth of interactions themselves, which require functionality, precise differentiation, intellectuality, exactitude, and calculability.[35] Thus the apparent tumult of the metropolis—its myriad abstract interactions and impressions, "the brevity and infrequency of meetings which are allotted to each individual," in short, what appears to be a chaos of impressions, shocks, and interactions—in fact results from "the *calculating exactness* of practical life" in the metropolis. This allows "the agglomeration of so many persons with such differentiated interests" to "intertwine with one another into a many-membered organism."[36]

The city's "rapid and unbroken change in external and internal stimuli" results in a dramatic "increase in *nervous* life," in the modern diseases of neurasthenia, agoraphobia, and hyperesthesia. The impossibility of otherwise retaining a stable subjectivity in the face of the endless shocks of metropolitan existence accounts for the "psychological distance" created by the intellect as a defense mechanism. The heightening of intellectual, "rational" defense mechanisms is matched by a heightening of emotional responses that remain unsatisfied by the "stimulations, interests, fillings in of time and consciousness" in the metropolis.

Simmel points here to the dialectic of subjective and objective culture: we can fully realize our subjectivity only in its externalization in objective cultural forms, yet the latter cannot fulfill our desires. Hence individuals experience a permanent "feeling of tension, expectation and unreleased intense desires," a "secret restlessness" that results in our endless neurotic search for "momentary satisfaction in ever-new stimulations, sensations and external activities.... We become entangled in the instability and helplessness that manifests itself as the tumult of the metropolis, as the mania for traveling, as the wild pursuit of competition, and as the typical modern disloyalty with regard to taste, style, opinions and personal relations."[37] This implies that "the *inner barrier* between people that is indispensable for the modern form of life, " "the mutual reserve and indifference" are never fully effective against the experience of modernity as discontinuity and disintegration of time, space, and causality. Hence alienated forms of existence can become the objective forms in which we live.

One such form, epitomizing urban society, is the blasé attitude, arising from "the rapidly changing and closely compressed contrasting stimulations of the nerves," which culminate in "an incapacity to react to new sensations with the appropriate energy." Thus where individuals are confronted with a mass of commodities and sensations and where all values are reduced to exchange values, the blasé individual "experiences all things as being of an equally dull and grey hue, as not worth getting excited about." Yet the unreleased desire for amusement and excitement remains, accounting for "the craving today for excitement, for extreme impressions, for the greatest speed in their change."[38] The metropolis does provide an "immense abundance of machines, products and supra-individual organizations" that offer the individual "endless habits, endless distractions and endless superficial needs," the "fillings in of time and consciousness."[39] This concentration of objective culture is dependent on the complex intersection of networks of circulation of commodities and individuals.

The metropolis is thus a center of the reification of a culture of things as the culture of human beings. Just as Weber proclaims the quasi autonomy of the technology of urban existence, so Simmel insists on the autonomy of the supra-individual objective culture: "In highly developed epochs with an advanced division of labor, cultural achievements mature and grow together into an autonomous realm."[40]

This increasing autonomy of objective culture provides the foundation for a prevalent pessimism with regard to modern culture, namely, "the ever-widening abyss between the culture of things and that of human beings."[41] Later Simmel brings together the apparently autonomous realm of circulation of commodities and individuals and the autonomy of the objective culture, declaring: "The 'fetishism' which Marx assigned to economic commodities represents only a special case of this general fate of contents of culture. With the increase in culture these contents more and more stand under a paradox:...originally created by subjects...in their intermediate form of objectivity...they follow an immanent logic of development...impelled not by physical necessities, but by truly cultural ones."[42] Similarly, within the cultural sphere itself there is a permanent struggle between life and form. Life generates form and struggles against that which it has created, impelled by an opposition to "form *as such*, against the *principle* of form."[43]

99
Walter Dexel
Sternenbrücke, 1919
(Starry bridge)
Cat. no. 14

Simmel gives an instance of this opposition to form in the artistic realm: "Of all the hotch-potch of aspirations covered by the general name of *Futurism*, only the movement described as *Expressionism* seems to stand out with a certain identifiable degree of unity and clarity...the point of Expressionism is that the artist's inner impulse is perpetuated in the work, or to be more precise, as the work, exactly as it is experienced. The intention is not to express or contain the impulse in a form imposed upon it by something external, either ideal or real." Expressionism relies upon "stimuli from objects in the external world" without Impressionism's "need for the identity between the form of the cause and that of its effect." And this new art "does not have a meaning by itself." It is "indifferent to the traditional standards of beauty or ugliness, which are connected with the primacy of form. Life, in its flow, is not determined by a goal but driven by a force." This accounts for "the desire for completely abstract art among some sectors of modern youth [which] may stem from passion for an immediate and naked expression of self."[44]

Elsewhere Simmel draws attention to an "unmistakable mechanizing, mathematizing tendency" in recent years:

> *All reconstruction of that which one terms the artist's "calculation"—the precise separation of "planes," the schemata of the horizontal and the vertical, the*

100
Paul Gangolf
Strassenszene, 1925
(Street scene)
Cat. no. 37

> *triangular and rectangular in composition, the determination of contrapposto, the theories of the golden section, of the visual arts as "spatial configuration," even the theory of complementary colors—all this breaks up the work of art into individual moments and elements and thereby strives to "explain" the work of art by putting it together again out of these partial regularities and demands.*[45]

The modern tendency toward the affirmation of the work of art as it is experienced by the artist, eschewing reliance on existing forms, accords with Simmel's insistence that life must assert itself continuously against reproduction of existing forms. In part this is a struggle of dynamic impulses against static form, spontaneity of expression against reproduced form. For Simmel, "the essence of life is intensification, increase, growth, of plenitude and power, strength and beauty from within itself—in relation not to any definable goal but purely to its own development."[46]

The city is the focal point of both objective culture and reified forms, including the formal intellectual distance and reserve that its inhabitants adopt as a barrier to immediate life impressions. Modern movements struggle against this rigidified objective culture and, in the case of Expressionism, seek to give substance to the immediate experience of metropolitan existence. It is the pieces and fragments of "the culture of things as the culture of human beings" that the Expressionists sought to represent in their streetscapes and cityscapes.[47]

There is another respect in which Expressionism's aim accords with Simmel's delineation of modern metropolitan existence, namely the attempt to represent artistically our inner experience of it. In a 1911 essay on Auguste Rodin, Simmel describes modernity as "psychologism, the experiencing and interpretation of the world in terms of the reactions of our inner life, and indeed as an inner world, the *dissolution of fixed contents* in the fluid element of the soul, from which all that is substantive is filtered and whose forms are merely *forms of motion*."[48] If we substitute *subjectivism* for *psychologism* and emphasize the shift to inner lived experience (*Erlebnis*), the destabilizing of content, the preponderance of fluid forms, and the domination of the fragmentary, then Simmel's delineation of metropolitan experience as the exemplar of the experience of modernity again becomes strikingly relevant for an understanding of at least some dimensions of Expressionism.

Finally Simmel illustrates both the ambivalence toward the metropolis and the recognition of its utopian potential characteristic of German Expressionism: "The atrophy of individual culture through the hypertrophy of objective culture is one reason for the bitter hatred which the preachers of the most extreme individualism, above all Nietzsche, harbor against the metropolis. But it is, indeed, also a reason why these preachers are so passionately loved in the metropolis and why they appear to the metropolitan person as the prophets and saviors of his or her unsatisfied yearnings."[49] But is the metropolis a site for the realization of "unsatisfied yearnings"? Simmel maintains that it is the site for the development, in often contradictory directions, of two forms of individualism: individual independence and the elaboration of individuality. The metropolis provides the arena for the struggle between these forms of individualism and for their reconciliation.

The engagement with Expressionism was continued by two of Simmel's students, Siegfried Kracauer and Ernst Bloch.[50] Whereas Kracauer developed a distinctive interest in deciphering the fields of signification in the modern metropolis that went far beyond Expressionism (though Expressionism remained a focus of some of his work on film), Bloch retained both a lifelong concern with the utopian possibilities embedded in modernity and a style of writing that displayed Expressionist impulses.

It is in Kracauer's early writings that we find his confrontation with Expressionism. Toward the end of World War I and in its immediate aftermath, he produced a series of unpublished manuscripts, one of which—"Über den Expressionismus: Wesen und Sinn einer Zeitbewegung" (On Expressionism: Essence and meaning of a movement of the times, 1918)[51]—is dedicated to investigating "wherein the *essence* of this new direction in art really lies. What is at issue is not the analysis of individual works but rather the investigation of those intellectual structures that make such works possible."

In order to understand Expressionism, one must have already confronted Impressionism: Impressionism's world is one that "knows no future; it is solely the contemporary moment"; typical "for the Impressionist ultimately is still the emphasis upon the basic principle of 'l'art pour l'art' [art for art's sake]." In contrast the Expressionist artist "always forcefully retains his or her active self." In relation to external reality Expressionist art "does not simply push reality aside but rather (primarily in painting) directly confronts it and battles with it. The Expressionist wants absolutely to destroy reality, and his or her work should not in the least be suggestive of it." Instead the goal of this new art is "to give expression to lived experience (*Erlebnis*) in its naked actuality as much as possible."[52]

Although Expressionist art is deeply caught up in contemporary life and its phenomena, nonetheless "a strong belief in the future and the victorious force of its nature unites the Expressionists. The Expressionist does indeed look forward, he never languishes in the past. An enemy of the present, an adversary of reality, he strives to overcome both. He is ready to engage in deeds; his basic attitude is affirmative." This longing for action, this waiting for genuine engagement are recurrent themes in Kracauer's early writings along with the problematic nature of the contemporary individual. Hence his view that "Expressionism, in fact, is essentially nothing other than a revolt, a cry of despair of the present-day personality, enslaved and condemned to powerlessness. It is above all, in the first instance, a *cultural movement*, in the second, an *artistic movement*." As for the latter: "A terrible danger appears to me bequeathed to Expressionist painting in particular—the danger of being unintelligible."[53]

Only two years later we find Kracauer, in "Schicksalswende der Kunst" (Art's turn of fate, 1920), declaring that "the *Expressionist movement in art*, distinctive to our times, is ripe for its demise." Whereas today "the experiences it embodies are no longer our experiences," before World War I Expressionism responded to an "epoch dominated above all by the spirit of the natural sciences and the spirit of the capitalist economic system," which together created an external reality of life (*Lebenswirklichkeit*) that was "so objective and so secured within itself like no other reality before it." The result was a transformation of "the Whole human environment" into "a structure of horrifying impersonality." Human beings were confronted with "a mechanized nature," with an atomized society locking them into "an invisible network of rational and objective-technical relations" devoid of fundamental elements of human community.[54]

With the individual condemned to a "God-estranged reality," as if encased in a "brazen solid wall," it was "Expressionism's historical merit to have forced a breach in this wall, to have reduced it to ruins." Thus even before the war Expressionism did in art that "which the great social revolutions of the present set as their task in the realms of real life: the destruction of the powers of existence that have hitherto been valid. First of all, Expressionism unmistakably took up battle against the average reality that surrounded it!"[55] Its aim was not merely the destruction of constraining forms or even the restoration of "differentiated and overrefined individual persons," but rather "the Expressionist artist felt and thought of himself or herself to some extent as a primal self (*Ur-ich*), filled with individual experiences of a totally elementary nature—a soul search of a God," with the attendant "ecstatic convulsions." The result was the emergence of a new art:

> *Paintings emerge that hardly still refer to the world of our senses. They transcend our accustomed space and the simultaneity* (Gleichzeitigkeit) *of appearances and press fragments of our perceptions into a texture of lines and bodylike forms, whose structure is almost exclusively determined by the inner needs of the human being transformed into a primal self. Painter and poet endeavor to strip existing reality of its power and to reveal it for what it actually is: a deceptive, shadowlike essence, a chaos without soul, without meaning. Here there appear things and human beings in an ostensibly known form, but their external form is only an empty mask, which the artist strips off or makes transparent so that the true face is revealed beneath.*

The human figures that appear in Expressionist art seem to be typical nighttime figures, but they "cast the burning torch into the buildings of our existence and inflame the ghosts into revolution. In the schematic personage of the 'father' the whole essence of the outlived epoch often takes on its form, and against him, as the symbol of tradition, the preserver of what exists, there arises the 'son,' prepared to murder."[56]

Kracauer saw Expressionism as having fulfilled its mission of representing, artistically at least, the "triumph of the soul over reality," the negation of the empty inner world and the awakening of "the need for new world formations." Although Expressionism produced new artistic means of expressing and representing reality, what was now required was to go beyond Expressionism, to realize "*the construction of a new reality in art*." Hence the realization of that which Expressionism proclaimed must be set in motion, the creation of a new reality "that no longer permits the advocacy, as does Expressionism, of the concerns of an abstract humanity by means of equally abstract types, but rather gives life to the general in the particular, embodying totally the human essence in accordance with its whole surging fullness."[57] This search for concretization is one that Kracauer himself engaged in, but only from around 1926 onward was it fully manifested in his rich constructions of metropolitan modernity that go far beyond the Expressionist impulses that he saw as ripe for realization in 1920.[58]

In contrast Ernst Bloch retained a commitment to at least the utopian impetus of German Expressionism long after its demise. Some of his works, especially *Geist der Utopie* (The spirit of utopia, 1918; see Appendix),[59] made a major contribution to the utopianism of Expressionism, traces of which can be found in later works such as *Erbschaff dieser Zeit* (Heritage of our times, 1935) and *Das prinzip Hoffnung* (The principle of hope, 1954).[60] Indeed, in its mode of presentation, with its "primacy of expression over signification," Bloch's whole philosophy is, according to Theodor Adorno, "that of Expressionism. It is preserved in the idea of breaking through the encrusted surface of life. Human immediacy wishes to make itself heard unmediated: Like the Expressionist human subject, Bloch's philosophy protests against the reification of the world."[61]

Geist der Utopie is a radical Expressionist assertion of "intellectual renewal," "self-confrontation [*Selbstbegegnung*]," and the development of a conception of utopia located in the here and now. As Arno Münster suggests, Bloch's notion of utopia does not presuppose any concretization in a specific sociohistorical context.[62] It does not presuppose a future state of affairs but is located, hidden, waiting to be drawn out, to be expressed now. Moreover Bloch not only rejects total utopian blueprints but also dismisses the notion that reality is a homogeneous totality. If it were, its seemingly insignificant utopian elements could never be brought to expression.

In this respect Bloch's work of this period, despite its affinities with Georg Lukács's *Geschichte und Klassenbewusstsein* (History and class consciousness, 1923) with regard to a romantic anticapitalism and variants of "messianic Marxism" (in Bloch's case, more messianism than Marxism), differs in its rejection of totalizations of society, reification, and utopia. For Bloch, "Actuality and utopia are not opposites, but 'the now' is finally the sole concern of utopia, whether one understands it as the constant demand to throw off masks, ideologies, and transit mythologies, or as premonition of the adequation of the process that recognizes both the driving tendency and the hidden genuine reality in the now."[63] That "now" of *Geist der Utopie* is one permeated by Expressionism. There and elsewhere is evidence of Bloch's reflections upon the metropolis, its buildings, its architecture.

An early chapter of *Geist der Utopie* titled "Die Erzeugung des Ornaments" (The creation of the ornament) is dominated by references to the Expressionism of Franz Marc, Wassily Kandinsky, Max Pechstein, and Oskar Kokoschka. Each of these artists—whether it be "Kandinsky, who has been called the intensive Expressionist; Pechstein, the extensive Expressionist; [or] Marc, the great, most subjectivist, and simultaneously most objectivist artist of the 'concept' of the thing"—is seeking "to anchor the fleeting element of feeling and to embody it purely economically in firm drawing, fixed spatial relations." Today "we seek the magical creator who allows us to confront ourselves, to encounter ourselves" in a new environment, with a new vision that "travels like a swimmer, like a cyclone through that which is there [*das Gegebene*]." In fact, for this new way of seeing things:

> *The cinematograph is the best picture gallery, the substitute for all the great general art exhibitions of the world. This should be kept in mind by all those who must ask with each Expressionist image what it represents, by what means, for instance, to their eye, that is like a mere photographic plate, hell can shrink back and resemble a street corner. For already since van Gogh, this has evidently changed; we are suddenly involved in things, and precisely this is what is painted; it is indeed still a visible tumult, still railings, underpasses, iron beams, brick walls, but suddenly all this overlaps in a remarkable manner, the discarded cornerstone lights up all at once, and what has been drawn in all appearances, that which is incomprehensibly related, that which is lost to us, the near, far, Sais-like aspect of the world, emerges in van Gogh's paintings.*

But it is not merely the cityscape that is transformed by Expressionism: "Grass is no longer grass, the multifarious disappears, and that which is facelike [*das Gesichthafte*] is victorious. The thing becomes a mask, a 'concept,' a fetish, a completely deformed, denaturalized formula of secret excitements toward a goal, the inner human being and the inside of the world move closer.... Suddenly I see my eyes, my place, my position: I am myself this drawer, and this fish, this kind of fish lying in the drawer."[64] Bloch highlights here the intense "materiality of things."

But it is not only the representation of still life—even in the "new Expressionism," which uses "things merely as memory stages of [our]...stubborn origins or as punctuation marks for keeping or storing their continuous recollection"—that is significant. Still life "can be superior to all cultures in its escapism and intensification of small things."[65] The "still life" of small things is also that with which we surround ourselves, the ornaments of our existence. They are the products of machines: "The machine knew how to make everything so lifeless, technical, and subhuman in individual elements, just as the streets of western Berlin are in their totality. Its actual goal is the bathroom and toilet, the most unquestionable and original achievements of this era.... Here the fact that things can be washed up reigns." These everyday objects were covered over with ornament and style in all their heterogeneity by historicism. And here there exists, "despite all antagonistic, malignant, and negative elements that can be read equally from the death of style in the mid-nineteenth century, the functional connection of this epidemic of styles with the positive forces of Expressionism."[66]

Such "positive forces," however, are contradictory, at least with respect to the tension between the functional and the ornamental that exists contemporaneously. For Bloch: "The birth of integral technology and the birth of integral expressionism, accurately kept apart from each other, arise from the same magic: complete void of ornament on the one hand, utmost superabundance of ornamentation on the other, but both are variables of the same exodus," Such tensions permeate architectural structures and the inability of functional form to expand stylistically. In this context,

101
Ludwig Meidner
Untitled (street scene), 1913
Cat. no. 137

There will never be any expressionist houses built if one attaches great importance to unified form. It is impossible to produce all of the rectangular shiny functional forms in an abundantly ornamental way, to break up and cover the firm windows, elevators, desks, the telephones with Lehmbruck's, with Archipenko's curves. The only contiguity, and in this instance only a seeming one, lies in places for celebrations, in exhibition halls, in the theatre, particularly when this space, as it does with Poelzig, shines into the stage itself, with the separate magic of its semblance.[67]

Later, in *Das Prinzip Hoffnung*, Bloch was to argue that the architecture of Bruno Taut's "House of Heaven" or that of the "pancosmist" Paul Scheerbart "remained fruitless." This was because architecture "is and remains a social creation, it cannot blossom at all in the hollow space of late capitalism."68 Nonetheless such fantasies as were sketched and sometimes completed, even in the age of functional technology, were the product of a remarkable concentrated outburst of fantasy, affirming Bloch's later statement that "ornament is the bad conscience of architecture."[69]

In the Expressionist decade and at least until his emigration in 1933, the site of Bloch's fantasies remained Berlin. As he stated in 1921, "I do indeed believe that Berlin, the forceful, the utopian, is still of all others my city."[70] He had already explored that utopian element in 1916 in the article "Das südliche Berlin" (Southern Berlin). Berlin was "on the way to a new exuberance, in some respects to breaking through the grey life." The city had been for a time "seductive, experimental." More than a decade later, in 1928, in "Berlin nach zwei Jahren" (Berlin two years later), despite the growing crisis, Bloch could assert that "the good element is, as we know, Berlin's dynamism, the journey into unknown stretches of heaven. To the citizen the treadmill, when it moves rapidly, appears to be an airstrip." Still later, in 1932, in "Berlin aus der Landschaft gesehen" (Berlin viewed from the landscape), he explored its contradictory newness, but whereas "other cities are often mere specters of a better past, the hollow Berlin is possibly—there is no other choice—the specter of a better future."[71]

102
Paul Klee
"Berlin dageggen unsere Hochburg buchte jähe Verzehnfachung seiner Bürger"; *Berlin als Zentrum*, 1919
("Berlin, however, our citadel, experienced a sudden decupling of its citizens"; Berlin as center)
Cat. no. 115

In Bloch's major published work of the 1930s, *Erbschaft dieser Zeit*, the utopian elements of the present become more difficult to detect and to defend, not merely against a destructive Nazism but also against ostensibly "progressive" commentators such as Lukács and others. Almost alone within this political discourse, Bloch defends what is valuable in "authentic Expressionism" as the "first and most genuine form of non-representational, different dream-montage of our times."[72] Originally Expressionism was "image explosion, was torn-up surface even starting with the original, namely with the subject which violently tore up and cross-connected. Thus this subject of bourgeois-aesthetic opposition... definitely sought contact with the world.... [It] covered the world with war, mounted its fragments into grotesque caricatures, mounted into the hollow spaces above all excesses and hopes of a substantial kind, archaic and utopian images." And though Expressionism sought to explode reification, it lacked contact with the concrete overcoming of this reification.

Nonetheless for Bloch the genuine elements of this movement still render cultural inheritance problematic, "simply because the Expressionist epoch so completely tore to shreds the casual routine, the conventional associations from the past." Its abrupt dislocations of the surface remain testimony to the negation of reality as homogeneity, as continuity, since "reality is never unbroken context...but always still—interruption and always still fragment." For Bloch, at least in 1938, "the inheritance of Expressionism is not yet at an end, because it has not yet been started on at all."[73] Is the same still true today?

NOTES

The author acknowledges the assistance of the staff of the Deutsches Literaturarchiv, Marbach, for access to material by Siegfried Kracauer, and of Dr. Karlheinz Weigand, director of the Ernst-Bloch-Archiv; Ludwigshafen, for access to material by Ernst Bloch.

1. Charles Baudelaire, "The Painter of Modern Life," in *The Painter of Modern Life and Other Essays*, trans. and ed. Jonathan Mayne (London: Phaidon, 1964), pp. 1–40.

2. Walter Benjamin, *Gesammelte Schriften*, vol. 1, pt. 3 (Frankfurt: Suhrkamp, 1980), p. 1152.

3. Baudelaire, "Painter of Modern Life," pp. 1, 4, 8, 9.

4. Ibid., p. 11.

5. Quoted in Walter Benjamin, *Charles Baudelaire: A Lyric Poet in the Era of High Capitalism*, trans. Harry Zohn (London: New Left Books, 1973), p. 74.

6. Friedrich M. Huebner, "Der Expressionismus in Deutschland" (1920), in *Expressionismus: Der Kampf um eine literarische Bewegung*, ed. Paul Raabe (Munich: Deutscher Taschenbuch Verlag, 1965), p. 136. The volume is a valuable source of documentation on Expressionism.

7. Jost Hermand, "Das Bild der 'grossen Stadt' in Expressionismus," in *Die Unwirklichkeit der Städte*, ed. Klaus R. Scherpe (Reinbek: Rowohlt, 1988), p. 66. On literary Expressionism and the metropolis, see Silvio Vietta and Hans-Georg Kemper, *Expressionismus* (Munich: Wilhelm Fink, 1975).

8. Reinhold Heller, "'The City Is Dark': Conceptions of Urban Landscape and Life in Expressionist Painting and Architecture," in *Expressionism Reconsidered*, ed. Gertrud Bauer Pickar and Karl Eugene Webb (Munich: Wilhelm Fink, 1979), p. 45; see also Christoph Brockhaus, "Die ambivalente Faszination der Grossstadterfahrung in der deutschen Kunst des Expressionismus," in *Expressionismus: Sozialer Wandel und künstlerische Erfuhrung*, ed. Horst Meixner and Silvio Vietta (Munich: Wilhelm Fink, 1982), pp. 84–106.

9. Ludwig Meidner, "An Introduction to Painting Big Cities," in *Voices of German Expressionism*, ed. Victor H. Miesel (Englewood Cliffs, N.J.: Prentice Hall, 1970), pp. 111–15; originally published as "Anleitung zum Malen von Grossstadtbilder," in "Das neue Programm," *Kunst und Künstler* 12 (March 1914): 299–314. The contrast with Impressionism could be extended beyond representation to social organization. Writing in 1917, Karl Scheffler argued that "expressionism...cannot really make use of this intimate group [the Berlin Secession]. The spirit that has captured our young artists and dominates them more every day rejects limits and boundaries, it seeks a direct link to the masses, it strives for breadth, universality, loudness—its essence is democratic, not patrician" (quoted in Peter Paret, *The Berlin Secession* [Cambridge, Mass.: Belknap, 1980], p. 233).

10. For a discussion of Meidner's text, see Heinz Brüggemann, "Grossstadt und neues Sehen," in *Ludwig Meidner: Zeichner, Maler, Literat, ed. Gerda Breuer and Ines Wagemann*, vol. 1 (Stuttgart: Hatje, 1991), pp. 48–56. For a more detailed examination, see Gerhard Leistner, *Idee und Wirklichkeit: Gehalt und Bedeutung des urbanen Expressionismus in Deutschland, dargestellt am Werk Ludwig Meidners* (New York: Peter Lang, 1986). More generally, on changes in perception, see Christoph Asendorf, *Ströme und Strahlen* (Glessen: Anabas, 1989).

11. Kurt Pinthus, "Rede für die Zukunft," in *Der Aktivismus, 1915–1920*, ed. Wolfgang Rothe (Munich: DTV, 1969), pp. 116–33, esp. p. 131.

12. Ferdinand Tönnies, *Gemeinschaft und Gesellschaft* (Leipzig: Fues's Verlag, 1887); translated by Charles P. Loomis, under the title *Community and Association* (London: Routledge, 1955). On representations of the city, see Andrew Lees, *Cities Perceived* (Manchester: Manchester University Press, 1985); Anthony Sutcliffe, ed., *Metropolis, 1890–1940* (London: Mansell, 1984), esp. pt. 2.

13. Ferdinand Tönnies, "Zur Einleitung in der Soziologie," *Zeitschrift für Philosophie und philosophische Kritik*, no. 115 (1899): 248.

14. Ibid., p. 242

15. Tönnies, *Community and Association*, p, 87.

16. Ibid., pp. 95–96.

17. Quoted in Harry Liebersohn, *Fate and Utopia in German Sociology, 1870–1923* (Cambridge: MIT Press, 1988), p. 36.

18. For example, see Donald E. Gordon, *Expressionism: Art and Idea* (New Haven, Conn.: Yale University Press, 1987), p. 136. On the sexual—and sexist—representations of "decay and degeneracy" in Expressionist and later portrayals of the city, see Beth I. Lewis, "*Lustmord*: Inside the Windows of the Metropolis," in *Berlin: Culture and Metropolis*, ed. Charles W. Haxthausen and Heidrun Suhr (Minneapolis: University of Minnesota Press, 1990), pp. 111–40.

19. Figures cited in Haxthausen and Suhr, *Berlin*, p. xxii, n. 13; for a detailed discussion of German urbanization, see *Jürgen Reulecke, Geschichte der Urbanisierung in Deutschland* (Frankfurt: Suhrkamp, 1985).

20. The Berlin Trade Exhibition of 1896 is discussed by, among others, Georg Simmel ("Berliner-Gewerbe Ausstellung," Die Zeit [Vienna] 8 [25 July 1896]; translated by Sam Whimster as "The Berlin Trade Exhibition,"*Theory, Culture, and Society* 8, no. 3 [1991]: 119–24).

21. Karl Baedeker, *Berlin and Its Environs*, 5th ed. (Leipzig: K. Baedeker, 1912), p. v.

22. [Walther Rathenau], "Die schönste Stadt der Welt," *Die Zukunft* 26 (1899): 37, 40, 41. For a fuller discussion of this article and of August Endell, see Lothar Müller, "The Beauty of the Metropolis: Toward an Aesthetic Urbanism in Turn-of-the-Century Berlin," in Haxthausen and Suhr, *Berlin*, pp. 37–57. The notion that Berlin and other cities were developing without a structure was widespread. Karl Scheffler saw the city as "an unnaturally extended, formless city economy" (*Die Architektur der Grossstadt* [Berlin: Bruno Cassirer, 1913], p. 21).

23. Walther Rathenau, *Zur Mechanik des Geistes* (Berlin: S. Fischer, 1913), pp. 40–41.

24. Egon Friedell, *Ecce Poeta* (Berlin: S. Fischer, 1912), p. 260.

25. August Endell, *Die Schönheit der grossen Stadt* (Stuttgart: Strecker und Schröder, 1908; Berlin: Archibook, 1984), p. 34.

26. Werner Sombart, *Die deutsche Volkswirtschaft im neunzehnten Jahrhundert*, 3d ed. (Berlin: G. Bondi, 1913), pp. 415, 416, 419, 420.

27. Werner Sombart, "Technik und Kultur," in *Verhandlungen des Ersten deutschen Soziologentages, 1910* (Tübingen: Mohr, 1911), pp. 80–97; on Expressionist literary responses to technology, see also Karlheinz Daniels, "Expressionismus und Technik," in *Technik in der Literatur*, ed. Harro Segeberg (Frankfurt: Suhrkamp, 1987), pp. 351–86.

28. Max Weber, "Diskussionsrede zu W. Sombarts Vortrag über Technik und Kultur," in *Gesammelte Aufsätze, zur Soziologie und Socialpolitik* (Tübingen: Mohr, 1988), p. 453; on Weber, see Sam Whimster, "The Secular Ethic and the Culture of Modernism," in *Max Weber: Rationality and Modernity*, eds. Sam Whimster and Scott Lash (London: Allen and Unwin, 1987), pp. 259–90.

29. Weber, "Diskussionsrede," pp. 453–54.

30. Kurt Pinthus, ed., *Menschheitsdämmerung: Symphonie jüngster Dichtung* (Berlin: Ernst Rowohlt, 1920), p. 26.

31. Georg Simmel, "The Metropolis and Mental Life," in *The Sociology of Georg Simmel*, ed. Kurt H. Wolff, trans. Hans Gerth (Glencoe, Ill.: Free Press, 1950), p. 409; originally published as "Die Grossstädte und das Geistesleben," in *Die Grossstadt*, special issue of *Jahrbuch der Gehe-Stiftung zu Dresden* 9 (1903): 185–206.

32. Huebner, "Expressionismus in Deutschland," p. 139.

33. See Georg Simmel, "Soziologie des Raumes," *Jahrbuch für Gesetzgebung, Verwaltung und Volkswirtschaft* 27 (1903): 27–71; for an English translation, see *Simmel on Culture*, ed. Mike Featherstone and David Frisby (forthcoming); see also idem, "Über räumliche Projektionen sozialer Formen," *Zeitschrift für Sozialwissenschaft* 6 (1903): 287–302. This discussion relies upon David Frisby, *Simmel and Since* (London: Routledge, 1992), pt. 2. Simmel's relevance for the interpretation of metropolitan art and architecture has been noted, for instance, by Manfredo Tafuri: "Simmel's considerations on the great metropolis...contained *in nuce* the problems that were to be at the center of concern of the historical avant-garde movements" (*Architecture and Utopia* [Cambridge: MIT Press, 1976], pp. 88–89; see also Michael Müller, *Schöner Schein* [Frankfurt: Athenäum, 1987], esp. p. 29ff.).

34. Simmel, "Metropolis and Mental Life," pp. 410, 422. The constellation of city, abstraction, and money economy was to receive a conservative interpretation in Oswald Spengler's highly popular volumes. Spengler's interpretation of the metropolis owes not a little to Simmel's themes (see *Der Untergang des Abendlandes*, vol. 2 [Munich: Beck, 1923], esp. pp. 101–31).

35. G. Simmel, *The Philosophy of Money*, 2d ed., trans. Tom Bottomore and David Frisby (London: Routledge, 1990), esp. chap. 6.

36. Simmel, "Metropolis and Mental Life," p. 412.

37. Simmel, *Philosophy of Money*, p. 484.

38. Ibid., pp. 256, 257. In "The Metropolis and Mental Life," Simmel equates the blasé attitude with "a faithful subjective reflection of a completely internalized money economy.... All things float with equal specific gravity in the constantly moving stream of money. All things lie on the same level." Commenting on this passage, Manfredo Tafuri writes: "The objects all floating on the same plane, with the same specific gravity, in the constant movement of the money economy: does it not seem that we are reading here a literary comment on a Schwitters *Merzbild*?... The problem was, in fact, how to render active the intensification of nervous stimulation...how to absorb the shock provoked by the metropolis by transforming it into a new principle of dynamic development; how to 'utilize' to the limit the anguish which 'indifference to value' continually provokes and nourishes in the metropolitan experience" (*Architecture and Utopia*, pp. 88–89).

39. Simmel, *Philosophy of Money*, p. 483; idem, "Metropolis and Mental Life," p. 422 (amended translation).

40. Georg Simmel, "Vom Wesen der Kultur," in *Brücke und Tür: Essays des Philosophen zur Geschichte, Religion, Kunst und Gesellschaft*, ed. Michael Landmann (Stuttgart: K. F. Koehler, 1957), p. 94.

41. Georg Simmel, "Die Zukunft unserer Kultur," in *Brücke und Tür*, p. 95.

42. Georg Simmel, "On the Concept and Tragedy of Culture," in *The Conflict in Modern Culture and Other Essays*, ed. and trans. K. Peter Etzkorn (New York: Teachers College Press, 1968), p. 42.

43. Georg Simmel, "The Conflict in Modern Culture," in *Conflict in Modern Culture*, p. 12.

44. Ibid., pp. 15–16, 18.

45. Georg Simmel, "L'art pour l'art," in *Zur Philosophie der Kunst* (Potsdam: Gustav Kiepenheuer, 1922), p. 79.

46. Quoted in Peter Lawrence, ed., *Georg Simmel: Sociologist and European*, trans. D. E. Jenkinson et al. (New York: Barnes and Noble, 1976), p. 228.

47. Georg Simmel, "Philosophie der Landschaft," in *Brücke und Tür*, p. 141.

48. Georg Simmel, "Rodin," in *Philosophische Kultur*, 3d ed. (Potsdam: Gustav Kiepenheuer, 1923), pp. 179–97, esp. p. 196.

49. Simmel, "Metropolis and Mental Life," p. 422.

50. On Kracauer, see Inka Mülder, *Siegfried Kracauer* (Stuttgart: Metzler, 1985); Frisby, *Fragments of Modernity*, chap. 3; Michael Kessler and Thomas Y. Levin, eds., *Siegfried Kracauer* (Tübingen: Stauffenburg, 1990). On Bloch, see Peter Zudeick, *Der Hintern des Teufels: Ernst Bloch: Leben und Werk* (Moos: Elster, 1987).

51. Siegfried Kracauer, "Über den Expressionismus: Wesen und Sinn einer Zeitbewegung," Siegfried Kracauer Nachlass, Deutsches Literaturarchiv, Marbach.

52. Ibid., pp. 18, 36.

53. Ibid., pp. 46, 72, 77.

54. Siegfried Kracauer, "Schicksalswende der Kunst" (1920), in *Schriften* 5.1 (*Aufsätze 1915–1926*), ed. Inka Mülder-Bach (Frankfurt: Suhrkamp, 1990), pp. 72, 73. The crisis in Expressionism around 1920 is also commented on by, among others, Kracauer's younger friend Theodor Adorno (see Theodor Wiesengrund, "Expressionismus und künstlerische Wahrhaftigkeit," *Die neue Schaubühne* 2 [1920]: 233–36).

55. Kracauer, "Schicksalswende der Kunst," p. 73.

56. Ibid., p. 75. For a more specific analysis of Expressionism by Kracauer, see his "Max Beckmann," *Die Rheinlande*

31 (July 1921): 93–96, in which he draws attention to Beckmann's depiction of "the thousand horrors of the street," "the wild chaos that unfolds itself between swaying buildings in streets and squares" (p. 95).

57. Ibid., p. 78.

58. See Frisby, *Fragments of Modernity*, chap. 3; Mülder, *Siegfried Kracauer*.

59. Ernst Bloch, *Geist der Utopie* (Munich: Duncker und Humblot, 1918). The second edition was published in 1923. The original was written between April 1915 and May 1917. There are significant differences in the two texts. Most references here are to the 1918 edition. Peter Zudeick has summarized the Expressionist content of this volume as follows: "In 'Geist der Utopie' Bloch played through the whole repertoire of the Expressionist sense of life, and he was master of this keyboard like hardly anyone else: critique of bourgeois society, mendacity, mediocrity, the constraint of bourgeois moral conceptions, anti-intellectualism, the mechanization and commercialization of society, the emptiness and anomic nature of human relationships, and out of all these things the longing for a new humanity, a new religiosity, a fraternal-socialistic future society" (*Der Hintern des Teufels*, pp. 66–67).

60. Ernst Bloch, *Erbschaft dieser Zeit* (Zurich: Oprecht und Helbling, 1935); translated by Neville and Stephen Plaice under the title *Heritage of Our Times* (Berkeley and Los Angeles: University of California Press, 1991); idem, *Das Prinzip Hoffnung*, 3 vols., rev. ed. (Frankfurt: Suhrkamp, 1959); translated by Neville Plaice, Stephen Plaice, and Paul Knight under the title *The Principle of Hope*, 3 vols. (Oxford: Blackwell, 1986).

61. Theodor W. Adorno, "Blochs Spuren," *Noten zur Literatür*, vol. 2 (Frankfurt: Suhrkamp, 1961), pp. 144–45.

62. Arno Münster, *Utopie, Messianismus und Apokalypse im Frühwerk von Ernst Bloch* (Frankfurt: Suhrkamp, 1982), p. 126.

63. Quoted in Wayne Hudson, *The Marxist Philosophy of Ernst Bloch* (New York: St. Martin's Press, 1982), p. 40.

64. Bloch, *Geist der Utopie*, pp. 44, 50–51; on Bloch's theory of ornament, see Gérard Raulet, *Natur und Ornament* (Darmstadt: Luchterhand, 1987), pp. 63–121.

65. Ernst Bloch, *The Utopian Function of Art and Literature: Selected Essays*, trans. Jack Zipes and Frank Mecklenburg (Cambridge: MIT Press, 1988), p. 101. This volume contains a translation of "Die Erzeugung des Ornaments" from the second edition of *Geist der Utopie*.

66. Bloch, *Geist der Utopie*, pp. 21, 22–23.

67. Bloch, *Utopian Function of Art and Literature*, pp. 82, 83.

68. Bloch, *Principle of Hope*, vol. 2, p. 737. Somewhat ironically Walter Benjamin, more critical of Expressionism, refers to Taut's *Alpine Architektur* as "a well-ventilated utopia." More significantly Benjamin sees Scheerbart's plea for glass architecture as a plea for an architectural material that leaves no traces: "Things made from glass have no 'aura.' Glass is everywhere the enemy of secrets. It is also the enemy of possession" ("Erfahrung und Armut," *Gesammelte Schriften*, vol. 2, pt. 1, pp. 213–19).

69. Ernst Bloch, "Architektur und Utopie" (Alpbach, 1972). Ernst-Bloch-Archiv, Ludwigshafen.

70. Quoted in Zudeick, *Hintern des Teufels*, p. 95.

71. Ernst Bloch, "Das sudliche Berlin," *Zeit-Echo*, no. 15 (1915–16): 235–38 (part of this text is incorporated into *Geist der Utopie*, pp. 303–4); idem, "Berlin nach zwei Jahren," *Die Weltbühne* 24 (3 January 1928): 32–33; idem, "Berlin aus der Landschaft gesehen," *Frankfurter Zeitung*, 7 July 1932.

72. Bloch, *Heritage of Our Times*, p, 204. The "dream-montage" is most often associated with Surrealism, which proved a major influence upon Walter Benjamin, despite his subsequent critical regard for it. Bloch too saw its possibilities, especially in the improvised revue form of Benjamin's *Einbahnstrasse* (One-way street, 1928), with its emphasis on the fragmentary. What Bloch found absent was the "concrete intention": "Even one-way streets have a destination." On Bloch's own fragmentary *Spuren*, see Klaus L. Berghahn, "A View through the Red Window: Ernst Bloch's *Spuren*," in *Modernity and the Text: Revisions of German Modernism*, ed. Andreas Huyssen and David Bathrick (New York: Columbia University Press, 1989), pp. 200–215.

73. Bloch, *Heritage of Our Times*, pp. 204–5, 240, 250, 253.

ARCHITECTURAL FANTASY

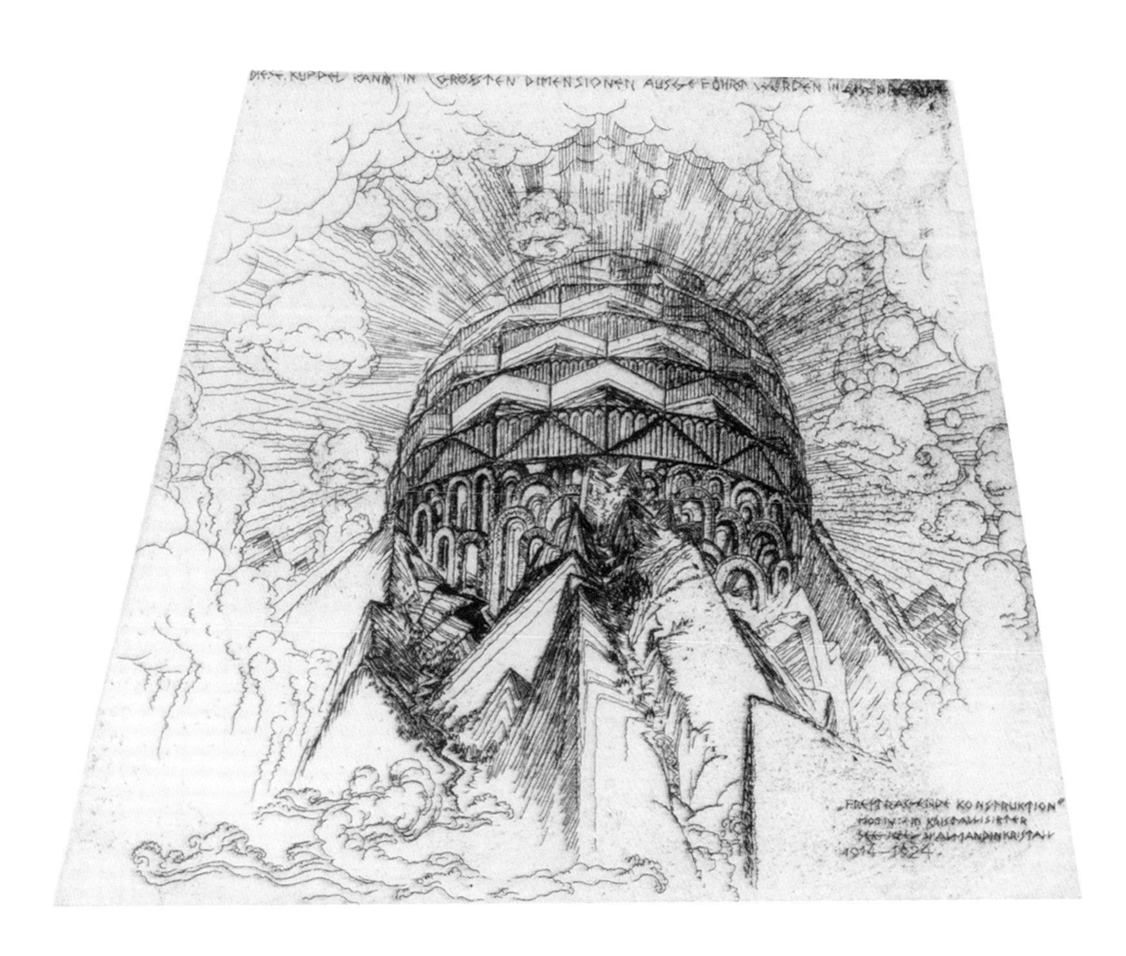

103
Hermann Finsterlin
Architektur—Kathedrale des Lichts, Serie IV, Blatt 4
(Architecture—cathedral of light, series IV, sheet 4)
Cat. no. 34

104
Wenzel Hablik
Freitragende Konstruktion, 1914–24
(Self-supporting construction)
Cat. no. 67

105
Hermann Finsterlin
Drei geometrische Phantasien,
1922–23
(Three geometric fantasies)
Cat. no. 31

106
Erich Mendelsohn
Architekturphantasie—
Perspektive, 1914
(Architectural fantasy—
perspective)
Cat. no. 139

107
Carl Krayl
Vision, 1920
(Vision)
Cat. no. 125

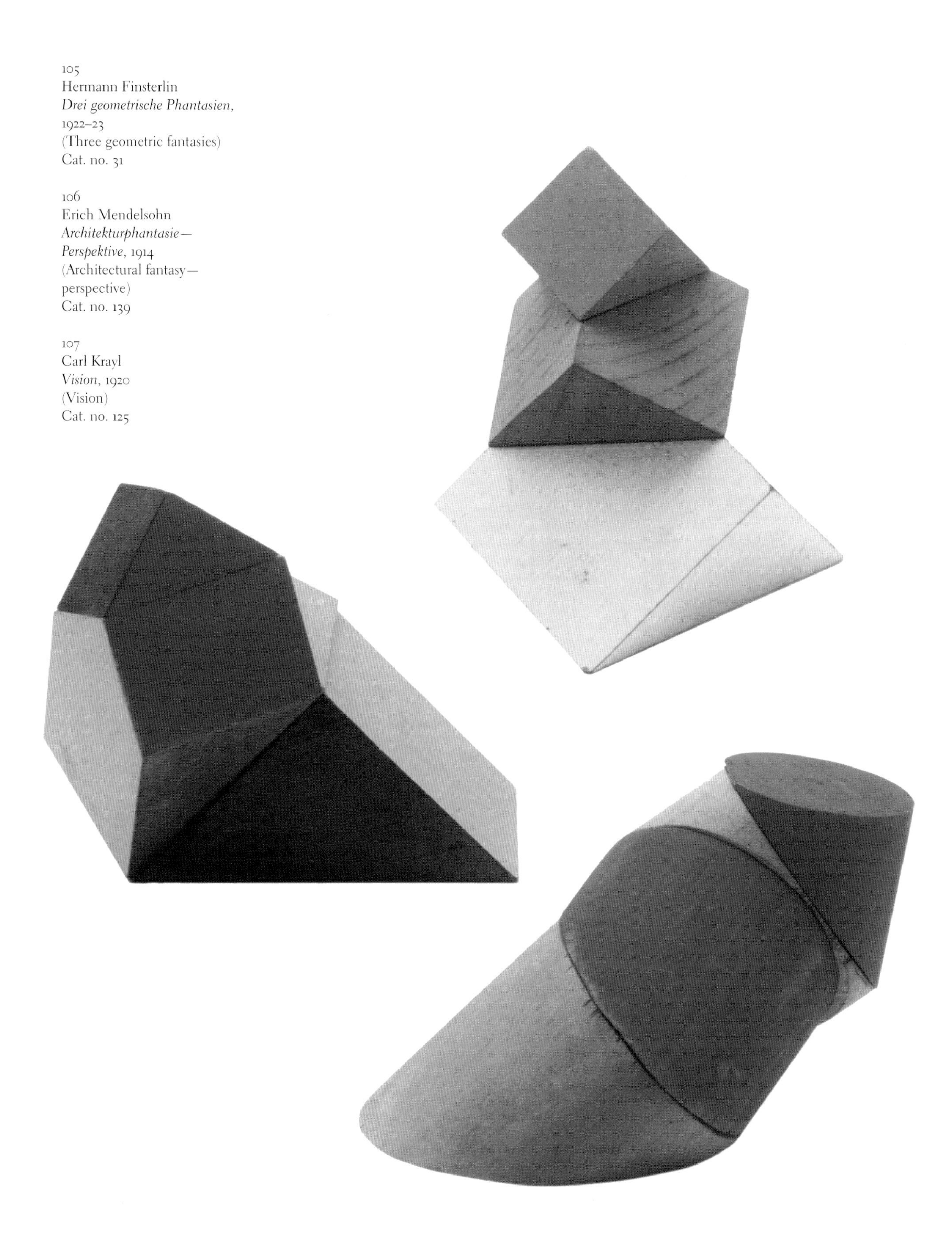

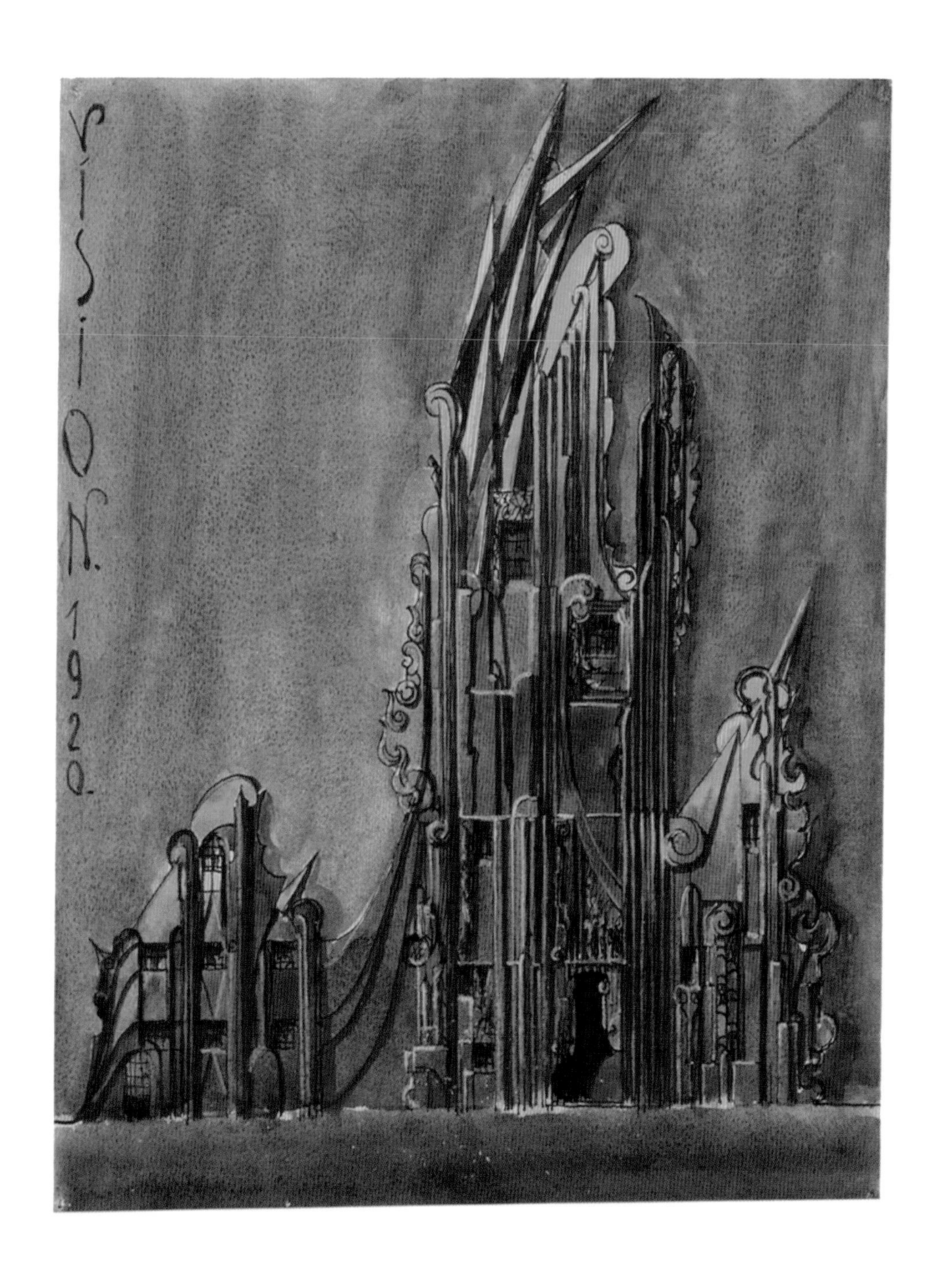
VISION. 1920

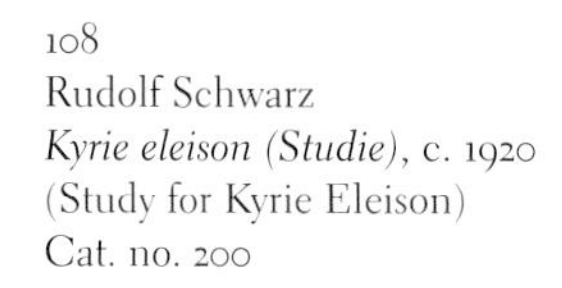

108
Rudolf Schwarz
Kyrie eleison (Studie), c. 1920
(Study for Kyrie Eleison)
Cat. no. 200

109
Rudolf Schwarz
Sanktus, c. 1920
Cat. no. 201

110
Ottheinrich Strohmeyer
Das Kreuz im Kreise, 1920
(The cross in the circle)
Cat. no. 205

111
Vlastislav Hofman
Projekt eines Friedhofs bei Prag, 1912
(Project for a cemetery near Prague)
Cat. no. 92

112
Paul Gösch
Untitled (fantasy architecture), c. 1919
Cat. no. 40

IAIN BOYD WHYTE

The Expressionist Sublime

Between 1914 and 1920 German Expressionism produced some of the most powerful utopian images in twentieth-century architecture. The most influential and archetypal of these images are the series of drawings entitled *Alpine Architektur* (Alpine architecture; see figs. 1 113, 114), produced by the architect Bruno Taut toward the end of World War I and published in book form in 1919. Taut's visionary images of glass cathedrals set high in the Alps and of cosmic constructions of colored glass speeding through the eternal night were conceived both as a protest against the insanity of the war and as a pointer to a better society, which would devote its energies to peace and understanding rather than self-destruction.

In common with Expressionist writing and painting, the visionary architecture of the Expressionist years has generally been explained in reactive terms, with the utopian visions defined as positive alternatives to negative aspects of German society as it had evolved following unification in 1871, The dreams of a new society and a new morality, to be embodied in a revolutionary architecture of light and color, were contrasted with the dystopian realities of contemporary Germany. It is a simple tale of good against bad, of architect dreamers against the forces of repression. Through well-practiced repetition these repressive forces align themselves in convenient ranks, braced for the historian's disapproval. They include the population explosion, rapid urban expansion in nineteenth-century Germany, and the resulting human degradation, illness, and mortality experienced by the overcrowded urban proletariat. The villains behind this scenario were the ruthless bankers and capitalist entrepreneurs, who themselves were looked down on by an aristocracy whose values and interests were inseparable from those of the Prussian military machine. Over this chaos of conflict and tension ruled a philistine monarchy that favored classicist kitsch and neo-Baroque bombast over the "truths" of the incipient modern movement. The scene is thus set for generational conflict between father and son, class conflict between the bourgeois and the proletarian, and cultural conflict between academician and pupil, professor and student. Fleeing from social repression, sexual hypocrisy, and cultural ennui, the artists and intellectuals reacted with a primal scream on the model of Edvard Munch, retreating into a private world of subjective fantasy and messianic speculation about a new and better society.

The historical data support this account. Conditions in the speculative housing blocks were appalling, infant mortality and prostitution were rampant, and the bourgeoisie was notably prosperous and self-satisfied. Moreover the apocalyptic prognoses offered around 1913 by painters such as Ludwig Meidner took on an awesome reality with the terrible losses and ultimate defeat of the German army in World War I, the collapse of monarchical government in November 1918, and the ensuing political unrest, which culminated in ferocious street fighting between communists and nationalists in the early months of

113
Bruno Taut
Kristallhaus in den Bergen, 1919
(Crystal house in the mountains)
Illustration from *Alpine Architektur*, p. 3
See Cat. no. 232

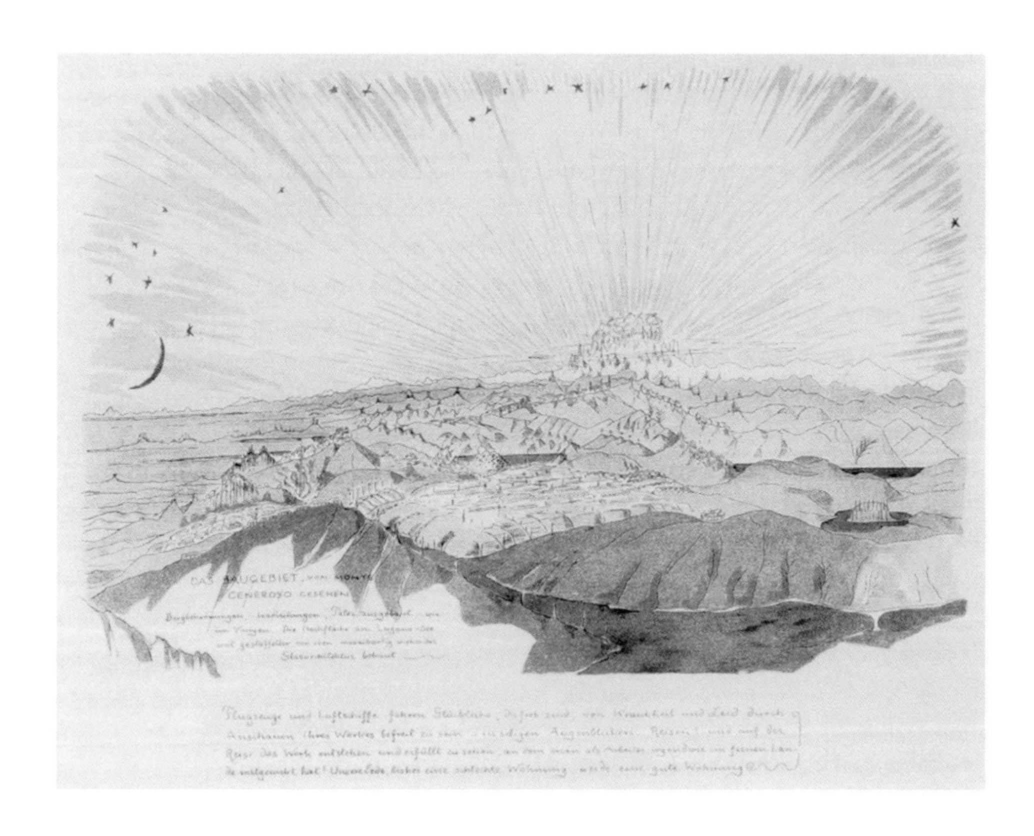

114
Bruno Taut
Das Baugebiet, vom Monte Generoso gesehen, 1919
(The building site seen from Monte Rosa)
Illustration from Alpine Architektur, p. 17
See cat. no. 232

1919. Against this background of military defeat and civil disorder, it is inevitable that the Expressionist interlude should be seen as a utopian escape from a mendacious reality.

This view has also informed the standard histories of twentieth-century architecture, in which the Expressionist contribution was invariably portrayed as an escapist, irrational interlude, a strange aberration in the steady progress toward functional modernism, explicable only in terms of the historical conditions of the moment. Nikolaus Pevsner, for example, called the Expressionists "ineffectual deviationists," and Sigfried Giedion insisted that "the Expressionist influence could not be healthy or perform any service for architecture."[1] While more recent scholarship has revised these damning judgments,[2] the reactive image of Expressionist architecture as a deviation from the modernist mainstream has exerted a lasting negative influence. Yet the reactive view fails on three counts. First, it does nothing to explain why Expressionist architecture took on the particular forms that it did, nor does it explain the aesthetic strategies employed, either wittingly or unwittingly, by the architects in framing their utopias. Second, it cuts off the Expressionist visionaries from their historical antecedents by interpreting their work as a unique reaction to a specific set of historical circumstances. Third, it isolates Expressionism as an irrationalist outburst, unrelated to any larger philosophical patterns or systems.

Looking back, however, with the perspective of seventy-five years, it becomes clear that many of the philosophical and aesthetic preoccupations of the Expressionist generation had been anticipated a century earlier in the emotive engagement with nature that characterized the work of German Romantic writers such as Ludwig Tieck and Novalis or of the painter Caspar David Friedrich (see fig. 115). The Romantic notion of beauty as a manifestation of a universal totality beyond human comprehension is perfectly captured in one of Novalis's "Blütenstaub" Fragments: "Fantasy sets the coming world either in the heights or in the depths, or in metempsychosis to ourselves. We dream of journeys through the cosmos; but is the cosmos not in us? We do not know the depths of our soul. The secret path leads inward. Eternity, with its worlds of past and future, exists either within ourselves or not at all."[3] To the Romantic mind nature in her most extreme manifestations offered moral and metaphysical insights into the human spirit. Creative engagement with the magnitude and power of natural phenomena offered the chance to link the individual soul and the universal spirit. This discourse, conducted in the language of the unportrayable and unrepresentable, echoed the philosophical investigations into the nature and qualities of the sublime pursued in the late eighteenth century by Edmund Burke and Immanuel Kant. The comparable use of sublime imagery in nineteenth-century Romanticism and twentieth-century Expressionism should not be ascribed to conscious imitation: the Expressionist visionaries and utopians did not keep Kant under their drawing boards. There was, however, in the first decade of this century a climate of ideas that was sympathetic to the aesthetic concerns and artistic production of Romanticism. Friedrich, for example, emerged as the undisputed star of the centenary exhibition held at the Nationalgalerie in Berlin in 1906, which launched a reappraisal of Romantic painting. Similarly the neo-Kantian movement that had originated in the 1860s blossomed around 1910. While it is highly unlikely that the artists or architects would have read the Kantian studies of Paul Gerhard Natorp, Wilhelm Windelband, or the young Ernst Cassirer, the broader intellectual climate of the first decade of this century was clearly receptive to Kantian echoes. As the painter Franz Marc wrote in 1915, "Kant looked far ahead, beyond the nineteenth century into the new age."[4]

Marc's contention finds support in recent studies of the sublime, which has been hailed

115
Caspar David Friedrich
Germany, 1774–1840
Das Eismeer, 1823–24
(The sea of ice)
Oil on canvas
38¹/16 x 50 in.
(96.7 x 127.0 cm)
Hamburger Kunsthalle

by Jean-François Lyotard as key to the understanding of twentieth-century art. "It is in the aesthetic of the sublime," he wrote in 1982, "that modern art (including literature) finds its impetus and the logic of the avant-gardes finds its axioms." In Lyotard's formulation the sentiment of the sublime is experienced "when the imagination fails to present an object which might, in principle, come to match a concept. We can conceive the infinitely great, the infinitely powerful, but every presentation of an object destined to 'make visible' this absolute greatness or power appears to us painfully inadequate."[5]

The sublime therefore operates in the no-man's-land between intuition and reason, at the point where one's instinctive ability to comprehend the scale of an object breaks down. In an article on the imagination written in 1712, which anticipated the eighteenth-century fascination with the sublime, Joseph Addison noted that:

> *The understanding, indeed, opens an infinite space on every side of us, but the imagination, after a few faint efforts, is immediately at a stand, and finds herself swallowed up in the immensity of the void that surrounds it: Our reason can pursue a particle of matter through an infinite variety of divisions, but the fancy soon loses sight of it, and feels in it self a kind of chasm, that wants to be filled with matter of a more sensible bulk. We can neither widen, nor contract the faculty to the dimensions of either extreme. The object is too big for our capacity, when we would comprehend the circumference of the world, and dwindles into nothing, when we endeavour after the idea of an atom.*[6]

Taken up by Kant as the *Grenze der Einbildungskraft*, the limit of our powers of imagination, this gap between the realms of reason and imagination has the potential to engender both fear and creativity. Confronted by the enormity or the minuteness of the object and the void of incomprehension, the observer experiences fear, which is then superseded by pleasure as new rational criteria are summoned to explain and contain that which had previously been beyond comprehension. In the process the power of imagination is extended to encompass new conceptions of space and time, and the power of reason generates visions of the world that extend to the limits of fiction. In thus confronting the abyss of incomprehension, the observer gains a heightened understanding of human potential and of the power of human rationality to overcome the chaos of creation and the intractability of nature.

As Kant makes clear, the sublime exists not in the observed object itself but in the response of the observer. Nevertheless certain phenomena are more likely to provoke sublime reactions than others, and Kant himself offers a list of likely candidates:

116
Hans Scharoun
"Glashausproblem,"
1920
(Glass house problem)
Cat. no. 184

117
Carl Krayl
Kosmischer Bau, c. 1919–20
(Cosmic building)
Cat. no. 123

> *Bold, overhanging, and, as it were, threatening rocks, thunderclouds piled up the vault of heaven, borne along with flashes and peals, volcanoes in all their violence of destruction, hurricanes leaving desolation in their track, the boundless ocean rising with rebellious force, the high waterfall of some mighty river, and the like, make our power of resistance of trifling moment in comparison with their might. But provided our position is secure, their aspect is all the more attractive for its fearfulness; and we readily call these objects sublime, because they raise the forces of the soul above the heights of the vulgar commonplace, and discover within us a power of resistance of quite another kind, which gives us courage to be able to measure ourselves against the seeming omnipotence of nature.*[7]

The sublime resides in our reaction to the abyss or the raging storm and in the attempt to master our fear through the redefinition of our rational perspectives. Aesthetic judgment is thus akin to moral judgment, and the wilderness of creation is given order by the intervention of free, rational man.

As the instrument that makes possible the victory of reason over nature or chaos, the sublime has always carried with it extra-aesthetic dimensions—social and political—that carry with them both the prospect of new perspectives and the dangers of authoritarianism. These dimensions can be sensed particularly strongly in the German word for the

sublime, *das Erhabene*, with its echoes of *Erhebung* (elevation) and *Erbauung* (in its original sense of building up, uplifting, or edifying). Writing in the mid-nineteenth century, the German aesthetician Theodor Vischer stressed the positive and constructive aspect of the sublime response to nature: “We feel ourselves elevated because we identify ourselves with the powers of nature, ascribing their vast impact to ourselves, because our fantasy rests on the wings of the storm as we roar into the heights and wander into the depths of infinity. Thus we ourselves expand into a boundless natural power.”[8] The notion of a sublime aesthetic that moves one to build or construct a nobler social, political, or moral order moves us closer to the glass temples of the Expressionist sublime (see figs. 116, 117).

The objects that stimulate the sequence of fear and awe, followed by pleasure and rational action, have changed over the centuries. “Awe, compounded of mingled terror and exultation, once reserved for God, passed over in the seventeenth century first to an expanded cosmos, then from the macrocosm to the greatest objects in the geocosm-mountains, ocean, desert.”[9] Thus discovered in the seventeenth century, the aesthetics of the infinite became a central preoccupation of the eighteenth century. As Addison insisted in his best-known text on the matter:

> *Our imagination loves to be filled by an object, or to grasp at anything that is too big for its capacity. We are flung into a pleasing astonishment at such unbounded views, and feel a delightful stillness and amazement in the soul at the apprehension of them. The mind of man naturally hates everything that*

118
Carl Blechen
Germany, 1798–1840
Schlucht bei Amalfi, 1831
(Ravine near Amalfi)
Oil on canvas
43 7/16 x 30 1/2 in.
(110.3 x 77.5 cm)
Nationalgalerie, Staatliche
Museen zu Berlin,
Preussischer Kulturbesitz

119
Ludwig Meidner
Apokalyptische Landschaft (Beim Bahnhof Halensee), 1913
(Apocalyptic landscape [near the Halensee railroad station])
Oil on canvas
32 1/16 x 38 3/16 in.
(81.5 x 97.0 cm)
Los Angeles County Museum
of Art. Gift of Clifford Odets

> *looks like a restraint upon it, and is apt to fancy itself under a sort of confinement, when the sight is pent up in a narrow compass, and shortened on every side by the neighbourhood of walls and mountains. On the contrary, a spacious horizon is an image of liberty, where the eye has room to expatiate at large on the immensity of its views.*[10]

In the mid-eighteenth century Edmund Burke added the emotion of terror to Addison's delight in limitless nature, prompting a taste for the morbid—graveyards, ruins, and natural disasters—that provided early Romantic art with a rich vein of literary and pictorial motifs.[11] Apocalyptic expectations derived from medieval theology lay behind the supernatural terrors of the charnel house and the graveyard.

With the emergence of industrial production and urban concentration in the nineteenth century, the inventions of man rather than nature offered a new focus for sublime contemplation. As Paul Crowther notes in his recent study of the Kantian sublime: "The structures of capitalism and the conflicts it engenders provide immediate and inescapable images that overwhelm our perceptual or imaginative powers, yet make the scope of rational comprehension or human artifice and contrivance all the more vivid."[12] In the nineteenth century industrial production, the speed and power of steam technology, and the burgeoning metropolis or industrial city stimulated the sensations of awe, terror, and exaltation previously associated with such natural phenomena as cliffs, waterfalls, and deserts. Carl Blechen's painting *Schlucht bei Amalfi* (Ravine near Amalfi, 1831; fig. 118) offers telling evidence of this realignment of sublime sentiment. Blechen sets a steam hammer above a roaring torrent, contrasting a symbol of mechanical power and danger with the same forces in nature. In the context of the cities of Victorian Britain, Nicholas Taylor lists among the sublime delights of the new century "the haranguing of the

Evangelical preacher; the ecstasy of the Anglo-Catholic Mass; the scientific wonders of panoramas and exhibition halls; the traveller's thrill in catching trains and climbing mountains; the capitalist's pride in the hum of mass production and hubbub of the market."[13] The city of brick and stone, driven by the limitless technological power of steam and iron, with its vast and ever-expanding scale and its brutal contrasts of splendor and deprivation, replaced the menacing mountains, crags, and cliffs of the eighteenth century. The conquest of the Alps and the conquest of the industrial city demanded similar qualities and provoked parallel aesthetic responses.

The metaphor of the city as an endless sea of stone recurs frequently in the literature of German Expressionism. In Gerrit Engelke's poem "Stadt" (City), the city appears as a man-made mountain, bristling with energy and menace:

> *Ten thousand staring, rigid blocks are built in the valley,*
> *Stone piled high upon stone on wood and iron frames;*
> *And block upon block pressed into a mountain,*
> *Spanned by steam pipe, tower, and railway,*
> *By wire spinning net over net.*
> *The mountain, cleft deep by many fissures:*
> *This is the great labyrinth*
> *Through which human destiny washes.*[14]

In a similar vein Alfred Wolfenstein saw in the city the ravines and cliffs of the sublime mountainscape:

> *Shyness looms and the blind parting!*
> *Still we stand in stony disguise,*
> *Escaped the chaos—are still in flight.*
> *Before us the city gapes in crag and chasm.*[15]

And just as the chaotic forces of nature exceed our powers of comprehension and threaten us with destruction, so the great urban centers of the late nineteenth century were invested with entropic qualities. Like an overheated boiler, these massive concentrations of energy carried in their very fabric the potential for self-destruction. The legacy of apocalyptic expectation passed down from medieval theology to the eighteenth-century theories of the sublime found a new resonance in early twentieth-century theories of urban degeneration and collapse. The city of stone would crush its inhabitants as surely as an avalanche.[16] This is the message of Ludwig Meidner's celebrated series of apocalyptic landscapes, created in 1912 and 1913 (see fig. 119).

The response of the Expressionist writers, painters, and architects to the nineteenth-century city was double-edged. As critics their starting point was rooted in the sublime response of incomprehension and fear: incomprehension at the physical scale of the city and its exploding population. This failure of the imagination to comprehend the extent of the city was reinforced on the human scale by disbelief at the overcrowded, tomblike conditions endured by the urban poor. At the microscopic scale recent advances in bacteriology drew attention to further hidden yet terrifying dangers such as cholera and tuberculosis, which lurked in the insanitary city streets.[17] As creative spirits, however, the same artists and intellectuals turned to the devices of the sublime to produce emotionally laden images intended to stimulate a rational reevaluation of how industrial society should progress. This complex interaction between reason and emotion was succinctly described by Kurt Hiller, one of the leading theorists of German Expressionism: "The source of all rationality lies not in knowledge, but in experience. Its deepest essence, therefore, is not to be comprehended quasi-mathematically, but mystically.... The impulse toward the benevolent, messianic reform of the world remains dark and inaccessible to all justification An intellectualism that lusts for proof—both pure and poor philosophy—fails here. For here rule the ardor and the assurance of more sacred, more profound powers."[18]

Expressionist reason was to be guided by emotion rather than the constraints of proof or objective analysis. As a symbol of messianic reform, the German Expressionists turned, as their Romantic forebears had before them, to the biblical symbol of purity, order, and indivisibility: the crystal. Stretching back to Saint John's Vision of the New Jerusalem in Revelation, the crystal has a long history as a symbol of utopian and millenarian faith in a perfectible society, moving from the Bible, via medieval mystics such as Schwester Hadewich and Wolfram von Eschenbach, to the Romanticism of Novalis and Tieck, and from there to the Holy Grail of Richard Wagner's *Parsifal*, first performed in 1882.[19]

The more immediate inspiration for the glass and crystalline fantasies proposed by Taut and developed in 1919 and 1920 by his associates in the Arbeitsrat für Kunst (Working council for art) and the Gläserne Kette (Crystal chain) group was the writer Paul Scheerbart. Scheerbart published a long succession of fantasy novels, articles, and poems between 1889 and his death in 1915, in which he insisted that the universe is far too rich and complex to be comprehended by reason alone. Only naive wonder—the basis of the sublime—could promote the development of higher forms of understanding. This position, of course, also had implications for artistic production; as one of the characters in his novel *Das Paradies, die Heimat der Kunst* (Paradise, the home of art, 1889) explained: "The concept of art is broadened here; the main issue is no longer representation but rather the invention of things that might be represented.... Our task is not the representation of comprehended perceptions, but a reorientation of comprehended perceptions. In this way we want to make it possible to comprehend new perceptions. You could call this the preparatory work for the artists who come later."[20] Rather than depict in minute and squalid detail the poverty and misery of the real world in the manner of naturalist writers such as Gerhart Hauptmann, Arno Holz, and Johannes Schlaf, who dominated German literature in the 1890s, Scheerbart described fantastic astral journeys and dispatched his readers to exotic locations on earth, where utopian existences were led under the beneficent shelter of a new architecture of color and transparency. The transparent envelope was intended to promote self-transcendence by allowing thought to move from the sensuous level to the universal, through the medium of endless space.

The moral implications of such a sequence had already been noted by Kant in a key passage in his *Kritik der Urteilskraft* (The critique of judgment, 1790): "The spontaneity in the play of the cognitive faculties whose harmonious accord contains the ground of this pleasure, makes the concept [of the finality of nature] in its consequences, a suitable mediating link connecting the concept of nature with that of the concept of freedom, as this accord at the same time promotes the sensibility of the mind for moral feeling."[21] In other words, moral and metaphysical insights were to be derived from natural excess. This link has already been seen in the context of German Romanticism. In the strictly architectural context a new morality was regarded as the product of new notions of space.

This was the message that first linked Scheerbart's writing to Taut's building, the nexus that generated Expressionist architecture. The first contact between the two men was made in 1912, through the circle of artists and intellectuals around Herwarth Walden's journal *Der Sturm* (The storm). In February 1914 Taut published an article entitled "Eine Notwendigkeit" (A necessity; see Appendix) in *Der Sturm*, which called for collaborative work on a great new building of glass, steel, and concrete, in which constructional virtuosity and the arts of painting and sculpture would be reunited again, as they were in the Gothic cathedrals. The building was to have no function beyond self-transcendence. The hymn to color and transparency was taken up again in Scheerbart's book *Glasarchitektur* (Glass architecture), which was published under the Sturm imprint in 1914 and dedicated to Taut. It contained 111 short texts on the virtues of glass as both material and symbol, the first of which proclaimed:

> *We live for the most part in enclosed spaces. These form for the most part the milieu in which our culture develops. Our culture is, so to speak, a product of our architecture. Should we wish to lift our culture to a higher level, then we are obliged, for better or worse, to transform our architecture. We shall only succeed in doing this when we remove the element of enclosure from the rooms in which we live. We can only do this, however, with glass architecture, which allows the light of the sun, moon, and stars to enter not merely through a few windows set in the wall, but through as many walls as possible—walls of colored glass. The new milieu created in this way must bring us a new culture.*[22]

120
Bruno Taut
Glashaus, Werkbund exhibition, Cologne, 1914

121
Bruno Taut
Glashaus, Werkbund exhibition, Cologne, 1914, cascade

This text also appeared in the pamphlet written by Taut describing his Glashaus (Glass house) at the 1914 Werkbund exhibition in Cologne, which was the first building to realize Scheerbart's vitreous vision. This little glass temple, set on a concrete plinth, had fourteen glazed sides, each with a motto from Scheerbart inscribed on the lintel, and was topped by a prismatic dome of double-skin glass (see fig. 120). The play of natural colored light was heightened in the interior by a water cascade on the lower level and a mechanical kaleidoscope (see fig. 121). Not only was the Glashaus the first Expressionist glass building, it also has the melancholy distinction of being the last, as the outbreak of war in August 1914 and the political and economic turmoil that followed for the next decade condemned the Expressionist vision to paper.

The war was welcomed by German youth as a catalyst for social and cultural change. The volunteers of 1914 saw the war as the ultimate realization of Nietzsche's vitalist philosophy, as the emancipation from the materialism of their fathers. Marc spoke for his generation in welcoming "this 'sublime feast' of the philosopher,"[23] whose destructive power created the conditions necessary for innovation and renewal. Yet as the war dragged on in sanguinary stalemate, the millenarian dreams of an age of the spirit that would be forged on the battlefield were replaced by ennui, despair, and increasing pacifist resistance. Fear of war and its consequences spread beyond the immediate confines of the two front lines to the entire population of Europe, which was threatened by hunger, illness, and economic hardship. The background to Taut's *Alpine Architektur* was the so-called turnip winter of 1916–17, marked by extreme food shortages and rationing among the civilian population in Germany. Toward the end of this winter of discontent, the Russian revolution broke out, bringing with it a new phase in the war and in European socialist politics.

Great, ill-defined ideas were in the air, visions of a world without war or nationalism, visions of universal brotherhood. Such visions are exactly what Kant pointed to in defining the aesthetic idea as "that representation of the imagination which induces much thought, yet without the possibility of any definite thought whatever, i.e., concept being adequate to it, and which language, consequently, can never get quite on level terms with or render completely intelligible."[24] The "brotherhood of man" is just such a notion that defies complete and convincing representation. Yet some image had to be found as a stimulus for the transformation of the world that was felt to be imminent and for the change in morality that was necessary for this transformation. As has already been noted, the aesthetic of the sublime offers a link between such strong human emotions as fear and the longing for self-transcendence and the moral goal of a free, rational man. In *Alpine Architektur* and its pendant, *Der Weltbaumeister* (The universal master builder; see Appendix), published in 1920, Taut created a series of gigantomanic visions that embodied almost all those qualities that Burke had linked to the sublime responses of "astonishment...admiration, reverence and respect."[25]

Although Taut's images are admittedly short on terror, the other Burkean qualities are to be found in rich abundance. High above the wartime trenches, technology and mechanical power over the material world are transformed into a constructive force, with airships, airplanes, and unspecified technological wonders employed to build glass temples on the Alpine peaks and launch glass satellites into space. Social progress was to be achieved through sublime inspiration, through engagement in a task of almost incomprehensible dimension: "Preach: be peaceable! Preach: the social idea: 'You are all brothers, organize yourselves and you could all live well, all be well educated and at peace!' As long as there are no tasks to be done, your preaching will echo emptily. Tasks that demand the last ounce of effort, the last drop of blood." The Burkean quality of astonishment is self-evident as the only possible response to these gigantic demands. As Taut admitted, "The execution will involve incredible difficulties and sacrifices but will not be impossible. 'The impossible is so rarely demanded of Man.' (Goethe)...But higher knowledge! The greatest work is nothing without the sublime. We must always recognize and strive for the unattainable if we are to achieve the attainable." The mountainscape and the cosmos guarantee, of course, Burke's demand for vastness, infinity, and the "privations [of] vacuity, darkness, solitude [and] silence." Taut's "crystal house in the mountains" is referred to as the temple of silence, the site of prayer and "inexpressible silence" (see fig. 113).[26]

122
Bruno Taut
Untitled, 1920
Illustration from *Der Weltbaumeister*, p. 8
See cat. no. 235

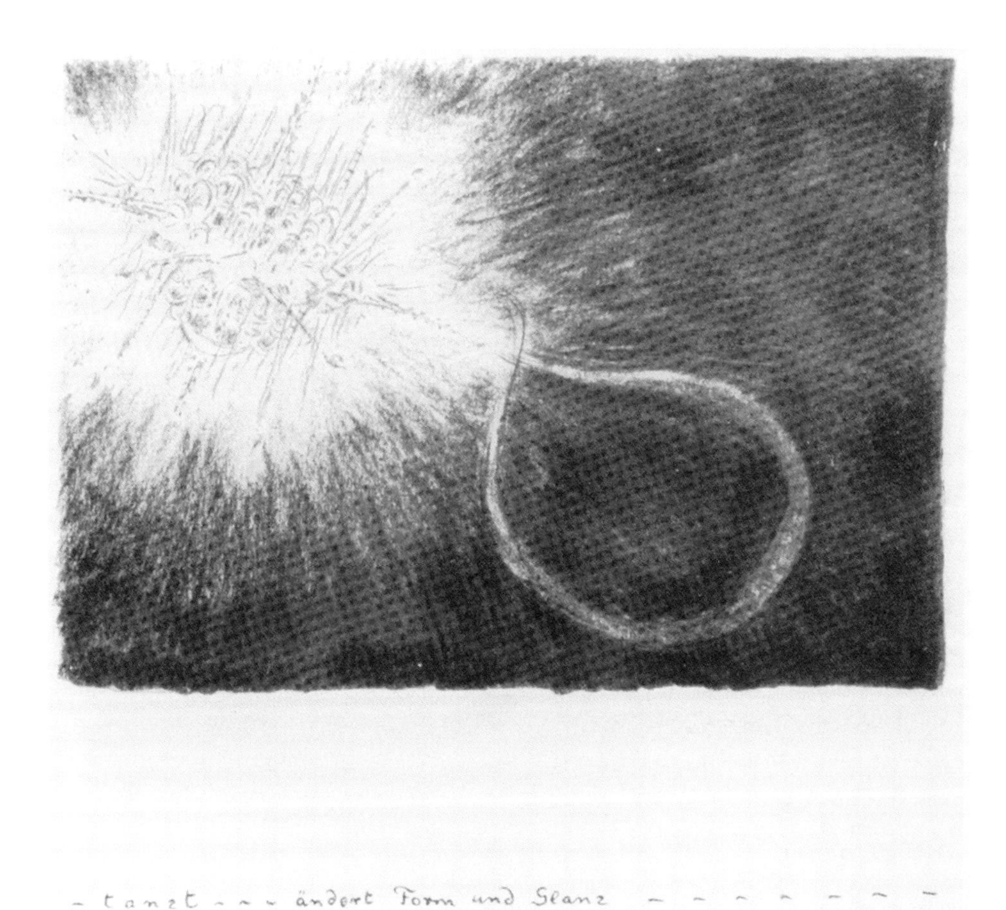

123
Bruno Taut
Untitled, 1920
Illustration from *Der Weltbaumeister*, p. 14
See cat. no. 235

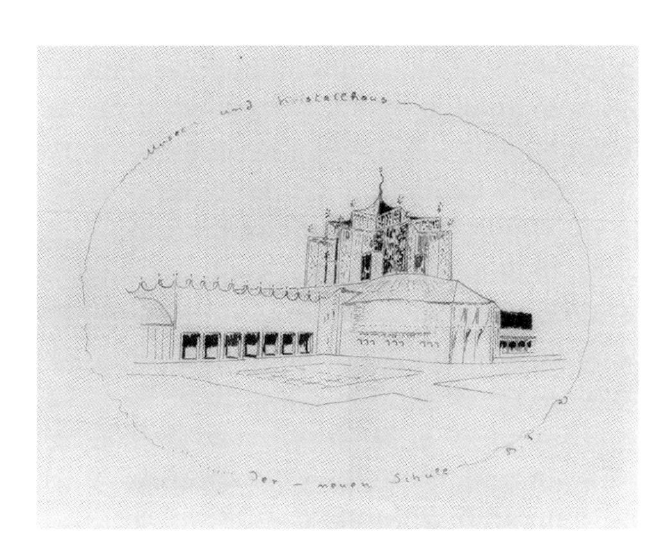

124
Wenzel Hablik
Der Weg des Genius, 1918
(The path of genius)
Oil on canvas
63³/16 x 37³/8 in.
(160.5 x 95.0 cm)
Wenzel-Hablik-Stiftung, Itzehoe

125
Bruno Taut
Museen und Kristallhaus der neuen Schule, c. 1920
(Museums and crystal house for the new school)
Cat. no. 211

The Burkean categories closest to architecture are magnitude in building, magnificence, and light in building, all of which are amply provided for in glass architecture. Indeed, in describing the beauty of the interior of the crystal house, Taut quotes a passage from Scheerbart's novel *Münchhausen und Clarissa* (Münchhausen and Clarissa), in which the architecture of a glass temple is specifically described as sublime (*erhaben*): "No one may speak in the temples, entry is always possible—even in the night. But there is nothing here that corresponds to our church services—the temples achieve their effect solely through their sublime architecture, and through their great silence, which is broken only from time to time by beautiful orchestral and organ music."[27]

In his attempts to show, rather inconsistently, that even finite objects can produce sublime responses in the observer, Kant had offered an architectural example, suggesting that when a visitor enters Saint Peter's in Rome, "a feeling comes home to him of the inadequacy of his imagination for presenting the idea of a whole within which that imagination attains its maximum, and, in its fruitless efforts to extend this limit, recoils upon itself, but in doing so succumbs to an emotional delight."[28] Crowther suggests that "this harmonious tension between what is perceptually overwhelming and what is nevertheless known to be artifice" provides the basis for a "specifically artistic sense of the sublime."[29] Taut's *Weltbaumeister*, an utterly fantastic and largely incomprehensible series of drawings conceived as stage drops for an "Architectural Drama for Symphonic Music—Dedicated to the Spirit of Paul Scheerbart," might be seen as exemplifying this tension. The plot, reflecting the workings of the sublime, involves a rocket cathedral hurtling through space—perhaps symbolizing the limits of human imagination—and then, at the most distant point of cosmic blackness, transforming itself into a star (see figs. 122, 123). Terrified, thrilled, and mystified by this performance, the architecture on earth is transformed, as reason creates a new paradise and houses of glass grow like mushrooms out of the earth's crust. Burke's suggestions on obscurity, light, and color are all followed here, no doubt unwittingly. He recommended that "in buildings where the highest degree of the sublime is intended, the materials and ornaments ought to be…of sad and fuscous colours, as black, or brown, or deep purple, and the like."[30] At the moment of transfiguration in *Der Weltbaumeister*, when the star disappears and our attention is redirected to earth, Taut's text specifies that "empty space becomes purple-red."

Booming around the mountaintops and across the cosmos, Taut's plea for the transcendental sublime carries unmistakable echoes of Nietzsche's demand for man to replace the deist god of nature: "We want to suffuse nature with humanity and free it from godly mummery. We want to extract what we need from nature in order to dream beyond man. Something should yet emerge that is more magnificent than storm, mountain, and ocean—but as the progeny of man!"[31] The driving force behind the Nietzschean revolution would be the will of the individual, more specifically the will of the most gifted individual, the genius, who goes to new heights where mere mortals fear to tread. Nietzsche's vision of the artist as superman is perfectly encapsulated in a painting by Wenzel Hablik, one of Taut's companions in the Gläserne Kette group. Entitled *Der Weg des Genius* (The path of genius, 1918; fig. 124), Hablik's painting shows the lone figure of the artist-genius reach-

126
Paul Gösch
Untitled (fantasy architecture),
c. 1921
Cat. no. 43

127
Paul Gösch
Untitled (fantasy architecture),
1920–29
Cat. no. 41

128
Wenzel Hablik
Canonbauten, 1925
(Canonical buildings)
Cat. no. 66

129
Wenzel Hablik
Original Skizze des Inneren eines Schautempels, 1914
(Original sketch of the interior of a display temple)
Cat. no. 58

ing the New Jerusalem, while the merely mortal lie broken on the mountain peaks below.

In the heady, chaotic months that followed the military defeat, the abdication of the Kaiser, and the German revolution of November 1918, it appeared to the radical artists and intellectuals that their dreams had been realized: the age of materialism, nationalism, and hate had been superseded by the age of the spirit. Political and artistic ambitions were fused in the many groups of artists and intellectuals that sprung up throughout Germany in 1918 and 1919 in parallel to the workers' and soldiers' councils that launched the revolution in November 1918. In December 1918 the Arbeitsrat für Kunst in Berlin published a program that insisted: "Art and the people must form a unity. Art should no longer be the delight of the few, but the good fortune and the life of the masses. The aim is the fusion of arts under the wing of a great architecture."[32] The favored symbol for this new architecture was the crystal; the favored model, the Gothic cathedral. Both became mainstays of Expressionist rhetoric in the immediate postwar years. In Ernst Toller's play *Die Wandlung* (Transfiguration), for example, which was published in 1919, the hopes for the future are symbolized by the *Menschheitskathedrale*, the cathedral of humanity, and voiced in the convoluted, emotionally charged syntax of Expressionism: "Born from the universal womb, the high-vaulted portal of the cathedral of humanity opens wide. The youth of all nations stride ablaze into the shrine of glowing crystal. Violently I behold radiant visions. No more misery, no war, no hate."[33]

For the architects in the Arbeitsrat für Kunst and its successor, the Gläserne Kette group, the cathedral, temple, or cult building symbolized both the infinite totality of humankind and the benevolent domination of architecture over the new world of social harmony and equality. Just as Kant saw in Saint Peter's the possibility of a sublime build-

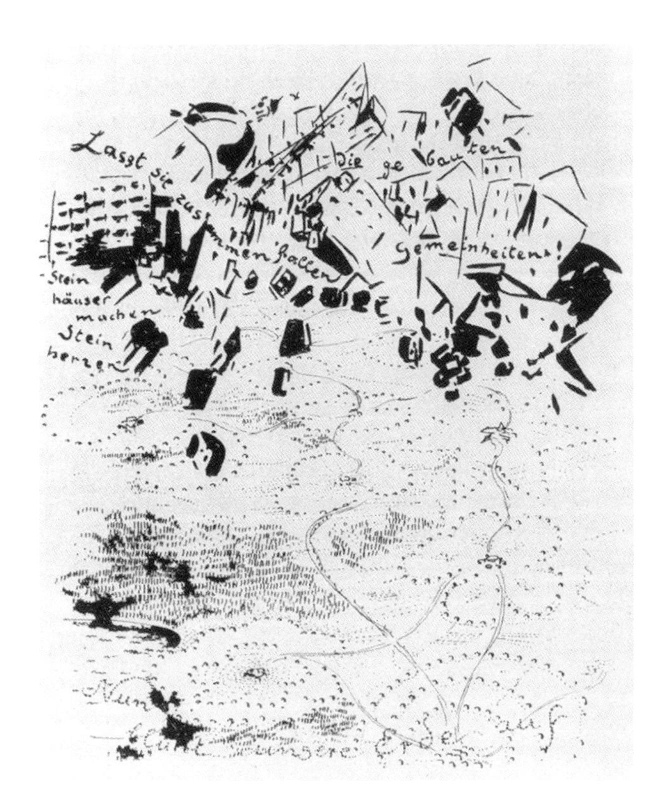

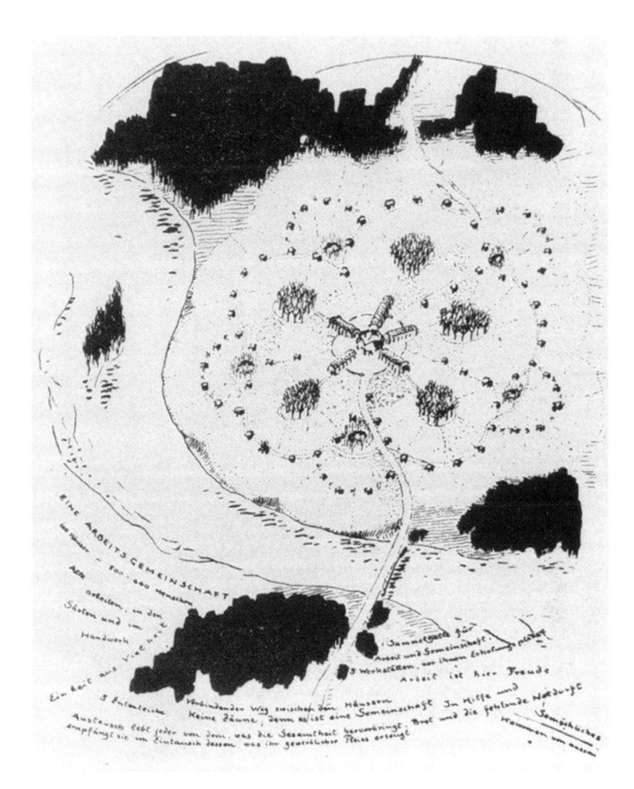

130
Bruno Taut
Untitled, 1920
Illustration from *Die Auflösung der Städte*, p. 1
See cat. no. 234

131
Bruno Taut
Eine Arbeitsgemeinschaft, 1920
(A working community)
Illustration from *Die Auflösung der Städte*, p. 2
See cat. no. 234

ing, so the Expressionist visionaries planned their utopias around a great architectural focus, the crystal shrine proposed by Taut and Scheerbart in 1914. The temple appears in endless guises as the *axis mundi* of the new utopia: in Taut's crystal house (fig. 125); in oriental garb, with theosophical overtones, in the variations by Paul Gösch (see figs. 126, 127); and in crystalline geometric fantasies by Hablik (see figs. 128, 129). Most famously Feininger chose the Gothic cathedral to symbolize the totality of the arts in his woodcut for the founding manifesto of Walter Gropius's Bauhaus, released in April 1919 to mark the opening of the new school in Weimar (fig. 26).

Around the temple the utopian community spread out in the regular formations favored in humanist utopias from Thomas More on. Antiurbanism and the desire to escape from the dystopian city were major themes of the political programs of the radical architects and artists. These programs focused on vague, utopian socialist ideals of decentralization, the replacement of the money economy with a mutualist system, and the economic autonomy of the rural community. Taut inevitably offered the most fantastic and eloquent vision of these ideas in his book *Die Auflösung der Städte* (The dissolution of the cities, 1920). The first two pages tell the political parable. In the first the city of stone is collapsing in sublime and apocalyptic chaos. Relief rather than fear should be the response, however, and Taut urges: "Let them collapse, these man-built acts of meanness! Stone houses create stone hearts. Now our soil is in bloom!"[34] Nature wins the battle against the barren city of stone, and in the second image a series of small communities grows out of the soil in a petallike pattern, reminiscent of a protozoan seen under a microscope (see figs. 130, 131).

The image of cellular development also goes back to the sublimity of the minute scale—Kant pointed to both the telescope and the microscope—and the fear of the unseen and the unknowable. The overcoming of this fear was also part of the Expressionist program, and the highly inventive images of single-cell creatures—polyps, corals, rhizopods, and the like—published at the turn of the century by Ernst Haeckel in his book *Kunstformen der Natur* (Art forms of nature) provided a rich hunting ground for the Expressionist visionaries. Hermann Finsterlin, one of the most prolific members of the Gläserne Kette, produced countless drawings of snaillike and polyplike forms as prototypes of the new glass architecture (see fig. 132). In the drawings of the Gläserne Kette the protozoan and the crystal were joined together as the archetypal foundations for growth, a linkage made explicit in Hablik's plans to fuse sand into glass houses resembling trees and flowers (see figs. 133, 134). This monist belief in a single, irreducible law uniting all matter, all faith, and all belief can be discerned in Taut's assurance in 1920 that "the great, all embracing element is discoverable. We flutter around it like amoebas, like coral polyps or salt atoms at the creation of rock or crystal."[35] In *Die Auflösung der Städte* Taut combined crys-

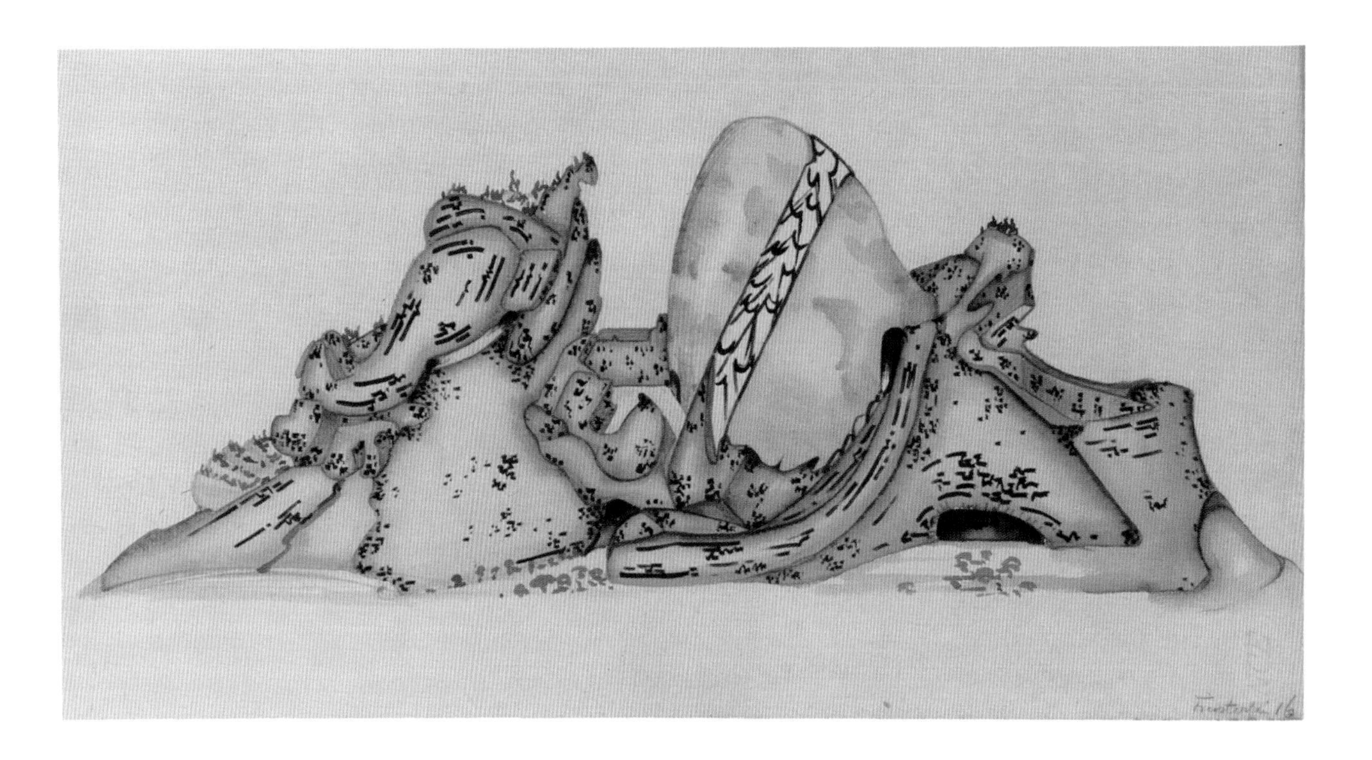

Hermann Finsterlin
Die Stadt, Serie IV, Blatt 8.
1920–24
(The city, series IV, sheet 8)
Cat. no. 27

talline dreams of glass temples in the Alps with a celebration of organic reproduction. His *Die grosse Blume* (The great flower; fig. 135) depicts a giant vitreous phallus and vagina floating on the endless ocean—the sublime triumph over the *Schornsteinzeit*, the stone age of the factory chimney.

Taut concluded *Die Auflösung der Städte* with a farewell to utopia that points to Lyotard's definition of the sublime: "Can one draw happiness? We can all live it and build it. Utopia? Is not utopia the 'certain' and the 'real,' swimming in the mire of illusion and indolent habit! Is not the content of our aspirations the true present, resting on the rock of faith and knowledge!"[36] This conscious return to the tangible, concrete, and comprehensible marked one of the most significant turning points in the evolution of architectural modernism. The elements of fear, uncertainty, and self-overcoming were willfully abandoned in favor of the mechanical and physical certainties on which functionalist modernism was grounded. A simplistic view of human existence as something reducible to the

133
Wenzel Hablik
Da wohnten Menschen auf kristall'nen Bäumen, 1925
(There humans lived on crystal trees)
Cat. no. 69

134
Wenzel Hablik
"Ziele" für die Jugend (schwer zu erreichen im Gebirge. Wunder-Bauten), 1920
("Goals" for youth [difficult to reach in the mountains. Miracle buildings])
Cat. no. 64

135
Bruno Taut
Die grosse Blume, 1920
(The great flower)
Illustration from *Die Auflösung der Städte*, p. 14
See cat. no. 234

optimal provision of shelter, light, and air by definition excluded any attempt to portray absolute greatness, power, or awe, either in nature or in architecture. Banished from the architectural discourse, the sublime, particularly in its Burkean variation, entered a new realm of operation in the cinema, where it lurked omnipresent behind the shadows of the Expressionist horror films.[37] Watching the vertiginous rooftop scenes in *Das Cabinet des Doktor Caligari* (The cabinet of Doctor Caligari, 1919; see fig. 136) or the demonic vaults of the rabbi's laboratory in *Der Golem* (The golem, 1920), the viewer in the back row of a warm cinema must have shared, however unwittingly, Burke's conviction that:

> *Whatever is fitted in any sort to excite the ideas of pain, and danger, that is to say, whatever is in any sort terrible, or is conversant about terrible objects, or operates in a manner analogous to terror, is a source of the sublime; that is, it is productive of the strongest emotion which the mind is capable of feeling....*

136
Scene from *Das Cabinet des Doktor Caligari* (The cabinet of Doctor Caligari), 1919
Cat. no. 218

> *When danger and pain press too nearly, they are incapable of any delight, and are simply terrible; but at certain distances, and with certain modification, they may be, and they are delightful, as we every day experience.*[38]

While the film industry adopted the strategies of the sublime to manipulate the emotions of its audience, the modern movement in architecture abandoned emotion in favor of reason, defined in the narrowest sense as the satisfaction of functional demands. The victory of functionalism over the emotionally charged architecture of Expressionism was seen as a triumph of reason over irrationality, of light over dark. As Giedion insisted in the passage from *Space, Time, and Architecture* quoted at the beginning of this essay: "Faustean outbursts against an inimical world and the cries of outraged humanity cannot create new levels of achievement."[39] But devoid of the emotional charge of power, awe, mystery, and fear on which Expressionist architecture thrived, the white architecture of the modern movement fell prey to the anodyne certainties of the sociologist and the economist. Indeed the very comprehensibility of the International Style—the antithesis of the Expressionist sublime—might be seen as a weakness. No uncertainties remained about the contours or dimensions of a building, the repeatability of its elements, its materials, or its economies of space and materials. With the powers or limits of imagination unchallenged, the result was ennui. As Cassirer has noted in the context of Kantian aesthetics, "Within phenomena themselves the infinite complexity which every organic natural form possesses for us points to the limit of the powers of mechanical explanation."[40] In architecture, as in nature, the merely mechanistic explanation is woefully inadequate.

NOTES

1. Nikolaus Pevsner, "Architecture in Our Time," *The Listener*, 29 December 1966, p. 953; Sigfried Giedion, *Space, Time, and Architecture* (Cambridge: Harvard University Press, 1949), p. 418.

2. See Wolfgang Pehnt, *Expressionist Architecture* (New York: Praeger, 1973); Iain Boyd Whyte, *Bruno Taut and the Architecture of Activism* (Cambridge: Cambridge University Press, 1982); idem, *The Crystal Chain Letters: Architectural Fantasies by Bruno Taut and His Circle* (Cambridge: MIT Press, 1985).

3. Novalis, "Blütenstaub," Fragment no. 16, in *Werke und Briefe* (Munich: Winkler, 1962), p. 342.

4. Klaus Lankheit, ed., *Franz Marc: Schriften* (Cologne: DuMont, 1978), p. 194.

5. Jean-François Lyotard, "What Is Postmodernism," in *The Postmodern Condition: A Report on Knowledge* (Manchester: Manchester University Press, 1986), pp. 77, 78.

6. Joseph Addison, in *The Spectator*, no. 420 (2 July 1712).

7. Immanuel Kant, *The Critique of Judgement*, trans. J. C. Meredith (Oxford: Oxford University Press, 1973), pp. 109–10.

8. Friedrich Theodor Vischer, *Über das Erhübene und Komische und andere Texte zur Äthetik* (Frankfurt: Suhrkamp, 1967), p. 155.

9. Marjorie Nicholson, *Science and the Imagination* (Ithaca, N.Y.: Cornell University Press, 1956), p. 96.

10. Joseph Addison, in *The Spectator*, no. 412 (23 June 1712).

11. Edmund Burke, *A Philosophical Enquiry into the Origin of Our Ideas of the Sublime and Beautiful* (London: R. and J. Dodsley, 1757; London: Routledge and Kegan Paul, 1958).

12. Paul Crowther, *The Kantian Sublime* (Oxford: Clarendon Press, 1989), pp. 164–65.

13. Nicholas Taylor, "The Awful Sublimity of the Victorian City," in *The Victorian City: Images and Realities*, ed. H. J. Dyes and Michael Wolff, 2 vols. (London: Routledge and Kegan Paul, 1973), p. 434.

14. Gerrit Engelke, "Stadt," in *Rythmus des neuen Europa* (Jena: Eugen Diederichs, 1921); reprinted in Wolfgang Rothe, ed., *Deutsche Grossstadtlyrik vom Naturalismus bis zur Gegenwart* (Stuttgart: Reclam, 1973), pp. 185–86.

15. Alfred Wolfenstein, "Neue Stadt," in *Menschlicher Kämpfer* (Berlin: S. Fischer, 1919); reprinted in Rothe, *Deutsche Grossstadtlyrik*, p. 194.

16. For a fascinating essay on the sublimity of stone, see Hartmut Böhme, "Das Steinerne: Anmerkungen zur Theorie des Erhabenen aus dem Blick des Menschenfremdeaten," in *Das Erhabene: Zwischen Grenzerfahrung und Grtissenwahn*, ed. Christine Pries (Weinheim: VCH Acta Humanoria, 1989), pp. 119–42.

17. It was in Berlin that Robert Koch identified the tuberculosis bacillus in 1882 and the cholera bacillus in 1883.

18. Kurt Hiller, "Ortsbestimmung des Aktivismus," *Die Erhebung* 1(1919): 366.

19. On the crystal theme, see Rosemarie Haag Bletter, "The Interpretation of the Glass Dream: Expressionist Architecture and the History of the Crystal Metaphor," *Journal of the Society of Architectural Historians* 40 (March 1981): 20–43; Regine Prange, *Das Kristalline als Kunstsymbole: Bruno Taut und Paul Klee* (Hildesheim: Georg Olms, 1991).

20. Paul Scheerbart, *Das Paradies, die Heimat der Kunst*, 2d ed. (Berlin: Verlag deutscher Fantasten, 1893), p. 170.

21. Kant, *Critique of Judgement*, p. 39

22. Paul Scheerbart, *Glasarchitektur* (Berlin: Verlag "Der Sturm," 1914; Munich: Rogner und Bernhard, 1971), p. 25.

23. Lankheit, *Franz Marc: Schriften*, p. 194.

24. Kant, *Critique of Judgement*, p. 175.

25. Burke, *Philosophical Enquiry* (1958), p. 57.

26. Bruno Taut, *Alpine Architektur* (Hagen: Folkwang, 1919), pls. 3, 10, 16, 21.

27. Ibid., pl. 4.

28. Kant, *Critique of Judgement*, p. 100.

29. Crowther, *Kantian Sublime*, pp. 153–54.

30. Burke, *Philosophical Enquiry (1958)*, p. 82.

31. Friedrich Nietzsche, "Nachgelassene Fragmente, Sommer 1883," no. 13 (1), in *Kritische Gesamtausgabe*, vol. 7, pt. 1 (Berlin: Walter de Gruyter, 1980), p. 450.

32. Arbeitsrat für Kunst, Programme (December 1918), in *Mitteilungen des Deutschen Werkbundes*, no. 4 (1918): 14.

33. Ernst Toller, *Die Wandlung* (Potsdam: Gustav Kiepenheuer, 1919), p. 77.

34. Bruno Taut, *Die Auflösung der Städte; oder, Die Erde, eine gute Wohnung* (Hagen: Folkwang, 1920), p. 1.

35. Bruno Taut, "Architektur neuer Gemeinschaft," *Die Erhebung* 2 (1920): 271.

36. Taut, *Auflösung der Städte*, p. 30.

37. As if to avert the impending schism, Bruno Taut, Hermann Finsterlin, and Hans Poelzig penned film scenarios in 1920. Poelzig was also responsible for the sets of Paul Wegener's film *Der Golem*, also made in 1920.

38. Burke, *Philosophical Enquiry* (1958), pp. 39–40.

39. Giedion, *Space, Time, and Architecture*, p. 418.

40. Ernst Cassirer, *Kant's Life and Thought*, trans. J. Haden (New Haven, Conn.: Yale University Press, 1981), pp. 346–47.

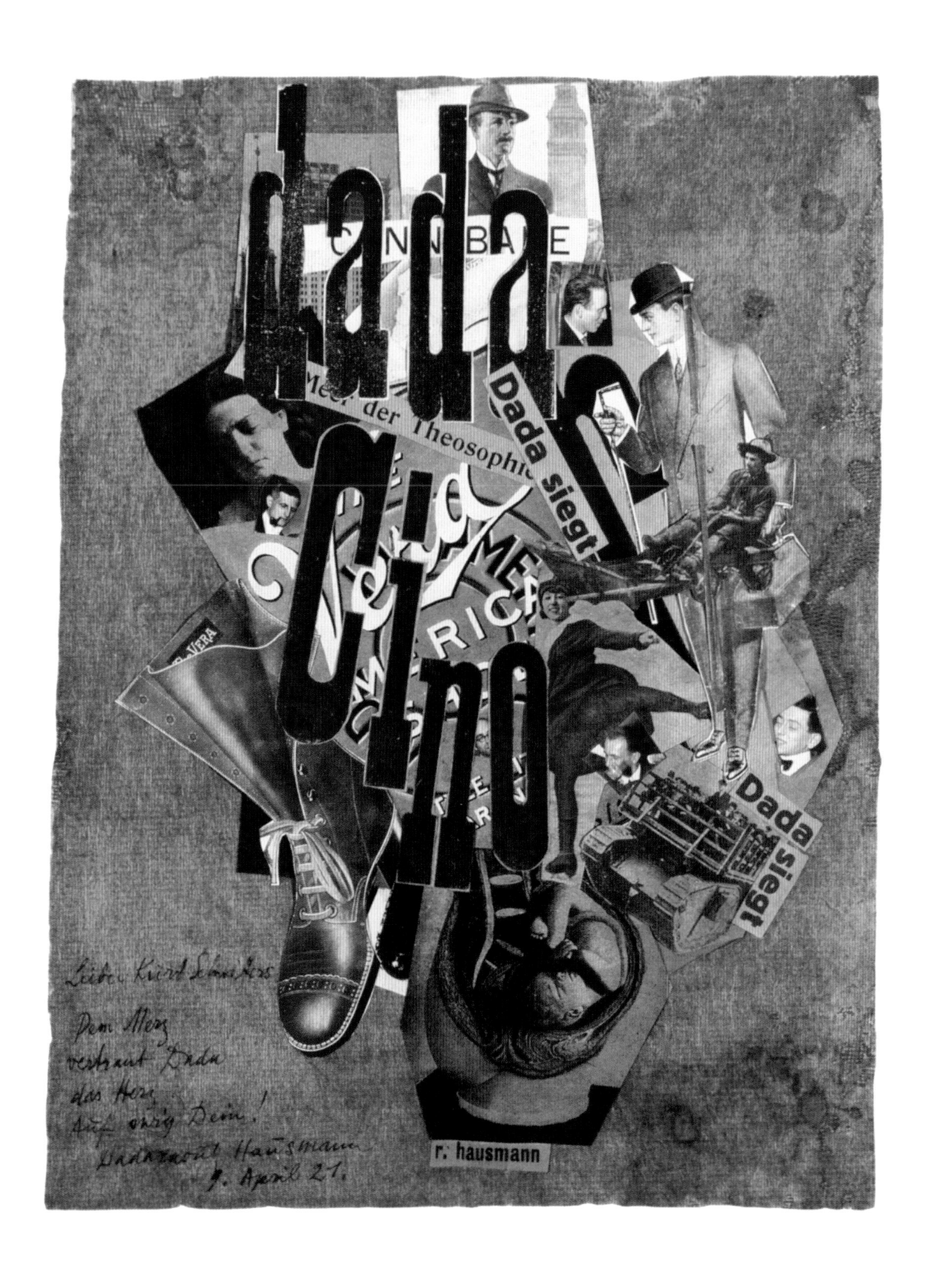

FILM AND STAGE

137
Raoul Hausmann
Dada Cino, 1920
Cat. no. 77

138
Erich Kettelhut
Metropolis: Turm Babel, 1925
(Metropolis: Tower of Babel)
Cat. no. 107

182
Hans Richter
Fugue, 1920
(Fugue)
Cat. no. 182

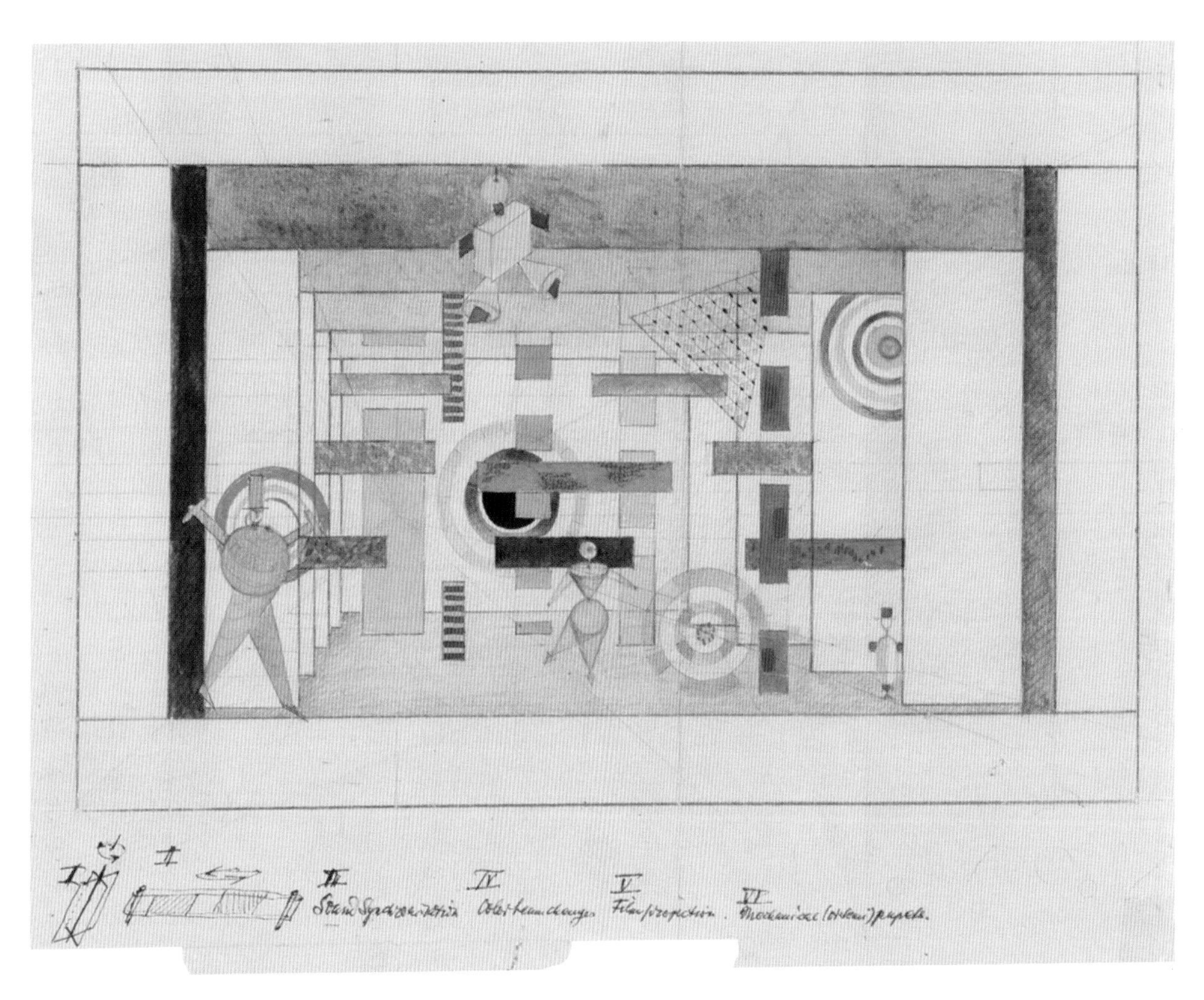

140
Andor Weininger
Mechanische Bühnen-Revue,
1923
(Mechanical stage review)
Cat. no. 219

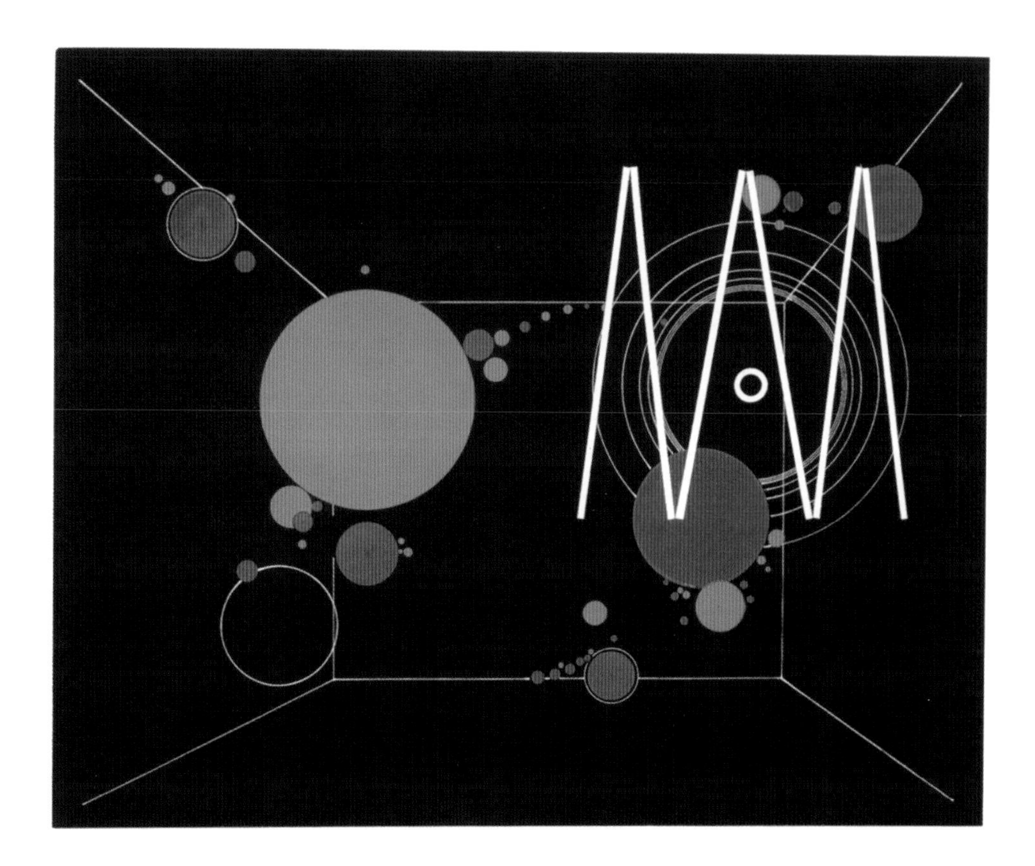

141
Roman Clemens
"Russisches": Bühnenbild zum "Spiel aus Form, Farbe, Licht und Ton," 1929
("Russian": Stage design for "Play of form, color, light, and sound")
Cat. no. 13

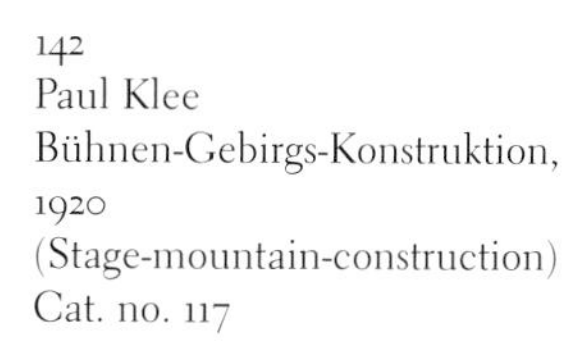

142
Paul Klee
Bühnen-Gebirgs-Konstruktion, 1920
(Stage-mountain-construction)
Cat. no. 117

NSU
VICTOR

143
Wassily Kandinsky
Das grosse Tor von Kiev (Szenenbild zu "Bilder einer Ausstellung," Bild XVI), 1928
(The great gate of Kiev [stage design for *Pictures at an Exhibition*, picture XVI])
Cat. no. 105

144
László Moholy-Nagy
Photomontage "Berlin" zum Schauspiel "Der Kaufmann von Berlin" von Water Mehring, 1929
(Berlin photomontage for "The merchant of Berlin" by Walter Mehring)
Cat. no. 152

145
Hannah Höch
Kabarett Bühne I, 1924–25
(Cabaret stage I)
Cat. no. 90

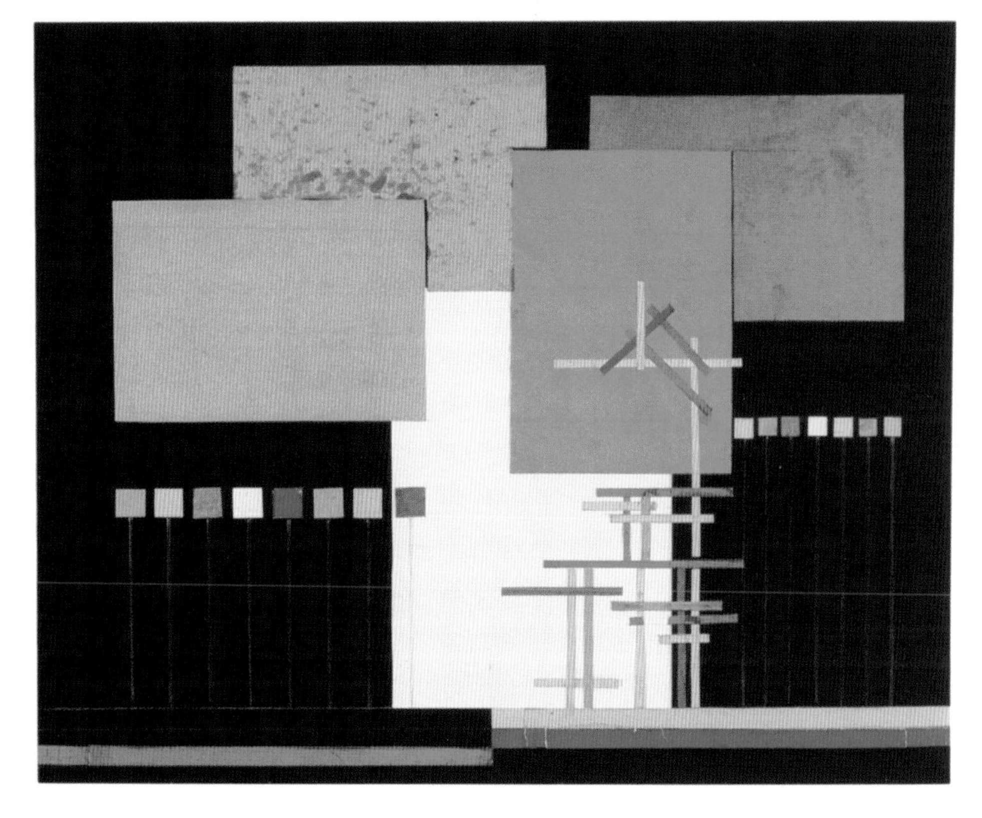

146
Oskar Schlemmer
Die Nachtigall: Thronsaal des Kaisers van China, 1929
(The nightingale: Throne room of the Chinese emperor)
Cat. no. 191

147
Walter Reimann
Untitled (woman on couch), c. 1919
Cat. no. 181

148
Walter Reimann
Untitled (café scene), c. 1919
Cat. no. 180

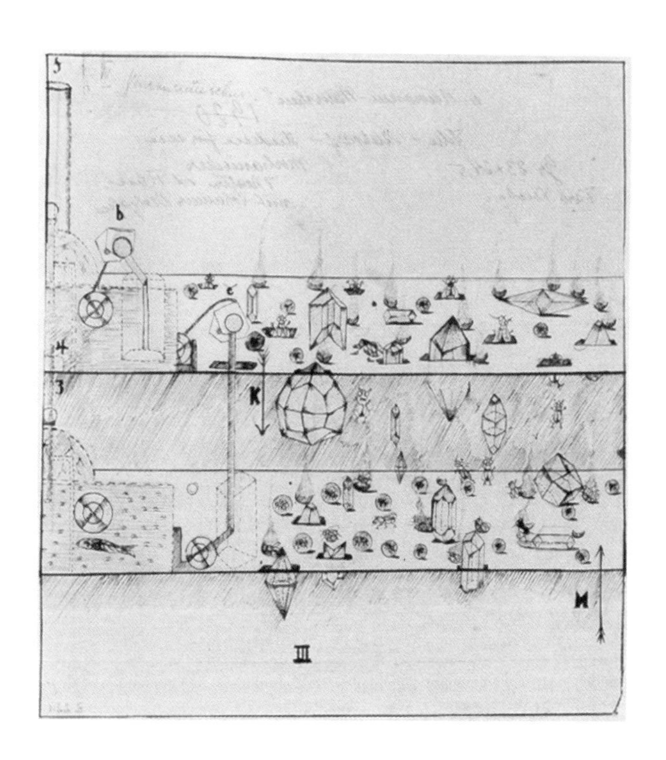

149
Ella Bergmann
Neuronen-Menschen / Idee-Entwurf-Studien für ein mechanisches Theater oder Film mit Johannes Molzahn, 1920
(Neurons-human beings / idea sketches for a mechanical theater or film with Johannes Molzahn)
Cat. no. 8

150
César Klein
Salon der "Genuine," 1920
(Salon for *Genuine*)
Cat. no. 11

ANTON KAES

Metropolis: City, Cinema, Modernity

ONE OF THE CRUCIAL ANTINOMIES OF ART TODAY IS THAT IT WANTS TO BE AND MUST BE SQUARELY UTOPIAN, AS SOCIAL REALITY INCREASINGLY IMPEDES UTOPIA, WHILE AT THE SAME TIME IT SHOULD NOT BE UTOPIAN SO AS NOT TO BE FOUND GUILTY OF ADMINISTERING COMFORT AND ILLUSION, IF THE UTOPIA OF ART WERE ACTUALIZED, ART WOULD COME TO AN END.

THEODOR W. ADORNO, AESTHETIC THEORY[1]

OPENING NIGHT

On January 10, 1927, all of Berlin's forty newspapers were abuzz with anticipation and excitement. *Metropolis*, the monumental new film by Fritz Lang, one and a half years in the making, was finally to open following an unprecedented advertising campaign that had run for several months. Everyone must have known by then that *Metropolis* was the most expensive and ambitious European film production to date, with an unheard-of cost of 5.3 million Reichsmark (more than three times its budget); that its shooting ratio was 1:300 (with more than one million meters of film exposed); and that it employed thirty-six thousand extras, including seventy-five hundred children and one thousand unemployed whose heads had been shaved by one hundred hairdressers for a scene that in the final cut lasted less than a minute. "A film of titanic dimensions," "the greatest film ever made, one of the most eternal artworks of all times," an "Über-film," and other slogans promised a film that could compete with such American high-culture spectacles as D. W. Griffith's *The Birth of a Nation* (1915) and *Intolerance* (1916) or Raoul Walsh's three-hour extravaganza, *The Thief of Bagdad* (1924), which had been shown in Berlin just a few years earlier.

Metropolis was also eagerly awaited as a sequel to Lang's successful megaproduction of 1924, the two-part *Die Nibelungen* (The Nibelungs), which established him as the most daring filmmaker of the 1920s both in visual style and ideological ambition. Dedicated to the German people, *Die Nibelungen* translated the archetypal German myth into stunning images of architectural excess, flaunting gigantic medieval castles and complete prehistoric forests made of concrete.[2] The son of an architect, Lang, who had studied painting before he turned to filmmaking, infused all of his films with a rich spatial imagination; he molded his characters and their fictional world to fit his architectural design. Not surprisingly it was the big-city architecture of New York that struck him when he toured the United States in 1924. His first glimpse of the New York skyline at night from a ship near Ellis Island in fact inspired him to make *Metropolis*:

> *I saw a street lit as if in full daylight by neon lights and, topping them, oversized luminous advertisements moving, turning, flashing, on and off, spiraling…something that was completely new and nearly fairy-tale-like for a European in those days.... The buildings seemed to be a vertical veil, shimmering, almost weightless, a luxurious cloth hung from the dark sky to dazzle, distract, and hypnotize. At night the city did not give the impression of being alive; it lived as illusions lived. I knew then that I had to make a film about all of these sensations.*[3]

151
Erich Kettelhut
Metropolis: Morgendämmerung, 1925
(Metropolis: Dawn)
Cat. no. 106

Upon his return Lang's wife, the novelist and screenwriter Thea von Harbou, furnished him with a script that envisioned a futuristic city of the year 2000 as the setting for a story that dramatized the latent social, sexual, and aesthetic conflicts of the 1920s. Serialized in the magazine *Das illustrierte Blatt* (The illustrated paper) and published as a novel at the time of the film's premiere, von Harbou's narrative, like Lang's film, extended over a broad intellectual terrain, touching on almost every issue that was discussed during the Weimar period. Placed in the artistic and social context of the modern era, *Metropolis* is Janus-faced, looking back to the rebellious Expressionist avant-garde and looking ahead to quiet submission under a fascist leader. The film displays the modernist dimension in fascism and the fascist dimension in modernism; it creates a site where modernism clashes with modernity.

After its premiere at the Ufa Palast am Zoo, which was attended by twenty-five hundred guests, among them the Reichskanzler and the leaders of finance and industry, *Metropolis* played at the refurbished Ufa Pavillion at the Nollendorfplatz for several months. The theater's exterior walls were covered with a gleaming silver coating. Brilliantly shimmering at night and faintly glistening during the day, the building radiated an eerie otherworldliness. Advertising gimmick as well as technological feat, the silvery theater projected a modernity associated with metal machinery. Futuristic technology was displayed not only in the film's fictional world but also outside, in the public space, which thus became an extension of the movie set. Upon approaching the theater, Berliners were also confronted with a gigantic steel sculpture that had been taken from the film set and mounted above the entrance. The gonglike sculpture represented a beating heart, offering a humanistic counterpoint to the cold, mechanical appearance of the exterior walls. The film's central conflict, between machinelike modernity and the sentimentality of the heart, was alluded to even before one entered the theater.

METROPOLIS, THE FILM

Metropolis, the event, clearly overshadowed *Metropolis*, the film. After a yearlong barrage of advertising and publicity, expectations were so great that probably no film could fulfill them. The papers on the morning following the premiere were almost unanimous in their criticism, pointing out the glaring contradiction between the film's strikingly innovative visual style and its atavistic, if not reactionary, ideology. The utopian solution to the plight of the working class (namely, to be oppressed by a kinder, gentler management) seemed either too facile or too cynical, and the Expressionist love story (Oedipal son rebels against rich father to win the hand of a working-class girl) seemed incongruous with the technical fetishism characteristic of this film as of all science fiction films.

"There is altogether too much of *Metropolis*," the exasperated film critic of *Life* commented when the film opened in New York in March 1927, only two months after its premiere in Berlin, "too much scenery, too many people, too much plot and too many platitudinous ideas."[4] It is true that intertextual references and resonances abound. The set design, for instance, runs the gamut from abstract cityscapes in the tradition of the Futurist architect Antonio Sant'Elia to cavernous Christian catacombs, from Art Deco interiors to the mythical Tower of Babel, from the abstract moving machine parts at the beginning of the film to the Gothic cathedral at the end (see figs. 156, 152). It was as if Erich Kettelhut, the set designer, were presenting his own entry in the famous architectural competition of 1921–22, in which more than a hundred architects (among them Ludwig Mies van der Rohe, Hans Poelzig, and Hans Scharoun) presented plans for a *Turmhaus* (skyscraper), the ultimate emblem of modernity, at the Friedrichstrasse station (see fig. 153).[5] And Kettelhut's plan, unlike those of the architects, was actually realized. The film

152
Scenes from *Metropolis*, 1927

153
Ludwig Mies van der Rohe
Friedrichstrasse Skyscraper: Presentation Perspective (North and East Sides), 1921
Charcoal, pencil on brown paper
68¼ x 48 in.
(173.5 x 122.0 cm)
Collection, Mies van der Rohe Archive, the Museum of Modern Art, New York. Gift of Ludwig Mies van der Rohe

154
Scene from *Metropolis*, 1927

reaches back into the mythical past and forward into the year 2000; its buildings stretch to the sky, and its lower reaches go deep into the bowels of the earth. This overdrawn vertical structure (in the tradition of Expressionist architecture) is meant to underscore the contrast between the wealthy, in their timeless pleasure gardens high above, and the working class, languishing in subterranean darkness, where time is measured in ten-hour shifts.

The bodies of the workers, depersonalized to the point of blending into the film's architectural design, are choreographed in the tradition of the agitprop and *Sprechchor* theater of Erwin Piscator, forming what Siegfried Kracauer has called a "mass ornament," in which the individual is radically submerged in highly structured formations. Kracauer saw the same process at work in the marching columns of the military as well as in the synchronized dancing style of the popular American girl revues, which mesmerized Berlin in the mid-1920s.[6] These lavish revues often featured more than one hundred dancers, all performing identical movements; they were, in his words, veritable "girl machines."[7] Less than a decade later Leni Riefenstahl would organize the masses similarly in her documentary of the Nazi Party Congress, *Triumph des Willen* (Triumph of the will, 1935).

"Metropolis, the city of the future," proclaimed the advertising material sent to movie theaters in 1927, "is the city of eternal social peace—the city of cities in which there is no animosity, no hatred, but only love and understanding."[8] Having gone into production only six years after the failed workers' revolution of 1918–19, *Metropolis* is clearly utopian in its keen desire for social peace. While it was true that relations between the classes had become relatively stable following the hyperinflation of 1923–24, the reconciliation between labor and management at the conclusion of the film still seemed like a happy ending made in Hollywood. In an interview published in the 1960s, Lang recalled: "The main thesis was Mrs. Lang's but I am least fifty percent responsible because I made the film. You cannot make a social-conscious picture in which you say that the intermediary between the hand and the brain is the heart—I mean that's a fairy tale—definitely. But I was very interested in machines."[9]

155
Scene from *Metropolis*, 1927

MACHINE AESTHETICS

"But I was very interested in machines." Lang's statement reveals precisely his contribution to the novel's predictable love story. In fact, the machine represents the underlying metaphor that places the film within the 1920s discourse on modernity and technology. The city, the workers' bodies, and the film itself are all associated with the machine (see figs. 154, 155). The city draws its energy from machines below ground; lights flicker, and flashes of lightning shoot across the sky after the workers destroy the gigantic generator that powers the city. And the city itself is organized like a machine that self-destructs as soon as any part malfunctions. When the workers rebel against their dehumanized status, they are presented as malfunctioning cogs in the city's machinery. Thus management's plan to replace them with robots is only logical: "Machines will be the workers of the future," proclaims Rotwang, the cabalistic scientist, voicing a utopian sentiment already uttered in Filippo Tommaso Marinetti's first Futurist manifesto.

Metropolis begins with an abstract montage of machinery in motion, set against tall skyscrapers that fill the entire frame (see fig. 156). Close-ups of moving pistons and a turbine engine turning in opposite directions build to a crescendo as more gears and movements are incorporated. The sequence is punctuated by the intercut image of a ten-hour clock, yet another machine, indicating the imminent start of a new shift. The steam whistle sounds, releasing the pressure that has built up, and—as a title card announces—a new shift begins. These machines move by themselves; we do not know what they produce or generate, nor do we know who set them in motion.

This fascination with mechanization, which Lang shared with the Russian Constructivists and Fernand Léger (whose film *Ballet mécanique* [Mechanical ballet] appeared in 1924), also found expression in the work of Ernst Jünger, who hailed the cold elegance and metallic energy of the impersonal machine. In 1925 Jünger wrote: "Standing in great glass-roofed halls, amid pistons and gleaming flywheels, where the mercury columns of manometers rose and fell, the red dials of dynamometers quivered against the white

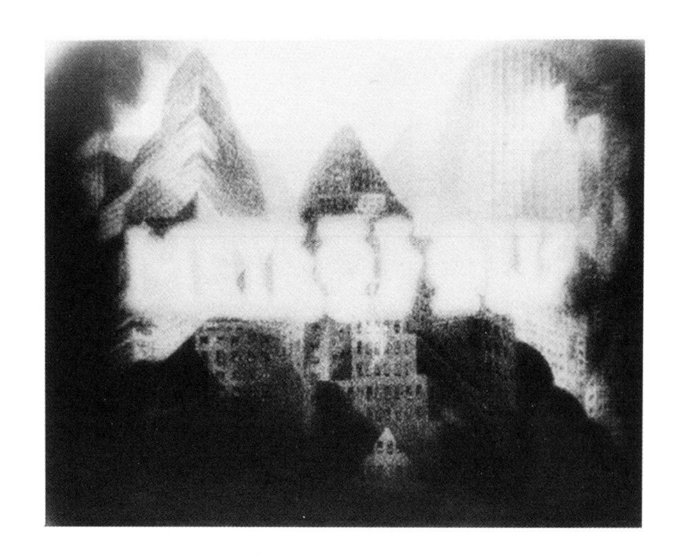

156
Opening montage from
Metropolis, 1927

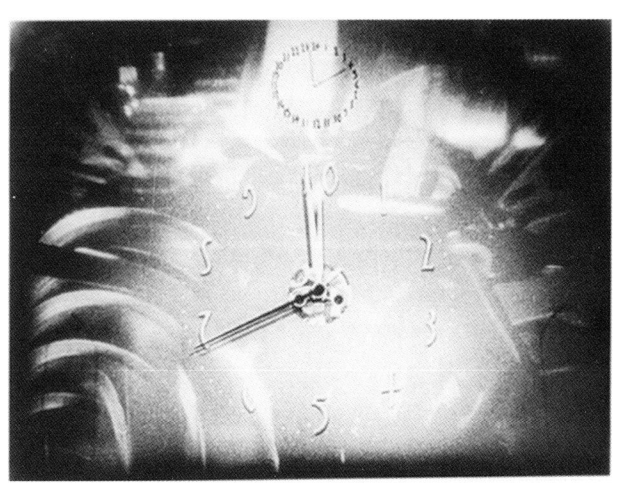

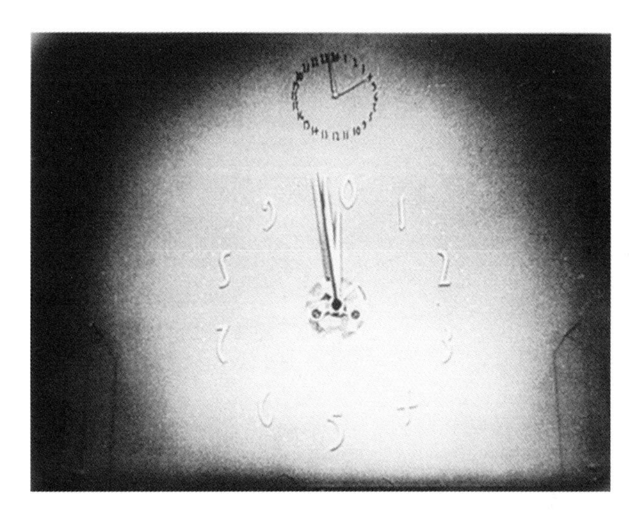

157
Otto Dix
Lens wird mit Bomben belegt, 1924
(Lens being bombed)
Cat. no. 16

marble of wall panels, we sensed that some surplus lived and breathed there, a luxury, an excess of energy, a will to transform all of life into energy."[10] This fusion of technology and vitalistic Nietzschean *Lebensphilosophie* (life philosophy) corresponds to what Joseph Goebbels would later call "stählerne Romantik" (steely romanticism). It was an intoxicating mixture. Jünger and Goebbels—and, one might add, Lang—reinvested modernity with the mythical dimension that had been repressed since the eighteenth century.

"Ours is the first generation to begin to reconcile itself to the machine and to see in it not only the useful but the beautiful as well," Jünger wrote in 1925, referring to the front generation of World War I, which experienced and survived the new symbiosis of human being and machine in the trenches. This generation was one that "builds machines and for whom machines are not dead iron but rather an organ of power, which it dominates with cold reason and blood."[11] In his view the war transformed a group of individuals into a cohesive mass that left behind the "gray, frightful world of utilitarianism" for the sake of higher values, community, and primordial passion.

Wartime mobilization, in which the soldier sacrificed his individual freedom to the demands of autocratic planning, also seemed the ideal model for industrial production; it was Jünger's contention, as expressed in his 1932 book-length treatise *Der Arbeiter* (The worker), that one day the worker would in fact become a worker-soldier of the type depicted in *Metropolis*. Jünger's futuristic project blended feudal imagery of service and sacrifice with a modern celebration of efficiency and vitality.

It was precisely the war, however, that also showed the destructive potential of modern technology, and it was the experience of bombing raids, machine-gun fire, and poison gas (invented and first used by Germans in 1917) that informed the deep split in the 1920s between technology and humanity (see fig. 157). As Jünger put it:

> *The war battle is a frightful competition of industries, and victory is the success of the competitor that managed to work faster and more ruthlessly. Here the era from which we come shows its cards. The domination of the machine over man,*

> *of the servant over the master, becomes apparent, and a deep discord, which in peacetime had already begun to shake the economic and social order, emerges in a deadly fashion. Here the style of a materialistic generation is uncovered, and technology celebrates a bloody triumph. Here a bill is paid, one that seemed old and forgotten.*[12]

In 1927, more than eight years after the war was over, the bill was still being paid. The images of large numbers of men in dark uniforms shuffling along in formation in *Metropolis* must have evoked memories of soldiers marching off to the front. It was the first modern war in which machines (from machine guns to bomber planes) decided the outcome. The consequences of World War I—thirteen million dead, eleven million crippled—were not forgotten by the mid-1920s. Millions of veterans with prostheses and mechanical body parts—half machine, half human—walked the streets, as we know from photographs and from George Grosz's paintings and drawings.[13] The war and its aftermath provided the ultimate context for modernism.

Metropolis offers a hallucinatory vision of the relationship between humanity and machine. The gigantic turbine that dominates the machine room transforms itself before the horrified eyes of Freder into the gaping jaws of a monster, identified in a title card as the biblical god Moloch (see fig. 159). Taking the visual motif of the man-eating machine from the famous 1914 Italian film *Cabiria*, the film uses superimposition to make the machine take on the features of a fuming god.[14] This sudden metamorphosis reveals *Metropolis*'s underlying ideology, which associates machines with man-eating monsters and the inventor Rotwang with black magic. Reminiscent in both dress and demeanor of Rabbi Loew in Paul Wegener's film *Der Golem* (The golem, 1920), Rotwang displays on his door and in his laboratory a five-pointed star, a pentagram associated with the occult and only vaguely with the star of David, even though von Harbou's novel wrongly identifies it as "the seal of Solomon" (i.e., star of David). The film dramatizes Rotwang's outsider status by linking him to a tiny, bizarre-looking medieval house surrounded by huge skyscrapers. Inventor of the artificial machine-human as well as sorcerer and magician, he represents the repressed archaic and nonsynchronous dimension of modernity.

"The more plain and advanced the technology," Ernst Bloch wrote in his perceptive essay "Die Angst des Ingenieurs" (The engineer's fear, 1929), "the more mysteriously it intersected with the old taboo region of vapors, supernatural velocity, Golem-robots, blue thunderbolts. Thus it touched what was once thought of as the realm of magic. An Edison is much closer to Doctor Faustus than to Herbert Spencer. Much of what the old fairy tales of magic promised has been realized by the most modern technology."[15] Situated between fairy tale and high-tech machinery, the film medium was predestined to represent technical progress and modernization as the intrusion of the horrific and uncanny.

Like most science fiction films, *Metropolis* is highly self-conscious about the representation of technology, because it is technology that produces the special effects and tricks that have characterized the genre ever since Georges Méliès made his first science fiction film, *Le voyage dans la lune* (Trip to the moon), in 1902. It was paradoxically the status of the camera as a machine that kept film for a long time, particularly in Germany, from being admitted to the temple of art: how can a machine produce more than a mechanical reproduction of reality? The invention of moving pictures itself was seen at the time as a fiction of science, and it is no coincidence that H. G. Wells's classic science fiction novel *The Time Machine* appeared in 1895, the same year moving pictures were inaugurated.[16]

In what is probably the most stunning scene in *Metropolis*, Rotwang's transformation

158
Scene from *Metropolis*, 1927

159
Scene from *Metropolis*, 1927

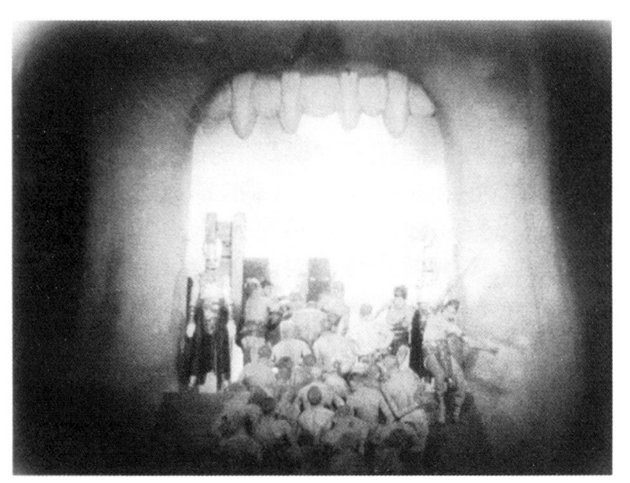

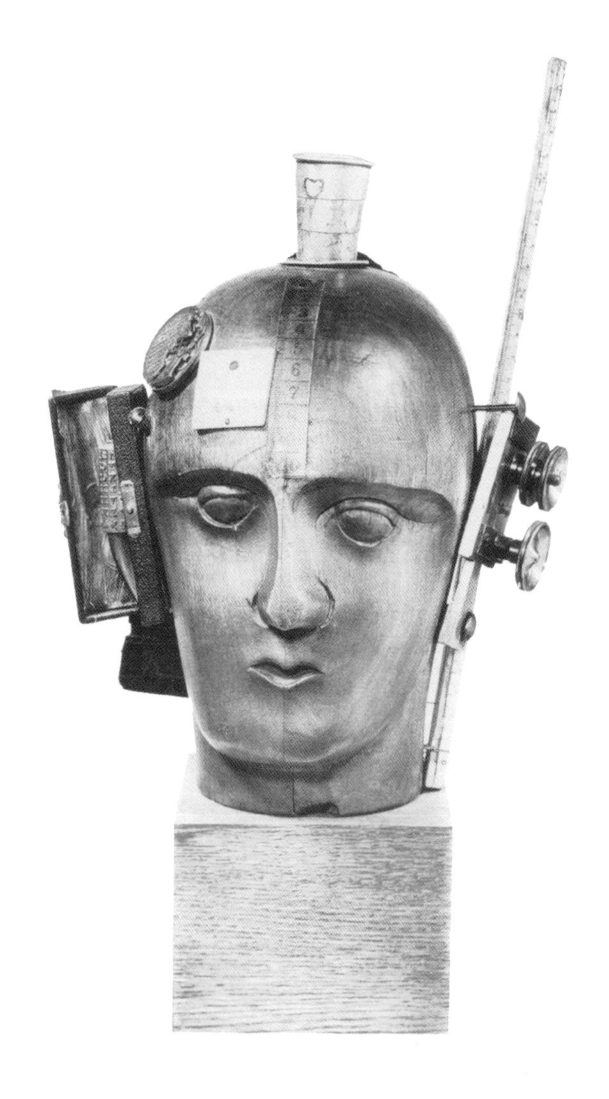

160
Scene from *Metropolis*, 1927

161
Raoul Hausmann
Mechanischer Kopf: Der Geist unserer Zeit, c. 1921
(Mechanical head: The spirit of our time)
Assemblage of wood, leather, cardboard, and other materials
12½ x 7½ x 7½ in.
(31.8 x 19.0 x 19.0 cm)
Musée National d'Art Moderne, Centre Georges Pompidou, Paris

of the robot into the likeness of Maria, mentioned briefly in von Harbou's novel, a replica is created with the help of enormous electrical machines and chemical apparatuses, a dazzling display of both scientific and cinematic magic (see fig. 160). The process involves machines, electricity, and chemistry—elements that are also needed to create a lifelike image on photographic film. Technology has the ability to conjure up simulacra, machine-made images indistinguishable from reality.[17] When the robot performs a lascivious dance before a male audience, attracting the spectators' desiring gaze and at the same time deceiving them, she becomes an emblem for the cinema as such: a product of technical ingenuity, an incarnation of visual pleasure, and a temptress out to delude anyone who falls for the illusion of a replica.[18]

The split of Maria into an asexual "good" Maria and an oversexed "bad" Maria, which Andreas Huyssen has perceptively analyzed,[19] can also be read as a reworking of historical developments that von Harbou and Lang may have regarded as a threat: the emergence of emancipated and sexually liberated women as well as organized feminist activity in the mid-1920s. The robot Maria, as the "new woman," rips the social fabric asunder, inciting

162
Scene from *Metropolis*, 1927

the workers to rebel and seducing them into self-destructive acts. Her punishment, once she is uncovered as an agent provocateur, is to be burned at the stake. The machine woman as witch: the film collapses the fear of women and machines into one. This nexus of technology, visual pleasure, simulation, and fantasy was also at the core of modern American mass culture, which, according to some cultural critics, had seduced Germany into renouncing its classical canon of high culture. While American modernity conquered the economy, culture, and life-style of the entire Western world in the 1920s, German intellectuals appeared powerless, vacillating between fascination and repulsion. Raoul Hausmann's famous sculpture, which bears a striking resemblance to the robot's head in *Metropolis*, is tellingly entitled *Mechanischer Kopf: Der Geist unserer Zeit* (Mechanical head: The spirit of our time, c. 1921; fig. 161).

"The number of people who see films and never read books is in the millions," theater critic Herbert Jhering wrote in despair in 1926. "They are all subordinated to American taste, they are made identical.... The American film is the new world militarism, which inexorably marches forward. It is more dangerous than Prussian militarism because it devours not only single individuals but whole countries."[20] The fear that mass culture might be a secret American weapon, one that would enslave the world by distracting it, found a particular resonance in Germany, where for too long cultural identity compensated for a lack of national identity. Linked to technology, mass consumption, and mass media, American modernity became a powerful agent in the economic and cultural modernization of Germany after the war.

AMERICAN MODERNITY

"How boring Germany is," wrote Bertolt Brecht in a short diary entry dated June 18, 1920. After finding fault with all classes of German society—peasants, middle class, and intellectuals—he concluded, "Only America remains."[21] For Brecht, as for other avant-garde writers of the early 1920s, America was the only progressive alternative to the still semifeudal life-style of Germany. America, more than Russia, was consistently represented as the New World, the alternative, the other. The relationship between Germany and America was understood as a historically momentous encounter between two radically different cultures, two ways of perceiving and interpreting the world, two divergent cultural languages and systems of signs. The Berlin avant-garde circles of Brecht and Grosz saw American mass culture as a vehicle for the radical modernization and democratization of German life and culture (see fig. 163). American mass culture stood for Charlie Chaplin and the movies, for jazz and Charleston, for boxing and other spectator sports; above all, it represented modernity and the ideal of living in the present (see fig. 164).

No other country embraced American modernity more feverishly than did Germany after the war. "America was a good idea," a German intellectual remarked, looking back in 1930:

> *It was the land of the future. It was at home in its century. We were too young to know it firsthand; nevertheless we loved it. Long enough had the glorious discipline of technology appeared only in the form of tanks, mines, poison gas, for the purpose of annihilating humankind. In America it was at the service of human life. The sympathy expressed for elevators, radio towers, and jazz demonstrated this. It was like a creed. It was the way to beat the sword into a plowshare. It was against cavalry; it was for horsepower.*[22]

By the mid-1920s, however, at the beginning of a five-year period of relative political and economic stability, a noticeable shift in the image of America began to take place in Germany. It continued to represent the mass culture of jazz, sports, and cinema, but it increasingly became associated with inhuman technological progress and industrial rationalization as well (see fig. 165). Americanism in the economic sphere meant efficiency, discipline, and control, and both the right and the left began criticizing what they considered the encroachment of instrumental rationality and cost effectiveness into all areas, including culture, which in Germany had always been defined as antithetical to the world of commerce. Adolf Halfeld, a conservative cultural critic, states this unmistakably on the cover of his polemical book *Amerika und der Amerikanismus* (America and Americanism), published in 1927, the year of *Metropolis*'s release: "Indebted to tradition, the culture of Europe, in particular of Germany, is threatened by America, with its focus on materialism and the mechanization of life. Rationalization in the American example triumphs, even if it kills the human side of humankind."[23] And in 1928, when asked by the avant-garde journal *Transition* about the influence of the United States on Europe, the German poet Gottfried Benn answered: "[The American] influence is enormous. There is a group of lyric poets, who think they have composed a poem by writing 'Manhattan.' There is a group of playwrights, who think they reveal the modern drama by having the action take place in an Arizona blockhouse and by having a bottle of whiskey on the table. The entire young German literature since 1918 is working under the slogan of tempo, jazz, cinema, overseas, technical activity by emphasizing the negation of an ensemble of psychic problems."[24] He particularly objected to "the purely utilitarian, the mass article, the collective plan," concluding, not surprisingly, by stating, "Personally I am against Americanism." In Benn's view Americanism had conspired with communism in promot-

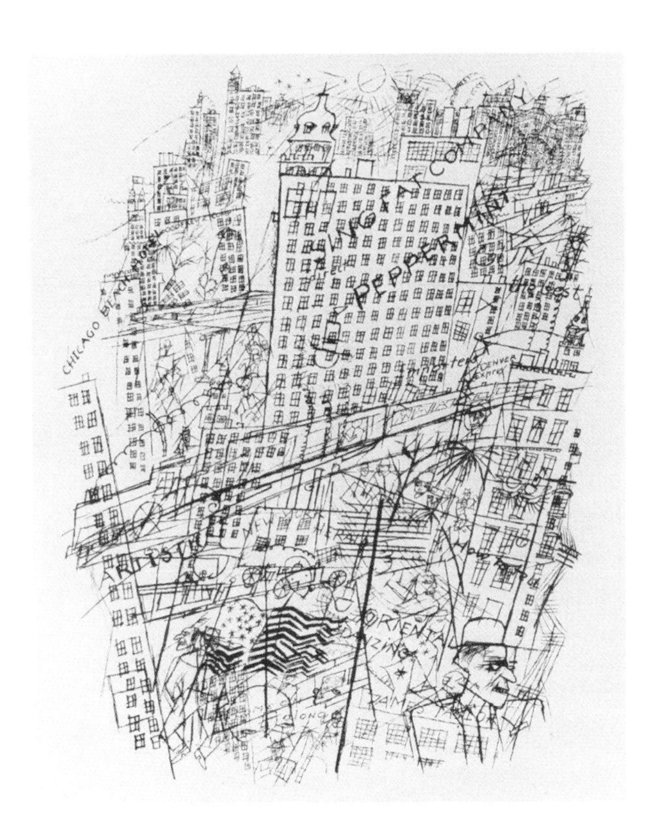

163
George Grosz
Erinnerung an New York,
1915–16
(Memory of New York)
Cat. no. 50

164
Marianne Brandt
Untitled, c. 1924
Cat. no. 10

ing collectivism and crass materialism at the expense of the German ideals of individualism and idealism, a polemical juxtaposition that structured the cultural debates of the Weimar era and also inscribed itself in *Metropolis*.

By the mid-1920s the term *Americanism* had come to signify two intricately related phenomena: scientific management of labor and industrial mass production (known as Taylorism and Fordism, respectively), on the one hand, and commercial mass culture, on the other. To speak of America was to evoke an image of a country in which economic productivity, technology, modernity, and democracy went hand in hand with a new urban culture. But to speak of America was also to conjure up a nightmarish picture of a materialistic, mechanized society ruled by exploitation, commercialism, and a lowbrow mass culture cynically catering to the largest possible audience. These contradictory attitudes prevailed throughout the Weimar era, with the critical view becoming dominant after the stock market crash of 1929.

Henry Ford, car manufacturer and popular philosopher, was generally regarded as the official spokesman for American big business. His 1922 autobiography, *My Life and Work*, was an instant bestseller in Germany and became a bible for all those who wanted to emulate America's economic success and thus lift Germany out of its backwardness. Ford preached the gospel of scientific instrumental rationality couched in humanitarian terms. In a chapter entitled "The Terror of the Machine, " he writes: "I have not been able to discover that repetitive labour injures a man in any way. I have been told by parlour experts that repetitive labour is soul- as well as body-destroying, but that has not been the result of our investigations." He goes on to explain:

> *There were 7,882 different jobs in the factory. Of these, 949 were classified as heavy work requiring strong, able-bodied, and practically physically perfect men; 3,338 required men of ordinary physical development and strength. The remaining 3,595 jobs were disclosed as requiring no physical exertion and*

165
Gerd Arntz
Fabrik, 1927
(Factory)
Cat. no. 2

> *could be performed by the slightest, weakest sort of men. In fact, most of them could be satisfactorily filled by women or older children. The lightest jobs were again classified to discover how many of them required the use of full faculties, and we found that 670 could be filled by legless men, 2,637 by one-legged men, 2 by armless men, 715 by one-armed men, and 10 by blind men.*[25]

Ford prides himself on the employment of the deaf and mute as well as the tubercular, who, he suggests, should be used mainly outdoors. He concludes, "Yet it is not true that men are mere machines."[26] Between 1912 and 1914, however, following the introduction of the assembly line, the time required to assemble a car was cut from fourteen hours to ninety-three minutes. By 1925, after further refinement and the addition of more conveyor belts, a new car rolled off the assembly line every ten seconds.

Metropolis's highly stylized, almost dancelike image of rationalized and fully alienated labor visualizes and critiques basic principles of Taylorism and Fordism: repetitive work under the dictates of the clock is bound to create pressure that can be released only in an explosive revolution, which the film represents as a natural catastrophe on the order of an earthquake or flood. Technology's repressed other returns with a vengeance.

THE DIALECTICS OF MODERNITY

The much-maligned ending of *Metropolis*—the reconciliation between capital and labor, which has been called simplistic, foolish, reactionary, and worse[27]—is in fact an accurate expression of contradictory tendencies in the mid-1920s that have to do with German reactions to modernity, technological progress, and instrumental rationality. Modernity, in Max Weber's often-quoted definition, means above all the progressive disenchantment (*Entzauberung*) of the world, a result of myth and religion being superseded by rational and secular thought. Intertwined with the rise of capitalism, free-market economy, democracy, and mass culture, modernity had a more destabilizing effect in Germany than in France, England, and the United States because Germany lacked an established democratic tradition. Everything capitalist modernity stood for—its challenge to authority, its drive for unbridled economic competition, its disavowal of spiritual and religious values, and its commercialization of culture—collided head-on with still intact patriarchal, feudal, and authoritarian structures.

Although the German battle against modernity goes back to the mid-nineteenth century (culminating in World War I), it was the Weimar Republic, Germany's first democratically elected government, that revealed the contradictions within modernity itself. In their magisterial *Dialektik der Aufklärung* (Dialectic of enlightenment, 1947), Theodor W. Adorno and Max Horkheimer voiced the suspicion that the rationality characteristic of the joint projects of enlightenment and modernity might rest on a logic of domination and oppression. Writing in the aftermath of two world wars, of Hiroshima and the Holocaust, they argued that the desire to dominate nature entailed the domination of human nature; the quest for human emancipation was thus transmuted and hardened into a system of universal oppression. The legacy of the Enlightenment spirit that informed modernity meant, in short, the triumph of instrumental rationality.[28]

Metropolis lays out a host of reactions to the nexus of modernity, capitalism, and rationality—including religion, superstition, irrationalism, sexual abandon, Expressionist idealism, and revolutionary zeal—only to reaffirm in the end a somewhat modified instrumental rationality. Both the failed socialist revolution of 1918–19 and the successful fascist takeover in 1933 responded to forces unleashed by modernity in Germany. *Metropolis* incorporates both reactions to modernity, the failed workers' revolt (in the film cynically masterminded by capital) as well as the insidious right-wing takeover that stands for what might be called "oppression with a heart." At the end the workers again march in formation to watch their foreman shake hands with management, as Freder and Maria, the idealistic young couple, look on (see fig. 166).

Who then is excluded from this harmonious ending? Rotwang falls to his death from the rooftop of the Gothic cathedral while fighting with Freder, and the female robot is burned at the stake. What remains is a transformed community that again embraces technology, a technology that is now free, the film insinuates, from "Jewish control" and infused instead with German spirituality. It is the kind of community (*Gemeinschaft*, not *Gesellschaft*) that reactionary modernists such as Jünger, Werner Sombart, and Oswald Spengler had emphatically valorized in their writings throughout the 1920s. *Metropolis*'s linkage of modern technology, cultural pessimism, and totalitarian ideology prefigures the National Socialists' resolve to emancipate technology from capitalist exchange and "Jewish materialism."[29] Hitler, who once defined Aryan culture as a synthesis of "the Greek spirit and Germanic technology,"[30] did not oppose modernity (unlike *völkisch* ideologues). Goebbels summed up the official Nazi position on technology in a speech at the opening of the Berlin Auto Show on February 17, 1939:

> *National Socialism never rejected or struggled against technology. Rather, one of its main tasks was to consciously affirm it, to fill it inwardly with soul, to discipline it and to place it in the service of our people and their cultural level. We live in an age that is both romantic and steel-like, that has not lost its depth of feeling. On the contrary, it has discovered a new romanticism in the results of modern inventions and technology. While bourgeois reaction was alien to and filled with incomprehension, if not outright hostility to technology, and*

166
Scenes from *Metropolis*, 1927

while modern skeptics believed the deepest roots of the collapse of European culture lay in it, National Socialism understood how to take the soulless framework of technology and fill it with the rhythm and hot impulses of our time.[31]

This romanticized vision of modernity was meant to obscure the contradictions of a regime that built high-tech weapons systems while insisting on the values of blood and soil.

Metropolis's ideological trajectory is part of a larger debate among German sociologists and philosophers about the "intellectual and spiritual revolution," which, Ernst Troeltsch stated in 1921, was a "revulsion against drill and discipline, against the ideology of success and power...against intellectualism...against the big metropolis and the unnatural... against the rule of money and prestige."[32] This reaction against capitalist modernity was itself perceived as revolutionary and utopian in the 1920s. Troeltsch put his hopes in the youth movement, and it is no coincidence that *Metropolis* also places the task of spiritual renewal in the hands of the young.

Lang's *Metropolis* offers one of the most fascinating and complex contributions to the vigorous 1920s discourse on modernity. Its message is ambivalent, suggesting that the undoing of modernization and technological progress would bring only self-destruction. This ambivalence is evident in the images that fetishize technology even as they display its cataclysmic power. The machine is the object of fascination and terror, of savagery and myth; its faceless power contrasts with the individualism of the German Expressionist narrative, in which a son rebels against his father and an entire industrial system. Clearly the Expressionist utopia of Georg Kaiser's Gas plays and Ernst Toller's *Die Maschinenstürmer* (The machine wreckers), which advocate revolution and a radically antitechnological humanism, had itself become dystopian in the context of the modern industrial society that Germany unquestionably was in 1927. Still it was impossible to dismiss utopian Expressionism, with its idealistic, impractical, and old-fashioned emphasis on the heart (and, in a wider sense, on community) and its rebellion against unrestrained instrumental rationality. The idealism of *Metropolis* should be seen, however, not as a "fault" of the film but as a historically explainable and valid attempt to fight those tendencies of modernity that have undeniably shown themselves to be cruel and dehumanizing. Viewed in its historical context, the film thus dramatizes the reaction of German modernism against an overpowering modernity, one that had undermined and negated its emancipatory and utopian potential.

NOTES

1. Theodor W. Adorno, *Aesthetic Theory*, trans. C. Lenhardt (Boston: Routledge and Kegan Paul, 1984), p. 47.

2. See Sabine Hake, "Architectural Histories: Fritz Lang and *The Nibelungs*," *Wide Angle* 12 (July 1990): 38–57.

3. Fritz Lang, "Was ich in Amerika sah," *Film-Kurier*, 11 December 1924.

4. R. E. Sherwood, "The Silent Drama: Metropolis," *Life*, 24 March 1927, p. 24.

5. See Florian Zimmermann, ed., *Der Schrei nach dem Turmhaus: Der Ideenwettbewerb Hochhaus am Bahnhof Friedrichstrasse Berlin*, 1921/22 (Berlin: Argon, 1988).

6. "The structure of the mass ornament reflects that of the general contemporary situation. Since the principle of the capitalist production process does not stem purely from nature, it must destroy the natural organisms which it regards either as a means or as a force of resistance. Personality and national community perish when calculability is demanded" (Siegfried Kracauer, "The Mass Ornament," *New German Critique* 5 [Spring 1975]: 69).

7. See Siegfried Kracauer, "Girls und Krise," *Frankfurter Zeitung*, 27 April 1931. The workers' automatized movements also recall the "mechanical ballets" performed at the Bauhaus theater (Oskar Schlemmer's *Triadisches Ballett* [Triadic ballet], for instance) in the early and mid-1920s.

8. Publicity brochure for *Metropolis* (1927).

9. Cited in Peter Bogdanovich, *Fritz Lang in America* (New York: Praeger, 1967), p. 124. For the production history of *Metropolis* and interviews with Lang, see also Fred Gehler and Ulrich Kasten, *Fritz Lang: Die Stimme von Metropolis* (Berlin: Henschel, 1990); Enno Patalas, "Metropolis, Scene 103," *Camera Obscura* 15 (Fall 1986): 165–73.

10. Ernst Jünger, "Feuer und Blut: Fin kleiner Ausschnitt aus einer grossen Schlacht" (1925), in *Tagebücher* (Berlin, 1926; Stuttgart: Klett, 1960),

p. 465; see also Klaus Theweleit, "The Soldierly Body, the Technological Machine, and the Fascist Aesthetic," in *Male Fantasies*, vol. 2, *Male Bodies: Psychoanalyzing the White Terror*, trans. Erica Carter and Chris Turner (Minneapolis: University of Minnesota Press, 1989), pp. 197–210.

11. Quoted in Jeffrey Herf, *Reactionary Modernism: Technology, Culture, and Politics in Weimar and the Third Reich* (Cambridge: Cambridge University Press, 1984), pp. 79, 81.

12. Jünger, "Feuer und Blut," p. 466.

13. See Peter Sloterdijk, *Critique of Cynical Reason*, trans. Michael Eldred (Minneapolis: University of Minnesota Press, 1987), pp. 443–59.

14. Chaplin alludes to this motif in a more playful, fairy-tale-like way in a scene from *Modern Times* (1936) in which the machine he operates first devours him and then spits him out.

15. Ernst Bloch, "Die Angst des Ingenieurs," in *Gesamtausgabe*, vol. 9 (Frankfurt: Suhrkamp, 1965), p. 353; see also idem, "Nonsynchronism and the Obligation to Its Dialectics," *New German Critique* 11 (Spring 1977): 23–38.

16. On *Metropolis* within the context of science fiction and utopia in Germany, see Peter S. Fisher, *Fantasy and Politics: Visions of the Future in the Weimar Republic* (Madison: University of Wisconsin Press, 1991); Götz Müller, *Gegenwelten: Die Utopie in der deutschen Literatur* (Stuttgart: Metzler, 1989), pp. 212–17.

17. On the importance of the motif of the machine-woman in Auguste de Villiers de L'Isle-Adam's 1886 novel *L'ève future* for cinema, see Annette Michelson, "On the Eve of the Future: The Reasonable Facsimile and the Philosophical Toy," in *October: The First Decade, 1976–1986*, ed. Annette Michelson et al. (Cambridge: MIT Press, 1987), pp. 417–34; Raymond Bellour, "Ideal Hadaly," *Camera Obscura* 15 (Fall 1986): 111–34.

18. For a discussion of the sexual politics of *Metropolis* in general and the nexus between machine and female sexuality in particular, see Andreas Huyssen, "The Vamp and the Machine," in *After the Great Divide: Modernism, Mass Culture, Postmodernism* (Bloomington: Indiana University Press, 1986), pp. 65–81; Patricia Mellencamp, "Oedipus and the Robot in Metropolis," *Enclitic* 5 (Spring 1981): 20–42; Stephen Jenkins, "Lang: Fear and Desire," in *Fritz Lang* (London: British Film Institute, 1981); Roger Dadoun, "*Metropolis*: Mother—City—'Mittler'—Hitler," *Camera Obscura* 15 (Fall 1986): 137–64; Peter Wollen, "Cinema / Americanism / the Robot," *New Formations, no.* 8 (Summer 1989): 7–34.

19. See Huyssen, "The Vamp and the Machine."

20. Herbert Jhering, "UFA und Buster Keaton," in *Von Reinhardt bis Brecht*, vol. 2 (Berlin: Aufbau-Verlag, 1961), p. 509.

21. Bertolt Brecht, *Gesammelte Werke*, vol. 20 (Frankfurt: Suhrkamp, 1967), p. 10.

22. Hans A. Joachim, "Romane aus Amerika," *Die neue Rundschau* 41 (September 1930): 397–98. On the extensive debate over cultural Americanism, see *Weimarer Republik: Manifeste und Dokumente zur deutschen Literatur, 1918–1933*, ed. Anton Kaes (Stuttgart: Metzler, 1983), pp. 265–86; see also Anton Kaes, "Mass Culture and Modernity: Notes toward a Social History of Early American and German Cinema," in *America and the Germans: An Assessment of a Three-Hundred-Year History*, eds. Frank Trommler and Joseph McVeigh, vol. 2 (Philadelphia: University of Pennsylvania Press, 1988), pp. 317–31. On Americanism in the economic sphere, see Charles S. Maier, "Between Taylorism and Technocracy: European Ideologies and the Vision of Industrial Productivity in the 1920s," *Journal of Contemporary History* 5 (April 1970): 27–61.

23. Adolf Halfeld, *Amerika und der Amerikanismus* (Jena: Eugen Diederichs, 1927).

24. Gottfried Benn, "Inquiry," *Transition* 13 (1928): 251ff.; reprinted in *Gesammelte Werke* (Wiesbaden: Limes, 1968), p. 2218.

25. Henry Ford, *My Life and Work* (Garden City, N.Y.: Doubleday, Page, 1922), pp. 105, 108.

26. Ibid., p, 209.

27. H. G. Wells, for instance, begins his 1927 review as follows: "I have recently seen the silliest film. I do not believe it would be possible to make one sillier.... It gives in one eddying concentration almost every possible foolishness, cliché, platitude, and muddlement about mechanical progress and progress in general served up with a sauce of sentimentality that is all its own" (quoted in *Authors on Film*, ed. Harry M. Geduld [Bloomington: Indiana University Press, 1972], p. 59).

28. See Max Horkheimer and Theodor W. Adorno, *Dialectic of Enlightenment*, trans. John Cumming (New York: Seabury Press, 1972); see also Jürgen Habermas, *The Philosophical Discourse of Modernity*, trans. Frederick Lawrence (Cam-bridge: MIT Press, 1987); Michael E. Zimmerman, *Heidegger's Confrontation with Modernity: Technology, Politics, and Art* (Bloomington: Indiana University Press, 1991).

29. The relationship between Fritz Lang and National Socialism is still under debate. Hitler and Goebbels liked *Die Nibelungen* as well as *Metropolis* and wanted to make Lang the head of the entire Nazi film production in 1933. He declined and went to Hollywood instead. His passport shows, however, that he actually returned to Germany on several brief sojourns after 1933 (see Gösta Werner, "Fritz Lang and Goebbels: Myth and Facts," *Film Quarterly* 43 [Spring 1990]: 24–27; Willi Winkler, "Ein Schlafwandler bei Goebbels," *Spiegel* 48 [26 November 1990]: 236–42).

30. Adolf Hitler, *Mein Kampf*; quoted in Eberhard Jäckel, *Hitler's World View: A Blueprint for Power*, trans. Herbert Arnold (Middletown, Conn.: Wesleyan University Press, 1972), p. 28.

31. Quoted in Herf, *Reactionary Modernism*, p. 196.

32. Ernst Troeltsch, "Die geistige Revolution," *Kunst wart und Kulturwart* 34 (January 1921): 231; translated in Fritz Ringer, *The Decline of the German Mandarins: The German Academic Community, 1890–1933* (Cambridge: Harvard University Press, 1969).

Galerie Berinson, Berlin

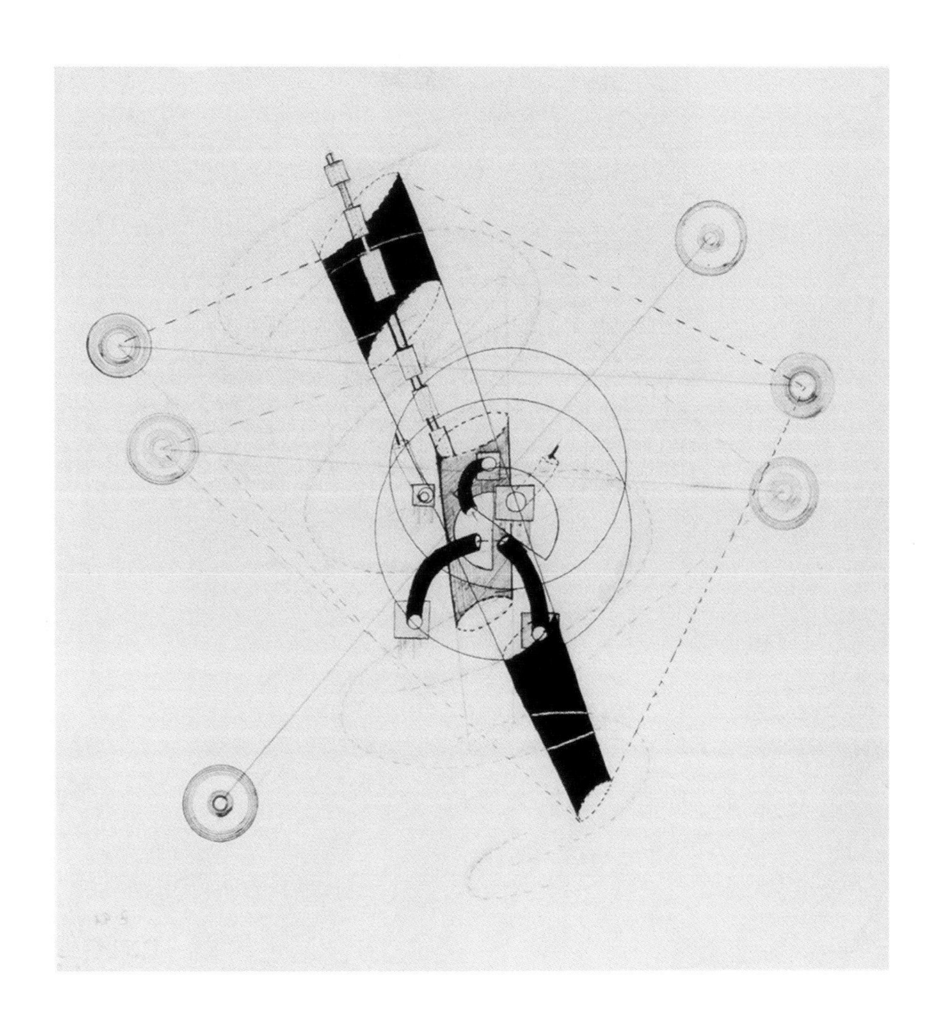

167
Hannah Höch
Hochfinanz, 1923
(High finance)
Cat. no. 89

168
Ella Bergmann
Untitled (spiral construction),
1922
Cat. no. 9

170
Johannes Molzahn
Zeit-Taster: Eine kleine Kollektion utopisch-phantastischer Maschinen und Apparate, 1921
(Time-feeler: A small collection of utopian fantastic machines and apparatuses)
Portfolio of six etchings
Cat. nos. 159–61

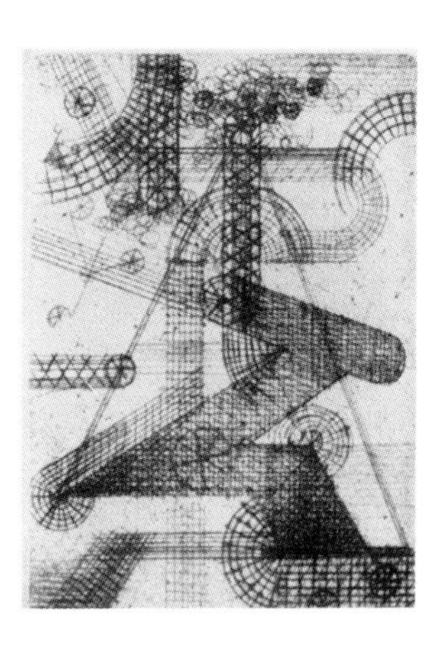

169
Franz Maria Jansen
Untitled (workers arriving), 1921
Cat. no. 99

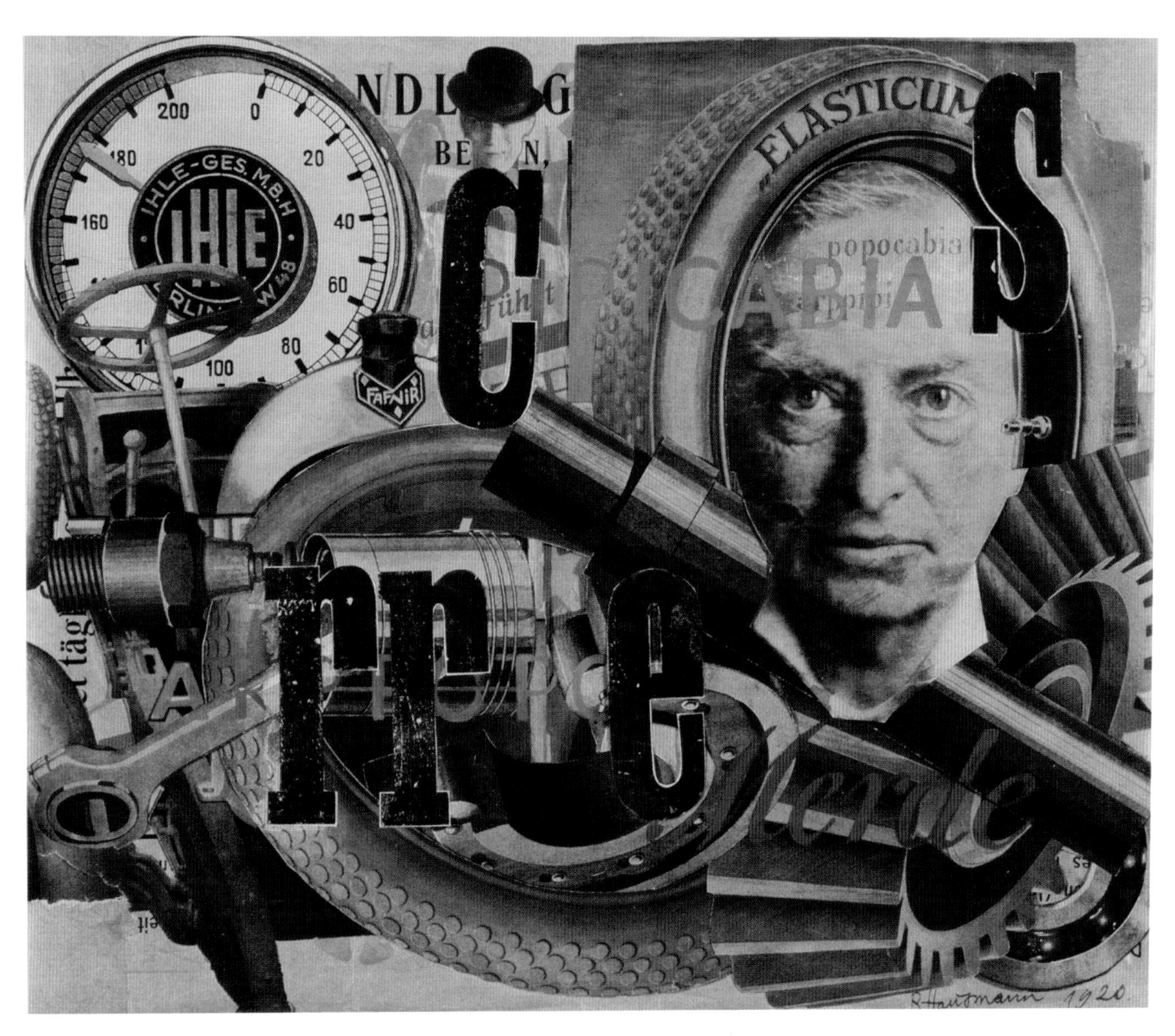

Galerie Berinson, Berlin

171
Raoul Hausmann
Elasticum, 1920
Cat. no. 78

172
Wenzel Hablik
Wohnhaus und Atelier, 1921
(Residence and studio)
Cat. no. 65

LIQUID

SPACE

EDWARD DIMENDBERG

The Museum as Liquid Space:

A Conversation with Wolf D. Prix on the Coop Himmelblau Design of the *Expressionist Utopias* Exhibit

INTRODUCTION

Although many devotees of contemporary architecture will already be acquainted with the work of the Viennese architectural firm Coop Himmelblau, the following remarks may prove helpful to those encountering it for the first time. Wolf D. Prix and Helmut Swiczinsky, the two principals of the office, were commissioned by Curator Timothy O. Benson of the Los Angeles County Museum of Art (LACMA) to design the *Expressionist Utopias* exhibition mounted in the museum's W. M. Keck Foundation Gallery from October 21, 1993, to January 16, 1994, and documented in this book.[1]

Together with contemporary architects such as Daniel Libeskind, Peter Eisenman, Zaha Hadid, Thom Mayne, Ricardo Scofidio, and Elizabeth Diller, Coop Himmelblau share an unyielding commitment to formal innovation and intellectual reflection. Their work challenges the dominant conception of architecture as subservient to the rote functions that buildings are expected to perform. These practitioners of the avant-garde embrace political or social criticism in their projects, which typically examine the tacit assumptions of everyday life no less than those of their profession. For more than thirty years Prix and Swiczinsky have withstood evanescent trends and changes in fashion so as to remain true to their ideals. Their built work and writings generate continual debate and provide a moral and aesthetic compass for several generations of architects.

Few visitors and critics failed to remark upon the powerful and suggestive design of the *Expressionist Utopias* exhibition, the first project realized by Coop Himmelblau in the United States. Its precariously balanced, freestanding, tilted columns, massive elongated walls, and transparent panels and display cases resembled few other exhibitions. Bold projections of cubes of light onto the ceiling and the titles of the five exhibition sections (Paradise, Metropolis, Architectural Fantasy, Anti-Utopia, Film and Stage) onto the floor were equally remarkable and unusual in a museum setting.

Beyond the four perimeter walls painted gray with white "clouds" stenciled with wire mesh to achieve an "incidental" quality, only pure unpainted materials were used: gray concrete board, Plexiglas, wood, stainless steel and aluminum flashing, and light itself. Organized in a labyrinth-like pattern, the space presented itself as a challenge to be negotiated, more resonant of an industrial setting than a typical art exhibition. Coop Himmelblau radically contested the traditional purity of the gallery cube that Brian O'Doherty calls "a white, ideal space that, more than any single picture, may be the archetypal image of twentieth century art."[2] That their design for *Expressionist Utopias* never overwhelmed the art and provided a kaleidoscopic array of positions from which to consider its significance further enhanced the magnitude of the architects' achievement.

Previous Page:
Wolf D. Prix (top)
Metropolis section (bottom)

Yet anyone familiar with the prior accomplishments of Himmelblau would have expected nothing less. The office was founded in the tumultuous year of 1968. Since then, its contributions to the built environment and theoretical debates in architecture and urbanism have consistently questioned the status quo and created forms of striking force and imagination. In their Austrian buildings such as the Red Angel Wine Bar and Song Club (Vienna, 1981), the SEG Apartment Tower (Vienna, 1994), the Seibersdorf Office and Research Center (Seibersdorf, 1995), and a score of other projects, provocative design solutions coexist with equally provocative formal and political metaphors.

The Reiss Bar (Vienna, 1977) includes a prominent crack that extends over the wall, ceiling, and floor. In The Blazing Wing (Graz, 1980), a steel wing fifteen meters high and weighing 1.5 tons was suspended over the courtyard of the Technical University of Graz and equipped with gas jets that were ignited. "Architecture must burn," Prix and Swiczinsky famously proclaimed of their project, in a simultaneous declaration as radicalized architects of their generation and an attack upon the stultifying character of tradition.[3] Intensely aware of the transformation of the political aspirations of early modernism into an inert style for producing corporate and consumer identities, Coop Himmelblau reject any notion of architecture as usual.

Included in the *Deconstructivist Architecture* exhibition curated by Philip Johnson and Mark Wigley at The Museum of Modern Art, New York, in 1988, the asymmetrical designs of Coop Himmelblau question the belief in unity and balance at the basis of the classical rules of architectural composition.[4] They reject hierarchically deployed forms and distinctions between inside and outside. Such aversion to the reassuring stability of the geometrically pure box evident throughout the work of Coop Himmelblau could well seem tailor made for classification under the rubric of architectural deconstruction. Yet this label, like all labels applied to their work, fits uncomfortably and conceals perhaps more than it reveals.

If formal exploration remains essential to Prix and Swiczinsky, their architecture is equally concerned with urban issues and with the lived experience of city-dwellers, an interest conveyed by their 1987 plan for the Melun-Sénart area on the southern edge of Paris. Scrutinize the interview that follows and one cannot help but be struck by the frequency with which phrases such as "synergy," "dynamic space," "fluid context," "living flow," "vibrant representation of life," and "vitality" are appropriated by Prix to describe the work of Coop Himmelblau. At once evoking the long tradition of vitalism, the *Lebensphilosophie* of Friedrich Nietzsche and Georg Simmel, whose valorization of life force inspired German cultural modernism, this concern with life and movement pervades the architectural conceptions of Himmelblau[5] (see Appendix, pages 282–84). Haunted by the nightmare of a fixed architecture of reified forms (to which a project such as the Open House [Malibu, California, 1983], with its flexible interior plan, provides an ambitious foil), for Prix and Swiczinsky the static is the status quo.

Their architecture entails a playful and democratic appeal to vital forces. The life to be celebrated and enhanced by architecture is that of the ordinary urbanite, rather than any lofty *Übermensch*. Few architects would applaud, as does Prix, the decision of the Groninger Museum to allow teenagers to roller-skate or ride their skateboards in the exhibition space of the East Pavilion designed by Himmelblau. A similar commitment to the design of a vibrant public space is evident in their UFA Cinema Center (Dresden, 1994), whose open lobby and generous circulation scheme remedies the paucity of gathering spots and public places in the surrounding neighborhood. At times Prix and Swiczinsky appear to echo the views of the Dutch Constant and the French situationist Guy Debord, for whom vital movement was manifested in the mobile architecture of the "New Babylon" or the *dérive* through the city, respectively.[6]

UFA Cinema Center, Dresden, Germany, 1994

Yet the distinct accomplishment of Coop Himmelblau is to have resisted the pressures of literalization that would privilege a specific formal device as the basis for an architecture of dynamic movement. Openness, as Prix notes, also signifies conceptual openness and cannot be reduced to a design element such as transparency, just as mobility and vitality cannot be guaranteed by movable walls or ramps. At once optimistic yet lacking in nostalgia, Coop Himmelblau practice an architecture that rejects recipes and stale platitudes. Their dedication to the avant-garde project of overcoming the separation between art and life criticizes "aestheticism" and the belief in art as an autonomous social realm that arose in the eighteenth century.

In contrast to the decorative or reassuring function of much aesthetic production since the advent of industrial capitalism (including modern architecture), Coop Himmelblau might well accept Peter Bürger's definition of avant-garde culture as art "not simply to be destroyed, but transferred to the praxis of life where it would be preserved, albeit in a changed form."[7] Unlike visual arts such as painting or cinema in which contemplative separation cannot be overcome, the programmatic dimension of architecture, its design and realization for a specific function, renders it uniquely suited to inject aesthetic force into life in a beneficial, rather than a socially conservative, sense. Here Coop Himmelblau avoid prescriptive formulas. Their work emphasizes the strategic role of irony (suggested by the hourglass-shaped cage of the UFA Cinema Center where spectators can sip cappuccinos) and the continual need to rework degraded concepts into knowledge.[8]

In *Architecture is Now* (1983), Coop Himmelblau wrote, "Architecture lives for the blink of an eye at the moment of the conception. . . The moment of the conception differentiates and decides. If it is free from compulsions, clichés, ideologies, and formalisms, then architecture will become free. Inherent necessities crumble. Causality is inverted."[9] Evoking the fragile temporality of the "constructed situation" explored by Debord and the situationists, the moment of the conception (der *Entwurf*) refers concretely to the initial sketch drawn by Prix or Swiczinsky (often with eyes closed) from which the subsequent design develops.[10]

Analogous to the surrealist technique of automatic writing, the energy captured in this first drawing reveals "the psychic planes of the space" as well as the subconscious of the architect.[11] Temporarily freed of circumstantial pressures, the drawing facilitates the gestation of a space of emotional resonance. It realizes what Prix and Swiczinsky call an open system, a notion that enters their work around 1983. "We cannot prove it," the architects write, "but we strongly suspect that the more intensely the designer experiences the design the more experiential the building will be."[12] But the moment of conception realized on paper simultaneously comprehends the energy of psyche and space as a means of grasping complexity, the concatenation of small events studied by chaos theory. In the eloquent words of Michael Sorkin:

> *The Open House is a shrine to the sensitive dependence on initial conditions. The impetus to retain—with utter fidelity—the character of the first sketch is exactly this. Instead of trying to smooth things out, rationalize an impulse without ready quantification, Himmelblau trusts the evidence of their sensibility, and then struggles to retain it—whatever the consequences. "All the lines in the drawing have been built" they write in guarantee of a project. Clearly, this is the terrain of their art. Instead of retreating into the tactic of the impossibility of building, they attempt to build the impossible.*[13]

The preliminary drawing evokes the energy and complexity in the architects' psyches and the space under design, but it also creates a set of initial conditions that inform the design process. One tiny line or squiggle can fundamentally shape the finished building. Similarly, in complex systems such as the weather, economic cycles, or patterns of urban growth the interaction of numerous causal variables, some perhaps quite small in themselves, challenges the possibility of our systematic comprehension of these phenomena. Himmelblau seek to engage these dynamic forces of complexity through the employment of open complex systems. Prix writes, "Architecture, as was proposed in the nineteenth century, is over. We have to go for a complexity that mirrors the diversity of world society. Interlaced and open buildings have no divisions: they challenge the user to take over space."[14]

In the earliest projects of Coop Himmelblau, their actions and installations of the late 1960s and 1970s, appropriating space commenced with the body of the user, now conceived as architecture. In *Heart Space* (1969), a plastic membrane was dynamized by a heartbeat. "Our architecture has no physical ground plan, but a psychic one. Walls no longer exist. Our spaces are pulsating balloons. Our heartbeat becomes room, our face is the building facade."[15] A later project, *Feedback Vibration City* (1971), modifies the form of the metropolis in response to the constantly changing heartbeats, brain waves, and bodily rhythms of its inhabitants. Developing in dialogue with the work of the British group Archigram as well as Viennese and international artists simultaneously exploring issues of corporeality, feedback cycles, and technology, this early interactive conception of architecture would decisively inflect the subsequent work of Coop Himmelblau.[16]

It conspicuously reappears in the design concept of their East Pavilion of the Groninger Museum (1994) in Groningen, the Netherlands. Once again, the body provides the

East Pavilion, Groninger Museum, Groningen, the Netherlands, 1995 (left)

Design models for the Anselm Kiefer studio (unbuilt), 1990 (right, top and bottom)

armature for a dynamized space of interactive architecture. Yet here embodiment involves neither the pneumatic environments of the 1960s projects nor the violent metaphorical displacement of the domesticated body in the burning form of the Hot Flat (Vienna, 1978).[17] Anthony Vidler has perceptively analyzed the work of Himmelblau with respect to its "apparent desire to merge the body completely with the design and its context."[18] *The Dissolution of Our Bodies into the City* (1980), a tantalizing allusion to Bruno Taut's manifesto "The Dissolution of the Cities" (1920, Cat. no. 234), realizes this aspiration literally in the transformation of a photograph of Prix and Swiczinsky into a sketch and later a three-dimensional model of an urban plan.

In their work on the East Pavilion, Himmelblau developed a concept of spatial flow that they call "liquid space." Paraphrasing the title of their earlier project, one might describe its ambition as the dissolution of the body into the museum. The gallery space is radically fractured and fissured, divided and channeled into smaller flowing spaces. No single position dominates; no view is superior to any other. The visitor is encouraged to move around an exhibition area stripped of its traditional function as the ground against which art works constitute the figure. Varying levels provide for multiple points of view, a strategy that the architects had already begun to employ in their unbuilt design for a studio commissioned by the artist Anselm Kiefer (1990).

For their design of the *Expressionist Utopias* exhibition, Prix and Swiczinsky appropriated their initial sketch for the East Pavilion, using it as well for the design of a stage set for a theatrical production of Bruno Taut's "The Universal Master Builder" that took place in the Schauspielhaus Graz on October 8, 1993[19] (see figs. 122, 123, and Appendix, page 312). Like the Groninger Museum, the *Expressionist Utopias* exhibition vertiginously multiplied points of view. As though driven by a deranged Hegelian logic, it insistently undercut the superiority of any particular vantage point, encouraging the viewer to continually move throughout its interlaced spaces. Time inflects this process no less than space. Few architects today more effectively deploy an understanding of cinema in the design of built space than Coop Himmelblau.

As Prix suggests, an overview is not immediately granted the viewer of the *Expressionist Utopias* exhibition. This suggests their design is more akin to the intellectually rigorous narration through montage in a film such as *The Passion of Joan of Arc* (Carl Theodor Dreyer, 1928) than the typical Hollywood blockbuster film edited to provide the most effortless possible overview of the action. In fact, obtaining such a unified view becomes difficult, if not impossible, anywhere in the exhibition, a fact confirmed in nearly all photographs of the installation and their blocked and foreshortened perspectives. (Can it be an accident that one's gaze toward the "Paradise" section is occluded by an element protruding from the wall?)

While the "liquid space" of Himmelblau's exhibition design may appear less overtly confrontational than some of their earlier projects, the reality of moving one's body through its sharp-edged walls and frequently constricted spaces evoked the simultaneous experiences of discovery and anxiety, freedom and menace, feelings often elicited by their architecture.[20] A video made by the museum using a steadycam moving through the installation confirms this complex blend of emotions provoked by the exhibition. This sense of spatial disquiet is also implicit in the intentional overlapping of its five categories, conceived as fluid and ambiguous, rather than sharp and distinct, a curatorial statement on the permeable contours of history intensified by Himmelblau's visual and spatial presentation.

Here, one might best discern the influence of the exhibition's subject matter upon the Himmelblau design, if not upon the larger corpus of the architects' work. While some critics have attempted to literalize the installation, discerning in its columns a specific reference to *The Cabinet of Dr. Caligari* (Robert Wiene, 1919), or reading its deployment of materials as an homage to architectural expressionism, these efforts appear unconvincing. How could they not given that many of the elements in the *Expressionist Utopias* design had already been explored by the architects in very different contexts? Similarly problematic are those interpretations of Coop Himmelblau's architecture that understand its glass or crystalline forms in relation to the aesthetics of dematerialization and dissolution of architectural Expressionism. Prix offers a patient and convincing rejoinder to such arguments in the conversation that follows.

A helpful clue appears in his concluding remark that treating the museum as a display case for finished products reflects a nineteenth-century conception of culture. Read in conjunction with David Frisby's observation that Expressionism "sought to explode reification," Prix's comment directs our attention away from style toward cultural and political critique.[21] In their exhibition design that frustrates thoughtless consumption and acknowledges the labor entailed by a surfeit of perspectives, Himmelblau realize an immanent critique of the museum as the great, reified form of our age. Unlike the expressionists who discerned technology and the metropolis as their primary battlegrounds, Prix and Swiczinsky take aim at the complicity of traditional museum design with the cultural politics of the status quo. By so doing they substantiate Prix's claim that attentiveness to the political context links Coop Himmelblau to Expressionism and pay fitting tribute to its utopian legacy.

NOTES

1. Coop Himmelblau were also commissioned by Curator Stephanie Barron of the Los Angeles County Museum of Art to design an exhibition of photomontages by the German artist John Heartfield that was on view from October 21, 1993, to January 2, 1994 at the museum.

2. Brian O'Doherty, *Inside the White Cube: The Ideology of Gallery Space* (Santa Monica and San Francisco: The Lapis Press, 1986; Berkeley and Los Angeles: University of California Press, 2001), 14.

3. Coop Himmelblau, "Architektur muss brennen" (1980) in *Architecture is Now. Projects, (Un)buildings, Actions, Statements, Sketches, Commentaries, 1968–1983* (New York: Rizzoli, 1983), 91. Translation mine.

4. See Philip Johnson and Mark Wigley, *Deconstructivist Architecture* (New York and Boston: The Museum of Modern Art/New York Graphic Society, 1988).

5. See Herbert Schnädelbach, *Philosophy in Germany: 1831–1933*, trans. Eric Matthews (Cambridge and New York: Cambridge University Press, 1984); Christoph Asendorf, *Batteries of Life: On the History of Things and their Perception in Modernity*, trans. Don Reneau (Berkeley and Los Angeles: University of California Press, 1993); Steven Aschheim, *The Nietzsche Legacy in Germany* (Berkeley and Los Angeles: University of California Press, 1994); and Alexandre Kostka and Irving Wohlfarth, eds., *Nietzsche and "An Architecture of Our Minds"* (Los Angeles: Getty Research Institute, 2000).

6. See Libero Andreotti, ed., *Theory of the Dérive and other Situationist Writings on the City* (Barcelona: Museu d'Art Contemporani de Barcelona, 1996), and Mark Wigley, *Constant's New Babylon: The Hyperarchitecture of Desire* (Rotterdam: Witte de With Center for Contemporary Art and 0.10 Publishers, 1998).

7. Peter Bürger, *Theory of the Avant-Garde*, trans. Michael Shaw (Minneapolis: University of Minnesota Press, 1984), 49.

8. See my forthcoming essay "Excluded Middle: Toward a Reflective Architecture and Urbanism" for a more extensive treatment of this topic.

9. Coop Himmelblau, *Architecture is Now: Projects, (Un)buildings, Actions, Statements, Sketches, Commentaries 1968-1983* (New York: Rizzoli, 1983), 11. Translation mine.

10. The German word *Entwurf* can mean also sketch, draft, outline, sketch, plan, or blueprint. Prix and Swiczinsky are playing on the prefix "Ent," comparable to the English prefix "de" as in the German verbs *entscheiden* (to decide) or *entwickeln* (to develop) and the root *Wurf* relates the activity of throwing (*werfen*) or a die (*Würfel*).

11. "Wolfgang Prix and Helmut Swiczinsky in Conversation with Alvin Boyarsky," *AA Files* 19 (Spring 1990): 71.

12. Coop Himmelblau, "Capturing Architecture in Words," *Pratt Journal of Architecture* 1 (Fall 1985): 45.

13. Michael Sorkin, "Post Rock Propter Rock: A Short History of the Himmelblau" (1988), in *Exquisite Corpse: Writings on Buildings* (London and New York: Verso, 1991), 347.

14. Wolf Prix, Coop Himmelblau, "On the Edge," *Architectural Design Profile No. 87 Deconstruction III* (1990): 65.

15. Coop Himmelblau, *Architecture is Now*, 182.

16. For discussions of related tendencies see Peter Cook, ed., *Archigram* (New York: Praeger, 1973), and Douglas Davis, *Art and the Future* (New York: Praeger, 1973).

17. See Anthony Vidler, "Architecture Dismembered," in *The Architectural Uncanny: Essays in the Modern Unhomely* (Cambridge, Mass.: The MIT Press, 1992), 69–82.

18. Ibid., 75.

19. See Kristiana Hartmann, "Der Weltbaumeister," *Bauwelt* 84, no. 44 (1993): 2380–2381. See the translation of Taut's scenario on page 294 of the present volume.

20. See in this regard Anthony Vidler, "Angelus Novus: Coop Himmelblau's Expressionist Utopia" in *Warped Space: Art, Architecture, and Anxiety in Modern Culture* (Cambridge, Mass.: The MIT Press, 2000), 186–192.

21. David Frisby, "Social Theory, the Metropolis, and Expressionism," 108 (this volume).

Left: Architectural Fantasy section

A CONVERSATION WITH WOLF D. PRIX

The following conversation with Wolf D. Prix was recorded in German and English on December 4, 2000, in Guadalajara, Mexico. Preliminary research for it was conducted as a Visiting Scholar in the Study Centre of the Canadian Centre for Architecture in Montreal. I am grateful to Wolf D. Prix for his generous engagement and to Alexander Alberro (University of Florida, Gainesville), Timothy O. Benson, Stephanie Emerson (LACMA), Garrett White (Whitney Museum of American Art) , Pierre-Edouard Latouche, and Eva Marie Neumann (CCA) for their invaluable assistance and suggestions.

WHAT DOES IT MEAN TO CONCEPTUALIZE ARCHITECTURE AS AN ACTION?

This entails a conception of interactive architecture. In *Heart Space* (1969) we translated our heartbeat into light and sound in order to create a space; this was the first example in our work of truly interactive architecture. *Face-Space* (1969), which translated facial expressions into colors and sounds produced by a facade, was another. The opening of the inner (the internal) to the outer (the external) was a very important theme in the 1960s. We later said that the feeling of the internal expands the skin of the external. It "pushes the envelope" of the skin.

HOW DO YOU UNDERSTAND THE NOTION OF AN OPEN COMPLEX SYSTEM?

Scientists claim that our brains are incapable of comprehending complex systems. We think it possible, however, by consciously utilizing emotion and working with the unconscious. Open systems emerge in the moment of the conception (*Entwurf*). A liberation of space takes place, if one does not impede the gestation of open systems through economic or legal constraints and other rational considerations or constructions. These become important later when the space—the ideal space—becomes a reality. Still, these structures must be challenged in order to generate new ideas.

IS IT ACTUALLY POSSIBLE TO REALIZE AN OPEN COMPLEX SYSTEM IN A MUSEUM EXHIBITION? IS THIS NOT A PARADOX?

Yes, of course it is. Nonetheless, I think it possible if one employs the concept of spatial flow, what we call "liquid space." This is a space that allows various viewpoints; it permits the gaze to travel, so to speak, "behind the scenes." One does not simply hang pictures on the wall, but rather creates spaces where pictures are suspended so that one can perceive them from other points of view. This is a project that we pursue.

DOES TRANSPARENCY PLAY A ROLE HERE? I THINK OF YOUR DESIGN FOR THE *EXPRESSIONIST UTOPIAS* EXHIBITION WITH ITS TRANSPARENT LABELS AND GLASS DISPLAY CASES VISIBLE FROM MANY PERSPECTIVES.

Glass, of course, plays a role but it is not the essential element in architecture. Openness also signifies intellectual and conceptual openness.

THIS SEEMS A CRUCIAL POINT. OPENNESS CANNOT BE REDUCED TO A SINGLE ELEMENT.

That I can see through something means absolutely nothing. Glass architecture was a consequential phase in the history of architecture. Its introduction as a building material was important, and its expressive significance captivated Bruno Taut and the members of the Crystal Chain. But the ability to see through something (*Durchsichtigkeit*) does not itself yield transparency (*Transparenz*).

Architectural Fantasy section

TRANSPARENT ARCHITECTURE SHOULD NOT BE CONFLATED WITH FREEDOM, FOR IT WILL NOT BRING ABOUT A REVOLUTION.

Correct. That would require transparent concepts.

BEFORE LACMA APPROACHED YOU TO DESIGN *EXPRESSIONIST UTOPIAS* HAD YOU THOUGHT MUCH ABOUT EXPRESSIONIST ARCHITECTURE? DID YOU IN FACT HAVE ANY INTEREST IN IT?

Yes, but only a superficial interest because the formal demands and aspirations of the Expressionists no longer satisfied us. As students we had studied the work of Bruno Taut and Hans Scharoun. Yet at a certain point we came to regard Expressionist architecture as representing an insufficient stage of formal advancement. We acquired few influences or prototypes from it, deriving them rather from works by Constantin Brancusi, Cubist painters, Le Corbusier, Frederick Kiesler, and last but not least, Giovanni Battista Piranesi. Nonetheless, Expressionism remains an important element in our theoretical work, even though we perceive our roots to lie elsewhere.

FOR MANY YEARS EXPRESSIONIST ARCHITECTS WERE MARGINALIZED IN STANDARD HISTORIES OF TWENTIETH-CENTURY ARCHITECTURE. THESE FIGURES WERE OFTEN PRESENTED (WHEN THEY WERE MENTIONED AT ALL) AS THE LOSING SIDE IN A WAR ALLEGEDLY WON BY THE BAUHAUS, LE CORBUSIER, AND VARIOUS FUNCTIONALISTS. IS THIS AN ACCURATE VIEW OF HISTORY, OR HAS THE INFLUENCE OF FIGURES SUCH AS TAUT, SCHAROUN, AND FINSTERLIN ACTUALLY BEEN GREATER THAN IS COMMONLY THOUGHT?

Art historians discern a similar opposition in the conflict between the Romanesque and Gothic styles. I believe that the Bauhaus proved so successful because it complied with the capitalist control of society, unlike the Expressionists, who sought to create an additional value that could not be measured in monetary terms. Although the architec-

Architectural Fantasy section, view through wall with drawing (left)

Preliminary sketch for *Expressionist Utopias* installation by Coop Himmelblau (right)

tural principles of the Bauhaus are simpler to understand, their intellectual claim is mediocre by comparison with the more complex and emotionally subtle ideas of the Expressionists. One sees this easier comprehensibility revealed today in the success of many contemporary Dutch architects who very cleverly and with great commercial savvy fulfill the demands of "turbo capitalism."

The works on paper by many Expressionist architects seem to suggest that valid architecture need not always be built, that the process of exploration also has a role to play.

This is very important. Jacques Derrida once said to us that a drawing or a line in a poem is more significant than tons of built space. The drawing or the line of verse can be more influential than a widely read novel. The same is true of a giant building whose particular features interest no one. Drawing is thinking. Building should also mean thinking. Sketching, if one analyzes it, also means complex thinking.

Could it be that one link between the work of Coop Himmelblau and that of the Expressionist architects consists in their shared uncertainty about the nature of space?

I am reluctant to emphasize Expressionism here, for the fourth and fifth dimensions in architecture, time and consciousness, should also be mentioned in this context. It is very important that we sharply analyze and introduce time as a concept in architecture. Time elapses while the body passes through and apprehends space, and this must be taken into account. The body must exist in space, for without it space does not exist. An interesting psychological investigation ascertained that a region of the brain defines space as something through which one must move. Without movement, there is no space. This is very suggestive, because according to this definition, virtual space (an imprecise linguistic expression) would not count as space at all.

Is there a political parallel between the work of Coop Himmelblau and that of a figure such as Bruno Taut? Your work also emerged during a charged political moment, and it continued with great optimism (as did Taut's) despite the subsequent failure of many hopes.

The refusal to exclude the political context remains an important parallel between our work and that of the Expressionists. Many people say that one can separate aesthetics from politics. We prefer to say that the aesthetic is political.

Has the moment of German Expressionist architecture been overly romanticized?

I see no signs among contemporary architects of an excessive interest in the work of the Expressionists. The minimalists dominate and obediently fulfill the requirements of capitalism.

Are you suggesting that something dangerous and subversive is still contained (perhaps hiding) in Expressionist architecture?

Without question. If one interprets deconstruction in this direction, one notes that someone such as our colleague Zaha Hadid has fewer opportunities to build than others, because the aesthetic of subversion is always feared.

In what does the subversive quality of this aesthetic consist?

In the nonrecognition of clichés and in conceptual advancement. A demand to think further and not simply manifest the status quo. "Pushing the envelope," as one says.

Your design for the *Expressionist Utopias* exhibition did in effect "push the envelope" by demonstrating the possibility of an alternative to the sterile "white cubes" of most gallery and museum spaces. Why do you think that this approach continues to exercise such a powerful hold upon the art world?

It often seems that artists and curators value aesthetic creativity only after the artist is dead. One might say that every exhibition celebrates the burial of the artist. We think, however, that a vast synergy potentially exists between art and architecture and that when we design exhibitions we must reveal this synergy. One does not simply hang pictures on the wall in a didactic sequence. Rather, one places pictures in the space with particular attentiveness to releasing them from a context that has become a cliché, so as to present them in a new light, so to speak. This was the task of our work on the *Expressionist Utopias* exhibition.

Did your design oppose the tendency to "functionalize" art and treat it as the manifestation of an underlying thesis that one encounters in many contemporary exhibitions?

Didactic preparation must, of course, take place but new points of view can always be emphasized through the design of the exhibition space.

How did you begin the task of conceptualizing the design of the *Expressionist Utopias* exhibition?

In our work on the East Pavilion of the Groninger Museum (1993–94) we first conceptualized in drawings and study models the notion of liquid space. We thought it would be an interesting experiment to reinterpret the sketch for the museum as a design for the LACMA exhibition. We sought to create a spatial flow that does not simply mimic the four walls of the gallery but creates situations where pictures and objects could be shown in a

Wall supports and shadows in the installation (left)

Anti-Utopia section (right)

more fluid context. What interested us was light as a design element. We employed light in order to create space, but not just light alone. The body and light were very important in the design of the exhibition, and thereby engage a theme long familiar in Expressionism.

Did you view the objects in the exhibition before you began your design?

Yes, we had access to reproductions of most of the objects in the exhibition.

Was this helpful?

Sometimes it was a nuisance.

Why?

If one begins to interpret objects and represent them literally, for example, if we had taken the Glass Chain literally as the basis for our design, it would have been catastrophic. Many exhibition and stage designers do precisely this, but I believe that one must produce synergy through a different relation to the material.

Was the studio you designed for Anselm Kiefer (1990) influential upon your conception of the *Expressionist Utopias* design?

Our work on the studio for Anselm Kiefer taught us a great deal about different points of view. For example, Kiefer views his paintings from different angles and sometimes climbs a ladder in order to study them. He perceives them in a dynamic spatial flow. Artworks exhibited in a conventional museum space produce a static status quo, yet art as a vibrant representation of life requires a dynamic spatial flow. This means that the

image can be seen from different points of view and thereby becomes part of a dynamic space. Such dynamism is visible in film, as well as in our architecture and in Kiefer's art.

IS IT POSSIBLE THAT THE KIEFER STUDIO WILL BE BUILT?

We designed the studio for Kiefer in Buchen, Germany. He later went through a divorce and moved to France. Although we have not yet designed anything for him there, we did complete a preliminary sketch for a studio in France. Our work with Kiefer is a process that gradually develops over the course of years. The exchange of ideas is actually more important than the finished building will be.

WHAT ABOUT THE RAMP AND THE MOBILITY IT AFFORDED THE VISITOR TO THE *EXPRESSIONIST UTOPIAS* EXHIBITION?

It is a trick that allows things to be viewed from above and enables the visitor to get a grip on the space. One should be able to look down at the art from above, not only from eye level, but also from other positions. The ramp displaces the perspective of the normal visitor to the exhibition and provides many possible points of view.

THE DESIGN OF THE EXHIBITION MADE IT DIFFICULT TO MOVE IN A STRAIGHT TRAJECTORY THROUGH THE SPACE OF THE GALLERY, AS ONE DOES IN MANY MUSEUMS. WAS THIS INTENTIONAL?

Liquid space conceals various elements of surprise. As in a labyrinth, one must discover certain elements of the exhibition for oneself. One does not immediately have an overview; one must search for things.

WHAT LED TO THE AESTHETIC DECISION TO PAINT THE WALLS OF THE MUSEUM GALLERY GRAY?

White is a color of indecision and background in three-dimensional form. We attempted to produce a deliberate background and to emphasize its three-dimensional qualities and thus painted everything gray in order not to differentiate between the two colors. The gray is an aesthetic element intended to produce a context in lieu of the absence of a traditional background.

IS THIS CONCERN WITH THREE-DIMENSIONAL FORM REFLECTED IN YOUR DESIGN OF THE TILTED WALLS AND THE UNEVEN COLUMNS?

They also exemplify the three-dimensional dynamization of space, and maintain it as a fluid, dynamic element, almost like a river. We learned that these design choices produce energy that allows the visitors to be pulled along by a current and drift through the exhibition.

Architectural Fantasy section (far left)

Film and Stage section (left)

Paradise section (above)

WAS THERE A SPECIFIC EXPERIENCE OR IMPRESSION THAT YOU HOPED VISITORS TO THE EXHIBITION WOULD HAVE?

No. We do not work this way. We refuse to become preachers or instructors. We offer possibilities, open landscapes. The visitor, the inhabitant, the user of the space is free to discover favorite elements within them.

MANY OF YOUR EARLY PROJECTS WERE SCULPTURES AND ENVIRONMENTS FOR MUSEUMS. HOW DOES THE EXPERIENCE OF WORKING AS AN ARTIST DIFFER FROM THAT OF WORKING AS AN EXHIBITION DESIGNER?

The processes are very different. As an artist, you alone are responsible for the object exhibited in the museum space. By contrast, working on an exhibition design one becomes part of a team (the same is true when designing a building), and one must be ready to accept the ideas of other people in one's conception.

COULD YOU IMAGINE DESIGNING AN EXHIBITION ON ANY TOPIC, OR IS SOME AFFINITY TO THE SUBJECT MATTER A NECESSARY PREREQUISITE?

We must be able to establish a relation to the theme. This applies to museum exhibition design or stage set design for theater. It is different, however, in architecture, where I can build a cinema or a supermarket without the need for this affinity. Exhibition design is not my primary sphere of activity, thus I require an emotional connection to the subject matter in order to be able to enter it.

THE *EXPRESSIONIST UTOPIAS* EXHIBITION WAS THE FIRST PROJECT YOU REALIZED IN AMERICA. WHAT WAS IT LIKE TO WORK IN THE UNITED STATES?

It was a very pleasant experience. I love Los Angeles and the atmosphere there. The team at the museum was extraordinary. We could actually do more there than we could have done elsewhere.

DID YOU LEARN OR DISCOVER ANYTHING THROUGH YOUR WORK ON THE *EXPRESSIONIST UTOPIAS* EXHIBITION?

Through the process of designing the exhibition, I obtained confirmation of the energy of art and architecture.

HAS YOUR ATTITUDE TOWARD THE MUSEUM AS A CULTURAL INSTITUTION CHANGED OVER THE MORE THAN THIRTY YEARS OF YOUR CAREER?

Unfortunately, the museum as a cultural institution has not changed. It is still the display case of the nineteenth-century. It still has not developed a viable approach to representing art in a living flow. There have been some attempts in this direction but the vitality of art that one notices in the studios of artists no longer exists (or is destroyed) in the nineteenth-century exhibition space of the museum. There are very few museums that allow this vitality. I was extremely pleased by the decision of the Groninger Museum to permit the use of roller-skates and skateboards in an art exhibition held in our East Pavilion. It suggested that art and life need not be separated by the walls of the museum.

WOULD IT BE CORRECT TO DESCRIBE THE MUSEUM AS A NECESSARY EVIL OF OUR CONTEMPORARY CIVILIZATION?

Yes. I think that many of the spaces now being built, the boxes of the new Tate Gallery in London for example, are in fact storage rooms where art is warehoused in preparation for real exhibitions in spaces that must be built or invented.

DOES THE MUSEUM STILL HAVE ANY POSITIVE ROLE TO PLAY?

Of course it does. The museum has the task of representing art as a contribution to culture and vitality.

IS IT THEN A UTOPIA OR A UTOPIAN SPACE?

No, I think not. Contemporary museums may concern themselves with utopias and demonstrate why their survival remains important without necessarily favoring the past over the present. "Don't look back," I would say.

YOUR APPROACH TO ARCHITECTURE HAS OFTEN OPPOSED "ACCOMMODATION" (ANPASSUNG) AND "ADJUSTMENT" (EINORDNUNG) AND CLAIMED THEM AS INIMICAL TO THE REALIZATION OF BUILDINGS WITH INTEGRITY AND VITALITY. IS IT POSSIBLE TO AVOID THESE IMPERATIVES IN MUSEUM DESIGN?

I have difficulties with the conception of the museum as a box. I know only few examples (Daniel Libeskind's addition to the Jewish Museum in Berlin or our Pavilion of the Groninger Museum or maybe some spaces in Frank Gehry's Bilbao Museum) of museums which challenge the belief in accommodation. It is not accidental that in these museums the curators have had major problems hanging pictures.

HOW WOULD YOU RESPOND TO THE CLAIM THAT SUCH ARCHITECTURE IS ANTITHETICAL TO ART?

Art and architecture produce synergy. A good museum and bad art are incompatible, just as a good space immediately reveals a bad piece of art. Our museum in Groningen or Libeskind's addition to the Jewish Museum both contain spaces that set a high standard for art. One must invite artists to grapple with these spaces rather than deliver finished products. The notion of the finished product is a nineteenth-century idea. Jannis Kounellis exhibits his work in a ship, Rebecca Horn exhibits her projects in hotels. They both produce installations that need not, a priori, take place in a museum. We once worked on a project in Helsinki where the museum was designed to dissolve in fifteen years, leaving only the administrative offices and releasing the art in the city. The exhibition space is only a point of departure.

Catalogue of the Exhibition

NOTE TO THE READER

The works of art in the exhibition are arranged alphabetically by artist; within each artist's oeuvre works are listed chronologically, with undated works placed at the end. When there is more than one work by an artist from a given year, they are listed alphabetically by title, with untitled works following those with titles. Prints from portfolios are listed in the order of their arrangement in the portfolio. Books, periodicals, and ephemera are listed separately at the end of the catalogue.

A biography is included for each artist whose work is represented. The authors of the biographies are:

A.S.	Annelisa Stephan
F.V.H.	Frauke von der Horst
S.C.T.	Susan C. Trauger
T.B.	Timothy O. Benson
V.H.	Virginia Haddad

Dimensions are given in inches and centimeters in the following order: height, width, depth. For drawings and collages, sheet size is used; for intaglio prints, plate size; for woodcuts and lithographs, image size.

Gerd Arntz

BORN 1900 REMSCHEID ✣ DIED 1988 THE HAGUE

1. *Militarischer Film*, 1921
(Military film)
Woodcut
8³/8 x 5⁷/8 in. (21.3 x 15.0 cm)
Collection Haags Gemeentemuseum, The Hague, Netherlands

2. *Fabrik*, 1927
(Factory)
Woodcut
9⁷/8 x 6³/8 in. (25.1 x 16.2 cm)
From the portfolio Zwölf Häuser der Zeit (1927)
Collection Haags Gemeentemuseum, The Hague, Netherlands

3. *Krise*, 1931
(Crisis)
Woodcut
11⁷/8 x 8¹/4 in. (30.1 x 21.0 cm)
Collection Haags Gemeentemuseum, The Hague, Netherlands

Working in a precise, almost geometric style, Gerd Arntz concentrated throughout his long career on social and economic issues, making diagrammatic works depicting the injustices and ironies of industrialized society. His flat, carefully composed paintings and woodcuts were influenced by Cubism and Constructivism. A political activist and a pioneering developer of international symbols as well as a painter and graphic artist, he was committed to the use of art as a forum for social analysis and was vocal in his opposition to totalitarianism and in his support of the workers' movement.

The offspring of a middle-class merchant family in Remscheid, Westphalia, Arntz lived in a remarkable number of cities during the course of his life, including Düsseldorf, Cologne, Vienna, Moscow, and The Hague. This not only enabled him to meet numerous fellow artists and political activists but also no doubt contributed to his interest in portraying life in the metropolis. Educated at a private academy in Düsseldorf before attending the school of applied arts in Barmen in 1921, he took over Otto Dix's studio in 1925, when Dix left Düsseldorf for Berlin.

In the early 1920s, as a member of the group Das junge Rheinland (Young Rhineland), which also included the artists Adolf Uzarski and Gert Wollheim, Arntz came into contact with other Cologne-based groups, such as Stupid, which counted among its members Heinrich Hoerle and Anton Räderscheidt, and the Progressiven (Progressives), who worked in a politically charged Cubo-Constructivist vein. Arntz collaborated from 1929 to 1933 on the Progressiven journal A–Z, which championed the avant-garde in the conservative Rhineland. He and other members of the group helped develop statistical symbols to present information clearly without using language. In one of his graphs, for example, Arntz used the same neutral figure to represent entrepreneurs, managers, workers, and the unemployed but varied the clothing and manner to identify each group.

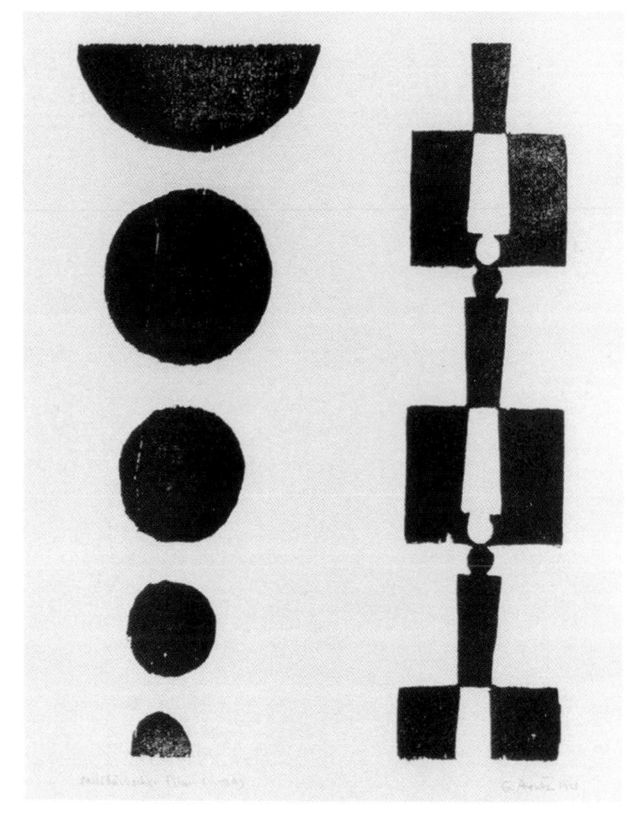

Cat. no. 1

Cat. no. 3

After his first solo exhibition, in 1925, Arntz participated in a number of group exhibitions such as the 1926 *Grosse Kunstausstellung Düsseldorf* (Great Düsseldorf art exhibition) and the *Ausstellung revolutionärer Kunst des Westens* (Exhibition of the revolutionary art of the West) in Moscow, which included the works of Dix, Hoerle, Conrad Felixmüller, Käthe Kollwitz, and Franz Seiwert, among others. From 1929 until 1931 Arntz was director of graphic design of the Gesellschafts- und Wirtschaftsmuseum (Museum of society and economy) in Vienna. In his frequent travels to Moscow as a member of the Allgemeine Arbeiterunion (General workers' union) and as an employee from 1931 to 1934 of the Moscow Isostat, a museum similar to the one where he had worked in Vienna, he came into contact with members of the Russian Constructivist avant-garde, including El Lissitzky and Vladimir Tatlin.

In 1934 Arntz took up residence in The Hague, where he was associated with the communist group De Arbeidersraad (The workers' council) and worked at the Mundaneum statistical institute. During the war he continued to work, using the pseudonym A. Dubois. In 1943, however, he was forced into military service and became a prisoner of war, first in France and later in Münster. After his return to The Hague in 1946, he continued to produce graphic art, becoming an honorary member of the group De Grafische (The graphic artists) and working for UNESCO.

A.S.

BIBLIOGRAPHY
Gerd Arntz, Zeit unterm Messer (Cologne: Leske, 1988); Eckhart Gillen, "Von der symbolischen Repräsentation zur Rekonstruktion der Wirklichkeit: Das Verhältnis von Bildstatistik und politischer Grafik bei Gerd Arntz," in *Politische Konstruktivisten: Die "Progressiven," 1919–1933*, exh. cat. (Berlin: Nationalgalerie, 1975).

■ ■ ■

Johannes Baader

BORN 1875 STUTTGART ✣ DIED 1956 ADLDORF

4. *Architektur für Svoboda* (Andruck aus dem "Dadaco"), 1919
Architecture for Svoboda [Dadaco proof]
Offset lithograph, trial proof
Sheet: 12 11/16 x 9 3/16 in. (32.2 x 23.4 cm)
Berlinische Galerie, Berlin, Museum für Moderne Kunst, Photographie und Architektur

The son of a metalworker for the royal buildings in Stuttgart, Johannes Baader studied at the state trade school there from 1892 to 1895 and then at the technical college. In 1903 he began working as a mortuary architect in Dresden. By 1905 he was in Berlin, where he met Raoul Hausmann, beginning a friendship that would eventually be at the center of Berlin Dada. In 1906 he conceived his utopian interdenominational "world temple," drawing on various forms, including Greek and Indian archetypes. Described in sketches and writings, the world temple in its grandest form was to be fifteen hundred meters high and unify all of humanity in its building.

In 1914 Baader published a treatise on monism entitled *Vierzehn Briefe Christi* (Fourteen letters of Christ) and during the next several years contributed to the journals *Die freie Strasse* (Free street) and *Der Dada*. In 1917 he was certified legally insane, a designation he used as a license for outrageous public performances parodying public and mythic identities. Also in 1917 he ran for the Reichstag in Saarbrücken and, with Hausmann, founded Christus GmbH (Christ Inc.), offering membership to pacifists, who, upon being certified with the identity of Christ, were to be exempted from the draft. In 1918 Baader wrote his quasi-religious tract *Die acht Weltsätze* (Eight world theses), and in 1919 he declared his own "resurrection" as the Oberdada, president of the earth. He expounded on this cosmic identity in texts and collages (for example, *Dada Milchstrasse* [Dada Milky Way, 1919]). His *Grosse Plasto-Dio-Dada-Drama* (Great plasto-dio-Dada-drama), an assemblage envisioned as a model for Dada architecture, was shown in Berlin at the 1920 *Erste internationale Dada-Messe* (First international Dada fair). He also produced sketches of visionary architecture, which, like those of Hausmann and Jefim Golyscheff, sometimes involved proto-Constructivist girderlike structures. In the 1920s he continued to produce collages and to practice as an architect.

T.B.

BIBLIOGRAPHY
Johannes Baader, *Oberdada: Schriften, Manifeste, Flugbätter, Billets, Werke und Taten*, ed. Hanne Bergius, Norbert Miller, and Karl Riha (Lahn-Giessen: Anabas-Kämpf, 1977); idem, *Das Oberdada: Die Geschichte einer Bewegung von Zürich bis Zürich*, ed. Karl Riha, Vergessene Autoren der Moderne, no. 31 (Siegen: Universität-Gesamthochschule Siegen, 1987); Stephen Foster, "Johannes Baader: The Complete Dada," in *Dada/Dimensions* (Ann Arbor, Mich.: UMI Research Press, 1985), pp. 249–71.

■ ■ ■

Max Beckmann

BORN 1884 LEIPZIG, GERMANY ✣ DIED 1950 NEW YORK

5. *Adam und Eva*, 1917
(Adam and Eve)
Drypoint
9 x 63/4 in. (22.9 x 17.1 cm)
Los Angeles County Museum of Art. Gift of Rabbi William Kramer

Both of Max Beckmann's parents descended from farming families in the Brunswick area, and his life and art reflected this heritage. He was solitary, uncompromising, and persistent. Despite the protests of his family, he attended the academy in Weimar from 1900 to 1903, then spent six months in Paris before settling in Berlin in 1904. After winning the prestigious Villa Romana prize, which enabled him to live in Florence for half a year, he returned in 1907 to Berlin, where he established a reputation as one of the leading painters of the Secession.

In the prewar years Beckmann's work was thematically and stylistically conservative. He painted a number of heroic, large-scale compositions depicting biblical or mythological subjects and natural or man-made disasters. These canvases, like his numerous portraits and landscapes, were painted in a rich, dark Impressionist style. His wartime service as a medical orderly in Belgium and East Prussia radically changed his life and his art. Subject matter became paramount as he began to incorporate his own experiences into his work and to define his personal and social consciousness. In hard, angular, often brutal images recurring themes emerged: the folly and inhumanity of war, violence, sexuality, alienation, and class intolerance.

Beckmann significantly increased his graphic output during this period. Although he began and completed his graphic oeuvre with lithographs and produced a small number of superb woodcuts, he is best remembered for the drypoints that he created between 1912 and 1923. His graphic production virtually ceased from 1925 to 1937, when he devoted more of his attention to painting.

In 1925 Beckmann moved to Frankfurt, where he was prominent among the artistic and literary establishment. His work was exhibited widely, and he was sought after as a portraitist and held a prestigious professorship at the Städelschule (municipal school). Between the years 1925 and 1932 his subject matter became milder, and his style was characterized by exuberance and vibrant color. Although Beckmann was not a member of any group or school, he was classified with the artists of the Neue Sachlichkeit (New objectivity), since he painted with much the same literalness as Otto Dix, George Grosz, and Rudolf Schlichter. Between 1932 and 1950 Beckmann created symbolic paintings, including the nine completed triptychs. Although he utilized a powerful range of symbolism in which reality was fused with vision, myth, and theater, the human figure remained his central subject.

In 1933 Beckmann was fired from his teaching post in Frankfurt by the Nazis. He moved to Berlin, where, because of the Nazi persecution of the avant-garde, he found himself isolated from the men and institutions that had made his success possible. He endured great personal hardship during these years. In 1937 he permanently left Germany and emigrated to Amsterdam. The outbreak of war prevented him from realizing his desire to move to America until 1947. The last three years of his life were his happiest. He taught at Washington University in Saint Louis and at the Brooklyn Museum Art School, exhibited his work throughout America and Europe, won numerous prizes and honors, led an active and personally meaningful social life, and maintained his creative productivity until his death.

S.C.T.

BIBLIOGRAPHY

Lothar-Günther Buchheim, *Max Beckmann: Holzschnitte, Radierungen, Lithographien* (Feldafing: Buchheim, 1954); Klaus Gallwitz, *Max Beckmann: Die Druckgraphik: Radierungen, Lithographien, Holzschnitte*, exh. cat., 2d rev. ed. (Karlsruhe: Badischer Kunstverein, 1962); James Hofmaier, *Max Beckmann: Catalogue Raisonné of His Prints*, 2 vols. (Bern: Kornfeld, 1990); Anne Röver and Bernhard Schnackenburg, *Max Beckmann in der Sämmlung Piper: Handzeichnung, Druckgraphik, Dokumente, 1910–1923*, exh. cat. (Bremen: Kunsthalle Bremen, 1974); Carla Schulz-Hoffmann and Judith C. Weiss, eds., *Max Beckmann: Retrospective*, exh. cat. (Saint Louis: Saint Louis Art Museum, 1984); Richard Vogler, ed., *Max Beckmann, Graphics: Selected from the Ernest and Lilly Jacobson Collection*, exh. cat. (Tucson: Tucson Art Center, 1972).

■ ■ ■

Peter Behrens

BORN 1868 HAMBURG ✣ DIED 1940 BERLIN

6. *Cover for Das Plakat*, 1920
Offset lithograph
Sheet: 11 x 8½ in. (27.9 x 21.6 cm)
From *Das Plakat*, no. 6 (June 1920)
Los Angeles County Museum of Art. The Robert Gore Rifkind Center for German Expressionist Studies, gift of Robert Gore Rifkind

Peter Behrens was a pioneer of modern architecture and industrial design. In his pre-World War I designs he successfully took advantage of new technology, using concrete, glass, steel, and other synthetic materials in an approach that was functional yet unbegrudging of ornamentation.

Behrens studied painting and graphic art at the school of applied arts in Hamburg, then at the art school in Karlsruhe, and finally at the Düsseldorf academy. He moved to Munich in 1890 and in 1893 became a cofounder of the Munich Secession and the Freie Vereinigung Münchner Künstler (Free union of Munich artists). In 1897 he cofounded the Vereinigte Werkstätten für Kunst im Handwerk (Union of arts and crafts workshops). As a collaborator on the journal *Pan*, he gained renown for his woodcuts and ornaments.

In 1899 Behrens was among a group of artists invited by the grand duke of Hesse-Darmstadt, Ernst Ludwig, to form an artists' colony in Darmstadt and to organize the exhibition *Ein Dokument deutscher Kunst* (A document of German art), which opened to great acclaim in 1901. In the Darmstadt colony Behrens, who was self-taught as an architect, designed his own house, which manifests influences as diverse as contemporary Jugendstil design and the medieval architecture of his native northern Germany. He left the colony, which had become the object of caricature and criticism, in 1903 to assume the directorship of the Düsseldorf school of applied arts.

During his Düsseldorf years, between 1903 and 1907, Behrens formed relationships with industrialists and received his first commissions from the Allgemeine Elektricitäts Gesellschaft (AEG), eventually becoming the company's artistic consultant. He has often been described as the first industrial designer because he attempted to create an overall image for AEG that would convey the company's strengths. His first major architectural commission from AEG, and perhaps his most significant accomplishment, was the 1909 turbine factory in Berlin. He was also a founding member of the Werkbund in 1907.

After World War I Behrens's work was altered by his involvement with Expressionism. By the 1920s he was designing in what came to be known as the International Style, as exemplified by his office buildings on the Alexanderplatz in Berlin (1929–31) and his tobacco factory in Linz, Austria (1932–34). He designed a German embassy for Washington, D.C., under the National Socialist regime, but it was never realized. He also held professorships at the academies in Vienna (1922–27) and Berlin (1936–40).

V.H.

BIBLIOGRAPHY

Peter Behrens, *Der moderne Garten*, 1911 (Berlin: Pückler Gesellschaft, 1981); Bernhard Buderath, ed., *Peter Behrens—Umbautes Licht: Das Verwaltungsgebäude der Hoechst AG* (Munich: Prestel, 1990); Hans-Joachim Kadatz, *Peter Behrens: Architekt, Maler, Grafiker und Formgestalter, 1868–1940* (Leipzig: E. A. Seemann, 1977); Wilhelm Weber, *Peter Behrens, 1868–1940: Gedenkschrift mit Katalog aus Anlass der Ausstellung*, exh. cat. (Kaiserslautern: Pfalzgalerie Kaiserslautern, 1966); Alan Windsor, *Peter Behrens: Architect and Designer* (New York: Whitney Library of Design, 1981).

■ ■ ■

Ella Bergmann

BORN 1895 PADERBORN ✣ DIED 1971 VOCKENHAUSEN

7. Untitled, 1917
Woodcut
14 x 5 15/16 in. (35.5 x 15.1 cm)
Sprengel Museum Hannover. Nachlass Ella Bergmann-Michel

8. *Neuronen-Menschen / Idee-Entwurf-Studien für ein mechanisches Theater oder Film mit Johannes Molzahn*, 1920
(Neurons-human beings/idea sketches for a mechanical theater or film with Johannes Molzahn)
Pencil, black and colored inks
9 13/16 x 9 1/8 in. (25.0 x 23.2 cm)
Sprengel Museum Hannover. Nachlass Ella Bergmann-Michel

9. Untitled (spiral construction), 1922
Black and colored inks
14 5/16 x 13 3/4 in. (36.3 x 35.0 cm)
Sprengel Museum Hannover. Nachlass Ella Bergmann-Michel

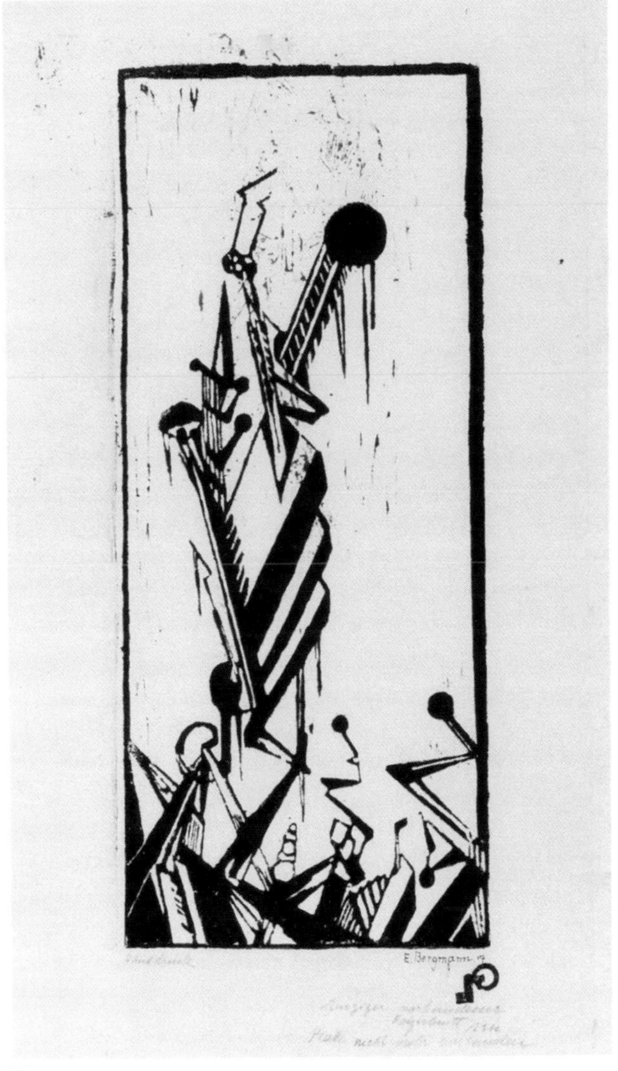

Cat. no. 7

Ella Bergmann received an education that was typical for girls from German upper-middle-class families. She attended a girls' school and studied music and foreign languages at home. Yet uncharacteristically she also learned the fundamental techniques of the emerging field of photography from her father, a druggist.

From 1915 to 1918 Bergmann studied art at the school of applied arts in Weimar. Two years into her studies she joined a group of students and architects associated with the Belgian architect and designer Henry van de Velde, among them Robert Michel, whom she married in 1919. Together they established connections with the Bauhaus, but she worked as an independent artist in Weimar until the couple settled on a remote estate near Frankfurt in 1920.

Influenced by van de Velde's philosophy, Bergmann was interested in the relationship between nature and technology. By 1917 she had abandoned her realistic style of oil painting and began to develop a distinctive montage and collage style, influenced by Futurism and Constructivism. Through her friendship with Kurt Schwitters, she established contacts with a number of Dada artists and with Katherine Dreier and the Société Anonyme. Bergmann participated in a variety of exhibitions, among them shows at the Sturm gallery in Berlin, the 1927 Werkbund exhibition in Stuttgart, and a traveling exhibition in the United States organized by the Société Anonyme in 1928.

Bergmann's oeuvre includes drawings, collages, graphic design, photography, and film. Of special interest to her were the social problems of the underprivileged. Her work on a documentary film on the campaign propaganda used by the National Socialists was interrupted by their rise to power. During the Third Reich her production and participation in the art scene became sparse. While her work was exhibited again after the war, Bergmann concentrated on promoting art and art films.

F.v.H.

BIBLIOGRAPHY

Norbert Nobis and Ute Pollmann, eds., *Ella Bergmann-Michel, 1895–1971: Collagen, Malerei, Aquarelle, Zeichnungen, Druckgraphik, Fotos, Reklame, Entwürfe*, exh. cat. (Hannover: Sprengel Museum, 1990); *Pioniere der Bildcollage: Ella Bergmann und Robert Michel: Werke von 1917 bis 1962*, exh. cat. (Leverkusen: Städtisches Museum Leverkusen, 1963).

■ ■ ■

Uriel Birnbaum

BORN 1894 VIENNA ✣ DIED 1956 AMERSFOORT, THE NETHERLANDS

See cat. no. 222

Uriel Birnbaum's highly imaginative graphics and paintings convey a vivid sense of fantasy that also permeates his poems and stories. His art education is said to have consisted of a single month spent studying at a Berlin art school in 1913. He illustrated many books, including works by Edgar Allan Poe and Lewis Carroll (*Alice im Wunderland* [Alice in Wonderland], 1923), biblical texts (*Das Buch Jona* [The book of Jonah], 1921), as well as his own writings (*Weltuntergang* [End of the world], 1921). Religious themes became more prevalent in Birnbaum's work after 1917, when he sustained a severe injury in World War I. He also created series of bright, decorative watercolors and participated in various group exhibitions, including one in 1916 at the Kunstsalon Heller in Vienna and the Wiener Zeitkunst shows of 1919 and 1924. He emigrated to the Netherlands in 1938.

T.B.

BIBLIOGRAPHY
Abraham Horodisch, *Die Exlibris von Uriel Birnbaum* (Zurich: Safaho-Stiftung, 1957); *Hodilz Polzer, Uriel Birnbaum: Dichter, Maler, Denker* (Vienna: Kommissions Verlag Dr. H. Glanz, 1936).

■ ■ ■

Marianne Brandt

BORN 1893 CHEMNITZ ✣ DIED 1983 HALLE

10. Untitled, c. 1924
Photocollage
25³/16 x 19⁵/16 in. (64.0 x 49.0 cm)
Created for László Moholy-Nagy's Bauhaus course
Prof. Eckhard Neumann, Frankfurt am Main

11. *Unsere irritierende Grossstadt*, 1926
(Our irritating metropolis)
Collage
25 x 19¹/18 in. (63.5 x 48.5 cm)
Galerie Berinson, Berlin

One of the few prominent women artists at the Bauhaus and the only woman in the metal workshop there, Marianne Brandt became so accomplished in metalwork and other media that she eventually became head of that workshop. Born Marianne Liebe, she studied painting and sculpture from 1911 to 1917 at the school of fine arts in Weimar before coming to the Bauhaus in 1924. A student in Joseph Albers's and László Moholy-Nagy's basic courses, Brandt also studied with Paul Klee and Wassily Kandinsky. She joined the metal workshop in April 1927 on Moholy-Nagy's recommendation.

Initially Brandt was not well received by the other students. "There was no place for a woman in a metal workshop," she wrote. "They admitted this to me later and meanwhile expressed their displeasure by giving me all sorts of dull, dreary work. How many little hemispheres did I most patiently hammer out of brittle new silver, thinking that was the way it had to be and all beginnings are hard. Later things settled down, and we got along well together" ("Letter to the Younger Generation," p. 98). By April 1928 she had replaced Moholy-Nagy as head of the workshop, continuing his emphasis on industrial design and the "functional but aesthetic assembly line." He had resigned when the new director of the school, Hannes Meyer, merged the metal workshop with the interior design workshop. Brandt remained titular head of the workshop until 1932.

During this interval Brandt also worked on other projects, as a designer for Gropius's architecture firm in Berlin and as an industrial designer for the Rüppelberg metalworks in Gotha. In 1933 she returned to Chemnitz, remaining there until 1949, when she accepted a position as lecturer in the metal, wood, and ceramics division of the school of fine arts in Dresden. In 1951 she moved to East Berlin to work as an industrial designer at the school of applied arts, where she remained until 1954. For the last thirty years of her life, she worked privately at her home in Chemnitz (which was renamed Karl-Marx-Stadt in 1953).

Brandt is best known for her work in metal but was accomplished in photography and photomontage as well as the applied arts. Her metal works, particularly the lamps and silver services made at the Bauhaus, are characterized by elegance and extreme simplicity of form. Many of her pieces were successful on the market; her bedside lamp of 1928, for example, became the prototype for the ubiquitous modern gooseneck desk lamp. She later wrote of the metal workshop: "If we had even dreamed at that time of plexiglass and the other plastics, I don't know to what utopian heights we would have aspired. But good enough: those who come after us must have something to do, too!" (ibid., p. 98).

Sometimes described as imitative of Moholy-Nagy's style, Brandt's photomontages focus on themes such as male-female relations, industry, the metropolis, and power relationships. With their humorously critical view of the big city and its diversions, these works constitute a reappraisal of the metropolis and an ironic commentary on its eclectic blend of "natural" and "industrial" aesthetics. Her photographs, which include numerous self-portraits, are characterized by both experimentation and incisive self-examination.

A.S.

BIBLIOGRAPHY

Marianne Brandt, "Letter to the Younger Generation," in *Bauhaus and Bauhaus People*, ed. Eckhard Neumann, trans. Eva Richter and Alba Lorman (New York: Van Nostrand Reinhold, 1970), pp. 97–101; *Marianne Brandt, Hajo Rose, Kurt Schmidt: Drei Künstler am Bauhaus*, exh. cat. (Dresden: Kupferstichkabinett der Staatlichen Kunstsammlungen, 1978); "Omaggio a Marianne Brandt," *Forme*, no. 110 (1985): 13–14.

■ ■ ■

Heinrich Campendonk

BORN 1889 KREFELD ✣ DIED 1957 AMSTERDAM

12. *Adam und Eva*, c. 1925
(Adam and Eve)
Woodcut
13⅞ x 13⅛ in. (35.2 x 33.3 cm)
Collection Grunwald Center for the Graphic Arts, UCLA.
Fred Grunwald bequest

Born into the family of a textile merchant, Heinrich Campendonk attended the textile industry trade school and the school of applied arts in Krefeld, where he studied under the newly arrived Dutch Art Nouveau painter Jan Thorn-Prikker, who introduced him to the work of Paul Cézanne and Vincent van Gogh. In 1911 he was invited by Wassily Kandinsky and Franz Marc to Sindelsdorf, Bavaria, and he joined their group, the Blaue Reiter (Blue rider), later that year.

While Campendonk's harmonious and often transparent application of luxurious Fauvist colors reflects the influence of Robert Delaunay and August Macke, the influence of Marc's geometric compositional approach is unmistakable in the still experimental style of such paintings as *Springendes Pferd* (Leaping horse, 1911), shown in the first Blaue Reiter exhibition in Munich in 1911–12 and illustrated in the group's almanac, *Der blaue Reiter*. Unlike Marc, Campendonk included the human figure in his mystical portrayals of animals in nature, as can be seen in his first tentative graphic works, published in 1912 in *Der Sturm* (The storm).

Continuing to experiment with Cubism, Futurism, and Orphism, Campendonk exhibited with Das junge Rheinland (Young Rheinland) before World War I. The war and the deaths of Marc and Macke were a turning point for Campendonk. In 1916, after two years of military service, he moved to Seeshaupt and destroyed much of his earlier work. His new paintings moved decisively toward representational fantasy influenced by Marc Chagall. Concurrently his woodcuts evolved to maturity with heraldic presentations of fish, cats, goats, cows, figures, and profuse vegetative ornament in a style having sources in African tribal art, Egyptian shadow-play figures, and Russian folk prints. Many of the woodcuts have black backgrounds, which contrast with radiant accents of watercolor that evoke the luminosity of stained glass and accrue symbolic power.

In 1920 Campendonk traveled to Italy to study the frescoes of Giotto and Fra Angelico as well as the Early Christian mosaics in Ravenna. Subsequently an architectonic construction of space entered his paintings (far example, *Interieur* [Interior], 1920). He returned to Krefeld in 1922 and moved toward a more abstract and decorative style while producing the stage designs for the Krefeld theater as well as boldy simplified woodcuts. He took the position vacated by Thorn-Prikker at the Dusseldorf academy in 1926 and concentrated on public art and stained glass. In 1933 he emigrated to Belgium, where he worked on an unfinished series of stained-glass icons of the Stations of the Cross. In 1935 he took a position at the academy of fine arts in Amsterdam, where he lived for the rest of his life. In 1937 his Passion window, shown at the Dutch pavilion at the Paris World's Fair, won the Grand Prix. Often praised for his dreamlike imagery, Campendonk blended fantasy with a reserved and exacting precision, creating work that is both imaginative and concrete.

T.B.

BIBLIOGRAPHY

Georg Biermann, *Heinrich Campendonk*, Junge Kunst, no. 17 (Leipzig: Klinkhardt und Biermann, 1921); Aurel Bongers, Dierk Stemmler, and Joachim Heusinger van Waldegg, eds., *Die rheinischen Expressionisten: August Macke und seine Malerfreunde*, exh. cat. (Recklinghausen: Aurel Bongers, 1979); Mathias T. Engles, *Heinrich Campendonk, Monographien zur rheinisch-westfälischen Kunst der Gegenwart*, no. 9 (Recklinghausen: Aurel Bongers, 1958); idem, *Campendonk: Holzschnitte: Werkverzeichnis* (Stuttgart: W. Kohlhammer, 1959); idem, *Campendonk als Glasmaler* (Krefeld: Scherpe, 1966); Andrea Firmenich, *Heinrich Campendonk: Leben und expressionistisches Werk: Mit Werkkatalog des malerischen Oeuvres* (Recklinghausen: Aurel Bongers, 1989); Paul Wember, *Heinrich Campendonk* (Krefeld: Scherpe, 1960).

■ ■ ■

Roman Clemens

BORN 1910 DESSAU ✣ DIED 1992 ZURICH

13. *"Russisches": Bühnenbild zum "Spiel aus Form, Farbe, Licht und Ton,"* 1929
("Russian": Stage design for "Play of form, color, light, and sound")
Tempera on black board
12 5/8 x 15 3/4 in. (32.0 x 40.0 cm)
Theaterwissenschaftliche Sammlung, Universität zu Köln

Roman Clemens was a key proponent of innovation in the German theater. He participated in Oskar Schlemmer's stage workshop at the Bauhaus, which worked to revolutionize notions about the theater and to pioneer new communication techniques for the stage. His abstract theater designs functioned as exercises in color and composition and are akin to Wassily Kandinsky's experiments with synesthesia.

Clemens came to the Bauhaus in the summer of 1927, joining the small group of stage workshop students there, which included Lukas (Lux) Feininger, Wolfgang Hildebrandt, and Andor Weininger. In a performance presented by the students in November 1927 to raise money for their program, Clemens created a *Lichtstück* (light piece) in which white and colored lights were projected on a moving figure before a backdrop. When opposition to Schlemmer's direction began to be felt both inside and outside the theater workshop, Clemens was among those who continued to support him. Along with Lyonel Feininger and Hermann Röseler, he drafted a letter to Schlemmer expressing support for his teaching. "We have decided," they wrote, "that instead of occupying ourselves with this activity [of the opposition], we will occupy ourselves with theater theory and will show the result of this work in an exhibition before the summer vacation" (quoted in Dirk Scheper, *Oskar Schlemmer: Das triadische Ballett und die Bauhausbühne* [Berlin: Akademie der Künste, 1988], p, 329). For this exhibition, held in July 1929, Clemens created a series of five designs entitled *Spiel aus Form, Farbe, Licht und Ton* (Play of form, color, light, and sound), described by critic Wilhelm van Kempen as the high point of the show. In the accompanying manuscript Clemens described the music corresponding to each geometric design. These five pieces were conceived both as designs for the theater and as abstract exercises that combined the elements of the theater—sound, motion, light, line, and color—in a two-dimensional format.

Clemens continued his work in theater after leaving the Bauhaus. From 1929 to 1931 he served as assistant set painter at the Friedrich-Theater in Dessau and from 1932 to 1943 was head set painter and designer of the Zurich opera house. He continued to investigate the "reality" of the theater as a physical space. In his 1953 *Theater "B"* he designed a semicircular theater incorporating a peep show. By using movable walls on the stage and modular sets that could be dismantled and reassembled to create new performance spaces, he aspired to unify spectator areas and foyers designed as side stages. His goal was to open up new possibilities for the theater by freeing it from the limitations of traditional design. Although this project was feasible, it was never realized; Clemens wrote that "a solution to our problems with theater sets is perhaps only to be found in utopia" ("Hinweis auf die Darinstädter Ausstellung 'Theaterbau,'" *Baukunst und Werkform* 8, no. 4 [1955]: 255). In the 1950s and 1960s he organized several traveling exhibitions to publicize the theater and aspects of Weimar culture, including *Theaterbau* (Theater sets) in 1955, *Bauhaus* in 1961, and *Thomas Mann* in 1962.

A.S.

BIBLIOGRAPHY
Marianne Herold, *Roman Clemens* (Zurich: ABC, 1991); Hannelore Kersting and Bernd Vogelsang, eds., *Raumkonzepte: Konstruktivistische Tendenzen in Bühnen- und Bildkunst, 1910–1930*, exh. cat. (Frankfurt: Städtische Galerie im Städelschen Kunstinstitut, 1986).

■ ■ ■

Walter Dexel

BORN 1890 MUNICH ✣ DIED 1973 BRUNSWICK

14. *Sternenbrücke*, 1919
(Starry bridge)
Woodcut
10 1/2 x 7 13/16 in. (26.6 x 19.8 cm)
Los Angeles County Museum of Art. The Robert Gore Rifkind Center for German Expressionist Studies

As an artist and art historian, Walter Dexel was an active participant in the art world of the Weimar era. He contributed to the articulation and dissemination of ideas evolving at that time among various groups, including De Stijl, the Bauhaus, the Novembergruppe (November group), and the circle around Kurt Schwitters in Hannover.

Dexel studied art history in Munich from 1910 to 1914; the theoretician Heinrich Wölfflin was among his teachers. In 1912 and 1913 he also attended a private drawing school. He traveled to Italy, where he was particularly impressed by the art and architecture of Florence. He produced his first pictures during this period. After 1914 he continued his studies in Paris but was called to Jena in 1916 to work at the war archive. In spite of the war, he was able to complete his doctoral degree at the university in Jena. He became the exhibition director for the Kunstverein (art association) there in 1916, maintaining that position until 1928.

In 1918 his work was exhibited with that of Heinrich Campendonk at the Sturm gallery in Berlin. In the ensuing years he established connections with the masters of the Bauhaus and had a particularly productive dialogue on De Stijl with Theo van Doesburg in the years 1921 to 1923. He maintained a membership in the Novembergruppe (November group) from 1923 to 1927.

Dexel was also active as a designer. In 1916 he began to design illuminated outdoor advertising, and in 1928 he became a member of the Ring neuer Werbegestalter (Circle of new advertising designers), founded by Schwitters. Also in 1928 he published the first of a series of books on interior design and the applied arts and was appointed to a teaching position in 1928 at the Magdeburg school of applied arts. He was fired from this post in 1935, when the Nazis purged educational institutions of "degenerate" artists. At the same time he was terminated as set designer for the Stadttheater in Jena. He was, however, able to secure a teaching position in Berlin from 1936 to 1942 at the Staatliche Hochschule für Kunsterziehung (State institute for art education) and from 1942 to 1955 assembled and directed the Historische Formsammlung (Historical collection of design) for the city of Brunswick.

F.V.H.

BIBLIOGRAPHY
Walter Vitt, *Walter Dexel: Werkverzeichnis der Druckgrafik von 1915–1971* (Cologne: W. König, 1971); Ruth Wöbkemeier and Siegfried Salzmann, eds., *Walter Dexel: Bild, Zeichen, Raum*, exh. cat. (Bremen: Kunsthalle Bremen, 1990).

■ ■ ■

Otto Dix

BORN 1891 UNTERMHAUS ✣ DIED 1969 SINGEN

15. *Elektrische*, 1920
(Streetcar)
Woodcut
11 x 9 3/8 in. (28.0 x 23.7 cm)
From the portfolio Neun Holzschnitte (1922)
Los Angeles County Museum of Art. The Robert Gore Rifkind Center for German Expressionist Studies

16. *Lens wird mit Bomben belegt*, 1924
(Lens being bombed)
Etching with aquatint
11 3/4 x 9 11/16 in. (29.8 x 24.6 cm)
From the portfolio Der Krieg (1924)
Los Angeles County Museum of Art. The Robert Gore Rifkind Center for German Expressionist Studies

Otto Dix may be best known for effectively portraying humanity's painful transition to the modern era through the horrific world war made possible by industrialization. Yet he held tradition in high esteem, venerating above all the art of the Renaissance and its revival during the early nineteenth century by the Nazarenes, a circle of German painters inspired primarily by religious art. Throughout his career he sought to portray the modern experience using traditional means derived from earlier artists such as Lucas Cranach, Albrecht Dürer, Hans Baldung Grien, and Francisco Goya, while also incorporating influences from such contemporaries as Conrad Felixmüller, George Grosz, and Gino Severini.

Dix received his early training with Carl Senff in Gera as an apprentice painter and decorator from 1905 to 1909, then attended the school of applied arts in Dresden from 1910 to 1914. He enlisted in an artillery regiment in 1914 and saw action as a machine gunner in France, Poland, and Russia. He created hundreds of war sketches in the dynamic style of the Italian Futurists, whose celebration of change confirmed beliefs derived from his intensive reading of Friedrich Nietzsche. Yet six years of artistic development were required before Dix could render the somber and moving testimony of his celebrated suite of fifty etchings entitled *Der Krieg* (War, 1924), which may be the most powerful antiwar statement produced by a modern artist.

During the tumultuous period following the 1918 armistice, Dix became a cofounder of the left-wing Gruppe 1919 (Group 1919) of the Dresden Secession and also exhibited with the Berlin Dadaists at the *Erste internationale Dada-Messe* (First international Dada fair) in 1920. This association led to his experimentation with collage, which clearly influenced the fragmented imagery of the portfolio Neun Holzschnitte (Nine woodcuts), executed in 1919–20 and published in 1922. After studying painting at the academy in Dresden from 1919 to 1922, Dix moved in 1922 to Düsseldorf to study painting under Heinrich Nauen and intaglio techniques under Wilhelm Herberholz at the academy. His confident handling of etching and drypoint is evident in his flamboyant and imaginative portfolio Zirkus (Circus, 1922), in which he invoked the melancholy presence of death and the grotesque absurdity of human behavior. While in Düsseldorf he joined the group Das junge Rheinland (Young Rhineland), through which he met the artists Gert Wollheim and Otto Pankok and the art dealer and patron Johanna Ey.

Moving to Berlin in 1925, Dix abandoned printmaking to concentrate on the veristic style of painting that had won him prominence in the 1925 Neue Sachlichkeit (new objectivity) exhibition in Mannheim. Using the traditional religious format of the triptych to secular ends, he realized such profound works of social criticism as his paintings *Grossstadt* (Metropolis, 1928) and *Der Krieg* (1932), produced during his tenure as a professor at the Dresden academy from 1927 to 1933, when he was expelled by the Nazis and prohibited from exhibiting. Dix endured an "internal exile" in Hemmenhofen at Lake Constance, painting primarily landscapes; was included in the infamous 1937 exhibition *Entartete Kunst* (Degenerate art) in Munich; and was briefly arrested in 1939. In 1945 he served in the Volkssturm (people's storm), Germany's last-ditch effort to defend itself against the Allies, and was interned in France as a prisoner of war.

Dix resumed printmaking in 1948, working almost exclusively in lithography and continuing his exploration of religious imagery, as exemplified by his illustrations for *Das Evangelium nach Matthäus* (The Gospel according to Matthew, 1960).

T.B.

BIBLIOGRAPHY

Keith Hartley, ed., *Otto Dix, 1891–1969*, exh. cat. (London: Tate Gallery, 1992); Wulf Herzogenrath and Johann-Karl Schmidt, eds., *Dix*, exh. cat. (Stuttgart: Galerie der Stadt Stuttgart, 1991); Florian Karsch, ed., *Otto Dix: Das graphische Werk* (Hannover: Fackelträger-Verlag Schmidt-Küster, 1970); Hans-Ulrich Lehmann, ed., *Otto Dix: Die Zeichnungen im Dresdner Kupferstich-Kabinett: Katalog des Bestandes*, exh. cat. (Dresden: Kupferstich-Kabinett der Staatlichen Kunstsammlungen, 1991); Fritz Löffler, *Otto Dix: Leben und Werk* (Vienna: Schroll, 1967); idem, *Otto Dix, 1891–1969: Oeuvre der Gemälde* (Recklinghausen: Aurel Bongers, 1981).

■ ■ ■

Siegfried Ebeling

BORN 1894 RÄTZLINGEN ✣ DIED 1963 HAMBURG

See cat. no. 224

Cat. no. 224

Siegfried Ebeling's life, like those of many Germans during the period framed by the two world wars, was characterized by restlessness and searching. His education covered a variety of subjects, from theology to architecture, and he worked as a dancer, laborer, artist, and architect. His views on architecture, published as theoretical treatises in the 1920s, added a new perspective to the field.

Ebeling started out in 1912 as a student of philosophy and theology at the university in Heidelberg. His education was disrupted by military service in World War I, then by his retention in an English prisoner-of-war camp until 1920. When he resumed his studies, from 1920 to 1923, he majored in Christian archaeology in Jena, later studying art history in Leipzig and also spending some time as an exchange student in Sweden. In 1924 he became a student of Wassily Kandinsky at the Bauhaus and started publishing articles in the periodical *Junge Menschen* (Young people). In 1925 he worked in the advertising department of the Junkers company in Dessau, returning to the Bauhaus in Weimar and in Dessau in 1925–26. There he made a significant contribution to the theory of architecture with his publication of "Der Raum als Membran" (Space as membrane) in 1926.

After leaving the Bauhaus, he served as director of a private research institute in Hamlin from 1927 to 1928. During this time he was also engaged as a dancer with Rudolf Laban in Berlin and worked as a laborer in factory. In 1929 he was hired as private secretary to a sugar manufacturer in Lausanne.

The recognition he received for his rotating Ganzmetall-Rundhaus (All-metal round house) of 1930 allowed him to settle in Bielefeld and, from 1939, in Hamburg, where he worked as a free-lance architect. His career was once again disrupted by military service and retention as a prisoner of war from 1941 to 1945. He devoted his final years, from the 1950s until his death in 1963, to painting at his home near Hamburg.

F.v.H.

■ ■ ■

Viking Eggeling

BORN 1880 LUND, SWEDEN ✣ DIED 1925 BERLIN

17. *Horizontal-vertikal Orchester I*, c. 1921
(Horizontal-vertical orchestra I)
Photomechanical reproduction
12 x 9¼ in. (30.5 x 23.5 cm)
Cover for *MA* 6, no. 8 (1921)
The Resource Collections of the Getty Center for the History of Art and the Humanities

18. *Diagonalsymphonie IV (Rolle)*, c. 1923
(Diagonal symphony IV [scroll])
Pencil
Approx. 19¹¹⁄₁₆ x 119 in. (50.0 x 303.2 cm)
Kunstmuseum Basel. Depositum Maja Sacher-Stehlin

19. *Studie für "Diagonalsymphonie I" (Rolle 1, Blatt 7)*
(Study for "Diagonal symphony I" [roll 1, sheet 7])
Pencil
8⁹⁄₁₆ x 6¼ in. (21.8 x 15.9 cm)
Emanuel Hoffmann-Stiftung. Depositum Kunstmuseum Basel

20. Studie für "Diagonalsymphonie I" (Rolle 1, Blatt 8)
(Study for "Diagonal symphony I" (roll 1, sheet 8])
Pencil
8⁹⁄₁₆ x 6¼ in. (21.8 x 15.9 cm)
Emanuel Hoffmann-Stiftung. Depositum Kunstmuseum Basel

Viking Eggeling's lifelong aspiration was to create an abstract artistic language capable of restoring contact between the artist and the public. He preferred to leave his works unsigned and undated as a protest against what he saw as the individualism and corruption inherent in the art of his time. Influenced by the ideas of Wassily Kandinsky as set forth in *Über das Geistige in der Kunst* (On the spiritual in art, 1912) and by Paul Klee's painting, Eggeling believed in the importance of the spiritual and worked to create a universal language based on a harmony of forms. His scroll paintings for his first film effort, *Horizontal-vertikal Symphonie* (Horizontal-vertical symphony, 1920–23), on which he collaborated with his friend and colleague Hans Richter, represent the first attempt to introduce abstraction into film. Eggeling viewed his experiments in film in almost mystical terms and thus differed somewhat from Richter, who, influenced by Constructivist ideas, was interested in pure, abstract form.

Eggeling immigrated to Germany to embark on an artistic career at the age of sixteen; both his parents had died before he was fifteen. From 1901 to 1907 he studied art history in Milan in the evenings while working as a bookkeeper by day. From 1911 to 1915 he lived in Paris, where he met Jean Arp, Amedeo Modigliani, and other artists. After moving to Zurich in 1915, he met Tristan Tzara, cofounder of the Dada Cabaret Voltaire, who introduced him to Richter. Over the next two years Eggeling made designs for his *Rollenbilder* (scroll pictures), thought to be preliminary drawings for the films *Horizontal-vertical Symphonie and Diagonalsymphonie* (Diagonal symphony, 1922). In 1919 he joined the artists' group Das neue Leben (The new life), started in Basel by Arp and Marcel Janco among others; this group later became Radikale Künstler

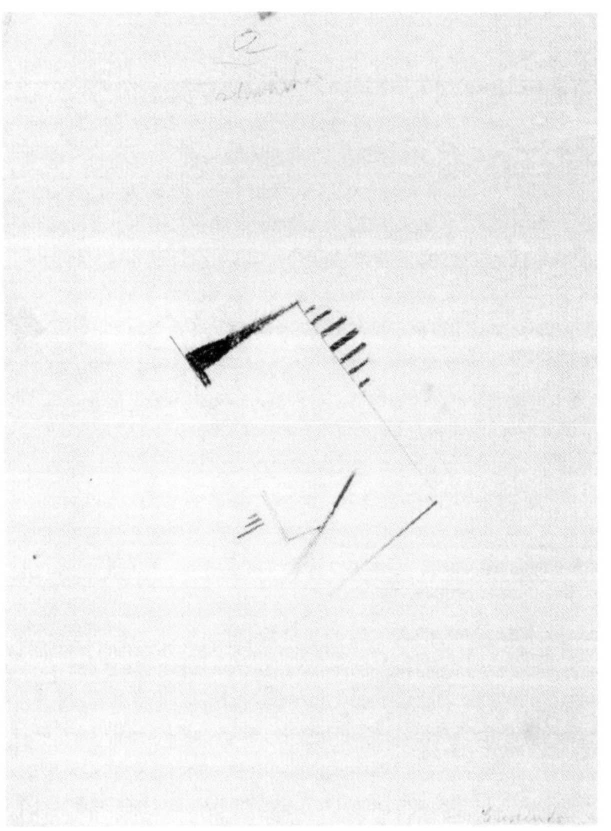

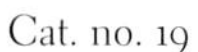

Cat. no. 19

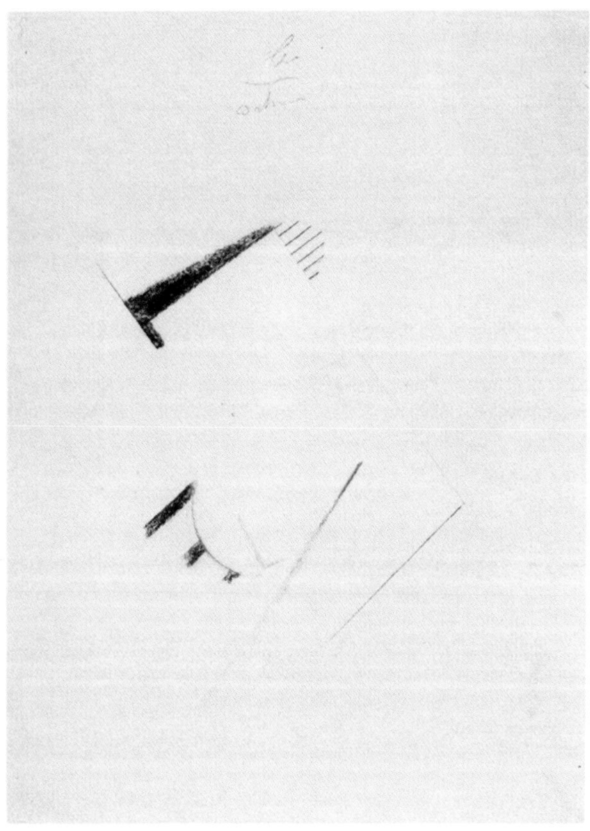

Cat. no. 20

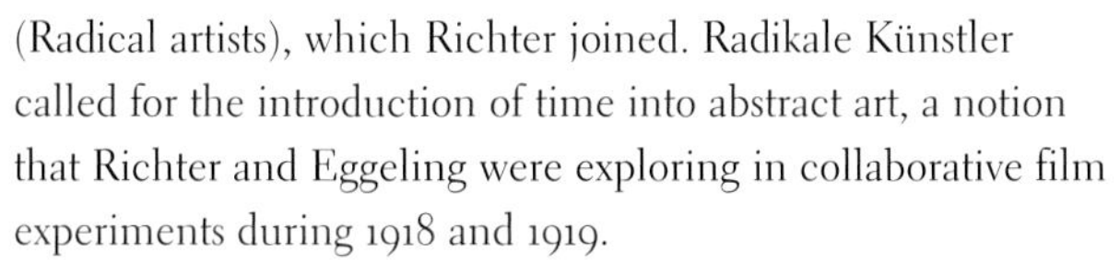

(Radical artists), which Richter joined. Radikale Künstler called for the introduction of time into abstract art, a notion that Richter and Eggeling were exploring in collaborative film experiments during 1918 and 1919.

In his voluminous sketchbooks Eggeling laid out a blueprint for his film experiments and plans for a universal language of form and wrote of the necessity of a transformation of human consciousness. "No utopia, " he wrote. "The material creation of utopia. No living against each other. Our common goal: the actualization of the existence of the human being as a spiritual being. The construction of a new spiritual and simple life" (quoted in O'Konor, *Viking Eggeling*, p. 102). Richter later wrote of Eggeling that "he had an 'all-embracing philosophy' which had led him to formulate rules of everyday conduct which had, for him, absolute validity" (Hans Richter, *Dada: Art and Anti-Art*, trans. David Britt [London: Thames and Hudson, 1965], p. 63).

Eggeling published declarations in 1921 and 1923 with Raoul Hausmann, calling for artists to adapt to changing technology by creating art that would capture "images of a world that is real, a synthesis of the spirit and of the material," and that would put art in the service of contemporary concerns. After 1919 Eggeling continued his film work, first alone and then from 1923 in collaboration with Erna Niemeyer. The pair worked on his last film, *Diagonalsymphonie*, which was shown publicly for the first time in May of 1925, the month Eggeling died.

A.S.

BIBLIOGRAPHY

Viking Eggeling, 1880–1925, exh. cat. (Stockholm: Nationalmuseum, 1950); Louise O'Konor, *Viking Eggeling, 1880–1925, Artist and Filmmaker: Life and Work*, trans. Catherine G. Sundström and Anne Bibby, Stockholm Studies in the History of Art, no. 23 (Stockholm: Almqvist and Wiksell, 1971).

■ ■ ■

Lyonel Feininger

BORN 1871 NEW YORK ✣ DIED 1956 NEW YORK

21. *Das Tor*, 1912
(The gate)
Etching
16 1/8 x 12 5/8 in. (41.0 x 32.0 cm)
Los Angeles County Museum of Art, The Robert Gore Rifkind Center for German Expressionist Studies

22. *Rathaus, Zottelstedt*, 1918
(Town hall, Zottelstedt)
Woodcut
4 1/2 x 5 1/2 in. (11.4 x 14.0 cm)
From *Ja! Stimmen des Arbeitsrates für Kunst in Berlin* (1919)
Los Angeles County Museum of Art, The Robert Gore Rifkind Center for German Expressionist Studies, purchased with funds provided by Anna Bing Arnold, Museum Acquisition Fund, and deaccession funds

23. *Kathedrale*, 1919
(Cathedral)
Woodcut
12 x 7 3/8 in. (30.5 x 18.7 cm)
Title page from the *Programm des Staatlichen Bauhauses in Weimar* (1919)
Los Angeles County Museum of Art, The Robert Gore Rifkind Center for German Expressionist Studies, purchased with funds provided by Anna Bing Arnold, Museum Acquisition Fund, and deaccession funds

Well known as a cartoonist in Germany in the early years of the century, the German-American painter and graphic artist Lyonel Feininger did not make his first painting until 1907, at the age of thirty-five. Many of the characteristics of his style, however—the dramatic angular forms, the sense of motion, the play with depth, the contrasts of black and white—were already present, developed over years of drawing for magazines. Fascinated by landscape as well as architecture, he used intersecting planes and sharp lines of force to represent the effects of light, carefully building his compositions from overlapping surfaces. Inspired by French novelists Eugène Sue and Victor Hugo, Feininger examined wide-ranging themes such as revolution and industrialization, modern technology, bourgeois promenades, landscapes, villages, and imaginary views of the "city at the end of the world." Although he used nature as a basis for his imagery, he believed that Expressionist artists must go beyond nature to "portray our inner vision, find our ultimate form uninfluenced by nature in order to express our longing" (Lyonel Feininger, "Credo of Expressionism: Letter to Paul Westheim," in Ness, *Lyonel Feininger*, p. 27).

Feininger was the child of German parents who were both musicians. He grew up in New York but in 1887, at the age of sixteen, traveled by boat to Germany, where his parents intended that he study music. Two weeks after his arrival, however, he enrolled at the general vocational school in Hamburg, where he studied drawing. In 1888 he moved to Berlin to attend the academy, where he received traditional artistic training, even though he had already begun to work as a cartoonist.

In the following years Feininger became well known for his cartoons and illustrations, publishing numerous drawings in such satirical magazines as *Ulk* (Fun) and *Lustige Blätter* (Funny papers) in Berlin and *Le témoin* (The witness) in Paris. Partially motivated by his relationship with the painter Julia Berg and weary of constantly producing commercial work, he decided to pursue his own artistic impulses and began to devote more time to nature drawing. A visit to Paris in 1905 introduced him to the work of Robert Delaunay and the Postimpressionists and furthered his interest in painting. In 1910 Feininger exhibited his "Fantastic Series" drawings at the Berlin Secession, which included the portfolios Montmartre, Die Stadt am Ende der Welt (The city at the end of the world), Lokomotiven (Locomotives), and Workers.

Feininger's growing familiarity with Cubism led to a greater use of overlapping planes and a concern with pictorial volume, which he explored in the years following another trip to Paris in 1911. A solo exhibition at the Sturm gallery in 1917 brought his work to the attention of other artists and critics. After the war he was a member of both the Novembergruppe (November group) and the Arbeitsrat für Kunst (Working council for art), although he took little part in their activities, preferring to work in solitude. Walter Gropius appointed him head of the graphics workshop at the Weimar Bauhaus in 1919 and asked him to design the cover of the Bauhaus manifesto. Feininger's woodcut *Kathedrale* (Cathedral, 1919) referred to the past in its use of Gothic architecture while projecting a sense of modernity.

In 1926 Feininger was given an honorary post at the Bauhaus, then in Dessau, without teaching duties, enabling him to continue his work without the usual financial worries. In the early 1930s, faced with his own dwindling resources and appalled by the political situation in Germany, he considered emigrating. Still an American citizen, he fled for New York with Berg in 1937.

A.S.

BIBLIOGRAPHY

T. Lux Feininger, *Lyonel Feininger: City at the Edge of the World* (New York: Praeger, 1965); Hans Hess, *Lyonel Feininger* (New York: Harry N. Abrams, 1961); Ulrich Luckhardt, *Lyonel Feininger*, trans. Eileen Martin (Munich: Prestel, 1989); June L. Ness, ed., *Lyonel Feininger, Documentary Monographs in Modern Art* (New York: Praeger, 1974); Leona E. Prasse, *Feininger: A Definitive Catalogue of His Graphic Work: Etchings, Lithographs, Woodcuts* (Cleveland: Cleveland Museum of Art, 1972); Ernst Scheyer, *Lyonel Feininger: Caricature and Fantasy* (Detroit: Wayne State University Press, 1964).

■ ■ ■

Hermann Finsterlin

BORN 1887 MUNICH ✣ DIED 1973 STUTTGART

24. *Architektur*, 1920
(Architecture)
Watercolor, graphite, and india ink
7 3/8 x 11 7/6 in. (18.8 x 29.0 cm)
Graphische Sammlung, Staatsgalerie Stuttgart

25. *Hygiene Museum*, 1920
Plaster, painted white and yellow-brown
14 9/16 x 10 1/4 x 9 1/16 in. (37.0 x 26.0 x 23.0 cm)
Gabriele Reisser-Finsterlin

26. *Traum aus Glas*, 1920
(Glass dream)
Watercolor, graphite, and india ink
7 3/8 x 11 7/16 in. (18.8 x 29.0 cm)
Graphische Sammlung, Staatsgalerie Stuttgart

27. *Die Stadt, Serie IV, Blatt* 8, 1920–24
(The city, series IV, sheet 8)
Watercolor over pencil
12 1/4 x 18 7/8 in. (31.0 x 48.0 cm)
Graphische Sammlung, Staatsgalerie Stuttgart

28. *Plan des "Stilspiels" zur Edition*, c. 1921
(Plan of "The style game" for the edition)
Pencil and ink on paper on board
14 3/8 x 19 7/8 in. (36.5 x 50.5 cm)
Gabriele Reisser-Finsterlin

29. *Grundriss, Serie III, Blatt* 7, c. 1922
(Ground plan, series III, sheet 7)
Black, red, and blue ink over graphite
7 5/16 x 10 1/4 in. (18.1 x 26.2 cm)
Collection Centre Canadien d'Architecture/Canadian Centre for Architecture, Montreal

30. *Das Stilspiel 1921*, 1922
(The style game, 1921)
Ninety-five single blocks of painted wood of different shapes and sizes
Graphische Sammlung, Staatsgalerie Stuttgart

31. *Drei geometrische Phantasien*, 1922–23
(Three geometric fantasies)
Painted wood
(a) 3 15/16 x 4 1/8 x 5 1/8 in. (10.0 x 10.5 x 13.0 cm.); (b) 4 7/8 x 2 3/4 x 3 15/16 in. (12.4 x 7.0 x 10.0 cm); (c) height: 3 9/16 in. (9.0 cm), diam: 3 5/8 in. (9.2 cm)
Graphische Sammlung, Staatsgalerie Stuttgart

32. *Didym-Durchdringungen geometrischer Körper*, 1922–23
(Didym-penetrations of geometric bodies)
Seven blocks of painted wood
Each: 2 3/4 x 2 3/4 x 2 3/4 in. (7.0 x 7.0 x 7.0 cm)
Graphische Sammlung, Staatsgalerie Stuttgart

33. *Geometrische Durchdringungen*, 1922–23
(Geometric penetrations)
Watercolor, pencil, whitening on transparent paper
10 1/4 x 15 1/4 in. (26.0 x 38.8 cm)
Graphische Sammlung, Staatsgalerie Stuttgart

34. *Architektur-Kathedrale des Lichts, Serie IV, Blatt* 4
(Architecture-cathedral of light, series IV, sheet 4)
Watercolor and white paint over pencil on brown paper
13 1/2 x 7 3/16 in. (34.2 x 18.2 cm)
Graphische Sammlung, Staatsgalerie Stuttgart

35. *Architekturentwürfe*
(Architectural sketches)
Pencil, black and green inks
8 7/8 x 11 ? in. (22.5 x 28.5 cm)
Graphische Sammlung, Staatsgalerie Stuttgart

Hermann Finsterlin—visionary architect, painter, sculptor, and toy maker—saw himself as "the Darwin of architecture," though he never built a permanent structure. His studies at the university in Munich reveal an extraordinarily catholic sensibility: chemistry, physics, medicine, philosophy, and Indology. In 1913 he studied painting at the academy in Munich under the famed teacher Franz von Stuck.

Cat. no. 25

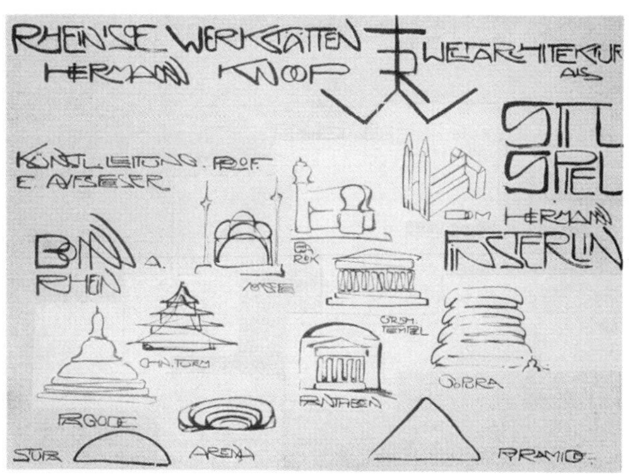

Cat. no. 28

Finsterlin executed some five hundred watercolors and ink sketches of isolated structures bearing anthropomorphic designs, which architectural historian Wolfgang Pehnt has described as "a cross between Bomarzo and Walt Disney." Forty of these architectural sketches were shown in 1919 at the *Ausstellung für unbekannte Architekten* (Exhibition of unknown architects), and Finsterlin also participated in the 1920 *Neues Bauen* (New building) exhibition, likewise organized by the Arbeitsrat für Kunst (Working council for art). He occasionally contributed articles to Bruno Taut's periodical *Frühlicht* (Daybreak) and to pamphlets published by the Arbeitsrat für Kunst, which he joined in 1919. Though he professed indifference to Expressionist social vision and utopianism, Finsterlin was an active contributor to the Gläserne Kette (Crystal chain) correspondence under the pseudonym *Prometh* (Prometheus). He also taught briefly at the Bauhaus (c. 1930).

Under the National Socialist regime Finsterlin was, through a misunderstanding, commissioned to create frescoes for state buildings and official portraits of leading figures, including Hitler. For years he declined, feigning illness, until he consented under the threat of internment in a concentration camp. Many of his works were destroyed when his house was bombed in 1944, although about 500 watercolors and ink drawings were spared, including 185 architectural drawings. In response to renewed interest in his work, he began to redraw his earlier architectural fantasies in the 1960s. Several of these and his paintings are in the collection of the Kunstverein (art association) in Stuttgart, where he continued to write and paint until his death.

V.H.

BIBLIOGRAPHY

Franco Borsi, *Hermann Finsterlin: Idea dell'architettura* (Florence: Stabilimento, 1963); Reinhard Döhl, *Hermann Finsterlin: Eine Annäherung*, exh. cat. (Stuttgart: Staatsgalerie Stuttgart, 1988); Hermann Finsterlin, "Innenarchitektur," *Frühlicht* (Winter 1921–22): 35–37.

■ ■ ■

Paul Gangolf

BORN 1879 BERLIN ✣ DIED 1940 NEAR THE FRENCH-GERMAN BORDER

36. *Seiltänzerin*, c. 1922
(Tightrope walker)
Hand-colored lithograph
Sheet: 19 x 14½ in. (48.3 x 36.8 cm)
From the portfolio Metropolis (1922)
Ruth and Jacob Kainen

37. *Strassenszene*, 1925
(Street scene)
Lithograph
Sheet: 16 x 12 in. (40.6 x 30.5 cm)
Ruth and Jacob Kainen

Like many of his colleagues, Paul Gangolf was self-taught as a graphic artist and painter. A member of the circle of artists and writers in Berlin around the Sturm gallery and Malik Verlag, the publishing house founded by Wieland Herzfelde and John Heartfield, Gangolf was described by his contemporary Ernst Rathenau as a penniless bohemian who roamed from café to café, frequently on the edge of starvation: "Gangolf was often absent-minded, restless, undisciplined, he got into muddles when he spoke—which only makes more astounding the concentration of many of his works, in which a visionary power reveals itself" (*In Memoriam*, p. 5).

Represented in the 1920 Berlin Secession exhibition by a group of lithographs, Gangolf focused on graphic art throughout his career. He favored etching, which allows for greater intricacy and fluidity of line than woodcut, although he also executed numerous cross-hatched woodcuts. His work was published by Paul Westheim in his journal *Das Kunstblatt* (The art paper) and was the subject of a retrospective in Hamburg in 1931. Westheim wrote of the artist that he was someone "who cannot make peace with a world that will always be a problem for him and...who tries to decipher meaning or nonsense in the midst of chaos" (quoted in Rathenau, *In Memoriam*, p. 7).

Gangolf was fascinated by the American West, with its cowboys and Indians, and by the big city, with its dark alleys, skyscrapers, and entertainment-hungry mobs. In Metropolis, a portfolio of ten lithographs published in 1922 by Malik Verlag, he portrayed the various diversions of the city: the cinema, the circus, street life. Using large areas of black and strong hatched lines, he created an environment in which the transitory excitement of big-city diversions mingles with fear, claustrophobia, and an urge to escape.

After the National Socialist takeover, Gangolf was denounced for mumbling a comment critical of the regime and spent several months interned in a concentration camp, from which he retained a mangled finger. He traveled to Portugal but on his return trip in 1940, while trying to cross the French border into Germany, was shot to death. Ironically he had written to an acquaintance in 1932 that "Benes, the leader of Czechoslovakia and one of the sharpest minds in Europe, just wrote that everything will soon sort itself out, although adventures like Hitler delay things for Germany" (letter to Gustav Schiefler, 1 October 1932, quoted in Rathenau, *In Memoriam*, p. 14).

A.S.

BIBLIOGRAPHY

Ernest Rathenau, ed., *In Memoriam: Paul Gangolf* (New York: Ernest Rathenau, 1964).

■ ■ ■

Jefim Golyscheff

BORN 1897 KHERSON, UKRAINE ✣ DIED 1970 PARIS

38. Untitled, 1918
Ink
5 5/16 x 5 15/16 in. (13.5 x 15.0 cm)
Lent anonymously

39. Untitled, 1918
Watercolor
8 5/8 x 11 13/16 in. (21.9 x 30.0 cm)
Lent anonymously

A provocative artist from his earliest years, Jefim Golyscheff began playing the violin at age five and started drawing lessons a year later under the direction of his father, a friend of Wassily Kandinsky. In 1911 Golyscheff set off on a two-year world tour with the Odessa Symphony Orchestra as a wunderkind violin soloist. From 1909 to 1933 he resided in Berlin, where he studied music theory and composition at the Stern'schen Konservatorium. At the age of seventeen he developed his principle of "dodecaphonic duration," contributing to the evolution of twelve-tone music. He came under the influence of Ferruccio Busoni, Arnold Schoenberg, and Richard Strauss; Golyscheff's twelve-tone compositions, however, antedated those of Schoenberg and his protégés Anton von Webern and Alban Berg by six years. As did a few other avant-garde composers, Golyscheff developed his own system of musical notation; he also invented musical instruments, wrote poetry, and made children's toys and craft objects.

Golyscheff's signature is found in a 1917 guest book of the Sturm gallery, but it was not until 1919 that he became actively involved with the avant-garde. He was one of two artists to show at both the *Ausstellung für unbekannte Architekten* (Exhibition of unknown architects) in April 1919 and the first Berlin Dada exhibition the following month at I. B. Neumann's Graphisches Kabinett. He showed at the 1921 *Grosse Berliner Kunst-Ausstellung* (Greater Berlin art exhibition) with what had become a less-politicized Novembergruppe (November group), even though he had signed a Berlin Dada manifesto that satirized the group's ideals in 1919. In that year he was also part of the elite artists' workshop group of the Arbeitsrat für Kunst (Working council for art). In a letter to Golyscheff, Walter Gropius remarked: "We have hung a series of your fascinating drawings in the unknown architects exhibition—let the bourgeois think what he will about them. We finally came to the conclusion that your works belong in the domain of architecture. They really are ultimate examples of what we want: utopia" (quoted in Ockman, "Reinventing Jefim Golyscheff," p. 75). He created mushroomlike structures in which bourgeois conventions found no place. The critic Adolf Behne believed that Golyscheff's colorful, childlike creations would inspire the proletariat, who would see that they too could make simple, beautiful art.

Although Golyscheff had been very active in Berlin Dada through his association with Raoul Hausmann, his distancing from the movement is evident in his manifesto *Aismus*, published late in the summer of 1919. In this work he opposed all "isms," all partisanship, and the tendency of individuals to unite under a banner. Nevertheless he continued to participate in Novembergruppe exhibitions until 1922, when he stopped exhibiting his work and devoted his time to composing music (all of which is lost). During the late 1920s and early 1930s he worked as a film sound engineer in Berlin and Russia.

After the Nazis confiscated his works in 1933, Golyscheff and his wife fled to Barcelona, where he worked as a chemist and began to paint again. At the end of the Spanish Civil War the couple sought refuge in France, where they were eventually interned in labor camps. After the war he worked as a chemical engineer for a French firm, then settled in São Paulo, Brazil, where he worked as a chemist and painted. In 1960–61 he returned to Germany in a vain effort to locate his works in museums and private collections. He reestablished his friendship with Hausmann but left Germany in September 1961 because he feared the outbreak of war upon the erecting of the Berlin Wall. He made great efforts to reestablish himself as an artist through articles and exhibitions in Europe and Brazil. His late paintings exhibit elements of Expressionism and Surrealism.

V.H.

BIBLIOGRAPHY

Adolf Behne, "Werkstattbesuche: II, Jefim Golyscheff," *Der Cicerone* 11, no. 22 (1919): 722–26; Detlef Gojowy, "Jefim Golyscheff: Der unbequeme Vorläufer," *Melos: Neue Zeitschrift für Musik* 1, no. 5 (May–June 1975): 188–93; Joan Ockman, "Reinventing Jefim Golyscheff: Lives of a Minor Modernist," *Assemblage* 11 (April 1990): 71–106.

■ ■ ■

Paul Gösch

BORN 1885 SCHWERIN ✣ DIED 1940 HARTHEIM

40. Untitled (fantasy architecture), c. 1919
Watercolor and india ink
8 1/8 x 13 in. (20.6 x 33.0 cm)
Ungers collection

41. Untitled (fantasy architecture), 1920–29
Gouache over ink
6 7/16 x 8 1/8 in. (16.3 x 20.7 cm)
Collection Centre Canadien d'Architecture/Canadian Centre for Architecture, Montreal

42. Untitled (fantasy architecture), c. 1921
Watercolor, gouache, and gum arabic over graphite
6 7/16 x 8 1/4 in. (16.3 x 20.9 cm)
Collection Centre Canadien d'Architecture/Canadian Centre for Architecture, Montreal

43. Untitled (fantasy architecture), c. 1921
Watercolor, gouache, and glaze over ink
8 1/8 x 12 7/8 in. (20.6 x 32.8 cm)
Collection Centre Canadien d'Architecture/Canadian Centre for Architecture, Montreal

44. Untitled (fantasy architecture), 1921
Watercolor and gouache over ink
8 3/16 x 6 7/16 in. (20.8 x 16.3 cm)
Collection Centre Canadien d'Architecture/Canadian Centre for Architecture, Montreal

45. Untitled (fantasy architecture)
Carbon (dark blue on white tissue paper)
5 11/16 x 4 3/16 in. (14.5 x 10.6 cm)
Wenzel-Hablik-Stiftung, Itzehoe

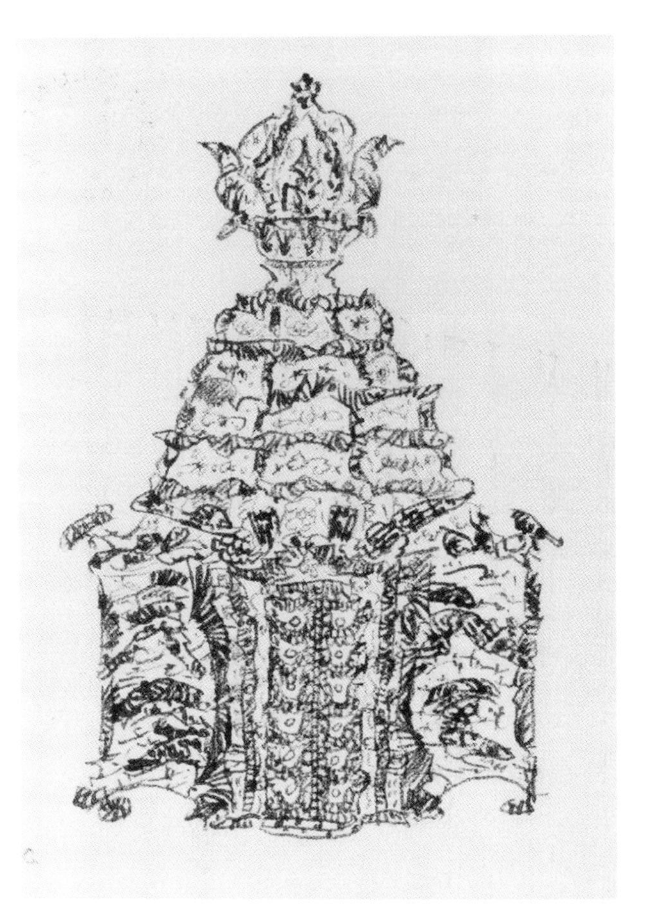

Cat. no. 45

Cat. no. 44

Despite his physical and emotional frailty, Paul Gösch demonstrated a robust determination to create prolifically and to further the utopian causes of the avant-garde of his time. He entered the technical college in Berlin-Charlottenburg in 1903 to pursue architectural studies, associated with the Friedrichshagen writers' colony, and met Sigmund Freud and apparently Rudolf Steiner. Upon completing his studies, he decided against establishing a private practice because of his delicate health and took a position as the city architect of Kulm. He made his first drawings and watercolors between 1914 and 1916.

In 1919 Gösch moved to Berlin-Friedenau, where he became a member of the Gläserne Kette (Crystal chain), using the pseudonym *Tancred*, after the hero of Voltaire's *Tancrède* (1760), and joined the Arbeitsrat für Kunst (Working council for art) and the Novembergruppe (November group), participating in their exhibitions. In 1920 he worked with Bruno Taut in Magdeburg on a restoration project and contributed essays and drawings to the latter's journal, *Frühlicht* (Daybreak).

In 1921 Gösch developed intermittent nervous problems and began several extended periods of treatment in the psychiatric institutes of Göttingen and Teupitz. In 1940 he was seized by SS officers at Teupitz, taken to Hartheim, and murdered. His psychosis had not interfered with his productivity; left behind were hundreds of drawings and watercolors of mythological and religious subjects (particularly depictions of the Madonna), in addition to his fantasy-world columns, pinnacles, and doorways. Gösch, who also wrote and illustrated fairy tales, explored an architectural dreamland with a childlike abandon quite unexpected from a government architect. Insisting that in art contrived principles of organization are tantamount to deception —a conviction shared by other architects of this genre—Gösch declared, "Above all, don't lie!"

V.H.

BIBLIOGRAPHY

Paul Gösch, 1885–1940: Aquarelle und Zeichnungen, exh. cat. (Berlin: Berlinische Galerie, 1976).

Gottfried Graf

BORN 1881 MENGEN, SWABIA ✣ DIED 1938 MENGEN

46. Untitled (standing nude woman), 1918
Woodcut
87/8 x 515/16 in. (22.5 x 15.0 cm)
Frontispiece from the deluxe edition of Das Kunstblatt 2, no. 8 (1918)
Los Angeles County Museum of Art. The Robert Gore Rifkind Center for German Expressionist Studies, purchased with funds provided by Anna Bing Arnold, Museum Acquisition Fund, and deaccession funds

Gottfried Graf was an advocate, practitioner, and teacher of the woodcut medium and an outspoken proponent of modern art in his native Swabia. Inspired by the landscape of the region, which he described in his memoirs as an important factor in his artistic formation, he championed what he termed *Schwäbischer Expressionismus* (Swabian Expressionism). His devotion to the region—he remained in and around Stuttgart throughout his career—was unusual at a time when the cultural centers of Berlin, Dresden, and Munich exerted such a strong pull on young artists.

As a cofounder and member of the artist's association Üechtgruppe from 1919 until its dissolution in 1924, Graf worked to encourage innovative art outside the control of the academy, challenging conservative critics favoring naturalism. His work was strongly influenced by Cubism and French art (Albert Gleizes, for example, was a close lifelong friend) and also bears the imprint of Jugendstil and the Brücke; his ideas about art were characterized by an idealistic, almost mystical belief in the new spirit sweeping art following the *Wende* (change) from naturalism to abstraction and the development of a new artistic language.

A student at the academy and the school of applied arts in Stuttgart during leaves of absence from the Württemburg post office, where he worked until 1913, Graf began to study intensively with Adolf Hölzel, a painter and glass designer, just before the outbreak of World War I. In 1916, during the wartime lull in artistic activity in Stuttgart, he began to experiment with woodcut and to prepare his book *Der neue Holzschnitt und das Problem der künstlerischen Gestaltung* (The new woodcut and the problem of artistic design), published in 1927. He took part in the three Herbstschaue neuer Kunst (Fall shows of new art) in 1919, 1920, and 1924 with the Üechtgruppe. In the introduction to the catalogue of the second of these exhibitions, Graf wrote of the "new life feeling," the "antithesis of dogmatism and rationalism" affecting the culture of the time. The new art, he wrote, "is a new language which has never been spoken before. Its grammar is about to be built and can be learned. But this new language came only out of a new world view.... It is a profound necessity, unwanted, imperative, the destiny of our time" ("Zur zweiten Herbstschau neuer Kunst," unpaginated). In *Der neue Holzschnitt* Graf emphasized the importance of contemporaneity in art and underscored the versatility of the woodcut and its ability to express the "artistic standpoints of the present."

In 1937 Graf's works were removed from museum collections, and he was forced to disavow his earlier work and ideas, writing: "The war and its necessity pushed the mind to the other side, to the supernatural. A new mysticism appeared in religion and philosophy, and even in art, people took refuge in a transcendental idealism" (quoted in Werner P. Heyd, "Gottfried Graf: Zwischen 1905 und 1925," in *Arbeiten auf Papier*, p. 11). He died of lung cancer the following year.

A.S.

BIBLIOGRAPHY

Gottfried Graf, 1881–1938: Arbeiten auf Papier, 1915–1925, exh. cat. (Grafenau: Galerie Schlichtenmaier, 1987); *Gottfried Graf, 1881–1938: Lagerkatalog: Aquarelle, Zeichnungen, Holzschnitte, Lithographien, Radierungen*, exh. cat. (Grafenau: Galerie Schlichtenmaier, 1990); Gottfried Graf, "Zur zweiten Herbstschau neuer Kunst," in *Zweite Herbstschau neuer Kunst*, exh. cat. (Stuttgart: Kunstgebäude Stuttgart, 1920); idem, *Der neue Holzschnitt und das Problem der künstlerischen Gestaltung* (Heilbronn: E. Salzer, 1927); Norbert Hüll, *Gottfried Graf, 1881–1938: Maler und Graphiker, Mitglied des Hölzelkreises* (Sigmaringen: Jan Thorbecke, 1986).

■ ■ ■

Cat. no.46

Walter Gropius

BORN 1883 BERLIN ✣ DIED 1969 BOSTON

47. *Grabdenkmal der Märzgefallenen*, 1923
(Grave monument to the March dead, Weimar)
Lithograph
5 3/8 x 8 5/8 in. (13.7 x 22.0 cm)
Print by Farkas Molnár (1898–1944)
The Resource Collections of the Getty Center for the History of Art and the Humanities

A progressive architect with both functionalist and experimental leanings, Walter Gropius studied at the technical colleges in Munich and Berlin-Charlottenburg, then worked as an assistant in the office of Peter Behrens, where Le Corbusier and Ludwig Mies van der Rohe also worked. Gropius is credited with initiating the development of modern architectural consciousness and mass industrial production. His reputation was established with the Fagus shoe factory (1911) at Alfeld-an-der-Leine, which he designed in collaboration with Adolf Meyer.

In both residential and commercial commissions, Gropius designed to allow the maximum admittance of natural light. His use of the glass curtain wall is best exemplified by the workshops of the Bauhaus building (1926) at Dessau. Also innovative was his insistence on considering the laborer's perspective in the design of working environments. He advocated standardization, prefabrication, dry assembly, and teamwork as means of saving both time and money in construction, although this earned him considerable censure by domestic and international critics of less pragmatic convictions. Despite Gropius's renown as a progressive architect, a relatively classical approach to design characterizes structures in all phases of his career, from the Bauhaus faculty residences of 1925–26 to the American embassy in Athens of 1956.

Gropius formed an alliance with the Expressionists during the period of revolutionary fervor following World War I, when he took a leading role in the Arbeitsrat für Kunst (Working council for art) and Der Ring (The ring). He participated in the Gläserne Kette (Crystal chain) correspondence (under the pseudonym *Mass* [measure or proportion]) and propounded his theme of "the cathedral of the future" in a visionary pamphlet for the *Ausstellung für unbekannte Architekten* (Exhibition of unknown architects). In 1918 he and Bruno Taut produced a manifesto advocating sweeping changes in urban planning. The following year Gropius wrote the Bauhaus manifesto, which expounded the ideals of the Arbeitsrat für Kunst. As founder and director of the Bauhaus, he assembled an outstanding faculty that included Marcel Breuer, Mies van der Rohe, László Moholy-Nagy, and Expressionist artists Lyonel Feininger, Wassily Kandinsky, and Paul Klee. The influence of Expressionism is evident in Gropius's first postwar projects, the Weimar monument (1922) and the Sommerfeld and Otte houses (1921–22) in Berlin. Stylistically these houses had little in common with each other and were much different from anything he later built.

After the Nazis closed the Bauhaus in 1933 and attacked Gropius personally, the architect emigrated, first to England in 1934 and then to the United States in 1937. From 1938 to 1952 he taught at Harvard's Graduate School of Design and served as director of the architecture department. Thereafter he established a private practice and, unlike other German visionary architects of his time, became widely recognized for his achievements during his lifetime, receiving numerous honors, including more than sixty honorary degrees.

V.H.

BIBLIOGRAPHY

Marcel Franciscono, *Walter Gropius and the Creation of the Bauhaus* (Urbana: University of Illinois Press, 1971); Walter Gropius, *Architecture and Design in the Age of Science* (New York: Spiral, 1952); idem, *Scope of Total Architecture*, ed. Ise Gropius (New York: Collier, 1962); idem, *The New Architecture and the Bauhaus*, trans. P. Morton Shand (Cambridge: MIT Press, 1965); Reginald Isaacs, *Gropius: An Illustrated Biography of the Creator of the Bauhaus* (Toronto: Little, Brown, 1991); Hartmut Probst and Christian Schädlich, *Walter Gropius*, 2 vols. (Berlin: Ernst, 1986).

■ ■ ■

George Grosz

BORN 1893 BERLIN ✣ DIED 1959 BERLIN

48. *Mondnacht*, 1915–16
(Moonlit night)
Transfer lithograph
14 11/16 x 11 5/8 in. (37.4 x 29.6 cm)
From the portfolio Erste George Grosz-Mappe (1917)
Los Angeles County Museum of Art. The Robert Gore Rifkind Center for German Expressionist Studies

49. *Vorstadt*, 1915–16
(Suburb)
Transfer lithograph
14 5/8 x 12 3/16 in (37.1 x 31.0 cm)
From the portfolio Erste George Grosz-Mappe (1917)
Los Angeles County Museum of Art. The Robert Gore Rifkind Center for German Expressionist Studies

50. *Erinnerung an New York*, 1915–16
(Memory of New York)
Transfer lithograph
14 7/8 x 11 5/8 in. (37.8 x 29.6 cm)
From the portfolio Erste George Grosz-Mappe (1917)
Los Angeles County Museum of Art. The Robert Gore Rifkind Center for German Expressionist Studies

51. *Strasse*, 1915–16
(Street)
Transfer lithograph
9 3/8 x 6 3/16 in. (23.8 x 15.7 cm)
From the portfolio Kleine Grosz Mappe (1917)
Los Angeles County Museum of Art. The Robert Gore Rifkind Center for German Expressionist Studies

See also cat. no. 79

The self-proclaimed saddest man in Europe, George Grosz transcended his innate pessimism through a profound investigation of human nature. A born draftsman, he developed a linear style with a sharp satirical edge, creating an art that is as ruthless it is refined, at once misanthropic and whimsical.

Born in Berlin, Georg Ehrenfried Gross was raised primarily in the provincial town of Stolp in Pomerania. His interest in art blossomed when the head of a local decorating firm gave him lessons in the elegant linear techniques of Jugendstil. He studied classical drawing at the academy in Dresden in 1909 but was attracted to the popular art and satire of such periodicals as *Simplicissimus*. Soon he was publishing caricatures while consuming pulp novels portraying a demimonde of illicit and often violent relationships between the sexes, later reflected in such favorite Grosz subjects as the *Lustmord* (crime of passion). His fascination with America is seen in his portrayals of New York and the "Wild West" as well as in personas he enacted publicly, such as the prizefighter and the gun-wielding urban cowboy.

Back in Berlin in 1912, Grosz studied intermittently at the school of applied arts until 1916 under Emil Orlik, who was sympathetic to modern art and introduced him to the linear arabesques of Jules Pascin and the sparsely delineated planes of Ferdinand Hodler. During a brief sojourn in Paris in 1913, Grosz learned to sketch fleeting poses at the Atelier Colarossi and used this technique to portray Berlin's bustling streets and café life.

Grosz's development was irreversibly altered by World War I, which brought two medical discharges and treatment for psychological disorders in 1917. During this period he established a close relationship with Wieland Herzfelde and his brother Helmut, who, like Grosz, anglicized his name (to John Heartfield) in opposition to anti-British propaganda. Committed pacifists, the two brothers were becoming involved in publishing and eventually established Malik Verlag. Impressed by Grosz's reeling urban scenes imbued with the dynamism and fragmentation of Italian Futurism, they featured his work in their earliest publications and produced his first portfolios, Erste George Grosz-Mappe (First George Grosz portfolio, 1917) and Kleine Grosz Mappe (Little Grosz portfolio, 1917).

During the political and social upheaval that followed the armistice of 1918, Grosz refined the sparse linear gestures of graffiti and caricature in his mordant observations of human behavior, producing his most politically effective works. They include the portfolios Gott mit uns (God with us, 1920), directed against militarism, and Die Räuber (The robbers, 1922), presenting exploitative capitalists and exploited workers, as well as the books *Das Gesicht der herrschenden Klasse* (The face of the ruling class, 1921) and *Ecce Homo* (1922–23), portraying the dehumanization and moral depravity of bourgeois society. The publication of Hintergrund (Background, 1928), a set of stage designs for Erwin Piscator's production of a play based on Jaroslav Hasek's novel *The Good Soldier Schweik*, like that of Gott mit uns and *Ecce Homo*, resulted in legal proceedings against Grosz and Herzfelde, which served to increase the artist's notoriety and political effectiveness. Nonetheless Grosz remained deeply skeptical of political ideology, placing his faith solely in art as a means of revealing the hypocrisy and injustice he saw around him.

T.B.

BIBLIOGRAPHY

Alexander Dückers, *George Grosz: Das druckgraphische Werk* (Frankfurt: Propyläen, 1979); M. Kay Flavell, *George Grosz: A Biography* (New Haven, Conn.: Yale University Press, 1988); George Grosz, *The Autobiography of George Grosz: Small Yes and a Big No*, trans. Arnold J. Pomerans (London and New York: Allison and Busby, 1982); Hans Hess, *George Grosz* (London: Studio Vista, 1974); Beth Irwin Lewis, *George Grosz: Art and Politics in the Weimar Republic*, rev. ed. (Princeton, N.J.: Princeton University Press, 1991).

■ ■ ■

Wenzel Hablik

BORN 1881 BRUÜX, BOHEMIA (NOW MOST, CZECHOSLOVAKIA) ✣ DIED 1934 ITZEHOE

---

52. *Kristallschloss*, 1903
(Crystal castle)
Watercolor and pencil
$7^{15}/16$ x $5^{15}/16$ in. (20.1 x 15.1 cm)
Wenzel-Hablik-Stiftung, Itzehoe

53. *Der Bau der Luftkolonie*, 1908
(The construction of the air colony)
Pencil
$8^{11}/16$ x $7^{1}/8$ in. (22.0 x 18.1 cm)
Wenzel-Hablik-Stiftung, Itzehoe

54. Untitled, 1909
Etching
$7^{1}/2$ x $7^{1}/2$ in. (19.0 x 19.0 cm)
Plate 1 from the portfolio Schaffende Kräfte (1909)
Wenzel-Hablik-Stiftung, Itzehoe

55. Untitled, 1909
Etching
$7^{5}/8$ x $7^{5}/8$ in. (19.4 x 19.4 cm)
Plate 2 from the portfolio Schaffende Kräfte (1909)
Wenzel-Hablik-Stiftung, Itzehoe

56. Untitled, 1909
Etching
$7^{1}/2$ x $7^{1}/2$ in. (19.0 x 19.0 cm)
Plate 4 from the portfolio Schaffende Kräfte (1909)
Wenzel-Hablik-Stiftung, Itzehoe

57. Untitled, 1909
Etching
$7^{5}/8$ x $7^{5}/8$ in. (19.3 x 19.3 cm)
Plate 7 from the portfolio Schaffende Kräfte (1909)
Wenzel-Hablik-Stiftung, Itzehoe

58. *Original Skizze des Inneren eines Schautempels*, 1914
(Original sketch of the interior of a display temple)
Ink, pencil, and watercolor on board
$19^{5}/8$ x $12^{13}/16$ in. (49.8 x 32.5 cm)
Wenzel-Hablik-Stiftung, Itzehoe

59. *Festbauten: "Triumpf der Gesetze in der Natur!"* 1920
(Festival buildings: "Triumph of the laws of nature!")
Watercolor
$25^{3}/8$ x $19^{3}/8$ in. (64.4 x 49.2 cm)
Wenzel-Hablik-Stiftung, Itzehoe

60. *Hochschulen für Mineralogie im Gebirge*, 1920
(Institutes for mineralogy in the mountains)
Ink and watercolor on parchment
$25^{5}/8$ x $19^{11}/16$ in. (65.0 x 50.0 cm)
Wenzel-Hablik-Stiftung, Itzehoe

61. *Kristalline Schlucht*, c. 1920
(Crystalline chasm)
Graphite
$12^{7}/8$ x $9^{3}/4$ in. (32.6 x 24.8 cm)
Wenzel-Hablik-Stiftung, Itzehoe

62. *Siedlungsanlage einer Familie*, c. 1920
(Family housing plan)
Blueprint (white on blue)
$9^{1}/16$ x 12 in. (23.0 x 30.5 cm)
Wenzel-Hablik-Stiftung, Itzehoe

63. *Siedlung Schwarzwald*, 1920
(Black Forest settlement)
Ink on vellum, glued to board
$22^{5}/8$ x $19^{5}/8$ in. (57.5 x 49.8 cm)
Wenzel-Hablik-Stiftung, Itzehoe

64. *"Ziele" für die Jugend (schwer zu erreichen im Gebirge. Wunder-Bauten)*, 1920
("Goals" for youth [difficult to reach in the mountains. Miracle buildings])
Pencil, colored pencil, and ink on vellum
$16^{3}/8$ x $23^{5}/8$ in. (41.5 x 60.5 cm)
Wenzel-Hablik-Stiftung, Itzehoe

65. *Wohnhaus und Atelier*, 1921
(Residence and studio)
Colored pencil and pencil on cardboard
$25^{5}/8$ x $19^{11}/16$ in. (65.1 x 50.0 cm)
Wenzel-Hablik-Stiftung, Itzehoe

66. *Canonbauten*, 1925
(Canonical buildings)
Etching
$9^{7}/8$ x $7^{11}/16$ in. (25.0 x 19.5 cm)
Plate 4 from the portfolio Cyklus Architektur—Übergangsbauten (1925)
Wenzel-Hablik-Stiftung, Itzehoe

67. *Freitragende Konstruktion*, 1925
(Self-supporting construction)
Etching
$7^{5}/8$ x $9^{3}/4$ in. (19.4 x 24.7 cm)
Plate 11 from the portfolio Cyklus Architektur—Utopie (1925)
Wenzel-Hablik-Stiftung, Itzehoe

68. *Museum im Hochgebirge*, 1925
(Museum in the high mountains)
Etching
$9^{7}/8$ x $7^{11}/16$ in. (25.0 x 19.5 cm)
Plate 15 from the portfolio Cyklus Architektur—Utopie (1925)
Wenzel-Hablik-Stiftung, Itzehoe

69. *Da wohnten Menschen auf kristall'nen Bäumen*, 1925
(There humans lived on crystal trees)
Etching
$11^{1}/4$ x 11 in. (28.5 x 28.0 cm)
Plate 17 from the portfolio Cyklus Architektur—Utopie (1925)
Wenzel-Hablik-Stiftung, Itzehoe

70. *Fliegende Siedlung*, 1925
(Flying settlement)
Etching
$9^{13}/16$ x $7^{1}/2$ in. (24.9 x 19.1 cm)
Plate 19 from the portfolio Cyklus Architektur—Utopie 1925)
Wenzel-Hablik-Stiftung, Itzehoe

71. *Entdecker-Siedlung*, 1925
(Explorers' colony)
Etching
$7^{5}/8$ x $9^{13}/16$ (19.3 x 24.9 cm)
Plate 20 from the portfolio Cyklus Architektur—Utopie (1925)
Wenzel-Hablik-Stiftung, Itzehoe

Wenzel Hablik's occasional boyhood walks through the mountains near Bruüx—and one outing in particular, during which he discovered a fascinating quartz crystal—inspired his lifelong obsession with crystals and other geological formations. His fanciful Schaffende Kräfte (Creative forces, 1909), a portfolio of twenty etchings portraying a voyage through an imaginary universe of crystalline structures, represents the most significant accomplishment of his career. He later made two additional portfolios of etchings: Das Meer (The sea, 1918) and Cyklus Architektur—Utopie (Architectural cycle—utopia, 1925). The former was inspired by his experience of living for a few months in art critic Ferdinand Avenarius's artists' colony on the north Frisian island of Sylt. The latter work is a manifesto and collection of characteristic architectural images: the airborne colony, the exhibition temple, the domed building, and the tower.

Although Hablik is best known for the architectural fantasies he created after 1918—mainly in association with the Arbeitsrat für Kunst (Working council for art) and as W.H. in the Gläserne Kette (Crystal chain) correspondence—he was originally a master cabinetmaker, having studied at the trade school in Teplitz, the school of applied arts in Vienna, and the academy in Prague. After 1907 he settled in Itzehoe, where he and his wife, Lisbeth Lindemann, established the Werkstatt für Handweberei (Atelier for hand weaving) in 1927. The architectural projects that he was able to realize were interior design and redesign schemes in Itzehoe, including the restaurant at the Hotel Central, the town hall, and several private residences.

V.H.

Cat. no. 54

Cat. no. 56

BIBLIOGRAPHY

Ewald Bender, "Radierungen von Wenzel Hablik," *Deutsche Kunst und Dekorution* 26 (1910): 165–70; Axel Feuss, "Zu Wenzel Habliks frühen Architekturphantasien," in *Steinburger Jahrbuch* 1987 31 (1986): 50–67; idem, "Auf dem Weg in die Utopie: Architekturphantasien, Innenräume und Kunsthandwerk von Wenzel Hablik," Ph.D. diss., Universität Hamburg, 1989; *Hablik: Designer, Utopian, Architect, Expressionist, Artist, 1881–1934*, exh. cat. (London: Architectural Association, 1980); Wolfgang Reschke, "Wenzel Hablik: The 'Schaffende Kräfte' Folio and Its Relationship to Expressionist Aims and Ideals," *The Architectural Association Quarterly* 12, no. 3 (1980): 25–38; Heinz Spielmann and Susanne Timm, *Wenzel Hablik* (Schleswig: Schleswig-Holsteinisches Landesmuseum, 1990); Anthony Tischhauser, "Wenzel Hablik: Crystal Utopias," *Architectural Association Quarterly* 12, no. 3 (1980): 18–24; *Wenzel Hablik: Attraverso l'espressionismo / Wenzel Hablik: Expessiomismus und Utopie*, exh. cat. (Florence: Museo Mediceo, Palazzo Medici Riccardi, 1989).

■ ■ ■

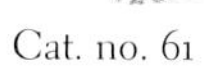

Cat. no. 61

Cat. no. 60

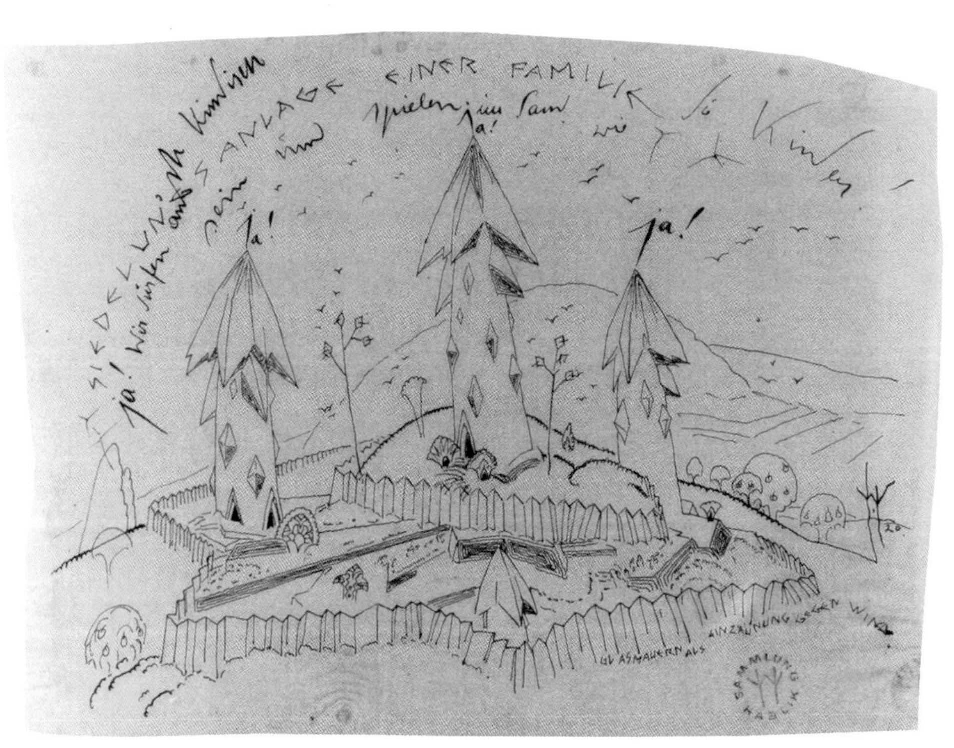

Cat. no. 63

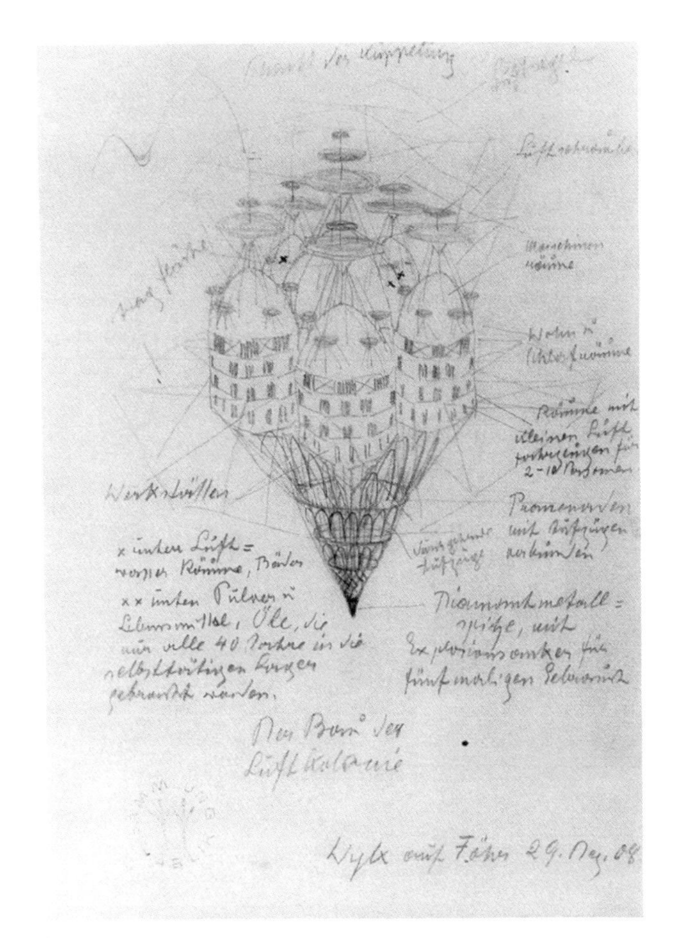

Cat. no. 53

Cat. no. 70

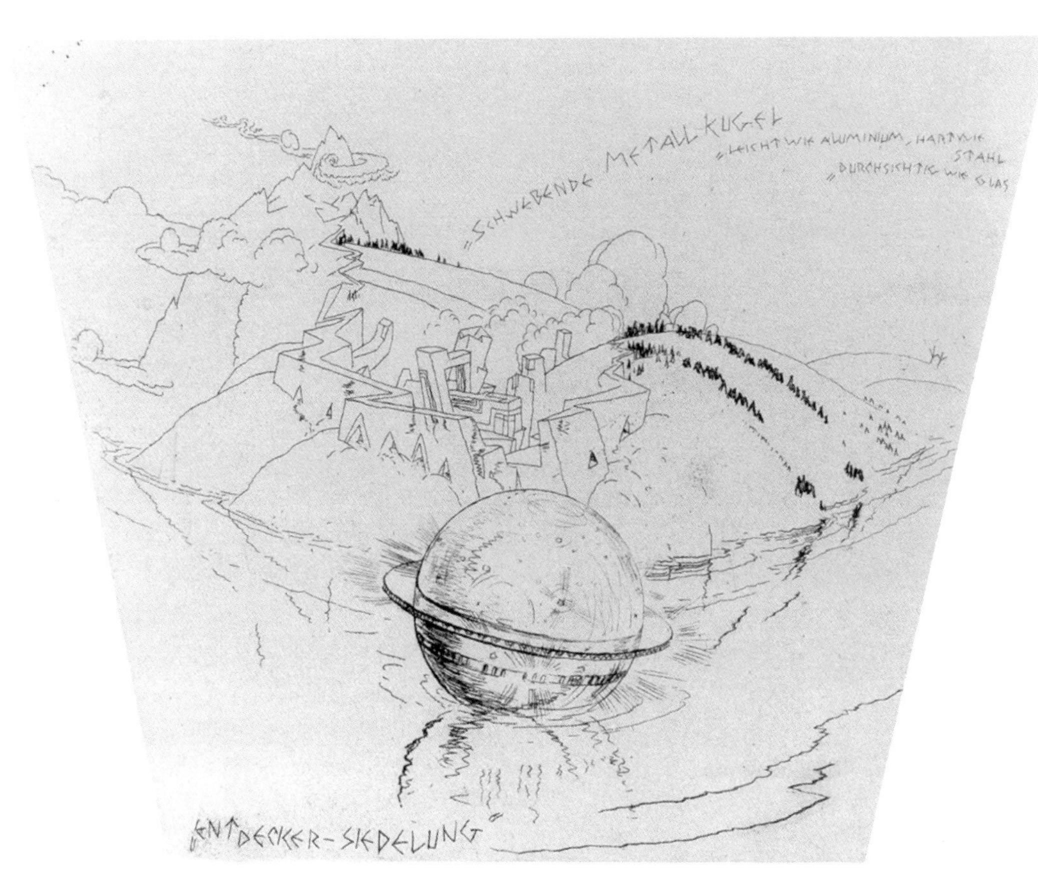

Cat. no. 71

Raoul Hausmann

BORN 1886 VIENNA ✣ DIED 1971 LIMOGES, FRANCE

72. Untitled, c. 1917
Woodcut
5 9/16 x 2 1/2 in. (14.1 x 6.4 cm)
Proof apart from edition published in Raoul Hausmann, *Material der Malerei, Plastik, Architektur* (1918)
Private collection

73. Untitled, 1918
Hand-colored woodcut
12 7/16 x 6 7/8 in. (31.5 x 17.5 cm)
From Raoul Hausmann, *Material der Malerei, Plastik, Architektur* (1918)
Berlinische Galerie, Berlin, Museum für Moderne Kunst, Photographie und Architektur

74. *Abstrakte Bildidee [Andruck aus den "Dadaco")*, 1919
(Abstract picture idea [Dadaco proof])
Offset lithograph
Sheet: 12 5/8 x 9 1/16 in.(32.1 x 23.0 cm)
Berlinische Galerie, Berlin, Museum für Moderne Kunst, Photographie und Architektur

75. *Jelzöállomás*, 1919
Photomechanical reproduction
8 x 8 in. (20.3 x 20.3 cm)
From *MA* 7, no. 5–6 (1922): 5
The Resource Collections of the Getty Center for the History of Art and the Humanities

76. Untitled, 1919
Watercolor
8 3/4 x 5 13/16 in. (22.0 x 14.7 cm)
Proposed cover for Adolf Behne, *Volk, Kunst und Bildung: Eine Flugschrift*
Berlinische Galerie, Berlin, Museum für Moderne Kunst, Photographie und Architektur

77. *Dada Cino*, 1920
Collage
12 1/2 x 8 7/8 in. (31.7 x 22.5 cm)
Private collection

78. *Elasticum*, 1920
Collage
12 3/16 x 14 9/16 in. (31.0x 37.0 cm)
Galerie Berinson, Berlin

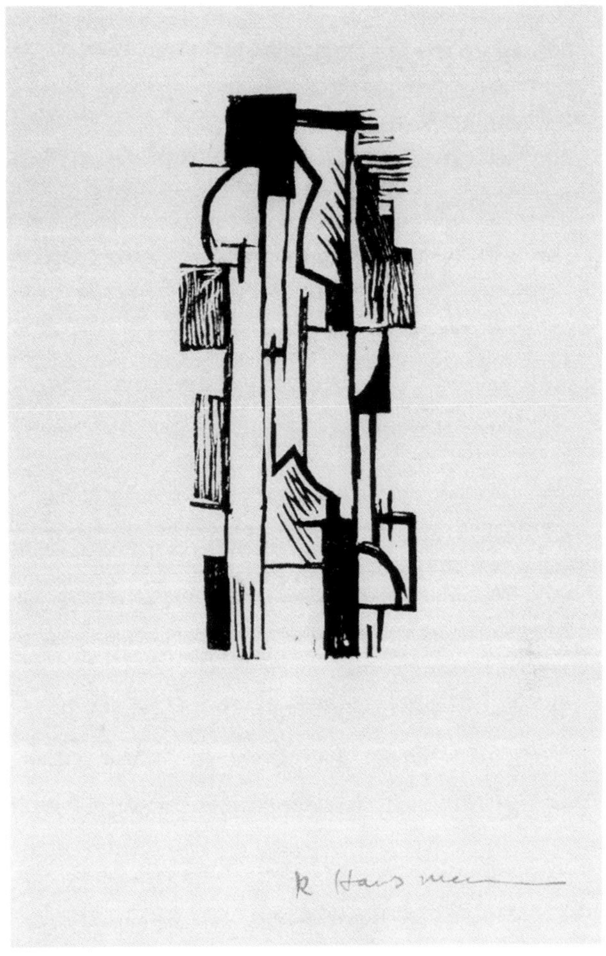

Cat. no. 72

Raoul Hausmann received his early training in the academic tradition from his father, painter Victor Hausmann. In 1900 he moved to Berlin, where he later became a central figure in the Dada movement. His important friendship with the eccentric architect and artist Johannes Baader began in 1905. In the first years of the following decade he was associated with Erich Heckel and Ludwig Meidner, producing numerous Expressionist paintings and woodcuts, several of which were published in his book *Material der Malerei, Plastik, Architektur* (Material of painting, sculpture, architecture, 1918). These works incorporated influences of artists shown at Herwarth Walden's Sturm gallery, including Alexander Archipenko, Robert Delaunay, Sonia Delaunay, Fernand Léger, and Arthur Segal. Around 1915 Hausmann's widening contacts with writers such as Salomo Friedländer and Franz Jung led him to begin publishing his prolific theoretical and satirical writings in *Der Sturm* (The storm), *Die Aktion* (Action), *Die freie Strusse* (Free street), and other avant-garde periodicals. Also in 1915 he met Hannah Höch, who was his companion and collaborator until 1922.

By 1917 Hausmann was associated with George Grosz, John Heartfield, Wieland Herzfelde, and Richard Huelsenbeck, who formed the nucleus of Dada in Berlin during 1918–20. In 1918 Hausmann advocated automatism in his "Manifest von der Gesetzmässigkeit des Lautes" (Manifesto on the lawfulness of sound) and the use of new materials in art in his Dada manifesto *Synthetisches Cino der Malerei* (Synthetic cinema of painting). His innovative art forms included "poster-poems" and "optophonetic" poetry, which presented random sequences of letters as phonetic sounds (for example, "OFFEAHBDC," 1918, and "L'inconnu" [The unknown], 1919); assemblages made of objets trouvés; and photocollages that combined fragments of photographs, typography, woodcuts, and other materials. Although his works were often ironic celebrations of modern technology, mass media, and the world of fashion, his message followed the monist mystical tradition, in which all matter is viewed as inextricably bound with spirit.

Hausmann's architectonic compositions of repeated forms anticipated the functionalist aesthetic of Constructivism, simultaneously retaining the irregularities and coincidences found in nature. Around 1920 he adopted the ambiguous spatial effects of Giorgio de Chirico's metaphysical works, using precise, realistic technical drawing combined with watercolor to extol the engineer and technician.

During the 1920s Hausmann embraced physiology under the influence of neo-Kantian philosopher Jacob Ernst Marcus, proposing biologically based "presentism" as an alternative to technologically inspired Constructivism. His associates at this time included Theo van Doesburg, Viking Eggeling, Werner Graeff, Lajos Kassák, László Moholy-Nagy, Hans Richter, and Kurt Schwitters. By the late 1920s Hausmann was working primarily in photography, and his preoccupation with the fundamental unity of the senses led to the development of the optophone, a device intended to convert light into sound. In 1933 he fled to Ibiza, where he wrote ethnographic studies of indigenous architecture. Eventually settling in Limoges, he resumed painting, produced his first photograms, and created gestural pictograms in drawings, gouaches, and collages. For all its diversity, Hausmann's art was consistently directed toward the attainment of a new language of forms and signs appropriate to the modern psyche.

T.B.

BIBLIOGRAPHY
Timothy O. Benson, *Raoul Hausmann and Berlin Dada* (Ann Arbor, Mich.: UMI Research Press, 1987); Michael Erlhoff, *Raoul Hausmann, Dadasoph: Versuch einer Politisierung der Äkhetik* (Hannover: Zweitschrift, 1982); Michel Giroud, *Raoul Hausmann: "Je ne suis pas un photographe"* (Paris: Chêne, 1975); Raoul Hausmann, *Courrier Dada* (Paris: Terrain Vague, 1958); idem, *Am Anfang war Dada*, ed. Karl Riha and Günter Kämpf, 2d ed. (Giessen: Anabas, 1980); idem, *Texte bis 1933*, ed. Michael Erlhoff, 2 vols. (Munich: Text und Kritik, 1982); Raoul Hausmann, exh. cat., Malmö Konsthalls Katalog no. 67 (Malmö: Konsthall, 1980).

■ ■ ■

Cat. no. 73

Cat. no. 76

John Heartfield

BORN 1891 BERLIN-SCHMARGENDORF ✣ DIED 1968

BERLIN

79. With George Grosz
Leben und Treiben in Universal-City, um 12 Uhr 5 Mittags, c. 1919
(Life and times in universal city at five past noon)
Photomechanical reproduction
13 x 15 11/16 in. (33.0 x 39.9 cm)
Lost collage reproduced on the cover of the exhibition catalogue *Erste internationale Dada-Messe* (1920)
Special Collections Department of the Northwestern University Library

John Heartfield is best known for his mastery of photomontage, a medium that he helped develop as part of the Berlin Dada movement during the 1910s and that he used as a vehicle for biting political satire over the subsequent two decades. Born Helmut Herzfelde, he was the son of a socialist poet father (who wrote under the pseudonym Franz Held) and a textile worker mother. Orphaned in 1898, he and his younger brother, Wieland, were raised by a foster family in Austria. After a brief stint as an apprentice in a relative's bookstore in Wiesbaden in 1905, Heartfield began to pursue his interest in art. He studied privately with Hermann Bouffier, then attended the state school of applied arts in Munich (1908–11) before moving to Berlin, where he attended the school of applied arts from 1912 until the outbreak of war in 1914.

After a brief military career that ended in early 1915, when he feigned insanity in order to receive a discharge, Heartfield returned to Berlin, where he met George Grosz, with whom he began making collaged postcards (purportedly designed for mailing to the front). By 1916 both artists had anglicized their names in protest against German war propaganda, and when Wieland Herzfelde departed for the front that year, they took over his little magazine, *Die neue Jugend* (New youth), which was soon banned on account of its subversive content. This prompted the two brothers in 1917 to found Malik Verlag, an activist publishing house in which Grosz became a principal participant, creating his portfolios Erste George Grosz-Mappe (First George Grosz portfolio, 1917) and Kleine Grosz Mappe (Little Grosz portfolio, 1917). At about this time Heartfield worked as a film director and designer, creating special effects for (intentionally unfinished) government propaganda films. Also in 1917 he began a long career as a designer of book covers, producing numerous covers for Malik Verlag publications by Upton Sinclair and other popular socialist writers in the 1920s.

In 1918 Heartfield joined the radical Spartacist League and the Communist party, editing its satirical periodical *Der rote Knüppel* (The red cudgel) and contributing photomontages to its ideological organ *Die rote Fahne* (The red flag). In 1919 he was the first to publish a Dada photomontage (on the cover of the periodical *Jedermann sein eigner Fussball* [Everyone his own football]). Proclaiming himself the "Dadamonteur" (or Dada assembler), he created photomontages for Dada publications, including the periodical *Der Dada*, which he edited with Grosz and Raoul Hausmann. Together with Grosz, Heartfield created the photocollage *Leben und Treiben in Universal-City, um 12 Uhr 5 Mittags* (Life and times in universal city at five past noon, c. 1919), which was reproduced on the cover of the 1920 *Erste internationale Dada-Messe* (First international Dada fair) exhibition catalogue, as well as many other photocollages, which the two artists signed "Grosz-Heartfield Concern" as a protest against elitism and the cult of artistic genius.

During the 1920s and 1930s Heartfield became more conservative artistically while maintaining his radical communist philosophy, which he expounded in innumerable photomontages directed toward the working class and in his 1929 book written in collaboration with dramatist Kurt Tucholsky, *Deutschland, Deutschland über alles* (Germany, Germany above all). His most widely known photomontages appeared in the 1930s on the covers of *AIZ* (*Arbeiter-illustrierten Zeitung* [Workers' illustrated newspaper]), which was based first in Berlin, then in Prague, to which Heartfield immigrated in 1933. In 1938 he fled to England, where he was interned in 1940. In 1950 he returned to East Germany, where he designed stage sets and later produced photocollages protesting the Vietnam War.

T.B.

BIBLIOGRAPHY

David Evans, John Heartfield, *AIZ: Arbeiter-illustrierte Zeitung, Volks illustrierte*, 1930-38, ed. Anna Lundgren (New York: Kent, 1992); John Heartfield, *Der Schnitt entlang der Zeit: Selbstzeugnisse, Erinnerungen, Interpretationen: Eine Dokumentation*, ed. Roland März (Dresden: VEB Verlag der Kunst, 1981); idem, *John Heartfield: Leben und Werk*, ed. Wieland Herzfelde (Dresden: VEB Verlag der Kunst, 1976); Douglas Kahn, *John Heartfield: Art and Mass Media* (New York: Tanam Press, 1985); Peter Pachnicke and Klaus Honnef, eds., *John Heartfield*, exh. cat. (New York: Harry N. Abrams, 1992); Eckhard Siepmann, *Montage, John Heartfield: Vom Club Dada zur Arbeiter-illustrierten Zeitung: Dokumente, Analysen, Berichte*, 7. Aufl., 2. Aufl. der gekützen Sonderausg. (Berlin: Elefanten, 1988).

■ ■ ■

Erich Heckel

BORN 1883 DÖBELN ✣ DIED 1970 RADOLFZELL

(LAKE CONSTANCE)

80. *Stehendes Kind*, 1910
(Standing child)
Color woodcut
14 3/4 x 10 13/16 in. (37.5 x 27.4 cm)
From the portfolio *Brücke VI* (1911)
Los Angeles County Museum of Art. The Robert Gore Rifkind Center for German Expressionist Studies

81. *Szene im Wald*, 1910
(Scene in the woods)
Lithograph
11 x 13 3/4 in. (28.0 x 34.9 cm)
From the portfolio *Brücke VI* (1911)
Los Angeles County Museum of Art. The Robert Gore Rifkind Center for German Expressionist Studies

82. *Badende am Teich*, 1912
(Bathers at the pond)
Woodcut
5 3/16 x 4 5/16 in. (13.1 x 11.0 cm)
From the exhibition catalogue *Ausstellung van Künstlergruppe Brücke* (1912)
Los Angeles County Museum of Art. The Robert Gore Rifkind Center for German Expressionist Studies

83. *Ballspielende*, 1912
(Ball players)
Woodcut
7 5/8 x 10 3/4 in. (19.3 x 27.3 cm)
Granvil and Marcia Specks collection

84. *Kniende am Stein*, 1913
(Woman kneeling near a rock)
Woodcut
19 3/4 x 12 3/4 in. (50.2 x 32.3 cm)
Granvil and Marcia Specks collection

85. *Parksee*, 1914
(Lake in a park)
Drypoint
9 3/4 x 7 13/16 in. (24.8 x 19.9 cm)
Granvil and Marcia Specks collection

86. *Sonnenaufgang*, 1914
(Sunrise)
Woodcut
9 7/8 x 12 11/16 in. (25.2 x 32.3 cm)
Los Angeles County Museum of Art. Gift of Dr. Ernest Schwarz

87. *Zwei am Meer*, 1920
(Two by the sea)
Woodcut
7 x 5 5/16 in. (17. 8 x 13.5 cm)
From the deluxe edition of Paul Westheim, *Das Holzschnittbuch* (1921)
Los Angeles County Museum of Art. The Robert Gore Rifkind Center for German Expressionist Studies, purchased with funds provided by Anna Bing Arnold, Museum Acquisition Fund, and deaccession funds

Cat. no. 87

Like his Brücke (Bridge) colleagues Otto Mueller, Ernst Ludwig Kirchner, and Karl Schmidt-Rottluff, Erich Heckel was fascinated by the nude as a symbol of nature. His aspiration to endow his works with monumental content, expressing the essence of what he depicted and not simply his feelings, may have stemmed from his early passion for literature. The writings of Friedrich Nietzsche and Fyodor Dostoyevski in particular absorbed him from his high school days onward. Kirchner called Heckel "the most intense one of us," and he was perhaps also the least theoretically inclined Brücke member. In 1914 he wrote: "The formulation of a program is...better left to those who will come later, who work theoretically and scientifically, not creatively. The unknown, as well as the unwanted, is the source of artistic power" ("Das neue Programm," *Kunst und Künstler* 12 [March 1914]: 309).

Heckel's family was solidly middle class. His father was a railway engineer, and his family moved frequently during his youth. A student at the vocational high school in Chemnitz, Heckel met Karl Schmidt (later Schmidt-Rottluff) in 1901 while the latter was attending the more prestigious humanistic high school, and together they participated in a literary debating society.

After leaving Chemnitz in 1904 to study architecture at the technical college in Dresden, Heckel met Kirchner and the following year formed the Brücke with Kirchner, Fritz Bleyl, and Schmidt-Rottluff. Heckel assumed the role of manager of the group, arranging for the four to work in his studio, a refurbished butcher's shop, until 1906, when he found a more conventional space. It was also largely due to his influence that Max Pechstein joined the group in 1906. Unlike the other Brücke artists, who devoted themselves entirely to personal artistic pursuits, Heckel continued his involvement with architecture, working as an assistant in the office of the architect Wilhelm Kreis until 1907. With the aid of Heckel's acquaintance Karl Ernst Osthaus, the Brücke was able to participate in the 1910 Sonderbund exhibition in Düsseldorf. Two years later the group participated in the Sonderbund's international exhibition, for which Heckel and Kirchner painted part of the exhibition space.

With the outbreak of World War I in 1914, Heckel volunteered for service in the Red Cross. He spent most of the war in Flanders, continuing to paint and draw (although with limited supplies necessitated by the war). In 1922 he undertook a monumental project lasting nearly two years, which he titled *Stufen des Daseins* (Steps of consciousness), painting the walls and ceiling of a medieval house in the town of Erfurt. During the remainder of the 1920s, he traveled throughout Europe with his wife, Siddi, concentrating on the depiction of landscape. Like his Brücke colleagues, Heckel was forbidden to work by the National Socialists and was represented in the *Entartete Kunst* (Degenerate art) exhibition in Munich in 1937. After the war he accepted a position at the academy in Karlsruhe and continued to travel.

A.S.

BIBLIOGRAPHY
Annemarie Dube and Wolf-Dieter Dube, *Erich Heckel: Das Graphische Werk*, 3 vols. (New York: E. Rathenau, 1974); Karlheinz Gabler, ed., *Erich Heckel und sein Kreis: Dokumente, Fotos, Briefe, Schriften* (Stuttgart: Belser, 1983); idem, *Erich Heckel: Zeichnungen, Aquarelle*, exh. cat. (Stuttgart: Belser, 1984); *Prints by Erich Heckel and Karl Schmidt-Rottluff: A Centenary Celebration*, exh. cat. (Los Angeles: Los Angeles County Museum of Art, 1985); Magdalena M. Moeller, *Erich Heckel: Aquarelle, Zeichnungen, Druckgraphik aus dem Brücke-Museum Berlin* (Berlin: Brücke-Museum, 1991); Paul Vogt, *Erich Heckel* (Recklinghausen: Aurel Bongers, 1965).

■ ■ ■

Hannah Höch

BORN 1889 GOTHA ✣ DIED 1978 BERLIN

88. *Mechanischer Garten*, 1920
(Mechanical garden)
Watercolor 28¾ x 18½ in. (73.0 x 47.0 cm)
H. Marc Moyens, Alexandria, Virginia

89. *Hochfinanz*, 1923
(High finance)
Collage
14³⁄₁₆ x 12³⁄₁₆ in. (36.0 x 31.0 cm)
Galerie Berinson, Berlin

90. *Kabarett Bühne I*, 1924–25
(Cabaret stage I)
Watercolor
13¾ x 19⁹⁄₁₆ in. (35.0 x 49.7 cm)
Berlinische Galerie, Berlin, Museum für Moderne Kunst, Photographie und Architektur

91. *Raum für ein Kabarett*, 1924–25
(Room for a cabaret)
Woodcut with watercolor and collage
7⁹⁄₁₆ x 11⁷⁄₁₆ in. (19.2 x 29.0 cm)
Berlinische Galerie, Berlin, Museum für Moderne Kunst, Photographie und Architektur

Affiliated with the rambunctious Berlin Dadaists, the circle around Kurt Schwitters in Hannover, and later the Dutch De Stijl group, Hannah Höch developed a collage style that bears the imprint of Dadaism yet differs markedly in technique and subject matter from the work of other artists associated with the movement. In her collages she explored the roles and representation of women, notably during the Weimar era.

In 1912 Höch began her studies at the school of applied arts in Berlin. She studied painting with Emil Orlik in 1915. In that year she also became acquainted with Raoul Hausmann. They soon formed an intimate friendship and lived together until 1922. In 1916 Höch began to experiment with new art forms, creating her first abstract collages and making dolls. She later ventured into photomontage, a technique she developed in collaboration with Hausmann in 1918. Her encounter with Schwitters at the Sturm gallery in 1918 led to a lifelong friendship. They later collaborated on Dada performances, and Höch contributed to his first *Merzbau* assemblage in Hannover in 1922.

In 1919 Höch participated in the first Dada exhibition at I. B. Neumann's Graphisches Kabinett. She contributed to the journal *Der Dada* and regularly exhibited with the Novembergruppe (November group). In 1920 she participated in the *Erste internationale Dada-Messe* (First international Dada fair) in Berlin. As the Berlin Dada movement began to wane in 1921, she went with Hausmann and Schwitters to Prague, where they gave "anti-Dada" and Merz performances.

During Höch's first stay in Paris, in 1924 she had been introduced to Piet Mondrian. Their acquaintance was renewed during her second sojourn there, and this led to contacts with the other members of the De Stijl group. Höch lived in the Netherlands from 1926 to 1929. There she met the Dutch writer Til Brugman, with whom she returned to Berlin in 1929. Several of her photomontages were included in the 1929 exhibition *Film und Foto* (Film and photography) in Stuttgart, organized by the Werkbund. Her work began to be shown internationally, but the National Socialists' rise to power forced her into seclusion. She was one of the first so-called degenerate artists to exhibit after the war.

F.V.H.

BIBLIOGRAPHY
Götz Adriani, *Hannah Höch: Fotomontagen, Gemälde, Aquarelle* (Cologne: DuMont, 1980); Maud Lavin, *Cut with the Kitchen Knife: The Weimar Photomontages of Hannah Höch* (New Haven, Conn.: Yale University Press, 1993); Elisabeth Moortgat and Cornelia Thater-Schulz, *Hannah Höch, 1889–1978: Ihr Werk, ihr Leben, ihre Freunde*, exh. cat. (Berlin: Berlinische Galerie, 1989); Cornelia Thater-Schulz, ed., *Hannah Höch: Eine Lebenscollage*, 2 vols. (Berlin: Argon, 1989).

■ ■ ■

Vlastislav Hofman

BORN 1884 JIČIN, BOHEMIA ✣ DIED 1964 PRAGUE

92. *Projekt eines Friedhofs bei Prag*, 1912
(Project for a cemetery near Prague)
Linocut with printed text on verso
9⁵/8 x 12¹⁵/16 in. (24.4 x 32.9 cm)
Proof apart from edition published in *Der Sturm* 5, no. 3 (1914): 21
Collection Centre Canadien d'Architecture/Canadian Centre for Architecture, Montreal

Known primarily as a Cubist architect, Vlastislav Hofman also produced outstanding work in the areas of stage design, painting, and graphics and wrote extensively on political themes and the philosophy of art. From 1902 to 1907 he studied architecture in Prague. He was self-taught as a visual artist. In 1911–12 he cofounded Skupina vytvarych umelcu (Avant-garde artists' group) in Prague. He was also a member of the Manes art union and of the Tvrdsijny (Stubborn) group and wrote for the social democratic journal *Provo lidu* (Human rights). He was represented in the 1914 Cubist exhibition in Prague.

Hofman's linoleum cuts were published in *Der Sturm* (The storm) in 1914 and 1928, and from about 1918 he submitted drawings to *Die Aktion* (Action). Outstanding among his graphic works is his portfolio Das Hochzeitshemd (The wedding shirt). He also produced numerous stage designs, particularly for the Vinohrader theater in Prague.

V.H.

BIBLIOGRAPHY
Douglas Cooper, *The Cubist Epoch* (London: Phaidon Press in association with the Los Angeles County Museum of Art and the Metropolitan Museum of Art, New York, 1970).

■ ■ ■

Karl Hubbuch

BORN 1891 KARLSRUHE ✣ DIED 1979 KARLSRUHE

93. *Probe im Grossen Schauspielhaus*, 1922
(Rehearsal in the Grosses Schauspielhaus)
Drypoint
5⁵/8 x 7¹/2 in. (14.3 x 19.0 cm)
Berlinische Galerie, Berlin, Museum für Moderne Kunst, Photographie und Architektur

Karl Hubbuch was a tireless observer of the metropolis and its inhabitants. Recording the social inequity and squalor of life in Berlin in a style akin to that of George Grosz and Otto Dix, he focused on the life of the street, with its crime, violence, and greed. Hubbuch often chronicled the way the city's architectural and public spaces affected the people living there. Although he was born in Karlsruhe and spent most of his life there—he was a professor at the Karlsruhe academy from 1925 until 1933 and again from 1948 until 1957—his frequent trips to Berlin and Paris helped form his vision of the city as a place of entrapment and confusion. He often portrayed the metropolis as a corrupting force, one that warped relations between individuals, turning business into exploitation and profiteering; turning romance into rape, crimes of passion, and prostitution; and turning ordinary citizens into voyeurs. In one of his many chalk drawings, for example, a woman squints along a deserted train platform near an enormous sign reading *Kein Ausweg* (no exit), while curious eyes peer out at her from high apartment building windows in the background.

Trained at the Karlsruhe academy and subsequently at the school of the Kunstgewerbemuseum in Berlin from 1912 until he was drafted in 1914, Hubbuch was a schoolmate of fellow Neue Sachlichkeit (new objectivity) artists Grosz, Georg Scholz, and Rudolf Schlichter. The latter described Hubbuch as reserved, noting that he seldom associated with his fellow students but that his work astounded them with its "mysterious, empty rooms, in which ghostlike furniture stood or horrifying instruments were lying around, crushed beds, which looked more like the teleplasm of spiritual apparitions than like real human dwellings...bleak big-city alley buildings, facades with repugnant ornamentation and gaping black window holes.... The very sober precision of his strokes intensified the effect to that of gruesome fantasy" (quoted in *Karl Hubbuch zum 100. Geburtstag*, pp. 87–88).

Removed from his professorship and forbidden to work by the National Socialists in 1933, Hubbuch took various jobs until the end of the war. After 1945 he once again took up political caricature and portraits of the city, such as his 1970 series of drawings of Paris, entitled Die Hauptstadt (The capital).

A.S.

BIBLIOGRAPHY

Wolfgang Hartmann, *Karl Hubbuch: Der Zeichner*, exh. cat. (Hannover: Wilhelm Busch Museum, 1991); *Karl Hubbuch, 1891–1979: Germälde, Zeichnungen, Druckgraphik: Gedächtnisausstellung zum 100. Geburtstag*, exh. cat. (Grafenau: Galerie Schlichtenmaier, 1991); *Karl Hubbuch zum 100. Geburtstag*, exh. cat. (Munich: Galerie Michael Hasenclever, 1991); Hans Kinkel, *Der frühe Hubbuch: Zeichnungen und Druckgraphik, 1911 bis 1925*, exh. cat. (Bremen: Kunsthalle Bremen, 1973); Diether Schmidt, *Karl Hubbuch*, exh. cat. (Milan: Galleria del Levante, 1976); Michael Schwarz and Beatrice Vierneisel, eds., *Karl Hubbuch, 1891–1979*, exh. cat. (Karlsruhe: Badischer Kunstverein, 1981).

■ ■ ■

Johannes Itten

BORN 1888 SÜDEREN-LINDEN, SWITZERLAND ✣ DIED 1967 ZURICH

94. *Rhythmen*, 1916
(Rhythms)
Pencil
9½ x 7⅝ in. (24.1 x 19.4 cm)
Kuntsmuseum Bern, Johannes Itten-Stiftung, Bern, Schenkung von Anneliesse Itten, Zurich

95. *Der Turm*, 1917
(The tower)
Watercolor
10⅛ x 7¼ in. (25.7 x 18.5 cm)
Private collection

96. *Komposition*, 1919
(Composition)
Lithograph
23⅝ x 17¾ in. (60.0 x 45.0 cm)
Plate 8 from the portfolio Johannes Itten: 10 Original-Lithographien (1919)
Kunstmuseum Bern, Johannes Itten-Stiftung, Bern, Schenkung von Anneliesse Itten, Zurich

97. *Analysen alter Meister*, 1921
(Analyses of old masters)
Offset lithograph
13¹⁄₁₆ x 9¾ in. (33.2 x 24.8 cm)
From Bruno Adler, ed., *Utopia: Dokumente der Wirklichkeit* (1921)
(see also cat. no. 190)
The Resource Collections of the Getty Center for the History of Art and the Humanities

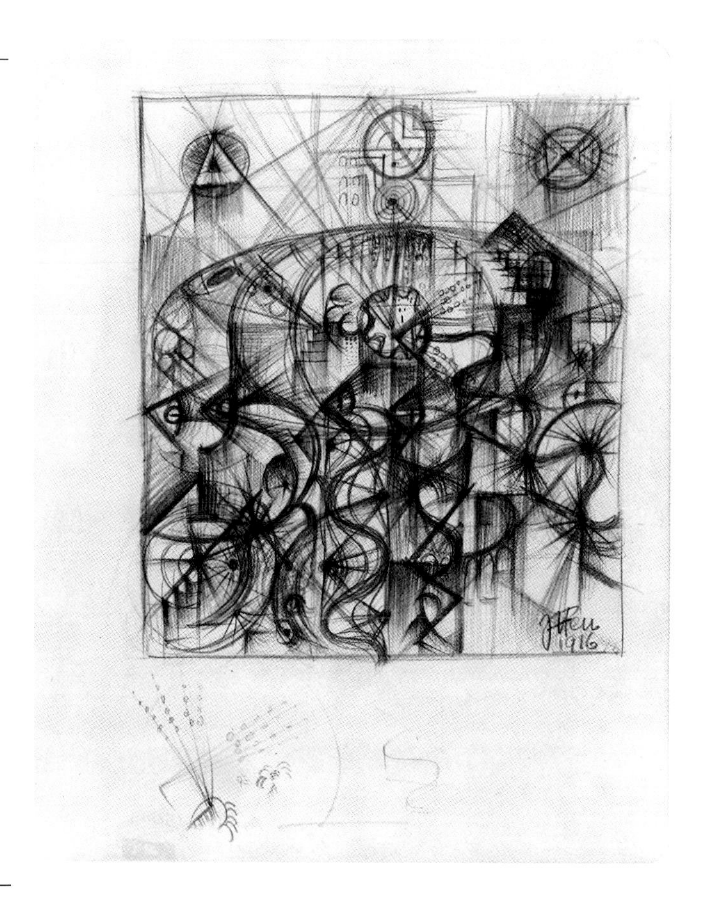

Cat. no. 94

Johannes Itten's introspective, philosophical temperament shaped the Bauhaus in its early years in Weimar. He was an odd figure, with his funnel-shaped monk's costume, his shaved head, and an interest in Eastern religion bordering on obsession. He was idolized by students and reviled by critics for his unconventional teaching methods, which included breathing exercises and physical acting out of shapes such as squares and circles. Yet he contributed much of lasting value not only to the Bauhaus but also to the discipline of art instruction itself.

In 1904 Itten entered the teacher training college for the canton of Bern in Hofwil, where his teachers included Hans Klee, Paul Klee's father, who encouraged his interest in piano, and the drawing teacher Emil Prochaska, who invited Itten to pursue his interest in visual art. After two years he moved to Bern, where he continued his studies and, in 1908, found work as a primary school teacher. During this period he began to develop his teaching methods. He encouraged students to derive emotional inspiration from artists of earlier eras, with the aim of "freeing and deepening [their] expressive ability" (*Design and Form*, p. 147).

In 1909 Itten decided to become an artist and enrolled in the school of fine arts in Geneva. The education he received there was disappointingly traditional, however, and in 1910 he signed up for a secondary-school teacher preparation program at the university in Bern. After his graduation in 1912 he had his first opportunity to travel to Europe's art capitals. Impressed by the work of Wassily Kandinsky and the pioneering styles of the Impressionists, Postimpressionists, and Cubists, Itten decided to continue his art studies in Geneva for another semester.

Back in Bern in 1913, Itten saw an exhibition of work by the painter Adolf Hölzel, which so deeply impressed him that he decided to undertake the journey to Hölzel's studio in Stuttgart on foot. Hölzel refused to accept him as a student, and Itten was sent to study with one of his students, although he was able to attend Hölzel's lectures. In 1916 the prominent art dealer Herwarth Walden exhibited fifty-seven of Itten's works at the Sturm gallery in Berlin, where he met Georg Muche, a future Bauhaus colleague. Later that year Itten moved to Vienna, where he resumed teaching and came into contact with Gustav Klimt, Oskar Kokoschka, Adolf Loos, Arnold Schoenberg, and Alma Mahler-Gropius, whose husband, Walter Gropius, would invite him to be one of the first teachers at the Bauhaus in 1919.

As the leader of the six-month basic course at the Bauhaus, Itten set goals that would remain in place even after his departure from the school: to free the students' creative powers, to introduce them to various art materials, and to convey the fundamental principles of design. His interest in Eastern religion, however, led him to adopt a persona increasingly resembling

Cat. no. 95

Cat. no. 96

that of a cult leader. His followers were induced to fast, torture themselves, and dress in a cloak of his design. Itten's enormous influence on the students—he not only ran the basic course but oversaw the sculpture, glass, painting, and metal workshops as well—and his dreamy notions, such as those expressed in his 1921 book *Utopia: Dokumente der Wirklichkeit* (Utopia: Documents of reality), made Gropius uneasy. The inevitable conflict between the two led to Itten's resignation in March 1923. Of his years at the Bauhaus, he wrote: "If new ideas are to take the shape of art, it is necessary to prepare and coordinate physical, sensual, spiritual, and intellectual forces and abilities. This insight largely determined the subject and method of my Bauhaus teaching. The task was to build the whole man as a creative being" (*Design and Form*, pp. 10–11).

After leaving the Bauhaus, Itten taught at the Moderne Kunstschule (modern art school), which he founded in Berlin in 1926 (and which was closed by the Nazis in 1934), and at the institute for textile design in Krefeld from 1932 to 1938, when he was fired by the Nazis. He fled to Amsterdam, where he continued to teach. After the war he settled in Zurich, where he was active as an artist and teacher.

A.S.

BIBLIOGRAPHY

Marion Agthe, ed., *Johannes Itten: Zwischen Expression und Konstruktion: Tuschen, Aquarelle und Gemälde der fünfziger Jahre*, exh. cat. (Essen: Galerie Neher, 1989); Josef Helfenstein and Henriette Mentha, eds., *Johannes Itten: Das Frühwerk 1907–1919: Mit dem überarbeiteten und ergänzten Werkverzeichnis 1907 bis 1919*, exh. cat. (Bern: Kunstmuseum, 1992); *Johannes Itten, Design and Form: The Basic Course at the Bauhaus*, trans. John Maass (New York: Reinhold Publishing, 1964); idem, *Tagebücher: Stuttgart, 1913–1916; Wien, 1916–1919*, 2 vols., ed. Eva Badura-Triska (Vienna: Löcker, 1990); idem, *Utopia: Dokumente der Wirklickkeit I/II*, ed. Bruno Adler (Weimar: Utopia, 1921); Willy Rotzler, ed., *Johannes Itten: Werke und Schriften* (Zurich: Orell Füssli, 1971); Hans Christoph von Tavel and Josef Helfenstein, eds., *Johannes Itten: Künstler und Lehrer*, exh. cat. (Bern: Kunstmuseum, 1984).

■ ■ ■

Franz Maria Jansen

BORN 1885 COLOGNE ✣ DIED 1958 BÜCHEL

98. Untitled (frontispiece), 1921
Etching, drypoint
$9^{11}/_{16}$ x $13^{3}/_{4}$ in. (24.5 x 34.9 cm)
From the portfolio Industrie 1920 (1921)
Los Angeles County Museum of Art. The Robert Gore Rifkind Center for German Expressionist Studies, purchased with funds provided by Anna Bing Arnold, Museum Acquisition Fund, and deaccession funds

99. Untitled (workers arriving), 1921
Etching, drypoint
$10^{1}/_{8}$ x $7^{11}/_{16}$ in. (25.7 x 19.6 cm)
From the portfolio Industrie 1920 (1921)
Los Angeles County Museum of Art. The Robert Gore Rifkind Center for German Expressionist Studies, purchased with funds provided by Anna Bing Arnold, Museum Acquisition Fund, and deaccession funds

Cat. no. 98

Franz Maria Jansen's work demonstrates the conflicting attractions exerted on artists in the early decades of the century by the unspoiled, ideialized landscape and by its antithesis, industrialized society, with its despoiled cities and wars. While many of his series of woodcuts and lithographs, such as Industrie 1920 (Industry 1920, 1921), Die Grossstadt (The metropolis, 1920-21), and Der Krieg (War, 1916-18), reveal a horrified fascination with the darker aspects of modern life, he also maintained his early interest in peaceful, almost idyllic landscapes of his native Rhineland, depicting them in paintings as well as series of lithogrtaphs such as Die Ernte (The Harvest, 1914) and Der Rhein (The Rhine, 1925).

Like the founding members of the Brücke (Bridge), Jansen studied architecture before turning to painting and the graphic arts, in which he was self-taught. He ascribed his decision to becoming an artist to his travel to Hungary, Italy, and the Balkans; he later wrote, "In the fantastic exuberance of the color in Dalmatia, in the bacchanalian color contrasts, the transition took place" ("Selbstbiographie," p. 197). In 1911 he helped found the short-lived Gereonsklub (Gereon club) and the Cologne Secession, both of which were exhibiting societies devoted to the promotion of the avant-garde in the Rhineland, which until then had played a minor role in the German art scene. Through the influence of August Macke, who joined the Gereonsklub in 1912, the group was able to exhibit paintings by the Brücke artists, whose landscapes and figures doubtless made an impression on Jansen.

Jansen's prewar works consisted primarily of landscapes. Some of them were shown in the 1913 Bonn exhibition *Die rheinischen Expressionisten* (Rhenish Expressionists), in which other artists working in a similar vein, such as Heinrich Campendonk and the group's leader, Macke, also participated. From 1912 Jansen exhibited yearly with the Berlin Secession and contributed to Franz Pfemfert's liberal journal *Die Aktion* (Action), which helped further his interest in socially critical art. Jansen expressed his commitment to and belief in the social power of art in a manifesto of 1918 entitled "Über den Expressionismus" (On Expressionism), which was published in the Bonn newspaper *Volksmund.* He rejected the formal school of Expressionism he described as "closely tied to five o'clock tea, the cult of the aesthetic, Poiret-ladies, astute debates" in favor of the school concerned with content. "We give up being called artists," he wrote. "We want instead to be humans, brothers, those aware of their responsibilities, with a total devotion to life" (reprinted *Ausgewählte Werke*, p. 4). This conviction is reflected both in his graphic images of urban alienation and in works that capture the regenerative, almost magical quality of the landscape. In his autobiography he wrote, "In painting there lies the liberating discovery that the Rhinelander has a landscape [that is] set free from the world" ("Selbstbiographie," p. 197). This faith in art inspired him to continue painting until his death in 1958.

A.S.

BIBLIOGRAPHY

Franz M. Jansen (1885–1958): Ausgewählte Werke, exh. cat. (Düsseldorf: Galerie Remmert und Barth, 1983); Carl A. Haenlein, ed., *August Macke und die rheinischen Expressionisten aus dem Städtischen Kunstmuseum Bonn*, exh. cat. (Hannover: Kestner-Gesellschaft, 1978); Franz Maria Jansen, "Selbstbiographie" and "Von damals bis Heute," reprinted in *Die rheinischen Expressionisten: August Macke und seine Malerfreunde*, exh. cat., ed. Aurel Bongers, Dierk Stemmler, and Joachim Heusinger von Waldegg (Recklinghausen: Aurel Bongers, 1979), pp. 196–99; *Unbekannte Zeichnungen des rheinischen Expressionismus aus der Sammlung des Museums Schloss Moyland*, exh. cat. (Bonn: Verein August Macke Haus, 1992).

■ ■ ■

Wassily Kandinsky

BORN 1866 MOSCOW ✣ DIED 1944 NEUILLY-SUR-SEINE, FRANCE

100. *Orientalisches*, 1911
(Oriental)
Color woodcut
4⅞ x 7½ (12.4 x 19.0 cm)
From Wassily Kandinsky, *Klänge* (1913)
Los Angeles County Museum of Art. The Robert Gore Rifkind Center for German Expressionist Studies, purchased with funds provided by Anna Bing Arnold, Museum Acquisition Fund, and deaccession funds

101. *Paradies*, 1911–12
(Paradise)
Watercolor and ink over pencil, mounted on board
9 7/16 x 6 5/16 in. (24.0 x 16.0 cm)
Städtische Galerie im Lenbachhaus, Munich

102. *Kleine Welten* X, 1922
(Small worlds X)
Drypoint
9⅜ x 7¾ in. (23.8 x 19.7 cm)
From the portfolio Kleine Welten (1922)
Collection Grunwald Center for the Graphic Arts, UCLA. Fred Grunwald bequest

103. *Fröhlicher Aufstieg*, 1923
(Joyful ascension)
Color lithograph
9 5/16 x 7 9/16 in. (23.7 x 19.2 cm)
The Museum of Modern Art, New York. Larry Aldrich Fund

104. *Postkarte für die Bauhaus-Ausstellung*, 1923
(Postcard for the Bauhaus exhibition)
Color lithograph
5⅜ x 3 9/16 (13.7 x 9.0 cm)
Los Angeles County Museum of Art. The Robert Gore Rifkind Center for German Expressionist Studies

105. *Das grosse Tor von Kiev (Szenenbild zu "Bilder einer Ausstellung," Bild XVI)*, 1928
(The great gate of Kiev [stage design for *Pictures at an Exhibition*, picture XVI])
Watercolor and ink
15½ x 22 7/16 in. (39.4 x 57.0 cm)
Set design for *Pictures at an Exhibition* by Modest Mussorgski, created for the Friedrich Theater in Dessau
Theaterwissenschaftliche Sammlung, Universität zu Köln

Consistently pursuing a synthesis of the arts, Wassily Kandinsky was equally effective as an artist, philosopher, educator, and organizer. From 1886 to 1893 he studied law and economics at the university in Moscow. He was also an accomplished amateur musician. When he arrived in Munich in 1896, determined to become an artist, he had left behind a promising legal and academic career. At Anton Azbé's school of painting, he befriended his Russian compatriots Alexej Jawlensky and Marianne von Werefkin. After two years he was admitted to the class of Franz von Stuck.

In 1901 Kandinsky cofounded the Phalanx group, whose purpose was to promote artistic ideas that were not fostered by the conservative academies. He soon became the group's president and a teacher at the Phalanx school. One of his students there, Gabriele Münter, became his companion until he was forced to return to Russia during World War I. The group organized twelve exhibitions before it dissolved in 1904. Over the next few years Kandinsky traveled extensively but continued to work and participated in the Salon d'automne in Paris from 1905 to 1910.

Settled in Munich again, Kandinsky reacted to the need for exhibition space by founding the Neue Künstlervereinigung (New artists' association) in 1909 with Adolf Erbslöh, Alexander Kanoldt, Alfred Kubin, Münter, and Werefkin, who elected him president. The group's first exhibition, at the Thannhauser gallery in 1910, led to a meeting with August Macke and Franz Marc. When an abstraction by Kandinsky was rejected by the jury for the group's third exhibition in 1911, he and Marc left the Neue Künstlervereinigung and founded the Blaue Reiter (Blue rider). In 1912 they published an almanac of the same name. Concurrently Kandinsky articulated his reflections on the implications of abstraction in his book *Über das Geistige in der Kunst* (On the spiritual in art, 1912).

With the outbreak of war in 1914 Kandinsky returned to Russia. From 1917 to 1921 he held various administrative positions, teaching at the academy and at the university in Moscow, serving as director of the Museum of Creative Arts in Moscow, and participating in the establishment of museums in other cities in the Soviet Union.

In 1921, with the support of the Russian revolutionary government, Kandinsky accepted a teaching position at the Bauhaus, which he held from 1922 to 1933. In 1923 he was appointed an honorary vice president of the Société Anonyme in New York. His important theoretical work *Punkt und Linie zur Fläche* (Point and line to plane) was published in the Bauhaus series in 1926. After the National Socialists came to power, he was removed from his teaching position, and in 1934 he left for France, where he spent the remainder of his life.

F.V.H.

BIBLIOGRAPHY

John E. Bowlt and Rose-Carol Washton Long, eds., *The Life of Vasilii Kandinsky in Russian Art: A Study of "On the Spiritual in Art,"* 2d ed. (Newtonville, Mass.: Oriental Research Partners, 1984); Ulrika-Maria Eller-Rüter, *Kandinsky: Bühnenkomposition und Dichtung als Realisation seines Synthese-Konzepts* (Hildesheim: Georg Olms, 1990); Jelena Hahl-Koch, ed., *Arnold Schoenberg, Wassily Kandinsky: Letters, Pictures, and Documents*, trans. John C. Crawford (London: Faber and Faber, 1984); Rose-Carol Washton Long, *Kandinsky: The Development of an Abstract Style* (New York: Oxford University Press, 1980); idem, "Occultism, Anarchism, and Abstraction: Kandinsky's Art of the Future," *Art Journal* 46, no. 1 (1987): 38–45; Hans Konrad Roethel, *Kandinsky: Das graphische Werk*, 2 vols. (Cologne: DuMont, 1970); Peg Weiss, *Kandinsky in Munich: The Formative Jugendstil Years* (Princeton, N.J.: Princeton University Press, 1970).

■ ■ ■

Erich Kettelhut

BORN 1893 BERLIN ✣ DIED 1979 HAMBURG

106. *Metropolis: Morgendämmerung*, 1925
(Metropolis: Dawn)
Oil on board
15 3/8 x 21 7/16 in. (39.0 x 54.5 cm)
Set design for the film *Metropolis* (1927), directed by Fritz Lang
Stiftung Deutsche Kinemathek, Berlin

107. *Metropolis: Turm Babel*, 1925
(Metropolis: Tower of Babel)
Oil on board
17 3/16 x 21 3/4 in. (43.6 x 55.2 cm)
Set design for the film *Metropolis* (1927), directed by Fritz Lang
Stiftung Deutsche Kinemathek, Berlin

108. *Metropolis: II. Fassung*, 1925
(Metropolis: Second version)
Ink and gouache
18 1/8 x 21 5/8 in. (46.0 x 55.0 cm)
Set design for the film *Metropolis* (1927), directed by Fritz Lang
Stiftung Deutsche Kinemathek, Berlin

Erich Kettelhut was one of the most innovative designers of German silent film. Working on a wide range of projects and not bound to a particular style, he came into contact with many of the major figures of Weimar cinema, including directors Fritz Lang, Joe May, and Walter Ruttmann; fellow designers Hans Poelzig, Walter Röhrig, and Karl Vollbrecht; and experimental filmmakers Viking Eggeling and Hans Richter. Following an apprenticeship as a set painter and decorator, Kettelhut trained at the Berlin school of applied arts and worked as a set decorator for the Berlin Staatsoper before being called up for military service in 1914. After his discharge in 1918 he accepted the offer of set painter Otto Hunte, whom he had met before the war, to work with him on films for May. At May's studios in Weissensee, Kettelhut met Lang, who was writing scripts for May at the time. Although Kettelhut designed a number of successful May films, including *Das indische Grabmal* (The Indian grave, 1921), *Die Herrin der Welt* (The mistress of the world, 1919–20), and *Asphalt* (1928–29), he is best known for his collaboration with Hunte and Vollbrecht on such Lang productions such as *Dr. Mabuse, der Spieler* (Dr. Mabuse, the gambler, 1922), the two-part *Die Nibelungen* (The Nibelungs, 1924), and *Metropolis* (1927). After completing *Metropolis*, Kettelhut left the Lang team to create the sets for Ruttmann's 1927 film *Berlin, die Sinfonie der Grossstadt* (Berlin, the symphony of a big city), an experimental effort to document the life of Berlin from morning until night.

Kettelhut's involvement with *Metropolis* began directly after the premiere of *Die Nibelungen*, when Lang invited him to his apartment to read the script of the film. In his drawings for *Metropolis*, Kettelhut created an urban world that is overwhelming in its scale, one that pulsates with the impersonal energy of the big city. The film's lavish sets reflect an ambivalence toward the metropolis: the worker's city is a dehumanizing machine that enslaves its inhabitants, yet it is also a fascinating, visually complex maze that seems alive.

In his unpublished memoirs Kettelhut described the laborious process of designing and shooting the film, complicated by lack of space at the site and constant disputes between Lang and Hunte, Kettelhut's collaborator. "Especially for Hunte and me, but also for the costume designer Anne Willkomm [whom he later married]," he wrote, "indescribably tiring months passed as we had already experienced with *Die Nibelungen*. Sessions until late into the night, during the days afterward the working of what we had discussed into designs and ground plans; in the following days more filming sessions until the appointed afternoon hour. An unforgiving cycle with no consideration for Sundays" ("Aus der Erinnerungen des Filmarchitekten Erich Kettelhut," *EPD Film 4* [October 1987]: 26–27). He also commented on the underappreciated role of the designer in the production of a film: "When the actual work on the film begins, the film architect is the one who puts up the sets, since he is the first one in the studio. When the work ends, he bears the responsibility for his production company for dismantling the decorations and for turning over the studio to his successor" (quoted in Grünwald, "Expressionistischer Dekor," p. 84).

Kettelhut's career in film design waned with the rise of sound pictures, which relied less on sets to enhance story line and atmosphere than did silent films. Although he continued to work in film after 1933 with directors Herbert Maisch and Georg Jacoby and had a second career in television after the war, Kettelhut's best-known work remains his designs from the 1920s.

A.S.

BIBLIOGRAPHY

EPD Film 4 (October 1987) (special issue on Kettelhut); Gabriela Grünwald, "Expressionistischer Dekor im deutschen Stummfilm," Ph.D. diss., Cologne, 1984–85; Walter Kaul, *Schöpferische Filmarchitektur* (Berlin: Deutsche Kinemathek, 1971).

■ ■ ■

Cat. no. 108

Ernst Ludwig Kirchner

BORN 1880 ASCHAFFENBURG ✣ DIED 1938 FRAUENKIRCH, SWITZERLAND

109. *Mit Schilf werfende Badende*, 1910
(Bathers tossing reeds)
Color woodcut
7 7/8 x 11 7/16 in. (20.0 x 29.0 cm)
From the portfolio Brücke V (1910)
Los Angeles County Museum of Art. The Robert Gore Rifkind Center for German Expressionist Studies

110. *Das Stiftsfräulein im See*, 1912
(The retired spinster in the lake)
Woodcut
4 1/2 x 3 1/16 in. (11.5 x 7.8 cm)
From Alfred Döblin, *Das Stiftsfräulein und der Tod* (1913)
Los Angeles County Museum of Art. The Robert Gore Rifkind Center for German Expressionist Studies, purchased with funds provided by Anna Bing Arnold, Museum Acquisition Fund, and deaccession funds

111. *Frauen am Potsdamer Platz*, 1914–15
(Women at Potsdamer Platz)
Woodcut
19 11/16 x 14 9/16 in. (50.0 x 57.0 cm)
Private collection

112. *Fünf Kokotten*, 1914–15
(Five tarts)
Woodcut
19 x 14 9/16 in. (48.5 x 37.0 cm)
National Gallery of Art, Washington, Ruth and Jacob Kainen Collection

113. *Stadtbahnbogen*, 1915
(Tramway arch)
Color lithograph
19 7/8 x 23 1/4 in. (50.5 x 59.1 cm)
Collection Grunwald Center for the Graphic Arts, UCLA. Gift of Mr. Virgil Whirlaw

The eldest of the founding members of the Brücke (Bridge) and its self-appointed leader and spokesperson, Ernst Ludwig Kirchner was one of the most prolific and vocal of the Expressionists. Like the group's other members, he was fascinated by nature and the nude form, but he also created an extensive body of work dealing with the life of the metropolis. Behind both subjects lies the impulse to escape societal conventions and the vice and hostility of the city, as well as the belief in a paradisiacal world in which men and women could live free from moralistic constraints, an amalgam of both nostalgic and forward-looking utopian ideas.

Born in the small town of Aschaffenburg, Kirchner moved a number of times in his youth, first to Frankfurt, then to Perlen, near Lucerne, and later to Chemnitz. He studied briefly at the Lehr- und Versuchsateliers für angewandte und freie Kunst (Teaching and experimental studios for applied and fine arts) in Munich before taking up the study of architecture at the technical college in Dresden in 1901. Immediately before receiving his diploma in June 1905, however, he joined with fellow students Fritz Bleyl, Erich Heckel, and Karl Schmidt-Rottluff to form the Brücke, a group inspired by "belief...in a new generation of creators as well as appreciators" (see Appendix). With the other Brücke members, Kirchner sketched nude models outdoors, experimented with new techniques (particularly in graphic art), organized several exhibitions, designed invitations and publications, and attempted to draw new members into the group.

After moving to Berlin in 1911, Kirchner continued to work with the other Brücke members, although less frequently. During this period he met Erna Schilling, who would become his lifelong companion and the woman he would consider his wife. The gradual breakup of the Brücke, hastened by Kirchner's often distant personality, was finalized by his drafting of the *Chronik KG Brücke* (Chronicle of the artists' group Brücke) in 1913, which emphasized his own creative role. He wrote in the *Chronik* that the group "radiates its new values for artworks onto modern artistic creativity throughout Germany.... It struggles for a humane culture, which will be the source of a true art" (translated in Reinhold Heller, *Brücke: German Expressionist Prints from the Granvil and Marcia Specks Collection*, exh. cat. [Evanston, Ill.: Mary and Leigh Block Gallery, Northwestern University, 1988], p. 16). Called up for military service in mid-1915, Kirchner was discharged following a nervous breakdown in the fall and went to a sanatorium in Königstein. From this time on, he was in frequent care of psychiatrists and was

Cat. no. 110

often in sanatoriums in Switzerland, where he settled in 1917.

Throughout the 1920s and 1930s Kirchner received increasing critical attention and was represented in a series of solo and group exhibitions. His mental state, however, continued to decline. Partly out of despair over Germany's social and artistic situation—he was represented by thirty-two works in the *Entartete Kunst* (Degenerate art) exhibition in Munich in 1937—and partly as a result of his longstanding psychological troubles, Kirchner committed suicide on June 15, 1938.

A.S.

BIBLIOGRAPHY

Rosalyn Deutsche, "Alienation in Berlin: Kirchner's Street Scenes," *Art in America* 71 (January 1983): 64–72; Annemarie Dube and Wolf-Dieter Dube, *E. L. Kirchner: Das graphische Werk*, 2d rev. ed., 2 vols. (Munich: Prestel, 1980); Annemarie Dube-Heynig, *Kirchner: His Graphic Art* (Greenwich, Conn.: New York Graphic Society, 1961); *Ernst Ludwig Kirchner, 1880–1938*, exh. cat. (Berlin: Nationalgalerie, 1979); Donald E. Gordon, *Ernst Ludwig Kirchner: Mit einem kritischen Katalog sämtlicher Gemälde* (Munich: Prestel, 1968); idem, *Ernst Ludwig Kirchner: Meisterwerke der Druckgraphik*, exh. cat. (Stuttgart: Gerd Hatje, 1990); Eberhard W. Kornfeld, *Ernst Ludwig Kirchner: Nachzeichnung seines Lebens: Katalog der Sammlung von Werken von Ernst Ludwig Kirchner im Kirchner-Haus Duvos*, exh. cat. (Basel: Öffentliche Kunstsammlung, 1979); Ewald Rathke, ed., *Ernst Ludwig Kirchner: Strassenbilder*, Werkmonographien zur bildenden Kunst, no. 136 (Stuttgart: Reclam, 1969).

■ ■ ■

Paul Klee

BORN 1879 MÜNCHENBUCHSEE, SWITZERLAND ✣ DIED 1940 MURALTO, SWITZERLAND

114. *Phantastische Architektur mit dem Reiter*, 1918
(Fantastic architecture with rider)
Pencil on writing paper
6 7/16 x 8 1/8 in. (16.4 x 20.7 cm)
Kunstmuseum Bern. Paul Klee—Stiftung

115. *"Berlin dagegen unsere Hochburg buchte jähe Verzehnfachung seiner Bürger"; Berlin als Zentrum*, 1919
("Berlin, however, our citadel, experienced a sudden decoupling of its citizens"; Berlin as center)
Ink on writing paper
11 3/8 x 8 5/8 in. (28.9 x 22.0 cm)
Illustration for Curt Corrinth, *Potsdamer Platz* (see cat. no. 226)
Kunstmuseum Bern. Paul Klee—Stiftung

116. *Zahlenbaumlandschaft*, 1919
(Number-tree landscape)
Lithograph
6 7/8 x 4 15/16 in. (17.5 x 12.6 cm)
From the deluxe edition of *Münchner Blatter für Dichtung und Graphik* 1, no. 9 (1919): 142
Los Angeles County Museum of Art. The Robert Gore Rifkind Center for German Expressionist Studies, purchased with funds provided by Anna Bing Arnold, Museum Acquisition Fund, and deaccession funds

117. *Bühnen-Gebirgs-Konstruktion*, 1920
(Stage-mountain-construction)
Oil, gouache, and ink on paper mounted on cardboard
13 x 16 1/2 in. (33.0 x 41.9 cm)
The Metropolitan Museum of Art. The Berggruen Klee Collection, 1987

118. *Die erhabene Seite: Postkarte für die"Bauhaus-Ausstellung Weimar 1923,"* 1923
(The raised facade: Postcard for the Bauhaus exhibition, Weimar 1923)
Lithograph with watercolor
5 5/8 x 2 7/8 (14.2 x 7.4 cm)
Kunstmuseum Bern. Paul Klee—Stiftung

See also cat. no. 223

Paul Klee was already an accomplished violinist performing in a Bern orchestra—his Bavarian father and Swiss mother were both professional musicians—when he went to Munich in 1898 to study art, first with Heinrich Knirr and later at the academy under Franz von Stuck. In 1901–2, after concluding his studies, he traveled in Italy with his friend the sculptor Hermann Haller. From 1903 to 1905 Klee lived with his parents in Bern but made several trips to Paris, Munich, and Berlin and began to exhibit his etchings. Following his marriage to pianist Lily Stumpf in 1906, he settled in Munich, where he resided until 1920.

In Klee's early work his primary concern was the expressive potential of line. His growing admiration for the work of Paul Cézanne, Vincent van Gogh, and especially Henri Matisse between 1908 and 1910 led to an increasing interest in color. Klee met Wassily Kandinsky and August Macke in 1911 and became affiliated with their group, the Blaue Reiter (Blue rider), participating in the group's second exhibition in 1912. He shared with Kandinsky an interest in the synthesis of the arts, particularly the relationship between music and color.

New impulses arose from Klee's introduction to the Parisian avant-garde during his stay there in 1912, when he met Guillaume Apollinaire, Robert Delaunay, Sonia Delaunay, and Pablo Picasso. His exhibition activities in Germany resumed in 1914 with shows at Herwarth Walden's Sturm gallery and at the New Munich Secession, of which he was a founding member.

Klee served in the army from 1916 to 1918. In 1920 Hans Goltz showed 362 of his works at his Munich gallery. Later that year Klee was invited by Walter Gropius to become a professor at the Bauhaus in Weimar, along with Kandinsky and Lyonel Feininger. The Société Anonyme organized his first solo exhibition in New York in 1924. Also in that year Klee entered into an agreement with Feininger, Kandinsky, and Alexej Jawlensky to form the Blue Four, represented in the United States by Emmy ("Galka") Scheyer.

Klee's travels to Tunisia in 1914 and to Egypt in 1928 had a lasting impact on his use of color, and he continued to collect new impressions on his 1931 trip to Sicily. His exhibition activity testified to his growing reputation: in 1928 he had his first solo show in Paris; in 1929, several fiftieth-birthday exhibitions in German and Swiss museums; in 1930, a solo exhibition at the Museum of Modern Art in New York. He was appointed to a teaching position at the Düsseldorf academy in 1931 but was dismissed in 1933 when the National Socialists assumed power. In 1934 he returned to Bern, remaining there until his death in 1940.

F.V.H.

BIBLIOGRAPHY
Marcel Franciscono, Paul Klee: *His Work and Thought* (Chicago: University of Chicago Press, 1991); Stefan Frey and Josef Helfenstein, *Paul Klee: Verzeichnis der Werke des Jahres 1940* (Stuttgart: Gerd Hatje, 1991); Will Grohmann, *Paul Klee* (New York: Harry N. Abrams, 1954); Eberhard W. Kornfeld, *Verzeichnis des graphischen Werkes von Paul Klee* (Bern: Kornfeld und Klipstein, 1963); Richard Verdi, *Klee and Nature* (New York: Rizzoli, 1985); Otto K. Werckmeister, *The Making of Paul Klee's Career, 1914–1920* (Chicago: University of Chicago Press, 1988); Bonnie Yochelson, "Paul Klee and Architecture," *Marsyas* 20 (1980): 61–70.

■ ■ ■

Cat. no. 114

Cat. no. 118

César Klein

BORN 1876 HAMBURG ✣ DIED 1954 PANSDORF

119. *Salon der "Genuine,"* 1920
(Salon for *Genuine*)
Colored chalk over pencil on board
10 13/16 x 12 13/16 in. (27.5 x 32.5 cm)
Set design for the film *Genuine* (1920), directed by Robert Wiene
Theaterwissenschaftliche Sammlung, Universität zu Köln

César Klein's career reflects the proliferation of new media and the overlapping of established ones in the first decades of the twentieth century. Because he worked in media that appealed to a mass audience, such as architectural decoration, applied arts, poster design, and theater and film design, his work was probably better known during his lifetime than that of some artists who are more prominent today. Through his varied activities Klein expressed his idealistic belief in the necessity of giving art both an aesthetic and a communicative function.

At the insistence of his parents, Klein was apprenticed as a craft painter at the age of seventeen. Subsequently, in 1895, he enrolled in the Hamburg school of applied arts. After briefly attending the Düsseldorf academy, he was awarded a scholarship to study at the school of the Königliches Kunstgewerbemuseum (Royal museum of applied arts) in Berlin, where he had his first contact with mosaic and glass painting.

Klein's first major commission, the one that introduced his art to the public, consisted of the painting and decoration of the lobby and auditorium of the Marmorhauskino, a Berlin movie theater, in 1913, Although his decorative art is not typically Expressionist, with its ordered compositions and wide tonal range, he was considered an Expressionist by contemporary critics because of his painting, which shares stylistic elements with the work of the Brücke (Bridge) artists. Paul Westheim wrote rather unflatteringly of Klein's easel painting in 1919, noting that he "paints such a true Expressionism, Expressionism like in the books.... He stands in the same relation to the Noldes, Kirchners, and Heckels in which E. R. Weiss stood to the leading Impressionists and to Cézanne in his day" ("César Klein," p. 246).

After World War I Klein substituted temporarily for Walter Gropius as the leader of the Arbeitsrat für Kunst (Working council for art), which brought him into contact with personalities such as Adolf Behne and Bruno Taut, and was a principal founding member of the Novembergruppe (November group) in 1918. Along with other members of the Arbeitsrat, Klein designed a series of political posters urging worker solidarity and support for the Weimar Republic in the period immediately following its establishment. This idealism carried over as well into his ideas on reform in the arts. In a text written in 1919 for an Arbeitsrat publication, Klein called for reform in children's education, for "free play of the imagination, " and for the "overlapping of the professions" (*Ja! Stimmen des Arbeitsrates für Kunst*, p. 48). Although he shared many of the ideals of the Bauhaus, Klein turned down Gropius's invitation to join its faculty, instead accepting a teaching position at the Kunstgewerbemuseum in Berlin. During the 1920s Klein also collaborated on set designs for the cinema and theater, including those for Robert Wiene's 1920 film *Genuine*, a production inspired by the success of the director's film of the previous year, *Das Cabinet des Doktor Caligari* (The cabinet of Doctor Caligari). Klein created an extravagant, shadowy world inspired by the designs for *Caligari* but also reflecting his own interest in surface pattern.
In 1931 Klein was appointed to the highest professorship at the German state schools but in April 1933 was suspended from his post and subsequently labeled "degenerate." Going into internal exile in Pansdorf during the war, he resumed designing for the theater in 1945.

A.S.

BIBLIOGRAPHY

Ruth Irmgard Dalinghaus, "César Klein (1876–1954): Angewandte Kunst: Werkmonographie mit Katalog," Ph.D. diss., Freie Universität, Berlin, 1990; idem, *Lieber Rhythmus: César Klein, 1876–1954: Bilder und Gouachen, Skizzen und Werkkartons*, exh. cat. (Niebüll: Kunstverein Niebüll, 1990); César Klein, in *Ja! Stimmen des Arbeitsrates für Kunst in Berlin* (Berlin-Charlottenburg: Photographische Gesellschaft, 1919), pp. 47–49; Johann Schlick, "César Klein: 'Genuine,'" *Nordelbingen* 47 (1978): 141–51; Paul Westheim, "César Klein," *Das Kunstblatt* 3, no. 8 (1919): 244–46.

■ ■ ■

Otto Kohtz

BORN 1880 MAGDEBURG ✣ DIED 1956 BERLIN

120. *Reichshaus am Königsplatz*, 1920
(Reichshaus on the Königsplatz)
Photostat with pencil and ink wash
21¹/4 x 27³/16 in. (54.0 x 69.0 cm)
Plansammlung der Universitätsbibliothek der Technischen Universität, Berlin

See also cat. no. 228

It seems that within Otto Kohtz's soul there dwelt two architects. One produced monumental public buildings of brick and stone in repetitive rhythms, reflective of a Wilhelmine Germany that strove to communicate its imperial power and cultural primacy through dramatic and massive edifices. His alter ego called for a new poetry of architecture and, in never-realized sketches of fanciful structures, drew upon such divergent sources as Byzantine, oriental, Mayan, classical, and Expressionist designs as well as the natural world.

Kohtz began his architectural training at the school of applied arts, then attended the school for building trades in Berlin, and finalized his studies at the technical college in Berlin-Charlottenburg. He designed many Berlin office buildings and residences with his partner, E. Schütze. His most renowned independent projects were the administration building of the Imperial Farmer's Union in Berlin-Friedenau (1911–12), the home for bachelors in Berlin-Moabit (1913–14), and the offices of the Scherl publishing house in Berlin (1925–28). The designs of these divergent structures are unified by a consistent adherence to academic compositional principles and historical models and motifs.

Kohtz occasionally contributed essays to various trade journals and published three books: *Gedanken über Architektur* (Thoughts about architecture, 1909), *Das Reichshaus in Berlin* (The Reichshaus in Berlin, 1920), and *Büroturmhäuser in Berlin* (High-rise office buildings in Berlin, 1921). The latter two texts are studies and commentaries on traditional structures built or planned; *Gedanken über Architektur* contains an essay and a series of fifty-five drawings of uncommissioned fantasy buildings that nevertheless exhibit the sequential arrangement of units, severity of style, and enormity of scale seen in Kohtz's built designs.

Inspired by Expressionist poet Paul Scheerbart, Kohtz believed that in the future architecture would be designed to exist harmoniously with nature and that just as the structures of plants and animals are adapted to their environment, this architecture would include a land style, an air style, and a water style. Despite the seeming disparity between Kohtz's realized architecture and the architecture of his fantasies, his example clearly illustrates the conflict between modernism and the steadfast persistence of tradition.

V.H.

BIBLIOGRAPHY
Werner Hegemann, ed., *Otto Kohtz* (Berlin: J. E. Hübsch, 1930); Otto Kohtz, *Gedanken über Architektur* (Berlin: O. Baumgärtel, 1909); idem, *Büroturmhäuser in Berlin* (Berlin: Privately printed, 1921).

■ ■ ■

Cat. no. 120

Oskar Kokoschka

BORN 1886 PÖCHLARN, AUSTRIA ✣ DIED 1980

MONTREUX, SWITZERLAND

121. *Das Mädchen Li und ich*, 1906–8
(The girl Li and I)
Color lithograph
9 7/16 x 9 1/16 in. (24.0 x 23.0 cm)
From Oskar Kokoschka, *Die träumenden Knaben*, 2d ed. (1917)
Los Angeles County Museum of Art. The Robert Gore Rifkind Center for German Expressionist Studies, purchased with funds provided by Anna Bing Arnold, Museum Acquisition Fund, and deaccession funds

Equally noted as an iconoclastic and pioneering painter and as an outspoken critic and writer, Oskar Kokoschka made significant contributions to Expressionist literature and art. He evolved a thickly painted, psychologically potent style, which he used to explore his lifelong passion, the human image. His numerous portraits aimed to capture, in his words, "the distillation of a living being."

Born in a small town in Austria, Kokoschka studied at the school of applied arts in Vienna from 1904 to 1909, during which time he designed posters and other items for the Wiener Werkstätte, including his book of poetry and prints *Die träumenden Knaben* (The dreaming boys), completed in 1908. His play *Mörder, Hoffnung der Frauen* (Murderer, hope of women), first performed in 1909, is considered an inaugural work of German Expressionist drama, with its archetypal characters and violent view of male-female relations. In Berlin the following year, twenty-five of his drawings were reproduced in Herwarth Walden's periodical *Der Sturm* (The storm), and he secured gallery representation with Paul Cassirer.

Influenced by Symbolism and Jugendstil in his youth, Kokoschka shared these movements' interest in line and in dreamlike visions of the human condition, as is evident in the drawings he created around 1910 for *Der Sturm*. Fascinated by the utopian architectural theories of Paul Scheerbart, Kokoschka was also impressed by artists as diverse as Robert Delaunay, El Greco, and Venetian painters of the Renaissance such as Giorgione, Tintoretto, and Titian. He defined his work by its message rather than by its style. Expressionism, he wrote in his autobiography, "was meant as a moral and cultural awakening of the true nature of man, and a political commitment. Essentially, Expressionism must be seen as a revolutionary movement, a compulsive need to communicate with the masses" (*My Life*, p. 66).

The years from 1912 until the war, during which Kokoschka created some of his most introspective work, were consumed by his legendary affair with Alma Mahler, widow of composer Gustav Mahler and future wife of Walter Gropius. After the dissolution of their relationship in 1914 he volunteered for the war effort and was sent to the Russian front, where he was severely wounded. He spent the end of 1916 and much of 1917 recovering from his physical and mental injuries and in 1919 accepted a professorship at the Dresden academy, which he held until 1923.

Embarking on an extended period of travel in 1927, Kokoschka executed numerous landscapes and fell in love with London, to which he would return during World War II. Spending the early 1930s in Paris, Vienna, and finally Prague, he fled to London in 1938 with his wife, a Czech. During the war he worked to raise money for war victims, creating political works satirizing the war and condemning fascism. Kokoschka, who received British citizenship in 1947, continued to work and travel throughout Europe for the remainder of his life, returning to Austria permanently only in 1975. He maintained his belief in the didactic function of art and argued for the validity of figuration at a time when many younger artists were exploring abstraction.

A.S.

BIBLIOGRAPHY

Richard Calvocoressi and Katharina Schulz, *Oskar Kokoschka, 1886–1980*, exh. cat. (New York: Solomon R. Guggenheim Museum, 1986); Oskar Kokoschka, *A Sea Ringed with Visions*, trans. Eithne Wilkins and Ernst Kaiser (New York: Horizon, 1962); idem, *Das schriftliche Werk*, 4 vols. (Hamburg: H. Christians, 1973–76); idem, *My Life*, trans. David Britt (New York: Macmillan, 1974); idem, *Letters, 1905–1976*, trans. Mary Whittall (London: Thames and Hudson, 1992); Erika Patka, *Oskar Kokoschka: Symposion* (Salzburg: Residenz, 1986); Frank Whitford, *Oskar Kokoschka: A Life* (New York: Atheneum, 1986); Hans Maria Wingler, *Oskar Kokoschka: The Work of the Painter*, trans. Frank S. C. Budgen et al. (Salzburg: Galerie Welz, 1955); Hans Maria Wingler and Friedrich Welz, *Oskar Kokoschka: Das druckgraphische Werk*, 2 vols. (Salzburg: Galerie Welz, 1975–81).

■ ■ ■

Carl Krayl

BORN 1890 WEINSBERG ✝ DIED 1947 WERDER

122. *Traumstadt*, c. 1919
(Dream city)
Graphite
12 15/16 x 8 1/4 in. (32.8 x 21.0 cm)
Page from a sketchbook
Collection Centre Canadien d'Architecture/Canadian Centre for Architecture, Montreal

123. *Kosmischer Bau*, c. 1919–20
(Cosmic building)
Graphite, ink, and watercolor
21 1/4 x 18 7/8 in. (54.0 x 48.0 cm)
Ungers collection

124. *Einen Licht Gruss aus meinem Sternenhaus*, 1920
(Light greetings from my star house)
Blueprint (purple on white)
8 1/4 x 6 5/16 in. (21.0 x 16.1 cm)
Wenzel-Hablik-Stiftung, Itzehoe

125. *Vision*, 1920
(Vision)
Watercolor
12 13/16 x 9 11/16 in. (32.5 X 24.7 cm)
Ungers collection

After studying from 1910 to 1912 at the school of applied arts and the technical college in Stuttgart, Carl Krayl was employed for two years by the architects Meckel in Freiburg and Brendel in Nuremberg. During World War I Krayl worked as a technician in Ingolstadt. After the war he returned to work with Brendel and became involved with groups such as the Arbeitsrat für Kunst (Working council for art), the Novembergruppe (November group), the Gläserne Kette (Crystal chain)—using the pseudonym *Anfang* (beginning)—and later *Der Ring* (The ring). Bruno Taut published Krayl's articles in *Frühlicht* (Daybreak) and obtained for him a position on the board of works in Magdeburg, where he lived from 1921 to 1938.

After 1923 Krayl worked independently, completing a number of private and public commissions, mainly in Magdeburg. These included apartment buildings, a union office, and the bureau of health insurance. In 1933 the Nazis falsely accused him of being a Bolshevik. From 1938 to 1946 he was employed as a technical draftsman with the national railway office. He died shortly before he was to begin working in the office of Hans Scharoun.

V. H.

■ ■ ■

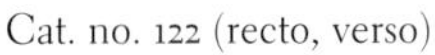

Cat. no. 122 (recto, verso)

Fritz Levy

BIRTH DATE UNKNOWN ✣ DEATH DATE UNKNOWN

126. *Grossstadt*, c. 1920
(Metropolis)
Woodcut
7³/8 x 4 ³/8 in. (18.8 x 11.7 cm)
From *Das Kunstfenster* 1, no. 4 (1920)
Los Angeles County Museum of Art. The Robert Gore Rifkind Center for German Expressionist Studies, purchased with funds provided by Anna Bing Arnold, Museum Acquisition Fund, and deaccession funds

■ ■ ■

El (Eliezer Marcovich) Lissitzky

BORN 1890 POCHINOK, RUSSIA ✣ DIED 1941 MOSCOW

127. With Kurt Schwitters
Untitled, c. 1924
Photomechanical reproduction
12 x 18¹/2 in. (30.5 x 47.0 cm)
From *Merz* 2 (April–July 1924)
Los Angeles County Museum of Art. The Robert Gore Rifkind Center for German Expressionist Studies, gift of Robert Gore Rifkind

In spite of his multifarious activities in Western Europe as an artist, architect, typographer, and photographer, El Lissitzky is best known for his contributions to Russian culture. After attending high school in Smolensk, he studied architectural engineering at the technical college in Darmstadt from 1909 to 1914. At the outbreak of World War I he was forced to return to Moscow, where he completed his degree in architecture in 1915 and began to establish a career. He illustrated books and participated in art exhibitions, and in 1917 he became a member of the revolutionary commission for the arts. Marc Chagall offered him a position as a professor of architecture at the Vitebsk art school in 1919, Lissitzky's first Constructivist compositions, which he called Prouns, date from this period. In 1921 he went to Moscow to teach architecture.

During the 1920s Lissitzky focused on designing exhibition spaces. His desire to minimize the psychological distance between the viewer and the artwork inspired the design of the Raum der Abstrakten (abstract gallery) at the Provinzial Museum in Hannover, where he was artist in residence at the Kestner-Gesellschaft in 1927 at the invitation of Kurt Schwitters. Lissitzky frequently visited Germany during the 1920s. In 1922 he helped organize the first exhibition of Soviet art in Berlin, which introduced Suprematism and Constructivism to Western Europe and opened up opportunities for cooperation between the Russian and German avant-gardes.

Lissitzky spent the last decade of his life primarily in Moscow, where he continued to design innovative exhibition spaces as well as posters and graphics.

F.V.H.

BIBLIOGRAPHY

El Lissitzky: Maler, Architekt, Typograf, Fotograf, exh. cat. (Halle: Staatliche Galerie Moritzburg; Leipzig: Galerie der Hochschule für Grafik und Buchkunst, 1982); Sophie Lissitzky-Küppers, ed., *El Lissitzky: Life, Letters, Texts*, trans. Helene Aldwinckle and Mary Whittall (London: Thames and Hudson, 1967); Peter Nisbet, ed., *El Lissitzky, 1890–1941: Catalogue for an Exhibition of Selected Works from North American Collections, the Sprengel Museum Hanover, and the Staatliche Galerie Moritzburg Halle*, exh. cat. (Cambridge: Harvard University Art Museums, Busch-Reisinger Museum, 1987).

■ ■ ■

Hans Luckhardt

BORN 1890 BERLIN ✣ DIED 1954 BAD WIESSEE

128. *Konzert Saal*, c. 1919
(Concert hall)
Hectograph
13 x 8¼ in. (33.1 x 21.0 cm)
Fragment of a letter from the Gläserne Kette correspondence
Collection Centre Canadien d'Architecture/Canadian Centre for Architecture, Montreal

Cat. no. 128

After completing his studies at the technical college in Karlsruhe, Hans Luckhardt entered private practice with his brother Wassili in 1921. The brothers' main collaborator was Alfons Anker, with whom they worked from 1924 to 1937. In the period immediately following World War I, Hans Luckhardt joined both the Novembergruppe (November group) and the Arbeitsrat für Kunst (Working council for art). He participated in the Gläserne Kette (Crystal chain) correspondence under the pseudonym Angkor, after the temples at Angkor Wat, Cambodia. In Bruno Taut's utopian journal *Frühlicht* (Daybreak), the Luckhardts published illustrations that reflected their interest in the interplay of sharp, angular forms.

At a time when economic conditions permitted young architects to do little more than express their aspirations on paper, the Luckhardt brothers drew imaginary projects for theaters, cultural halls, and monuments. Their style was generally geometric and blocky, although they sometimes experimented with curved facades, as in the 1929 Telschow-Haus department store in Berlin. Hans Luckhardt designed a concert hall with spiral rooms inspired by Hans Poelzig's Salzburg Festspielhaus project. Stalactitelike structures hang from the ceiling of Luckhardt's 1920 Konzertsaalgebäude (concert hall), recalling Poelzig's Grosses Schauspielhaus theater in Berlin. The Luckhardt brothers collaborated with Anker on the book *Zur neuen Wohnform* (On new dwelling forms, 1930), the most significant of their many publications.

V.H.

BIBLIOGRAPHY

Marita Gleiss et al., eds., *Brüder Luckhardt und Alfons Anker: Berliner Architekten der Moderne*, exh. cat., *Schriftenreihe der Akademie der Künste*, no. 21 (Berlin: Akademie der Künste, 1990); Hans Luckhardt, Wassili Luckhardt, and Alfons Anker, *Zur neuen Wohnform*, Der wirtschaftliche Baubetrieb, no. 3 (Berlin: Bauwelt, 1930).

■ ■ ■

Wassili Luckhardt

BORN 1889 BERLIN ✣ DIED 1972 BERLIN

129. *Denkmal der Arbeit*, c. 1920
(Monument to work)
Charcoal and pencil
20¼ x 42⅛ in. (51.5 x 107.0 cm)
Akademie der Künste, Berlin. Sammlung Baukunst

Wassili Luckhardt worked in Berlin with his brother Hans from 1921 until the latter's death in 1954 and in partnership with Alfons Anker from 1924 to 1937, as Brüder Luckhardt and Anker. Together they were well-known participants in Bruno Taut's avant-garde circle.

Wassili Luckhardt was educated at the technical colleges in Berlin-Charlottenburg and Dresden and served in the army from 1914 to 1918. Caught up in the wave of visionary and utopian Expressionism following World War I, he participated in the Gläserne Kette (Crystal chain) correspondence under the pseudonym *Zacken* (spikes). In Bruno Taut's periodical *Frühlicht* (Daybreak), he published bold Expressionist designs for theaters and cinemas, highly stylized crystalline temples, and a monument to labor. He was a member of the Arbeitsrat für Kunst (Working council for art), the Novembergruppe (November group), and Der Ring (The ring) and was included in the *Ausstellung für unbekannte Architekten* (Exhibition of unknown architects).

The Luckhardt brothers and Anker showed great interest in adapting new materials for construction, especially steel and glass, producing fresh design concepts characterized by openness, clarity, simplicity, and light. They designed one of the first modern housing estates in Berlin in 1924 and continued to build residences. Their inclination was toward blocky, geometric structures accented by horizontal bands of windows. Construction of the 1951 Berlin Pavilion was interrupted by World War II, and it became their first major postwar building. After Hans's death in 1954, Wassili completed the Bavarian welfare office in Munich, his own home in Berlin, and other civil, university, and business structures. He was awarded the Berlin Kunstpreis in 1958. He continued his work through the 1960s and is considered one of the founders of modernism.

V.H.

BIBLIOGRAPHY

Udo Kultermann, *Wassili und Hans Luckhardt: Bauten und Entwürfe* (Tübingen: E. Wasmuth, 1958); Wassili Luckhardt, *Wassili Luckhardt*, ed. Helga Kliemann (Tübingen: E. Wasmuth, 1973).

■ ■ ■

Cat. no. 129

Franz Marc

BORN 1880 MUNICH ✣ DIED 1916 VERDUN, FRANCE

130. *Versöhnung*, 1912
(Reconciliation)
Woodcut
7⅞ x 10⅛ in. (20.0 x 25.7 cm)
Los Angeles County Museum of Art. Given anonymously

131. *Geburt der Pferde*, 1913
(The birth of horses)
Color woodcut
8½ x 5¾ in. (21.5 x 14.5 cm)
Los Angeles County Museum of Art. The Robert Gore Rifkind Center for German Expressionist Studies

132. *Zaubriger Moment: Blatt 21 des "Skizzenbuchs aus dem Felde,"* 1915
(Magical moment: Page 21 from "Sketchbook from the field")
Pencil
6⅜ x 3⅞ in. (16.1 x 9.9 cm)
Staatliche Graphische Sammlung, Munich

Known for his images of animals and landscapes painted in strong Expressionist colors, Franz Marc studied theology in Munich before deciding to become an artist. In 1900 he began studying painting at the academy in Munich. His travels to Italy in 1902 and to Paris and Brittany in 1903 gave him the opportunity to encounter old and new masters. At Durand-Ruel in Paris he discovered the Impressionists Edouard Manet, Claude Monet, and Pierre-Auguste Renoir. On a trip in 1906 to Salonika and Mount Athos, Marc explored the traditions of Greek art. With a solid knowledge of classical art, he created arrangements of form and color that carried a powerful emotional charge. Following this period of travel, he retreated in 1909 to a farmhouse in Sindelsdorf, a small town in Bavaria, where he worked independently.

Through August Macke, who had been a close friend since 1910, Marc became associated with the Neue Künstlervereinigung (New artists' association) in Munich in 1911. Wassily Kandinsky recognized in him a kindred spirit, and together they edited the almanac *Der blaue Reiter* (The blue rider). Marc was able to convince Reinhard Piper to publish this eclectic project, to which he contributed three essays, including one on the younger generation of German artists. The first and last volume of the planned series appeared in 1912. Marc participated in the two Blaue Reiter exhibitions, in 1911 and 1912, and in Herwarth Walden's *Erster deutscher Herbstsalon* (First German autumn salon) in Berlin in 1913.

Marc was called up for military service in 1914 and he recorded his wartime experiences in his letters and sketches from the field. He was killed in action at Verdun in 1916.

F.V.H.

BIBLIOGRAPHY

Klaus Lankheit, *Franz Marc: Katalog der Werke* (Cologne: DuMont, 1970); idem, *Franz Marc: Sein Leben und seine Kunst* (Cologne: DuMont, 1976); idem, *Franz Marc: Schriften* (Cologne: DuMont, 1978); Frederick S. Levine, *The Apocalyptic Vision: The Art of Franz Marc as German Expressionism* (New York: Harper and Row, 1979).

■ ■ ■

Gerhard Marcks

BORN 1889 BERLIN ✣ DIED 1981 BURGBROHL

133. *Landschaft mit Turmarchitekturen*, 1919
(Landscape with tower architecture)
Ink
8¹¹/16 x 12⁵/8 in. (22.1 x 32.0 cm)
Gehard Marks Stiftung, Bremen

Gerhard Marcks is best known as a sculptor, yet he did not limit himself to any medium or subject nor to any of the many artistic schools that flourished during his ninety-two years. He had no formal training but received a classical education at the Bismarck Gymnasium in Berlin, which instilled a lifelong love of Greek culture. He began to make drawings as a very young child, and drawing remained the foundation of his work. His sculptures were created not directly from models but from two-minute sketches.

From 1907 to 1912 Marcks studied and shared a studio with painter-turned-sculptor Richard Scheibe, and from 1914 to 1918 he fought in World War I. Following his release from service, Marcks taught at the school of applied arts in Berlin. In 1919 he exhibited several architectural sketches in the *Ausstellung für unbekannte Architekten* (Exhibition of unknown architects) in Berlin. From 1919 to 1925 he taught ceramics at the Bauhaus, although he rejected Gropius's concept of relating art and technology. It was there that he met Lyonel Feininger, Paul Klee, and Oskar Schlemmer. In 1925 Marcks obtained a teaching position at the school of applied arts at Schloss Giebichenstein, near Halle, later becoming the school's director. In 1933 the Nazis removed him from this position and later placed his works in the *Entartete Kunst* (Degenerate art) exhibition. Forbidden to exhibit, he became one of the "internal exiles," living in and around Berlin. During World War II his son was killed in Russia, and his home was bombed, destroying years of accumulated work. In 1946 Marcks was able to return to teaching, becoming a professor at the state art school in Hamburg.

The postwar years brought Marcks scores of commissions for monuments, restorations, tributes, and memorials, which gave him the means to travel abroad. He visited Greece (1954), southwestern and southern Africa (1955), the United States (1963), and Mexico (1963). The persecution, poverty, and loss that he had experienced only seemed to strengthen his conviction that the artist is "the sense organ of humanity."

V.H.

BIBLIOGRAPHY
Günter Busch and Martina Rudloff, *Gerhard Marcks: Das plastische Werk* (Frankfurt: Propyläen, 1977); Detlef Hamer, ed., *Gerhard Marcks: Bilder aus Niehagen, Briefe nach Mecklenburg* (Restock: Hinstorff, 1989); Kurt Lammek, ed., *Gerhard Marcks: Das druckgraphische Werk* (Stuttgart: E. Hauswedell, 1990); Martina Rudloff, ed., *Gerhard Marcks, 1889–1981: Retrospektive* (Munich: Hirmer, 1989).

■ ■ ■

Ludwig Meidner

BORN 1884 BERNSTADT ✣ DIED 1966 DARMSTADT

134. *Strasse in Wilmersdorf*, 1913
(Street in Wilmersdorf)
Drypoint
8⁵/8 x 5¹/2 in. (21.9 x 14.0 cm)
Collection of the Grunwald Center for the Graphic Arts, UCLA. Gift of Mr. and Mrs. Stanley I. Talpis

135. *Wannsee Bahnhof*, 1913
(Wannsee train station)
Black ink heightened with white
18¹/4 x 23¹/4 in. (46.4 x 59.0 cm)
Los Angeles County Museum of Art. The Robert Gore Rifkind Center for German Expressionist Studies

136. *Wogende Menge*, 1913
(Surging crowd)
Etching
10¹¹/16 x 8⁵/16 (27.1 x 21.2 cm)
Städtische Kunstsammlungen, Darmstadt

137. Untitled (street scene), 1913
Black ink and white gouache
18⁷/8 x 16 in. (47.9 x 40.6 cm)
Los Angeles County Museum of Art. Gift of Rabbi William Kramer

Although he belonged to none of the major Expressionist artists' groups, Ludwig Meidner was one of the movement's most individualistic and prolific painters and graphic artists. He maintained a lifelong interest in literature, associating more frequently with poets and writers than with other visual artists and publishing a number of his own collections of texts, such as *Im Nacken das Sternemeer* (The sea of stars at my back, 1918) and *Septemberschrei* (September cry, 1920). Meidner was born in Bernstadt, a Silesian town he characterized as "terribly provincial" but whose geography contributed to his interest in landscape. Although his parents wanted him to be an architect and were opposed to his studying art, he was accepted in 1903 to the school of applied arts in Breslau, then under the direction of Hans Poelzig. In 1905 he moved to Berlin and the following year journeyed to Paris, where he made the acquaintance of Amedeo Modigliani, who was to be an inspirational figure to him throughout his life.

Between 1907 and 1911 Meidner spent most of his time in Berlin, living in squalid conditions. In 1911 he received a stipend through the intervention of Max Beckmann, which helped him concentrate more fully on his work. The next year he began to produce what are now known as his apocalyptic landscapes, the works for which he is most frequently recognized. During this period he moved in the circle of the Neue Club (New club)—composed mainly of writers such as Alfred Döblin, Carl Einstein, Georg Heym, and Jacob van Hoddis—and published numerous illustrations in *Die Aktion* (Action). With the painters Richard Janthur and Jakob Steinhardt, Meidner formed the short-lived group Die Pathetiker (The pathetic ones) in 1912 and exhibited with the group at Herwarth Walden's Sturm gallery.

Along with the powerful imagery of the Expressionist poets, the work of the Italian Futurists, the French painter Robert

Delaunay, and the English artist William Blake influenced Meidner's work, which became more abstract in the years leading up to 1916. The influence of the Futurists is apparent in an essay from 1914 entitled "Anleitung zum Malen von Grossstadtbildern" (An introduction to painting big cities), in which he exhorted artists to turn their attention to the urban world around them and abandon Impressionist plein air painting. Unlike other Expressionist painters, Meidner displayed little interest in ethnographic art and stressed the urgency of treating contemporary themes.

In December 1912 Meidner had a "revelation" that he knew to be religious. Although he was raised a Jew, he did not believe in God. Three years later, however, he wrote in his journal of "a proof of the existence of God: the general harmony (the greatest artists were Christians)" (*Dichter, Maler und Cafés*, p. 30). Meidner's religious fervor and fascination with both Christian and Jewish religious figures grew during the 1910s and 1920s, and he produced numerous paintings of prophets and saints. Although Meidner's work is often characterized as apocalyptic because of his tumultuous landscapes (the artist himself used the term to describe these works in 1918, when they were shown together for the first time), his style and themes owe more to his religious beliefs and interest in theories of the apocalypse than to nihilism. While he was fascinated by the dystopian notion of the apocalypse, he also believed in the possibility of utopia, which he conceived of in vaguely religious terms.

In 1939, as the Nazi persecution of Jews intensified, Meidner fled to England. In 1952 he returned to Germany, where he received increasing recognition.

A.S.

BIBLIOGRAPHY
Gerda Breuer and Ines Wagemann, *Ludwig Meidner: Zeichner, Maler, Literat, 1884–1966*, exh. cat., 2 vols. (Darmstadt: Mathildenhöhe, 1991); Carol S. Eliel, *The Apocalyptic Landscapes of Ludwig Meidner*, exh. cat. (Los Angeles: Los Angeles County Museum of Art, 1989); Thomas Grochowiak, *Ludwig Meidner* (Recklinghausen: Aurel Bongers, 1966); Klaus Hoffmann, ed., "Ausstellungsverzeichnis," *in Ludwig Meidner, 1884–1966*, exh. cat. (Wolfsburg: Kunstverein Wolfsburg, 1985); Gerhard Leistner, *Idee und Wirklichkeit: Gehalt und Bedeutung des urbanen Expressionismus in Deutschland, dargestellt am Werk Ludwig Meidners*, Europäische Hochschulschriften, Reihe 18, no. 66 (Frankfurt: Peter Lang, 1986); Ludwig Meidner, "Anleitung zum Malen von Grossstadtbildern," *Kunst und Künstler* 12 (March 1914): 312–14; translated under the title "An Introduction to Painting Big Cities," in *Voices of German Expressionism*, ed. Victor H. Miesel (Englewood Cliffs, N.J.: Prentice Hall, 1970), pp. 111–15; idem, "An alle Künstler," *Das Kunstblatt* 3, no. 1 (1919): 29–30; idem, *Dichter, Maler und Café*, ed. Ludwig Kunz (Zurich: Arche, 1973).

■ ■ ■

Moriz Melzer

BORN 1877 ALBENDORF, BOHEMIA ✣ DIED 1966 BERLIN

138. Untitled (abstract composition), c. 1919
Woodcut
5 15/16 x 7 1/16 in. (15.0 x 18.0 cm)
From *Der schwarze Turm*, no. 6 (1919)
Los Angeles County Museum of Art. The Robert Gore Rifkind Center for German Expressionist Studies, purchased with funds provided by Anna Bing Arnold, Museum Acquisition Fund, and deaccession funds

Moriz Melzer was a prolific graphic artist and an active participant in artists' groups and contributor to periodicals in the early decades of the century. Initially trained as a porcelain painter at the academy in Weimar, he moved to Berlin in 1908, shifting his focus to fine and graphic art and coming into contact with the German artistic and literary leftist avant-garde, of which he was to become a prominent member. First showing his work at the Berlin Secession in 1909, he helped found the New Secession the following year, after his work was rejected by the secession's jury. He took part in the New Secession's first graphic art exhibition and was a member of the group's work committee. During this period Melzer and Georg Tappert founded the Schule für freie und angewandte Kunst (School of fine and applied art) in Berlin, to provide an alternative to the conservative academic instruction offered by established institutions.

In Paris in 1912 Melzer participated in the Salon d'automne as well as the Sonderbund exhibition in Cologne. Back in Berlin in 1913, he showed his work at the Free Secession and contributed graphics to the periodicals *Die Aktion* (Action), *Der Sturm* (The storm), *Die weissen Blätter* (The white papers), and *Die schöne Rarität* (The beautiful curio). The drawings and prints he published in these journals are tumultuous works with an almost painterly quality of line. His subjects range from scenes of combat to studies of nudes in landscapes.

In 1914 Melzer voyaged to Montreux at the invitation of a friend and subsequently traveled in Italy, receiving the Villa Romana prize from the city of Florence. Beginning in 1922, he served as chair of the Novembergruppe (November group) and was a member of the Arbeitsrat für Kunst (Working council for art), in whose publication *Ja! Stimmen des Arbeitsrates für Kunst* (Yes! Voices of the Working council for art) he was represented by a print, Melzer also held professorships at the Reimann school in Berlin and at the institute of fine arts in Berlin from 1921 until the National Socialist takeover in 1933, when he joined the ranks of "degenerate" artists and was forbidden to work.

A.S.

BIBLIOGRAPHY
Helga Kliemann, *Die Novembergruppe, Bildende Kunst in Berlin*, no. 3 (Berlin: Mann, 1969); *Moriz Melzer zum 80. Geburtstag*, exh. cat. (Berlin: Kunstamt Wedding, 1957).

■ ■ ■

Erich Mendelsohn

BORN 1887 ALLENSTEIN, EAST PRUSSIA ✣ DIED 1953 SAN FRANCISCO

---

139. *Architekturphantasie—Perspektive*, 1914
(Architectural fantasy—perspective)
Ink
4 15/16 x 7 3/16 in. (12.5 x 18.3 cm)
Staatliche Museen zu Berlin, Kunstbibliothek

140. *Skizze für ein Bahnhofsgebäude—Perspektive*, 1914
(Sketch for a railroad station—perspective)
Pencil, ink
3 7/16 x 7 7/16 in. (8.7 x 18.2 cm)
Staatliche Museen zu Berlin, Kunstbibliothek

141. *Skizze für eine Halle(?)—Perspektive*, c. 1915
(Sketch for a hall[?]—perspective)
Ink
2 5/8 x 6 1/8 (6.7 x 15.5 cm)
Staatliche Museen zu Berlin, Kunstbibliothek

142. *Skizze für ein Glashaus*, 1917
(Sketch for a glass house)
Ink
3 1/4 x 3 7/8 in. (8.3 x 9.8 cm)
Staatliche Museen zu Berlin, Kunstbibliothek

143. *Einsteinturm: Drei Skizzenblätter mit je einer Perspektive (von Nordwesten und Nordosten) in verschiedenen Fassungen*, 1920
(Einstein tower: Three sketches with one perspective each [from northwest and northeast] in different versions)
Ink
3 x 5 3/8 in. (7.7 x 13.6 cm); 3 x 5 3/8 in. (7.6 x 13.5 cm); 3 1/16 x 5 1/4 in. (7.8 x 13.3 cm)
Staatliche Museen zu Berlin, Kunstbibliothek

144. *Skizze einer Dünenarchitektur*, 1920
(Sketch of dune architecture)
Pencil
4 3/4 x 8 13/16 in. (12.0 x 22.4 cm)
Staatliche Museen zu Berlin, Kunstbibliothek

145. *Skizze zum Kino "Universum,"* 1927
(Sketch for the Universum cinema)
Pencil, red pencil
3 7/16 x 9 1/4 in. (8.7 x 23.5 cm)
Staatliche Museen zu Berlin, Kunstbibliothek

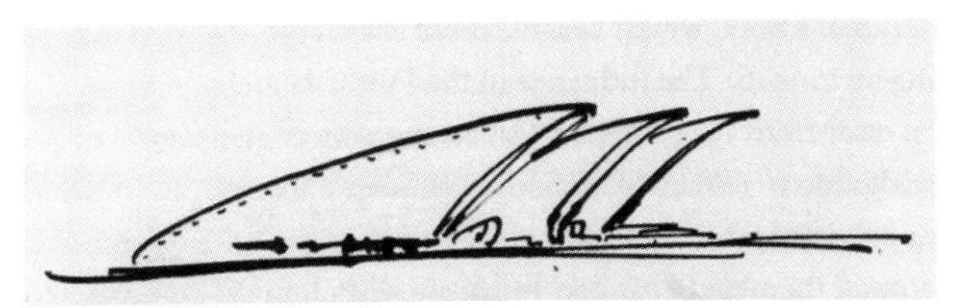

Cat. no. 141

Cat. no. 142

Cat. no. 144

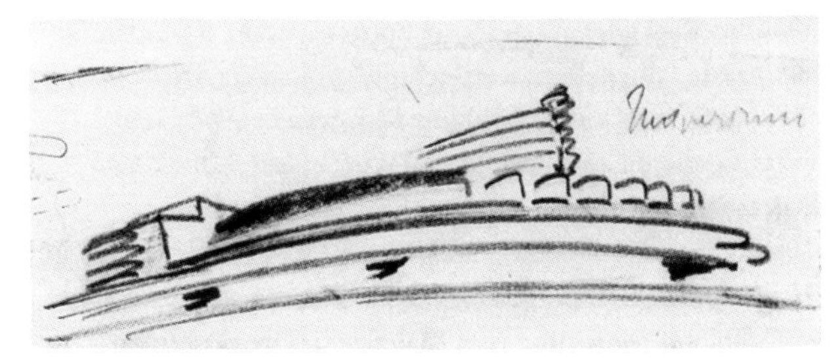

Cat. no. 145

Erich Mendelsohn absorbed a diverse array of influences to develop a highly individualized style that made him one of the foremost contributors to modern architecture in Germany in the 1920s. His family recalled that he was already determined to be an architect at the age of five, when he would build with whatever materials he could find. Mendelsohn himself credited the natural beauty of the area around Allenstein with instilling in him a love of nature. His designs were often based on organic forms and patterns of growth.

After receiving a classical education at the humanistic gymnasium in Allenstein (1892–1907), Mendelsohn attended classes in natural economy at the university in Munich. In 1908 he transferred to the technical college in Berlin to study architecture, returning to the university in Munich to complete his architectural studies. From 1912 to 1914 he worked as a private architect in Munich. In 1916 he was sent to the Russian front but made an agreement with a superior officer to allow him to sketch during his night watch, resulting in his "trench sketches" (1917) and his design for the Einsteinturm (Einstein tower). In 1919 many of these sketches were included in the exhibition In *Eisen und Beton* (In iron and concrete) at Paul Cassirer's gallery in Berlin.

After completing his military service, Mendelsohn established an architectural practice in Berlin in 1919 and formed close relationships with the Blaue Reiter (Blue rider) painters. His Einsteinturm in Potsdam (1919–21) and other early works exhibited his new Expressionist outlook. Unlike most Expressionist architects, however, Mendelsohn was neither impoverished nor unknown; his Berlin office was one of the busiest and most successful in Germany. During the 1920s he began to incorporate elements of Constructivism and moved away from Expressionism toward what became known as the International Style. Major works from this period include the Herman and Company hat factory in Luckenwalde (1921–23), the Schocken department store in Stuttgart (1926–28), and the Universum cinema in Berlin (1926–29).

Mendelsohn was compelled to leave Germany in 1933, when Hitler came to power. He emigrated to England and later became a British subject. He was invited to Palestine, where he designed several residences, hospitals, and other structures, which he adapted not only to the climate and available building materials but also to the landscape and culture. In 1941 he moved to San Francisco, where he again made spontaneous, unrestrained sketches reminiscent of his early work. His commissions there included the Maimonides Medical Center (1946–50).

V.H.

BIBLIOGRAPHY

Sigrid Achenbach, ed., *Erich Mendelsohn, 1887–1953: Ideen, Bauten, Projekte*, exh. cat. (Berlin: Staatliche Museen Preussischer Kulturbesitz, 1987); Susan King, *The Drawings of Eric Mendelsohn* (Berkeley and Los Angeles: University of California Press, 1969); Erich Mendelsohn, *Briefe eines Architekten*, ed. Oskar Beyer (Munich: Prestel, 1961); translated by Geoffrey Strachan as *Letters of an Architect* (London: Abelard-Schumann, 1967); idem, *Erich Mendelsohn: Complete Works of the Architect: Sketches, Designs, Buildings*, trans. Antje Fritsch (New York: Princeton Architectural Press, 1991); Hans R. Morgenthaler, *The Early Sketches of German Architect Erich Mendelsohn (1887–1953): No Compromise with Reality* (Lewiston, N.Y.: E. Mellen Press, 1992); Julius Posener, ed., *Erich Mendelsohn*, exh. cat. (Berlin: Akademie der Künste, 1968); Arnold Whittick, *Eric Mendelsohn*, 2d ed. (New York: F. W. Dodge, 1956); Bruno Zevi, *Erich Mendelsohn: Opera completa, architetture e immagini architettoniche* (Milan: Etas Kompass, 1970); idem, *Erich Mendelsohn* (London: Architectural Press, 1985).

■ ■ ■

Carl Mense

BORN 1886 RHEINE ✣ DIED 1965 KÖNIGSWINTER

146. *Strasse mit Fahnen*, 1913
(Street with flags)
Chalk and watercolor
10 1/4 x 8 1/8 in. (26.0 x 20.6 cm)
Rheinisches Landesmuseum, Bonn

147. *Stadt am Fluss*, 1918
(City on the river)
Lithograph
12 x 14 3/8 in. (30.5 x 36.5 cm)
Staatliche Graphische Sammlung, Munich

Cat. no. 147

Upholding, perhaps unconsciously, the traditions of north Rhenish painting, painter and graphic artist Carl Mense created dreamlike, visionary scenes. Although he began his career working in an Expressionist style, he later incorporated elements of Futurism and eventually, in 1918–19, made the transition to Neue Sachlichkeit (new objectivity).

From 1905 to 1908 Mense studied at the academy in Düsseldorf, and in 1909 he studied under Lovis Corinth in Berlin. Mense's work was published in *Der Sturm* (The storm) and *Die Aktion* (Action), but he maintained close ties with his native region, participating in the 1913 exhibition *Die rheinischen Expressionisten* (Rhenish Expressionists) in Bonn, joining the Rhenish Secession, and participating in several exhibitions organized by Das junge Rheinland (Young Rhineland).

From 1914 to 1918 Mense was a soldier. After the war he joined the Novembergruppe (November group). From 1924 to 1932 he was a professor at the academy in Breslau but began traveling through Europe in 1933. He continued to exhibit under the Third Reich, and from 1939 to 1945 he served as a soldier. After 1945 he resided in Bad Honnef.

V.H.

BIBLIOGRAPHY

Oskar Maria Graf, "Der Maler Carl Mense," *Der Cicerone* 15, no. 8 (1923): 380–86.

■ ■ ■

Robert Michel

BORN 1897 VOCKENHAUSEN ✣ DIED 1983 NEUSTADT

148. *Für Hans Godbard II*, 1921
(For Hans Godbard II)
India ink
21 5/8 x 26 3/8 in. (55.0 x 67.0 cm)
Sprengel Museum Hannover. Nachlass Robert Michel

Robert Michel's work reflects a fascination with machine technology, particularly the airplane. His early training was in engineering. A test pilot during World War I, he crashed his plane in 1916. After his recuperation he was released from military service in the winter of 1917, and he enrolled at the school of applied arts in Weimar, where he was part of a circle of students and architects around the Belgian architect and designer Henry van de Velde, with whom he shared an enthusiasm for modern technology and architecture. Among the students in this group was Ella Bergmann, whom he married in 1919. A year later the couple settled at his family estate in Vockenhausen.

Michel's broad education allowed him to pursue his own artistic work as well as endeavors in typography, design, advertising, and architecture. His art was frequently exhibited during the 1920s. In 1925 his work was shown at the Kunstverein (art association) in Wiesbaden alongside that of El Lissitzky and Kurt Schwitters, artists with whom he shared a breadth of skills and interests. Schwitters became a close friend of Michel and Bergmann and a frequent visitor at their home. He suggested that they send samples of their work to American collector Katherine Dreier. She bought one of Michel's drawings, which was included in a Societe Anonyme exhibition in 1928. His advertising designs were included in an exhibition organized by the Ring neuer Werbegestalter (Circle of new advertising designers), a group founded by Schwitters, in 1930 and in the *Internationale Ausstellung Kunst der Werbung* (International exhibition of advertising art) in Essen in 1931.

In 1927 Schwitters introduced Michel to Lucy Hillebrandt, an established architect in Frankfurt. They worked together until 1930. In 1932 and 1933 he also participated in exhibitions of the Bund deutscher Architekten (Association of German architects), of which he was a member until 1933. For the duration of the Third Reich he retreated to his country estate. In the postwar period he was slow to reemerge into the public arena, but his work has gained increasing recognition since the 1960s.

F.V.H.

BIBLIOGRAPHY

Norbert Nobis and Christian Grohn, eds., *Robert Michel, 1897–1983: Collagen, Malerei, Aquarelle, Zeichnungen, Druckgraphik, Reklame, Typographie, Entwürfe*, exh. cat. (Hannover: Sprengel Museum, 1988); *Pioniere der Bildcollage: Ella Bergmann und Robert Michel: Werke von 1917 bis 1962*, exh. cat. (Leverkusen: Stadtisches Museum, 1963).

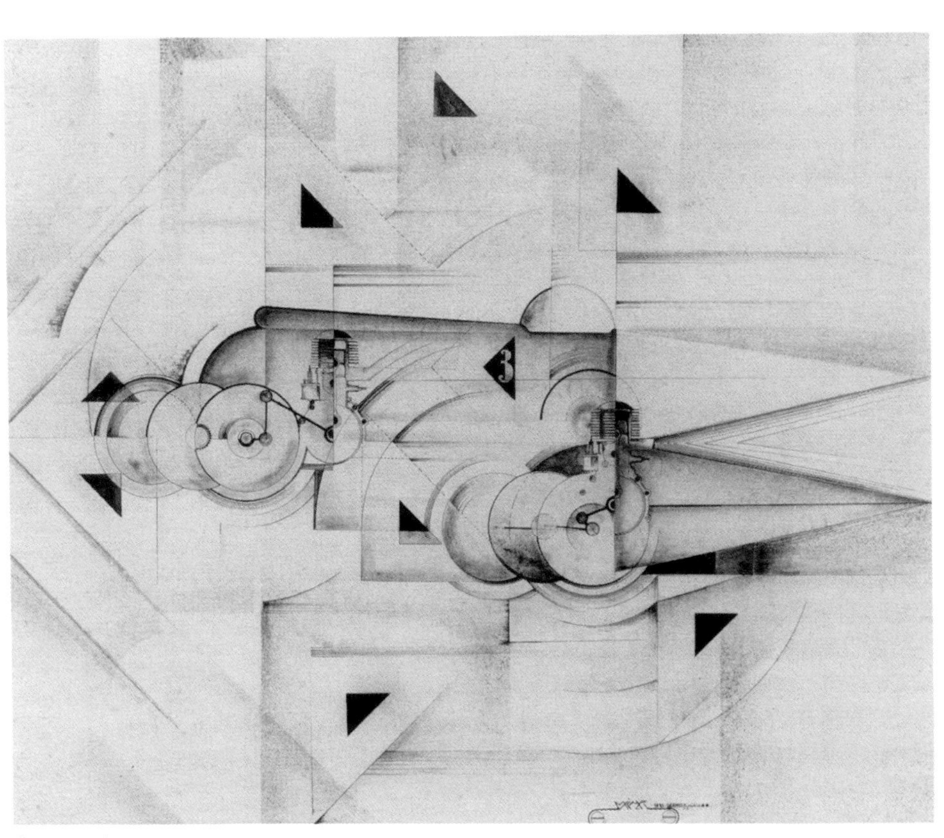

Cat. no. 148

Ludwig Mies van der Rohe

BORN 1886 AACHEN ✣ DIED 1969 CHICAGO

149. Cover for G, c. 1924
Photomechanical reproduction
9 7/8 x 6 7/8 in. (25.1 x 17.5 cm)
From G: *Zeitschrift für elementare Gestaltung*, no. 3 (June 1924)
The Resource Collections of the Getty Center for the History of Art and the Humanities

Ludwig Mies van der Rohe is considered a founder of the modern movement in architecture and furniture design. Among the diverse factors that influenced him were neoclassicism, the Dutch De Stijl movement, and the belief in a zeitgeist. His success was attained without the benefit of a formal education in architecture. Born into a family of stonemasons in Aachen, he attended the trade school there, then served as an apprentice to the architect and cartoonist Bruno Paul from 1905 to 1907. Along with Walter Gropius and Le Corbusier, Mies worked in the office of Peter Behrens from 1908 to 1911. He opened his own office in Berlin in 1913.

Mies's vision and craftsmanship mark him as an artist rather than a practitioner; this is especially evident in his spectacular drawings. His glass towers were precursors of American skyscrapers. Miesian architecture is characterized by vast expanses of glass with slender steel supports in buildings of exacting proportions which reflect his desire to achieve "a clear construction."

In the years following World War I Mies joined the activist Novembergruppe (November group), although some have speculated that his involvement was motivated as much by professional ambition as by political conviction at a time when even conservative architects lacked outlets to expose their work. He served as director of the group's architectural exhibitions from 1923 to 1925. Many of the early projects that helped establish his reputation—the crystalline office towers, the brick and concrete houses—were shown in exhibitions sponsored by the Novembergruppe and other organizations. In 1923 he cofounded the design periodical G with Hans Richter, and in 1925 he helped form the architects' organization Der Ring (The ring). From 1926 to 1932 Mies served as the first vice president of the Werkbund, organizing the group's 1927 exhibition in Stuttgart. Only a few of Mies's early designs were actually built; they include the German pavilion for the Barcelona exposition (1929) and the Tugendhat house (1928–30) in Brno, Czechoslovakia. During this period he also developed a line of tubular steel furniture, which included the first true cantilevered chair.

Upon Walter Gropius's recommendation, Mies was appointed director of the Bauhaus following the dismissal of Hannes Meyer in 1930, remaining there until its closure in 1933. Amid great controversy he strove to free the school of militant factions. In 1937 he immigrated to the United States and the following year became head of the Armour Institute (later Illinois Institute of Technology) in Chicago.

V.H.

BIBLIOGRAPHY

Werner Blaser, *Mies van der Rohe: The Art of Structure* (New York: Praeger, 1965); idem, *Mies van der Rohe: Less Is More* (New York: Waser, 1986); Arthur Drexler, *Ludwig Mies van der Rohe* (New York: George Braziller, 1960); Philip Johnson, *Mies van der Rohe*, 3d rev. ed. (New York: Museum of Modern Art, 1978); *Mies Reconsidered: His Career, Legacy, and Disciples*, exh. cat. (Chicago: Art Institute of Chicago, 1986); Fritz Neumeyer, *The Artless Word: Mies van der Rohe on the Building Art* (Cambridge: MIT Press, 1991); Franz Schulze, *Mies van der Rohe: A Critical Biography* (Chicago: University of Chicago Press, 1985); David A. Spaeth, *Mies van der Rohe* (New York: Rizzoli, 1985); A. James Speyer, *Mies van der Rohe* (Chicago: Art Institute of Chicago, 1968); Paul Westheim, "Mies van der Rohe: Entwicklung eines Architekten," *Das Kunstblatt* 11, no. 2 (1927): 55–62.

■ ■ ■

Constantin von Mitschke-Collande

BORN 1884 COLLANDE ✣ DIED 1956 NUREMBURG

150. Untitled (nude man with animals), c. 1923
Color woodcut
4 3/8 x 3 3/8 in. (11.1 x 8.0 cm)
From Walther Georg Hartmann, *Die Tiere der Insel* (1923)
Los Angeles County Museum of Art. The Robert Gore Rifkind Center for German Expressionist Studies, purchased with funds provided by Anna Bing Arnold, Museum Acquisition Fund, and deaccession funds

Conrad Felixmüller once remarked, "Besides Mitschke-Collande I was the only one in the political organization, movement, and struggle" (quoted in *Kunst im Aufbruch*, p. 50). Mitschke-Collande's political interests commanded a pivotal role in his art. After studying architecture at the technical college in Munich from 1905 to 1907, he studied painting at the academy in Dresden from 1907 to 1910, spent a year in Italy, returned to Dresden to study under Otto Gussman from 1912 to 1913, then spent a year in Paris as a student of Maurice Denis and Fernand Léger.

Mitschke-Collande served in World War I from 1914 to 1918, but in 1917 he, Felixmüller, Peter August Böckstiegel, and Otto Lange exhibited together as Gruppe 1917 (Group 1917) at the Kunstsalon Richter in Dresden. In 1919 he was a founding member of the Dresden Sezession Gruppe 1919 (Secession group 1919), which exhibited works with elements of Expressionism, Dadaism, and Futurism, some containing political imagery. Mitschke-Collande and a few others had expected the group to be more politically engaged, however, and they left in 1920. Despite being one of the few artists of his time to join the Communist party and one of the most radical of the Expressionists, Mitschke-Collande seems to have lost his political zeal with the dissolution of the Sezession Gruppe, a transition his art reflected. While he was a member, his vibrant art combined elements of the late Brücke style and Cubism; his later works were characterized by a stylized realism.

In the mid-1920s Mitschke-Collande worked as a set designer at the Staatliches Schauspielhaus in Dresden, where he designed the first production of Georg Kaiser's *Gas* (1925). In 1930 he established a private painting school. Several of his works were included in a 1933 National Socialist exhibition of "degenerate" art at the Neue Rathaus in Dresden, and two of his works were included in the 1937 *Entartete Kunst* (Degenerate art) exhibition in Munich. From that time on, he was forbidden to exhibit his work or seek public commissions.

Much of Mitschke-Collande's early work was destroyed in the bombing of Dresden during World War II. He resumed working after the war, first in Rothenburg, then in Nuremberg.

V.H.

BIBLIOGRAPHY

Constantin von Mitschke-Collande, exh. cat. (Regensburg: Ostdeutsche Galerie, 1975); *Dresdner Sezession, 1919–1923* (Milan: Galleria del Levante, 1977); *Kunst im Aufbruch: Dresden, 1918–1933*, exh. cat. (Dresden: Staatliche Kunstsammlungen, Gemäldegalerie Neue Meister, 1980); Lothar Lang, *Expressionist Book Illustration*, trans. Janet Seligman (Greenwich, Conn.: New York Graphic Society, 1976); *Revolution und Realismus: Revolutionäre Kunst in Deutschland 1917 bis 1933*, exh. cat. (Berlin: Staatliche Museen Preussischer Kulturbesitz, 1979).

■ ■ ■

László Moholy-Nagy

BORN 1895 BÁSBOKOD, HUNGARY ✣ DIED 1946 CHICAGO

151. *Dynamik der Metropol*, 1921–22
(Dynamic of the metropolis)
Photomechanical reproduction
9 x 14⁷⁄₈ in. (23.0 x 37.7 cm)
Illustrated screenplay from László Moholy-Nagy, *Malerei, Fotographie, Film*, 2d ed. (1925), pp. 120–21
Los Angeles County Museum of Art. The Robert Gore Rifkind Center for German Expressionist Studies, purchased with funds provided by Anna Bing Arnold, Museum Acquisition Fund, and deaccession funds

152. *Photomontage "Berlin" zum Schauspiel "Der Kaufmann von Berlin" von Water Mehring*, 1929
(Berlin photomontage for "The merchant of Berlin" by Walter Mehring)
Photomontage
11³⁄₄ x 15³⁄₈ in. (29.8 x 39.0 cm)
Theaterwissenschaftliche Sammlung, Universität zu Köln

See also cat. no. 230

An outstanding figure both for his teaching at the Bauhaus and for the extraordinary breadth of his work, László Moholy-Nagy was one of a large group of Hungarian émigrés (including Bela Balázs, Marcel Breuer, and Andor Weininger) who contributed to the cultural avant-garde of Weimar Germany. Moholy-Nagy is best known for his experimental photography and montage and his 1925 book *Malerei, Fotographie, Film* (Painting, photography, film), in which he set forth his theories on the potential of mechanical media to extend "the limits of the depiction of nature and the use of light as a creative agent" (*Painting, Photography, Film*, p. 7). He also worked in typography, stage design, and film and headed the metal workshop at the Bauhaus from 1923 until 1928.

Moholy-Nagy began law studies in Budapest, interrupting his education to serve in World War I from 1914 to 1917. Upon his return he came into contact with the circle around the liberal art journal *MA* (Today), which was published in Budapest until 1919, when its editorial staff moved to Vienna. In 1919 he left Hungary, moving first to Vienna and then, in 1920, to Berlin, where he worked as a correspondent for the magazine. After meeting El Lissitzky in 1921, he took part in Theo van Doesburg's Constructivist congress in Weimar and worked with other Hungarian artists, among them László Péri, with whom he exhibited at the Sturm gallery in 1922.

Invited by Walter Gropius to teach at the Bauhaus in 1923, Moholy-Nagy took over the teaching of the basic course from Johannes Itten and the leadership of the metal workshop from Paul Klee. Moholy-Nagy was fascinated by the possibilities of light as a medium in itself, exploring still photography as well as film, whose "essential medium," he wrote, "is *light* not pigment" (Kostelanetz, *Moholy-Nagy*, p. 131). For the stage he proposed a "total theater," which would eliminate "all that is logical-intellectual (literature)," using light, sound, form, and motion as interdependent elements. In his essay "Theater, Zirkus, Varieté" (Theater, circus, variety show), published in 1927, he emphasized formal elements rather than content: "Even if conflicts arising from today's complicated social patterns, from the world-wide organization of technology, from pacifist-utopian and other kinds of revolutionary movements, can have a place in the art of the stage, they will be significant only in a transitional period, since their treatment belongs properly to the realms of literature, politics, and philosophy" (translated in Gropius and Wensinger, *Theater o f the Bauhaus*, p. 62).

Although Moholy-Nagy designed a number of theatrical productions in the early 1920s—such as Upton Sinclair's *Prince Hagen* in 1921 and Walter Hasenclever's *Die Menschen* (The people) and Shakespeare's *Othello* in 1923—his most ambitious projects were for the Berlin Krolloper, founded in 1927, where he was able to implement his ideas on a grander scale, despite the traditional material he was given. For his first commission, *Hoffmanns Erzählungen* (The tales of Hoffmann), performed in 1929, he created imaginary spaces with scaffolding, used light and color to accentuate parts of the drama, and employed steel sets (designed by Breuer) for the first time on the stage. That year Moholy-Nagy received a commission from radical theater director Erwin Piscator to design Walter Mehring's *Der Kaufmann von Berlin* (The merchant of Berlin). Moholy-Nagy also designed Paul Hindemith's *Hin und Zurück* (There and back) in 1930 and Giacomo Puccini's *Madama Butterfly* in 1931 for the Krolloper.

After the National Socialist takeover Moholy-Nagy immigrated first to Amsterdam, then to London, and finally to Chicago, where he cofounded the New Bauhaus design school.

A.S.

BIBLIOGRAPHY

Walter Gropius and Arthur S. Wensinger, eds., *The Theater of the Bauhaus*, trans. Arthur S. Wensinger (Middletown, Conn.: Wesleyan University Press, 1961); Eleanor M. Hight, *Moholy-Nagy: Photography and Film in Weimar Germany*, exh. cat. (Wellesley, Mass.: Wellesley College Museum, 1985); Richard Kostelanetz, ed., *Moholy-Nagy, Documentary Monographs in Modern Art*, ed. Paul Cummings (New York: Praeger, 1970); *László Moholy-Nagy, Painting, Photography, Film*, trans. Janet Seligman (Cambridge: MIT Press, 1969); Sibyl Moholy-Nagy, *Moholy-Nagy: Experiment in Totality*, 2d ed. (Cambridge: MIT Press, 1969); Krisztina Passuth, *Moholy-Nagy*, trans. Eva Grusz et al. (New York: Thames and Hudson, 1985); Leland D. Rice and David W. Steadman, eds., *Photographs of Moholy-Nagy from the Collection of William Larson*, exh. cat. (Claremont, Calif.: Galleries of the Claremont Colleges, 1975).

■ ■ ■

Otto Möller

BORN 1883 SCHMIEDEFELD ✣ DIED 1964 BERLIN

153. *Berliner Expression*
(Berlin expression)
Lithograph
9 15/16 x 8 1/16 in. (25.2 x 20.5 cm)
Los Angeles County Museum of Art, The Robert Gore Rifkind Center for German Expressionist Studies

Otto Möller devoted most of his career to teaching, although he was also a prolific artist and played a role in the Novembergruppe (November group) from its founding in 1919 until 1932. Having studied with renowned German Impressionist Lovis Corinth, he began working in a modified Impressionist style but, like many other German artists of his generation, was influenced by Cubism and Futurism and drew inspiration from Robert Delaunay's use of color.

In a group of works from the 1910s and 1920s Möller depicted the city as a series of colored geometric forms, using fragments of words drawn from daily life and from advertising, such as *café* and *cigarette*. With their densely overlapping groups of stores, vehicles, and industrial objects, his cityscapes communicate both the excitement and the disorienting nature of the metropolis. His themes were wide-ranging, however, and he produced numerous semiabstract woodcuts, watercolors, and drawings as well as realistic landscapes in a more Fauvist vein.

From 1904 to 1907 Möller studied at the royal school of art in Berlin, where he received classical training in draftsmanship and painting. Beginning in 1909, he taught art in Berlin; he exhibited with the Berlin Secession from 1910 until 1912, showing mostly lithographs, drawings, and woodcuts. In 1919 he was represented in a Novembergruppe exhibition along with eighteen other artists, including César Klein and Moriz Melzer, and participated in most of the group's exhibitions until 1931. In 1927 Möller was also a member of the group's jury and exhibition committee. In the mid-1920s his style became more representational, resembling that of the Neue Sachlichkeit (new objectivity) artists.

From 1920 Möller taught methodology and artistic pedagogy at the institute of art education in Berlin, where he and the painter Bernhard Hasler shared responsibility for developing new teaching programs, Although he maintained this post until 1940, he was forbidden to exhibit after the National Socialist takeover in 1933. After the war, from 1946 to 1955, he was a professor of art education at the institute of fine arts in Berlin.

A.S.

BIBLIOGRAPHY

Peter Hopf, ed., *Die Novembergruppe: Teil I: Die Maler*, exh. cat., *Tendenzen der zwanziger Jahre* (Berlin: Kunstamt Wedding, 1977); *Künstler der Novembergruppe*, exh. cat. (Berlin: Galerie Nierendorf, 1985).

■ ■ ■

Johannes Molzahn

BORN 1892 DUISBURG ✝ DIED 1965 MUNICH

154. *Schöpfung*, 1917
(Creation)
Watercolor
17 5/8 x 12 1/8 in. (44.8 x 30.8 cm)
Loretto Molzahn

155. *Spingende Pferde (Tierformen)*, 1919
(Jumping horses [animal forms])
Woodcut
13 11/16 x 10 in. (34.8 x 25.3 cm)
Wilhelm Lehmbruck Museum, Duisburg

156. *Sternbewegung*, 1919
(Star movement)
Woodcut
8 7/16 x 5 13/16 in. (21.5 x 14.8 cm)
Wilhelm Lehmbruck Museum, Duisburg

157. *Sternendröhnen*, 1919
(Roar of the stars)
Woodcut
13 3/4 x 8 11/16 in. (35.0 x 22.0 cm)
Wilhelm Lehmbruck Museum, Duisburg

158. *Zeit-Taster: Eine kleine Kollektion utopisch-phantastischer Maschinen und Apparate*, 1921
(Time-feeler: A small collection of utopian fantastic machines and apparatuses)
Color lithograph
Sheet: 12 7/8 x 10 in. (32.7 x 25.4 cm)
Cover from the portfolio Zeit-Taster: Eine kleine Kollektion utopisch-phantastischer Maschinen und Apparate (1921)
Wilhelm Lehmbruck Museum, Duisburg

159. *Grundriss der Mechanik und Festigkeitslehre*, 1921
(Blueprint of mechanics and tensile strength)
Etching
3 3/8 x 4 3/8 in. (8.6 x 12.0 cm)
From the portfolio Zeit-Taster: Eine kleine Kollektion utopisch-phantastischer Maschinen und Apparate (1921)
Wilhelm Lehmbruck Museum, Duisburg

160. *Industrie-Denkmäler*, 1921
(Monuments for industry)
Etching
4 3/4 x 3 3/4 in. (12.0 x 8.6 cm)
From the portfolio Zeit-Taster: Eine kleine Kollektion utopisch-phantastischer Maschinen und Apparate (1921)
Wilhelm Lehmbruck Museum, Duisburg

161. *Atom-Zerstäuber, die neue Kraft-Zentrale*, 1921
(Atom smasher, the new power plant)
Etching
6 15/16 x 4 7/8 in. (17.6 x 12.5 cm)
From the portfolio Zeit-Taster: Eine kleine Kollektion utopisch-phantastischer Maschinen und Apparate (1921)
Wilhelm Lehmbruck Museum, Duisburg

162. *Konstruktion eines Milchstrassen-Elevators*, 1921
(Construction of an elevator for the Milky Way)
Etching
10 11/16 x 4 13/16 (27.2 x 12.2 cm)
From the portfolio Zeit-Taster: Eine kleine Kollektion utopisch-phantastischer Maschinen und Apparate (1921)
Wilhelm Lehmbruck Museum, Duisburg

163. *Höhen-Lokomobilchen*, 1921
(Little height locomobiles)
Etching
4 5/8 x 4 1/2 in. (11.8 x 11.5 cm)
From the portfolio Zeit-Taster: Eine kleine Kollektion utopisch-phantastischer Maschinen und Apparate (1921)
Wilhelm Lehmbruck Museum, Duisburg

164. *James Watt, dem Erfinder der Dampfmaschine*, 1921
(To James Watt, the inventor of the steam engine)
Etching
7 1/2 x 5 5/8 in. (19.1 x 14.3 cm)
From the portfolio Zeit-Taster: Eine kleine Kollektion utopisch-phantastischer Maschinen und Apparate (1921)
Wilhelm Lehmbruck Museum, Duisburg

Johannes Molzahn spent his youth in Weimar, where he attended drawing school. In 1915 he was called up for military duty and served on the German-Danish border. His best-known early paintings, *Schöpfung I* (Creation I) and *Schöpfung II* of 1916, manifest a pantheistic perspective. His first exhibition was in 1917 at Herwarth Walden's Sturm gallery in Berlin. In 1918 he returned to Weimar, where he was active in the founding and early phases of the Bauhaus. In 1919 he published "Das Manifest des absoluten Expressionismus" (The manifesto of absolute Expressionism) in *Der Sturm* (The storm).

Foremost a painter, "the German Boccioni" also created architectural fantasies in charcoal and graphite and participated in the 1919 *Ausstellung für unbekannte Architekten* (Exhibition of unknown architects) in Berlin. Bruno Taut, who was serving as Magdeburg's city-planning officer, chose Molzahn to teach advertising, graphics, typesetting, printing, and lithography at the school of applied arts there. His later works show the influence of film, for example, his 1921 *Die Rollschuhläufer* (The roller skaters), a homage to Charlie Chaplin, and the 1925 *Porträt-Kinema* (Cinema portrait). Erotic and mythological images were likewise subjects for works such as *Männliche Kurve—Urtierchen* (Masculine curve—protozoan, 1921); *Frauenspiegel II* (Lady's looking glass II, 1928); and *Heroische Geste (Apollo)* (Heroic gesture [Apollo], 1933). From 1928 to 1932 Molzahn was a professor at the academy in Breslau.

The Nazi's 1937 exhibition *Entartete Kunst* (Degenerate art) included six paintings and one woodcut by Molzahn. With the help of Walter Gropius, who was then a professor of architecture at Harvard, he emigrated to the United States in 1938. From 1938 to 1952 Molzahn lectured and held professorships in Seattle, Chicago, and New York, obtaining American citizenship in 1949. His works after 1950 were often on religious subjects, reflecting his growing interest in Catholicism. In 1959 he returned to Germany and was named a full member of the academy in Berlin.

V.H.

BIBLIOGRAPHY
Christoph Brockhaus and Barbara Lepper, *Johannes Molzahn: Das malerische Werk*, exh. cat. (Duisburg: Wilhelm Lehmbruck Museum, 1988); Siegfried Salzmann and Ernst-Gerhard Güse, *Johannes Molzahn: Das druckgraphische Werk*, exh. cat. (Duisburg: Wilhelm Lehmbruck Museum, 1976); Herbert Schade, *Johannes Molzahn: Einführung in das Werk und die Kunsttheorie des Malers* (Munich: Schnell und Steiner, 1972)

■ ■ ■

Cat. no. 155

Cat. no. 156

Otto Mueller

BORN 1874 LIEBAU ✣ DIED 1930 BRESLAU

165. *Knabe zwischen Blattpflanzen*, 1912
(Youth seated between large plants)
Woodcut
11 x 14¹/16 in. (27.9 x 37.3 cm)
Los Angeles County Museum of Art. The Robert Gore Rifkind Center for German Expressionist Studies

166. *Badende*, 1920
(Bathers)
Lithograph
6 7/8 x 9 5/16 in. (17.5 x 23.7 cm)
From Kurt Pfister, *Deutsche Graphiker der Gegenwarf* (1920)
Los Angeles County Museum of Art. The Robert Gore Rifkind Center for German Expressionist Studies, purchased with funds provided by Anna Bing Arnold, Museum Acquisition Fund, and deaccession funds

167. *Adam und Eva*, 1920–23
(Adam and Eve)
Lithograph
17³/16 x 13 in. (43.6 x 33.1 cm)
Los Angeles County Museum of Art. The Robert Gore Rifkind Center for German Expressionist Studies

Otto Mueller, like fellow members of the Brücke (Bridge) Erich Heckel, Ernst Ludwig Kirchner, and Karl Schmidt-Rottluff, was fascinated by the portrayal of landscape and the human form in harmony with nature. Unlike his colleagues, however, Mueller was engaged almost exclusively with this motif and showed comparatively little interest in portraying the city. His numerous depictions of female figures in nature not only display a fascination with arcadian symbolism but also present the female form as the incarnation of, and perhaps a necessary condition for, this preindustrial idyll. While his female figures are almost always depicted in groups, secluded from men and modern society, they are also highly erotic.

Another subject frequently depicted in Mueller's work is gypsies. It is probable that gypsies intrigued him for many of the same reasons that African and Oceanic art interested Kirchner; they represented the fringe of German society. Culturally, racially, and often linguistically isolated, they may have appealed to Mueller's sense of himself as an outsider.

Born in a small town in Silesia to a civil servant father and a mother whom he claimed was part gypsy, Mueller had an unusual upbringing. A childhood friend of the writer Gerhart Hauptmann, he moved in avant-garde literary circles early in his life. Mueller's education was a patchwork of schooling and self-training: he began an apprenticeship in lithography in the town of Görlitz, then entered the academy in Dresden in 1894, again leaving before completing his studies. Planning to study in Munich in 1898, he changed his mind again and worked independently for a year, after which he returned to Dresden. From 1900 to 1908 he lived in various parts of Silesia with Maschka Mayerhofer, who later became his first wife.

Mueller's move to Berlin in 1908 brought contacts with the artists with whom he would join in founding the New Secession and with the Brücke, which he joined in 1910, becoming the last member to join before the group's dissolution in 1913. For the next few years he was the friend and colleague of the Brücke artists, who learned from him the technique of distemper, a painting method that allowed them to work more spontaneously. From 1916 to 1918 Mueller served in World War I, resuming work after his return to Berlin in 1918 and traveling frequently to Eastern Europe. He taught at the academy in Breslau from 1919 until his death there in 1930.

A.S.

BIBLIOGRAPHY

Lothar Günther Buchheim, *Otto Mueller: Leben und Werk: Mit einem Werkverzeichnis der Graphik Otto Muellers von Florian Karsch* (Feldafing: Buchheim, 1963); idem, *Otto Mueller* (Feldafing: Buchheim, 1968); *Otto Mueller zum hundertsten Geburtstag: Das graphische Gesamtwerk*, exh. cat. (Berlin: Galerie Nierendorf, 1974).

■ ■ ■

Hermann Obrist

BORN 1862 KILCHBERG, SWITZERLAND ✣ DIED 1927 MUNICH

168. *Felsgrotte mit loderndem Fluss II*, c. 1895–1900
(Rock grotto with blazing river II)
Tempera over pencil on gray paper glued to board
11 3/16 x 7 7/16 in. (28.4 x 18.8 cm)
Staatliche Graphische Sammlung, Munich

169. *Entwurf zu einem Denkmal II*, c. 1898–1900
(Sketch for a monument II)
Pencil
5 11/16 x 4 in. (14.5 x 10.1 cm)
Staatliche Graphische Sammlung, Munich

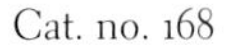

Cat. no. 168

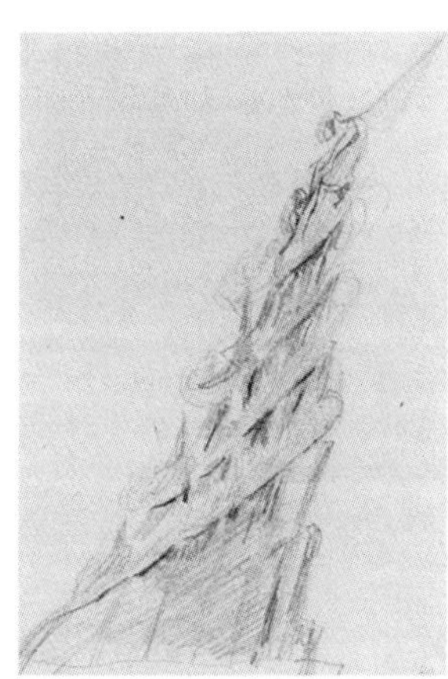

Cat. no. 169

From his early schooldays through his final years Hermann Obrist experienced visions of architectural forms, city plans, fairy-tale buildings, and religious edifices of inconceivable beauty, accompanied by an inner voice exclaiming, "Go and build this!" Although he was never commissioned to design a building, he expressed his innovative architectural concepts in models and exceptionally imaginative fountains and funerary monuments, which inspired a new approach to art and architecture in the pre-World War I years. He explored the "possibilities of new shapings of space, new static effects, new constructions, new forms, new methods, and new ornamentation."

As a sculptor, designer, and teacher Obrist based his works and writings on the psychological theories of empathy taught by Theodor Lipps, seeking through his art to transcend bourgeois concerns and encounter an object's inner essence. Born to a Swiss physician father and a Scottish mother, he entered Heidelberg University in 1885 to study medicine and natural sciences but left a year later, traveling to Berlin, England, and then Scotland. In the fall of 1887 he entered the school of applied arts in Karlsruhe to study ceramics. After winning a gold medal at the 1889 Paris Exposition for his unusual ceramic and furniture designs, he went to Paris, where he studied sculpture. In 1892 he moved to Florence to study marble craftsmanship and established an embroidery studio, which he transferred to Munich in 1895.

Obrist gained notoriety as an inspiring lecturer advocating the reform of arts and crafts education. In 1897 he became the leading organizer of the Vereinigte Werkstätten für Kunst im Handwerk (Union of arts and crafts workshops) in Munich. In 1902 he and Wilhelm von Debschitz opened the Lehr- und Versuchsateliers für angewandte und freie Kunst (Teaching and experimental studios for the applied and fine arts) in Munich, which was one of the first schools in Germany to emphasize the interdependence of the fine and applied arts.

Throughout his career Obrist had erratic contacts with a variety of groups. He was associated with the Munich Jugendstil and joined the Munich Secession but attacked the latter for its conservatism and resigned. He took delight in the visionary works of the participants in the 1919 *Ausstellung für unbekannte Architekten* (Exhibition of unknown architects). The show was organized by the Arbeitsrat für Kunst (Working council for art), which honored Obrist by including photographs of his sketches for funerary monuments. As an advocate of private initiative, however, Obrist shunned the group's social ideals and argued that the true artist should avoid any organizational or committee affiliation. Nevertheless the Expressionists, considerably younger than he, looked upon Obrist as a prophet, a spiritual father. Although he felt that his fantasy work surpassed that of the Expressionists, Obrist shared their utopian yearnings. In 1919 he predicted that in three decades Germany would lead triumphantly in the arts. He did not associate with the postwar phase of Expressionism, having withdrawn into a private world.

V.H.

BIBLIOGRAPHY

Silvie Lampe-von Bennigsen, *Hermann Obrist: Erinnerungen* (Munich: Herbert Post Presse, 1970); *Hermann Obrist, Neue Möglichkeiten in der bildenden Kunst: Essays* (Leipzig: Eugen Diederichs, 1903); Hans Christoph von Tavel, *Hermann Obrist, 1862–1927; Louis Soutter, 1871–1942; Jean Bloé Niestlé, 1884–1942; Kurt Seligmann, 1900–1962*, exh. cat. (Bern: Kunstmuseum, 1967); Siegfried Wichmann, *Hermann Obrist: Wegbereiter der Moderne*, exh. cat. (Munich: Stuck-Jugendstil-Verein, 1968).

■ ■ ■

Max Pechstein

BORN 1881 ZWICKAU ✝ DIED 1955 BERLIN

170. *Erlegung des Festbratens*. 1911
(Killing of the banquet roast)
Hand-colored woodcut on newsprint
8 7/8 x 10 1/4 in. (22.5 x 26.0 cm)
Proof apart from the edition published in *Der Sturm* 2, no. 93 (1912)
Los Angeles County Museum of Art. The Robert Gore Rifkind Center for German Expressionist Studies

171. *Tanzende und Badende am Waldteich*, 1912
(Dancers and bathers at a forest pond)
Hand-colored lithograph
17 1/16 x 2 13/16 in. (43.5 x 32.5 cm)
From the portfolio Brücke VII (1912)
Los Angeles County Museum of Art. The Robert Gore Rifkind Center for German Expressionist Studies

172. Attributed to Max Pechstein
Cover for *Arbeitsrat für Kunst Berlin*, 1919
Woodcut on green paper
7 5/8 x 12 1/2 in. (19.4 x 31.7 cm)
The Resource Collections of the Getty Center for the History of Art and the Humanities

Max Pechstein was one of the most politically active and vocal of the Expressionists, believing in the power of revolutionary socialism to provide a new ground for artistic creativity. Surprisingly, however, he was also one of the most publicly accepted of the Expressionists, receiving a number of government prizes during the 1910s and 1920s, exhibiting with the Berlin Secession, and managing to live at least partially from the sale of his works. Cofounder of the New Secession as well as the Novembergruppe (November group) and the Arbeitsrat für Kunst (Working council for art), he played an important role in the Berlin art community both before and after World War I.

The son of a textile worker, Pechstein left school at age fifteen to study painting with a local mural painter. This apprenticeship—four years of drawing "a draft animal in front of a cart"—bored him, however, and in 1900 he moved to Dresden, where he enrolled at the school of applied arts. Meeting Erich Heckel in 1906 on the occasion of an applied arts show for which he created a mural, Pechstein joined the Brücke (Bridge) that year. He wrote of his relationship with Heckel: "We recognized our common longing, our similar enthusiasm for the van Goghs and Munchs we had seen.... A shared love of the woodcut also bonded us" ("Autobiographie," in *Max Pechstein: Zeichnungen und Aquarelle*, exh. cat., ed. Jürgen Schilling [(Hamburg?), 1987], p. 6).

From 1908 Pechstein lived in Berlin, where his studio provided a meeting place for the Brücke during stays in the city. Along with a number of other artists, such as César Klein, Moriz Melzer, and Georg Tappert, he founded the New Secession as an alternative exhibition society after a number of artists had been rejected by the Berlin Secession's jury. After Pechstein exhibited with the Berlin Secession in 1912, which the Brücke members had agreed not to do, he was expelled from the group, bringing it closer to its final breakup in 1913, When he returned to Germany in 1915 after a journey to Palau that ended with imprisonment in Japan and a long voyage home under a false passport, he was called up for military service.

After the war Pechstein was instrumental in founding the Arbeitsrat für Kunst and the Novembergruppe in Berlin, whose stated goal was "to dedicate all our energies to the moral regeneration of a young and free Germany" ("The November Group Manifesto," in *Voices of German Expressionism*, p. 169). For a book published by the Novembergruppe entitled *An alle Künstler!* (To all artists), Pechstein designed the cover and drafted the central essay, "Was wir wollen" (What we want). He called for students to break away from the conservative *Scheinkunst* (sham art) taught at the academies and voiced the hope that the future socialist republic would provide fertile ground for artistic development and cultural renewal. He demanded a greater voice for artists in society and access to art and art education for all citizens: "The beginning of a new unity of *Volk* and art will be heralded on the basis of craft, with each artist working in his own fashion.... Art is no game, but a duty to the *Volk!* It is a matter of public concern.... This we demand as the most important aspect of our right to self-determination, and this is how we shall demonstrate that we are important not merely for art lovers but for society as a whole" ("What We Want," ibid., p. 179).

Pechstein was appointed to a professorship at the academy in Berlin in 1922, which he held for eleven years before being removed from his post by the National Socialists. He spent the war years in Pomerania, where he was eventually taken prisoner by the Russians. After the war he returned to Berlin to resume teaching at the academy.

A.S.

BIBLIOGRAPHY

Paul Fechter, *Das graphische Werk Max Pechsteins* (Berlin: Fritz Gurlitt, 1921); Günter Krüger, "Der Maler Max Pechstein als Graphiker," *Zeitschrift des Deutschen Vereins für Kunstwissenschaft* 40 (1986): 115–35; idem, *Das druckgraphische Werk Max Pechsteins* (Tökendorf: R. C. Pechstein, 1988); Wolfgang Werner, ed., *Max Pechstein: Brücke Period and Works by Heckel, Nolde, Kirchner, Schmidt-Rottluff*, exh. cat. (New York: Helen Serger/La Boetie, 1984); Max Pechstein, "Was wir wollen," in *An alle Künstler!* (Berlin: W. Simon, 1919), pp. 18–22; translated under the title "What We Want," in *Voices of German Expressionism*, ed. Victor H. Miesel (Englewood Cliffs, N.J.: Prentice Hall, 1970); idem, *Erinnerungen*, ed. Leopold Reidemiester (Wiesbaden: Limes, 1960); Jürgen Schilling, ed., *Max Pechstein*, exh. cat. (Unna: Schloss Cappenberg, 1989).

■ ■ ■

Wilhelm Plünnecke

BORN 1894 HANNOVER ✣ DIED 1954 STUTTGART

173. *Häuser, Bäume, Menschen*, 1919
(Houses, trees, people)
Lithograph
9 7/8 x 8 7/16 in. (25.1 x 21.4 cm)
Cover for the portfolio Häuser, Bäume, Menschen (1921)
Los Angeles County Museum of Art. The Robert Gore Rifkind Center for German Expressionist Studies

174. Untitled (factory), 1919
Lithograph
13 1/8 x 9 3/4 in. (33.3 x 24.8 cm)
From the portfolio Häuser, Bäume, Menschen (1921)
Los Angeles County Museum of Art. The Robert Gore Rifkind Center for German Expressionist Studies, purchased with funds provided by Anna Bing Arnold, Museum Acquisition Fund, and deaccession funds

The little-known painter and graphic artist Wilhelm Plünnecke was trained at the Kunstgewerbemuseum (Museum of applied arts) in Berlin. He illustrated books and from 1919 to 1920 contributed illustrations to the Hannover avant-garde journal *Das hohe Ufer* (The high bank).

V.H.

■ ■ ■

Hans Poelzig

BORN 1869 BERLIN ✣ DIED 1936 BERLIN

175. Untitled (interior perspective sketch looking toward the stage, for the concert hall project, Dresden), c. 1918
Graphite on tracing paper
Image: 10 1/16 x 12 7/8 in. (25.6 x 32.8 cm)
Collection Centre Canadien d'Architecture/Canadian Centre for Architecture, Montreal

176. Untitled (sketch of the interior of the Grosses Schauspielhaus, Berlin), c. 1919
Graphite and crayon on tracing paper
Image: 10 1/4 x 12 7/8 in. (26.1 x 32.8 cm)
Collection Centre Canadien d'Architecture/Canadian Centre for Architecture, Montreal

177. *Festspielhaus Salzburg, erste Fassung: Zuschauerraum*, 1920–21
(Salzburg festival hall, first version: Auditorium)
Charcoal on tissue paper
21 7/8 x 27 15/16 in. (55.6 x 71.0 cm)
Plansammlung der Universitäsbibliothek der Technischen Universität, Berlin

178. *Festspielhaus Salzburg, erste Fassung: Aussenansicht mit Treppenanlage*, 1920–22
(Salzburg festival hall, first version: Exterior view with stairway)
Chalk on tissue paper
15 3/8 x 27 7/8 in. (39.1 x 70.8 cm)
Plansammlung der Universitätbibliothek der Technischen Universität, Berlin

179. *Modell für eine Wegkapelle*, 1921
(Model for a way chapel)
Plaster
16 1/8 x 13 3/16 x 9 13/16 in. (40.0 x 33.5 x 25.0 cm)
Badisches Landesmuseum, Karlsruhe

An architect who created some of the most personal Expressionist works, Hans Poelzig was the son of a countess, whose maiden name he retained. He studied architecture at the technical college in Berlin-Charlottenburg, worked as an assistant to Hugo Häring in the Berlin building office between 1894 and 1895, and began working in the technical office of the Prussian ministry of public works in 1899. Poelzig taught for most of his life, placing the highest value upon his role as a teacher. He worked tirelessly, incessantly making sketches of people, animals, and landscapes as well as architectural forms and ornamental motifs, Two common themes in his works are the cave and the tower. The cave became a leitmotif that was adopted by other architects (for example, in Bruno Taut's 1914 Glashaus [Glass house]). The tower was also a common Expressionist theme. Poelzig's 1910 water tower at Posen was perhaps his most significant early work. During World War I he proposed many projects, few of which were built.

In 1918 Poelzig joined both the Arbeitsrat für Kunst (Working council for art) and the Novembergruppe (November group). He became chairman of the Werkbund in 1919, later joined Der Ring (The ring), and by 1924 was an active participant in the Kreis der Freunde des Bauhauses (Circle of friends of the Bauhaus). Although Poelzig and Taut belonged to some of the same organizations, their relationship was not amicable. Taut attacked Poelzig on many occasions, almost causing him to resign from the Arbeitsrat. The brunt of his criticism targeted Poelzig's use of repeating patterns in his structures, yet what was for Taut redundancy was for Poelzig resonance.

Poelzig's best-known work was his 1919 Grosses Schauspielhaus theater in Berlin. Combining the concept of the "people's theater" with nineteenth-century utopian socialism, the Schauspielhaus manifested the Expressionist concern for the social usefulness of art, uniting actors and audience in an arena defined by imposing stalactite ceiling projections.

Director Paul Wegener's 1920 *Der Golem* (The golem) was the first and most significant of Poelzig's three film commissions (followed by Wegener's *Lebende Buddhas* [Living Buddhas, 1923–24], a financial failure, and Arthur von Gerlach's *Zur Chronik von Grieshuus* [Chronicles of Grieshuus, 1924–25]). Unlike other designers, who created the illusion of space, Poelzig used scaffolding, wooden lath, and plaster to create three-dimensional space, a concept foreign to motion pictures up to that time. Describing the set of *Der Golem*, Wegener stated: "It isn't Prague...not Prague or any other town. Rather it is a poetic townscape" (quoted in *Der dramatische Raum*, p. 109). Poelzig assembled palpable dream scenes: winding passages, distorted rib vaults, twisting and turning stairs—externalized symbols of the inner psychology of an enclosed ghetto.

Harassed by the Nazis because of his friendships, architecture, and principles, Poelzig left Germany for Turkey in 1936. There he was granted responsibility for the design of public works and was offered a professorship at the school of architecture in Ankara. In spite of his successes—he won first place in a 1935 competition for an academy of music and theater in Istanbul—Poelzig returned to Germany because of ill health, dying soon thereafter.

V.H.

BIBLIOGRAPHY
John R. Clarke, "Expressionism in Film and Architecture: Hans Poelzig's Sets for Paul Wegener's *The Golem*," *Art Journal* 34 (Winter 1974–75): 115–24; *Der dramatische Raum: Hans*

Cat. no. 178

Poelzig: Malerei, Theater, Film, exh. cat. (Krefeld: Museum Haus Lange, 1986); Heinrich de Fries, "Raumgestaltung im Film," *Wasmuths Monatshefte für Baukunst* 5, no. 3–4 (1920–21): 63–82; *Hans Poelzig: Ein grosses Theater und ein kleines Haus*, exh. cat. (Berlin: Aedes Galerie für Architektur und Raum, 1986); Theodor Heuss, *Hans Poelzig: Bauten und Entwürfe: Das Lebensbild eines deutschen Baumeisters* (1939: Stuttgart: Deutsche Verlags-Anstalt, 1985); Herta Elisabeth Killy, Peter Pfankuch, and Dirk Scheper, eds., *Poelzig, Endell, Moll und die Breslauer Kunstakademie, 1911–1932*, exh. cat. (Berlin: Akademie der Künste, 1965); Wolfgang Pehnt, "Hans Poelzig's Film Sets for *Der Golem*, 1920," *Domus*, no. 688 (November 1987): 81–84; Hans Poelzig, "Architektur," in *Das deutsche Kunstgewerbe*, exh. cat. (Dresden: Staatliche Kunstsammlungen, 1906); Julius Posener, *Hans Poelzig: Reflections on His Life and Work*, ed. Kristin Feireiss, trans. Christine Charlesworth (Cambridge: MIT Press, 1992); Paul Westheim, "Eine Filmstadt von Poelzig," *Das Kunstblatt* 4 no. 11 (1920): 325–33

■ ■ ■

Cat. no. 175

Cat. no. 176

Walter Reimann

BORN 1887 BERLIN ⁜ DEATH DATE UNKNOWN

180. Untitled (café scene), c. 1919
Pastel
12 x 13¾ in. (30.5 x 34.9 cm)
Set design for the film *Das Cabinet des Doctor Caligari* (1919)
directed by Robert Wiene
Department of Special Collections, University of Southern California

181. Untitled (woman on couch), c. 1919
Pastel
12 x 13¾ in. (30.5 x 34.3 cm)
Set design for the film *Das Cabinet das Doktor Caligari* (1919),
directed by Robert Wiene
Department of Special Collections, University of Southern California

See also cat. no. 218

A member of the design trio that helped create *Das Cabinet des Doktor Caligari* (The cabinet of Doctor Caligari, 1919), Walter Reimann is credited by his partners, Hermann Warm and Walter Röhrig, with introducing Expressionism into film decoration. Reimann studied in Berlin, Düsseldorf, and Hamburg and is thought to have been a fringe member of the Sturm group. Before World War I he worked as a newspaper illustrator, as did many artists. After the war he met Warm at the Armee-Theater in Wilna, and together they set up a studio with Robert Herlth. In 1919 Warm introduced Reimann to the film industry by asking him to help paint sets. Later that year Reimann served as one of the designers for *Caligari*, providing the initial impetus for its Expressionist style as well as designing the costumes.

A fervent believer in the expressive capabilities of scenic design, Reimann worked on more than twenty-five films during the Weimar period, including *Die Pest in Florenz* (The plague in Florence, 1919), directed by Otto Rippert and with a script by Fritz Lang, on which he also collaborated with Warm and Röhrig; Arthur von Gerlach's *Vanina* (1922); and Henrik Galeen's *Alraune* (Mandrake, 1928). On many of his projects Reimann worked with other film designers, illustrating the importance of the collaborative effort of design teams in film at the time. In *Vanina*, on which he worked independently, he dreamed up "dark, multiple, inextricable corridors—created with all the fervor of Expressionism" (Lotte Eisner, *The Haunted Screen* [Berkeley and Los Angeles: University of California Press, 1973], p. 63).

In an enthusiastic manifesto entitled "Filmbauten und Raumkunst" (Film sets and the art of space), published in 1926, Reimann delineated his ideas on film decor. On the stage, he wrote, a person "can be everything, for he lives there in his words and works by his personality. But in film, words and personality are taken from him, as are all other things; he works only through photographic communication." Set design is "not merely a decorative accessory, as is generally assumed; it replaces the explicatory word with silent demonstration." In film, the "silent fine art…the decoration, the theatrical properties, the costumes, the masks; in short, the visible materiality must replace the word! Film is a language of signs that must be seen" (reprinted in Walter Kaul, *Schöpferische Filmarchitektur* [Berlin: Deutsche Kinemathek, 1971], p. 11).

Reimann continued to work in film design through 1936. After a possible flirtation with Nazism (he published an article in *Deutsche Kultur-Wacht* in 1933 entitled "Dem deutschen Film gewidmet" [To the German cinema]), he appears to have stopped working in film. The details of his later years are unknown.

A.S.

BIBLIOGRAPHY

Richard Burdick Byrne, "German Cinematic Expressionism, 1919–1924," Ph.D. diss., State University of Iowa, Iowa City, 1962; Klaus Peter Hess, *Das Cabinet des Dr. Caligari: Materialien zu einem Film von Robert Wiene* (Duisburg: Atlas Film, 1988), p. 53.

■ ■ ■

Hans Richter

BORN 1888 BERLIN ✣ DIED 1976 LOCARNO, SWITZERLAND

182. *Fuge*, 1920
(Fugue)
Pencil on scroll
$18^{1/2}$ x 110 in. (47.0 x 279.4 cm)
Sketch for a film
The Museum of Modern Art, New York. Gift of Mr. and Mrs. Irvin Shapiro

Hans Richter's multifaceted career exemplifies the broad range of artistic experimentation that engaged European artists in the first decades of the twentieth century. A participant in Zurich Dada and the author of numerous books on the movement, he was an artist, writer, publisher, and experimental filmmaker who, along with Swedish artist Viking Eggeling, is credited with creating the first abstract film.

A contributor to the journal *Dada* in Zurich from 1916 to 1918 and to the Dutch Constructivist periodical *De Stijl* from 1921 to 1927 as well as the artistic director for the film periodical *Lichtbildbühne* (Screen) in 1926 and 1927, Richter also founded and published the periodical G from 1923 until 1926. He called G, whose pithy title stands for *Gestaltung* (design) "the first modern art periodical in Germany." It published contributions from artists and theoretical articles on avant-garde art in Europe. In 1926 he devoted a full issue to film, being among the first to treat the medium as an independent art form. Richter and Eggeling proposed that film, instead of being representational, could develop its own formal language. Richter wrote in *De Stijl* in 1921 that film is "evolution and revolution in the sphere of the purely artistic (abstract forms), somewhat analogous to the familiar effects of music on our ear." For the new art of film, he stated, "it is absolutely essential to have unambiguous elements. Without these a play of forms can certainly be brought about (and a seductive one), but never a language" (translated in Louise O'Konor, *Viking Eggeling, 1880–1925: Artist and Filmmaker: Life and Work*, trans. Catherine G. Sundström and Anne Bibby, Stockholm Studies in the History of Art, no. 23 [Stockholm: Almqvist and Wiksell, 1971], pp. 128–29).

Richter began, like many experimental artists of his generation, by studying architecture. He subsequently attended the institute of fine arts in Berlin and the academy in Weimar in 1908 and 1909. In Berlin in 1912 he was introduced to avant-garde circles through the Sturm gallery; he distributed Filippo Tommaso Marinetti's first Futurist manifesto in Berlin and contributed to the periodical *Die Aktion* (Action) beginning in 1914. After serving in the army from 1915 to 1916, Richter joined the Dada group around the Cabaret Voltaire in Zurich. He met Eggeling there two years later, and they began to collaborate on theoretical film projects. Richter created his first *Rollenbilder* (scroll pictures), abstract paintings in a long, thin, horizontal format similar to a series of film stills, which explored the possibilities of abstract film. He followed his first abstract film, *Rhythmus 21* (1921), which explored the development over time of geometric forms, with two films based on the same concept, *Rhythmus 23* and *Rhythmus 25*. In 1920 he joined the Novembergruppe (November group) and participated in the Berlin Dada movement. After Eggeling's death in 1925, Richter continued to work in film and helped make known his friend's contributions to the medium.

Beginning in the 1920s, Richter published numerous texts on cinema, such as the 1929 theoretical book *Filmgegner von heute—Filmfreunde von morgen* (Today's film foes—tomorrow's film friends). Throughout the 1930s he continued to lecture and write on film in Europe. In 1940 he immigrated to the United States, where he became the head of the film institute at the City College of New York in 1942, teaching and producing films. In 1964 he published his classic work on the Dada movement, *Dada: Art and Anti-Art.*

A.S.

BIBLIOGRAPHY

Herbert Gehr and Marion von Hofacker, eds., *Hans Richter: Malerei und Film*, exh. cat., Schriftenreihe des Deutschen Filmmuseums, Kinematograph no. 5 (Frankfurt: Deutsches Filmmuseum, 1989); Hans Richter, *Dada: Art and Anti-Art*, trans. David Britt (London: Thames and Hudson, 1965); idem, "My Experience with Movement in Painting and in Film," in *The Nature and Art of Motion*, ed. Gyorgy Kepes (New York: George Braziller, 1965), pp. 142–57; idem, *Hans Richter*, ed. Cleve Gray (New York: Holt, Rinehart and Winston, 1971); idem, *Der Kampf um den Film: Für einen gesellschaftlich verantwortlichen Film* (Munich: Hanser, 1976); Barbara Volkmann, ed., *Hans Richter, 1888–1976: Dadaist, Filmpionier, Maler, Theoretiker*, exh. cat. (Berlin: Akademie der Künste, 1982).

■ ■ ■

Walter Röhrig

BORN 1897 BERLIN ✣ DIED 1945 POTSDAM

See cat. no. 218

Although Walter Röhrig was a prolific film designer and a member of the teams that created such pioneering films as Robert Wiene's *Das Cabinet des Doktor Caligari* (The cabinet of Doctor Caligari, 1919) and Fritz Lang's *Der müde Tod* (released in English-speaking countries as *Destiny*, 1921), relatively little is known about his life. Röhrig's first film assignment was *Caligari*, on which he worked with designers Hermann Warm and Walter Reimann. He is usually assumed to have been a member of the Sturm group, although little evidence exists to support such a claim. During the Weimar years he worked on more than forty films, often collaborating with Robert Herlth, as he did on F. W. Murnau's *Der letzte Mann* (released in English-speaking countries as *The Last Laugh*, 1924), *Tartüff* (Tartuffe, 1925), and *Faust* (1925–26), as well as Arthur von Gerlach's *Zur Chronik von Grieshuus* (Chronicles of Grieshuus, 1924–25), Lang's *Der müde Tod*, G. W. Pabst's *Der Schatz* (The treasure, 1922–23), and Erik Charell's *Der Kongress tanzt* (The congress dances, 1931).

Röhrig's role in the making of *Caligari* is, like much else about the film, uncertain. Erich Pommer, the film's producer, stated that "the two art directors, Herlth and Röhrig, proposed the style and treatment which then made the film world famous" (quoted in Mike Budd, "The Moments of Caligari," in *The Cabinet of Dr. Caligari: Texts, Contexts, Histories*, ed. Mike Budd [New Brunswick, N.J.: Rutgers University Press, 1990], p. 35). This account conflicts with Warm's assertion that Reimann, not Röhrig or Herlth (who is not even listed in the credits), conceived the film's Expressionist style. Pommer also claimed, perhaps with tongue in cheek, that the three artists proposed painting lights and shadows on the set because the studio had run out of money to pay for electricity. In search of a way to create lighting without electricity, they came up with the idea of painted light and shadows.

After 1933 Röhrig designed a series of Nazi propaganda and entertainment films, including works directed by Karl Ritter, such as *Patrioten* (Patriots) and *Urlaub auf Ehrenwort* (On furlough) of 1937 and *Über alles in der Welt* (Above all in the world) of 1941. He collaborated with director Gustav Ucicky on *Unter heissem Himmel* (Under a hot sky, 1936) and *Heimkehr* (Return home, 1941). He also worked on Hans Steinhoff's *Rembrandt* of 1942, which portrayed the artist as a misunderstood genius.

A.S.

BIBLIOGRAPHY

Richard Burdick Byrne, "German Cinematic Expressionism, 1919–1924," Ph.D. diss., State University of Iowa, Iowa City, 1962; Klaus Peter Hess, *Das Cabinet des Dr. Caligari: Materialien zu einem Film von Robert Wiene* (Duisburg: Atlas Film, 1988), p. 53.

■ ■ ■

Hans Scharoun

BORN 1893 BREMEN ✣ DIED 1972 BERLIN

183. *3 x 3 dimensionales Glashaus*, 1920
(3 x 3-dimensional glass house)
Iron-based cyanotype
13 7/16 x 8 7/8 in. (34.1 x 22.5 cm)
Letter from the Gläserne Kette correspondence
Collection Centre Canadien d'Architecture/Canadian Centre for Architecture, Montreal

184. *"Glashausproblem,"* 1920
(Glass house problem)
Iron-based cyanotype
13 1/8 x 8 5/8 in. (33.4 x 22.0 cm)
Letter from the Gläserne Kette correspondence
Collection Centre Canadien d'Architecture/Canadian Centre for Architecture, Montreal

185. Untitled (architectural fantasy), 1920
Iron-based cyanotype
13 7/16 x 12 13/16 in. (34.1 x 32.5 cm)
Letter from the Gläserne Kette correspondence
Collection Centre Canadien d'Architecture/Canadian Centre for Architecture, Montreal

186. Untitled (design for a glass house)
Iron-based cyanotype
14 3/16 x 9 3/16 in. (36.1 x 23.3 cm)
Letter from the Gläserne Kette correspondence
Collection Centre Canadien d'Architecture/Canadian Centre for Architecture, Montreal

Hans Scharoun's work can be divided into his accomplishments before and after World War II. Much of his early work is a mixture of international modernism and Expressionism, integrated with Hugo Häring's "neues Bauen" (new building) design philosophy. Scharoun spent his youth in the port city of Bremerhaven, which undoubtedly inspired the marine imagery sometimes appearing in his designs. He studied at the technical college in Berlin before entering the military in 1915. While working in the division of reconstruction in East Prussia, he established contact with Bruno Taut and other young, idealistic Berlin architects.

After completing his military service, Scharoun joined the Arbeitsrat für Kunst (Working council for art) and Der Ring (The ring) and participated in the Gläserne Kette (Crystal chain) correspondence under the pseudonym Hannes. The influence of the latter group can be seen in his designs for the Gelsenkirchen cultural center (1920) and the Matheus Müller works extension (1920), which display characteristic, though nonfunctional, crystalline shapes. For the 1929 Werkbund exhibition *Wohnung und Werkraum* (Home and workplace) in Breslau, he built a large residential complex. Under the Nazis Scharoun was barred from undertaking major projects, although he was permitted to build several private residences in and around Berlin, in which Expressionist designs are skillfully concealed behind

Cat. no. 183

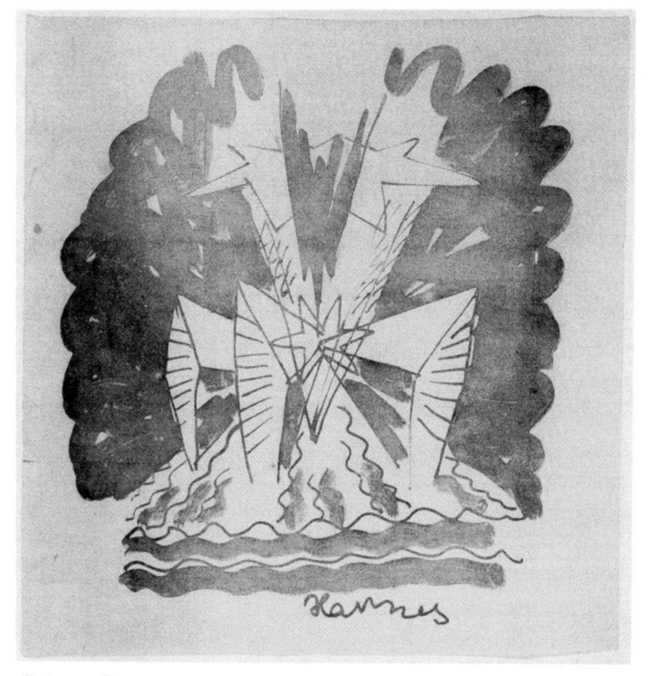

Cat. no. 185

traditional exteriors. During this period he also painted utopian fantasies in watercolor and worked on many designs that influenced later projects.

After World War II Scharoun was recognized as one of the few architects still practicing in the Expressionist tradition. His work from this period includes not only homes but also projects such as the unrealized city theater for Kassel (1952), the Romeo and Juliet apartments in Stuttgart-Zuffenhausen (1959), and his most famous work, the Philharmonie Berlin (Philharmonic hall, 1963). Posthumously completed works include the Staatsbibliothek (National library; with Edgar Wisniewski, 1978) in Berlin.

V.H.

BIBLIOGRAPHY

J. Christoph Bürkle, *Hans Scharoun und die Moderne: Ideen, Projekte, Theaterbau, Wolfsburger Beiträge zur Stadtgeschichte und Stadtentwicklung* (Frankfurt: Campus, 1986); Eckehard Janofske, *Architektur-Raume: Idee und Gestalt bei Hans Scharoun* (Wiesbaden: Vemey, 1984); Peter Blundell Jones, *Hans Scharoun: Eine Monographie* (Stuttgart: K. Kramer, 1979); Peter Pfankuch, ed., *Hans Scharoun: Bauten, Entwürfe, Texte*, exh. cat., Schriftenreihe der Akademie der Künste, no. 10 (Berlin: Akademie der Künste, 1974).

■ ■ ■

Oskar Schlemmer

BORN 1888 STUTTGART ✣ DIED 1943 STUTTGART

187. *Das Nusch-Nuschi: Gerichtssaal beim Kaiser II*, 1921
(The Nusch-Nuschi: The emperor's courtroom II)
Watercolor, gold-bronze, and pencil on paper mounted on cardboard
9⅞ x 13⅜ in. (25.0 x 34.0 cm)
Set design for an opera by Paul Hindemith, based on a text by Franz Blei
Private collection, courtesy C. Raman Schlemmer

188. *Das Nusch-Nuschi: Gerichtssaal beim Kaiser IV*, 1921
(The Nusch-Nuschi: The emperor's courtroom IV)
Watercolor, silver-bronze, and pencil on paper mounted on cardboard
8⅛ x 10 13/16 in. (20.6 x 27.5 cm)
Set design for an opera by Paul Hindemith, based on a text by Franz Blei
Private collection, courtesy C. Raman Schlemmer

189. *Szene mit verwandelbarer Architektur, Turm*, 1921
(Scene with convertible architecture, tower)
Ink
11⅝ x 16⅞ in. (29.6 x 42.8 cm)
Set design for the play *Mörder, Hoffnung der Frauen* (1907) by Oskar Kokoschka
The Oskar Schlemmer Theatre Estate, Collection UJS, courtesy C. Raman Schlemmer

190. *Utopia: Dokumente der Wirklichkeit*, 1921
(Utopia: Documents of reality)
Lithograph with watercolor and gold and silver paint on parchment
13 1/16 x 9¾ in. (33.2 x 24.8 cm)
Cover for a book with lithographs by Johannes Itten (see also cat. no. 97)
Los Angeles County Museum of Art. The Robert Gore Rifkind Center for German Expressionist Studies, purchased with funds provided by Anna Bing Arnold, Museum Acquisition Fund, and deaccession funds

191. *Die Nachtigall: Thronsaal des Kaisers von China*, 1929
(The nightingale: Throne room of the Chinese emperor)
Collage and white pencil on black paper
15 13/16 x 23 13/16 in. (40.2 x 60.5 cm)
Set design for the opera *Le rossignol* (The nightingale) by Igor Stravinsky
The Oskar Schlemmer Theatre Estate, Collection UJS, courtesy C. Raman Schlemmer

See also cat. no. 230

The death of his middle-class parents while he was still a child forced Oskar Schlemmer to enter the building trade at the age of fifteen, as an apprentice in a Stuttgart wood-inlay shop. By 1913 he had attended the school of applied arts and the academy in Stuttgart and had spent some time in Berlin in Herwarth Walden's Sturm circle. Under the direction of his teacher Adolf Hölzel, he and his fellow students Willi Baumeister and Hermann Stenner painted murals for the main pavilion of the 1914 Werkbund exhibition in Cologne. After interrupting his studies to serve in World War I, Schlemmer returned to the academy and in 1919 served as a student delegate to the Rat geistiger Arbeiter (Council of intellectual workers).

Cat. no. 187

Cat. no. 188

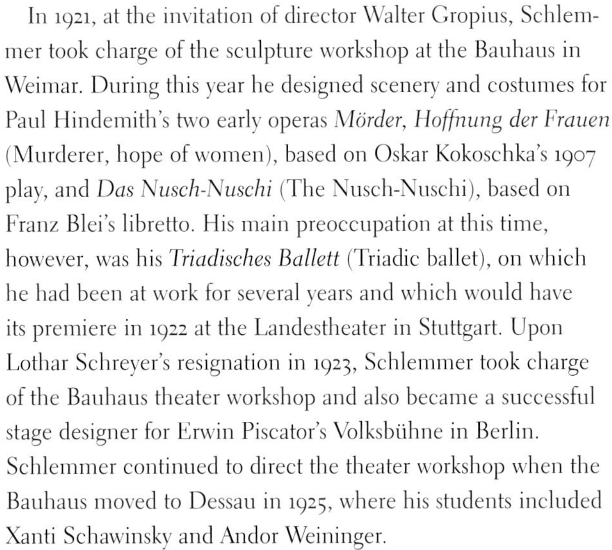

In 1921, at the invitation of director Walter Gropius, Schlemmer took charge of the sculpture workshop at the Bauhaus in Weimar. During this year he designed scenery and costumes for Paul Hindemith's two early operas *Mörder, Hoffnung der Frauen* (Murderer, hope of women), based on Oskar Kokoschka's 1907 play, and *Das Nusch-Nuschi* (The Nusch-Nuschi), based on Franz Blei's libretto. His main preoccupation at this time, however, was his *Triadisches Ballett* (Triadic ballet), on which he had been at work for several years and which would have its premiere in 1922 at the Landestheater in Stuttgart. Upon Lothar Schreyer's resignation in 1923, Schlemmer took charge of the Bauhaus theater workshop and also became a successful stage designer for Erwin Piscator's Volksbühne in Berlin. Schlemmer continued to direct the theater workshop when the Bauhaus moved to Dessau in 1925, where his students included Xanti Schawinsky and Andor Weininger.

Schlemmer's activities in the 1920s included organizing the 1927 *Deutsche Theater-Ausstellung* (German theater exhibition) in Magdeburg and winning the competition for the painting of the rotunda murals at the Folkwang Museum in Essen in 1928. In 1929 he look a position at the academy in Breslau, where he also designed sets for productions of Igor Stravinsky's operas *Renard* (The fox) and *Le rossignol* (The nightingale). In 1930 he staged Arnold Schoenberg's musical drama *Die glückliche Hand* (The fortunate hand) for the Krolloper in Berlin and in 1931 worked on sculptural wall designs for Erich Mendelsohn. Partly, as a result of the favorable reception of his lecture "Bühnenelemente" (The elements of theater), Schlemmer received a position at the state schools of art in Berlin, an appointment he lost with the Nazi seizure of power in 1933. In his final years he was considered a degenerate artist and eked out a living painting exterior murals and camouflaging barracks.

T.B.

Cat. no. 189

BIBLIOGRAPHY

Wulf Herzogenrath, *Oskär Schlemmer: Die Wandgestaltung der neuen Architektur* (Munich: Prestel, 1973); Arnold L. Lehman and Brenda Richardson, eds., *Oskar Schlemmer*, exh. cat. (Baltimore: Baltimore Museum of Art, 1986); Karin von Maur, *Oskar Schlemmer*, 2 vols. (Munich: Prestel, 1979); idem, *Oskar Schlemmer: Der Maler, der Wandgestalter, der Plastiker* (Munich: Prestel, 1982); Dirk Scheper, *Oskar Schlemmer: Das triadische Bullett und die Bauhausbühne*, exh. cat., Schriftenreihe der Akademie der Künste, no. 20 (Berlin: Akademie der Künste, 1988).

■ ■ ■

Kurt Schmidt

BORN 1901 LIMBACH ✝ LIVES(?) GERA

192. *Bühnenwerkstatt: Bühnenentwurf für "Das mechanische Ballett,"* c. 1923
(Theater workshop: Stage design for "The mechanical ballet")
Lithograph
8¼ x 9¹/16 in. (21.0 x 23.0 cm)
From *Staatliches Bauhaus in Weimar, 1919–1923* (1923)
Los Angeles County Museum of Art. The Robert Gore Rifkind Center for German Expressionist Studies, purchased with funds provided by Anna Bing Arnold, Museum Acquisition Fund, and deaccession funds

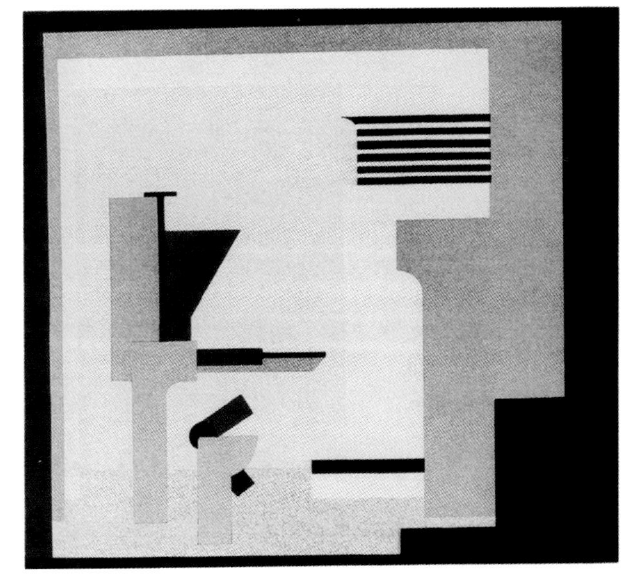

Cat. no. 192

Kurt Schmidt was a participant in the Bauhaus theater workshop and an innovator in stage and costume design. He created machinelike characters and figurines that embodied the basic theatrical elements of motion, light, sound, and color while adding a humorous note to Bauhaus stage performances.

Schmidt briefly attended the school of applied arts in Hamburg in 1919. The following year he went to the Bauhaus, where he studied under Johannes Itten and Lyonel Feininger and became a student in Wassily Kandinsky's popular mural-painting workshop. A member of the De Stijl circle in Weimar, Schmidt participated in Theo van Doesburg's *Stijlkurse* (Stijl courses), offered from March through July of 1922 in Max Burchartz's Weimar studio. Schmidt was also a member of the Constructivist student group known as KURI, standing for *Konstruktiv-Utilitar-Rationell-International* (Constructive-utilitarian-rational-international), whose manifesto was written in 1922 by the Hungarian Bauhaus students Farkas Molnár and Andor Weininger.

Schmidt's approach to design was personal and sometimes eccentric. Although he advocated Constructivist principles, a postcard he created as one of a series of invitations designed by Bauhaus students and teachers for the school's 1923 exhibition is a hand-drawn map of the town of Weimar executed in an unconventional, almost childlike style. A set of figures he designed the same year for *Die Abenteuer des kleinen Bucklingen* (The adventures of the little hunchback), an episode from *A Thousand and One Nights*, are humorous, whimsical little personalities designed to play on mechanical, multipurpose stages. Although this project was never realized, Schmidt and Georg Teltscher were able to mount a performance of another of Schmidt's projects, the *Mechanisches Ballett* (Mechanical ballet), in 1923 during the Bauhaus exhibition. In the performance abstract two-dimensional forms were moved by invisible actors to the beat of a kettledrum, emphasizing shape and color rather than traditional dramatic elements. The exhibition also included Schmidt's sketches for Oskar Schlemmer's *Figurales Kabinett* (Figural cabinet). Schmidt's *Der Mann am Schaltbrett* (The man at the switchboard)—a pantomime of a man battling (and losing to) a huge, futuristic control panel—was repeated almost exactly in a scene of Fritz Lang's 1927 film *Metropolis*.

Schmidt left the Bauhaus in 1925 for Stuttgart and later settled in Gera, where he worked independently until 1941, when he entered World War II. Released from war imprisonment in 1945, he resumed work, designing furniture and painting.

A.S.

BIBLIOGRAPHY

Marianne Brandt, Hajo Rose, Kurt Schmidt: Drei Künstler am Bauhaus, exh. cat. (Dresden: Kupferstichkabinett der Staatlichen Kunstsammlungen, 1978).

Karl Schmidt-Rottluff

BORN 1884 ROTTLUFF ✣ DIED 1976 BERLIN

193. *Berliner Strasse in Dresden*, 1909
Lithograph
15¾ x 13¼ in. (40.0 x 33.7 cm)
From the portfolio Brücke IV (1909)
Los Angeles County Museum of Art. The Robert Gore Rifkind Center for German Expressionist Studies

194. *Bucht im Mondschein*, 1914
(Bay in moonlight)
Woodcut
15½ x 19½ in. (39.4 x 49.5 cm)
Los Angeles County Museum of Art. The Robert Gore Rifkind Center for German Expressionist Studies

195. *Menschenpaar*, 1917
(Couple)
Woodcut
7¹⁵⁄₁₆ x 5¹³⁄₁₆ in. (20.1 x 14.8 cm)
From the deluxe edition of *Das Kunstblatt* 2, no. 2 (1918)
Los Angeles County Museum of Art. The Robert Gore Rifkind Center for German Expressionist Studies, purchased with funds provided by Anna Bing Arnold, Museum Acquisition Fund, and deaccession funds.

Cat. no. 195

Karl Schmidt-Rottluff was a founding member of the Brücke (Bridge) and is credited with providing the group with its name, supposedly drawn from a passage of Friedrich Nietzsche's *Also sprach Zarathustra* (Thus spoke Zarathustra). Although he had studied at the Kunstverein (art association) in Chemnitz during his high-school years, Schmidt-Rottluff dated his real artistic beginnings to 1905, the year of the Brücke's founding. Erich Heckel, a fellow Brücke member and lifelong friend, credited him with bringing "glowing and pure color from Chemnitz" to the group; it was apparently Ernst Ludwig Kirchner, however, who encouraged Schmidt-Rottluff to take up the woodcut, in which he would execute some of his finest work. While his earliest efforts in the medium reveal the influence of Impressionism, he soon developed a stark, arresting style, employing large areas of black and simple, commanding forms.

Both before and after World War I Schmidt-Rottluff produced many woodcuts, concentrating from 1917 to 1919 on a series treating New Testament themes, which exemplifies his angular, emotional style, In his paintings he combined this formal language with bright, Fauve-inspired colors. His approach to art was spontaneous and unprogrammatic. Responding in 1914 to a questionnaire about the "new program" for art devised by the periodical *Kunst und Künstler* (Art and artists), he stated, "I don't have any program, only an inexplicable yearning to lay hold of what I see and feel and then to find the most direct expression possible for such experience" ("The New Program," in *Voices of German Expressionism*, ed. Victor H. Miesel [Englewood Cliffs, N.J.: Prentice Hall, 1970], p. 29).

Born Karl Schmidt in Rottluff, near Chemnitz in Saxony, Schmidt-Rottluff took on the name of his town in 1905. A schoolmate of Erich Heckel, he met Kirchner briefly in 1904 before moving to Dresden to study architecture at the technical college the following year. In Berlin before the war he contributed drawings and prints to periodicals such as Franz Pfemfert's liberal *Die Aktion* (Action) and joined the New Secession in 1910. He was drafted into the army in 1915 and served on the eastern front until the end of the war, when he returned to Berlin. Joining the *Arbeitsrat für Kunst* (Working council for art) in 1919, he published a short text that year in its publication *Ja! Stimmen des Arbeitsrates für Kunst* (Yes! Voices of the Working council for art), in which he appealed for art education to be based on a solid knowledge of craft and expressed the hope that a socialist state would allow artists creative freedom.

Schmidt-Rottluff was named an associate of the Prussian academy in Berlin in 1931 but was labeled degenerate in 1933 and expelled from his post. More than six hundred of his works were seized from museums in 1937, and four years later he was forbidden to paint. He was reappointed to a professorship at the Berlin academy in 1947.

A.S.

BIBLIOGRAPHY

Ludwig Coellen, "Karl Schmidt-Rottluff," *Das Kunstblatt* 11, no. 11 (1917): 321–28; Will Grohmann, ed., *Karl Schmidt-Rottluff* (Stuttgart: W. Kohlhammer, 1956); *Karl Schmidt-Rottluff zum einhundertsten Geburtstug: Holzschnitte, Lithographien, Radierungen*, exh. cat. (Berlin: Galerie Nierendorf, 1984); Magdalena Moeller, ed., *Karl Schmidt-Rottluff: Aquarelle* (Stuttgart: Gerd Hatje, 1991); *Prints by Erich Heckel and Karl Schmidt-Rottluff: A Centenary Celebration*, exh. cat. (Los Angeles: Los Angeles County Museum of Art, 1985); Ernest Rathenau, *Karl Schmidt-Rottluff: Das graphische Werk seit 1923* (New York: Ernest Rathenau, 1964); Rosa Schapire, *Karl Schmidt-Rottluffs graphisches Werk bis 1923* (1924; Hamburg: Hauswedell, 1965); Gunther Thiem and Armin Zweite, eds., *Karl Schmidt-Rottluff: Retrospektive*, exh. cat. (Bremen: Kunsthalle Bremen, 1989); Gerhard Wietek, *Schmidt-Rottluff: Graphik* (Munich: K. Thiemig, 1971).

■ ■ ■

Arnold Schoenberg

BORN 1874 VIENNA ✣ DIED 1951 LOS ANGELES

196. *Szenenentwurf für "Die glückliche Hand": 2. Bild: "Beleuchtungsquelle"*
(Sketch for "The fortunate hand": Scene 2, "The source of light")
Oil on pasteboard
85/8 x 115/8 in. (22.0 x 30.0 cm)
Set design for Schoenberg's drama with music
Lawrence Schoenberg, Los Angeles

Arnold Schoenberg's contribution to the development of modern music— he was a pioneer of atonal music and invented a twelve-tone method of composition—has been widely acknowledged. His compositions have been performed and recorded by the major orchestras, and the debt owed to him by his pupils Alban Berg and Anton von Webern has been analyzed at length. Schoenberg was not only a musician, however, but a painter as well. His view of the relationship between the two arts is suggested in the recollection of a student who took his composition master class in 1930: "On the first day...he really didn't talk about music. He talked about other arts—about architecture, about painting, about everything that there was and not at all about music, and one was always conscious of it anyway.... It is all one thing, and not music here and something else there, but all one thing, one idea" (Smith, *Schoenberg and His Circle*, p. 232).

Schoenberg's visual art often involved this idea of the *Gesamtkunstwerk* (total work of art), as can be seen in his stage sets for his monodrama *Erwartung* (Expectation, 1907–8) and his drama with music *Die glückliche Hand* (The fortunate hand, 1909–13). Although somewhat influenced by the German painter Richard Gerstl, he was largely self-taught, producing direct, nondecorative self-portraits he called Visions. Schoenberg's paintings so impressed Wassily Kandinsky that they were included in the first Blaue Reiter (Blue rider) exhibition in Munich in 1911 and were illustrated in the almanac *Der blaue Reiter*, which also included Schoenberg's important essay "Das Verhältnis zum Text" (The relationship to the text).

Schoenberg was also self-taught as a musician. He worked in a bank until he joined a chamber group led by Alexander von Zemlinsky. Schoenberg married Zemlinsky's sister Mathilde in 1901, and his brother-in-law became his friend and mentor. From 1901 to 1903 Schoenberg taught at the Stern'schen Konservatorium in Berlin. He continued his professional career in Vienna as a composer, conductor, and teacher but returned to Berlin twice more, in 1911 and 1926. In 1933 he was dismissed from his post at the Prussian academy. With Austria under National Socialist rule, Schoenberg emigrated via Paris to New York and finally settled in Los Angeles in 1934. Two years later he obtained a teaching position at the University of California, Los Angeles, which he held until 1944.

F.V.H.

BIBLIOGRAPHY

Jelena Hahl-Koch, ed., *Arnold Schoenberg, Wassily Kandinsky: Letters, Pictures, and Documents*, trans. John C. Crawford (London: Faber and Faber, 1984); Jane Kallir, *Arnold Schoenberg's Vienna* (New York: Galerie St. Etienne, 1984); Joan Allen Smith, *Schoenberg and His Circle: A Viennese Portrait* (New York: Schirmer, 1986); Hans Heinz Stuckenschmidt, *Schoenberg: His Life, World, and Work*, trans. Humphrey Searle (New York: Schirmer, 1978); Thomas Zaunschirm, ed., *Arnold Schönberg: Das bildnerische Werk / Arnold Schoenberg: Paintings and Drawings*, exh. cat. (Vienna: Museum des 20. Jahrhunderts, 1991).

■ ■ ■

Lothar Schreyer

BORN 1886 BLASEWITZ ✣ DIED 1966 HAMBURG

197. *Geliebte/Mutter*, c. 1920
(Lover/mother)
Color woodcut
8 7/16 x 12 3/16 in. (21.5 x 30.9 cm)
From Lothar Schreyer, *Kreuzigung: Spielgang Werk VII* (1921)
Los Angeles County Museum of Art. The Robert Gore Rifkind Center for German Expressionist Studies, purchased with funds provided by Anna Bing Arnold, Museum Acquisition Fund, and deaccession funds

Lothar Schreyer communicated his intense desire to express mystical themes and discovery through bold manifestations in painting, poetry, essays, and especially dramaturgy. He was the son of a landscape painter. While studying art history and law at the universities of Heidelberg, Berlin, and Leipzig, he encountered a mystical interpretation of art through long discussions with a student from Japan who convincingly argued that European art had been stagnant since A.D. 1000. After receiving his degree in law, Schreyer pursued his interests in art and the theater. He gravitated to stage art, in which he sought to demonstrate the interrelationship of the arts and the universality of human experience.

In 1911 Schreyer obtained his first position as a dramaturge and assistant director at the Deutsches Schauspielhaus theater in Hamburg, where he remained until 1918. Meanwhile in 1914 he began an absorbing study of medieval and Eastern mystics, concentrating on the works of Meister Eckhart and Jakob Böhme, considered the father of theosophy, a form of spiritualism that many German Expressionists embraced. In 1915 Schreyer became part of the Sturm circle. He was a contributor to and editor of Herwarth Walden's journal *Der Sturm* (The storm) and worked as its chief editor from 1916 to 1918. He founded the Sturmbühne theater in Berlin in 1917 and headed it until 1921. From 1919 to 1921 he concentrated on making masks, figurines, and marionettes for the stage.

Walter Gropius was so impressed by Schreyer's stage production that he recruited him as the supervisor of the Bauhaus theater workshop and as an arts and crafts teacher. About that time Schreyer and Walden had begun to drift apart as Walden found a new political mission in Bolshevik Russia while Schreyer turned toward Christianity. By 1921 Schreyer and Lyonel Feininger, dubbed "Masters of Form" by Gropius, were working together at the Bauhaus. Schreyer remarked, "We did not build the Cathedral of Socialism, but we lived the Cathedral." His immersion in mysticism and his Expressionist dramaturgy did not follow the more pragmatic ideology of the Bauhaus, however, and he was dismissed from his position in 1923.

From 1924 to 1927 Schreyer codirected the art school Der Weg (The way) in Berlin and Dresden and became involved with the Zentralinstitut für Erziehung und Unterricht (Central institute for education and instruction) in Berlin. From 1928 to 1932 he worked as the chief reader and cultural and literary editor for the Hanseatische Verlagsanstalt publishing house in Hamburg and lectured throughout Germany. Increasingly drawn to mysticism, he converted to Catholicism in 1933. At a 1933 convention of ecclesiastical architects he met radical church architect Rudolf Schwarz. Schreyer stated that the turning point of his life was Schwarz's remark, "The essential question begins only when art is consummated." Schreyer contended that such a concept could not have come from either the Sturm circle or the Bauhaus. Writing in 1933 for the Caritas publications under the pseudonym Angelus Pauper, he began researching and compiling accounts of holy legends. The years from 1948 to 1950 became for Schreyer a period of intense research into literature and art history. Despite great financial hardships, he rejected an offer to be the chief dramaturge of Hamburg. In 1950 he resumed his painting, but from 1953 he struggled with chronic health problems leading to crippling arthritis. One of his final public appearances was his participation in the ground breaking of the church of Saint Agnes in Hamburg-Tonndorf, where a copy of his *Agnes und die Söhne der Wölfin: Ein Prozess* (Agnes and the sons of wolves: A trial, 1956) was placed in the cornerstone.

V.H.

BIBLIOGRAPHY

Herwarth Walden und "Der Sturm": Konstruktivisten, Abstrakte: Eine Auswahl, exh. cat. (Cologne: Galerie Stolz, 1987); M. S. Jones, *Der Sturm: A Focus of Expressionism* (Columbia, S.C.: Camden House, 1984); Lothar Schreyer, *Erinnerungen an Sturm und Bauhaus: Was ist des Menschen Bild?* (Munich: A. Langen, G. Müller, 1956).

■ ■ ■

Georg Schrimpf

BORN 1889 MUNICH ✣ DIED 1938 BERLIN

198. Untitled (two nudes in landscape), c. 1918
Woodcut
5 1/8 x 7 3/16 in. (13.0 x 18.2 cm)
From deluxe edition of *Das Kunstblatt* 2, no. 3 (1918)
Los Angeles County Museum of Art. The Robert Gore Rikind Center for German Expressionist Studies, purchased with funds provided by Anna Ring Arnold, Museum Acquisition Fund, and deaccession funds

Cat. no. 198

Throughout his relatively short career Georg Schrimpf was fascinated by interactions among figures, especially women and children. His earliest works display the influence of late Cubism, particularly as practiced by Fernand Léger, while his paintings from the late 1910s are reminiscent of those of a number of German contemporaries, such as Franz Marc, Conrad Felixmüller, and Oskar Schlemmer. During the 1920s Schrimpf constantly reworked images of female figural groups and the Madonna and Child. He painted numerous variations of the latter subject with simple outdoor backdrops that recall those used by Italian artists of the Renaissance. Although many of his themes are similar to those explored a decade earlier by the Brücke (Bridge) artists, such as peaceful scenes of women alone in the woods, his treatment of them is more sculptural, displaying a concern with volume and composition; he described the lines of his figures as "embodied melodies." He also worked extensively in woodcut during the late 1910s in a stark, dramatic style reminiscent of the work of Karl Schmidt-Rottluff.

Schrimpf was inspired to begin painting partially through his involvement in 1913 with an anarchist colony, which he described in 1920: "Everything brought me to the conclusion that man is the kernel of all happening: if I change myself first from the ground up and look into myself, the transformation of the whole world and salvation is there.... We lived there as if in paradise" ("Der Künstler über sich," in *Graf, Georg Schrimpf*, p. 15; reprinted in Storch, *Georg Schrimpf und Maria Uhden*, p. 18). Although he did not start painting until 1915, while working in a chocolate factory in Berlin, Schrimpf quickly became a prominent figure in the art world, publishing woodcuts in *Die Aktion* (Action) and *Der Sturm* (The storm) and exhibiting at the Sturm gallery in 1916.

Married from 1917 until her death in 1918 to the painter Maria Uhden, who also exhibited at the Sturm gallery, Schrimpf lived in Munich after the war and was a member of the Aktionsausschuss revolutionärer Künstler (Action committee of revolutionary artists). With a group of other young artists, including Georg Kaiser and Gottfried Graf, he cofounded the Munich group Der Morgen (Morning), dedicated to "new writing and art." Schrimpf also associated with the circle around the Italian journal *Valori plastici* (Plastic values), which espoused a classicizing "return to order." In 1925 he was represented in the exhibition *Neue Sachlichkeit: Deutsche Malerei seit dem Expressionismus* (New objectivity: German painting since Expressionism), organized by Gustav Hartlaub in Mannheim, which proclaimed the resurgence of interest in representational art. He was one of four painters—along with Alexander Kanoldt, Franz Radziwill, and Albert Renger-Patsch—whose work was included in the 1929 traveling exhibition *Die neue Romantik* (The new Romanticism), which presented their work as a search for "confirmation of an inwardly seen picture."

Having taught sporadically from 1925, Schrimpf was transferred in October 1933 to the state institute for art education in Berlin, where he taught for four years. Esteemed for his landscapes, he may have chosen to concentrate on this subject at least in part to avoid political controversy. One of his paintings was included in the Nazi's 1937 show *Entartete Kunst* (Degenerate art) but was taken out of the show by Rudolf Hess, Hitler's deputy, undoubtedly to avoid the awkwardness of the government condemning Schrimpf's art at the same time that he was working for its school system. Later that year, however, Schrimpf was fired from his position on the grounds that he had been involved, albeit temporarily, with the Communist party and the Rote Hilfe (Red help). He died soon after in Berlin.

A.S.

BIBLIOGRAPHY
Oskar Maria Graf, *Georg Schrimpf*, Junge Kunst, no. 37 (Leipzig: Klinkhardt und Biermann, 1923); Georg Schrimpf, *An dich—Erde!* (Berlin: Freie Strasse, 1915); Wolfgang Starch, ed., *Georg Schrimpf und Maria Uhden: Leben und Werk* (Berlin: Charlottenpresse, 1985).

■ ■ ■

Rudolf Schwarz

BORN 1897 STRASSBURG ✣ DIED 1961 COLOGNE

199. *Gloria*, c. 1920
Watercolor
127/8 x 83/8 in. (32.7 x 21.2 cm)
Dipl. -Ing. Maria Schwarz

200. *Kyrie eleison (Studie)*, c. 1920
(Study for Kyrie Eleison)
Watercolor
165/16 x 117/16 in. (41.5 x 29.0 cm)
Maria Elisabeth Stapp

201. *Sanktus*, c. 1920
Watercolor
161/8 x 111/16 in. (41.0 x 28.0 cm)
Maria Elisabeth Stapp

Rudolf Schwarz is considered one of the twentieth century's most innovative church architects, a designer whose structures were infused with a personal metaphysical viewpoint, elaborated in his 1938 master text, *Vom Bau der Kirche* (published in English under the title *The Church Incarnate*). After studying at the technical college in Berlin from 1915 to 1919, he became a student of Hans Poelzig at the academy in Berlin. From 1927 until 1934 Schwarz was director of the school of applied arts in Aachen.

Schwarz's greatest inspiration came from the early Christian and medieval churches, which he revered as "the true churches. We have not surpassed them in the least." He envisioned an intimate interrelationship between the structure and the congregation, which together formed the true constituents of the church building. In his search for "sacred forms," he viewed churches as "life-size parables" and the church architect as one guided not by magic or mathematics, but by the life of Christ. Schwarz's most significant contribution is arguably the 1930 Fronleichnameskirche (Corpus Christi church) in Aachen, which elicited great controversy because of its stark simplicity. From 1946 to 1952 he headed the planning department in Cologne, restoring the war-devastated city. From 1952 until his death he was professor of city planning at the academy in Düsseldorf. His last churches were completed by his architect wife, Maria Lang Schwarz, and his pupils. His legacy includes more than sixty churches in Germany.

V.H.

BIBLIOGRAPHY
Hans-Dieter Dyroff and Paul Tümena, eds., *Rudolf Schwarz*, exh. cat. (Düsseldorf: Akademie der Architektenkammer Nordrhein-Westfalen, 1981); *Rudolf Schwarz: Gedächtnisausstellung des BDA Köln*, exh. cat. (Berlin: Akademie der Künste, 1963); Rudolf Schwarz, *Vom Bau der Kirche* (Heidelberg: Schneider, 1938); translated by Cynthia Harris as *The Church Incarnate: The Sacred Function of Christian Architecture* (Chicago: H. Regnery, 1958); idem, Kirchenbau: Welt vor der Schwelle (Heidelberg: E H. Kerle, 1960).

■ ■ ■

Martel Schwichtenberg

BORN 1896 HANNOVER ✣ DIED 1945 SULZBURG

202. *Torsäule*, c. 1915–18
(Portal column)
Woodcut printed in red on brown paper
9 9/16 x 12 7/8 in. (24.3 x 32.7 cm)
Schleswig-Holsteinisches Landesmuseum, Schloss Gottorf, Schleswig

Martel Schwichtenberg worked in a wide range of media, from woodcut, lithography, and wood relief to mural painting, stained glass, and package design. Partly because a fire in 1938 destroyed her home and many of her works from the preceding fifteen years, she has been little studied. She remains best known for her rough wood reliefs and woodcuts, often portraying female figures characterized by strong, blocklike forms; massive heads; large, commanding eyes; and a resolute bearing.

Schwichtenberg studied privately in Hannover before attending the Kunowsky art school in Düsseldorf from 1913 to 1916. She later studied at the school of applied arts in Düsseldorf, completing her studies in 1924 at the studio of the French landscape painter Eugène Kissling in Paris. Early in her career she was known primarily for her mural paintings, such as those executed for the Hermann Bahlsen biscuit factory in Hannover in 1917 and 1918. Working with the architect and sculptor Bernhard Hoetger—from whom she is sometimes described as having adopted her energetic, often linear style—Schwichtenberg also designed packaging and advertising for the factory's products as well as stained-glass windows and wall decorations for the building itself.

Schwichtenberg spent the summers of 1918 and 1919 in the Worpswede artists' colony, and in 1919 she married the painter Willy-Robert Huth. From 1920 she lived in Berlin, where her circle of friends included Tilla Durieux, Karl Ernst Osthaus, Max Pechstein, Fritz Radziwill, Karl Schmidt-Rottluff, Kurt Schwitters, and Milly Steger as well as Nell Walden, the second wife of art dealer and publisher Herwarth Walden. Schwichtenberg published a number of prints in contemporary art publications such as *Das Kunstblatt* (The art paper), *Kündung* (Annunication), and *Junge Berliner Kunst* (New Berlin art). In the third portfolio of Die Schaffenden (The creators), Paul Westheim wrote rather derisively of her "typical womanly talent; elegant and impressionable, she knows how to adapt to the currents of the time.... She needed and still needs more than others do the energy to arrive at her own style" (Beate Jahn and Friedemann Berger, eds., *Die Schaffenden: Eine Auswahl der Jahrgänge I bis III und Katalog des Mappenwerkes* [Leipzig: Gustav Kiepenheuer, 1984], p. 216).

Schwichtenberg exhibited her works in Berlin at the Möller gallery in 1922 and 1924 and at the Flechtheim gallery in 1930 and 1931. During the 1920s she traveled extensively, visiting Denmark, Italy, Spain, and North Africa as well as France, where she spent part of 1924 and 1927. In the latter year she separated from her husband. In 1933 she immigrated to Italy and subsequently to Johannesburg, South Africa, where she set up a potter's studio with Franz Goldschmidt. She spent part of 1935 in Europe and part of 1939 in New York and Connecticut. In 1940 she returned to Germany to spend the last five years of her life in the Black Forest.

A.S.

BIBLIOGRAPHY

Silvia von Bennigsen, *Martel Schwichtenberg (1896–1945): Ihr Frühwerk von 1913–1923* (Hamburg: Kunstgeschichtliches Seminar der Universität, 1986); Joachim Kirchner, *Junge Berliner Kunst*, Wasmuths Kunsthefte, no. 6 (Berlin: Ernst Wasmuth, [1919?]); Ursula März and Ulrike Mond, "Marianne Werefkin, Gabriele Münter, Lou Albert-Lasard, Martel Schwichtenberg," *Du: Die Zeitschrift für Kunst und Kultur* 49 (July 1989): 31–37; Christian Rathke, "Martel Schwichtenberg," *Die Weltkunst* 22 (November 1982): 3302–3; "Unterm Kreuz des Südens: Sterne und Whisky—Eine Frau erlebt Afrika," *Die Welt*, 16 and 18 June 1949.

■ ■ ■

Kurt Schwitters

BORN 1887 HANNOVER ✣ DIED 1948 KENDAL, ENGLAND

203. Untitled (abstract composition), c. 1920
Lithograph
8 7/16 x 5 5/16 in. (21.4 x 13.5 cm)
From the picture book *Die Kathedrale* (1920)
Los Angeles County Museum of Art. The Robert Gore Rifkind Center for German Expressionist Studies, purchased with funds provided by Anna Bing Arnold, Museum Acquisition Fund, and deaccession funds

See also cat. no. 127

Kurt Schwitters's most widely discussed and elusive project was his *Merzbau*, an assemblage of found objects, both cultural artifacts and personal memorabilia, which expanded through several rooms of his home in Hannover. Constructed between 1920 and 1937, when the artist had to abandon it to escape Nazi persecution, the *Merzbau* was destroyed by bombing in 1943 but is preserved in narratives and photographs. Even as myth, it comprises the essential components that gave Schwitters his place in art history as a transitional figure between Dadaism and Constructivism.

Schwitters acquired the skills to undertake this massive construction through his studies at the school of applied arts in Hannover in 1908, at the academy in Dresden from 1904 to 1914, and at the technical college in Hannover, where he studied architecture in 1918. After taking up residence in an apartment building owned by his parents in Hannover, he became actively involved in the city's uncharacteristically lively art scene and publishing activities after the war.

In his collages of around 1918–19, known as Merz, Schwitters created a distinct form of Dada. His glued and nailed bits and pieces often veil very personal narratives in his artworks. To connect all aspects of life in art was a goal that he articulated: "Establish connections, preferably among all things." Consequently his artistic production included drama, poetry, prose, typography, stage design, sculpture, painting, drawing, collage, and montage. Many of his works combined several genres, and some were produced in collaboration with other artists.

Beginning in the early 1920s, Schwitters sought to formalize his connections with other artists as a founding member of associations such as Die Abstrakten Hannover (Hannover abstract artists) and the Ring neuer Werbegestalter (Circle of new advertising designers). From 1923 to 1932 he published sixteen issues of the periodical *Menz*, their topics ranging from poetry and fairy tales to typography, modern advertising, and architecture. His circle included Jean Arp, Ella Bergmann, Walter Dexel, Theo van Doesburg, Raoul Hausmann, Hannah Höch, El Lissitzky, and Robert Michel.

Under the threat of arrest by the National Socialists, Schwitters went to Norway, where he had spent his summers

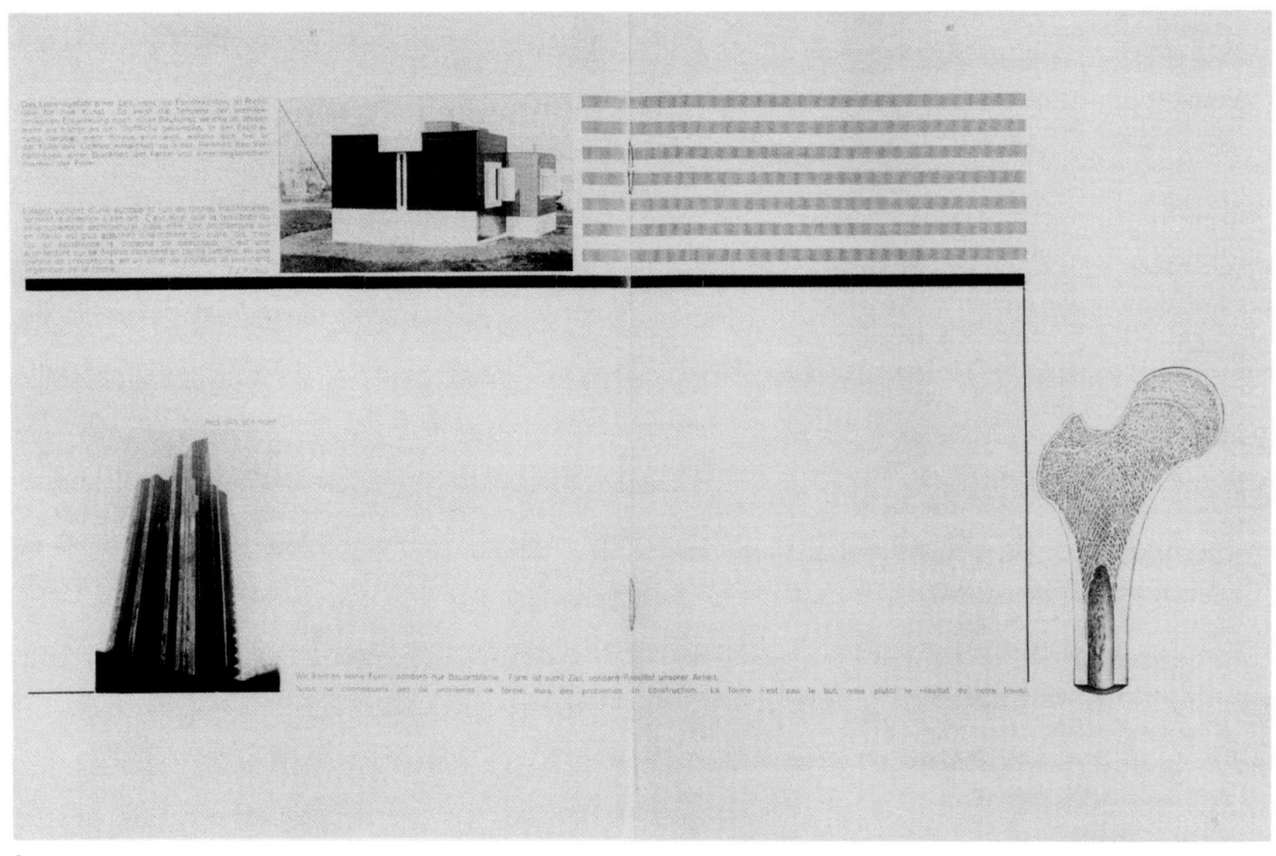

Cat. no. 127

since 1934. When German troops invaded Norway in 1940, he escaped to England, leaving behind another *Merzbau* (which was accidentally burned down in 1951). A grant from the Museum of Modern Art in New York enabled him to begin a third *Merzbau* in a barn in Ambleside in the Lake District in 1945. It remained incomplete at the time of his death in 1948.

F.V.H.

BIBLIOGRAPHY

John Elderfield, *Kurt Schwitters* (London: Thames and Hudson, 1985); Dietmar Elger, *Der Merzbau: Eine Werkmonographie* (Cologne: W. König, 1984); Annegreth Nill, "Decoding Merz: An Interpretive Study of Kurt Schwitters' Early Work, 1918–1922," Ph.D. diss., University of Texas, Austin, 1990; Ernst Nündel, *Kurt Schwitters in Selbstzeugnissen und Bilddokumenten, Rowohlts Monographien*, no. 296 (Reinbek bei Hamburg: Rowohlt, 1981); Werner Schmalenbach, *Kurt Schwitters* (New York: Harry N. Abrams, 1967); Kurt Schwitters, *Kurt Schwitters: Das literarische Werk*, ed. Friedhelm Lath, 5 vols. (Cologne: DuMont, 1973–78).

■ ■ ■

Cat. no. 203

Richard Seewald

BORN 1889 ARNSWALDE (NEUMARKT) ✣ DIED 1976

MUNICH

204. *Paradies*, 1914
(Paradise)
Woodcut with watercolor
7 1/8 x 5 1/2 in. (18.1 x 14.0 cm)
From the portfolio Zehn Holzschnitte zur Bibel (1916)
Los Angeles County Museum of Art, The Robert Gore Rifkind Center for German Expressionist Studies

Although his work had much in common with that of the Expressionists, Richard Seewald considered himself a classical artist and gradually distanced himself from Expressionism. Many of his works from the 1910s, however—particularly his woodcuts, which resemble Karl Schmidt-Rottluff's in their severe lines and dramatic use of black—are clearly Expressionist in origin and share the movement's interest in modified religious themes and apocalyptic musings. Revering Giotto (he wrote a book on the artist, which he titled *Eine Apologie des Klassischen* [An apology for the classical]) and drawing inspiration from the landscape of the Mediterranean, which he often visited, Seewald synthesized classical and avant-garde ideals.

It was the work of Emil Nolde that turned Seewald away from Expressionism in 1913. After visiting the Neue Kunstsalon (New art salon) in Munich, he wrote: "My separation from Expressionism was completed by the confrontation with the violent work of Emil Nolde.... It is not surprising that after only two years, I painted that little still life with the cigarette packets on a chess board. I had rediscovered space and the third dimension, which Expressionism, with its two-dimensional painting, had given up" ("Der Standpunkt," in 85 *Jahre Bilder, Zeichnungen, Graphik*, unpaginated). Perhaps the strongest current in Seewald's art was his interest in religious themes, which manifested itself in early woodcuts treating biblical subjects and became stronger during his later years, when he worked almost exclusively on church commissions.

Like the artists of the Brücke (Bridge), Seewald began studying architecture, at the technical college in Munich, but abandoned it in favor of painting, in which he had no formal instruction. He nevertheless quickly received critical attention and took part in the Salon d'automne in Paris in 1911 and 1912 and in Herwarth Walden's *Erster deutscker Herbstsalon* (First German autumn salon) in Berlin in 1913. A member of the Munich New Secession, the Berlin Free Secession, and the Deutsche Künstlerbund (German artists' society), he was a professor at the trade school in Cologne from 1924 until 1931, when he took up temporary residence in Italy, a country that he had visited many times, with whose artistic tradition he felt an affinity, and where he had converted to Catholicism two years earlier. From this time on, he executed many commissions for the Church, including several large altarpieces in Switzerland during the war.

For the remainder of his career, Seewald continued to create and lecture about religious art, giving talks such as "Über die Möglichkeit einer neuen Kunst in der Kirche" (On the possibility of a new art in the Church) in 1950 and "Moderne religiöse Kunst im kultischen und privaten Raum" (Modern religious art in the ritual and private sphere) in 1953. Summing up his ideals, he wrote, "It is in accordance with the idea of classicism that...the heroic and the idyllic exist side by side" ("Der Standpunkt," unpaginated).

A.S.

BIBLIOGRAPHY

Ralph Jentsch, *Richard Seewald: Das graphische Werk* (Esslingen: Kunstgalerie Esslingen, 1973); *Richard Seewald: 85 Jahre Bilder, Zeicknungen, Graphik, 1912–1973*, exh. cat. (Munich: Galerie Wolfgang Ketterer, 1973); Richard Seewald, *Glanz des Mittelalters* (Feldafing: Buchheim, 1956).

■ ■ ■

Ottheinrich Strohmeyer

BIRTH DAYE UNKNOWN ✣ DEATH DATE UNKNOWN

205. *Das Kreuz im kreise*, 1920
(The cross in the circle)
Linocut
7 3/4 x 6 1/4 in. (19.7 x 15.9cm)
From *Eos* 2, no. 4 (1920)
Los Angeles County Museum of Art. The Robert Gore Rifkind Center for German Expressionist Studies, purchased with funds provided by Anna Bing Arnold, Museum Acquisition Fund, and deaccession funds

■ ■ ■

Bruno Taut

BORN 1880 KÖNIGSBERG ✣ DIED 1938 ORTAKÖY, TURKEY

206. *Bewegungsspiel fürs Weimarer Bauhaus*, 1919
(Exercise for the Weimar Bauhaus)
Iron-based cyanotype
13¾ x 9¼ in. (34.9 x 23.4 cm)
Letter from the *Gläserne Kette* correspondence
Collection Centre Canadien d'Architecture/Canadian Centre for Architecture, Montreal

207. *Dandanah, the Fairy Palace*, 1919
Set of fifty-one building blocks of different shapes and sizes, cast from blue, red, yellow, green, and clear glass, housed in rare box, which also contains five diagrams showing how to display the blocks and one showing how to store them in the box
Box: 10¼ x 10 x 1⅝ in. (26.0 x 25.4 x 4.1 cm); rectangular blocks: 2 x ¾ x ¾ in. (5.0 x 1.9 x 1.9 cm); balls (diam): ¾ in. (1.9 cm); triangular blocks: ⅝ x 1 x ⅞ in. (1.6 x 2.5 x 2.2 cm); cubes: ¾ x ¾ x ¾ in. (1.9 x 1.9 x 1.9 cm)
Building block collection of Arlan Coffman, Santa Monica

208. *Vivat Stella MDCCCCXXI*, 1919
Iron-based cyanotype
13 7/16 x 9⅞ in. (34.2 x 25.1 cm)
Letter from the Gläserne Kette correspondance
Collection Centre Canadien d'Architecture/Canadian Centre for Architecture, Montreal

209. *Weinachts Grüsse: "Monument des neuen Gesetzes,"* 1919
(Christmas greeting: "Monument to the new law")
Iron-based cyanotype
13 9/16 x 9⅜ in. (34.4 x 23.8 cm)
Letter from the Gläserne Kette correspondence
Collection Centre Canadien d'Architecture/Canadian Centre for Architecture, Montreal

210. Untitled (community hall), 1919–20
Iron-based cyanotype
13⅞ x 9⅛ in. (35.2 x 23.1 cm)
Letter from the Gläserne Kette correspondence
Collection Centre Canadien d'Architecture/Canadian Centre for Architecture, Montreal

211. *Museum und Kristallhaus der neuen Schule*, c. 1920
(Museums and crystal house for the new school)
Ink on tracing paper
12 x 15¾ in. (30.5 x 40.0 cm)
Ungers collection

212. *Watz Paar Konzert*, 1922
(Watz pair concert)
Ink on red paper
8⅞ x 11 5/16 in. (22.6 x 28.7 cm)
Graphische Sammlung, Staatsgalerie Stuttgart

See also cat. nos. 231–35

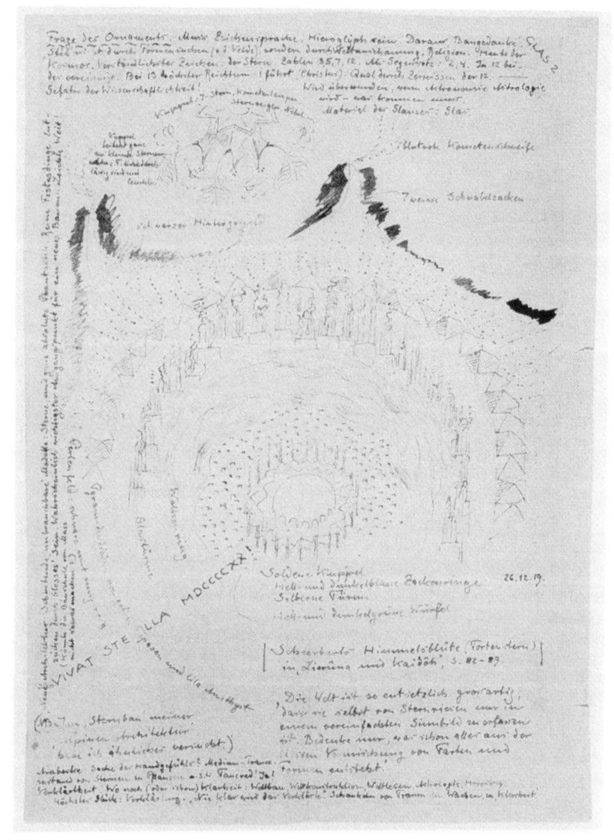

Cat. no. 208

A leading exponent of Expressionist ideals in architecture, Bruno Taut may be better known for his utopian visions than for his buildings. Although his early industrial and residential designs manifest little Expressionist influence, his pavilions for the 1913 *Internationale Baufachausstellung* (International building exhibition) in Leipzig and the 1914 Werkbund exhibition in Cologne, particularly his Glashaus (Glass house) for the latter, typify his Expressionist style.

Taut attended the gymnasium and the school of building trades in Königsberg. Like many of his contemporaries, he was disillusioned by the historicism prevalent in German architecture around the turn of the century. His meeting in 1913 with art critic Adolf Behne and Expressionist poet Paul Scheerbart led to a lifelong friendship and mutual inspiration. Scheerbart's influence is evident throughout Taut's works. His verses inspired the architect to embark on a personal mission to promulgate a quasi mythology of glass.

A prolific writer, Taut published books, articles, pamphlets, and manifestos. His major books include *Die Stadtkrone* (The city-crown, 1919), *Alpine Architektur* (Alpine architecture, 1919), and *Die Auflösung der Städte* (The dissolution of the cities, 1920). He crusaded for land reform, environmental preservation, and the abolition of war through massive "impossible tasks" such as rebuilding the Alps. His social commentary has made him one of the most widely read and studied architects of the first third of the twentieth century. He believed that new communal structures such as sparkling cities would create a new social order founded on cooperation and love. His sketches were as much social fantasies as they were architectural fantasies.

Taut's idealism also took more practical forms. He founded the Arbeitsrat für Kunst (Working council for art) in 1918, with the goal of promoting cooperation between intellectuals and the proletariat in the building of a new community, and joined the Novembergruppe (November group). He was also active in the Werkbund. In 1919 he initiated the Gläserne Kette (Crystal chain) correspondence (writing under the pseudonym *Glas*

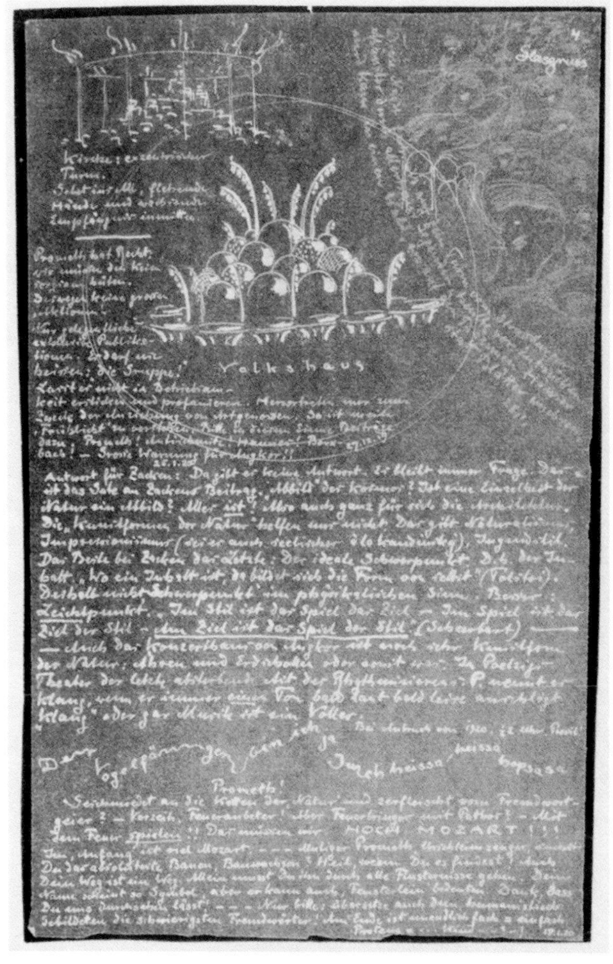

Cat. no. 210

[glass]), considered the most significant dialogue on architectural theory in the twentieth century. In 1921 and 1922 he edited and published four issues of *Frühlicht* (Daybreak), a journal of the modern movement. In 1925 he organized Der Ring (The ring), a diverse group of architects who united in the search for a new, progressive *Baukultur* (building culture).

From 1930 to 1932 Taut served as professor at the technical college in Berlin. With great hopes of building utopia, he moved to Russia in 1932 and worked as a consulting architect in Moscow. He left in 1933, frustrated by the government's firm doctrinal resistance to change. Soon after his return to Germany, he discovered that the Nazis were about to arrest him as a cultural Bolshevik. He fled to Japan and lived there for three years, until his asthma forced him to seek a drier climate in Turkey, where he spent the last two years of his life. During this time Taut immersed himself in his work, becoming a professor at the academy of fine arts in Istanbul and head of the architectural office of the Turkish ministry of education. He continued to design, combining indigenous elements with modernism. His most important building of this period is the faculty of languages at the university in Ankara (1936–38). He completed a summary of his architectural ideas, which served as a text for his classes. He died of an asthma attack, likely provoked by his exhausting work habits.

V.H.

BIBLIOGRAPHY

Kurt Junghanns, *Bruno Taut, 1880–1938*, 2d rev. ed., Schriften des Instituts für Städtebau und Architektur (Berlin: Elefanten, 1983); Julius Posener, *Bruno Taut: Eine Rede zu seinem fünfzigsten Todestag*, Anmerkungen zur Zeit, no. 28 (Berlin: Akademie der Künste, 1989); Bruno Taut, *Alpine Architektur* (Hagen: Folkwang, 1919); idem, *Die Stadtkrone* (Jena: Eugen Diederichs, 1919); idem, *Der Weltbaumeister: Architektur-Schauspiel für symphonische Musik* (Hagen: Folkwang, 1920); idem, "Mein Weltbild," *Feuer* 3, no. 1 (1922): 277–84; idem, *Architekturlehre: Grundlagen, Theorie und Kritik, Beziehung zu den anderen Künsten und zur Geschichte*, ed. Tilmann Heinisch and Goerd Peschken (Hamburg: VSA, 1977); Barbara Volkmann, ed., *Bruno Taut, 1880–1938* (Berlin: Akademie der Künste, 1980); Iain Boyd Whyte, "Bruno Taut und die sozialistischen und weniger sozialistischen Wurzeln des sozialen Wohnungsbaues," *Neue Heimat Monatshefte* 5, no. 27 (1980): 28–37; idem, *Bruno Taut and the Architecture of Activism* (Cambridge: Cambridge University Press, 1982).

■ ■ ■

Cat. no. 212

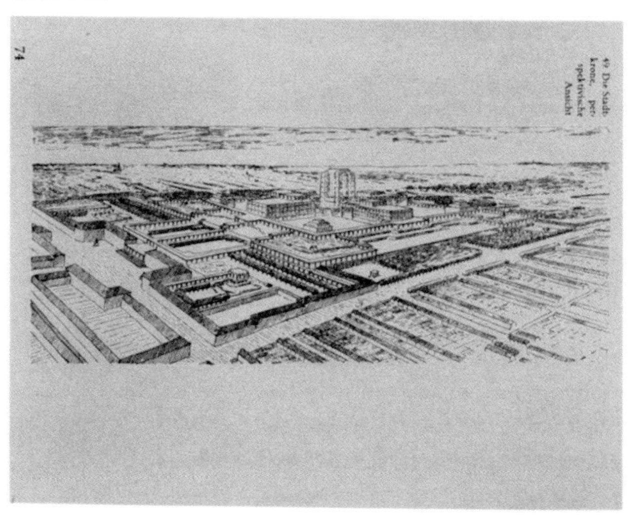

Cat. no. 233

Max Taut

BORN 1884 KÖNIGSBERG ✣ DIED 1967 BERLIN

213. *Betonhallen*, c. 1919
(Concrete halls)
Photographic process
7 15/16 x 6 3/4 in. (20.2 x 17.1 cm)
Collection Centre Canadien d'Architecture/Canadian Centre for Architecture, Montreal

214. *Das drehbare Haus in den Sand Dünen der Curischen Nehrung bei Cranz*, c. 1919
(The rotating house in the sand dunes of Kurland Spit, near Cranz)
Brown cyanotype
13 11/16 x 13 11/16 in. (34.8 x 34.7 cm)
Letter from the Gläserne Kette correspondence
Collection Centre Canadien d'Architecture/Canadian Centre for Architecture, Montreal

215. Untitled (form fantasy), c. 1919
Photographic process
7 1/2 x 8 1/4 in. (19.1 x 22.3 cm)
Letter from the Gläserne Kette correspondence
Collection Centre Canadien d'Architecture/Canadian Centre for Architecture, Montreal

The younger and more pragmatic of the Taut brothers, Max Taut attended the school of building trades in Königsberg. He worked in the office of Ludwig Mies van der Rohe in 1905, then with Hermann Billing in 1906, and in 1911 he opened an independent practice. After World War I he formed a partnership with his brother Bruno and Franz Hoffmann. With his brother and Walter Gropius, Taut founded the Arbeitsrat für Kunst (Working council for art) in 1918. He was also a member of Der Ring (The ring) and participated in the 1914 Werkbund exhibition in Cologne. He contributed drawings to Bruno Taut's Gläserne Kette (Crystal chain) correspondence, in which he risked using his own name. His sketch of the Wissinger family tomb (1920) was the only Gläserne Kette drawing to be built.

Unlike his brother, Max Taut showed no interest in didacticism, polemics, or theoretical speculation. He gained a reputation during the Weimar era as the architect of the labor unions, creating projects such as buildings for the Deutsche Gewerkschaftbund (Federation of German trade unions) in Düsseldorf (1926) and Frankfurt (1929–31). Another significant project was his 1920 revolving house, built on the dunes of Kurland Spit.

With the rise of the National Socialists, Taut was barred from public commissions and was able to complete only a few residential buildings. After World War II he became a professor at the academy in Berlin and, with Wilhelm Büning, established a new school of architecture. He also resumed designing; outstanding examples of his postwar work include the Ludwig-Georg-Gymnasium in Darmstadt (1953) and the Renter housing estate in Bonn (1949–52). His projects from this latter period tended toward large housing developments and apartment buildings. He shared with other Expressionist architects a conceptual boldness and daring yet refrained from exaggeration.

V.H.

BIBLIOGRAPHY
Barbara Volkmann and Rose-France Raddatz, eds., *Max Taut, 1884–1967: Zeichnungen, Bauten*, exh. cat., Akademie-Katalog no. 142 (Berlin: Akademie der Künste, 1984).

■ ■ ■

Cat. no. 214

Cat. no. 215

Max Thalman

BORN 1890 THÜRINGISCHEN ✣ DIED 1944 WEIMAR

216. *Der Dom,* 1920
(Cathedral)
Woodcut
26½ x 19 in. (67.3 x 48.3 cm)
Plate 8 from the portfolio Der Dom (1920)
Los Angeles County Museum of Art. Gift of Ernest Raboff

Little-known painter and graphic artist Max Thalman was educated at the school of applied arts in Weimar. After World War I he was active as a book illustrator. He is also noted for his woodcut series. A trip to New York in 1923–24 inspired his book *Amerika in Holzschnitt* (America in woodcut).

V.H.

BIBLIOGRAPHY
Wilhelm Michel, "Gott und die Sprache," *Feuer* 3, no. 2–3 (1922): 56–64.

■ ■ ■

Cat. no. 216

Heinrich Vogeler

BORN 1872 BREMEN ✣ DIED 1942 KARAKHSTAN, U.S.S.R.

217. *Die sieben Schalen des Zorns (Offenbarung Johannis),* 1918
(The Seven Bowls of Wrath [Revelation to John])
Etching
14³/16 x 10⅛ in. (36.0 x 25.8 cm)
Staatliche Graphische Sammlung, Munich

Like many young German artists of his time, Heinrich Vogeler was a utopian idealist. He was a prolific member of the Worpswede artists' community, and his early work—characterized by Jugendstil-inspired swerving lines, soft rhythms, and his celebrated feather images—seemed to depict a fairy-tale world. During World War I, however, his life and art underwent a transformation with his conversion to communism. From that point on he devoted his many artistic talents to disseminating communist ideals and eventually settled in the Soviet Union.

Vogeler began his formal artistic training in 1890 at the academy in Düsseldorf, and in 1894 he traveled to Worpswede, where he joined Fritz Mackensen, Otto Modersohn, and others to form the Künstlervereinigung Worpswede (Worpswede artists' alliance). Vogeler, in contrast to the others, made few landscapes but explored many different subjects and disciplines: still life, portraiture, circle motifs, book illustration, commercial graphics, furniture, and architecture, among others. In 1898 he traveled to Florence, where he began a long friendship with the poet Rainer Maria Rilke, who published an essay on the artist in 1903. By this time Vogeler's primary interest was etching. In 1899 he, Modersohn, and Fritz Overbeck left the Worpswede community, precipitating its dissolution.

By 1900 Vogeler had achieved renown as an illustrator, particularly for the journal *Die Insel* (The island) and its publishing house. He was thoroughly impressed with British book art, especially the use of the ornamental framework. On a 1909 trip to England he became acquainted with the socialist physician Emil Löhnberg. Vogeler was so deeply affected by a tour of the blighted slums of Glasgow and Manchester that he decided to dedicate himself to social reform. He designed a workers' settlement for Worpswede, which was never realized, and houses for workers, of which only a few were constructed. In August 1914 he volunteered as a draftsman for the army. From 1915 to 1917 he recorded his wartime experiences in drawings. His initial idealization of the conflict was eventually overcome by growing antiwar sentiment as he became aware of Germany's territorial objectives and encountered the propaganda of the revolutionary Russian army.

After making an appeal to the Kaiser for peace, Vogeler was released from the army, placed under psychiatric observation, and reported to the police. After the war he formed close associations with German socialists and in 1923 took the first of many trips to the Soviet Union. He 1925 he published *Reise durch Russland: Die Geburt des neuen Menschen* (Journey through Russia: The birth of the new man). He lectured, exhibited, created propaganda art, wrote, and affiliated with many organizations, among them the Assoziation revolutionärer bildender Künstler Deutschlands (Association of revolutionary German visual artists), the most significant organization of communist visual artists in the Weimar Republic, which he cofounded in 1928. Because of his years of intensive devotion to the communist effort in the Soviet Union, Vogeler was chronically impoverished. German writer friends in Moscow donated a large sum of money to liquidate his debts, but he died a month later.

V.H.

BIBLIOGRAPHY
David Erlay, *Vogeler: Ein Maler und seine Zeit* (Fischerhude: Atelier im Bauernhaus, 1981); Rainer Maria Rilke, *Heinrich Vogeler* (Lilienthal: Worpsweder Verlag, 1986); Bernd Stenzig, ed., *Worpswede Moskau: Das Werk von Heinrich Vogeler*, exh. cat. (Worpswede: Worpsweder Kunsthalle, 1989); Johann Heinrich Vogeler, *Werden: Erinnerungen: Mit Lebenszeugnissen aus den Jahren 1923–1942* (Fischerhude: Atelier im Bauernhaus, 1989).

■ ■ ■

Hermann Warm

BORN 1889 BERLIN ✣ DIED 1976 BERLIN

218. With Walter Röhrig and Walter Reimann
Untitled, 1919
Silver print
9 15/16 x 13 in. (25.3 x 33.0 cm)
Set design for the film *Das Cabinet des Doktor Caligari* (1919), directed by Robert Wiene (photographer unknown)
Los Angeles County Museum of Art. The Robert Gore Rifkind Center for German Expressionist Studies

Hermann Warm, like his colleagues Walter Röhrig and Walter Reimann, is probably best known for his contribution to the scenic design of *Das Cabinet des Doktor Caligari* (The cabinet of Doctor Caligari). Warm worked on more than 160 other productions during his lifetime, however, and was one of the most distinguished film designers in Europe in the early decades of the century. His credits include some of the preeminent films of the Weimar era, such as F. W. Murnau's *Phantom* (1920), Fritz Lang's *Der müde Tod* (released in English-speaking countries as *Destiny*, 1921), and Henrik Galeen's *Der Student von Prag* (The student from Prague, 1926), as well as two French films for the director Carl Dreyer, *La passion de Jeanne d'Arc* (released in English-speaking countries as *The Passion of Joan of Arc*, 1928) and *Vampyr* (1932). In Warm's own view he worked on only twenty good films and two especially good ones: *Caligari* and *Jeanne d'Arc*.

Although Warm is usually described as a member of the circle around the Sturm gallery, little evidence exists to support such a claim. He studied theatrical painting at the school of arts and crafts in Berlin from 1905 until 1907, then trained in stage design at the Szenograph theater in Berlin from 1908 until 1909 and at the Schauspielhaus theater from 1910 until 1911. He subsequently entered the film industry, working first with Vitascop in 1912 and then with the Decla-Bioscop, Union, and Greenbaum production companies.

According to the critic Siegfried Kracauer, Warm believed that "films must be drawings brought to life" (Siegfried Kracauer, *From Caligari to Hitler: A Psychological History of the German Cinema* [Princeton, N.J.: Princeton University Press, 1947], p. 68). Speaking later of his work as a film designer, Warm recalled: "At that time there was still a close working relationship between the director, film artist, and cameraman, especially in the area of the silent film. The picture was the language of the film; the composition of the image and the style were dependent on the film designer" (quoted in Gabriela Grunwald, "Expressionistischer Dekor im deutschen Stummfilm," Ph.D. diss., Cologne, 1984–85, p. 79).

Warm's precise role in the conception of *Caligari* is uncertain. According to Warm's account, the producer Rudolf Meinert gave the script to Warm, and he then shared it with Röhrig and Reimann, who had worked with him on previous films. Warm knew that the images had to be "visionary, nightmarish" but had not developed a style for the film. Reimann apparently suggested that "this theme had to have an Expressionist style for the sets, costumes, actors, and direction" (Hess, *Das Cabinet des Dr. Caligari*, p. 53). The film's producer, Erich Pommer, by contrast, recalled that three artists—Robert Herlth and two others—brought him the "absurd proposition" that the set for *Caligari* be painted with lights and shadows. Herlth then attempted to sway Pommer by stating, "We are living in an age of Expressionism" (quoted in Byrne, "German Cinematic Expressionism," p. 162).

During the actual production of *Caligari*, Warm seems to have worked mainly on the sets, while Röhrig did the painting and Reimann was responsible for the costumes. In addition to the films already mentioned, Warm claims to have designed sets for Lang's *Dr. Mabuse, der Spieler* (Dr. Mabuse, the gambler, 1922) along with Otto Hunte and Stahl-Urach, although his name is not listed in the film's credits. Warm worked as a freelance designer in Hungary, France, and England from 1924 until 1933 and then in Switzerland from 1941 until 1944.

A.S.

BIBLIOGRAPHY

Richard Burdick Byrne, "German Cinematic Expressionism, 1919–1924," Ph.D. diss., State University of Iowa, Iowa City, 1962; Klaus Peter Hess, *Das Cabinet des Dr. Caligari: Materialien zu einem Film von Robert Wiene* (Duisburg: Atlas Film, 1988), p. 53; Hermann Warm, "Gegen die Caligari-Legenden," in *Caligari und Caligarismus*, ed. Walter Kaul (Berlin: Deutsche Kinemathek, 1970), pp. 11–19.

■ ■ ■

Andor Weininger

BORN 1899 KARANCS, HUNGARY ✣ DIED 1986 NEW YORK

219. *Mechanische Bühnen-Revue*, 1923
(Mechanical stage review)
Watercolor, black ink, wash, and graphite
11 5/8 x 17 3/4 in. (29.5 x 45.1 cm)
The Metropolitan Museum of Art. Gift of Cornelia Weininger, 1992

Like most of the theater designs devised by students and professors at the Bauhaus, Andor Weininger's ambitious plans for a *Mechanische Bühne* (Mechanical theater) and a *Kugeltheater* (Spherical theater) were never realized. He worked on the concept of a *Gesamtkunstwerk* (total work of art), even though, as he wrote, the idea "was made fun of at the Bauhaus and viewed as romantic" (quoted in Michaelsen, "Andor Weiningers Bühnenprojekte," p. 430). His visionary *Kugeltheater*, a spherical building with hanging stages for the actors and rows of spectator seating on the inside of the ball, was designed to eliminate the spatial limitations imposed by the proscenium of a traditional theater. Noted for his theoretical contributions, Weininger was also a valuable member of the Bauhaus stage workshop because of his singing and piano playing and was a key member of the Bauhaus Band, popular in Dresden, Berlin, and Munich as well as at the school itself.

Weininger began his studies in law, first at the university in Pécs for two semesters beginning in 1917 and then at the technical university in Budapest for another two terms. In 1921—along with a number of other young Hungarian artists, including Farkas Molnár and Henrik Stefán—Weininger was able to enroll at the Bauhaus in Weimar, where he studied with Johannes Itten and Georg Muche and participated in Wassily Kandinsky's mural-painting workshop until 1925. He took part in the informal Weimar De Stijl group and joined Theo van Doesburg's *Stijlkurse* (Stijl courses), offered from March until July of 1922. Weininger also helped form the student group known as KURI, standing for *Konstruktiv-Utilitar-Rationell-International* (Constructive-utilitarian-rational-international), which advocated Constructivist principles and was opposed to Itten's spiritual, dreamily utopian Mazdaznan group. In 1923 Weininger left the Bauhaus for five months to work as a set designer and musician at a nightclub in Hamburg, where he developed his idea for a *Mechanische Bühnen-Revue* (Mechanical stage revue), which involved the orchestration of abstract colored shapes on the stage. He later wrote of the project: "How it could be done technically was another question. But I solved that also, in theory, with rooms moving around an axis carrying moving bands. It is possible to carry this out in practice, but it is difficult" (ibid., p. 428).

In 1925, after the Bauhaus moved to Dessau, Weininger returned to Pécs, but in 1927 he went to Dessau at the request of Walter Gropius, receiving a monthly stipend and joining Oskar Schlemmer's theater workshop. In 1927 Weininger's *Mechanische Bühnen-Revue* and *Kugeltheater* designs were shown at the *Deutsche Theater-Ausstellung* (German theater exhibition) in Magdeburg, and the design for his *Kugeltheater* was published in the book *Die Bühne im Bauhaus* (The Stage at the Bauhaus), edited by Oskar Schlemmer and László Moholy-Nagy. Leaving the Bauhaus the following year to live in Berlin, Weininger collaborated during the 1930s on design projects with his future wife, Eva Fernbach. The pair moved to the Netherlands in 1938 and in 1951 immigrated to Canada and later the United States.

A.S.

BIBLIOGRAPHY

Eva Bajkay-Rosch, "Hungarians at the Bauhaus," *Bauhaus: International Centrum voor Structuuranalyse en Constructivisme*, no. 6–7 (1987): 97–117; Kathrin Michaelsen, "Andor Weiningers Bühnenprojekte am Bauhaus," in *Wechsel Wirkungen: Ungarische Avantgarde in der Weimarer Republik*, exh. cat., ed. Hubertus Gassner (Kassel: Staatliche Kunstsammlungen, 1986), pp. 427–30; Jiri Svestka, ed., *Andor Weininger: Vom Bauhaus zur konzeptuellen Kunst*, exh. cat. (Düsseldorf: Kunstverein für die Rheinland und Westfalen, 1990); Andor Weininger, "Kugeltheater," *Bauhaus: Zeitschrift für Gestaltung*, no. 3 (1927): 2; idem, "The Fun Department at the Bauhaus," *Mosaic* (November 1957): 15–17.

■ ■ ■

Gustav Wolf

BORN 1887 ÖSTRINGEN ✣ DIED 1947 EAST NORTHFIELD, MASSACHUSETTS

220. *Der vierte Tag*, c. 1913
(The fourth day)
Lithograph with watercolor
10⁵⁄₁₆ x 7 in. (26.2 x 17.8 cm)
From the portfolio Am Anfang: Genesis (1913)
Los Angeles County Museum of Art. The Robert Gore Rifkind Center for German Expressionist Studies, purchased with funds provided by Anna Bing Arnold, Museum Acquisition Fund, and deaccession funds.

Gustav Wolf was a painter, sculptor, and graphic artist whose work often addressed religious themes. Like other artists of his generation, such as Franz Marc, he often chose animals as his subjects, depicting them as peaceful, spiritual beings. Wolf painted and drew many landscapes, including naturalistic views of Lake Constance in southern Germany, where he lived, and also invented fantastic dream landscapes in bright, unreal colors.

Wolf studied at the school of applied arts in Karlsruhe from 1904 until 1906 on the advice of the artist Hans Thoma, then traveled through Europe until 1908. In that year Wolf exhibited his work in Paris. In the period before World War I he created numerous print portfolios, often based on biblical stories. In addition to his portfolio of seven lithographs Die sieben Schöpfungstage (The seven days of Creation), published in 1913 by Eugen Diederichs Verlag in Jena, Wolf made woodcut series entitled Confessio (1908), Das erste Flugblatt vom lebenden Sein (The first flier of the living soul, 1918), Die Blätter vom lebenden Sein (The pages of the living soul, 1919), Deutsche Landschaft (German landscape, 1922), and Kreaturen (Creatures, 1925). He also designed a cover for Alfred Mombert's book *Der Thron der Zeit* (The throne of time) and illustrated Jean Paul's treatise *Der grösste Gedanke der Menschen* (Humankind's greatest thought) with six color plates in 1925.

After the war Wolf was a founder of the artists' group Kunst und Kulturrats für Baden (Art and culture council for Baden) and was a professor of graphic art at the state art school of Baden in Karlsruhe from 1920 until 1921. In addition to his graphic work, Wolf made many small bronzes, particularly of animals, and seems to have been attracted to figures from Greek mythology as well as to non-Western cultures. His contemporary Max Raphael wrote of him in 1923 that his interest in animals stemmed from the difference in scale between the "mighty animal" and "tiny man." In 1933 Wolf painted a series of frescoes in the Karlsruhe Kunsthalle (now destroyed), his last commission before his immigration to Switzerland. Five years

Cat. no. 220

later he moved to the United States, where he executed drawings of New York and a series of etchings entitled Vision of Manhattan. In 1944 his Book of Job was selected as one of the best fifty books of the year by the American Institute of Graphic Art.

A.S.

BIBLIOGRAPHY

Richard Benz, "Die Zeichen-Sprache der Kunst: Betrachtungen zum Werk Gustav Wolfs," in *Jahrbuch der jungen Kunst*, 1921 (Leipzig: Klinkhardt und Biermann, 1921), pp. 47–55; Max Raphael, "Über Gustav Wolf," *Jahrbuch der jungen Kunst*, 1923 (Leipzig: Klinkhardt und Biermann, 1923), pp. 190–94.

■ ■ ■

Books, Periodicals, and Ephemera

221. *Ausstellung Für unbekannte Architekten*, 1919
(Exhibition of unknown architects)
Pamphlet
Catalogue for an exhibition organized by the Arbeitsrat Für Kunst
The Resource Collections of the Getty Center for the History of Art and the Humanities

222. Uriel Birnbaum
Der Kaiser und der Architekt: Ein Märchen in fünfzig Bildern, 1924
(The kaiser and the architect: A fairy tale in fifty pictures)
Illustrated book
Los Angeles County Museum of Art. The Robert Gore Rifkind Center for German Expressionist Studies, gift of Robert Gore Rifkind

223. Curt Corrinth
Potsdamer Platz; oder, Die Nächte des neuen Messias: Ekstatische Visionen, 1920
(Potsdamer Platz; or, The nights of the new Messiah: Ecstatic visions)
Book with illustrations by Paul Klee
Los Angeles County Museum of Art. The Robert Gore Rifkind Center for German Expressionist Studies, purchased with funds provided by Anna Bing Arnold, Museum Acquisition Fund, and deaccession funds

224. Siegfried Ebeling
Der Raum als Membran, 1926
(Space as membrane)
Pamphlet
Ungers collection

225. *Frühlicht* (Winter 1921–22)
Periodical
Los Angeles County Museum of Art. The Robert Gore Rifkind Center for German Expressionist Studies, purchased with funds provided by Anna Bing Arnold, Museum Acquisition Fund, and deaccession funds

226. *Frühlicht* (Fall 1921, Spring 1922, Summer 1922)
Periodicals
The Resource Collections of the Getty Center for the History of Art and the Humanities

227. *Für das neue Deutschland*, 1919
(For the new Germany)
Broadside
Los Angeles County Museum of Art. The Robert Gore Rifkind Center for German Expressionist Studies, gift of Robert Gore Rifkind

228. Otto Kohtz
Gedanken über Architektur, c. 1909
(Thoughts about architecture)
Illustrated book
Helen Topping Architecture and Fine Arts Library, University of Southern California

229. *Ruf zum Bauen*, 1920
(Call to building)
Book
Published to accompany an exhibition organized by the Arbeitsrat für Kunst
The Resource Collections of the Getty Center for the History of Art and the Humanities

230. Oskar Schlemmer and László Moholy-Nagy
Die Bühne im Bauhaus, 1924
(The stage at the Bauhaus)
Book
From the series Bauhausbücher, no. 4
Los Angeles County Museum of Art. The Robert Gore Rifkind Center for German Expressionist Studies, purchased with funds provided by Anna Bing Arnold, Museum Acquisition Fund, and deaccession funds

231. Bruno Taut
Ein Architekturprogramm, 1918
(A program for architecture)
Pamphlet
From the series Flugschriften des Arbeitsrates für Kunst, no. 1
The Resource Collections of the Getty Center for the History of Art and the Humanities

232. Bruno Taut
Alpine Architektur, 1919
(Alpine architecture)
Illustrated book
The Resource Collections of the Getty Center for the History of Art and the Humanities

233. Bruno Taut
Die Stadtkrone, 1919
(The city-crown)
Book
Los Angeles County Museum of Art. The Robert Gore Rifkind Center for German Expressionist Studies, gift of Robert Gore Rifkind

234. Bruno Taut
Die Auflösung der Städte, 1920
(The dissolution of the cities)
Illustrated book
The Resource Collections of the Getty Center for the History of Art and the Humanities

235. Bruno Taut
Der Weltbaumeister, 1920
(The universal master builder)
Illustrated book
Helen Topping Architecture and Fine Arts Library, University of Southern California

UTOPIA
DOKUMENTE

Appendix: Essays, Articles, Manifestos, Letters, and Other Writings

173
Johannes Itten
Untitled (proposed cover for *Utopia: Dokumente der Wirlichkeit*), 1921
Ink
13 x 97/16 in (33.0 x 24.0 cm)
Courtesy Itten Estate

Paradise

Program of the Brücke

The earliest Expressionist group in Germany, the Brücke (Bridge) artists celebrated youth and spontaneity of expression in their image of a community of artists defiantly creating the future. Their 1906 program is in the tradition of the avant-garde manifesto.

Translated in Reinhold Heller, Brücke: German Expressionist Prints from the Granvil and Marcia Specks Collection, *exh. cat. (Evanston, Ill.: Mary and Leigh Block Gallery, Northwestern University, 1988), p. 15; reprinted by permission of the publisher.*

With a belief in continuing evolution, in a new generation of creators as well as appreciators, we call together all youth. And as youth that is carrying the future, we intend to obtain freedom of movement and of life for ourselves in opposition to older, well-established powers. Whoever renders directly and authentically that which impels him to create is one of us.

Metropolis

AUGUST ENDELL

From *The Beauty of the Big City*

Endell (1871–1925) was a leading Jugenstil architect who broke with the contemporary view (voiced by Karl Scheffler and other architectural critics) that the city was inherently ugly. His portrayal of the city anticipates the Italian Futurists' bruitist glorification of cacophonous noise while also recalling the pastoral harmony of landscape painting.

Originally published as Die Schönheit der grossen Stadt *(Stuttgart: Strecker und Schröder, 1908), pp. 30–33; translated by David Britt.*

THE CITY AS NATURE

Alongside this hidden beauty [of work], which does not speak to the senses, which is accessible only to one who employs visualization—the thinking imagination—to explore the form that work has created, there is a second form of beauty, that of the city as nature. This may sound curious, but that is because this beauty is almost always overlooked; we are not used to looking at a city in the same way we look at forests, mountains, or the sea.

THE CITY OF NOISES

It is curious: the cawing of crows, the rushing of the wind, the roar of the sea, seem poetic, magnificent, and noble. But the sounds of the city do not even seem worthy of notice, and yet they in themselves create a remarkable world that must make the city appear, even to the blind, as a richly complex entity. We have only to listen and hearken to the city's voices. The light rolling of cabs; the ponderous rumble of mail vans; the clatter of hoofs on the asphalt; the quick, sharp, staccato of the trotter; the dragging pace of a cab horse: all have an individual character of their own, more subtly nuanced than we can express in words. Without really knowing how, we distinguish one vehicle from another; no eyes needed. These sounds are as familiar to us as old acquaintances. Often too loud, of course, even deafening at close quarters, but almost always beautiful as they fade gradually into the distance. How cheerful is the sound of wheels bowling along; with what strange suddenness they fall silent when the vehicle disappears round a corner. How insistent are the echoing footsteps of pedestrians. How trippingly quiet, even delicate, are the steps of multitudes in narrow streets where vehicles seldom pass, as often heard on Schloss-Strasse in Dresden. With what muted passion the waiting multitudes jostle and shuffle, and how varied are the voices of automobiles, their oncoming rush, the cry of the klaxons, and then, gradually emerging into audibility, the rhythmic throb of the pistons, sometimes a roar, sometimes a heavy thump, sometimes keeping time with a delicately metallic ring and finally, close by, the siren song of the wheels, as their spokes strike the air, and the quiet, slithering crunch of the rubber tires. How mysterious is the deep hum of the transformers hidden in the billboard columns, which nudge us with their barely audible sounds as a dog gently nudges its master from behind. How wonderful is the dark, suffused roar of a trolley at full speed, rhythmically punctuated by the heavy pounding of the car, then, gradually emerging, the hard beat on the tracks, the grinding of the gears, the whir of the roller, and the shiver in the wires, long after the car has passed. One can walk the streets of the city for hours on end, listening to its voices, loud and soft, and sense a strange and intricate life in the quiet of unfrequented places and in the roar of busy streets. There are no words to express the delight of all these things.

THE CITY AS LANDSCAPE

To the hearer the great city is an animated, richly detailed being; to the viewer it makes an inexhaustible gift of itself as landscape, as a colorful, ever-changing picture; it offers a bounty, a profusion, which generation after generation of humanity will never exhaust.

SIEGFRIED KRACAUER

"Locomotive over Friedrichstrasse"

Kracauer (1889–1966) was an eminent cultural critic for the Frankfurter Zeitung *who also wrote important sociological texts. His vignette on Berlin's bustling Friedrichstrasse as seen by a locomotive engineer is a succinct example of his fascination with the "exotic of the everyday," a phrase he used in describing his celebrated study of Germany's white-collar workers,* Die Angestellten *(The employees, 1930)*

Originally published as "Lokomotive über der Friedrichstrasse," in Frankfurter Zeitung, *28 January 1933; reprinted in Siegfried Kracauer,* Strassen in Berlin und anderswo *(Frankfurt: Suhrkamp, 1964, pp. 41–43; translated by David Britt.*

Crossing Friedrichstrasse toward the railroad station, one often sees a giant express locomotive halted above. It stands directly over the center of the street and belongs to some long-distance train that is arriving from the west or departing for the east. Does it engage the attention of the crowd? Nobody gives it a glance. Cafés, display windows, women, automats, headlines, luminous advertisements, cops, buses, vaudeville photographs, beggars—all these ground-level impressions preoccupy the passerby far too deeply for him to grasp the apparition on the skyline. Even the upper floors along this street are lost in a blur; the caryatids on the facades have no interlocutors, the dormers might as well be cardboard, and the roofs vanish into a void. The locomotive suffers the same fate. With its long body, its gleaming rods, and its array of red wheels, it is a wondrous sight to see, but it lingers, neglected, above the throng of vehicles and people that surges through the underpass. It is an alien visitant, arriving and gliding away amid the nocturnal vapors, as unnoticed as if it were always there—or never there at all.

But what a spectacle Friedrichstrasse itself presents to the man on the locomotive! Imagine that he may have been driving his machine through the darkness for hours on end. The open iron road still rings in his ears: tracks hurtling toward him, signals, block stations, forests, plowed fields, and pastures. He has passed through little depots and has brought his train to a halt for a few minutes at a time beneath the vast gloom of a station roof. Freight trains, local trains, lamplit parlors, church towers, voices calling. But, time and again, all this life has been swallowed up by the earth and lost in the sky. Towns? Brief interruptions. Villages? Scattered clusters in the countryside. Nothing has endured but embankments and telegraph poles, field patterns, endless spaces. Sometimes the fields have dropped away beneath the blaze of the firehole, to be replaced by the surface of a river. Carts and wagons have waited at level crossings, smokestacks have sliced across the landscape, childish hands have waved from below. And, always, looming masses of blackness, rapidly growing and instantly disappearing.

The man on the locomotive has just left all that behind him. After a journey on which everything but earth and sky has fled from him, he suddenly comes to a halt above Friedrichstrasse, which obliterates both sky and earth. To him it must seem like the axis of the world, stretching away to either side, dead-straight and immeasurable. For its brightness obliterates his memories, its din drowns out that of the railroad, and its activity is sufficient unto itself. This is no mere halt along the way, but a sojourn at the very center of life. Himself an alien visitant, the man above peers down at the street as if through a chink. His eyes, accustomed as they are to darkness, may fail to distinguish details, but he nevertheless perceives the turmoil that explodes out of this narrow canyon of buildings; he registers the glare that is redder than the wheels of his own machine. In his perception the glare and the turmoil mingle in an eruption of festivity that has—like the string of arc lights—no beginning and no end. It looms out of the distance, enfolding rich and poor, harlots and escorts, and lines the facades with a roof-high, tumultuous blaze of words and signs. The man feels as if he were invisible, with the street of streets surging over and past him. A chain that never breaks. A human ribbon that ceaselessly unrolls, through the flickering air, between one plowed field and the next.

When he moves on, the night seems darker than ever. Everywhere he looks, behind and before, he sees a glowing line. It haunts him, and soon it can no longer be reduced to time and space: it becomes an emblem of redly glowing life. On Friedrichstrasse no one has noticed the locomotive.

GEORG SIMMEL

From "The Metropolis and Mental Life"

Simmel (1858–1918) based his ground-breaking sociological theory on the experience of the city, using his native Berlin as his case study. Although his Jewish origins prevented him from obtaining a full professorship at the university there, his lectures and private seminars in his home were widely influential. They were attended by Ernst Bloch, Paul Ernst, Georg Lukács, and Rainer Maria Rilke among others. "The Metropolis and Mental Life" has become his best-known essay.

Originally published as "Die Grossstädte und das Geistesleben," in Die Grossstadt, *special issue of* Jahrbuch der Gehe-Stiftung zu Dresden 9 *(1903); translated by Hans Gerth, in* The Sociology of Georg Simmel, *ed. Kurt H. Wolff (Glencoe, Ill.: Free Press, 1950), pp. 409–24; reprinted by permission of the publisher.*

The deepest problems of modern life derive from the claim of the individual to preserve the autonomy and individuality of his existence in the face of overwhelming social forces, of historical heritage, of external culture, and of the technique of life.... An inquiry into the inner meaning of specifically modern life and its products, into the soul of the cultural body, so to speak, must seek to solve the equation which structures like the metropolis set up between the individual and the super-individual contents of life. Such an inquiry must answer the question of how the personality accommodates itself in the adjustments to external forces. This will be my task today.

The psychological basis of the metropolitan type of individuality consists in the *intensification of nervous stimulation* which results from the swift and uninterrupted change of outer and inner stimuli. Man is a differentiating creature. His mind is stimulated by the difference between a momentary impression and the one which preceded it. Lasting impressions, impressions which differ only slightly from one another, impressions which take a regular and habitual course and show regular and habitual contrasts—all these use up, so to speak, less consciousness than does the rapid crowding of changing images, the sharp discontinuity in the grasp of a single glance, and the unexpectedness of onrushing impressions. These are the psychological conditions which the metropolis creates. With each crossing of the street, with the tempo and multiplicity of economic, occupational and social life, the city sets up a deep contrast with small town and rural life with reference to the sensory foundations of psychic life.... Thus the metropolitan type of man—which, of course, exists in a thousand individual variants—develops an organ protecting him against the threatening currents and discrepancies of his external environment which would uproot him. He reacts with his head instead of his heart. In this an increased awareness assumes the psychic prerogative. Metropolitan life, thus, underlies a heightened awareness and a predominance of intelligence in metropolitan man. The reaction to metropolitan phenomena is shifted to that organ which is least sensitive and quite remote from the depth of the personality. Intellectuality is thus seen to preserve subjective life against the overwhelming power of metropolitan life, and intellectuality branches out in many directions and is integrated with numerous discrete phenomena.

The metropolis has always been the seat of the money economy. Here the multiplicity and concentration of economic exchange give an importance to the means of exchange which the scantiness of rural commerce would not have allowed. Money economy and the dominance of the intellect are intrinsically connected. They share a matter-of-fact attitude in dealing with men and with things; and, in this attitude, a formal justice is often coupled with an inconsiderate hardness. The intellectually sophisticated person is indifferent to all genuine individuality, because relationships and reactions result from it which cannot be exhausted with logical operations. In the same manner, the individuality of phenomena is not commensurate with the pecuniary principle. Money is concerned only with what is common to all: it asks for the exchange value, it reduces all quality and individuality to the question: How much?...

In certain seemingly insignificant traits, which lie upon the surface of life, the same psychic currents characteristically unite. Modern mind has become more and more calculating. The calculative exactness of practical life which the money economy has brought about corresponds to the ideal of natural science: to transform the world into an arithmetic problem, to fix every part of the world by mathematical formulas.... The relationships and affairs of the typical metropolitan usually are so varied and complex that without the strictest punctuality in promises and services the whole structure would break down into an inextricable chaos. Above all, this necessity is brought about by the aggregation of so many people with such differentiated interests, who must integrate their relations and activities into a highly complex organism. If all clocks and watches in Berlin would suddenly go wrong in different ways, even if only by one hour, all economic life and communication of the city would be disrupted for a long time....

The same factors which have thus coalesced into the exactness and minute precision of the form of life have coalesced into a structure of the highest impersonality; on the other hand, they have promoted a highly personal subjectivity. There is perhaps no psychic phenomenon which has been so unconditionally reserved to the metropolis as has the blasé attitude. The blasé attitude results first from the rapidly changing and closely compressed contrasting stimulations of the nerves. From this, the enhancement of metropolitan intellectuality, also, seems originally to stem. Therefore, stupid people who are not intellectually alive in the first place usually are not exactly blasé. A life in boundless pursuit of pleasure makes one blasé because it agitates the nerves to their strongest reactivity for such a long time that they finally cease to react at all. In the same way, through the rapidity and contradictoriness of their changes, more harmless impressions force such violent responses, tearing the nerves so brutally hither and thither that their last reserves of strength are spent; and if one remains in the same milieu they have no time to gather new strength. An incapacity thus emerges to react to new sensations with the appropriate energy. This constitutes that blasé attitude which, in fact, every metropolitan child shows when compared with children of quieter and less changeable milieus....

...For the reciprocal reserve and indifference and the intellectual life conditions of large circles are never felt more strongly by the individual in their impact upon his independence than in the thickest crowd of the big city. This is because the bodily proximity and narrowness of space make the mental distance only the more visible. It is obviously only the obverse of this freedom if, under certain circumstances, one nowhere feels as lonely and lost as in the metropolitan crowd. For here as elsewhere it is by no means necessary that the freedom of man be reflected in his emotional life as comfort....

...The metropolis reveals itself as one of those great historical formations in which opposing streams which enclose life unfold, as well as join one another with equal right. However, in this process the currents of life, whether their individual phenomena touch us sympathetically or antipathetically, entirely transcend the sphere for which the judge's attitude is appropriate. Since such forces of life have grown into the roots and into the crown of the whole of the historical life in which we, in our fleeting existence, as a cell, belong only as a part, it is not our task either to accuse or to pardon, but only to understand.

Architectural Fantasy

HERMANN OBRIST

From "The Future of Our Architecture"

A teacher of considerable influence and an innovative decorative artist and sculptor of the Jugendstil movement, Obrist explored fundamental issues in often provocative ways in his writings. In his book of essays, from which the following excerpt is taken, he also considered art and originality, the public's interest in art, and whether art should be practical or fanciful.

Originally published as "Die Zukunft unserer Architektur," in Neue Möglichkeiten in der bildenden Kunst: Essays *(Leipzig: Eugen Diederichs, 1903), pp. 112–14; translated by David Britt.*

For centuries architecture has known no progress even remotely comparable with the rest of civilized life, and the reason for this is summed up in a single phrase that we once heard from the lips of an artist: "ignominious dependency." (By which we mean, of course, not its dependency on function and material...but dependency in a purely social and civic sense.) The painter paints his picture the way he wants to paint it; he starves, maybe, but he can still paint it. What young architect can build himself a house or a church? He can only make sketches and designs (and in fact he ought to do more of them and show them more often than hitherto). No municipality, no government, no business community can be expected to take the initiative; they are dependent on countless contingencies of their own. There are nevertheless thousands of tasks that need to be done, given only a fair breath of wind from the courageous private initiatives of those men and women who are capable of thinking further ahead than the next instant or the next two years. Whence comes our deliverance, except it be from them? Rarely has the moment been more propitious than it is today, when the initiative of powerful and enterprising corporate bodies has rescued the outskirts of our cities from the speculative builders of bleak apartment houses and has made them available for the building of homes fit for human beings to live in. In many of these developments the practical conditions of life at least come very close to the ideal that previous generations vainly longed for. In this new century let us take the chance that offers itself: let us prove ourselves worthy of social progress, by making these homes solid, true, contemporary, and individual, so that we may take pleasure in them and so that we may leave our descendants a memorial, not of the things we most liked to imitate, but of the way we were at the onset of the new century. If we were to do that, there would be an unparalleled sprouting of green shoots, a true rebirth at last.

From *For the New Germany*

The armistice of November 1918 brought the end of the Wilhelmine empire and the opportunity for a new form of government in Germany. Many intellectuals and artists overcame their disagreements to unite around their hopes for a socialist government, as is evident in these selections from a broadside circulated during the election of delegates to the Weimar assembly in January 1919 (see fig. 23).

Originally published as Für das neue Deutschland *(January 1919); translated by David Britt.*

HANS BALUSCHEK (JANUARY 14, 1919)
I expect a new age to be entirely to the advantage of creative individuals: the freest development, the greatest protection, the greatest aid, and the most extensive influence on the people as a whole, whose natural aristocracy they are.

PETER BEHRENS (JANUARY 13, 1919)
Erect on the debris of the vanished age stand the emblems of the new. Let us cast doubt aside, set to work, and build that bright edifice.

HERBERT EULENBERG (JANUARY 17, 1919)
The socialist republic is the best form of government for this nation of poets and thinkers. Every free mind must salute the revolution of the German state, which began in November 1918, with hope and with joy. Our nation will once more be mindful of its mission, which is to help improve the life of the earth, not only through deeds and trade but also through poetry and thought.

GERHART HAUPTMANN (JANUARY 14, 1919)
Our renewal has been accomplished in a state of exhaustion. Our strength had turned to inner weakness—so much so that it collapsed inward upon itself. But at once the first shoots of the new began to sprout amid the ruins. The new is young and quite different from the old. Woe betide anyone who can find nothing better to do today than dig out ancestral lumber from beneath the dust and debris. Woe betide the national identity that was nothing more than a repository for all that ancestral lumber, accompanied by all the tired old political tunes and performers. Either a strong faith in the new will preside over a future gathering of the German clans—from which our German-Austrian brethren must not be absent—or else *lasciate ogni speranza!*

You believe in the resurrection of Germany, but do not imagine that we were united before just because we talked about the kaiser and the Reich. We were torn, fissured, ruptured beneath that unifying coat of bright new paint. Let there be no timorous quest for the old so-called union. Its deceptive gloss is gone forever. Such a union is not enough for the new Germany. Let us be united in the new; let us seek a new union, one that is closer, deeper, and more honest. God knows, this is a forlorn hope, but I can never abandon it as long as I live. You Germans, pursue the prize of union! Germania's tattered garment has hitherto been pinned together by a brooch. You talked of union, but you did not have it. This union must be discovered, felt, explored, recognized, experienced, invented; it must have its birth in a melting pot of universal fervor. Alas for all our wretched partisan divisions! A Frenchman may embrace a *Boche*,* but two Germans of different parties will slap each other's faces, irreconcilable in this world and in the next. Allow yourselves to be reconciled; make peace at long last, you countless feuding brothers! While the builders quarrel among themselves, nothing will ever be built. Without a word, but in present awareness of an overriding plan, we must set one stone upon another. For the first time the German genius is cast back entirely on its own resources to build its own country, its own house, its own temple. This must be recognized as a historic moment, one toward which Germany has grown and matured over many eventful centuries. Let us all be worthy of it!

*A pejorative French term for Germans. —E.D.

FELIX HOLLÄNDER (JANUARY 10, 1919)
If people of insight would only get it clear in their minds that this revolution had to come, that it was no accident but the outcome of an evolutionary process based on natural laws, then their courage would never again fail them. The idea of having a part in the building of a new and free Germany is so exhilarating that even the mentally inert should involve themselves with all their might.

KÄTHE KOLLWITZ (JANUARY 14, 1919)
Beauty of living, free play of individual powers, harmonious development of personality must no longer be built on a foundation of ugliness, misery, and disease. This sense of liberation is what the bourgeois stands to gain from socialism. He cannot expect to gain anything else. But in return for this gain he must be prepared to give up his previous, privileged life.

HEINRICH MANN (JANUARY 10, 1919)
The spiritual renewal of Germany, our natural task, is made easier for us by the revolution. At last we are walking hand in hand with the state.

THOMAS MANN (JANUARY 11, 1919)
It would certainly be wrong to see the revolution purely in terms of collapse and disintegration. The defeat of Germany is a highly paradoxical matter: it is not a defeat like any other, any more than the war that it brought to an end was a war like any other. Unless I am very much mistaken, the nation that has suffered this unparalleled defeat is not a broken nation; indeed, as in 1914, it still feels itself to have the future on its side. There can be no doubt (even for one who does not by any means subscribe to Marxist dogma and philosophy) that the political future, nationally and internationally, belongs to the social idea. The Western bourgeoisies will not enjoy their triumph for long. Once the social idea is embedded in the consciences of nations, it will not rest until it has been made reality—so far as any idea can be made reality by human beings. But the state morality to which it has longest been familiar is that of Germany. The social nation-state, such as now seeks to erect itself in our country, is part and parcel of German national evolution. I am equally certain that, in Germany above all, the social or socialist state could never survive or perform without an infusion of the bourgeois spirit. This has nothing to do with the imperialistic bourgeois ethos; it is none other than the spirit of German civilization. The pure workers' republic, the dictatorship of the proletariat, would be barbarism.

JULIUS MEIER-GRAEFE (JANUARY 15, 1919)
We have the revolution to thank for ridding us of a set of ignoble and mindless monarchs. Our attitude toward the republic is not so much governed by programs—whose social spirit has our assent—as by personalities who bring greater mental and spiritual qualities to their leadership than did the members of the former regime. Such are the leaders we expect above all. I consider unpatriotic experimenters or party hacks to be as disastrous as kaisers and kings.

FRANZ OPPENHEIMER (JANUARY 12, 1919)
Socialism is a free and equal society, freed from the taint of unearned income and therefore classless and therefore united in brotherhood. It is the highest aim of all religious and ethical systems. It brings harmony within and peace without and makes a reality of "The Kingdom of God on Earth." It is the task of humanity to find the pathway to this goal. It has not been found yet, but it will and must be found! The German revolution has removed the fetters that impeded us from seeking the path of salvation. And that is why it is a great sign of hope—in spite of everything.

KARL ERNST OSTHAUS (JANUARY 10, 1919)
No fate is undeserved. Anyone who sees the revolution as a misfortune must inquire as to his own guilt. He who feels himself to be free of guilt, let him hail the dawn, with its promise that the living seed will flourish.

WILHELM OSTWALD (JANUARY 10, 1919)
Now Germany will reveal what she wants and what she can do.

GABRIELE REUTER (JANUARY 12, 1919)
For anyone who lives the life of the mind, it must be a joy to participate in the moral renewal of one's own nation through a genuine social and fraternal process of resolve, creation, and consummation. The revolution has made this beautiful and worthy life accessible to us. Let us give thanks and set to work with all our might.

ERNST TROELTSCH (JANUARY 14, 1919)
The revolution has forcibly taken in hand a process that had become an inevitable consequence of the long war, with its destruction of property and transfer of wealth, a process that was massively reinforced by the growing awareness of the impossibility of victory: the process of democratization and socialization, by which I mean the equal participation of all in the formation of the will of the state and the meticulous organization of an economy excluded from world trade, which otherwise would have been unable to feed its densely packed masses. After long and embittered obstruction, this reform was already in train, then the defeat and the ensuing military revolution left everything in ruins, and chaos ensued. But in this situation especially the temptation to despair must be manfully resisted. Only he who gives himself up for lost is lost. Great things have been destroyed; a state that upheld its glory through growing hardships has been shattered, as has a valiant army. But so great a nation, with such a capacity for psychological and mental attainment—so hardworking and so educated a nation—can never perish. It must perform the vast task of reorganizing itself, using its own resources, politically, economically, spiritually, and intellectually; it must meet the new situation by giving itself a new army that will shield the new edifice and protect it against dangers both from without and from within. If this

can be done, there can be a massive unfolding of strength and greatness in which everyone can and must play a part. This must fill us with the sense of a great responsibility and with the strength for a totally committed achievement. Life will be hard for the men of the German mind and for the men of German art, but theirs will be the great task of restoring the German mind to a leading position, both at home and abroad. If life draws its value not from comfort but from the greatness of the task in hand, then our future life is of the utmost value. Out of our sufferings must come purity and grandeur of mind; our faith in God and in man must convince us that pure minds shall not work in vain. In this certainty we can and must live and hope; without it there is nothing but a vegetable existence, waiting for death, and then the work of rebirth would be left to later generations, generations of greater faith.

FRITZ VON UNRUH (JANUARY 18, 1919)
—Pile awesome impossibilities mountain-high—we feel the good cheer, the love for the work!

HEINRICH WÖLFFLIN (JANUARY 16, 1919)
No form of state is good or bad in itself. The socialist form will be the best form when every individual is prepared to take upon himself the greatest measure of moral responsibility.

From *Yes! Voices of the Working Council for Art in Berlin*

The German revolution of November 1918 spawned various artists' and writers' associations modeled on the revolutionary soldiers' and sailors' soviets. Chief among these were the Novembergruppe (November group) and the Arbeitsrat für Kunst (Working council for art), which merged in 1919. This Arbeitsrat questionnaire seeking a common basis for an artistic contribution to a hoped-for socialist state elicited 114 responses from artists, architects, and critics, a small sampling of which is presented below.

Originally published as Ja! Stimmen des Arbeitsrates für Kunst in Berlin *(Berlin-Charlottenburg: Photographische Gesellschaft, 1919).*

Questions translated in Victor H. Miesel, ed., Voices of German Expressionism *(Englewood Cliffs, N.J.: Prentice Hall, 1970), pp. 172–75; reprinted by permission of the publisher.*

QUESTIONS WHICH NEED CLARIFICATION

I. Curriculum. What must be done to reform thoroughly the education of all those who work in the visual arts?

II. State Support. In what ways should the socialist state aid art and artists? (Purchases, art commissions, museums, schools, exhibits, etc.)

III. Public Housing. What guarantees should one demand from the state so that housing in the future is planned in accord with far-reaching cultural considerations?

IV. The Transfer of Creators from the Fine Arts to the Crafts. How can the broad mass of the art proletariat be persuaded to enter the crafts and avoid destruction by the economic catastrophe which seems imminent? What must the state do so that the education of the next generation is based upon a thorough mastery of craft?

V. The Artist in the Socialist State.

VI. Art Exhibits. How can one interest the *Volk* once more in a total work of art—the unification of architecture, sculpture, and painting? State-supported testing places to take the place of salon art exhibitions.

VII. How can creators from the various arts unify the arts?

VIII. Color and the Image of the City. Ideas for the use of color in the city, bright colors for houses, painted facades and interiors, and the elimination of easel paintings.

IX. The Designing of Public Buildings by Artists. What practical demands must be made upon the government so that public buildings are designed by artists rather than, as is the case now, by engineers and building officials?

X. Harmony with the *Volk*. How can the efforts of modern artists reach the *Volk* and harmonize with it?

XI. What steps must be taken so that at the right moment the above material, which has been privately compiled, can be effectively publicized? Newspaper articles, lectures, exhibitions, sufficient press coverage.

XII. How shall the closest contact possible be established with foreign art associations which have similar ideals?

XIII. Point of view on the issue of artistic anonymity.

174
Lyonel Feininger
Rathaus, Zottelstedt, 1918
(Town hall, Zottelstedt)
Cat. no. 22

Responses translated by Christiane C. Collins and George R. Collins, in Ulrich Conrads and Hans G. Sperlich, The Architecture of Fantasy: Utopian Building and Planning in Modern Times *(New York: Praeger, 1962), pp. 138–41; reprinted by permission of the publisher.*

CÉSAR KLEIN (P. 49)

Ideal building project: We are arriving by ship. The town lies by the ocean. Two enormous double archways receive us. The harbor—gigantic silos, houses on the wharf. Behind this the quay-street with the offices, banks, and business buildings. In the center, the town hall. Carved into the rock: two huge staircases leading to the residential section above; elevator and elevator shafts. The whole is treated as though it were a sculptural creation. It is covered with terraces, hanging gardens. On top, the development of the City of Color. The green street, the red, blue, yellow street, the black house of the Artists' Lodge, run up to the center, crowned by a cathedral to the great unknown God. A steep gold-glass pyramid with a thousand crystal-like points. A magnet for the mariners: come inside! One's heart becomes solemnly still. The walls are of silver filigree, filled with shapes of colored glass. Rainbow rays from all sides. Dematerialization of man. Blue women, red men, green older people. Transparent luminous glass floor. Sonorous column of life, birth, and death. Furthermore: the theatre and art center in the park. Movable stage. Side-stages which can be lowered for shadow plays. Surrounding the town a marvelous flower garden with grottoes, fountains, and pavilions.

HERMANN OBRIST (PP. 63–64)

And now my last word: Long live Utopia! What I like is that in each of these writings the word "Utopia" occurs twice, from which we gather that it is employed intentionally. It is, in fact, the only thing that survives. Let us then live in Utopia, let us fabricate plans, castles in Spain; let us pretend and let us prepare for the time that will come thirty years hence, when Germany will triumphantly lead in the arts. This is precisely what I am doing. Never before have I lived so much in the realm of imagination as now. As my specialty of architectural sculpture has forever ended for me and for my lifetime, I have completely given up this calling—that is, sculpture—and I design, in solitude, fantasies (painted and drawn) which, I think, go well beyond the so-called Expressionist. They are only sketches, dreams, mere shadows, which I do not intend to show for another year or two. Then, however, I hope to be able to offer a surprise. In short, I work like the German poets and musicians of a hundred years ago, out of a longing, without any hope for realization. But this is a quiet, divine labor, removed from any quasi-organization, *Künstlerrat*, etc.

KARL SCHMIDT-ROTTLUFF (P. 91)

Ideal building project: Town on a mountain. The town is supposed to accommodate about 8,000 to 10,000 inhabitants. Town viewed from afar has large unified silhouette. On the top of the mountain stands a vast construction composed of powerful cubic masses whose white paint gleams far out into the countryside. United in this structure are all the major public buildings of the town. Schools, concert-, and festival-halls, theaters, a hall for worship by the new Christian community. Its large courtyard, which again is a unit in itself, is also used as a public meeting place; it is vividly colored and decorated with large mosaics. On the slopes of the hill are groups of single homes with gardens, and also compact row houses. The streets, rising sharply, are emphasized by thick walls, darting up to the top like white ribbons. In all other edifices the color white is avoided. Blue and red (rough walls), and here and there yellow, serve as colors for individual homes and row houses. Conifers provide sharp accents.

To carry out this plan the government would have to make available a wooded mountain, which would then be cleared wherever building is feasible. Building lots should be offered free of cost, under the condition that the person for whom the house is to be built will have it designed by a designated architect. Individual houses and rows of buildings are worked out independently by various architects—they are required only to harmonize with the total effect of the town.

GEORG TAPPERT (P. 97)

To begin with, in Gross-Berlin, all stucco ornaments should be removed from the buildings of the "fashionable" streets. All buildings to be painted the same on each thoroughfare: the red, the blue, the green street.

ADOLF BEHNE (P. 16)

Utopian building project: The most important thing seems to me to construct an ideal *House of God*, not a denominational one, but a *religious* work. We cannot go ahead without a reawakening of piety. We must not wait until a new religiosity is upon us, for it may be waiting for us while we are waiting for it. Architectural form shapes Man. If now the Church at last is going to separate—willingly or unwillingly—from the State, we have to prepare betimes so that the religious community which no longer belongs to governmental bureaucracy can find its own architects. We should seek a *de facto* commission for our association, which would provide work for everyone, and around which a school could develop. Building will not proceed in haste, but slowly and patiently, and laymen must not be left out. They should cooperate in the selection of the design, ground plan, etc.

WALTER GROPIUS

"New Ideas on Architecture"

In April 1919 Gropius and Bruno Taut organized the Ausstellung für unbekannte Architekten *(Exhibition of unknown architects) at I. B. Neumann's Graphisches Kabinett in Berlin. In lieu of a catalogue they published a manifesto-like pamphlet with statements by Gropius, Taut, and art critic Adolf Behne celebrating a unification of the arts around architecture. The following statement by Gropius corresponds closely to the founding manifesto for the Bauhaus, whose directorship he had just assumed.*

Originally published in the exhibition catalogue Ausstellung für unhbkannte Architekten *(1919); translated by Michael Bullock, in Ulrich Conrads, ed.,* Programs and Manifestoes on Twentieth-Century Architecture *(Cambridge: MIT Press, 1971), pp. 46–48; reprinted by permission of the publisher.*

What is architecture? The crystalline expression of man's noblest thoughts, his ardour, his humanity, his faith, his religion! That is what it once was! But who of those living in our age that is cursed with practicality still comprehends its all-embracing, soul-giving nature? We walk through our streets and cities and do not howl with shame at such deserts of ugliness! Let us be quite clear: these grey, hollow; spiritless mock-ups, in which we live and work, will be shameful evidence for posterity of the spiritual descent into hell of our generation, which forgot that great, *unique* art: *architecture*. Let us not deceive ourselves, in our European arrogance, that the wretched buildings of our era could alter the overall picture. All our works are nothing but splinters. Structures created by practical requirements and necessity do not satisfy the longing for a world of beauty built anew from the bottom up, for the rebirth of that spiritual unity which ascended to the miracle of the Gothic cathedrals. We shall not live to see it. But there is one consolation for us: the *idea*, the building up of an ardent, bold, forward-looking architectural idea to be fulfilled by a happier age that must come. Artists, let us at last break down the walls erected by our deforming academic training between the 'arts' *and all of us become builders again!* Let us together will, think out, create the new idea of architecture. Painters and sculptors, break through the barriers to architecture and become fellow builders, fellow strugglers for the final goal of art: the creative conception of the cathedral of the future, which will once again be all in one shape, architecture and sculpture and painting.

But ideas die as soon as they become compromises. Hence there must be clear watersheds between dream and reality, between longing for the stars and everyday labour. Architects, sculptors, painters, we must all return to the crafts! For there is no 'professional art.' Artists are craftsmen in the original sense of the word, and only in rare, blessed moments of revelation that lie outside the power of their will can art blossom unconsciously from the work of their hands. Painters and sculptors, become craftsmen again, smash the frame of salon art that is round your pictures, go into the buildings, bless them with fairy tales of colour, chisel ideas into the bare walls—and *build in imagination*, unconcerned about technical difficulties. The boon of imagination is always more important than all technique, which always adapts itself to man's creative will. There are no architects today, we are all of us merely preparing the way for him who will once again deserve the name of architect, for that means: *lord of art*, who will build gardens out of deserts and pile up wonders to the sky.

HANS HANSEN

"The Building Yard"

Hansen's (1889–1966) passion for architecture, expressed in his book Das Erlebnis der Architektur (The experience of *architecture, 1920), won him the praise of Bruno Taut. Hansen would later become one of the leading church architects in Germany. This essay appeared in the book* Ruf zum Bauen *(Call to building), published on the occasion of the exhibition* Neues Bauen *(New building) in May 1920, which also included texts by Adolf Behne, Hans Scharoun (see "Thoughts on Theatrical Space" below),* and Bruno Taut (*see* The Universal Master Builder *below*).

Originally published as "Der Bauhof," in Ruf zum Bauen *(Berlin: E. Wasmuth, 1920); translated by David Britt.*

A free-lance architect is an architect who is free to enter the service of a client, in order to have a chance of exercising his freedom as an architect.* There is thus no such thing as a free-lance architect, and yet thousands describe themselves as such. They unthinkingly

The German word freie *means both "free" and "free-lance."* —E.D.

describe themselves as free, when they are merely the servants of many paymasters; for all their freedom, they are not even the masters of all those who execute their ideas and their plans. And wherever they succeed, at great cost to themselves in time and energy, in making themselves the masters, their mastery turns into the emptiest tyranny over their clients. Every architect knows his own freedom and knows that it is an elaborately disguised servitude and tyranny.

I do not think that a man in bodily servitude can be free in spirit. Nor do I think that there can be any freedom in his work, just so long as those who execute it remain in servitude. So it is nonsense to speak of the freedom of the architect today.

In common with every living thing, architecture is not a self-sufficient object, i.e., one that finds its own perfection within itself. It forms a necessary part of the world as a whole and of the entirety of a civilization; it is the physical expression of an essence that is simultaneously expressed through culture, politics, and religion. In the phenomenal world body is the vehicle of mind. Matter is dead in itself. Mind gives it life. Matter endures, even after the creative mind has changed. Architecture is the connecting link between mind and body. It creates bodies: it takes something that first appeared, imageless, in the mind and frames it into an image. *It is the servant of mind.* And in this respect it is conceivable that architecture is free and sovereign on earth as the servant of mind, but not as expressed through the arbitrary will and illusory freedom of the individual.

The Building Yard is an attempt to make what has just been described into a reality by representing it through a *formula*. It cannot provide anything definitive but can only present in graphic terms what is here attempted in words.

The Building Yard presupposes that in the course of evolution a time will come when justification springs not from profitability but from the natural logic of the demands of human reason.

This new epoch will have no knowledge of any such thing as a free-lance architect in private practice. It will value architecture too highly to abandon it to the caprice of an individual and the tyranny of an owner. It will therefore make architecture sovereign. From this the freedom of the individual will grow as part of the crown of a many-branched tree. Now to the matter in hand.

The Building Yard is a single body that is a workshop, an architectural academy, a craft center, and a building administration for an urban or rural district, all rolled into one. The administration would be no more than a petty mechanism, were it not simultaneously the practical center of craftsmanship. A logical part and consequence of this is the academy of architecture and art, which would likewise be unthinkable in isolation from a center of work. Externally the workshop city takes the form of a cluster of workshops and studios grouped around courtyards; in turn the whole is grouped around a center that consists of the academy, as the crown of the whole, and adjacent schools and yards for the individual disciplines of construction and of art.

The inner structure of the Building Yard corresponds to this outer form. From the craftsmen's workshops come the students, who maintain the closest links with their shops during their time in the academy. At the same time the workshops produce the leaders and teachers, and at the head of the whole organization is the supreme council of masters, who are simultaneously the teachers in the art and architecture schools. The ablest master will emerge from the graded master groups, and so the whole organism will always be totally rooted in practical craft work and will never degenerate into artistic or historicist theory.

As the architectural focus of an urban or rural district, the Building Yard is as centrally placed as possible and enjoys good communications by rail and water. In direct contact with the railroad there are iron and wood assembly shops, boiler houses, and storehouses, all with plenty of space for expansion. The Building Yard as a whole is an organism with a head and a stomach and a heart. The head is the academy, the thousand arms and sinews are the workshops that extend from the yard in a circle, the stomach is the water-front, and the heart is the great courtyard that is used for experimental structures and exhibitions. In this new kind of working organism, the street serves only as a production line (a work city is not a city for traffic), and its external form is simply the architectural synthesis of the whole work city idea. It girdles the inner body and runs partly between the assembly buildings and partly over the roofs of the storage buildings between the work courts, before rising on an ascending bend to the center, the platform on which the academy stands.

This, as the showpiece of the work city, stands on a hill, either natural or created by the terracing of the work courts; its construction is impossible to foresee. Any prediction can be no more than formulaic, for the form will emerge from a new, rational, vitalized craft spirit and will come into being only when the thing itself does so. With the growth of architectural thought and consciousness, this building too will grow, and from year to year and from generation to generation human beings will build in commemoration of their own work and understanding and will cease to build only when for the tower-builders no problem remains, nothing higher to aspire to—or when a generation is brought low by the building of its own tower.

BRUNO TAUT

"A Program for Architecture"

Chief instigator and polemicist of the architects within the Arbeitsrat für Kunst, Taut launched its architectural program in this 1918 manifesto. His blending of all of the arts, as well as social reform, under the aegis of architecture harks back to his ground-breaking essay "Eine Notwendigkeit" (A necessity; see below), in which the cosmic and earthly realms find a creative unity in the model of the Gothic cathedral and in which the architect is advised to turn to painters for new structural forms.

Taut's view of a humanity transformed by architecture is much indebted to the writings of poet and novelist Paul Scheerbart (1863–1915), who presented the glass building as a primary metaphor for spiritual transcendence in his Glasarchitektur *(Glass architecture), which is in turn dedicated to Taut. The architect's homage to Scheerbart was the renowned Glashaus (Glass house) at the 1914 Werkbund exhibition in Cologne (see figs. 120, 121), which included on its exterior aphorisms on the virtues of glass composed by Scheerbart.*

Taut's "Die Erde eine gute Wohnung" (The earth, a good dwelling place; see below) anticipates his Die Auflösung der Städte *(The dissolution of the cities, 1920) in its plea for decentralization of habitation patterns. While he admits some contradiction to his contemporaneous* Die Stadtkrone *(The city-crown, 1919), his argument is imbued with the same faith that architectural planning will influence social and economic structures. Taut's "Haus des Himmels" (House of heaven; see below), published in his periodical* Frühlicht *(Day-*

break), conveys his image of architectural perfection as "a vessel for the divine." His numerological obsession, reminiscent of Early Christian architecture, is combined with a belief in the compatibility of technological advances indebted to Scheerbart.

Originally published by the Arbeitsrat für Kunst as "Architektur-Programm" *(1918); translated by Michael Bullock, in Ulrich Conrads, ed.,* Programs and Manifestoes on Twentieth-Century Architecture *(Cambridge: MIT Press, 1971), pp. 41–43; reprinted by permission of the publisher.*

UNDER THE WING OF A GREAT ARCHITECTURE

In the conviction that the political revolution must be used to liberate art from decades of regimentation, a group of artists and art-lovers united by a common outlook has been formed in Berlin. It strives for the gathering together of all scattered and divided energies which, over and above the protection of one-sided professional interests, wish to work resolutely together for the rebuilding of our whole artistic life. In close contact with associations with similar objectives in other parts of Germany, the Arbeitsrat für Kunst hopes in the not too distant future to be able to push through its aims, which are outlined in the following programme.

In the forefront stands the guiding principle:

Art and people must form a unity.

Art shall no longer be the enjoyment of the few but the life and happiness of the masses.

The aim is alliance of the arts under the wing of a great architecture.

On this basis six preliminary demands are made:

1. Recognition of the public character of all building activity, both State and private. Removal of all privileges accorded to Civil Servants. Unitary supervision of whole urban districts, streets, and residential estates, without curtailment of freedom over detail. New tasks: people's housing as a means of bringing all the arts to the people. Permanent experimental sites for testing and perfecting new architectural effects.

2. Dissolution of the Academy of Arts, the Academy of Building and the Prussian Provincial Art Commission in their existing form. Replacement of these bodies, accompanied by a redefining of their territories, by others drawn from the ranks of productive artists themselves and free from State interference. The changing of privileged art exhibitions into exhibitions to which entry is free.

3. Freeing of all training in architecture, sculpture, painting, and handicrafts from State supervision. Transformation of all instruction in the arts and handicrafts from top to bottom. State funds to be made available for this purpose and for the training of master craftsmen in training workshops.

4. Enlivenment of the museums as educational establishments for the people. Mounting of constantly changing exhibitions made to serve the interests of the people by means of lectures and conducted tours. Separation of scientific material in specially constructed buildings. Establishment of specially arranged collections for study by workers in the arts and crafts. Just distribution of State funds for the acquisition of old and new works.

5. Destruction of artistically valueless monuments as well as of all buildings whose artistic value is out of proportion to the value of their material which could be put to other uses. Prevention of prematurely planned war memorials and immediate cessation of work on the

war museums proposed for Berlin and the Reich.

6. Establishment of a national centre to ensure the fostering of the arts within the framework of future lawmaking.

PAUL SCHEERBART

From *Glass Architecture*

Originally published as Glasarchitektur *(Berlin: Verlag "Der Sturm," 1914); translated by James Palmer as* Glass Architecture, *ed. Dennis Sharp (New York: Praeger, 1972), pp. 41, 45, 47, 67; reprinted by permission of the publisher.*

1. ENVIRONMENT AND ITS INFLUENCE ON THE DEVELOPMENT OF CULTURE

We live for the most part in closed rooms. These form the environment from which our culture grows. Our culture is to a certain extent the product of our architecture. If we want our culture to rise to a higher level, we are obliged, for better or for worse, to change our architecture. And this only becomes possible if we take away the closed character from the rooms in which we live. We can only do that by introducing glass architecture, which lets in the light of the sun, the moon, and the stars, not merely through a few windows, but through every possible wall, which will be made entirely of glass—of coloured glass. The new environment, which we thus create, must bring us a new culture....

13. THE FUNCTIONAL STYLE

The reader might gain the impression that glass architecture is rather cold, but in warm weather, coolness is not unpleasant. Anyhow, let me make it clear that colours in glass can produce a most glowing effect, shedding perhaps a new warmth. What has been said up to now takes on a somewhat warmer atmosphere. I should like to resist most vehemently the undecorated "functional style,"* for it is inartistic. It has often been adopted before in other contexts, and this is happening once again.

The German word here is "Sachstil" (author's quotes). —E.D.

For a transition period, the functional style seems to me acceptable; at all events it has done away with imitations of older styles, which are simply products of brick architecture and wooden furniture. Ornamentation in the glass house will evolve entirely of its own accord—the oriental decoration, the carpets and the majolica will be so transformed that in glass architecture we shall never, I trust, have to speak of copying. At least, let's hope so!...

18. THE BEAUTY OF THE EARTH, WHEN GLASS ARCHITECTURE IS EVERYWHERE

The face of the earth would be much altered if brick architecture were ousted everywhere by glass architecture. It would be as if the earth were adorned with sparkling jewels and enamels. Such glory is unimaginable. All over the world it would be as splendid as in the gardens of the Arabian Nights. We should then have a paradise on earth, and no need to watch in longing expectation for the paradise in heaven....

83. AIRPORTS AS GLASS PALACES

For the building of airports, also, glass-iron construction has much to recommend it; airports must be visible and identifiable from far off and this is best achieved by coloured ornamental glass. This will reach its full effect at night, when the entire building is crowned by a diadem of projected lights, delighting not only the aeronauts, but also people who have no airship at their bidding.

BRUNO TAUT

From "The Earth, a Good Dwelling Place"

Originally published as "Die Erde eine gute Wohnung," in Die Volkswohnung *1, no. 4 (1919): 45ff.: translated by David Britt.*

Ideas are signposts, and the image of a remote future must light the way for us who strive .It cannot be too often shown to people, to make them tire of the present and ever more impatiently demand its fulfillment. As an architect, am I not working against my own art when I demand the dispersal of the cities? The most magnificent buildings have always grown out of cities, and in my own City-Crown project I have tried to devise a suitable culmination for the city of the future. The most magnificent buildings of all, the gigantic temple precincts of Asia—Angkor Wat, Borobudur, and the rest—stand in isolation, and as for my own City-Crown, there too I wanted to show the splendid isolation of my building in the midst of a widely scattered settlement and, above all, to awaken appreciation of the building that distinguishes itself from its surroundings.

Let us resolutely contemplate the new look of the earth: great estates like those of today but collectively owned and worked in such a way that more people than today cultivate them and live off them. Smallholdings and gardens, interspersed with woods, pastures, and lakes, occupy all the present wastelands. Scattered among these are extensive settlements of small houses, all with outbuildings and gardens of their own. Industry will automatically follow the same pattern, becoming scattered among numerous workshops, the more readily to respond to need. The process is hastened by new forms of transport: the main railroad lines wither away, and in their place is a dense network of lighter transport routes operated by mechanically propelled vehicles; raw materials are brought in almost exclusively by water. The markets become almost superfluous, as the population sustains itself almost entirely by its own efforts and lives by the natural bartering of home produce. The power of money dwindles, vanishes...vacation travel ceases...and people meet en masse only where they ought to meet, in the place of worship.... The rarity of travel will make it more highly valued, and for the rest, people will adopt Scheerbart's motto, "Do your traveling at home!"

But alas! What of the architectural character of the cities? Let us waste no tears on that. An entirely new one rises in its place. In the settlements "urban planning" disappears entirely, and the individual house takes on an entirely new significance. Likewise the isolated great building...It is the religious buildings, made of glass, that illuminate the night. Everything is opened up; at last people understand the necessity to isolate the architectural work of art, which blossoms here and there like some rare and precious flower. The stars in the sky and the stars on earth greet each other....

A new bond unites all men. Where will anyone draw a frontier, when the whole earth looks like this? Frontiers become impossible, and an entirely new form of human community must come into being. States disappear, and with them their armed might; they give way to a new form of human organization, one that may act to forestall trouble but no longer organizes or gives orders. The only institutions are voluntary ones, both in their nature and in their workings. For the city is the sign of the power of the state, and this and all it entails—politics, wars—will never disappear until the city disappears...For we want love and not hate. "Her foot is in the air, descending. When will she set it down?" At the start of the third millennium, will it be possible for the new Messiah to come?

BRUNO TAUT

"A Necessity"

Originally published as "Eine Notwendigkeit," in Der Sturm *4, no. 196–97 (1914): 174–75; translated by David Britt.*

It is a joy to be alive in our time, and anyone who cannot sense this is beyond help. Artists in all the arts have been overtaken by an intensity, a sacredness of feeling that is not content with nebulous impulses but strives for forms governed by law. Sculpture and painting are committed to purely synthetic and abstract paths; on every side there is talk of the construction of images. This is based on an architectural conception of the image, a conception that is no mere analogy but is based on architectural thinking in the plainest sense of the word. A secret architecture runs through all these works and holds them together, very much as it did in the age of the Gothic. The Gothic cathedral too is the sum of all of its artists; filled with a wondrous sense of union, they achieved an all-encompassing rhythm that rang through the architecture of the building.

And architecture is ready to respond. In the work of its best representatives, architecture too is filled with a new and profound intensity. In those great works that transcend mere economic considerations, architecture too seeks expression, dynamism, and a ringing rhythm. Even in the simplest buildings, strictly defined by economic constraints, the same tendency expresses itself with equal intensity through the quest for utter plainness that exalts the most primitive form into a symbol. Here too there is a kinship of meaning with the Gothic, which at its greatest combines a passion for structure with a quest for the simplest and most expressive combination of practicality and economy. This tendency has a structural intensity that far transcends the complacent classical ideal of harmony. Glass, iron, and concrete are the materials that equip the new architect for this greater intensity and lead him beyond merely material and functional architecture.

It is an inescapable necessity of the new art that architecture, painting and sculpture must join together in this way. Only by acknowledging this inevitable conjunction can modern architects design creatively and, in a higher sense, traditionally. There is more to this than making architectural forms assume the outward guise of painting. By its very essence, architecture is a Cubist thing. It would be perverse to make exclusive use of angular forms; the paintings of a Léger unite the angular and the soft within themselves. The architect must be on his guard against a purely superficial assimilation. He must absorb all possible architectural forms within his own creative scope, just as all possible pictorial forms are present in the inventive compositions of Kandinsky. And this is because, if its works are to endure, architecture must be broadly based: it must take account of all possible factors (artistic, structural, social, financial). The functions of the frame differ from those of the picture surface. And so the architect must recognize that architecture has within it the very quality that the new painting has had to create for itself: freedom from the confines of a single viewpoint. The buildings of the great ages of architecture were designed without benefit of perspective; it is perspective that has given us all those familiar buildings that look like stage sets.

This connection is worth understanding, and for us architects it is particularly fruitful. But something tangible must also take place: at some time the edifice of ideal architecture that the new art already represents must manifest itself in a visible building. And it is a necessity that this happen.

Let us work together on a magnificent building! One that is not architecture alone but in which everything—painting, sculpture, all together—forms a greater architecture, and in which architecture is once more subsumed into the other arts. Architecture must be both frame and content; it must be everything at once. The building need have no purely practical object. Architecture too can set itself free from utilitarian demands. It would be enough if a modern collection were to afford the occasion to create one space for the safekeeping of works of art and one adjoining hall suitable for all possible artistic purposes. The result will be a simple architectural organism, built close to the metropolis on an open site, so that its external manifestation too will be that of an artistic organism. The building must contain rooms that incorporate the characteristic manifestations of the new art: the luminous compositions of Delaunay in great stained-glass windows; on the walls Cubist rhythms, the painting of a Franz Marc, and the art of Kandinsky. The piers without and within must await the constructive sculptures of Archipenko; the ornament will be provided by Campendonk. This does not exhaust the roster of contributors. All original artists must play a part—as is entirely possible in any true architectural organism—so that the whole will ring with a single, magnificent harmony. This would be the necessary step that would free the arts from the confines of the salon, to which current aesthetics and practice have relegated them. It would put an end to all the chatter about "arts and crafts" elements in the new art.

The building need not be finished all at once. No harm is done if individual details are not completed for a generation or more.

Any idea of social purpose must be avoided. The whole must assert its exclusivity; for all great art initially exists solely within the artist. The people may then use it to educate themselves or else wait until their educators come.

BRUNO TAUT

"House of Heaven"

Originally published as "Haus des Himmels," in Frühlicht *(April 1920); reprinted in Bruno Taut, ed.,* Frühlicht, 1920–1922: Eine Folge für die Verwirklichung des neuen Baugedankens *(Berlin: Ullstein, 1963), pp. 33–35; translated by David Britt.*

THE ARCHITECT

A house that is intended for nothing but to be beautiful. It is there for no other purpose; it must stand empty in accordance with the saying of Meister Eckhart: "I never want to ask God to give himself to me. I want to ask him to make me empty and pure; for if I were empty and pure, God by his very nature would give himself to me and be enclosed within me."

The joy of architecture will fill the visitor, emptying his soul of all that is human and

HUMANITY IS THE HIGHER MEANING OF OUR PLANET, THE NERVE THAT CONNECTS THIS LIMB WITH THE WORLD ABOVE, THE EYE THAT IT RAISES TO HEAVEN.

NOVALIS

making it a vessel for the divine. This building is an image and a salutation of the stars. Its plan is star shaped, and in it the sacred numbers seven and three are united: seven in the great hall, three in the secondary rooms, arrayed like chapels, which accommodate human activities: teaching, lectures, all that relates to the life of human beings. The three large chapels are divided internally at ceiling level; within them side steps lead down to adjoining plazas. From the main entrance a wide flight of steps, flanked by the Pillars of Suffering and Prayer, leads down onto the terrace on which the house stands.

When the assembly mounts these steps in procession, the whole house rings like a bell. There are galleries in six of the triangles formed by the points of the seven-pointed star, and in their corners stand the separate registers of the great organ; there are openings to allow the sounds to be heard outside. When there is a concert within, the orchestra and the oratorio *[sic]* are similarly distributed; they can be overseen and conducted from the first pier. Seven stairways lead up to the galleries and connect them with one another.

The seventh triangle of the star has nothing built into it and no gallery, so that the upward view is unobstructed. In front of it are two sculptured, freestanding pillars, fifteen meters high, which rise to enmesh the crystals that hang from the ceiling. Between these, on those occasions when speech is called for in this place, an orator might stand, facing a stepped array of stone seating for his hearers. A curtain might be suspended between the pillars below, and cosmic dramas and mime shows (Stramm, Scheerbart) might be performed in the space behind, which extends to the full depth of the seventh niche of the star. All the walls, ceilings, and floors are of glass. The load-bearing framework is of reinforced concrete, and a space one meter deep between the inner and outer skins of glass serves to equalize the heat. Flying buttresses vary the abruptly terminating surfaces of the stellar vault.

Between the inner and outer skins of glass is the lighting. This can be switched from shining inward to shining outward, for happenings within and for effect without, and shines both inward and outward through many walls of colored glass. If one arrives at the house in an airplane by night, it shines from afar like a star. And it rings like a bell.

FIRST PAINTER: SCULPTURAL GLASS CEILING

The roof is built up of prisms of electrolytically bonded glass, the inner walls of cast prisms. Given a highly stable construction, the prisms in the roof too might be cast. In low relief, angular, and clear-cut, the roof and walls are to repeat the crystalline form of the exterior and will provide a rich and glittering setting for the deep glow of the stained-glass windows. These are not really windows in any real sense, for the roof and walls themselves will be not only colorful but also filled with light. The windows must therefore look more like brightly colored tapestries, somewhat darker and far more colorful still than the walls and ceilings.

SECOND PAINTER: PART OF A STAINED-GLASS WINDOW

All the forms rise, aspire, grow upward, drawn aloft by the star of the roof. Steep and hard, soft and tender, in manifold shifts of form. Seemingly endless in incessant motion. The colors are deep and luminous, mysteriously glowing: every point of the star is attuned to a single color of the rainbow. The angular wind bracing follows the powerful contours.* The verticals of the pillars bind the whole together and lend repose. Sunlight makes the colors shower sparks, a gray day speaks earnestly and weightily through them, and the stars chime their light like little silver bells through the colored glass.

* *"Die Windeisen zacken wuchtige Führung." I am grateful to Iain Boyd Whyte for his assistance with this translation.*

— E.D.

THE SCULPTOR

The Pillars of Suffering and Prayer begin at ground level in gloomy black (shading into intense blue) and terminate above in a blaze of gold. With the exception of the gold, all the colors are shot through with flecks and stripes of blood red.

Gläserne Kette Correspondence

Disillusioned with the Arbeitsrat für Kunst, Bruno Taut formed the Gläserne Kette (Crystal chain) in November 1919 as a closed brotherhood of architects and artists, most of whom were drawn from the ranks of the Arbeitsrat. Desiring secrecy, they employed such pseudonyms as Glas *("glass," Taut),* Prometh *("Prometheus," Hermann Finsterlin), and* Anfang *("beginning," Carl Krayl). Taut's initial letter conveys both his dismay over the widespread lack of commissions and his enthusiasm for an exchange of letters and drawings. In Taut's letter of December 23 and Hans Scharoun's undated letter, drawing plays an especially significant role. Wenzel Hablik's letter suggests the scope of the discourse, which ranged from philosophical speculation on the relationship between architecture and nature to communal projects for buildings, cities, schools, films, and a Bible-like "Book."*

While the exchange continued for a full year, Taut's letter of October 5, 1920, evidences a desire for a new realism and directness as an alternative to the fantasy images of the past.

From Iain Boyd Whyte, ed. and trans., The Crystal Chain Letters: Architectural Fantasies by Bruno Taut and His Circle *(Cambridge: MIT Press, 1985); reprinted by permission of the publisher.*

BRUNO TAUT (GLAS), 24 NOVEMBER 1919

From Whyte, Letters, *p. 19.*

Dear Friends,

I want to make this proposal to you: Today there is almost nothing to build, and if we can build anywhere, then we do it in order to live. Or are you lucky enough to be working on a nice commission? My daily routine almost makes me ill, and it is basically the same for all of you. As a matter of fact, it is a good thing that nothing is being built today. Things will have time to ripen, we shall gather our strength, and when building begins again we shall know our objectives and be strong enough to protect our movement against botching and degeneration.

Let us consciously be "imaginary architects"! We believe that only a total revolution can guide us in our task. Our fellow citizens, even our colleagues quite rightly suspect in us the forces of revolution. Break up and undermine all former principles! Dung! And we are the bud in fresh humus.

The individual personality will disappear with commitment to a higher task—if architecture reappears then the master builder will be anonymous.

I can see the beginning of this in our tendency to join and fuse together as a first cell, without asking—who did it? Instead, the idea exists in the realm of endless joy, remote and autonomous. The purpose of my proposal is to strengthen this existing unity. It is as follows:

Quite informally and according to inclination, each of us will draw or write down at regular intervals those of his ideas that he wants to share with our circle, and will then send a copy to each member. In this way an exchange of ideas, questions, answers, and criticism will be established. Above each contribution will be a pseudonym. The mutual sympathy within the circle and the use of terse language will make it difficult for outsiders to understand us. Nevertheless, we must agree not to reveal anything to uncomprehending eyes. Any request to expand the circle or to expel a member of the group should emerge from the contributions themselves. A single vote will suffice for an expulsion, unless all the other members veto it in their next letters.

Let it be a magnet, the snowy core of an avalanche! If nothing comes of the idea, if I am deluding myself, then at least it will be a beautiful memory for each of us.

By the way: Whoever leaves the group before the whole thing comes to an end is obliged to return all the contributions he has accumulated either to me or another member, or to destroy them.

If you agree, could you sign and return this to me as soon as possible, together with the desired pseudonym. I will let you have the result immediately and—the thing will be under way.

With color and glass greetings,
Glas

From Whyte, Letters, *pp. 23–24.*

BRUNO TAUT (GLAS), 23 DECEMBER 1919

STARS—WORLDS—DEATH—THE GREAT NOTHINGNESS—THE NAMELESS

"You may rob me of the earth,
but not the heavens."
— KARL LIEBKNECHT,
DECEMBER 1916

"Storm, my companion,
you call me!
Still I can do nothing,
still I am in chains!
Yes, I am also the storm,
part of you;
and the day will come again
when I shall break the chains.
I shall rage anew,
rage through the worlds,
storm around the earth.
Storm through the lands,
storm mankind,
his brain and heart,
storm-wind, I am like you."
— KARL LIEBKNECHT,
SPRING 1917

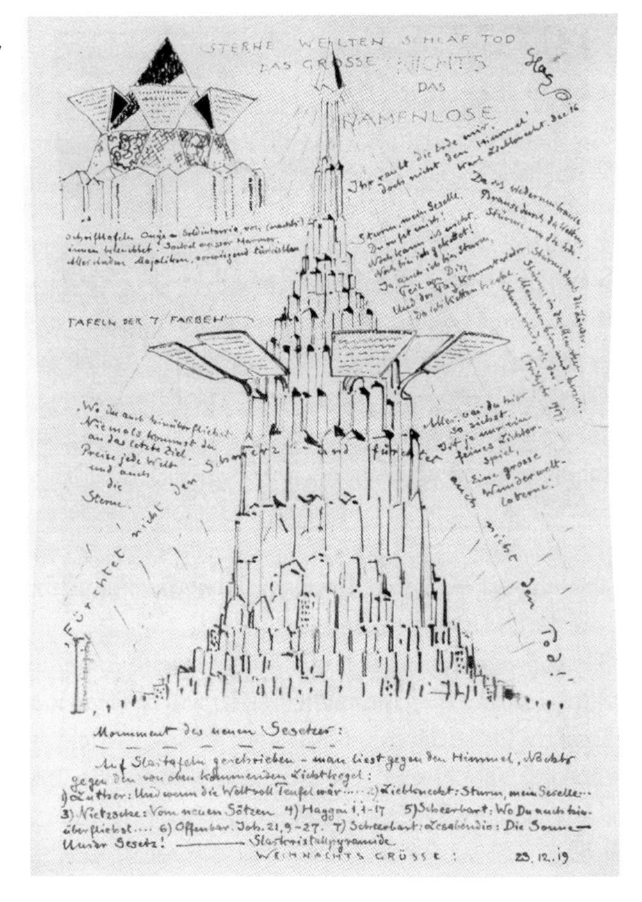

175
Bruno Taut
Weinachts Grüsse: "Monument des neuen Gesetzes," 1919
(Christmas greeting: "Monument to the new law")
Cat. no. 209

"Wherever you may roam
you will never reach the ultimate goal.
Extol every world and the stars too.
Everything you see here
is nothing but an elegant play of light,
an eternal magic lantern."

—PAUL SCHEERBART

Fear neither pain—nor death!

Glas,
Christmas Greetings

HANS SCHAROUN (HANNES), NO DATE

From Whyte, Letters, *p. 61.*

We must of course over and over again let hot-blooded thrusting out of the primeval slime stream out through concentrated form into eternity.

A thousand possibilities flow out of our fantasy. The one that remains will come into being overnight. Our ardent will should rage feverishly toward this night of unification with the primeval urge of the "Volk." Then once again will building have its function in the sensuality of mankind and its crown in the purity of the beyond. And once again we shall be rooted in reality.

Hannes

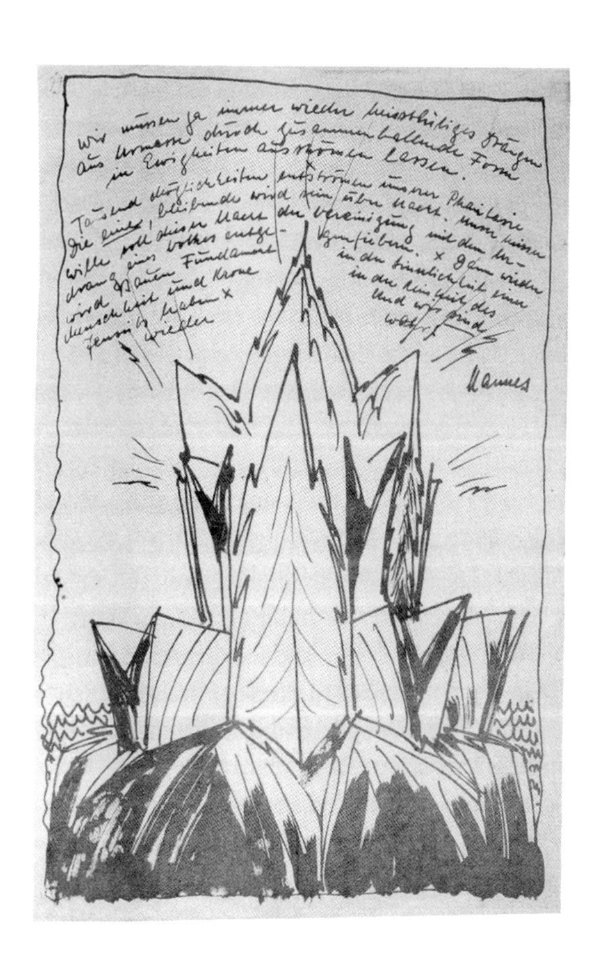

176
Hans Scharoun
Untitled (design for a glass house)
Cat. no. 186

From Whyte, Letters, *pp. 152–54.*

WENZIL HABLIK (W.H.), "DIE NEUE STADT" (THE NEW CITY), PENCIL DRAFT, NO DATE

Through The Book and the captivating lectures of the cultural leaders (our new poets!) millions of people have been inspired to work 6 hours each day for the *Idea*. Six hours of conscientious work done voluntarily in the knowledge that only joyful work can produce great results. Many rich people have donated the greater part of their wealth. A place has been found where the city is to be developed. Everything has been taken into account—water, woodland, green space. The roads and railway tracks for the building materials meet at the appointed place, bringing steel and stone, tools, and food from all over the land, a land inflamed with one idea. A great nation that has roused itself from the dead in order to build for its children and for their children the free city—the symbol of the new life, the new spirit, of new and divine perceptions. Here, in future, the "Yes" of human existence will be proclaimed, the positive truth revealed, which will free all humanity from the poverty of earthly existence, from the curse of endless war, from the bane of boredom and fraternal discord. There will be room for everyone. Each worker employed on the great project will be given a piece of land and will have to prove his seriousness and ability by clearing and cultivating the land around the site of his future house. Workshops would be built and workers' hostels, each with room for 1,000 people.

Keen, conscientious trade union leaders would supply the central authority with labor and would also have the power and responsibility to expel unworthy workers (idlers, thieves) from the community without mercy. The members of the community would have an identification mark and a password, without which no one would be able to enter the workshops and building sites.

The site plan is fixed and final. It would be drawn up by the council of ten masters, approved by the one hundred and twenty senior journeymen, and ratified by the one million workers. Only on the completion of the hostels, tool stores, and storehouses for materials would work begin on the project through which all are symbolically united, the task demanding the greatest devotion and the longest construction time. While the streets and squares for the whole city are being laid out and the foundations of the cityscape begun, the ground will be prepared for the central focus. On a site beside the water groups of trees will be planted, which will have reached maturity by the time the project is completed. The building itself will be of such dimensions that it could be achieved only by an army of workers fired by the joy of creation—unified by the *Idea*.

A self-supporting dome will rise up, 300 meters in diameter and 500 meters high, overshadowing everything that the inhabitants of the new city had regarded as noblest and most holy. After the foundations have been laid and the water and drainage, lighting, access, railway tunnels, and canals have been installed above and below ground level, the building will rise up without scaffolding as a series of columns and infill rings, like an amphitheater. Ring by ring the dome will be closed, regardless of ice and snow, sun and rain.

Ring by ring the electric railway will also climb up, taking the army of workers to and from their work each day. The lifting gear will also be moved upward so that the parts that have already been completed below can be hoisted up on cables.

Never will such a stable and enduring building have been constructed at such low cost and with such speed. The sons of those engaged on the project will already stand before the completed work when they are fifteen years old, although no worker had been younger than eighteen at the inception of the project. There will be no strikes, no disputes to be settled. Indeed, with the passing of the years and the increasing pleasure in the work, the majority of the workers will voluntarily suggest and achieve *longer* working hours.

Now the final ring has been completed —the last cable drops unimpeded to the ground far below—and the victorious symbol of the unified will for peace, for the positive new world-spirit stands free in space. Never has there been a more striking, more unanimous statement of the new spirit of peace.

Hundreds of thousands of men and women stream through the giant portals, lifting their eyes to the incredible glistening, sparkling spectacle, to the glowing colors and the radiant sunshine. In an ecstasy of joy their gaze soars upward into the heights, where heavenly tones are rejoicing.

Planets made of precious metals and stones swing in space on beautiful chains and complete the impression of weightlessness through which wafts the breath of God.

The breasts of the young swell more freely than ever before—the boys are conscious of the achievement, the girls see the work of real men—men worthy of their love, able to build a home for them, for their children, and for God. In the central space the people stream toward the sacrificial table and place there donations for the further development of the city, including the final embellishments of the apparently completed dome project. The donations will also go toward the welfare of the younger generation, who now have found their home, in appreciation of the older generation that created a new set of values.

Free cities for free people. Centers of spirituality and intellect that in the future shall alone decide the destiny of the world. All the nations of the earth must be made aware of the idea of community, of belonging to each other. Admittedly, we must first do all the hard groundwork. But what's wrong with that? We are thinking of those who will come *after* us.

BRUNO TAUT (GLAS), 5 OCTOBER 1920

From Whyte, Letters, *pp. 154–56.*

Friends!

Comrades in innovation! Our "gläserne Kette" [Crystal Chain], as its new link Cor (Alfred Brust) call it, needs tensile stress, even at the risk of an already flawed link breaking. We shall then forge a new one, and the chain will stretch out shining and multi-colored into our sun, moon, and star-lit ether....

Enough! Let them recognize us by our drawings and by our somnambulistic certainty.

Long live Utopia!—and long live that particular utopia that, to the great horror of the yapping critic, dares to reach right into the hornet's nest. The worst sort of troublemaker, we carry our light held high. In the realm of "pure" Utopia, the realm of the "Fantastic," it is a mere spark. Even the dear, upright and worthy fellow-citizen likes to gaze into the blue firmament. But when our torch is shone into the cozy, dark sulking-corner it becomes a terrible flame. Moths fly into it and burn their wings, vermin cower away, and the worthy citizen, blinded by the light, shrieks "Revolution!"

Hurrah!... In a word, I no longer want to draw Utopias "in principio," but absolutely palpable Utopias that "stand with both feet on the ground." I already indicated this in my last communication. Since then, the need for this change has led me to work out a specific project, about which I shall tell you later. Today in particular, the architect has three tasks. First: to build (there is little of that at present!); second: to create the new cultural image (the so-called pure Utopia); third: to awaken the demand for building (who should do this if not the architect?)....

Long live the eternal faith in the fire,
Glas

Anti-Utopia

JOHANNES BAADER

From "Germany's Greatness and Downfall; or, The Fantastic Life Story of the Supreme Dada"

Johannes Baader's humorous text was written to accompany his assemblage shown at the Erste internationale Dada-Messe *(First international Dada fair) at the Kunsthandlung Otto Burchard in Berlin from June 30 to August 25, 1920, and then reprinted in Richard Huelsenbeck's compendium of Dada writings. The* Dada-Messe *parodied German culture at large, including the avant-garde (and Expressionism in particular), while also advancing what the Dadaists saw as more promising new alliances between art and politics, technology, and the mass media. While lampooning the excesses of the utopian architects, the Dadaists nonetheless carried on their sweeping vision of social change by supplanting the cult of artistic genius with the more pragmatic personas of the engineer and the "monteur" (assembler).*

Originally published as "Deutschlands Grösse und Untergang; oder, Die phantastische Lebensgeschichte des Oberdada," in Dada Almanach, *ed. Richard Huelsenbeck (Berlin: E. Reiss, 1920), pp. 91–94: translated by David Britt.*

A Dadaistic Monumental Architecture in 5 upper stories, 3 complexes, 1 tunnel, 2 elevators, and 1 cylindrical superstructure. The first story, or the ground underfoot, is prenatal predestination and has nothing to do with the matter at hand.

The Description of the Upper Stories:
First Upper Story: The Preparation of the Supreme Dada.
Second Upper Story: The Metaphysical Test.
Third Upper Story: The Initiation.
Fourth Upper Story: The World War.
Fifth Upper Story: World Revolution.
Superstructure: The cylinder screws itself into the heavens and proclaims the fame of Teacher Hagendorf's Desk.

DETAILED DESCRIPTION

First Upper Story

From the metaphysical plane (also known as the 'Children's Pond') there gently arises on June 21, 1875, the day of the Supreme Dada's birth, the first hint of the pathological mentality that was a remnant from Pallas, the Dada Walrus (cf. Karl Hagenbeck's zoo), by way of the Asiatic Lion of the Pomeranian farmers without reference to any command economy (brass gold coins), adjacent to the demolished tower of the Kreuzkirche (Dresden) as a remnant of the competition for the new Dresden city hall. There are spent live

177
Johannes Baader with his assemblage *Das grosse Plasto-Dio-Dada-Drama* (The great plasto-dio-Dada-drama), 1920

cartridges in the tobacco pouch of the demolished church. On the large powder keg that looms in the center of the scene, its architectural detailing sculpturally reinforced right up to the pendant carbide lamp in which the original architectural idea, the work of the Dresden Association of Artists for Monumental Funerary Architecture (Baader, Metzner, Rössler, Hempel), was burned in Dresden in 1903–4.

Around the powder keg, deluded by the false hope of a far-ranging future between Schiller's poems with the motto "Dada Triumphs" and the first edition of the *Vierzehn Briefe Christi*,* there crawls the express train of Kaiser Wilhelm the Magnificent, which, symbolically circumscribed by the circular track, does nothing but circle the powder keg until it finally explodes.

"Fourteen letters of Christ," Baader's book published in 1914.

Second Upper Story
But first, in the tunnel of the doomed empire, there emerges the whole epoch of unified artistic culture. A museum of the masterpieces of the centuries opens, as the ancient Teutonic mousetrap twitches. The church is split in two down the middle, and the third part was demolished in accordance with its purpose and now stands on Alexanderplatz as a jailhouse (for a comfortable stay on all week-, Sun-, holi- and putschdays).

The green cloth beneath the mousetrap stands for unspoiled nature, while to one side the Wheel of Events (in order to continue the round tour of real life—still tied to the wheel) triumphantly passes the metaphysical test. The tunnel and the two devices are brimful of Platonic Ideas. When they grab, ravish, overpower the Supreme Dada, the phantom and the outcome of the world war appears, on January 19, 1908; April 8–9, 1910; September 4, 1912; August 13 and September 26, 1913. The exclamation mark that already appears on the geometry of the first upper story has become the beanstalk of Herr van Münchhausen, and he uses its flag (the Supreme Dada in person holds its flagpole in the cosine of the isosceles angle of all square triangles) to swing above all illusive pathology to the level of the third upper story, that of initiation.

Third Upper Story

Goethe reaches Weimar, drops his *Italienische Reise* on Teacher Hagendorf's Desk, and declares to the Swabian Pastor*: Without this desk no literature can ever be understood. The Asiatic Lion offers the second half to the public gaze. The last vestiges of Architecture are stowed away in a broken basket. The Angel of the Annunciation speaks: Lo, I bring you tidings of great joy, for unto you this day old Hagenbeck hath appeared. Paul Scheerbart too arrives in a crystal glass coach and plants himself as a bomb next to the dusty architecture basket. Meanwhile at the front elevator Woman makes her first appearance and unveils the naked secrets (only a whole man can become President). The Mine Engineers' Professional Association and Deutsche Bank take a dive, retrieve the Statement of August 2, 1914, from the depths of the Mother Mouth of the *Vagina sanguinalis protastata*, and thus emerges from the embryonic conception of the "W" (crowning glory and foundation of the cosmos; Cassiopeia; kaiser; airplane; streetcar line; the sum of all woe (Revelation 19.17 onward). Section Four, the world war.

**Baader.* –E.D.

RAOUL HAUSMANN

"In Praise of the Conventional"

Extolling art over fashion and scientific invention above artistic imagination, Hausmann carries on the legacy of Dadaist vitriol. Yet in its essential argument that traditions be replaced with conventions, Hausmann's text marks a fundamental shift away from the historicist assumptions of the modernist avant-garde. In this text and in his contemporaneous writings on "presentism," he emphasizes the practicality and simplicity of the moment.

Originally published as "Lob des Konventionellen," in Die Pille 3, *no. 1–2 (1922): 4–7; reprinted in Raoul Hausmann,* Sieg Triumph Tabak mit Bohnen: Texte bis 1933, *ed. Michel Erlhoff, vol. 2 (Munich: Text und Kritik, 1982), pp. 48–50; translated by David Britt.*

Hey, neighbor, haven't you noticed you're living in a museum? You look at old pictures; you read old books, which you claim are better than those of today; you live opposite old churches; you regale yourself with history that is full of the errors and shortcomings of the past. You know, man has invented law, beauty, harmony, and he tries so hard to live up to them that they eat him up. Hey, neighbor, hello there, rouse yourself, cheer up, let's live in the present! Our houses are awful, you say? Sure, they're conventional, but I ask nothing better. I like conventional furniture, and it's what I have; it would be interesting to have other kinds, no doubt, but then, after all, not everything has to be interesting. Sometimes on my travels I step down from an express train in a city that is like a museum, and there are antiquities standing around all over—I am not going to stay in some beautiful old Gothic house, I take a room in a convenient hotel with electric light, a bright toilet, and a bath. Of course, in the old Gothic house it would be more unconventional. I would fall over and break my neck in the dark, I would sit on a barrel instead of a toilet, and it would be very little consolation to me to know that the barrel in question—the ramshackle construction of which would very probably drown me—was first used in the year 1374 and was a pure example of the style. I would certainly have nightmares and end up doing battle with ghosts. I am no lover of ghosts, and before I decide to stop over in any house I look at the toilet first. I am so conventional that I am quite spoiled for the Gothic. I am quite spoiled for anything that is interesting, because my first thought is of its practical purpose. I am against the Werkbund, against Caligari, against the Golem, and against all attempts to make practical life into something interesting, to give it a spiritual polish. I am too conventional for Expressionism in any shape or form, old or new. If I want to make my life interesting or somber, I have to do it for myself, but I never use an Expressionist chamber pot. I am for the conventional imagination, that of the mason or the hairdresser, the truly influential, the patently obvious. What is a medieval saint to me? Our age needs the art that springs from hairdressers' models and tailors' mannequins and the pictures in the fashion magazines, all of which are entirely conventional and entirely contemporary! Is even one of your works of art more alive than a mannequin? What's that you say, neighbor? Spirituality in art? A dumb look in the eyes, to Hell with it. The imagination of the oxyacetylene torch, the hot-air hair dryer, and the electric iron is more necessary than the imagination of the artist—which irritates me because it is exceptional, because it is interesting, and because it seeks to seduce me away from my rightful place in modern life, away from the world of necessity, to a realm of abstraction and sheer debility where there are no railroads and none of the things we really need: things like electricity or motion-picture psychology, so universal and so utterly simple. The artistic imagination sabotages life; it is romantic, backward-looking, and stupid by comparison with the imagination of the technician or of the designer of machines or of the scientific experimenter—or even with the skill of a clock maker, welder, or locomotive engineer. No, take it away! If it's interesting, it's not for me. The word "interesting" stands for things like the magazine section of the *Berliner Tageblatt* or the novels in the *Wilmersdorfer Anzeiger* or the Dada carnival newspaper, all of which are inept efforts to make the imagination transcend the conventional. Efforts that are boring and stale. Arts and crafts are interesting, and therefore bad; take your fumbling hands off movies, fashion, and the manual trades! Why is the art of our time wretched? Why are exhibitions an abomination? Because gentlemen artists want to be a cut above sign painters or photographers; they all take such terrific pains to be interesting and unconventional. Than which nothing could be more ludicrous. Artists ought to be conclusively expressing the various manifestations of the age; they ought to be formulating the new conventionalism of plain, ordinary life; not all this abstruse philosophy and half-baked, soulful Romanticism! What is beautiful, really beautiful, huh, neighbor? Not your Böcklin postcard of Rügen in a Lake Hertha mood: an express train is beautiful; the locomotive roaring, steaming down the track is beautiful; the subway is beautiful; an ironworks is beautiful: all things conventional are wonderful! But then, my dear Puffke,* no doubt you flatter yourself that I think you beautiful too, because you are conventional! Relax, dear man, you are nothing of the sort. You try too hard to be something special, to have at least a little wooden plaque with interesting pyrography on it, or some other venial sin of unconventionality; no, I don't mean you. You don't appeal to me. You are thoroughly corrupted. I mean the genuinely conventional person, who can afford to be conventional because he does not need anything interesting: no arts and crafts, no oil painting, no plaster Venus de Milo, no *Berliner Tageblatt*, or any of the whatnots that you have so laboriously endowed with interest. A truly conventional person is one who does things quite simply for their own sake, without diversions or digressions. And so let us cultivate the soil, ride the subway, admire the beauty shops, and go to the telegraph office. Just spare me your interesting horse manure!

**Hausmann's bourgeois alter ego.* —E.D.

Film and Stage

BRUNO TAUT

The Universal Master Builder: An Architectural Drama for Symphonic Music

Taut intended his theatrical production to be performed to music composed by Heinz Tiessen (1887–1971) on the occasion of an exhibition of a Darmstadt group of architects he was attempting to establish under the name Bauwandlung (Building transformation). Although neither the group nor the performance ever materialized, Taut's text and accompanying sequence of spectacular images of a cosmic architecture in continual transformation (see figs. 122, 123) conveyed the hope for a Gesamtkunstwerk *(total work of art) shared by many of his colleagues in the Arbeitsrat für Kunst and the Gläserne Kette. The text reprinted here was also presented in the Arbeitsrat's book* Ruf zum Bauen *(see above). The epilogue appeared in the illustrated book published in the same year.*

Originally published as Der Weltbaumeister: Architektur-Schauspiel für symphonische Musik *(Hagen: Folkwang, 1920); translated by David Britt.*

The curtain rises.
THE WHOLE STAGE NOTHING BUT COLORED LIGHT—RADIANT YELLOW
Nothing else—no floor, no ceiling, no walls
MUSIC
no swelling, just a ringing in space—
long bright yellow brilliant RINGING....
from below forms emerge and with them figures in the music—with the forms the musical figures become richer more swelling more clamorous more colorful

It slowly emerges from below—

grows, forms an arch, other forms freely add themselves out of space—

it grows more and more—lively jostling of forms—until—

—it stands erect on the ground

Foot of an immense building, with a portal. The portal slides open—the whole building opens up and

—unfolds its halls—multicolored light—BELLS—

closes—revolves—a tremor runs through it—it leans, threatens to fall—

shatters—but the forms playfully detach themselves—

dance apart in a descending whirl—splinter—

become atoms and dissolve into the cosmos....
The light has grown darker—from light yellow to orange to moss-green—

and deep blue-green the void of space—MUSIC IN DISTANT SPACE

The space becomes deepest blue and stars begin to glimmer—

From the far distance two stars approach in a twirling dance—
—one disappears—

—the cathedral star comes closer—spins—dances—

dances—alters its form and light—

and soars away—a meteor—and once more dark blue space—without stars—for a longtime—
MUSIC. ETHEREALLY REMOTE

Empty space becomes purple-red—green leaf forms and flowers float down from above and from the sides—

The globe arches up—is decked by them in radiant green—
the sky grows oppressively violet—thunder—

—heavy rain—

—blue-yellow, red, green bow against azure blue—

summer sunlight—the bright green face of the earth rises up—from it human cabins grow—many-colored—like flowers—

—away as far as the horizon—the primeval green has turned into trees and gardens—afternoon light—
MUSIC OF EARTH'S JOY—CHILDREN'S VOICES—

On the hill THE HOUSE grows upward in the warm, yellow light—

—the radiant crystal house—in stage light, evening red—

—it opens up—shows its inner marvels—radiant cascades and fountains—glass flashing everywhere—against a deep red background—

Opening—unfolding of the building—movement and flow of all its elements—
Flashing and sparkling—all colors—in light turning to violet

Unfolding complete—stars glimmer through the crystal panels—
Architecture—Night—Cosmos—a Unity—
No more movement—the image stands still—THE MUSIC HANGS ON ONE ENDLESS TONE—

—the curtain slowly falls

BRUNO TAUT

From "On Stage and Music: An Epilogue to the Architectural Drama"

Originally published as "Über Bühne und Musik: Nachwort zum Architekturspiel." in Der Welthaumeiater: Architektur-Schauspiel für symphonische Musik *(Hagen: Folkwang, 1920); translated by David Britt.*

Color rings, forms ring—colors and forms as pure, unadulterated elements of the universe sustain tone. From them the musical work has an unforced birth, and equally unforced is the birth of forms and colors from the musical work. Not a forced conjunction of things related only by analogy: the color and form of the audible world sustains and creates, through a reciprocal action, the form and color of the visible world. Of the world!...of an all-embracing realm that abolishes all isolated, isolating, ego-separating and divisive feelings and thoughts. Audible, visible, and tangible forms unite freely and simply in the sphere of the cosmic element; they contract an alliance that knows no boundaries, internal or external: a mingling of the most intimate kind...a faithful image of the elements in the real world: earth, air, water, fire, sun, stars....

The boundaries stand out clearly. When a grand musical intermezzo is played, even in a traditional opera, the stage is left vacant. The strains of music put all fauna to flight. But they summon up elemental processes. Darkening, lightening, changes of color, non-anecdotal metamorphoses, are positively invoked by music from the depths of the stage.

This architectural play draws one logical conclusion from this observation. The effect may also be a purely dramatic one: an action with an inner logic of its own, based on causality, which is sustained not by one human being but by the whole stage itself. Of course anything that is done by human beings remains anthropomorphic, and even an action that is conceived in wholly cosmic terms must derive from human imagination, human emotion, and human thought. A projection of our human existence into the universe with the desire to lose ourselves therein. Woe betide art if it seeks to project the instinctual, ephemeral side of human nature onto the starry heavens!...

Art is the communication of emotions, and that defines its limits. Accordingly it has no place for any abstraction that does not lie within the nature of its own resources. Beyond this, any abstraction exceeds the limits of art, with the danger that it will appear as a product of intellect rather than of imagination.

Accordingly this play uses all its elements—even to the point of illusion—strictly as they serve the dramatic idea. The impersonal principle that makes and breaks, behind the visible world, the "universal master builder" who works within the cosmos, is the protagonist....

...Space in its inexhaustible depth is the womb that gives birth to everything—forms, colors, light—like the floating tone of the measureless ringing from which music takes its origin.

BRUNO TAUT

"Artistic Film Program"

Film was among the media Taut, Wenzel Hablik, and others discussed in the Gläserne Kette correspondence. In this essay Taut acknowledges the cinematic possibilities of his Der Weltbaumeister *and also touches on abstract film and experimentation with color kaleidoscopic projection.*

Originally published as "Künstlerisches Filmprogramm," in Das hohe Ufer 2 (1920): *86–88; translated by David Britt.*

The achievements of film, those that it may be expected to contribute to art, can basically be divided into three categories. By the nature of the subject, these three overlap and complement one another: for example, an instructive film, imaginatively presented, always affords artistic enjoyment; similarly, the film as an autonomous artistic creation is also instructive.

The three categories are as follows: (1) the generally stimulating film, which kindles the artistic imagination; (2) the instructive film, produced as an aid to the teaching of art, craft, or architecture; (3) the film as an autonomous work of art.

FIRST CATEGORY

For this, films from the whole field of the natural sciences, most of which have already been shot, should be selected and manufactured, not for their scientific or purely practical interest, but for that of the artistic beauty of natural forms, of their growth, etc., and of the image itself.

Examples: Crystal formations in ice, snow, minerals, etc. Growth of plants as seen in seeds, leaves, and whole trees. Zoological films, with particular emphasis on the beauty of animal form and motion. Use of time-lapse cinematography.

SECOND CATEGORY

Films of the making of works of art, and of good craftsmanship. The hands of the good craft worker are filmed in the act of making a beautiful piece.

Examples: The silversmith making a beautiful ring, the engraver at work, the pillow lace maker, the stained-glass artist, painting and inserting glass in cames, etc. We watch the pieces taking shape, they are turned around, etc., and then alongside them a piece is shown that merely imitates the good artistic forms and is badly made in itself. The difference between genuine and imitation lace—between a good and a bad piece of work in ceramics, metalwork, or whatever—will become clearly apparent, leading the viewer to conclude that a good piece, in spite of its higher purchase price, is essentially cheaper than a bad piece (Werkbund work). The same principle may be applied to purely artistic work: woodcut, linocut, lithography, etc.

Architecture: Films of buildings and groups of buildings, shot by moving the camera around them, coming closer to show the detail, and finally entering. The student of architecture, like the layman, will thus acquire a lively notion of the true essence of architecture. He will free himself of the pictorial notions fostered hitherto by perspectival renderings and will learn to comprehend the building as a unified organism that grows inevitably out of the determinant factors of function, location, and the rest. The significance of details and fittings, right down to the furniture, is made evident within their total context.

Examples: A filmed sequence of a residential neighborhood: first a walk though the streets, then around the outsides of individual houses, and finally inside individual homes. Likewise factories working, schools in use, railroad stations, churches, crematoria, theaters, etc. In the case of theaters, filming during performances, both in front of and behind the scenes, would demonstrate the close relationship between the architecture of the building and the drama. Complemented by sectional drawings with animation. The same principle for whole cities: Danzig, Goslar, etc., first from the air, then driving around in an automobile, then individual buildings as above—in short, a sightseeing tour of the whole town. Also bad examples, such as tenement areas and squalid housing.

Dance and Gymnastics: Films of dance schools to show the teaching method; use of slow-motion technique to evaluate various methods. Comparative sequences of animals filmed in slow motion, as in the first group.

THIRD CATEGORY

Film as art.

(a) Dance with music, as product of school of dance and gymnastics. Extension into filmed mime. Important to exert an influence on the existing dramatic film, in which whole scenes are ruined by characters who are seen speaking and writing, because the word is a medium completely alien to film.

(b) Mime without figures. Fantasy scenery in motion. Architectural drama and the like (cf. my own architectural drama, *Der Weltbaumeister*). Connection with symphonic music.

(c) "The mobile image." Abstract painting transposed into film by showing an image in which the forms are constantly in motion. Made from drawings by artists, technically, similar to the existing—mostly puerile—joke animations, as shown in the movie houses.

(d) The kaleidoscope. Camera points directly into the kaleidoscope tube. A projector adapted to show the kaleidoscope directly has the advantage of reproducing colors accurately, but it is expensive, and beyond a certain size of projected image (1.2 meters), it is blurred and unclear. The lack of color should be made up by skillful coloring; the same goes for (b) and (c). But the black-and-white image is also adequate in itself. When the tube is loaded by artists, the kaleidoscope can produce extraordinary artistic effects. (Glass house at Werkbund exhibition, Cologne 1914.)

LOTHAR SCHREYER

From "The Drama"

This text was written while Schreyer was working as a producer and assistant stage manager for the Deutsches Schauspielhaus in Hamburg between 1911 and 1918. His deeply mystical theory of the Bühnenkunstwerk *(theatrical work of art) drew on the telegraphic style of Expressionist poet August Stramm as well as the Wagnerian idea of the* Gesamtkunstwerk.

Originally published as "Das Drama," in Der Sturm *7, no. 10 (1917): 119; translated by David Britt.*

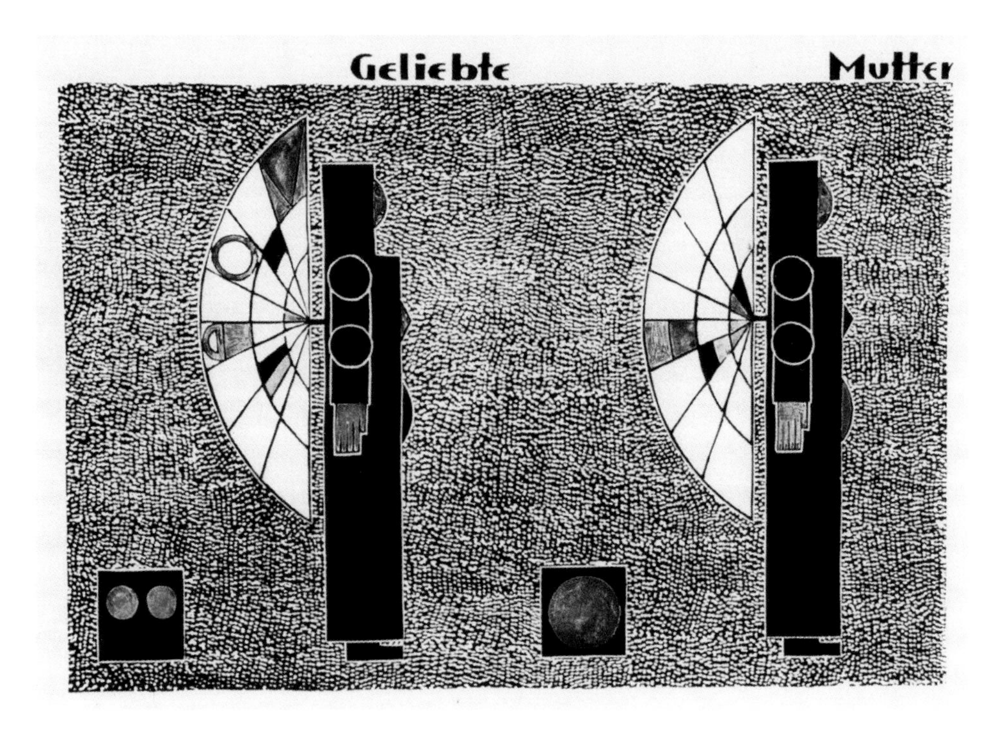

178
Lothar Schreyer
Geliebte/Mutter, c. 1920
(Lover/mother)
Cat. no. 197

The drama is dead. Long live the drama!

Performance is for the dead. The new work is shaped.

The new work is the theatrical work of art. It is the union and the shaping of the artistic media of form and color and movement and sound.

The tone of discourse, in the new theatrical work of art, is set by the word. Shaping words is poetry.

The new drama is the verbal shape taken by the vision of the theatrical work of art.

The new drama is not action. Poetry presents no action. Man acts. The work of art is. The drama does not signify the world. It does not interpret the world. Art is the world. The work of art is the finite shape of the infinite world. The artist beholds the face of infinity. The artist proclaims the vision.

The inner shape of drama is the cosmic experience. He who experiences this is not a human being. He and the cosmos are one. He has cosmic power....

The shape created by art is an organism. The work of art is organic and not abstract. There are no abstract organisms. The organism of the work of art proclaims the world of the spirit. The work of art is not an abstraction of the natural world. The concept within the work of art is a reality of the spirit. The concept has the form of its shaping. Once shaped, the concept is elusive, infinite. It is rhythmic.

The shape of the drama is not harmonic but rhythmic. Every shaped word, every shaped sentence, has its own rhythm. Every verbal shape is a rhythmic component of the rhythm of the work. Every verbal shape is a rhythmic unit.

The rhythmic verbal sequence of the drama is a rhythmic tone series.

The speech tone of the word is sonority and noise. The spoken vowels are sonority, the spoken consonants are noise.

The power of speech tone is governed by word tone. Every word has a specific tone that depends on the sonority of the vowels and the noise of the consonants.

The artistic power of vowels is the artistic power of their sounds.

The consonants transform the power of the vowels. The consonants are composite sounds, in which the partials combine not into sonorities but into noises.

Noises operate through the power of associations. Associations emerge from the similarity between natural sounds and those of the consonants. Associations derive from the content of the word and from its emotional implications. Associations between one verbal form and another are means to art only when they are also associations in terms of content....

The drama is the verbal shape of the theatrical work of art, which corresponds to its shape in terms of color and form. It is the verbal shape of the theatrical work of art, which corresponds to its shape in terms of movement and sound.

The drama is a part of the theatrical work of art; it is also extrinsic to it. The word sequences of the shapes created in color and form are part of the theatrical work of art. The totality of the verbal work of art is autonomous poetry: it is drama.

The drama cannot be played. It is recited. What is played is the theatrical work of art.

The drama lives.

The theatrical work of art lives.

The work of man dies.

The work of art never dies.

OSKAR SCHLEMMER

"The Painter and the Stage"

Schlemmer was a widely influential force in Bauhaus stage activities from 1923 to 1929. His vision of a liberated stage was premised on the dissolution of the boundaries between painting, architecture, and dance. Although not published until much later, the following text was part of his campaign for the abandonment of the traditional theatrical hierarchy.

Originally titled "Der Maler und die Bühne," from the unpublished first version of the essay "Kunst und Bühne" for the Bauhaus-Bühnenbuch *(1924); published in* Oskar Schlemmer und die abstrakte Bühne, *exh. cat. (Zurich: Kunstgewerbemuseum, 1961), p. 17; translated by David Britt.*

The painter, the longest enslaved in the theater of dramatists and actors, now vigorously claims his rights. He has long since transformed himself from a decorator and scene painter into an "artistic adviser." He declines to be a servant any longer, and he is setting out to conquer the stage. His demands are radical ones: just as the Futurists want to abolish museums and moonlight, he demands the demolition of all stagehouses. Such is the vitality and decisiveness with which borderline areas are being targeted in all the visual arts—and in painting above all—that the results are a blueprint for the theater as well.

ROMAN CLEMENS

Script for the *Play of Form, Color, Light, and Sound*

Clemens produced his set of five stage designs entitled Spiel aus Form, Farbe, Licht und Ton *(Play of form, color, light, and sound) for an exhibition at the Bauhaus in July 1929. Each design was set in motion to the accompaniment of music and lighting effects, as described in the following score. Included in the present exhibition is the design for part 2 (see fig. 140).*

Published in Dirk Scheper, Oskar Schlemmer: Das triadische Ballett und die Bauhausbühne, *exh. cat., Schriftenreihe der Akademie der Künste, no. 20 (Berlin: Akademie der Künste, 1988), p. 214; translated by David Britt.*

PART 1: FORTISSIMO

Movement 1

Vertical stripes on from left

Movement 2

Intersection of stripes

Movement 3

Blue stripes down from above

Movement 4

Red disk from below

Movement 5

Pink wall on from right / End

Climax at 1

Music: Foxtrot in E flat major. Full jazz orchestra with piano solo

PART 2: PLAY OF CIRCLES (Russian)

Vigorous movement of the various disks with complementary color shift. Projection of a light bulb. Powerful light. Big movements.

End

Climax at end

Music: The Russian in D minor. Piano, banjo, drums

PART 3: TANGO

Movement 1

4 black stripes on horizontally and off again

Movement 2

4 black stripes on horizontally and 7 wavy lines down from above

Movement 3

Intersection of horizontals

Movement 4

Motion of horizontals from center to top, then down, over the wavy lines

Movement 5

Left of stage rather dark. Red circle (projected) gently rotating in direction of arrow.

Movement 6

Disk grows brighter and three vigorous revolutions

Movement 7

Disk off, left-hand part lights up. Upward movement of wavy lines. Then off

Movement 8

4 horizontals to left. Then off. End

1st climax at 4

2nd climax at 6

Music: Tango in A minor. Piano, violin, drums, banjo

PART 4: MATCHSTICK GAME

Movement 1

Row on at bottom left and back

Movement 2

Row on at top right and [back] with series at bottom left

Movement 3

Wheel on from below and revolves in direction of arrow

Movement 4

From top left and bottom right, meeting above center / End

Climax at end

Music: Hobgoblins Mounting Guard. Clarinet, piano, and drums

PART 5: FINALE

Movement 1

Red stripe on from left

Movement 2

Blue-yellow from above

Movement 3

Pink wall from right

Movement 4

Red-yellow from top to bottom / End

Music: Slow foxtrot in C minor, full jazz orchestra

HANS SCHAROUN

"Thoughts on Theatrical Space"

Scharoun's essay echoes his exaltation of an architecture rooted in the senses in the Gläserne Kette correspondence. He finally received an opportunity to design a performance space with the commission of the Philharmonic Berlin in 1963.

Originally published as "Gedanken zum Theaterraum," in Ruf zum Bauen *(Berlin: E. Wasmuth, 1920); translated by David Britt.*

Turning our backs on the confines of conventional theatrical space—in which "the" person sits here, between walls decorated for his benefit, and events take place there, in a vision too spatially false and too pictorial ever to become a significant experience—we boldly put both space and spectacle over and into the person.

Form, collective consciousness, and collective experience—in building, object, and person—are the single reflection of our present-day yearning to unite art and life.

"One" person in sight of another, arrayed in circles, in a vast, curving arc around upthrusting crystal pyramids. Space, plunging out of black and blue through a thousand spurts of color, swinging aloft to a silver-yellow star, in arch and ribs, in swelling and hollow of dark mass probing upward to winged purity, marking for itself—and for the expectant crowd—both the upward path and the crowning glory.

Thus the space expands into nonspatial infinity and prepares the ground to receive the mysteries of color, word, and tone.

Space darkens; light from an unseen source floats aloft to coalesce within the dome. A flash of light within the crystal block, color and form, now breaking free of earthly gloom, now showering down from the dome of light, now licking tongues of red, now drops of silver-blue.

Form and color in the rhythm of the musical sounds that issue from somewhere unknown to fill the expanse of space. Punctuated, drowned, or accompanied by the sung or spoken words of unseen single performers or choral groups.

Orchestra, organ, and speakers are arrayed behind openings artfully disposed in the surrounding wall.

Utopian Theory and Philosophy

GUSTAV LANDAUER

From *A Rallying Cry for Socialism*

Landauer (1870–1919) was among the primary sources of the social idealism of Taut and his circle. Landauer had been a member of the Friedrichshagen group, a colony of poets advocating decentralized communities along the lines of the British Garden Cities Association, and had founded the Neue Gemeinschaft (New society) in 1990 and the Sozialistischer Bund (Socialist group) in 1908. His Aufruf zum Sozialismus *(A rallying cry for socialism) attacked the centralized state and presented his plans for the Sozialistischer Bund as an ideal communalist alternative to capitalism. His murder in connection with the military suppression of the Bavarian Socialist Councils Republic in Munich in 1919 made him a martyr among those in the avant-garde seeking radical alternatives to party politics.*

Originally published as Aufruf zum Sozialismua, *2d ed. (Cologne: F. J. Marcan, 1925), pp. 2–3; translated by David Britt.*

It is not that the ideal is becoming reality, but in these times of ours it is through the ideal, and through the ideal alone, that our reality will take shape. Before us stands something beyond which we can discern nothing further or better; we behold the ultimate, and we say, That is what I want! And then everything—but everything—is done to make it happen. The individual, to whom the ideal has come as a moment of revelation, seeks out companions; he finds that there are others to whom it has already come as an cataclysm, a tempest of the mind and heart; for him, and for all like-minded persons, it is in the air. He finds yet others who have been sleeping, but sleeping lightly, whose understanding is veiled only by the thinnest of membranes, whose energy is but slightly blunted, and now that they have come together, these companions find ways of their own and talk to many others, to the masses in the great cities, in the smaller towns, in the countryside. An outward crisis helps to arouse the inward need; a divine discontent stirs and rouses itself; something like a spirit—spirit is common spirit, spirit is community and freedom, spirit is the human bond, as we shall soon see even more clearly—a spirit takes possession of people. Where spirit is, there is a nation; where a nation is, there is a wedge that presses forward; there is a will. Where there's a will, there's a way: the saying is quite true. But this is also the only way. And the light grows stronger, and the compulsion ever deeper; the veil, the net, the matted roots of the swamp of dullness are cast further aside; a nation joins together, a nation awakens: deeds are done, action takes place; imagined obstacles are recognized for what they are, something to leap over; other obstacles are eliminated by the use of united strength. For spirit is gladness and power; it is a motion that nothing, nothing in the world can hold back. Thither will I!

ERNST BLOCH

From *Spirit of Utopia*

Although Bloch (1885–1977) was not a member of the same circle as Taut and the utopian architects, his views were known through their publication in Die weissen Blätter *(The white papers), which represented the Expressionist generation of poets, critics, dramatists, and artists. His* Geist der Utopie *(Spirit of utopia), written in the effusive style common to much Expressionist prose, represents the initial response of a highly educated intellectual to an awareness of social inequality indebted to Marxist materialism. Bloch's search for "that principle...the thing worth living for" would culminate in his three-volume treatise* Das Prinzip Hoffnung *(The principle of hope, 1954). Originally published as* Geist der Utopie *(Munich: Duncker und Humblot, 1918), pp. 9, 47–48; translated by David Britt.*

INTENTION

And now?

Enough. Now we have to make a start. Life is given into our hands. In itself it has long since become an empty thing. Life stumbles aimlessly to and fro, but we stand firm, and so let us be life's fist and its aims.

What has just happened will probably soon be forgotten. Only an empty, hideous memory still hangs in the air. Who was being defended? The idle, the contemptible, the usurers were being defended. The young were killed; the ignoble were saved and now sit by their own warm firesides. Not a single one of them has been lost; those who upheld other banners are dead. The painters have fought to defend the middlemen and have kept the hinterland warm for the stay-at-homes. There is no longer any point in speaking of it. A stifling compulsion, imposed by the mediocre, endured by the mediocre; the triumph of stupidity, protected by the gendarme, glorified by intellectuals who lacked even the brains for phrase making.

The one thing that counts is this. He who pays the piper calls the tune, but this abdication at the sound of a drum was surprising all the same. It means we have not one socialist idea in our heads. We have grown poorer than warm beasts: everyone worships either his own belly or the state, and everything beyond that has cheapened into fun and entertainment. We can give society no idea of what it ought to be for, and therefore we cannot build society. We have longings and a little knowledge but little by way of deeds and—a partial explanation for this lack—no breadth, no outlook, no goals, no inner boundary to be intuitively perceived and crossed, no utopian concept of principle. To find that principle, to find the right, the thing worth living for, to be organized, to have time: it is for this that we blaze the trails of the imagination, invoke the nonexistent, build out into the blue, build ourselves out into the blue; where the merely factual vanishes, let us seek the true and the real—*incipit vita nova*....

But is it still possible to "build"? It is here that the interpolation of an overriding craft mentality must justify itself. It is probable that the extraordinary pursuit of expressiveness will cause certain artisanal—and, in due course, sculptural and architectural—interpretations to exalt themselves over traditional pictorialism on the grounds that its reference is predominantly naturalistic. Which means that, seen in a future perspective—transcending craft in the narrow, socially conditioned, stylistic sense and thereby transcending ornament in the unilinear, nontranscendental sense—there is more aesthetic content in a Sheraton chair than in the sweetest Perugino or in some yet more celebrated piece of art-historical illusionism. There is already much that points in this direction, and things long lost or never understood are coming to light: dance masks, totems, carved balconies, frieze ornaments, altar tabernacles; the idea of a sculpture carved from the inside outward, whether Negroid, Nordic, Gothic, or Baroque; the nameless body of a sculpture as architecture. There consequently emerges the concept of a third, more abstract quality, beyond relief and beyond the various forms of sculpture in the round, which represents not merely the shell or vague antechamber of the physical, human, psychic entity but the best location for its paradoxically lifelike, metaphysical abstraction. We are therefore in a position to give "building" its due, without any sacrifice of psychic qualities.

ERNST BLOCH

From "On Preconscious Knowledge"

Originally published as "Über das noch nicht bewusste Wissen," Die weissen Blätter *6 (January–March 1919): 355–66; translated by David Britt.*

We live above and beyond ourselves. This is what makes us human; the body no longer forces the head down to ground level. If our own emptiness pains us, and if this makes us all the more aware of the emptiness that is outside ourselves, then—even in the pain—a red glow burns. Even the most despairing individual still has the strength to feel that he is in despair. That at least he does feel, and so his state is not a simple one: through it he perceives—he infers from it by reversal—the existence of the Other, without which he would not be aware of his own continued existence: this is the sense of knowing something better, the intuition that things might be better. In some way, somewhere, we are pristinely good, untouched, unknown, young. Whatever we may achieve in this world turns out not to be what we meant, and yet, however shattered by the wasted effort, we cannot completely succumb. There is a core within us that shines and reflects the light cast by things that have yet to be, things that already affect us although they have never yet entered our consciousness.

At this stage it is important to eliminate a few misconceptions from the concept of the unconscious in general in order to concentrate on the preconscious. I can never take possession of myself as the person who is experiencing. Not even the fact that I am now smoking and writing—this least of all—is consciously known to me in itself. I cannot represent such a thing to myself until immediately afterward, and so only the immediate past is present to me; this is what we ostensibly experience as the present. Again the willed, attentive gaze itself constantly shifts; all the things it observes sink from view, and I can no longer possess them as current information. They can no longer be willed, sensed, or felt, but only summoned up in my memory or—still more vividly—known about. Nevertheless past will and past experience do not cease to exist and to have effects, even when lost from the present field of view. In dreams, above all, the will that has vanished from waking life returns and, though devoid of muscular power, takes command of visualized memories, using them "symbolically" in pursuit of some desire that is forgotten or unresolved or discountenanced by the moral, waking, grown-up consciousness....

...Above all, it is in days of expectation, when we feel the influence not of things past but of things to come, in severe suffering, in the violent force of happiness, in the vision of love, in perhaps the most receptive state of all, through music, which invariably addresses the latent part of our psyche and seeks to give it utterance—but above all it is in creative work itself that we cross the awesome frontier into preconscious knowledge. It is a dawning, a growing light within, effort, darkness, the cracking of the ice, an awakening, an approaching perception: it is a state and a concept that (just as Leibniz showed the psychic roots and thus revealed to the Sturm und Drang movement the dark side of nature, the *fundus animalis* of the *petites perceptions*) makes accessible to the higher, aspiring mode of thought—to the soul bathed in the inchoate, in mystic trajectories, and in the swelling fires of futurity—the "unconscious" aspect of the organizational processes and makes accessible to the *fundus intimus* the creative unconscious of the crowning inner self.

But, to whatever heights this intuitive state may point, it encounters on the way—not only in its "unconscious" intention but also in its "adequation," on its *object side*—all manner of deceptive solutions that stop it short, that constantly breed static forms, discarding the utopian excess of this existence of ours and leveling it—stylistically—to a routine....

Philosophical knowing, in the sense that is meant here, is the lamp that can transmute objects into precious stones; it is the arrival of the minister in the prison of the demiurge Pizarro; it is the action of the great work, of the water of life, of the way of metal, of the word of redemption. It is magic idealism, from the depths of the prophetic dream that resides at the universal fountainhead, of the unconstruable question, of the thing in itself [*Ding an sich*]: it is what does not yet exist, the ultimate future, the ultimate and true present, the problem of identity manifesting itself within existence, the still-unknown, inchoate utopia. Once again philosophical thinking is revealed as turning toward myth: not myth as known before, but the final myth before the great corner is turned, the myth of utopia, which of its essence has preoccupied the Jews as well as the philosophers since time immemorial—and which makes both groups, as unquiet worshipers of the *invisible* God, of the utter absolute, suspect to all those theologians who preach that a halfway state is a finished image.

Selected Bibliography

Allen, Roy F. *Literary Life in German Expressionism and the Berlin Circles*. Göppingen: A. Kümmerle, 1974.

Altmeier, Werner. "Die bildende Kunst des deutschen Expressionismus im Spiegel der Buch- und Zeitschriftenpublikationen zwischen 1910 und 1925: Zur Debatte um ihre Ziele, Theorien und Utopien." Ph.D. diss., Universität des Saarlandes, Saarbrücken, 1972.

Andersen, Arne. "Heimatschutz: Die bürgerliche Naturschutzbewegung." In *Besiegte Natur: Geschichte der Umwelt im 19. und 20. Jahrhundert*. Edited by Franz-Josef Brüggemeier and Thomas Rommelspacher, pp. 143–57. Munich: C. H. Beck, 1987.

"Architecture Begins Where the Space Ends." *Architecture and Urbanism* (a+u) 7, no. 310 (1996): 112–113.

Architecture is Now: Projects, (Un)buildings, Actions, Statements, Sketches, Commentaries, 1968–1983 (New York: Rizzoli, 1983).

Asmus, Gesine, ed. *Berlin um 1900*. Exhibition catalogue. Berlin: Berlinische Galerie, 1984.

Autour de l'expressionisme allemand et du Caligarisme. Exhibition catalogue. Toulouse: Musée des Augustins, 1984.

Bahr, Hermann. "Der Betrieb der Grossstadt." *Die neue Rundschau* 23, pt. 1 (1912): 697–705.

——. *Expressionismus*. Munich: Delphin, 1916.

Bajkay-Rosch, Eva. "Die KURI-Gruppe." In *Wechsel Wirkungen: Ungarische Avantgarde in der Weimarer Republik*. Exhibition catalogue. Edited by Hubertus Gassner, pp. 260–66. Kassel: Staatliche Kunstsammlungen, 1986.

Banham, Reyner. "The Glass Paradise." *The Architectural Review* 125 (February 1959): 87–89.

——. *Theory and Design in the First Machine Age*. New York: Praeger, 1960.

——. *The Architecture of the Well-Tempered Environment*. London: Architectural Press, 1969.

Barlow, John D. *German Expressionist Film*. Boston: Twayne, 1982.

Barsacq, Léon. *Caligari's Cabinet and Other Grand Illusions: A History of Film Design*. 1st English-language ed. Revised and edited by Elliott Stein and translated by Michael Bullock. Boston: New York Graphic Society, 1976.

Bartmann, Dominik. "Das Grossstadtbild Berlins in der Weltsicht der Expressionisten." In *Stadtbilder Berlin in der Malerei vom 17. Jahrhundert bis zur Gegenwart*, pp. 243–94. Exhibition catalogue. Berlin: Berlin Museum, 1987.

Bathrick, David, Thomas Elsaesser, and Miriam Hansen, eds. *New German Critique*, no. 40 ("Special Issue on Weimar Film Theory") (Winter 1987) (later incorporated as vol. 14, no. 1).

Behne, Adolf. "Expressionistische Architektur." *Der Sturm* 5, no. 19–20 (1915): 135.

——. "Gedanken über Kunst und Zweck, dem Glashaus gewidmet." *Kunstgewerbeblatt* 27, no. 2 (1915–16): 1–4.

——. "Unsere Baukunst und das Morgenland." *Sozialistische Monatshefte* 22 (17 February 1916): 155–57.

——. "Kritik des Werkbundes." *Die Tat: Monatsschrift für die Zukunft deutscher Kultur* 9, no. 1 (1917): 430–38. Reprinted in Werkbund Archiv, no. 1 (1972): 118–28.

——. "Unbekannte Architekten." *Sozialistische Monatshefte* 25 (28 April 1919): 422–23.

——. "Wiedergeburt der Baukunst." In *Die Stadtkrone*. Edited by Bruno Taut. Jena: Eugen Diederichs, 1919.

——. *Die Wiederkehr der Kunst*. Leipzig: Kurt Wolff, 1919.

——. "Glasarchitektur." *Frühlicht* (January 1920). Reprinted in *Frühlicht, 1920–1922: Eine Folge für die Verwirklichung des neuen Baugedankens*. Edited by Bruno Taut, pp. 12–16. Bauwelt Fundamente, no. 8. Berlin: Ullstein, 1963.

——. "Die Zukunft unserer Architektur." *Sozialistische Monatshefte* 27 (31 January 1921): 90–94.

——. "Architekten." *Frühlicht* (Winter 1921–22): 55–60.

——. *Der moderne Zweckbau*. Frankfurt: Ullstein, 1964.

Ben, Michael, ed. *Weimarer Republik*. 2d ed. Berlin: Elefanten, 1977.

Benhabib, Seyla. *Critique, Norm, and Utopia: A Study of the Foundations of Critical Theory*. New York: Columbia University Press, 1986.

Berghahn, Klaus L., and Hans Ulrich Seeber, eds. *Literarische Utopien von Morus bis zur Gegenwart*. Königstein: Athenäum, 1983.

Berlage, Hendrik P. *Grundlagen und Entwicklung der Architektur*. Berlin: J. Bard, 1908.

"Berlin: Geschichte einer Grossstadt." *Du: Die Kunstzeitschrift* 39, no. 10 (1979): 16–83.

Betthausen, Peter. "Die 'Brücke': Künstlergemeinschaft und Kunstverein des Expressionismus." In *Expressionsten: Die Avantgarde in Deutschland, 1905–1920*, pp. 25–30. Exhibition catalogue. Berlin: Staatliche Museen zu Berlin, Kupferstichkabinett und Sammlung der Zeichnungen, 1986.

Blaubox (London: Architectural Association, 1988).

Bletter, Rosemarie Haag. "The Interpretation of the Glass Dream: Expressionist Architecture and the History of the Crystal Metaphor." *Journal of the Society of Architectural Historians* 40 (March 1981): 20–43.

——. "Expressionism and the New Objectivity." *Art Journal* 43 (Summer 1983): 108–20.

Bloch, Ernst. *Geist der Utopie*. Munich: Duncker und Humblot, 1918. Reprint. Frankfurt: Suhrkamp, 1977.

——. "Über das noch nicht bewusste Wissen." *Die weissen Blatter* 6 (August 1919): 355–66.

——. *Das Prinzip Hoffnung*. 3 vols. Berlin: Aufbau-Verlag, 1954, Translated by Neville Plaice, Stephen Plaice, and Paul Knight, under the title *The Principle of Hope*. 3 vols. 1st American ed. Studies in Contemporary German Social Thought. Cambridge: MIT Press, 1986.

——. *The Utopian Function of Art and Literature: Selected Essays*. Translated by Jack Zipes and Frank Mecklenburg. Cambridge: MIT Press, 1988.

Boberg, Jochen, Tilman Fichter, and Eckhart Gillen, eds. *Die Metropole: Industriekultur in Berlin im 20. Jahrhundert*. Industriekultur deutscher Städte und Regionen. Munich: C. H. Beck, 1986.

Böhme, Gernot. *Natürlich Natur: Über Natur im Zeitalter ihrer technischen Reproduzierbarkeit*. Neue Folge, no. 680. Frankfurt: Suhrkamp, 1992.

Bohnen, Hans U. *Das Gesetz der Welt ist die Änderung der Welt: Die rheinische Gruppe progressiver Künstler (1918–1933)*. Berlin: Kramer, 1976.

Bohrer, Karl-Heinz. *Plötzlichkeit zum Augenblick des ästhetischen Scheins*. Frankfurt: Suhrkamp, 1981.

——. "Schein and Chock: On Walter Benjamin's Esoteric Aesthetics." In *Zeitgeist: International Art Exhibition, Berlin 1982*. Exhibition catalogue, Martin-Gropius-Bau, Berlin. Edited by Christos M. Joachimides and Norman Rosenthal, pp. 25–37. NewYork: George Braziller, 1983.

Bollerey, Franziska. *Architekturkonzeption der utopischen Sozialisten: Alternative Planung und Architektur für den gesellschaftlichen Prozess*. Munich: H. Moos, 1977.

Borsi, Franco, and G. K. König. *Architettura dell'expressionismo*. Genoa: Vitali e Ghianda, 1967.

Brockhaus, Christoph. "Die ambivalente Faszination der Grossstadterfahrung in der deutschen Kunst des Expressionismus." In *Expressionismus: Sozialer Wandel und künstlerische Erfahrung*. Edited by Horst Meixner and Silvio Vietta, pp. 89–106. Munich: Wilhelm Fink, 1982.

Bronner, Stephen Eric. "Revolutionary Anticipation and Tradition." *Minnesota Review* (Spring 1976): 88–95.

Budd, Mike, ed. *The Cabinet of Dr. Caligari: Texts, Contexts, Histories*. New Brunswick, N.J.: Rutgers University Press, 1990.

Buddensieg, Tilmann, ed. *Berlin, 1900–1933: Architecture and Design*. Exhibition catalogue. New York: Cooper-Hewitt Museum, 1987.

Burger, Fritz. *Einführung in die moderne Kunst*. Berlin: Akademie Verlagsgesellschaft Athenaion, 1917.

Busch, Günter, ed. *Die Stadt: Bild-Gestalt-Vision: Europäische Stadtbilder im 19. und 20. Jahrhundert*. Exhibition catalogue. Bremen: Kunsthalle Bremen, 1973.

Byrne, Richard Burdick. "German Cinematic Expressionism, 1919–1924." Ph.D. diss., State University of Iowa, Iowa City, 1962.

"Capturing Architecture in Words." *Sites* 14 (1985):12-28.

Cassirer, Paul. "Utopische Plauderei." *Die weissen Blätter* 6 (March 1919): 105–17.

Chiarini, Luigi. "Il cinema espressionista." *Maggio musicale fiorentino* 27 ("L'espressionismo") (1964): 93–95.

Clark, Kenneth. *Landscape into Art*. Boston: Beacon, 1961.

Collins, George R. *Visionary Drawings of Architecture and Planning: Twentieth Century through the 1960s*. Exhibition catalogue. Cambridge: MIT Press, 1979.

Conrads, Ulrich, ed. *Programs and Manifestoes on Twentieth Century Architecture*. Translated by Michael Bullock. Cambridge: MIT Press, 1971.

Conrads, Ulrich, and Hans G. Sperlich. *The Architecture of Fantasy: Utopian Building and Planning in Modern Times*. Edited and translated by Christiane C. Collins and George R. Collins. New York: Praeger, 1962.

Coop Himmelblau Austria Biennale di Venezia 1996 (Klagenfurt: Ritter Verlag, 1996).

Deri, Max. *Naturalismus, Idealismus, Expressionismus*. Leipzig: E. A. Seemann, 1922.

Dückers, Alexander, ed. *Bilder aus der grossen Stadt: Eine Reportage von Gross-Berlin: Druckgraphik und Handzeichnungen*. Exhibition catalogue. Berlin: Staatliche Museen Preussischer Kulturbesitz, Kupferstichkabinett, 1977.

Duncan, Michael. "Deconstructing Display." *Art in America* (October 1994): 57–61.

Eberle, Matthias. *Individuum und Landschaft: Zur Entstehung und Entwicklung der Landschaftsmalerei*. Kunstwissenschaftliche Untersuchungen des Ulmer Vereins, Verband für Kunst- und Kulturwissenschaften, no. 8. Giessen: Anabas, 1980.

Eeden, Frederik van. *Het Godshuis in de Lichstad*. Amsterdam: W. Versluys, 1921.

Eisner, Lotte H. *The Haunted Screen: Expressionism in the German Cinema and the Influence of Max Reinhardt*. Berkeley and Los Angeles: University of California Press, 1973.

——. *Vingt ans de cinéma allemand, 1913–1933*. Paris: Centre National d'Art et de Culture George Pompidou, 1978.

Endell, August. "Möglichkeit und Ziele einer neuen Architektur." *Deutsche Kunst und Dekoration* 1 (March 1898): 141–53.

——. *Die Schönheit dergrossen Stadt*. Stuttgart: Strecker und Schröder, 1908.

Eschenburg, Barbara. *Landschaft in der deutschen Malerei*. Munich: C. H. Beck, 1987.

Eschmann, Karl. *Jugendstil: Ursprünge, Parallelen, Folgen*. Götingen: Muster-Schmidt, 1992.

The Fascination of the City (Darmstadt: Verlag der Georg Büchner Buchhandlung, 1988).

Fechter, Paul. *Die Tragödie der Architektur*. 2d ed. Weimar: E. Lichtenstein, 1922.

Filler, Martin. "Fantasms and Fragments: Expressionist Architecture." *Art in America* 71 (January 1983): 102–11.

Finkeldey, Bernd, et al., eds. *Konstruktivistische internationale schöpferische Arbeitsgemeinschaft, 1922–1927: Utopien für eine europäische Kultur*. Exhibition catalogue. Düsseldorf: Kunstsammlung Nordrhein-Westfalen, 1992.

Fletcher, Valerie. *Dreams and Nightmares: Utopian Visions in Modern Art*. Exhibition catalogue. Washington, D.C.: Hirshhorn Museum and Sculpture Garden, 1983.

Foucault, Michel. "Of Other Spaces." *Diacritics* 16 (Spring 1986): 22–27.

Freyer, Hans. "Landschaft und Geschichte." *In Mensch und Landschaft im technischen Zeitalter*. Jahrbuch Gestalt und Gedanke, no. 10. Munich: R. Oldenbourg, 1966.

Fricke, Roswitha, ed. *Bauhaus Fotografie*. Düsseldorf: Edition Marzona, 1982.

Friedländer, Salomo. "Absolutismus." *Der Sturm* 4, no. 194–95 (1914): 162.

Fritsch, Theodor. *Die Stadt der Zukunft*. Leipzig: T. Fritsch, 1896.

Furlon, Pierre, et al. *Réification et utopie: Ernst Bloch et György Lukács un siècle après*. Paris: Actes Sud, 1986. German-language edition: *Verdinglichung und Utopie: Ernst Bloch und Georg Lukács zum 100*. Geburtstag. Frankfurt: Sendler, 1987.

Gassen, Richard W., and Bernhard Holeczek, eds. *Apokalypse: Ein Prinzip Hoffnung? Ernst Bloch zum loo. Geburtstag*. Exhibition catalogue. Ludwigshafen am Rhein: Wilhelm-Hack Museum, 1985.

Gassner, Hubertus, Karlheinz Kopanski, and Karin Stengel, eds. *Die Konstruktion der Utopie: Ästhetische Avantgarde und politische Utopie in den zwanziger Jahren*. Schriftenreihe des Documenta Archivs, no. 1. Marburg: Jonas, 1992

Gersch, Wolfgang. *Film bei Brecht: Bertolt Brechts praktische und theoretische Auseinandersetzung mit dem Film*. Munich: Hanser, 1976.

Giovannini, Joseph. "Coop Himmelblau in Los Angeles." *Architecture* (December 1993): 24–25.

Godé, Maurice. "Der Sturm" *de Herwarth Walden: L'utopie d'un art autonome*. Nancy: Presses Universitaires de Nancy, 1990.

Gregotti, Vittorio. "L'architettura dell'espressionismo." *Casabella*, no. 254 (August 1961): 24–50.

Greve, Ludwig, Margot Pehle, and Heidi Westhoff, eds. *Hätte ich das Kino! Die Schriftsteller und der Stummfilm*. Exhibition catalogue. Sonderausstellungen des Schiller-Nationalmuseums, no. 27. Marbach: Schiller-Nationalmuseum, 1976.

"The Groninger Museum East Pavilion." *GA Document* 45 (1995): 48–65.

Haas, Patrick de. "Cinema: The Manipulation of Materials." In *Dada-Constructivism: The Janus Face of the Twenties*. Exhibition catalogue. Edited by Annely Juda and David Juda, pp. 53–71. London: Annely Juda Fine Art, 1984.

Hansen, Hans. *Das Erlebnis der Architektur*. Cologne: Kairos, 1920.

Hansen, Miriam. "Decentric Perspectives: Kracauer's Early Writings on Film and Mass Culture." *New German Critique*, no. 54 (Fall 1991): 47–76 (later incorporated as vol. 18, no. 3).

Harbison, Robert. *The Built, the Unbuilt, and the Unbuildable: In Pursuit of Architectural Meaning*. London: Thames and Hudson, 1991.

Haxthausen, Charles W. "Images of Berlin in the Art of the Secession and Expressionism." In *Art in Berlin, 1815–1989*. Exhibition catalogue. Edited by Kelly Morris and Amanda Woods, pp. 61–82. Atlanta: High Museum of Art, 1989.

Haxthausen, Charles W. and Heidrun Suhr, eds. *Berlin: Culture and Metropolis*. Minneapolis: University of Minnesota Press, 1990.

Hein, Birgit, and Wulf Herzogenrath, eds. *Film als Film, 1910 bis Heute: Vom Animationsfilm der zwanziger zum Filmenvironment der siebziger Jahre*. Exhibition catalogue. Cologne: Kölnischer Kunstverein, 1978.

Heiss, Robert. *Utopie und Revolution: Ein Beitrag zur Geschichte des fortschrittlichen Denkens*. Munich: R. Piper, 1973.

Heller, Reinhold. "'The City Is Dark': Conceptions of Urban Landscape and Life in Expressionist Painting and Architecture." In *Expressionism Reconsidered: Relationships and Affinities.* Edited by Gertrud Bauer Pickar and Karl Eugene Webb, pp. 42–57. Houston German Studies, no. 1. Munich: Wilhelm Fink, 1979.

Henn, Walter. "Die Künstler der 'Brücke' und ihre Architektur-Motive." In *Kunstmuseum Hannover mit Sammlung Sprengel: Die Künstlergruppe "Brücke," Ernst Ludwig Kirchner. Verzeichnis der Bestände*, pp. 17–26. Exhibition catalogue. Hannover: Kunstmuseum Harmover mit Sammlung Sprengel, 1982.

Hermand, Jost. "Brecht on Utopia." *Minnesota Review* (Spring 1976): 96–113.

Hermann, Georg. "Um Berlin." *Pan* 2, no. 2 (1911–12): 1101–6.

Herzog, Oswald. "Vom Ausdruck der Form." *Veröffentlichung der Novembergruppe*, no. 1 (May 1921): 32–34.

Herzogenrath, Wulf, ed. *Bauhaus Utopien: Arbeiten auf Papier.* Stuttgart: Cantz, 1988.

Hess, Klaus Peter. *Das Cabinet des Dr. Caligari: Materialien zu einem Film von Robert Wiene.* Atlas Forum. Duisburg: Atlas Film and AV, 1988.

Hilberseimer, Ludwig. "Grossstadtarchitektur." *Der Sturm* 15, no. 4 (1924): 177–89.

——. *Groszstadt Architektur.* Stuttgart: J. Hoffmann, 1927.

Hines, Thomas. "Danger: Walls With an Attitude." *Los Angeles Times* (December 19, 1993): 83–85.

Hirschbach, Frank D., et al., eds. *Germany in the Twenties: The Artist as Social Critic: A Collection of Essays.* New York: Holmes and Meier, 1980.

Hofmann, Werner. *Das irdische Paradies: Motive und Ideen des 19. Juhrhunderts.* 2d ed. Munich: Prestel, 1974.

Hübner, Herbert. *Die soziale Utopie des Bauhauses: Ein Beitrag zur Wissenssoziologie in der bildenden Kunst.* Darmstadt: Hoppenstedt, 1963.

Hull, David Stewart. *Film in the Third Reich: A Study of German Cinema, 1933–1945.* Berkeley and Los Angeles: University of California Press, 1969.

Hülsewig-Johnen, Jutta. *o meine Zeit! So namenlos zerrissen....* Exhibition catalogue. Bielefeld: Kunsthalle Bielefeld, 1985.

Huse, Norbert. *"Neues Bauen," 1918 bis 1933: Moderne Architektur in der Weimarer Republik.* Munich: H. Moos, 1975.

Illing, Werner. *Utopolis.* Berlin: Bücherkreis, 1930.

"Interview with Wolf D. Prix." *Progressive Architecture* (September 1991): 136.

Isaacs, Reginald R. "Das Bauhaus: Eine Utopie." In *Deutsches utoaisches Denken im 20. Juhrhundert.* Edited by Reinhold Grimm and Jost Hermand, pp. 70–81. Stuttgart: W. Kohlhammer, 1974.

Ja! Stimmen des Arbeitsrates für Kunst in Berlin. Berlin-Charlottenburg: Photographische Gesellschaft, 1919.

Jameson, Fredric. "Introduction/Prospectus: To Reconsider the Relationship of Marxism to Utopian Thought." *Minnesota Review* (Spring 1976): 53–58.

——. "Of Islands and Trenches: Neutralization and the Production of Utopian Discourse." *Diacritics* 7 (June 1977): 2–21.

——. "Progress versus Utopia; or, Can We Imagine the Future?" *Science-Fiction Studies* 9, no. 2 (1982): 147–58. Reprinted in *Art after Modernism: Rethinking Representation.* Edited by Brian Wallis and Marcia Tucker, pp. 239–52. New York: New Museum of Contemporary Art, 1984.

——. "Postmodernism and Utopia." In *Utopia Post Utopia: Configurations of Nature and Culture in Recent Sculpture and Photography.* Edited by Albert Bierstadt et al., pp. 11–32. Boston: Institute of Contemporary Art, 1988.

Joedicke, Jürgen. "Utopisten der zwanziger Jahre in Deutschland." *Bauen + Wohnen* 22 (May 1967): 193–97.

Johnson, Philip, and Mark Wigley. *Deconstructivist Architecture* (New York and Boston: The Museum of Modern Art/New York Graphic Society, 1988).

Jones, Michael. "Expressionism and Philosophical Aesthetics: Bloch's Geist der Utopie." In *Expressionism Reconsidered: Relationships and Affinities.* Edited by Gertrud Bauer Pickar and Karl Eugene Webb, pp. 74–79. Munich: Wilhelm Fink, 1979.

Kaes, Anton, ed. *Kino-Debatte: Texte zum Verhältnis von Literatur und Film, 1909–1929.* Munich: Deutscher Taschenbuch Verlag, 1978.

Kapner, Gerhart. *Architektur als Psychotherapie: Über die Rezeption von Studtbildern in Romanen des 20. Jahrhunderts.* Vienna: Böhlau, 1984.

Kaul, Walter, ed. *Caligari und Caligarismus. Deutsche Kinemathek Berlin, no.* 17. Berlin: Deutsche Kinemathek, 1970.

——. *Schöpferische Filmarchitektur.* Berlin: Deutsche Kinemathek, 1971.

Kessler, Charles S. "Sun Worship and Anxiety: Nature, Nakedness, and Nihilism in German Expressionist Painting." *Magazine of Art* 45 (November 1952): 304–12.

Klages, Ludwig. *Mensch und Erde.* Jena: Eugen Diederichs, 1933.

Kleindienst, Jürgen, ed. *Wem gehört die Welt: Kunst und Gesellschuft in der Weimarer Republik.* Exhibition catalogue. Berlin: Staatliche Kunsthalle, 1977.

Kliemann, Helga. *Die Novembergruppe.* Berlin: Mann, 1969.

Kohtz, Otto. *Gedanken über Architektur.* Berlin: o. Baumgärtel, 1909.

Kracauer, Siegfried. *From Caligari to Hitler: A Psychological History of the German Film.* Princeton, N.J.: Princeton University Press, 1947.

Krull, Wilhelm. "Vitalistische und utopische Prosa." In *Prosa des Expressionismus*, pp. 45–67, Sammlung Metzler, no. 210 (Abteilung D, Literaturgeschichte). Stuttgart: Metzler, 1984.

Krysmanski, Hans-Jürgen. *Die utopische Methode: Eine literatur- und wissenssoziologische Untersuchung deutscher utopischer Romane des 20. Juhrhunderts.* Dortmunder Schriften zur Sozialforschung, no. 21. Cologne: Westdeutscher, 1963.

Kurtz, Rudolf. *Expressionismus und Film.* Berlin: Verlag der Lichtbildbühne, 1926.

Kuspit, Donald. "Utopian Protest in Early Abstract Art." *Art Journal* 29 (Summer 1970): 430–37, Reprinted in Donald Kuspit, *The Critic Is Artist: The Intentionality of Art*, pp. 129–40. Ann Arbor, Mich.: UMI Research Press, 1984.

Landschaft: Gegenpol oder Fluchtraum? Exhibition catalogue. Leverkusen: Stadtisches Museum Leverkusen, Schloss Morsbroich, 1974.

Lane, Barbara Miller. *Architecture and Politics in Germany, 1918–1945.* Cambridge: Harvard University Press, 1968.

Lang, Fritz. *Metropolis: A Film by Fritz Lang.* Classic Film Scripts, no. 39. New York: Simon and Schuster, 1973.

Lange, Annemarie. *Berlin in der Weimarer Republik.* Berlin: Dietz, 1987.

Lasky, Melvin. *Utopia and Revolution: On the Origins of a Metaphor....* Chicago: University of Chicago Press, 1976.

Lawder, Standish D. *The Cubist Cinema.* Anthology Film Archives Series, no. 1. New York: New York University Press, 1975.

Leistner, Gerhard. *Idee und Wirklichkeit: Gehalt und Bedeutung des urbanen Expressionismus in Deutschland, dargestellt am Werk Ludwig Meidners.* New York: Peter Lang, 1986.

Levitas, Ruth. *The Concept of Utopia.* Syracuse: Syracuse University Press, 1990.

Liebersohn, Harry. *Fate and Utopia in German Sociology, 1870–1923.* Cambridge: MIT Press, 1988.

Lindahl, Göran. "Von der Zukunftskathedrale bis zur Wohnmaschine: Deutsche Architektur und Architekturdebatte nach dem ersten Weltkriege." *Acta Universitatis Upsaliensis*, n.s., 1 (1959): 226–82.

Long, Rose-Carol Washton. "Expressionism, Abstraction, and the Search for Utopia in Germany." In *The Spiritual in Art: Abstract Painting, 1890–1985.* Exhibition catalogue. Edited by Maurice Tuchman and Judi Freeman, pp. 201–17. Los Angeles: Los Angeles County Museum of Art, 1986.

——, ed. *German Expressionism: Documents from the End of the Wilhelmine Empire to the Rise of National Socialism.* New York: G. K. Hall, 1993.

Manheim, Ron. "Expressionismus—Zur Entstehung eines kunsthistorischen Stil- und Periodenbegriffes." *Zeitschrift für Kunstgeschichte* 49, no. 1 (1986): 73–91.

Mannack, Eberhard, ed. *Beiträge zur Literatur und Literaturwissenschaft des 20. Jahrhunderts.* Frankfurt: Peter Lang, 1982.

Mannheim, Karl. *Ideologie und Utopie.* 1929. Translated by Louis Wirth and Edward Shils, under the title *Ideology and Utopia: An Introduction to the Sociology of Knowledge.* New York: Harcourt, Brace, and World, 1968.

Manuel, Frank E., and Fritzie P. Manuel. *Utopian Thought in the Western World.* Cambridge, Mass.: Belknap, 1979.

Manvell, Roger, ed. *Masterworks of the German Cinema.* New York: Harper, 1973.

Marcuse, Herbert. "The End of Utopia." In *Five Lectures: Psychoanalysis, Politics, and Utopia.* Translated by Jeremy J. Shapiro and Shierry M. Weber. Boston: Beacon, 1970.

Marin, Louis. *Utopiques: Jeux d'espaces.* Paris: Editions de Minuit, 1973.

Mendelsohn, Everett, and Helga Nowotny, eds. *Nineteen Eighty-Four: Science between Utopia and Dystopia.* Sociology of the Sciences: A Yearbook, no. 8. Boston: D. Reidel, 1984.

Meuerburg, Waltraut. "Der graphische Zyklus im deutschen Expressionismus und seine Typen, 1905–1925." Ph.D. diss., Rheinische Friedrich-Wilhelms Universität, Bonn, 1976.

Michaud, Eric. "Das abstrakte Theater der zwanziger Jahre: Von der Tragik erlöste Figuren." In *Die Maler und das Theater im 20. Jahrhundert.* Exhibition catalogue. Edited by Erika Billeter, pp. 99–108. Frankfurt: Schirn Kunsthalle, 1986.

Monaco, Paul. *Cinema and Society: France and Germany during the Twenties.* New York: Elsevier, 1976.

Morris, Kelly, and Amanda Woods, eds. *Art in Berlin, 1815–1989.* Exhibition catalogue. Atlanta: High Museum of Art, 1989.

Müller, Götz. *Gegenwelten: Die Utopie in der deutschen Literatur.* Stuttgart: Metzler, 1989.

Müller-Wulckow, Walter. *Aufblau-Architektur!* Berlin: E. Reiss, 1919.

Muthesius, Hermann. "Wo stehen wir?" In *Die Durchgeistigung der deutschen Arbeit. Jahrbuch des Deutschen Werkbundes 1912.* Jena: Eugen Diederichs, 1912.

Naylor, Gillian. *The Bauhaus Reassessed: Sources and Design Theory.* New York: E. P. Dutton, 1985.

Neumann, Dietrich. "Deutsche Hochhäuser der zwanziger Jahre." Ph.D. diss., Technische Universität, Munich, 1989.

Offene Architektur, Wohnanlage Wien 2 (Munich: Architekturgallerie 8000, 1986).

Olbrich, Herald. "Faszination, Schock, Enthüllung, Widerstand: Zum expressionistischen Grossstadtbild." In *Expressionisten: Die Avantgarde in Deutschland, 1905–1920.* Exhibition catalogue. Edited by Roland März and Anita Kühnel, pp. 49–52. Berlin: Staatliche Museen zu Berlin, 1986.

"On the Edge." *Architectural Design Profile No. 87 Deconstruction III* (1990): 65–79.

"Open House." *Progressive Architecture* (January 1991): 85–86.

Osterwold, Klaus, ed. *Nutur und Bauen.* Vol. 2 of *Trilogie.* Exhibition catalogue. Stuttgart: Württembergischer Kunstverein, 1977.

Palmier, Jean Michel. *L'expressionnisme et les arts.* Vol. 2, Bibliothèque Historique. Paris: Payot, 1980.

Paris-Berlin, 1900–1933: Rapports et contrastes France-Allemagne, 1900–1933. Exhibition catalogue. Paris: Centre National d'Art et de Culture Georges Pompidou, 1978.

Pehnt, Wolfgang. *Expressionist Architecture.* London: Thames and Hudson, 1973.

——. *Expressionist Architecture in Drawings.* New York: Van Nostrand Reinhold, 1985.

——. "Verstummte Tonkunst: Musik und Architektur in der neueren Architekturgeschichte." In *Vom Klang der Bilder: Die Musik in der Kunst des 20. Jahrhunderts.* Exhibition catalogue. Edited by Peter Stepan, pp. 394–99. Stuttgart: Staatsgalerie Stuttgart, 1985.

Pesch, Ludwig. "Das Utopia der romantischen Kunsttheorie und die Moderne." In *Wandlungen des Paradiesischen und Utopischen: Studien zum Bild eines Ideals.* Edited by Hermann Bauer. Probleme der Kunstwissenschaft, no. 2. Berlin: W de Gruyter, 1966.

Peternák, Miklós. "Licht und Klang aus Ungarn: Bemerkungen zur Geschichte des Intermedia in den zwanziger Jahren." In *Wechsel Wirkungen: Ungarische Avantgarde in der Weimarer Republik.* Exhibition catalogue. Edited by Hubertus Gassner, pp. 456–60. Kassel: Staatliche Kunstsammlungen, 1986.

Piepmeier, Rainer. "Das Ende der ästhetischen Kategorie 'Landschaft.'" In *Westfälische Forschungen: Mitteilungen des Provinzialinstituts für westfälische Landes- und Volksforschung des Landesverbandes Westfallen-Lippe.* Vol. 30. Edited by Peter Schöller and Alfred Hartlieb van Wallthor, pp. 8–46. Münster: Aschendorffsche Verlagsbuchhandlung, 1980.

Pinthus, Kurt, ed. *Das Kinobuch.* 1913–14. Reprint. Zurich: Arche, 1963.

Pleister, Michael. *Das Bild der Grossstadt in den Dichtungen Robert Walsers, Rainer Maria Rilkes, Stefan Georges und Hugo von Hofmannsthals.* Hamburger philologische Studien, no. 53. Hamburg: H. Buske, 1982.

Reidemeister, Leopold. "Die 'Brücke' im Spiegel der Zeitschriftenkritik." *Brücke-Archiv,* no. 1 ([1968?]): 41–54.

——. *Künstler der Brücke an den Moritzburger Seen, 1909–1911: Erich Heckel, Ernst Ludwig Kirchner, Max Pechstein: Ein Beitrag zur Geschichte der Künstlergruppe Brücke.* Exhibition catalogue. Berlin: Brücke-Museum, 1970.

——. *Künstler der Brücke in Berlin, 1908–1914: Ein Beitrag der Künstlergruppe Brücke.* Exhibition catalogue. Berlin: Brücke-Museum, 1972.

Ribbe, Wolfgang, and Wolfgang Schäche, eds. *Baumeister, Architekten, Stadtplaner: Biographien zur baulichen Entwicklung Berlins.* Berlin: Historische Kommission zu Berlin, 1987.

Richter, Hans. "The Language of Paradise." In *Dada: Art and Anti-Art.* Translated by David Britt, pp. 44–50. London: Thames and Hudson, 1965.

——. ed. "Ausgabe 5–6, April 1926." In G.: *Material zur elementaren Gestaltung.* 1923–26. Reprint. Munich: Kern, 1986: 103–42.

Riha, Karl. *Die Beschreibung der "Grossen Stadt": Zur Entstehung des Grossstadtmotivs in der deutschen Literatur (ca. 1750 bis ca. 1850).* Bad Homburg: Gehlen, 1970.

Rischbieter, Henning, ed. *Art and the Stage in the Twentieth Century: Painters and Sculptors Work for the Theater.* Greenwich, Conn.: New York Graphic Society, 1968.

Roberts, David. "'Menschheitsdämmerung': Ideologie, Utopie, Eschatologie." In *Expressionismus und Kulturkrise.* Edited by Bernd Hüppauf, pp. 85–103. Heidelberg: Winter Universittäsverlag, 1983.

Rochard, Patricia, ed. *Der Traum von einer neuen Welt: Berlin, 1910–1933. 32. internationale Tage.* Exhibition catalogue. Ingelheim am Rhein: Museum-Altes-Rathaus, 1989.

Rölleke, Heinz. *Die Stadt bei Stadler, Heym und Trakl.* Berlin: E. Schmidt, 1966.

Roters, Eberhard. "Big-City Expressionism: Berlin and German Expressionism." In *Expressionism: A German Intuition, 1905–1920,* pp. 238–51. Exhibition catalogue. New York: Solomon R. Guggenheim Foundation, 1980. German-language edition: "Grossstadt-Expressionismus: Berlin und der deutsche Expressionismus." In *Deutscher Expressionismus, 1905–1920.* Edited by Paul Vogt, pp. 247–61. Munich: Prestel, 1981.

——, ed. *Berlin, 1910–1933.* New York: Rizzoli, 1982.

Roters, Eberhard, and Bernhard Schulz, eds. *Ich und die Stadt: Mensch und Grossstadt in der deutschen Kunst des 20. Jahrhunderts.* Exhibition catalogue. Berlin: Berlinische Galerie, 1987.

Rothe, Wolfgang, ed. *Deutsche Grossstadtlyrik vom Naturalismus bis zur Gegenwart.* Stuttgart: Reclam, 1973.

Rother, Rainer, ed. *Die UFA, 1917–1945: Das deutsche Bilderimperium.* Exhibition catalogue. Edited by Michael Töteberg and Klaus Kreimeier. Berlin: Deutsches Historisches Museum Berlin, 1992.

Ruf zum Bauen. Buchpublikation des Arbeiterrats für Kunst no. 2. Berlin: E. Wasmuth, 1920.

Ryan, Raymond. "When Vienna Starts to Dream of California." *Blueprint* (December/January 1994): 39.

Santomasso, Eugene Anthony. "Origins and Aims of German Expressionist Architecture: An Essay into the Expressionist Frame of Mind in Germany, Especially as Typified in the Work of Rudolf Steiner." Ph.D. diss., Columbia University, New York, 1973.

Sayag, Alain, ed. *Cinéma dadaiste et surrealiste.* Exhibition catalogue. Paris: Musée National d'Art Moderne, Centre National d'Art et de Culture Georges Pompidou, 1976.

Scheffler, Karl. *Moderne Baukunst.* Berlin: J. Bard, 1907.

——. *Berlin: Ein Stadtschicksal.* 2d ed. 1910. Reprint. Berlin: Fannei und Walz, 1989.

——. *Die Architektur der Grossstadt.* Berlin: B. Cassirer, 1913.

——. *Der Geist der Gotik.* Leipzig: Insel, 1917.

——. *Berlin: Wandlungen einer Stadt.* Berlin: B. Cassirer, 1931.

Scheper, Dirk. "Theater zwischen Utopie und Wirklichkeit." In *Tendenzen der zwanziger Jahre.* Exhibition catalogue. 2d ed. Edited by Stephan Waetzoldt and Verena Haas, vol. 1, pp. 192–98. Berlin: Neue Nationalgalerie, Akademie der Künste, 1977.

Schiff, Gert. "Arcadia and Human Wasteland." *Art Journal 41,* no. 1 (1981): 64–69.

Schlösser, Manfred, ed. *Arbeitsrat für Kunst: Berlin, 1918–1921.* Exhibition catalogue. Berlin: Akademie der Künste, 1980.

Schmidt, Paul F. "Das Recht auf Romantik." *Das Kunstblatt* 4 (November 1920): 321–25.

Schneider, Ludwig. *Zerbrochene Formen, Wort und Bild im Expressionismus.* Hamburg: Hoffmann und Campe, 1967.

Schneider, Martina. "Von der futuristischen zur funktionellen Stadt: Planen und Bauen in Europa von 1913 bis 1933." In *Tendenzen der zwanziger Jahre.* Exhibition catalogue. Edited by Stephan Waetzoldt and Verena Haas, vol. 2, pp. 1–47. Berlin: Neue Nationalgalerie, Akademie der Künste, 1977.

Schrader, Bärbel, and Jürgen Schebera. *Kunst-Metropole Berlin, 1918–1923: Dokumente und Selbstzeugnisse.* Berlin: Aufbau-Verlag, 1987.

Schulz, B. "La nostalgie de la nature et la fièvre de la grande ville: L'expressionisme allemand entre Brücke et Berlin." In *Expressionisme à Berlin, 1910–1920,* pp. 17–32. Exhibition catalogue. Brussels: Société des Expositions du Palais des Beaux-arts de Bruxelles, 1984.

Schumacher, Fritz. "Expressionismus und Architektur." Parts 1–3, *Dekorative Kunst* 23 (October–December 1919): 10–20, 62–72, 80–88.

Schumpp, Mechthild. *Stadtbau-Utopien und Gesellschaft: Der Bedeutungswandel utopischer Stadtmodelle unter sozialem Aspekt.* Gütersloh: Bertelsmann, 1972.

Sengle, Friedrich. "Wunschbild Land und Schreckbild Stadt: Zu einem zentralen Thema der neueren deutschen Literatur." *Studium Generale* 16 (1963): 619–31.

Seuter, Harald, ed. *Der Traum vom Paradies: Zwischen Trauer und Entzücken.* Vienna: Herder, 1983.

Sharp, Dennis, ed. *Glass Architecture by Paul Scheerbart and Alpine Architecture by Bruno Taut.* Translated by James Palmer and Shirley Palmer. New York: Praeger, 1972.

——. *Modern Architecture and Expressionism.* New York: George Braziller, 1967.

Siebenhaar, Klaus. *Klänge aus Utopia: Zeitkritik, Wandlung und Utopie im expressionistischen Drama.* Berlin: Agora, 1982.

Simmel, Georg. "Die Grossstädte und das Geistesleben." In *Die Grossstadt.* Special issue of *Juhrbuch der Gehe-Stiftung zu Dresden* 9 (1903): 185–206.

——. "Philosophie der Landschaft." In *Brücke und Tür: Essays des Philosophen zur Geschichte, Religion, Kunst und Gesellschaft.* Edited by Michael Landmann, pp. 141–52. 1957. Reprinted in *Das Individuum und die Freiheit: Essais.* Berlin: K. Wagenbach, 1984.

6 Projects for 4 Cities (Darmstadt: Verlag Jürgen Häuser, 1993).

Skyline (Berlin: Aedes Gallerie für Architektur, 1986).

Sorkin, Michael. "Post Rock Propter Rock: A Short History of the Himmelblau" (1988), in *Exquisite Corpse: Writings on Buildings* (London and New York: Verso, 1991), 347.

Die Stadt: Druckgraphische Zyklen des 19. und 20. Jahrhunderts. Exhibition catalogue. Bremen: Kunsthalle Bremen, 1974.

"Städtephantasien: Architekturutopien in der Literatur." *Du: Die Zeitschrift für Kunst und Kultur* 45, no. 2 (1985): 12–67.

"Stadtlandschaften." *Du: Die Zeitschrift fur Kunst und Kultur* 42, no. 2 (1982): 26–61, 95.

Stark, Michael. *Für und wider den Expressionismus: Die Entstehung der Intellektuellendebatte in der deutschen Literaturgeschichte.* Stuttgart: Metzler, 1982.

Steneberg, Eberhard. *Arbeitsrat für Kunst: Berlin, 1918–1921.* Düsseldorf: Edition Marzona, 1987.

Struck, Gabriele. "Glas-Architektur." In *Wände aus farbigem Glas: Das Archiv der vereinigten Werkstätten für Mosaik und Glasmalerei Puhl & Wagner, Gottfried Heinersdorff,* pp. 17–35. Exhibition catalogue. Berlin: Berlinische Galerie, 1989.

Szeemann, Harald, ed. *Der Hung zum Gesamtkunstwerk: Europäische Utopien seit 1800.* Exhibition catalogue. Zurich: Kunsthaus Zurich, 1983.

Szeemann, Harald, et al. *Monte Verità—Berg der Wahrheit: Lokale Anthropologie als Beitrag zur Wiederentdeckung einer neuzeitlichen sakralen Topographie.* Exhibition catalogue. Zurich: Kunsthaus Zurich, 1978.

Tafuri, Manfredo. *Architecture and Utopia: Design and Capitalist Development.* Translated by Barbara Luigia La Penta. Cambridge: MIT Press, 1976.

Taut, Bruno. "Zum neuen Theaterbau." *Das hohe Ufer* 1 (August 1919): 204–8.

——, ed. *Frühlicht, 1920–1922: Eine Folge für die Verwirklichung des neuen Baugedankens.* Bauwelt Fundamente, no. 8. Berlin: Ullstein, 1963.

Timms, Edward, and David Kelly, eds. *Unreal City: Urban Experience in Modern European Literature and Art.* New York: St. Martin's Press, 1985.

Tower, Beeke Sell. *Envisioning America: Prints, Drawings, and Photographs by George Grosz and His Contemporaries, 1915–1933.* Exhibition catalogue. Cambridge: Busch-Reisinger Museum, Harvard University, 1990.

Ueding, Gert, ed. *Literatur ist Utopie.* Frankfurt: Suhrkamp, 1978.

Ungers, Oswald Mathias, and Udo Kultermann, eds. *Die Gläserne Kette: Visionäre Architekturen aus dem Kreis um Bruno Taut, 1919–1920.* Exhibition catalogue. Berlin: Akademie der Künste, [1963?].

Vidler, Anthony. "Agoraphobia: Spatial Estrangement in Georg Simmel and Siegfried Kracauer." *New German Critique*, no. 54 (Fall 1991): 31–45 (later incorporated as vol. 18, no. 3).

——. "Architecture Dismembered," in *The Architectural Uncanny: Essays in the Modern Unhomely* (Cambridge, Mass.: The MIT Press, 1992), 69–82.

——. "Angelus Novus: Coop Himmelblau's Expressionist Utopia," in *Warped Space: Art, Architecture, and Anxiety in Modern Culture* (Cambridge, Mass.: The MIT Press, 2000), 186–192.

Vietta, Silvio. "Grossstadtwahrnehmung und ihre literarische Darstellung: Expressionistischer Reihungsstil mid Collage." *Deutsche Vierteljahrsschrift für Literaturwissenschaft und Geistesgeschichte* 48, no. 2 (1974): 354–73.

Vosskamp, Wilhelm, ed. *Utopieforschung: Interdisziplinäre Studien zur neuzeitlichen Utopie.* 3 vols. Stuttgart: Metzler, 1982.

Weinstein, Joan. "Expressionist Utopias: Paradise, Metropolis, and Architectural Fantasy." *Journal of the Society of Architectural Historians* 53, no. 3 (September 1994): 347–350.

Westheim, Paul. "Die Landschaft." *Das Kunstblatt* 4 (January 1920): 7–19.

Whitford, Frank. "Expressionism in the Cinema." *Studio International* 179 (January 1970): 24–27.

Whyte, Iain Boyd. "The End of an Avant-Garde: The Example of 'Expressionist' Architecture." *Art History* 3 (March 1980): 102–13.

——. "The Politics of Expressionist Architecture." *Architectural Association Quarterly* 12, no. 3 (1980): 11–17.

——, ed. and trans. *The Crystal Chain Letters: Architectural Fantasies by Bruno Taut and His Circle.* Cambridge: MIT Press, 1985.

——. "Expressionistische Architektur-der philosophische Kontext." In *Das Abenteuer der Ideen: Architektur und Philosophie seit der industriellen Revolution.* Exhibition catalogue. Edited by Josef Paul Kleihues, pp. 167–84. Berlin: Internationale Bauausstellung, 1987.

Wiedmann, August K. *Romantic Roots in Modern Art: Romanticism and Expressionism: A Study in Comparative Aesthetics.* Old Woking, England: Gresham Books, 1979.

Willett, John. *The Theatre of the Weimar Republic.* New York: Holmes and Meier, 1988.

"Wolf Prix and Helmut Swiczinsky in Conversation with Alvin Boyarsky." *AA Files* 19 (Spring 1990): 70–77.

"The Works of Coop Himmelblau 1968-1989." *Architecture and Urbanism* (a+u) 89:07 (July 1989), no. 226.

Worringer, Wilhelm. *Abstraction and Empathy: A Contribution to the Psychology of Style.* Translated by Michael Bullock. New York: International Universities Press, 1967.

Zimmermann, Florian, ed. *Der Schrei nach dem Turmhaus: Der Ideenwettbewerb Hochhaus am Bahnhof Friedrichstrasse, Berlin, 1921–22.* Exhibition catalogue. Berlin: Bauhaus-Archiv, Museum für Gestaltung, 1988.

Acknowledgments

Just as utopias are inherently expansive and communal visions, an exhibition on this theme could succeed only with the cooperation of many individuals and institutions. The enthusiastic support of the museum's director, Michael E. Shapiro, and the encouragement of his predecessor, Earl A. Powell III, made this collaboration possible. I am grateful to them and to the museum's board of trustees, under the direction of Daniel N. Belin and, subsequently, Robert E. Maguire III, for their sustained support. Crucial funding for the exhibition was received from the National Endowment for the Arts, the National Endowment for the Humanities, and the Design Arts division of the National Endowment for the Arts. This support was augmented by a generous grant from the Federal Republic of Germany, and I am indebted to Dr. Cornell Metternich, consul general; Dr. Stefan Schlüter, deputy consul; and his predecessor, Tius Fischer, for their efforts in securing this funding. I am also grateful to the Harry and Yvonne Lenart Charitable Foundation and the Andrew W. Mellon Foundation for providing additional support.

From its inception the project benefited from the resources of the Getty Center for the History of Art and the Humanities — not only its splendid research collections but also its visiting scholars program, which brought together an unparalleled assembly of distinguished experts on Expressionist art, architecture, music, and theater, among them Hartmut Frank, Peter Jelavich, Anton Kaes, Fritz Neumeyer, and Iain Boyd Whyte. Thanks in part to the interdisciplinary exchange at the Getty Center, this catalogue includes contributions by film historian Kaes and architectural historian Whyte as fitting complements to the perspectives offered by sociologist David Frisby and art historian Reinhold Heller. Nor could the detailed research for this project have been undertaken without the encouragement of Getty scholar Tilmann Buddensieg, who was my host while I was a visiting Humboldt scholar at the Kunsthistorisches Institut in Bonn. I am deeply grateful to him and to the Alexander von Humboldt-Stiftung for making my months of initial research and consultation in Germany possible.

My research for this exhibition was conducted at institutions in both Europe and the United States, and I am indebted to many colleagues who helped me find materials and often facilitated loans for the exhibition as well. My research in Berlin was aided by Dominick Bartmann, Berlin Museum; Alexander Dückers, Kupferstichkabinett; Bernd Evers, Kunstbibliothek; Helmut Geisert and Freya Mulhaupt, Berlinische Galerie; Magdalena Moeller, Brücke-Museum; Dieter Radicke, Technische Universität; Werner Sudendorf, Stiftung Deutsche Kinemathek; and Achim Wendschuh, Wolfgang Trautwein, and Matthias Schirren, Akademie der Künste. In Munich Annegret Hoberg, Städtische Galerie im Lenbachhaus; Eckehart Nölle, Deutsches Theatermuseum; Enno Patalas, Filmmuseum, Münchner Stadtmuseum; and Gisela Scheffler, Staatliche Graphische Sammlung, were all very helpful. In other cities in Germany, Elmar Buck and Bernd Vogelsang, Theaterwissenschaftliche Sammlung, Universität zu Köln, Cologne; Katharina Lepper, Wilhelm Lehmbruck Museum, Duisberg; Norbert Nobis, Sprengel Museum, Hannover; Peter Schmitt, Badisches Landesmuseum, Karlsruhe; Suzanne Klingeberg and Elisabeth Fuchs-Belhamri, Wenzel-Hablik-Stiftung, Itzehoe; Ulrike Gauss and Karin von Maur, Staatsgalerie Stuttgart; and Erich Franz, Westfälisches Landesmuseum für Kunst und Kulturgeschichte, Münster, provided valuable assistance. Virginia Sease, Freie Hochschule für Geisteswissenschaft at the Gotheanum, Dornach; Gillian Hartnoll and Bridget Kinally, British Film Institute, London; Nicholas Olsberg, Canadian Centre for Architecture, Montreal; Russell Maylone, Special Collections, Northwestern University Library, Evanston;

Magdalena Dabrowski and Matilda McQuaid, Museum of Modern Art, New York; Donald Anderle, Mel Edelstein, Irene Lotspeich-Phillips, Marcia Reed, and Brendt Sverdloff, Getty Center for the History of Art and the Humanities, Santa Monica; Cynthia Burlingham, Grunwald Center for the Graphic Arts, University of California, Los Angeles; Alison Pinsler, Academy of Motion Picture Arts and Sciences, Los Angeles; and Peter Nisbet, Busch-Reisinger Museum, Harvard University, Cambridge, furnished useful information.

In conceiving this project, I drew on the advice of those in the many fields in which the elusive concept of utopia manifests its myriad forms. I am especially indebted to Helen Atkins, Erhard Bahr, Rosemarie Haag Bletter, Uta Brandes, Ulrich Conrads, John Czaplicka, Ruth Irmgard Dalinghaus, Michael Erlhoff, Axel Feuss, Stephen C. Foster, Helmut Geisert, Maurice Godé, Peter Guenther, Charles W. Haxthausen, Michael Hayes, Berndt Heller, Marion von Hofacher, Klaus Itten, Annegreth Janda, Pamela Kort, Barbara Miller Lane, Heidi Lesemann, Karl Levin, Mario-Andreas von Lüttichau, Ron Manheim, Thomas Messer, Winfred Nerdinger, Wolfgang Pehnt, Jonathan Petropolis, Barton Phelps, Julius Posener, Hans-Peter Reisse, Karl Riha, Rainer Rumold, Louisa Stude Sarofim, C. Raman Schlemmer, Arturo Schwarz, Dennis Sharp, Richard Sheppard, Manfred Speidel, Ann Stacy, Carmen Stonge, Heinrich Taut, Oswald Matthias Ungers, Eva Weininger, Joan Weinstein, John Willett, and Barbara D. Wright.

At the Los Angeles County Museum of Art I have received much assistance and useful advice from curatorial colleagues Stephanie Barron, Victor Carlson, Bruce Davis, and Carol Eliel. I am also indebted to the staff of the Rifkind Study Center. Librarian Susan Trauger responded to many research requests, checked innumerable references, and helped prepare the bibliography for the exhibition catalogue. Assistant registrar Christine Vigiletti saw to the intricate details of loans, insurance, and shipping, while secretary Vicki Gambill cheerfully undertook endless tasks in connection with the exhibition preparations, including securing photographs for the catalogue. Additionally, Eleanor Hartmann and the staff of the Mr. and Mrs. Allan C. Balch Research Library helped me find many research materials, with Anne Diederich obtaining countless interlibrary loans.

This publication was designed by Robin Weiss, whose imaginative layouts capture the lively attitude toward the page of the Expressionists themselves. The editing and coordination of texts by various authors were masterfully handled by Karen Jacobson, whose sense of clarity and good judgment contributed greatly to the catalogue. The encouragement and advice of Mitch Tuchman, the museum's editor in chief, and Sandra Bell, head designer, have helped shape this volume from its inception to its final form. The museum's supervising photographer, Peter Brenner, and his staff supplied photographic material, often at a moment's notice. Virginia Haddad, Frauke von der Horst, and Annelisa Stephan researched and wrote most of the artists' biographies, which often required diligent sleuthing. In preparing the documents section, I benefited from the thoughtful suggestions of Hans Morgenthaler and Iain Boyd Whyte. David Britt undertook the challenging task of translating many of these Expressionist texts. Naomi Weiss helped develop the necessary photography research files, while volunteers Grete Wolf and Maria Steinberg made certain our correspondence with German colleagues was conveyed with tact and refinement.

As an intern during the early stages of the project, Nancy Perloff assisted me in developing an interdisciplinary bibliography on utopias, and her musicological expertise was crucial to the development of the film and stage section of the exhibition. The exploration of theater and music was expanded through the suggestions of Leonard Stein, former director of the Schoenberg Institute; Nancy and John Crawford of the University of California, Riverside; Peter Lackner of the University of California, Santa Barbara; as well as LACMA's own director of musical programs, Dorrance Stalvey.

I was privileged to work on the exhibition's installation with Wolf Prix and Frank Stepper of Coop Himmelblau, whose visionary approach rivals that of the utopian architects of the Expressionist era. I am grateful to project architect Jennifer Rakow for her attention to the minutest details of this complex endeavor. Jim Drobka created an elegant graphic design to complement the architectural setting. The construction of this environment and the mounting of the works of art were overseen by Art Owens, assistant director of operations, with the assistance of project manager Mee Mee Leong. Peggy Olson provided audiovisual expertise for the installation.

In budgeting the exhibition and arranging for many of the details of shipping, I relied on Elizabeth Algermissen, assistant director of exhibitions, and John Passi, head of exhibitions programs, as well as registrar Renée Montgomery. Careful attention to the proper handling of the often fragile materials in this show was provided by Victoria Blyth-Hill and Joanne Page of the conservation department, under the direction of Pieter Meyers.

The educational component was ably managed by Lisa Vihos, who wrote the visitors brochure. With Virginia Haddad and Annelisa Stephan, she also participated in preparing the didactic texts used in the exhibition installation. David Inocencio and Minette Siegel created a lively slide-tape presentation to orient the visitor to the historical context of the Expressionist era.

Christopher Ponce, director of development, and Tom Jacobson, head of grants and foundation giving, administered the grant proposals that led to the successful funding of the project. Lynn Terelle, Talbot Welles, Dana Hutt, and designer Brent Saville were instrumental in the process of providing granting agencies with budget details, clear descriptions, and a coherent layout for the show. Sarah Gallop of the public information office effectively communicated the scope and purpose of the project to the public.

Throughout the many stages of this project I have had the great privilege and pleasure of seven years' immersion in the extensive library and graphic collection of the museum's Robert Gore Rifkind Center for German Expressionist Studies. To Robert Gore Rifkind I am especially grateful, not only for the building of this extraordinary resource but also for his willing augmentation of its holdings with several important objects acquired specifically for this exhibition. My family and friends have patiently endured my excessive preoccupation and occasional utopian reveries. Most indulgent of all has been Susan Annett, whose pithy suggestions have added balance and perspective to this project. To my father, Donald R. Benson, a literary scholar who has brought many insights to our discussions of this topic, I dedicate this catalogue.

T.B.

Lenders to the Exhibition

Akademie der Künste, Berlin
Badisches Landesmuseum, Karlsruhe
Berlinische Galerie, Museum für Moderne Kunst, Photographie und Architektur, Berlin
Canadian Centre for Architecture, Montreal
Doheny Library, University of Southern California, Los Angeles
Galerie Berinson, Berlin
Gerhard Marcks Stiftung, Bremen
The Getty Center for the History of Art and the Humanities, Los Angeles
The Grunwald Center for the Graphic Arts, University of California, Los Angeles
Haags Gemeentemuseum, The Hague
Helen Topping Architecture and Fine Arts Library, University of Southern California, Los Angeles
Kunstmuseum, Basel
Kunstmuseum, Bern
Los Angeles County Museum of Art, Department of Prints and Drawings
Los Angeles County Museum of Art, The Robert Gore Rifkind Center for German Expressionist Studies
The Metropolitan Museum of Art, New York
The Museum of Modern Art, New York
The National Gallery of Art, Washington, D.C.
The Oskar Schlemmer Theatre Estate, Oggebbio
Plansammlung, Technische Universität, Berlin
Rheinisches Landesmuseum, Bonn
Schleswig-Holsteinisches Landesmuseum, Schleswig
Special Collections, Northwestern University, Evanston, Illinois
Sprengel Museum, Hannover
Staatliche Graphische Sammlung, Munich
Staatliche Museen zu Berlin, Kunstbibliothek
Staatsgalerie Stuttgart
Städtische Galerie im Lenbachhaus, Munich
Städtische Kunstsammlungen, Darmstadt
Stiftung Deutsche Kinemathek, Berlin
Theaterwissenschaftliche Sammlung der Universität, Cologne
Wenzel-Hablik-Stiftung, Itzehoe
Wilhelm Lehmbruck Museum, Duisberg

Arlan Coffman, Santa Monica, California
Ruth and Jacob Kainen, Chevy Chase, Maryland
Mrs. Loretto Molzahn, Munich
H. Marc Moyens, Alexandria, Virginia
Prof. Eckhard Neumann, Frankfurt am Main
Gabriele Reisser-Finsterlin, Stuttgart
Lawrence Schoenberg, Los Angeles
Frau Dipl.-Ing. Maria Schwarz, Cologne
Granvil and Marcia Specks, Evanston, Illinois
Maria Elisabeth Stapp, Germany
Prof. O. M. Ungers, Cologne
Several private collections

Photo Credits

Unless an acknowledgment appears below, the photographs in this volume have been provided by the owners of the works of art or by the Los Angeles County Museum of Art.

Jörg P. Anders, Berlin: figs. 87, 118
© Coop Himmelblau: p. 171 (top, photo by Aleksandra Pawloff; bottom, photo by Tom Bonner); 176 (left, photo by Margherit Spiluttni; right [both], photos by Markus Pillhofer); 178, 181 (right), 185 (178, 181 [right], 185, photos by Tom Bonner)
© Copyright und Werk-Documentation für Johannes Molzahn im Molzahn Centrum, Kassel: cat. nos. 155–164
Foto-Fachlabor Bachor: fig. 42
Fotoarchiv Bolliger-Ketterer: fig. 77
Marc Dachy Archives: fig. 177
Grossfoto, Berlin: p. 234
Kai Falck: figs. 38, 39, 40, 44, 48, 104, 124, 128, 129, 133, 134, 172; pp. 9, 194–96
Hamburger Kunsthalle, photo by Elke Wolford, Hamburg: p. 121
Markus Hawlik Fotografie: fig. 145
© Ingeborg & Dr. Wolfgang Henze-Ketterer, Wichtrach/Bern: cat. nos. 109–113
Hermann Kiessling: fig. 53
Bernd Kirtz BFF: figs. 7, 58, 170; p. 245
Jörg F. Klam: fig. 86
© Kupferstichkabinett—Sammlung der Zeichnungen und Druckgraphik—Staatliche Museen zu Berlin—Preussicher Kulturbesitz, KdZ/SZ/Inv: fig. 87
Marburg/Art Resource, New York: fig. 62
© Ludwig Meidner-Archiv, Jüdisches Museum der Stadt Frankfurt an Main: cat. nos. 134–137
Stefan Müller: figs. 107, 112, 117, 125; p. 188
Knud Peter Petersen: figs. 34, 36, 106; p. 238
© 2001 The Oskar Schlemmer Theater Estate, Bühnen Archiv, I-28824 Oggebio, Italy/Photo Archive C. Raman Schlemmer, I-28824 Oggebio, Italy: fig. 146, p. 240, cat. nos. 187–191
VAGA, New York: pp. 204, 205 (cat. no. 96), 211 (cat. no. 118)
Verlag am Goetheanum, Dornach: fig. 47
VG Bild-Kunst, Bonn: fig. 102, p. 227 (cat. no. 114)
Elke Walford: fig. 115
Mechthild Wilhelmi: figs 29, 31

Index

Numbers in *italics* refer to pages with illustrations.